Mathematics in Economics

Mathematics in Economics

Models and Methods

Adam Ostaszewski

Based on lecture notes by K. G. Binmore
and A. Ostaszewski

BLACKWELL
Oxford UK & Cambridge USA

First published 1993

Blackwell Publishers
108 Cowley Road, Oxford, OX4 1JF, UK

British Library Cataloguing in Publication Data

A CIP catalogue record for this book is available from the British Library.

Library of Congress Cataloging-in-Publication Data

Ostaszewski, Adam.
    Mathematics in economics : models and methods / Adam Ostaszewski.
        p.   cm.
    "Based on lecture notes by K. G. Binmore and A. Ostaszewski."
    Includes index.
    ISBN 0-631-18055-9. -- ISBN 0-631-18056-7 (pbk.)
    1. Economics--Mathematical models. I. Binmore, K. G., 1940–   .
    II. Title.
    HB135.0867 1993
    330'.01'5118--dc20   92-32454 CIP

ISBN 0–631–18055–9 0–631–18056–7(pb)

... And how will your night dances
Lose themselves. In mathematics?

Such pure leaps and spirals –
Surely they travel
The world for ever ...

Sylvia Plath, 'The Night Dances' from *Ariel*

To my students and to my teachers
Acknowledging a debt from generation to generation

Contents

Acknowledgements

It is a great pleasure to extend thanks to John Sutton and Stephen Glaister, colleagues in Economics, for reading parts of this book and also colleagues in Mathematics – especially Graham Brightwell and Elizabeth Boardman – for sharing in some of the chores associated with the production of the book. I am indebted to my erstwhile teaching assistant A. Brandolini.

The unsung heroes of the production saga are Philomena McNicholas and Pat Smith (Omega Scientific) who typed the majority of the book, aided in the closing stages by Alison Adcock. The skilful editorial judgement, watchful eye and patience of Christine Sharrock (Omega Scientific) have turned an often unruly manuscript to the ennobled words of print. Her superb work is very gratefully acknowledged.

Adam Ostaszewski

Note on Conventions

There are exercises at the end of each chapter – answers are provided to asterisked questions (in a later section) to help students in their first attempts at solutions. Often an asterisked question will be followed by a very similar question for which no answer is provided. Some chapters – especially those in Part II – have further exercise sets. Here the questions go beyond testing routine skills; they are a little harder, more theoretical and hopefully both challenging and interesting.

The reader may be amused somewhat to see certain economic agents referred to in the feminine and others in the masculine. This is not just in the interests of gender equality. The custom derives from a convention in game theory whereby, if there are two agents involved in a game, to distinguish between them more clearly one is a him and the other a her. Typically, firms are masculine and consumers feminine.

Some attempt has been made to denote functions of one variable, like $f(x)$, by lower case letters and functions of two variables, like $F(x, y)$, by upper case letters. Similarly a fixed value assumed by a variable will be given an upper case letter whereas the variable itself will be denoted by a lower case letter. Such rules are inevitably broken from time to time, especially if there are time-honoured denotations in economics (e.g. L for labour).

A few of the sections presented in this book are also marked with an asterisk. This is to signify that no loss in continuity of thought will occur if the reader decides to skip the section. The material is optional and is included either because it offers an interesting perspective on earlier material or because the authors could not resist writing the topic in. The optional reader will, hopefully, find them a good read.

Foreword

This is a book on elementary mathematics for students of economics who hope to use mathematics seriously. It is based on lectures given to undergraduate freshers at the London School of Economics by Adam Ostaszewski and myself – building on a tradition established by a sequence of teachers including Steve Glaister, Avner Shaked, Tony Shorrocks and Alisdair Smith.

Many introductory courses in mathematics for economists consist of little more than a menu of formulae that students are to learn by rote in order to establish their erudition at examination time. Personally, I see no point in turning out students who can write learnedly on such matters as the formal derivation of the Slutsky equations unless they have some understanding of what the mathematical manipulations they have learned to reproduce actually mean. When one teaches how things are done without explaining why they are done this way, one does worse than fill the heads of the weaker students with mumbo-jumbo, one teaches the stronger students something that is terribly wrong – that mathematics is a list of theorems and proofs that have no practical relevance to the person on the Clapham omnibus.

The attitude that mathematics is a list of theorems that ordinary mortals can only admire from afar is very common among those who know no mathematics at all. Research mathematicians, for example, are often greeted with incredulity when they reply to questions about what they do for a living. The man – and woman – in the street finds it very hard to come to grips with the fact that the mathematics we learn at school was not brought down from some mountain by a mathematical Moses engraved on tablets of stone. Such awe of mathematics creates a form of hysterical paralysis that must be overcome before a student can join the community of those of us who see mathematics as an ever-changing box of tools that an educated person can use to make sense of the world in which he or she lives.

Within this community, a model is not expressed in mathematical form in order to invite the applause of those who are easily impressed, or to obfuscate the issues in order to immunize the model from criticisms by uninitiated outsiders. Instead, the community that I represent is always anxious to find the *simplest* possible model that captures how a particular aspect of some economic process works. For us, mathematical sophistication is pointless unless it serves to de-mystify and to clarify what is going on. We do not see mathematical modelling as some grandiose activity that can only be carried out by professors at the blackboard. Mathematical modelling is what *everybody* should do when seeking to make sense of some problem. Beginners, of course, will only be able to construct very simple models – but a good teacher will only ask them very simple problems!

However, such an attitude to problem-solving in economics is not possible with students whose intellectual processes freeze at the mere mention of mathematics. The remedy for this species of mathematical paralysis, with which previous teachers have often infected our students, lies in teaching that mathematics is something that one *does* – not something that one just appreciates. Rather than offering them a cookbook, one needs to teach students to put together simple recipes of their own. Above all, they need confidence-enhancing therapy to persuade them that they are genuinely capable of thinking coherent mathematical thoughts *all by themselves*.

Such confidence comes from involving students in the mathematics as it is developed, using the traditional method of demanding weekly answers to carefully chosen sets of problems. The problems must not be too hard – but nor must they be too easy. Nobody gets their confidence boosted by being asked to jump through hoops that are held too low. On the contrary, if one only asks students to solve problems that they can see are trivial, one only confirms to them that their low opinion of their own mathematical prowess is shared by their teacher. Some hoops need to be held high enough that students get to feel that they have achieved something by jumping through them.

But it is not enough to build an obstacle course of just the right level of difficulty. The students have to see that it is taking them where they wish to go. The examples and problems used must therefore never stray too far from the applications in economics for which the student is learning mathematics.

This is the teaching philosophy on which Adam Ostaszewski's introduction to mathematics for economists is based. Those who want to learn the mathematical equivalent of painting by numbers should therefore look elsewhere for a textbook. Ostaszewski is anxious to tell his students more than the *how* of things – he also offers *whys*. Pure mathematicians sometimes think that the *why* that goes with a mathematical technique is a formal proof of the theorem that guarantees that the method always gives the right answer. But, although Ostaszewski is a mathematician, his *whys* are practical *whys* – the *whys* that a student will need to use the technique for more than supplying stereotyped answers to stereotyped examination questions. He puts the *whys* across partly by using geometry – the book has many diagrams – and partly by appealing to economic intuitions. The very large number of examples is also important, both for consolidating past gains and for breaking new ground. Above all, a great deal of thought has gone into a wide variety of highly instructive and original problems. These are an integral part of the text. To read the book without attempting as many problems as time allows is to waste one's time.

The second part of the book is its heart. It contains a comprehensive account of elementary calculus for potential users. Ostaszewski never talks down to his readers, and there are passages that some students will find challenging, but Ostaszewski's exuberant style never permits the suggestion that his material is dull! Students who read this introduction to calculus carefully will be rewarded with an unusually sound training in how to use mathematics to think seriously about serious matters.

The first part of the book provides the algebraic foundations for the second. Its pace is markedly slower, and there are lengthy stops along the way to explore how and why the ideas matter in economics. The intention is to seduce reluctant mathematicians into warming a little to the subject. Reluctant economists may also be surprised to find how much economics they have inadvertently picked up along the way while supposedly learning mathematics! I hope teachers will not be tempted to hurry this part of the course. Students really do need some time to learn that they can do mathematics as well as anyone else – and this is what the first part of the book has to offer.

In conclusion, let me say that Adam Ostaszewski and I were colleagues for many years at the London School of Economics. He is a good friend and a joy to teach with. I wish him good luck with this book. May it enjoy the success it deserves.

Ken Binmore
Professor of Economics
University of Michigan
Ann Arbor, MI 48109

Part I

Elementary Algebra

1

Sets and Numbers

1.1 Sets

A *set* is a collection of objects which are called its *elements*. If x is an element of the set S, we say that x belongs to S and write

$$x \in S.$$

If y does not belong to S, we write

$$y \notin S.$$

The simplest way of specifying a set is by listing its elements. We use the notation

$$A = \{1, 2, 4\}$$

to denote the set whose elements are the numbers 1, 2 and 4. Similarly,

$$B = \{\text{Romeo, Juliet}\}$$

denotes the set whose elements are Romeo and Juliet.

Sometimes we want to specify a set by describing its elements rather than listing them. For example, we use the notation

$$C = \{x : x^2 + 2x - 3 = 0\}$$

to denote the set of all solutions of the equation $x^2 + 2x - 3 = 0$. Thus $C = \{1, -3\}$. Similarly,

$$D = \{y : y \text{ loves Romeo}\}$$

denotes the set of those people who love Romeo. Juliet is an element of D and so, doubtless, is Romeo himself and probably his mother also.

In order for the notation used to define C and D to be properly meaningful, it is necessary to have a clear idea about the range of the variables x and y. For the set C, we may take the range of the variable x to be the set of all real numbers. For the set D, we may take the range of the variable y to be the set of all Shakespearian characters.

3

Some particular mathematical sets deserve special mention. The set $\mathbb{R}$ of all *real numbers* may be thought of as the collection of all points on a line which extends indefinitely in both directions (figure 1.1).

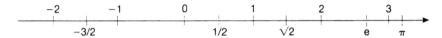

Figure 1.1 The real numbers.

The real numbers 1, 2, 3, 4, ... make up the set $\mathbb{N}$ of *natural numbers*. The real numbers ... −2, −1, 0, +1, +2, +3, ... constitute the set $\mathbb{Z}$ of *integers*. The set of all fractions, however vulgar or improper, such as 0, 1, 1/2, 22/7, −3/2, ... is called the set $\mathbb{Q}$ of rational numbers.

Not all real numbers are rational. Some examples of *irrational numbers* are $\sqrt{2}$, e and π. All real numbers have a decimal expansion which may or may not terminate. The rational numbers may be characterized as those real numbers whose decimal expansion terminates or else repeats itself over and over again. For example,

$$\frac{22}{7} = 3.142\ 857\ 142\ 857\ 142\ 857\ \ldots,$$

while

$$\pi = 3.141\ 592\ 653\ 589\ 793\ldots.$$

1.2 Venn diagrams

Venn diagrams illustrate the relationships that may hold between different sets. The outer represents the 'universal set' U to which all objects in the context under consideration belong. Figure 1.2 shows the relationship

$$S \subset T$$

which means that S is a *subset* of T in that each element of S is also an element of T.

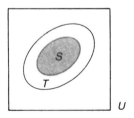

Figure 1.2 Venn diagram to illustrate $S \subset T$.

Figure 1.3 illustrates the *complement* $\tilde{S}$ of a set S. This is the set of all elements which are *not* elements of S, i.e.

$$\tilde{S} = \{x : x \notin S\}.$$

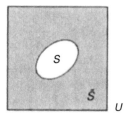

Figure 1.3   The complement $\tilde{S}$ of a set S.

Figure 1.4(a) illustrates the *union* $S \cup T$ of two sets, which consists of all elements which belong to at least one of the sets. Figure 1.4(b) shows the *intersection* $S \cap T$ of two sets, which consists of all elements which belong to both sets.

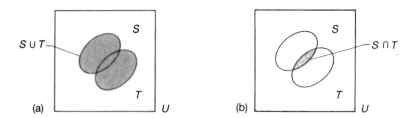

Figure 1.4   (a) The union $S \cup T$ of two sets; (b) the intersection $S \cap T$ of two sets.

It is useful to have a notation for the empty set $\varnothing$ which contains *no* elements. For example, if S and T have no elements in common, then we may write $S \cap T = \varnothing$.

Examples
Take $U = \{1, 2, 3, 4, 5, 6\}$ so that U is the set of numbers on the face of a die. Take $A = \{1, 3, 5\}$ and $B = \{1, 2, 3\}$. Then

1   $\tilde{A} = \{2, 4, 6\}$
2   $\tilde{B} = \{4, 5, 6\}$
3   $C = A \cap B = \{1, 3\}$
4   $D = A \cup B = \{1, 2, 3, 5\}$
5   $A \subset D$
6   $C \cap \tilde{B} = \varnothing$

1.3 Inequalities

Table 1.1 introduces the necessary notation. Note that the fact that $2 < 3$ does not make it false that $2 \leqslant 3$. Similarly, the fact that $-1 = -1$ does not make it false that $-1 \leqslant -1$. All the statements $2 < 3$, $2 \leqslant 3$, $-1 = -1$, $-1 \leqslant -1$ are true.

Table 1.1

Notation	Meaning	Examples
$a > b$	a is greater than b	$1 > 0$, $-2 > -3$
$a < b$	a is less than b	$2 < 3$, $-4 < -1$
$a \geqslant b$	a is greater than *or* equal to b	$1 \geqslant 0$, $-2 \geqslant -3$
		$1 \geqslant 1$, $-3 \geqslant -3$
$a \leqslant b$	a is less than *or* equal to b	$2 \leqslant 3$, $-4 \leqslant -1$
		$3 \leqslant 3$, $-1 \leqslant -1$

Intervals are sets of real numbers defined by inequalities as indicated in table 1.2. The first three types of interval are called open because their endpoints are excluded from the set. The remaining three types are called closed because their endpoints are included. Also counted as intervals are $\varnothing$ and $\mathbb{R} = (-\infty, \infty)$. These are deemed to be both open and closed! Finally there are the 'half-open' intervals of the form $[a, b)$ or $(a, b]$.

Table 1.2

Notation	Definition	Picture
(a, b)	$\{x: a < x < b\}$	
(a, ∞)	$\{x: a < x\}$	
$(-\infty, b)$	$\{x: x < b\}$	
$[a, b]$	$\{x: a \leqslant x \leqslant b\}$	
$[a, \infty)$	$\{x: a \leqslant x\}$	
$(-\infty, b]$	$\{x: x \leqslant b\}$	

Note that the 'infinity' symbol is only a notational convenience in all this. It does not represent a real number and should not be treated as though it did. Thus statements like $1/0 = \infty$ or $\infty - \infty = 0$ are meaningless and you will only confuse yourself by writing them down. In particular, since ∞ does not represent an actual object, it cannot be a candidate for an endpoint in the above discussion.

In manipulating inequalities, the most important thing to remember is that, although they remain valid when multiplied through by a *positive* constant, they are reversed when multiplied through by a *negative* constant.

For example, $3 > 2$ and hence $4 \times 3 > 4 \times 2$, i.e. $12 > 8$. On the other hand, $-3 < -2$ and hence $(-2) \times (-3) > (-2) \times (-2)$, i.e. $6 > 4$.

Example
Express the set

$$S = \left\{ x: 5 > \frac{x-1}{x+3} \geq 2 \right\}$$

in terms of intervals.

SOLUTION   Note first that $x = -3$ cannot belong to S because the expression $-4/0$ is meaningless and therefore cannot have any properties.

There are then two cases to consider, depending on whether $x + 3 > 0$ or $x + 3 < 0$. If $x < -3$, then multiplying the inequality in the definition of S by the negative quantity $x + 3$ gives

$$5x + 15 < x - 1 \leq 2x + 6,$$

which means that $5x + 15 < x - 1$ and $x - 1 \leq 2x + 6$. These inequalities reduce to

$$4x < -16 \qquad \text{and} \qquad -x \leq 7,$$

i.e.

$$x < -4 \qquad \text{and} \qquad x \geq -7,$$

i.e.

$$-7 \leq x < -4,$$

i.e.

$$x \in [-7, 4).$$

(Notice the reversal of the inequality $-x \leq 7$ to $x \geq -7$ on multiplication by -1.)

If $x > -3$, then multiplying the inequality in the definition of S by the positive quantity $x + 3$ gives

$$5x + 15 > x - 1 \geq 2x + 6,$$

which reduces to

$$4x > -16 \qquad \text{and} \qquad -x \geq 7,$$

i.e.

$$x > -4 \qquad \text{and} \qquad x \leq -7,$$

i.e.

$$-4 < x \leq -7,$$

which is impossible because $-7 < -4$.

We conclude that

$$S = \left\{ x: 5 > \frac{x-1}{x+3} \geqslant 2 \right\} = [-7, -4).$$

Such results are usually more easily seen with the help of a graph (figure 1.5). In sketching such a graph, it is usually best to begin as shown in figure 1.6.

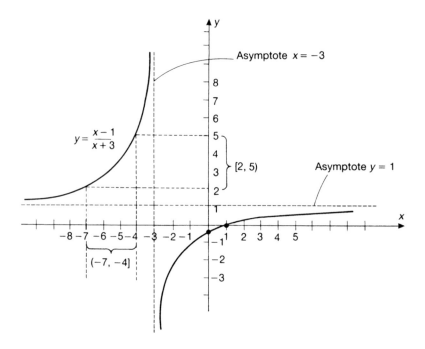

Figure 1.5 The graph identifies $(-7, -4]$ as those x for which $2 \leqslant y < 5$, where $y = (x-1)(x+3)$.

Plot only those points which are very easy to locate. Those on $x = 0$ and $y = 0$ are always easy. Then see what happens when x and y are very large.

When x is large and positive,

$$y = \frac{x-1}{x+3} = \frac{1 - 1/x}{1 + 3/x}$$

is less than but very close to 1. When x is large and negative,

$$y = \frac{x-1}{x+3} = \frac{1 + (1/-x)}{1 - (3/-x)}$$

is more than but very close to 1. If x is larger but very close to -3, then

$$y = \frac{x-1}{x+3}$$

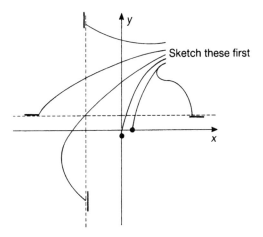

Figure 1.6   Curve sketching: first steps.

is large and negative. If x is smaller but very close to -3, then y is large and positive.

Simply plotting points often results in a completely wrong graph as indicated in figure 1.7.

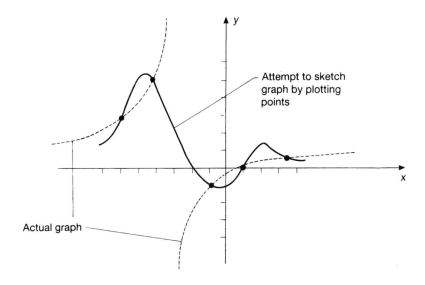

Figure 1.7   Plotting points and joining them is not enough.

1.4   Roots

For each real number $y \geqslant 0$, there is exactly one real number $x \geqslant 0$ such that

$$y = x^n.$$

We call x the nth root of y and write

$$x = y^{1/n} = \sqrt[n]{y}.$$

If n is even and $y > 0$, the equation $y = x^n$ has *two* real solutions for x. It is the *positive* solution which is denoted by $y^{1/n}$. The negative solution is simply $-y^{1/n}$ (figure 1.8).

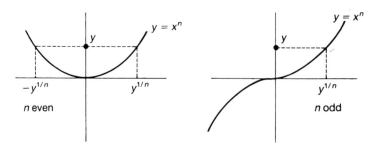

Figure 1.8   Solutions of $y = x^n$.

If $y \geqslant 0$ and $r = m/n$ is a rational number, we define

$$y^r = y^{m/n} = (y^{1/n})^m.$$

Note also that $y^0 = 1$ and $y^{-r} = 1/y^r$. These definitions ensure that the following laws are always satisfied when $a \geqslant 0$, $b \geqslant 0$ and r and s are rational numbers:

1 $(ab)^r = a^r b^r$
2 $a^r a^s = a^{r+s}$
3 $(a^r)^s = a^{rs}$

The equation $y = x^2$ is particularly important. It has two solutions when $y > 0$. The positive solution is denoted by $\sqrt{y}$ and the negative solution $-\sqrt{y}$. The notation $x = \pm\sqrt{y}$ simply means that 'either $x = \sqrt{y}$ or $x = -\sqrt{y}$'.

Consider the quadratic equation

$$ax^2 + bx + c = 0$$

in which $a \neq 0$. This may be solved by 'completing the square'. Multiply through by $4a$. Then

$$4a^2x^2 + 4abx + 4ac = 0$$
$$(2ax + b)^2 - b^2 + 4ac = 0$$
$$(2ax + b)^2 = b^2 - 4ac.$$

It follows that the quadratic equation has no real solutions if $b^2 - 4ac < 0$, one real solution if $b^2 - 4ac = 0$ and two real solutions if $b^2 - 4ac > 0$. (In the case when $b^2 - 4ac = 0$, mathematicians usually say that there are still two solutions but these are 'equal' or 'repeated'.)

If $b^2 - 4ac \geqslant 0$, the solutions are given by

$$2ax + b = \pm \sqrt{(b^2 - 4ac)}$$

$$x = \frac{-b \pm \sqrt{(b^2 - 4ac)}}{2a}.$$

When $b^2 - 4ac \geqslant 0$, it follows that the solutions (or roots) of the quadratic equation $ax^2 + bx + c = 0$ are given by

$$\alpha = \frac{-b + \sqrt{(b^2 - 4ac)}}{2a} \quad \text{and} \quad \beta = \frac{-b - \sqrt{(b^2 - 4ac)}}{2a}.$$

It is easy to check that, for all values of x,

$$ax^2 + bx + c = a(x - \alpha)(x - \beta).$$

The formula is helpful in drawing the graph of

$$y = ax^2 + bx + c.$$

We begin by observing that $y = 0$ when $x = \alpha$ or $x = \beta$. Next note that, provided a is positive, y is negative for $\beta < x < \alpha$ and positive for $x < \beta$ or $x > \alpha$. Finally,

$$y = x^2 \left(a + \frac{b}{x} + \frac{c}{x^2} \right)$$

and so, provided again that a is positive, y will be large and positive whenever x is large enough.

When a is negative, similar considerations apply.

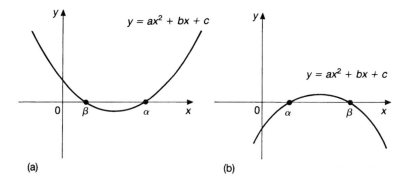

(a)   (b)

Figure 1.9 (a) $a > 0$, $b^2 - 4ac > 0$; (b) $a < 0$, $b^2 - 4ac > 0$.

The graphs in figure 1.9 are examples of *parabolas*. (Similar graphs are obtained if $b^2 - 4ac \leqslant 0$; however, if $b^2 - 4ac < 0$ the graph will not intersect the x axis, and if $b^2 - 4ac = 0$ the graph touches the x axis.)

A parabola is one of the 'conic sections'. The other curves in this class are the *ellipse* and the *hyperbola*. The circle drawn in figure 1.10 is a special kind of ellipse and the rectangular hyperbola (so called because its asymptotes are perpendicular) is a special kind of hyperbola.

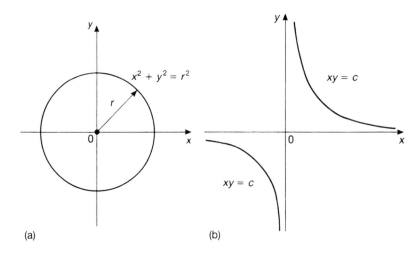

Figure 1.10 (a) Circle; (b) rectangular hyperbola, $c > 0$.

1.5 Exercises

Answers to asterisked questions are given in the next section as mentioned in the Note on Conventions (see p. xv). Obviously, however, there is no point in consulting the answer before attempting the problem. Usually, an even-numbered question is similar to its odd-numbered predecessor.

1* Which of the statements

$$1 \in S \qquad 0 \in S \qquad 2 \notin S \qquad -1 \notin S$$

are true and which are false in each of the following cases:

(a) $S = \{1, 2\}$
(b) $S = \{x: x \text{ is positive}\}$
(c) $S = \{x: x^2 + 2x - 3 = 0\}$
(d) $S = \{0, 1, 2\} \cup \{-1, 0\}$
(e) $S = \{0, 1, 2\} \cap \{-1, 0\}$

2 Repeat question 1 with

(a) $S = \{0, 1, 2\}$
(b) $S = \{x: x^2 = 1\}$
(c) $S = \{x: x^2 < 1\}$
(d) $S = \{x: x^2 > 1\}$
(e) $S = \{-1, 2\} \cup \{1, 2\}$
(f) $S = \{-1, 0\} \cap \{1, 2\}$

3* The following laws are always satisfied for any sets A, B and C. Illustrate the first of these with a Venn diagram.

$$A \cup (B \cap C) = (A \cup B) \cap (A \cup C)$$
$$A \cap (B \cup C) = (A \cap B) \cup (A \cap C)$$

4 Illustrate the first of the following laws for sets with a Venn diagram.

$$\widetilde{A \cup B} = \tilde{A} \cap \tilde{B}$$

$$\widetilde{A \cap B} = \tilde{A} \cup \tilde{B}.$$

5* Show that

$$S = \left\{ x: \frac{x^2 - x}{x^2 - 5x + 6} \leqslant \frac{1}{5} \right\} = \left[-\sqrt{\left(\frac{3}{2}\right)}, + \sqrt{\left(\frac{3}{2}\right)} \right] \cup (2, 3)$$

and illustrate the result using a sketch of

$$y = \frac{x^2 - x}{x^2 - 5x + 6}.$$

6 Show that

$$S = \left\{ x: \frac{1 - x}{x^2 - 5x + 6} \leqslant \frac{1}{5} \right\} = (-\infty, 2) \cup (3, \infty)$$

and illustrate the result using a sketch of

$$y = \frac{1 - x}{x^2 - 5x + 6}.$$

7* Condense the following expressions:

(a) $a \times a \times a \times a \times a \times a \times a \times a$
(b) $b^2 b^3$
(c) $c^5 \times c^{-6}/c^2$
(d) $(d^2)^3$
(e) $8^{2/3}$
(f) $e^{1/3} f^{1/3}$
(g) $g^{0.1} \times g^{0.9}/g^{-0.5}$

8 Complete the square in the expression

$$y = ax^2 + bx + c$$

and hence show, without using calculus, that y has a minimum value of $c - b^2/4a$ at $x = -b/2a$ when $a > 0$. What happens if $a < 0$ or $a = 0$?

1.6 Answers

These are outline answers to the asterisked problems of section 1.5.

1 (a) True, false, false, true.
  (b) True, false (zero is neither positive nor negative), false, true.
  (c) $S = \{1, -3\}$ (see section 1.1). Hence: true, false, true, true.

(d) $S = \{-1, 0, 1, 2\}$. Hence: true, true, false, false.

(e) $S = \{0\}$. Hence: false, true, true, true.

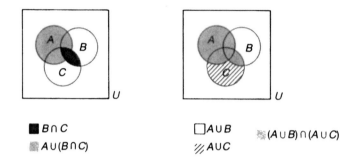

■ $B \cap C$

▨ $A \cup (B \cap C)$

☐ $A \cup B$

▨ $A \cup C$

▨ $(A \cup B) \cap (A \cup C)$

Figure 1.11 Illustration of $A \cup (B \cap C) = (A \cup B) \cap (A \cup C)$.

3 Consult figure 1.11.

5 Observe to begin with that

$$\frac{x^2 - x}{x^2 - 5x + 6} = \frac{x(x - 1)}{(x - 2)(x - 3)}.$$

Thus $x = 2$ and $x = 3$ cannot be in the set. Note also that $(x - 2)(x - 3) > 0$ when '$x < 2$ or $x > 3$' and $(x - 2)(x - 3) < 0$ when $2 < x < 3$ (figure 1.12).

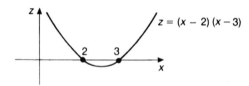

Figure 1.12 The sign of $(x - 2)(x - 3)$.

When $(x - 2)(x - 3) > 0$,

$$\frac{x^2 - x}{x^2 - 5x + 6} \leqslant \frac{1}{5}$$

is the same as

$$5x^2 - 5x \leqslant x^2 - 5x + 6$$

$$4x^2 \leqslant 6$$

$$x^2 \leqslant \frac{3}{2},$$

i.e.

$$-\sqrt{\left(\frac{3}{2}\right)} \leqslant x \leqslant +\sqrt{\left(\frac{3}{2}\right)}$$

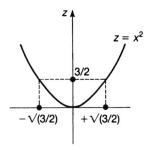

Figure 1.13 When $x^2 \leqslant 3/2$.

When '$x < 2$ or $x > 3$', the inequality in the definition of S therefore reduces to $-\sqrt{(3/2)} \leqslant x \leqslant +\sqrt{(3/2)}$. It follows that *no* values of x with $x > 3$ satisfy the inequality and that the only values of x with $x < 2$ which satisfy the inequality lie in the interval $[-\sqrt{(3/2)}, +\sqrt{(3/2)}]$.

What if $2 < x < 3$? Then $(x-2)(x-3) < 0$ and so the inequality in the definition of S becomes

$$5x^2 - 5x \geqslant x^2 - 5x + 6$$

$$x^2 \geqslant \frac{3}{2},$$

i.e.

$$x \leqslant -\sqrt{\left(\frac{3}{2}\right)} \quad \text{or} \quad x \geqslant +\sqrt{\left(\frac{3}{2}\right)}.$$

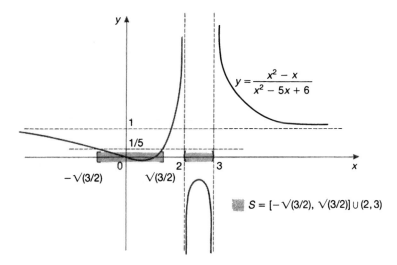

Figure 1.14 The graph identifies S as $[-\sqrt{(3/2)}, +\sqrt{(3/2)}] \cup (2, 3)$.

Observe that $x \leqslant -\sqrt{(3/2)}$ is incompatible with $2 < x < 3$ while $x \geqslant \sqrt{(3/2)}$ is automatically satisfied when $2 < x < 3$. Thus *all* values of x in the interval $(2, 3)$ satisfy the inequality in the definition of S (figure 1.14).

7 (a) a^8; (b) $b^{2+3} = b^5$; (c) $c^{5-6-2} = c^{-3}$; (d) $d^{2 \times 3} = d^6$; (e) $8^{2/3} = (2^3)^{2/3} = [(2^3)^{1/3}]^2 = 2^2 = 4$; (f) $(ef)^{1/3}$; (g) $g^{0.1 + 0.9 - (-0.5)} = g^{1.5} = g^{3/2}$.

2

Matrices and Vectors

2.1 Matrices

An $m \times n$ matrix is a rectangular array of numbers with m rows and n columns. Some examples are given below:

$$A = \begin{pmatrix} 1 & 2 & 3 \\ 4 & 5 & 6 \end{pmatrix} \qquad B = \begin{pmatrix} -1 & 5 & 0 \\ 0 & -2 & -4 \end{pmatrix}$$

$$C = \begin{pmatrix} 1 & 4 \\ 2 & 5 \\ 3 & 6 \end{pmatrix} \qquad D = \begin{pmatrix} -1 & 0 \\ 5 & -2 \\ 0 & -4 \end{pmatrix}.$$

Here A and B are 2×3 matrices while C and D are 3×2 matrices.

When working with matrices, it is important not to get confused about what is a matrix and what is a number, although the notation is not always helpful on this point. For example, the zero matrix, of whatever dimensions, is always denoted by 0. Thus we write

$$0 = \begin{pmatrix} 0 & 0 & 0 \\ 0 & 0 & 0 \end{pmatrix} \qquad \text{or} \qquad 0 = \begin{pmatrix} 0 & 0 \\ 0 & 0 \\ 0 & 0 \end{pmatrix}$$

and you are left to work out from the context whether 0 represents the zero number or a zero matrix (and, in the latter case, what its dimensions are).

To help emphasize the difference between matrices and numbers, the latter are often referred to as *scalars*. For our purposes, the scalars will be real numbers.

In order to do some algebra with matrices, we need to define matrix addition and other matrix operations. Only the simplest ideas will be presented in this section and we shall return to the subject later.

2.1.1 Matrix addition

Two matrices can be added if and only if they have the same dimensions. One simply adds the corresponding entries. For example,

$$A + B = \begin{pmatrix} 1 & 2 & 3 \\ 4 & 5 & 6 \end{pmatrix} + \begin{pmatrix} -1 & 5 & 0 \\ 0 & -2 & -4 \end{pmatrix} = \begin{pmatrix} 0 & 7 & 3 \\ 4 & 3 & 2 \end{pmatrix}$$

$$C + 0 = \begin{pmatrix} 1 & 4 \\ 2 & 5 \\ 3 & 6 \end{pmatrix} + \begin{pmatrix} 0 & 0 \\ 0 & 0 \\ 0 & 0 \end{pmatrix} = \begin{pmatrix} 1 & 4 \\ 2 & 5 \\ 3 & 6 \end{pmatrix} = C.$$

Note that, in the case $C + 0$, dimensions for the zero matrix are assumed which make the addition meaningful. An expression such as

$$A + D = \begin{pmatrix} 1 & 2 & 3 \\ 4 & 5 & 6 \end{pmatrix} + \begin{pmatrix} -1 & 0 \\ 5 & -2 \\ 0 & -4 \end{pmatrix}$$

is completely meaningless because the two matrices A and D do not have the same dimensions.

2.1.2 Scalar multiplication

Any matrix can be multiplied by any scalar. One simply multiplies each entry of the matrix by the scalar. For example,

$$3A = 3\begin{pmatrix} 1 & 2 & 3 \\ 4 & 5 & 6 \end{pmatrix} = \begin{pmatrix} 3 & 6 & 9 \\ 12 & 15 & 18 \end{pmatrix}$$

$$C - D = \begin{pmatrix} 1 & 4 \\ 2 & 5 \\ 3 & 6 \end{pmatrix} + (-1)\begin{pmatrix} -1 & 0 \\ 5 & -2 \\ 0 & -4 \end{pmatrix} = \begin{pmatrix} 2 & 4 \\ -3 & 7 \\ 3 & 10 \end{pmatrix}.$$

2.1.3 Transposition

The *transpose* M' of a matrix M is obtained by making the columns of M into the rows of M'. Thus

$$A' = \begin{pmatrix} 1 & 2 & 3 \\ 4 & 5 & 6 \end{pmatrix}' = \begin{pmatrix} 1 & 4 \\ 2 & 5 \\ 3 & 6 \end{pmatrix} = C$$

$$D' = \begin{pmatrix} -1 & 0 \\ 5 & -2 \\ 0 & -4 \end{pmatrix}' = \begin{pmatrix} -1 & 5 & 0 \\ 0 & -2 & -4 \end{pmatrix} = B.$$

It will be obvious that transposing the transpose just takes us back to where we came from, i.e.

$$(M')' = M.$$

2.1.4 Matrix multiplication

If R has the same number of columns as S has rows, then the matrix product RS is meaningful, but *not otherwise*. Thus it will often be the case that RS is meaningful but SR is not. And even if both RS and SR make sense, they will not usually be equal!

If R is an $m \times n$ matrix and S is an $n \times p$ matrix, then RS is an $m \times p$ matrix. The manner in which the entries of RS are calculated is indicated using the 2×3 matrix A and the 3×2 matrix D as examples. The matrix AD is then 2×2. We have

$$AD = \begin{pmatrix} 1 & 2 & 3 \\ 4 & 5 & 6 \end{pmatrix} \begin{pmatrix} -1 & 0 \\ 5 & -2 \\ 0 & -4 \end{pmatrix} = \begin{pmatrix} 9 & -16 \\ 21 & -34 \end{pmatrix},$$

where the entries of AD have been calculated as follows.

$$9 = (1 \times -1) + (2 \times 5) + (3 \times 0)$$
$$-16 = (1 \times 0) + (2 \times -2) + (3 \times -4)$$
$$21 = (4 \times -1) + (5 \times 5) + (6 \times 0)$$
$$-34 = (4 \times 0) + (5 \times -2) + (6 \times -4).$$

Let us look more closely at the entry -16 in AD. This is in the *first row* and *second column* of AD. It is therefore calculated from the *first row* of A and the *second column* of D.

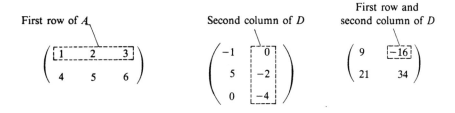

To get -16 from the first row of A and the second column of D, multiply the corresponding entries and then sum the result. Thus

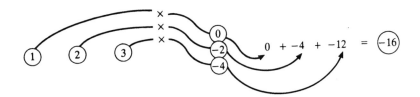

As another example, we have that

$$BC = \begin{pmatrix} -1 & 5 & 0 \\ 0 & -2 & -4 \end{pmatrix} \begin{pmatrix} 1 & 4 \\ 2 & 5 \\ 3 & 6 \end{pmatrix} = \begin{pmatrix} 9 & 21 \\ -16 & -34 \end{pmatrix}.$$

Notice that $BC = (AD)'$ and recall that $B = D'$ and $C = A'$. We therefore have an instance of the general rule that *transposition reverses the order* of a product, i.e.

$$(RS)' = S'R'.$$

We can also consider CB. Since C is 3×2 and B is 2×3, the result is a 3×3 matrix. We have that

$$CB = \begin{pmatrix} 1 & 4 \\ 2 & 5 \\ 3 & 6 \end{pmatrix} \begin{pmatrix} -1 & 5 & 0 \\ 0 & -2 & -4 \end{pmatrix} = \begin{pmatrix} -1 & -3 & -16 \\ -2 & 0 & -20 \\ -3 & 3 & -24 \end{pmatrix}.$$

Notice that BC is not the same as CB. They do not even have the same dimensions.

The zero matrix acts precisely as one would expect: the result of multiplying anything by a zero matrix is another zero matrix. There is also a unit matrix I with the properties one would anticipate. The unit matrix is always a square matrix but, as with the zero matrix, its precise size usually has to be deduced from the context. The 2×2 unit matrix is

$$I = \begin{pmatrix} 1 & 0 \\ 0 & 1 \end{pmatrix}.$$

The 3×3 unit matrix is

$$I = \begin{pmatrix} 1 & 0 & 0 \\ 0 & 1 & 0 \\ 0 & 0 & 1 \end{pmatrix}.$$

Observe that

$$AI = \begin{pmatrix} 1 & 2 & 3 \\ 4 & 5 & 6 \end{pmatrix} \begin{pmatrix} 1 & 0 & 0 \\ 0 & 1 & 0 \\ 0 & 0 & 1 \end{pmatrix} = \begin{pmatrix} 1 & 2 & 3 \\ 4 & 5 & 6 \end{pmatrix} = A.$$

Similarly,

$$IA = \begin{pmatrix} 1 & 0 \\ 0 & 1 \end{pmatrix} \begin{pmatrix} 1 & 2 & 3 \\ 4 & 5 & 6 \end{pmatrix} = \begin{pmatrix} 1 & 2 & 3 \\ 4 & 5 & 6 \end{pmatrix} = A.$$

2.1.5 Inverse matrices

Only sometimes is it possible to multiply matrices. For example, the product AB is meaningless. Even less often can matrices be divided. One can only divide by a square matrix and then only by a 'non-singular' square matrix. (Dividing by a singular matrix corresponds to dividing numbers by zero.)

To divide by an $n \times n$ square matrix M, we need to calculate its inverse matrix M^{-1}. For a 2×2 matrix

$$M = \begin{pmatrix} a & b \\ c & d \end{pmatrix}$$

we have that

$$M^{-1} = \frac{1}{ad - bc} \begin{pmatrix} d & -b \\ -c & a \end{pmatrix}.$$

It is easy to check that the requirement for an inverse matrix, namely

$$MM^{-1} = M^{-1}M = I$$

is satisfied. It is also easy to see that the condition that M be non-singular is that $ad - bc \neq 0$. The calculation of inverses of $n \times n$ non-singular matrices is left to a later stage (sections 6.9 and 6.11.4).

We close this section with some incidental results about inverses. Although it may not be true that $RS = SR$ even when both products make sense, it is always true that $(RS)T = R(ST)$ when the products make sense. Thus we can just write RST without specifying which product is to be calculated first.

Now suppose that P and Q are non-singular $n \times n$ matrices. Then,

$$(Q^{-1}P^{-1})(PQ) = Q^{-1}(P^{-1}P)Q = Q^{-1}IQ = Q^{-1}Q = I.$$

Also

$$(PQ)(Q^{-1}P^{-1}) = P(QQ^{-1})P^{-1} = PIP^{-1} = PP^{-1} = I.$$

Thus $Q^{-1}P^{-1}$ satisfies the requirement for an inverse to the $n \times n$ matrix PQ, i.e.

$$(PQ)^{-1} = Q^{-1}P^{-1}.$$

This is reminiscent of our earlier result about transposes, i.e. $(RS)' = S'R'$.

Finally, we note that a symmetric matrix S has the property that $S = S'$. A symmetric matrix is therefore necessarily square. An example of a symmetric matrix is

$$S = \begin{pmatrix} 1 & 3 & 2 \\ 3 & 2 & 4 \\ 2 & 4 & 3 \end{pmatrix}.$$

Any unit matrix I is, of course, symmetric. It follows, if M is any non-singular $n \times n$ matrix, that since

$$MM^{-1} = M^{-1}M = I$$

then

$$(MM^{-1})' = (M^{-1}M)' = I' = I$$
$$(M^{-1})'M' = M'(M^{-1})' = I.$$

Thus $(M^{-1})'$ satisfies the requirement for an inverse to the $n \times n$ matrix M', i.e.

$$(M')^{-1} = (M^{-1})'.$$

2.2   Vectors

An $n \times 1$ matrix

$$x = \begin{pmatrix} x_1 \\ x_2 \\ \vdots \\ x_n \end{pmatrix}$$

is called a *column vector*. The $1 \times n$ matrix

$$x' = (x_1, x_2, \ldots, x_n)$$

is called a *row vector*. Usually we work with column vectors for reasons which will emerge later.

A vector is essentially a list of n real numbers. It is therefore natural to denote the set of all n-dimensional vectors by $\mathbb{R}^n$. The figures below are all of $\mathbb{R}^2$ for obvious reasons, but the results they illustrate are true in general.

One can think of a vector x as specifying a location in $\mathbb{R}^n$ as in figure 2.1(a). Or one can think of x as specifying the displacement indicated by the arrow in figure 2.1(b). In the latter case, one need not draw the blunt end of the arrow at the zero vector 0.

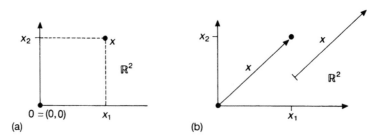

Figure 2.1   (a) Specifying location; (b) specifying displacement.

The description in terms of displacements provides an easily understood interpretation of the addition of two vectors and of the scalar multiplication of a vector. The sum $x + y$ of two vectors is simply the displacement obtained by making the displacement x followed by the displacement y (figure 2.2). This explains why the rule for calculating $x + y$ is called the parallelogram law. If λ (the Greek letter 'lambda') is a scalar, the vector λx is the displacement in the same direction as x whose magnitude is λ times that of x. (If λ is negative, this is to be understood as meaning that λx points in the opposite direction to x.)

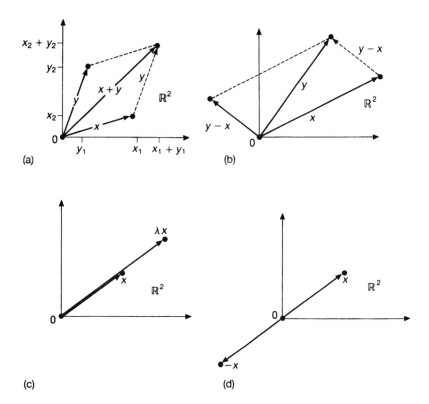

Figure 2.2 (a) Vector addition; (b) vector subtraction; (c) scalar multiplication; (d) scalar multiplication when $\lambda = -1$.

The length of the arrow representing the vector x is called its *norm* (or *absolute value* or *modulus*) and is denoted by $\|x\|$. Pythagoras's theorem tells us that

$$\|x\| = (x_1^2 + x_2^2 + \cdots + x_n^2)^{1/2}.$$

Consulting figure 2.2(b), we see that the distance between x and y (thought of as locations) must be

$$\|x - y\| = [(x_1 - y_1)^2 + (x_2 - y_2)^2 + \cdots + (x_n - y_n)^2]^{1/2}.$$

The norm of a vector allows us to deal with magnitudes. To deal with directions, the idea of the inner product of two vectors x and y is useful.

If x and y are two n-dimensional column vectors, then their *inner product* $x \cdot y$ is defined by

$$x \cdot y = x_1 y_1 + x_2 y_2 + \cdots + x_n y_n.$$

Thus

$$x \cdot y = x' y = (x_1, x_2, \ldots, x_n) \begin{pmatrix} y_1 \\ y_2 \\ \vdots \\ y_n \end{pmatrix}.$$

The following properties of inner products are easy to check:

1 $x \cdot x = \| x \|^2$
2 $x \cdot y = y \cdot x$
3 $x \cdot (\alpha y + \beta z) = \alpha (x \cdot y) + \beta (x \cdot z)$ (α and β scalars)

From these rules we can deduce that

$$\begin{aligned} \| x - y \|^2 &= (x - y) \cdot (x - y) \\ &= (x - y) \cdot x - (x - y) \cdot y \\ &= x \cdot (x - y) - y \cdot (x - y) \\ &= x \cdot x - x \cdot y - y \cdot x + y \cdot y \\ &= \| x \|^2 - 2 x \cdot y + \| y \|^2. \end{aligned}$$

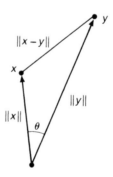

Figure 2.3 Computing $\| x - y \|$ by the cosine rule.

But the 'cosine rule' in figure 2.3 tells us that

$$\| x - y \|^2 = \| x \|^2 + \| y \|^2 - 2 \| x \| \cdot \| y \| \cos \theta$$

where θ (the Greek letter 'theta') is the angle between the vectors x and y. Thus

$$x \cdot y = \| x \| \cdot \| y \| \cos \theta.$$

In particular, we obtain the important condition for two vectors to be orthogonal (i.e. perpendicular, 'at right angles'). If θ is a right angle ($\theta = 90°$ or $\theta = \pi/2$ rad), then $\cos \theta = 0$. Two vectors x and y are therefore orthogonal when

$$x \cdot y = 0.$$

Examples
1 Find the distance between the vectors $x = (0, 1, 2)'$ and $y = (-1, 3, 4)'$ in $\mathbb{R}^3$.

We have that

$$\| x - y \| = [(0 - (-1))^2 + (1 - 3)^2 + (2 - 4)^2]^{1/2}$$
$$= (1 + 4 + 4)^{1/2} = \sqrt{9} = 3.$$

2 Find the angle between the vectors $x = (0, 3, 4)'$ and $y = (12, 5, 0)'$ in $\mathbb{R}^3$.

We have that

$$\| x \| = (0^2 + 3^2 + 4^2)^{1/2} = \sqrt{(25)} = 5$$
$$\| y \| = \{(12)^2 + 5^2 + 0^2\}^{1/2} = \sqrt{(169)} = 13$$
$$x \cdot y = 0 \times 12 + 3 \times 5 + 4 \times 0 = 15.$$

It follows that

$$\cos \theta = \frac{x \cdot y}{\| x \| \cdot \| y \|} = \frac{15}{5 \times 13} = \frac{5}{13}.$$

3 Prove that the vectors $x = (0, 1, -1)'$ and $y = (13, 2, 2)'$ are orthogonal in $\mathbb{R}^3$.

We have that

$$x \cdot y = 0 \times 13 + 1 \times 2 + -1 \times 2 = 0 + 2 - 2 = 0.$$

2.3 Lines and planes

Suppose that p is a fixed non-zero vector and that x_0 is any fixed vector. Consider the set of all vectors x which satisfy the equation

$$p \cdot (x - x_0) = 0.$$

This says that the vector p and the vector $x - x_0$ are orthogonal.

Figure 2.4 shows that, in $\mathbb{R}^3$, this means that x must lie in the plane through x_0 which is orthogonal to p. Writing $p \cdot x_0 = k$, we can therefore say that

$$p \cdot x = k,$$

i.e.

$$p_1 x_1 + p_2 x_2 + \cdots + p_n x_n = k,$$

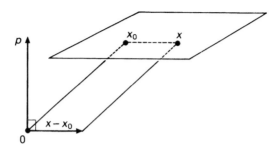

Figure 2.4 x lies on the plane through x_0 orthogonal to p.

where k is a constant, is the equation of a plane when $n = 3$. Moreover the vector p is a *normal* to this plane (i.e. it is orthogonal to the plane).

For general n we say that $p \cdot x = k$ is the equation of a 'hyperplane'. Let us concentrate, however, on the case $n = 2$. The equation then becomes

$$p_1 x_1 + p_2 x_2 = k$$

and we have the equation of a line in $\mathbb{R}^2$ (figure 2.5).

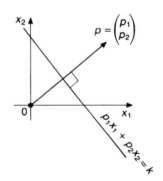

Figure 2.5 Equation of a hyperplane when $n = 2$.

This observation provides an opportunity to offer some reminders about straight lines in $\mathbb{R}^2$. If the equation of a straight line in $\mathbb{R}^2$ is given in the form

$$y = mx + c$$

then m is the *slope* of the line. This means that y increases m units for each unit that x increases (figure 2.6).

Sometimes it is more convenient to write the equation of a straight line in $\mathbb{R}^2$ in the 'intercept form'

$$\frac{x}{a} + \frac{y}{b} = 1.$$

The numbers a and b are then respectively the x and y intercepts (figure 2.7).

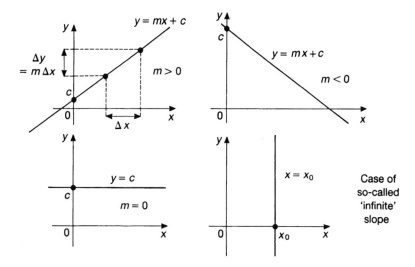

Figure 2.6 Graphs of straight lines for various slopes.

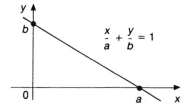

Figure 2.7 Graph of a line in intercept form:

$$\frac{x}{a} + \frac{y}{b} = 1$$

Returning to the equation $p_1 x_1 + p_2 x_2 = k$, we observe that, not only is the vector $\mathbf{p} = (p_1, p_2)'$ orthogonal to the line it represents, but also the line has slope $m = -p_1/p_2$ (unless $p_2 = 0$). The x_1 intercept is k/p_1 (unless $p_1 = 0$) and the x_2 intercept is k/p_2 (unless $p_2 = 0$) (figure 2.8).

Examples

1   What is the slope of a line in $\mathbb{R}^2$ with x intercept 2 and y intercept 4?

We can draw a picture from which the answer will be obvious, or observe that the intercept form of the line is

$$\frac{x}{2} + \frac{y}{4} = 1$$

which can be rewritten as

$$y = -2x + 4.$$

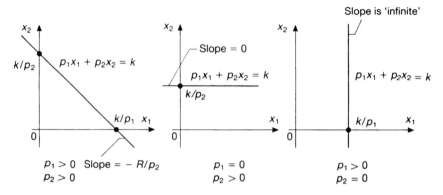

Figure 2.8 Computing the intercept.

The slope is therefore $m = -2$.

2 What is the equation of a line in $\mathbb{R}^2$ with slope -3 which passes through the point $(1, 1)'$?

We can observe immediately that the equation must be of the form

$$y = -3x + c.$$

To find c, we note that the point $(x, y)' = (1, 1)'$ must lie on the line and hence satisfy the equation. Thus

$$1 = -3 + c$$
$$c = 4.$$

The anwer is therefore

$$y = -3x + 4.$$

Alternatively, we can use the formula for the line of slope m through the point (x_1, y_1), i.e.

$$m = \frac{y - y_1}{x - x_1}$$

(figure 2.9). The same formula will also provide the equation for the straight line through $(x_1, y_1)'$ and $(x_2, y_2)'$. Because $m = (y_2 - y_1)/(x_2 - x_1)$, we obtain that

$$\frac{y_2 - y_1}{x_2 - x_1} = \frac{y - y_1}{x - x_1},$$

i.e.

$$\frac{y - y_1}{y_2 - y_1} = \frac{x - x_1}{x_2 - x_1}.$$

3 What is the equation of the plane in $\mathbb{R}^3$ which is orthogonal to the vector $u = (1, 1, 2)'$ and which passes through the point $v = (0, 1, 3)'$?

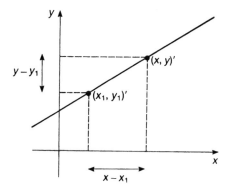

Figure 2.9 The slope is $(y - y_1)/(x - x_1)$.

The answer is

$$u \cdot (x - v) = 0,$$

i.e.

$$u_1(x_1 - v_1) + u_2(x_2 - v_2) + u_3(x_3 - v_3) = 0,$$

i.e.

$$1(x_1 - 0) + 1(x_2 - 1) + 2(x_3 - 3) = 0,$$

i.e.

$$x_1 + x_2 + 2x_3 = 7.$$

4   What is the equation of the hyperplane in $\mathbb{R}^5$ which is orthogonal to the vector $u = (1, 1, 2, 0, 1)'$ and which passes through the point $v = (0, 1, 3, 1, 0)'$?

The answer is

$$u \cdot (x - v) = 0,$$

i.e.

$$u_1(x_1 - v_1) + u_2(x_2 - v_2) + u_3(x_3 - v_3) + u_4(x_4 - v_4) + u_5(x_5 - v_5) = 0,$$

i.e.

$$1(x_1 - 0) + 1(x_2 - 1) + 2(x_3 - 3) + 0(x_4 - 1) + 1(x_5 - 0) = 0,$$

i.e.

$$x_1 + x_2 + 2x_3 + x_5 = 7.$$

The lesson is that a line, a plane or a hyperplane is specified by one 'linear' equation.

2.4 Exercises

1* Given

$$A = \begin{pmatrix} 0 & 1 \\ 2 & 3 \end{pmatrix} \qquad B = \begin{pmatrix} -1 & 2 \\ -2 & 1 \end{pmatrix} \qquad C = \begin{pmatrix} 1 & 2 \\ 2 & 4 \end{pmatrix}$$

find (a) $2A$, (b) $B + C$, (c) $A - B$, (d) $2A + 3B$.

2 Given

$$A = \begin{pmatrix} 1 & 0 & 4 \\ -2 & 1 & 3 \end{pmatrix} \qquad B = \begin{pmatrix} -1 & 0 & -2 \\ 2 & 0 & 1 \end{pmatrix} \qquad C = \begin{pmatrix} 0 & 1 & -3 \\ 0 & -1 & -3 \end{pmatrix}$$

find (a) $3A$, (b) $A + C$, (c) $B - C$, (d) $3A - 4C$.

3* Answer the following questions for the matrices

$$A = \begin{pmatrix} 2 & 5 \\ 0 & 1 \\ 1 & 2 \end{pmatrix} \qquad B = \begin{pmatrix} 1 & 2 \\ 0 & 1 \end{pmatrix} \qquad C = \begin{pmatrix} 2 & 1 \\ 1 & 0 \end{pmatrix}.$$

(a) Why is AB defined? Why is BA not defined? Calculate AB.
(b) Why are both BC and CB defined? Is it true that $BC = CB$?
(c) Work out $(AB)C$ and $A(BC)$ and show that these are equal.

4 Repeat question 3 for the matrices

$$A = \begin{pmatrix} 2 & 5 \\ 0 & 1 \end{pmatrix} \qquad B = \begin{pmatrix} 1 & 2 & 1 \\ 2 & 0 & 0 \end{pmatrix} \qquad C = \begin{pmatrix} 2 & 2 \\ 0 & 1 \\ 5 & 0 \end{pmatrix}.$$

5* For the matrices of question 3, find (a) A', (b) B', (c) C', (d) $(2B - 3C)'$, (e) $(B')'$, (f) $(AB)'$, (g) $(ABC)'$.
    Verify that C is symmetric, that $(2B - 3C)' = 2B' - 3C'$, that $(B')' = B$, that $(AB)' = B'A'$ and that $(ABC)' = C'B'A'$.

6 For the matrices of question 4, find (a) A', (b) B', (c) C', (d) $(2B' - 3C)'$, (e) $(BC)'$, (f) $(ABC)'$.
    Verify that $(2B' - 3C)' = 2B - 3C'$, that BC is symmetric and that $(ABC)' = C'A'B'$.

7* Find the inverse matrices of the 2×2 non-singular matrices A and B of question 1. Verify that $AA^{-1} = A^{-1}A = I$ and that $BB^{-1} = B^{-1}B = I$.
    Explain why the 2×2 matrix C of question 1 is singular. Check that the matrix equation

$$X^2 = 5X$$

is satisfied by the matrix $X = C$. Explain why the only non-singular matrix that satisfies this equation is $X = 5I$.

8   Given

$$A = \begin{pmatrix} 1 & 2 \\ 4 & 3 \end{pmatrix} \qquad B = \begin{pmatrix} 1 & 1 \\ 1 & 1 \end{pmatrix} \qquad C = \begin{pmatrix} 1 & -1 \\ 1 & -1 \end{pmatrix}$$

explain why A is non-singular and find its inverse. Check that $AA^{-1} = A^{-1}A = I$. Explain why the matrices B and C are singular. Verify that B and C satisfy the equation

$$CB = 0$$

where 0 is the zero matrix. (What will be its dimensions in this context?) Show that, if P and Q are $n \times n$ matrices and either P or Q is non-singular, then the equation $PQ = 0$ implies that the other matrix is the $n \times n$ zero matrix.

9*   Show that the system of 'linear equations'

$$-x_1 + 2x_2 = 3$$
$$-2x_1 + x_2 = 4$$

can be expressed in the form $Bx = b$, where B is as in question 1 and

$$x = \begin{pmatrix} x_1 \\ x_2 \end{pmatrix} \qquad b = \begin{pmatrix} 3 \\ 4 \end{pmatrix}.$$

Deduce that the system has a unique solution for x_1 and x_2 given by

$$x = B^{-1}b.$$

Use this formula to calculate the solution values (B^{-1} was found in question 7). Verify that these values are correct by substituting them in the equations.

10   Show that the left-hand system of 'linear equations'

$$x_1 + 2x_2 = 3 \qquad\qquad x_1 + 2x_2 = 0$$
$$2x_1 + 4x_2 = 4 \qquad\qquad 2x_1 + 4x_2 = 0$$

can be expressed in the form $Cx = b$, where C is as in question 1 and

$$x = \begin{pmatrix} x_1 \\ x_2 \end{pmatrix} \qquad b = \begin{pmatrix} 3 \\ 4 \end{pmatrix}.$$

Recall that C is singular (question 7). Explain why the left-hand system has *no* solutions and the right-hand system has *many* solutions.

11*   Why is the matrix $M'M$ always defined for any $m \times n$ matrix M? Why is $M'M$ always symmetric? If $M'M$ is non-singular (it need not be in the general case), show that $L = (M'M)^{-1}M'$ satisfies

$$LM = I.$$

Verify this formula in the case when M is the matrix A of question 3. The matrix ML is also defined, but verify that $ML \neq I$ when $M = A$.

12 Why is the matrix MM' always defined for any $m \times n$ matrix M? Why is MM' always symmetric? If MM' is non-singular (it need not be in the general case), show that $R = M'(MM')^{-1}$ satisfies

$$MR = I.$$

Verify this formula in the case when M is the matrix A of question 2. The matrix RM is also defined, but verify that $RM \neq I$ when $M = A$.

13* Given the 2×1 column vectors

$$x = \begin{pmatrix} 1 \\ 2 \end{pmatrix} \quad y = \begin{pmatrix} -3 \\ 4 \end{pmatrix} \quad z = \begin{pmatrix} 2 \\ 0 \end{pmatrix}$$

find (a) $x + y$, (b) $2y$, (c) $-3z$, (d) $x - z$, (e) $2x + y$. Illustrate each result geometrically.

14 Repeat question 13 for the 2×1 column vectors

$$x = \begin{pmatrix} 0 \\ 3 \end{pmatrix} \quad y = \begin{pmatrix} -1 \\ -2 \end{pmatrix} \quad z = \begin{pmatrix} -2 \\ 3 \end{pmatrix}.$$

15* If x and y are $n \times 1$ column vectors, explain why $x'y$ and xy' are both defined but $x'y \neq xy'$ unless $n = 1$. Show that it is always true that $x'y = y'x$.

16 Given the 3×1 column vectors

$$x = \begin{pmatrix} 1 \\ 2 \\ 3 \end{pmatrix} \quad y = \begin{pmatrix} -2 \\ 1 \\ -3 \end{pmatrix} \quad z = \begin{pmatrix} -2 \\ -1 \\ 1 \end{pmatrix}$$

find (a) $\|x\|$, (b) $\|x - y\|$, (c) $x \cdot x$, (d) $x \cdot y$, (e) $x \cdot z$, (f) $x \cdot (2y + 3z)$. Verify that $x \cdot x = \|x\|^2$ and that $x \cdot (2y + 3z) = 2x \cdot y + 3x \cdot z$.
 What is the distance from x to 0? What is the distance from x to y? Which two of the vectors are orthogonal?

17* Explain why the 'triangle inequality'

$$\|x + y\| \leq \|x\| + \|y\|$$

is satisfied.

18 Explain why the set of 2×1 column vectors x which satisfies the equation $\|x\| = r$ is a circle with centre 0 and radius r. What will the set be in $\mathbb{R}^3$?

2.5 Answers

1
(a)

$$2A = 2\begin{pmatrix} 0 & 1 \\ 2 & 3 \end{pmatrix} = \begin{pmatrix} 0 & 2 \\ 4 & 6 \end{pmatrix}.$$

(b)

$$B + C = \begin{pmatrix} -1 & 2 \\ -2 & 1 \end{pmatrix} + \begin{pmatrix} 1 & 2 \\ 2 & 4 \end{pmatrix} = \begin{pmatrix} 0 & 4 \\ 0 & 5 \end{pmatrix}.$$

(c)

$$A - B = \begin{pmatrix} 0 & 1 \\ 2 & 3 \end{pmatrix} - \begin{pmatrix} -1 & 2 \\ -2 & 1 \end{pmatrix} = \begin{pmatrix} 1 & -1 \\ 4 & 2 \end{pmatrix}.$$

(d)

$$2A + 3B = 2\begin{pmatrix} 0 & 1 \\ 2 & 3 \end{pmatrix} + 3\begin{pmatrix} -1 & 2 \\ -2 & 1 \end{pmatrix}$$

$$= \begin{pmatrix} 0 & 2 \\ 4 & 6 \end{pmatrix} + \begin{pmatrix} -3 & 6 \\ -6 & 3 \end{pmatrix} = \begin{pmatrix} -3 & 8 \\ -2 & 9 \end{pmatrix}.$$

3　(a) A is 3×2, B is 2×2. AB is defined because A has the same number of columns as B has rows, namely two. BA is not defined because B has two columns and A has three rows.

$$AB = \begin{pmatrix} 2 & 5 \\ 0 & 1 \\ 1 & 2 \end{pmatrix}\begin{pmatrix} 1 & 2 \\ 0 & 1 \end{pmatrix} = \begin{pmatrix} 2 \times 1 + 5 \times 0 & 2 \times 2 + 5 \times 1 \\ 0 \times 1 + 1 \times 0 & 0 \times 2 + 1 \times 1 \\ 1 \times 1 + 2 \times 0 & 1 \times 2 + 2 \times 1 \end{pmatrix} = \begin{pmatrix} 2 & 9 \\ 0 & 1 \\ 1 & 4 \end{pmatrix}.$$

(b)　BC and CB are both defined because B and C both have the same number of rows and columns, namely two. It is not true that $BC = CB$ because

$$BC = \begin{pmatrix} 1 & 2 \\ 0 & 1 \end{pmatrix}\begin{pmatrix} 2 & 1 \\ 1 & 0 \end{pmatrix} = \begin{pmatrix} 1 \times 2 + 2 \times 1 & 1 \times 1 + 2 \times 0 \\ 0 \times 2 + 1 \times 1 & 0 \times 1 + 1 \times 0 \end{pmatrix} = \begin{pmatrix} 4 & 1 \\ 1 & 0 \end{pmatrix}$$

and

$$CB = \begin{pmatrix} 2 & 1 \\ 1 & 0 \end{pmatrix}\begin{pmatrix} 1 & 2 \\ 0 & 1 \end{pmatrix} = \begin{pmatrix} 2 \times 1 + 1 \times 0 & 2 \times 2 + 1 \times 1 \\ 1 \times 1 + 0 \times 0 & 1 \times 2 + 0 \times 1 \end{pmatrix} = \begin{pmatrix} 2 & 5 \\ 1 & 2 \end{pmatrix}.$$

(c)　$(AB)C = A(BC)$ because

$$(AB)C = \begin{pmatrix} 2 & 9 \\ 0 & 1 \\ 1 & 4 \end{pmatrix}\begin{pmatrix} 2 & 1 \\ 1 & 0 \end{pmatrix} = \begin{pmatrix} 2 \times 2 + 9 \times 1 & 2 \times 1 + 9 \times 0 \\ 0 \times 2 + 1 \times 1 & 0 \times 1 + 1 \times 0 \\ 1 \times 2 + 4 \times 1 & 1 \times 1 + 4 \times 0 \end{pmatrix} = \begin{pmatrix} 13 & 2 \\ 1 & 0 \\ 6 & 1 \end{pmatrix}$$

$$A(BC) = \begin{pmatrix} 2 & 5 \\ 0 & 1 \\ 1 & 2 \end{pmatrix}\begin{pmatrix} 4 & 1 \\ 1 & 0 \end{pmatrix} = \begin{pmatrix} 2 \times 4 + 5 \times 1 & 2 \times 1 + 5 \times 0 \\ 0 \times 4 + 1 \times 1 & 0 \times 1 + 1 \times 0 \\ 1 \times 4 + 2 \times 1 & 1 \times 1 + 2 \times 0 \end{pmatrix} = \begin{pmatrix} 13 & 2 \\ 1 & 0 \\ 6 & 1 \end{pmatrix}.$$

5
(a)

$$A' = \begin{pmatrix} 2 & 5 \\ 0 & 1 \\ 1 & 2 \end{pmatrix}' = \begin{pmatrix} 2 & 0 & 1 \\ 5 & 1 & 2 \end{pmatrix}.$$

(b)

$$B' = \begin{pmatrix} 1 & 2 \\ 0 & 1 \end{pmatrix}' = \begin{pmatrix} 1 & 0 \\ 2 & 1 \end{pmatrix}.$$

(c)

$$C' = \begin{pmatrix} 2 & 1 \\ 1 & 0 \end{pmatrix}' = \begin{pmatrix} 2 & 1 \\ 1 & 0 \end{pmatrix} = C.$$

Thus, since $C' = C$, C is symmetric.

(d)

$$2B - 3C = 2\begin{pmatrix} 1 & 2 \\ 0 & 1 \end{pmatrix} - 3\begin{pmatrix} 2 & 1 \\ 1 & 0 \end{pmatrix} = \begin{pmatrix} -4 & 1 \\ -3 & 2 \end{pmatrix}$$

$$(2B - 3C)' = \begin{pmatrix} -4 & 1 \\ -3 & 2 \end{pmatrix}' = \begin{pmatrix} -4 & -3 \\ 1 & 2 \end{pmatrix}.$$

(e)

$$(B')' = \begin{pmatrix} 1 & 2 \\ 0 & 1 \end{pmatrix}'' = \begin{pmatrix} 1 & 0 \\ 2 & 1 \end{pmatrix}' = \begin{pmatrix} 1 & 2 \\ 0 & 1 \end{pmatrix} = B.$$

(f)

$$(AB)' = \begin{pmatrix} 2 & 9 \\ 0 & 1 \\ 1 & 4 \end{pmatrix}' = \begin{pmatrix} 2 & 0 & 1 \\ 9 & 1 & 4 \end{pmatrix}$$

(see question 3).

$$B'A' = \begin{pmatrix} 1 & 0 \\ 2 & 1 \end{pmatrix}\begin{pmatrix} 2 & 0 & 1 \\ 5 & 1 & 2 \end{pmatrix} = \begin{pmatrix} 2 & 0 & 1 \\ 9 & 1 & 4 \end{pmatrix} = (AB)'.$$

(g)

$$(ABC)' = \begin{pmatrix} 13 & 2 \\ 1 & 0 \\ 6 & 1 \end{pmatrix}' = \begin{pmatrix} 13 & 1 & 6 \\ 2 & 0 & 1 \end{pmatrix}$$

$$C'B'A' = C'(B'A') = \begin{pmatrix} 2 & 1 \\ 1 & 0 \end{pmatrix}\begin{pmatrix} 2 & 0 & 1 \\ 9 & 1 & 4 \end{pmatrix} = \begin{pmatrix} 13 & 1 & 6 \\ 2 & 0 & 1 \end{pmatrix}.$$

7   Using the formula given in section 2.1.5,

$$A^{-1} = \begin{pmatrix} 0 & 1 \\ 2 & 3 \end{pmatrix}^{-1} = \frac{1}{0 \times 3 - 2 \times 1}\begin{pmatrix} 3 & -1 \\ -2 & 0 \end{pmatrix} = -\frac{1}{2}\begin{pmatrix} 3 & -1 \\ -2 & 0 \end{pmatrix}$$

$$AA^{-1} = -\frac{1}{2}\begin{pmatrix} 0 & 1 \\ 2 & 3 \end{pmatrix}\begin{pmatrix} 3 & -1 \\ -2 & 0 \end{pmatrix} = -\frac{1}{2}\begin{pmatrix} -2 & 0 \\ 0 & -2 \end{pmatrix} = \begin{pmatrix} 1 & 0 \\ 0 & 1 \end{pmatrix} = I$$

$$A^{-1}A = -\frac{1}{2}\begin{pmatrix} 3 & -1 \\ -2 & 0 \end{pmatrix}\begin{pmatrix} 0 & 1 \\ 2 & 3 \end{pmatrix} = -\frac{1}{2}\begin{pmatrix} -2 & 0 \\ 0 & -2 \end{pmatrix} = \begin{pmatrix} 1 & 0 \\ 0 & 1 \end{pmatrix} = I$$

$$B^{-1} = \begin{pmatrix} -1 & 2 \\ -2 & 1 \end{pmatrix}^{-1} = \frac{1}{-1 \times 1 - 2 \times -2}\begin{pmatrix} 1 & -2 \\ 2 & -1 \end{pmatrix} = \frac{1}{3}\begin{pmatrix} 1 & -2 \\ 2 & -1 \end{pmatrix}$$

$$BB^{-1} = \frac{1}{3}\begin{pmatrix} -1 & 2 \\ -2 & 1 \end{pmatrix}\begin{pmatrix} 1 & -2 \\ 2 & -1 \end{pmatrix} = \frac{1}{3}\begin{pmatrix} 3 & 0 \\ 0 & 3 \end{pmatrix} = \begin{pmatrix} 1 & 0 \\ 0 & 1 \end{pmatrix} = I$$

$$B^{-1}B = \frac{1}{3}\begin{pmatrix} 1 & -2 \\ 2 & -1 \end{pmatrix}\begin{pmatrix} -1 & 2 \\ -2 & 1 \end{pmatrix} = \frac{1}{3}\begin{pmatrix} 3 & 0 \\ 0 & 3 \end{pmatrix} = \begin{pmatrix} 1 & 0 \\ 0 & 1 \end{pmatrix} = I.$$

The matrix C is singular because, if

$$C = \begin{pmatrix} 1 & 2 \\ 2 & 4 \end{pmatrix} = \begin{pmatrix} a & b \\ c & d \end{pmatrix},$$

then $ad - bc = 1 \times 4 - 2 \times 2 = 0$.

$$C^2 = C \cdot C = \begin{pmatrix} 1 & 2 \\ 2 & 4 \end{pmatrix}\begin{pmatrix} 1 & 2 \\ 2 & 4 \end{pmatrix} = \begin{pmatrix} 5 & 10 \\ 10 & 20 \end{pmatrix} = 5\begin{pmatrix} 1 & 2 \\ 2 & 4 \end{pmatrix} = 5C$$

and so $X = C$ satisfies the matrix equation $X^2 = 5X$.

If X is *non-singular* and $X^2 = 5X$, then X^{-1} exists. Multiplying both sides of $X^2 = 5X$ on the right by X^{-1}, we obtain

$$X \cdot X \cdot X^{-1} = 5X \cdot X^{-1}$$
$$X(XX^{-1}) = 5(XX^{-1})$$
$$XI = 5I$$
$$X = 5I.$$

(In this case we could equally well have multiplied both sides of $X^2 = 5X$ by X^{-1} *on the left*. But usually it will matter whether a multiplication is on the left or on the right, because AB need not be equal to BA.)

9

$$Bx = \begin{pmatrix} -1 & 2 \\ -2 & 1 \end{pmatrix} \begin{pmatrix} x_1 \\ x_2 \end{pmatrix} = \begin{pmatrix} -x_1 + 2x_2 \\ -2x_1 + x_2 \end{pmatrix} \qquad b = \begin{pmatrix} 3 \\ 4 \end{pmatrix}.$$

Thus $Bx = b$ if and only if

$$-x_1 + 2x_2 = 3$$
$$-2x_1 + x_2 = 4.$$

In question 7 we saw that B is non-singular and that

$$B^{-1} = \frac{1}{3} \begin{pmatrix} 1 & -2 \\ 2 & -1 \end{pmatrix}.$$

Multiplying both sides of the equation $Bx = b$ *on the left* (it would make no sense to multiply on the right), we obtain that

$$B^{-1}(Bx) = B^{-1}b$$
$$(B^{-1}B)x = B^{-1}b$$
$$Ix = B^{-1}b$$
$$x = B^{-1}b$$

and so $x = B^{-1}b$ is the unique solution of the system. The solution values of x_1 and x_2 are therefore given by

$$\begin{pmatrix} x_1 \\ x_2 \end{pmatrix} = x = B^{-1}b = \frac{1}{3} \begin{pmatrix} 1 & -2 \\ 2 & -1 \end{pmatrix} \begin{pmatrix} 3 \\ 4 \end{pmatrix} = \frac{1}{3} \begin{pmatrix} -5 \\ 2 \end{pmatrix} = \begin{pmatrix} -5/3 \\ 2/3 \end{pmatrix}$$

and so $x_1 = -5/3$ and $x_2 = 2/3$. To verify that these answers are correct, we substitute back in the original system to obtain

$$-x_1 + 2x_2 = -(-5/3) + 2(2/3) = 9/3 = 3$$
$$-2x_1 + x_2 = -2(-5/3) + (2/3) = 12/3 = 4.$$

11   If M is $m \times n$, then M' is $n \times m$. Thus $M'M$ is defined because M' has the same number of columns as M has rows, namely m. The matrix $M'M$ is symmetric because

$$(M'M)' = M'(M')' = M'M$$

(transposition reverses products). If $L = (M'M)^{-1}M'$, then

$$LM = ((M'M)^{-1}M')M = (M'M)^{-1}(M'M) = I.$$

When $M = A$ in question 3,

$$M'M = \begin{pmatrix} 2 & 0 & 1 \\ 5 & 1 & 2 \end{pmatrix} \begin{pmatrix} 2 & 5 \\ 0 & 1 \\ 1 & 2 \end{pmatrix} = \begin{pmatrix} 5 & 12 \\ 12 & 30 \end{pmatrix}$$

$$(M'M)^{-1} = \frac{1}{150 - 144}\begin{pmatrix} 30 & -12 \\ -12 & 5 \end{pmatrix} = \frac{1}{6}\begin{pmatrix} 30 & -12 \\ -12 & 5 \end{pmatrix}$$

$$L = (M'M)^{-1}M' = \frac{1}{6}\begin{pmatrix} 30 & -12 \\ -12 & 5 \end{pmatrix}\begin{pmatrix} 2 & 0 & 1 \\ 5 & 1 & 2 \end{pmatrix} = \frac{1}{6}\begin{pmatrix} 0 & -12 & 6 \\ 1 & 5 & -2 \end{pmatrix}$$

$$LM = \frac{1}{6}\begin{pmatrix} 0 & -12 & 6 \\ 1 & 5 & -2 \end{pmatrix}\begin{pmatrix} 2 & 5 \\ 0 & 1 \\ 1 & 2 \end{pmatrix} = \frac{1}{6}\begin{pmatrix} 6 & 0 \\ 0 & 6 \end{pmatrix} = \begin{pmatrix} 1 & 0 \\ 0 & 1 \end{pmatrix} = I$$

$$ML = \frac{1}{6}\begin{pmatrix} 2 & 5 \\ 0 & 1 \\ 1 & 2 \end{pmatrix}\begin{pmatrix} 0 & -12 & 6 \\ 1 & 5 & -2 \end{pmatrix} = \frac{1}{6}\begin{pmatrix} 5 & 1 & 2 \\ 1 & 5 & -2 \\ 2 & -2 & 2 \end{pmatrix} \neq I.$$

13
(a)

$$x + y = \begin{pmatrix} 1 \\ 2 \end{pmatrix} + \begin{pmatrix} -3 \\ 4 \end{pmatrix} = \begin{pmatrix} 1 - 3 \\ 2 + 4 \end{pmatrix} = \begin{pmatrix} -2 \\ 6 \end{pmatrix}.$$

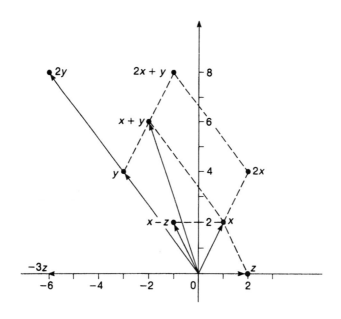

Figure 2.10 Examples of vector addition.

(b)

$$2y = 2\begin{pmatrix} -3 \\ 4 \end{pmatrix} = \begin{pmatrix} -6 \\ 8 \end{pmatrix}.$$

(c)

$$-3z = -3\begin{pmatrix} 2 \\ 0 \end{pmatrix} = \begin{pmatrix} -6 \\ 0 \end{pmatrix}.$$

(d)

$$x - z = \begin{pmatrix} 1 \\ 2 \end{pmatrix} - \begin{pmatrix} 2 \\ 0 \end{pmatrix} = \begin{pmatrix} -1 \\ 2 \end{pmatrix}.$$

(e)

$$2x + y = 2\begin{pmatrix} 1 \\ 2 \end{pmatrix} + \begin{pmatrix} -3 \\ 4 \end{pmatrix} = \begin{pmatrix} 2 \\ 4 \end{pmatrix} + \begin{pmatrix} -3 \\ 4 \end{pmatrix} = \begin{pmatrix} -1 \\ 8 \end{pmatrix}.$$

15   x' is a $1 \times n$ matrix and so has the same number of columns as y which is an $n \times 1$ matrix. The product $x'y$ is a 1×1 matrix, i.e. a number. On the other hand, x is an $n \times 1$ matrix, and so has the same number of columns as y' which is a $1 \times n$ matrix. The product xy' is an $n \times n$ matrix and so cannot be equal to $x'y$ unless $n = 1$. Also,

$$x'y = (x_1, x_2, \ldots, x_n) \begin{pmatrix} y_1 \\ y_2 \\ \vdots \\ y_n \end{pmatrix} = x_1y_1 + x_2y_2 + \cdots + x_ny_n = x \cdot y$$

$$y'x = (y_1, y_2, \ldots, y_n) \begin{pmatrix} x_1 \\ x_2 \\ \vdots \\ x_n \end{pmatrix} = y_1x_1 + y_2x_2 + \cdots + y_nx_n = y \cdot x.$$

It follows that $x'y = y'x$.

Alternatively, notice that a 1×1 matrix must be symmetric. Thus

$$x'y = (x'y)' = y'(x')' = y'x.$$

(Although it is not asked in the question, you may wonder whether it is always true that $xy' = yx'$. The answer is no. For example, when $n = 2$,

$$xy' = \begin{pmatrix} x_1 \\ x_2 \end{pmatrix}(y_1, y_2) = \begin{pmatrix} x_1y_1 & x_1y_2 \\ x_2y_1 & x_2y_2 \end{pmatrix}$$

$$yx' = \begin{pmatrix} y_1 \\ y_2 \end{pmatrix}(x_1, x_2) = \begin{pmatrix} y_1x_1 & y_1x_2 \\ y_2x_1 & y_2x_2 \end{pmatrix}.$$

What is always true is that $xy' = (yx')'$.)

17 The 'triangle inequality'

$$\| x + y \| \leqslant \| x \| + \| y \|$$

says that one side of the shaded triangle is less than the sum of the other two sides (figure 2.11), i.e. 'the shortest distance between two points is a straight line'.

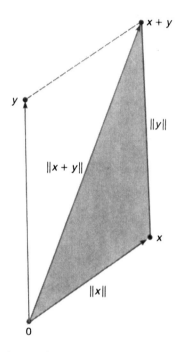

Figure 2.11 The triangle inequality.

3

Modelling Consumer Choice

3.1 Commodity bundles

The set $\mathbb{R}_+$ is the set of all non-negative real numbers, i.e. $\mathbb{R}_+ = [0, \infty) = \{x: x \geqslant 0\}$. The set $\mathbb{R}^n_+$ is the set of all 'non-negative' vectors of dimension n, i.e.

$$\mathbb{R}^n_+ = \{x: x_1 \geqslant 0, x_2 \geqslant 0, \ldots, x_n \geqslant 0\}.$$

The vectors in $\mathbb{R}^n_+$ can be used to represent *commodity bundles*. For example

$$q = \begin{pmatrix} 5 \\ 1 \\ 2 \\ 0.3 \end{pmatrix}$$

might be used to represent the purchases made by a housewife who visits the supermarket and buys the following items on her shopping list:

flour	5 kilos
sugar	1 kilo
milk	2 litres
yeast	0.3 kilos

In theoretical discussions, the space of commodities is often taken to be $\mathbb{R}^2_+$. Partly this is so that the results can be illustrated by diagrams. However, confining attention to only two commodities is not quite so restrictive as it may at first appear. This is because the second commodity can often be thought of as an 'aggregate' of all the commodities that a consumer might wish to buy, excluding the first commodity (figure 3.1).

3.2 Price vectors

The housewife of section 3.1 will have to pay for the commodity bundle q that she purchases. If the relevant prices are

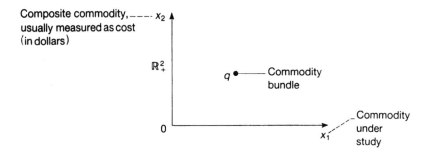

Figure 3.1 Commodity space.

flour	$2 per kilo
sugar	$3 per kilo
milk	$1 per litre
yeast	$30 per kilo

then the value of her commodity bundle is

$$(2 \times 5) + (3 \times 1) + (1 \times 2) + (30 \times 0.3) = \$24.$$

The form of this expression makes it natural to introduce the *price vector* $p \in \mathbb{R}^n_+$. Here

$$p = \begin{pmatrix} 2 \\ 3 \\ 1 \\ 30 \end{pmatrix}.$$

The *value* of the commodity bundle q is then the inner product

$$p \cdot q = p_1 q_1 + p_2 q_2 + \cdots + p_n q_n = 24.$$

3.3 Budget set

In choosing what to buy in the supermarket, the housewife will be constrained by how much money she can spend. The quantity of money she has available is usually called her *income* and denoted by I. Her *budget constraint* is then the inequality

$$p \cdot q \leqslant I.$$

This simply expresses the requirement that the value of what she purchases must not exceed her income.

The set of commodity bundles from which a consumer can choose given her budget constraint is called her *budget set*. This is illustrated in figure 3.2 for the case of two commodities.

The following observations are trivial, but they are still worth making.

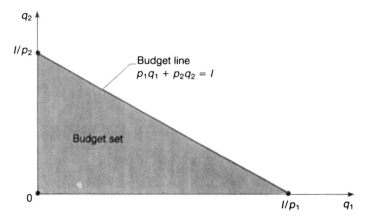

Figure 3.2 The budget set.

1 What happens if one of the prices goes up but everything else stays the same? (Economists say *ceteris paribus*, which means 'other things being equal'.) Obviously, the budget set will become smaller (figure 3.3).

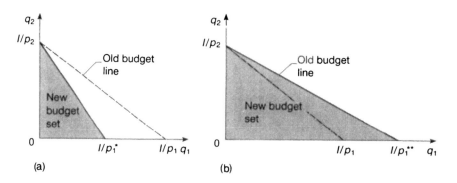

Figure 3.3 (a) Old price is p_1, new price is p_1^*, $p_1^* > p_1$; (b) old price is p_1, new price is p_1^{**}, $p_1 > p_1^{**}$.

2 What happens if the income goes up, but everything else stays the same? Obviously, the budget set will become larger (figure 3.4).
3 What happens if the prices are measured in Polish złotys instead of US dollars? The answer is that the budget set remains unchanged, provided that złotys can be exchanged for dollars at a fixed rate. Suppose that 1 dollar is equivalent to z złotys. Then an income of I dollars is equivalent to Iz złotys. Similarly, if 1 unit of commodity i costs p_i dollars, then it will cost zp_i złotys. The budget constraint in złotys is therefore

$$zp_1q_1 + zp_2q_2 \leqslant zI$$

which is just the same as $p_1q_1 + p_2q_2 \leqslant I$.

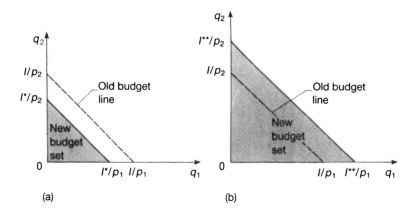

Figure 3.4 (a) Old income is I, new income is I^*, $I^* < I$; (b) old income is I, new income is I^{**}, $I^{**} > I$.

Sometimes it is convenient to take one of the commodities as *numeraire*. This means treating 1 unit of the commodity as the unit of currency. The price of that commodity is then pegged at 1 but, as we have seen, this does not affect the budget set at all.

3.4 Rationing, taxation and subsidies

Rationing If a consumer can buy at most q_1^* of the first commodity the budget set alters as indicated in figure 3.5.

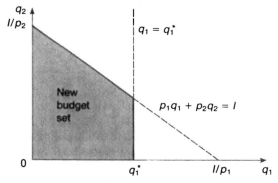

Figure 3.5 Budget set under rationing.

Income tax If income is taxed at a rate of 30 per cent, then a consumer will only have $I^* = 0.7 \times I$ to spend (figure 3.6).

Sales tax A sales tax of 15 per cent means that, if the manufacturer's price for the first commodity is p_1, then the price actually paid by the consumer is

$$p_1^* = p_1 + t_1 = 1.15 \times p_1.$$

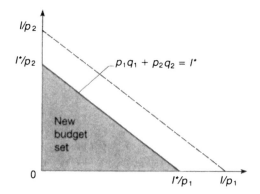

Figure 3.6 Budget set under income tax.

If the consumer buys a quantity q_1 at this price, the government gets t_1q_1 and the manufacturer gets p_1q_1 (figure 3.7).

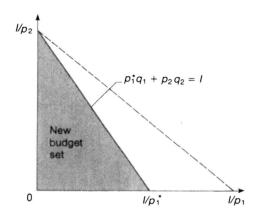

Figure 3.7 Budget set under sales tax.

If the sales tax is imposed only on quantities greater than some level $q_1{}^*$, then the budget set alters as indicated in figure 3.8. For $q_1 \leqslant q_1{}^*$, no taxation is imposed and so the budget constraint remains $p_1q_1 + p_2q_2 \leqslant I$. For $q_1 \geqslant q_1{}^*$, the quantity $q_1 - q_1{}^*$ is taxed and the budget constraint becomes

$$p_1q_1{}^* + p_1{}^*(q_1 - q_1{}^*) + p_2q_2 \leqslant I,$$

i.e.

$$p_1{}^*q_1 + p_2q_2 \leqslant I - p_1q_1{}^* + p_1{}^*q_1{}^* = I + t_1q_1{}^*.$$

Subsidies We shall do no more than comment that a government subsidy is a form of negative taxation. The considerations above therefore apply here also.

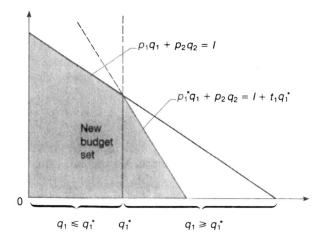

Figure 3.8 Budget set under sales tax on quantities above q^*.

3.5 Preferences

We have studied the consumer's budget set from which she must make a choice. The choice she makes will depend on her *preferences*. These can be described with the help of a *preference relation*.

We write

$$x \lesssim y$$

to mean that the consumer likes commodity bundle y at least as much as she likes x. It is usual to assume that consumers' preferences satisfy certain 'rationality conditions':

1 for each x and y, $x \lesssim y$ or $y \lesssim x$;
2 for each x, y and z, $x \lesssim y$ and $y \lesssim z$ implies $x \lesssim z$.

The first condition (completeness) says that the consumer can compare any two commodity bundles. For some bundles x and y, it will be the case that $x \lesssim y$ and $y \lesssim x$ (for example, if $x = y$). If y is liked at least as much as x and x is liked at least as much as y, we say that the consumer is *indifferent* between x and y and write

$$x \sim y.$$

If $x \lesssim y$ but it is not true that $x \sim y$, then we say that y is strictly preferred to x and write

$$x < y.$$

The second of the two rationality conditions (transitivity) has more substance. If it were false, then it would be possible to find bundles x, y and z such that

$$x \lesssim y \lesssim z < x.$$

A consumer in possession of x would then be ready to exchange x for y, then y for z and then z for x. Moreover, since strict preference holds at the last stage, the consumer would be prepared to pay a small amount, perhaps one penny, to exchange z for x. But the result of these transactions is just to return the irrational consumer to her starting point but one penny the poorer.

Let us call a set of the form

$$S = \{x : x \gtrsim y\}$$

a preference set. The set S contains all bundles that the consumer likes at least as much as y. Figure 3.9 shows a preference set for 'well-behaved' preferences.

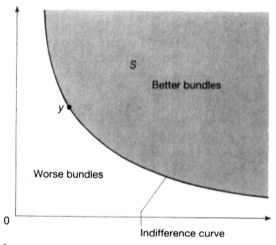

Figure 3.9   A preference set.

It implicitly incorporates a number of assumptions of which the more important are the following.

1   The boundary of S is a smooth *indifference curve*. The consumer is indifferent between any two bundles on the same indifference curve.
2   Preferences are *monotone*. This means that the commodities are always to be regarded as 'goods' and so, other things being equal, more is always better (figure 3.10).
3   Preferences are *convex*. Mathematically, this means that S is a convex set. This in turn means that, if a and b are in the set S, then so is the line segment which joins them (figure 3.11).

A bundle x on the line segment joining a and b can be expressed in the form

$$x = \alpha a + (1 - \alpha)b$$

where $0 \leq \alpha \leq 1$ (figure 3.12). Observe that x is therefore a *mixture* of the bundles a and b, in that a fraction α of each of the commodities making up a is mixed with a fraction $1 - \alpha$ of each of the commodities making up b.

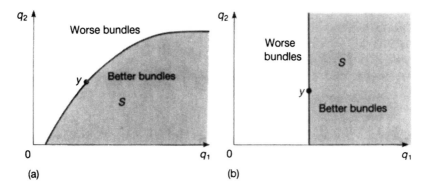

(a)   (b)

Figure 3.10   (a) q_1 is a 'good', q_2 is a 'bad' (e.g. pollution); (b) q_1 is a 'good', q_2 is 'neutral'.

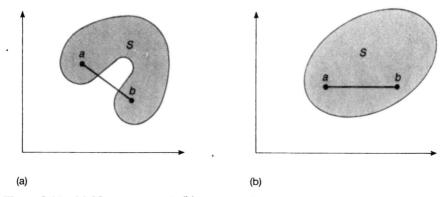

(a)   (b)

Figure 3.11   (a) Non-convex set; (b) convex set.

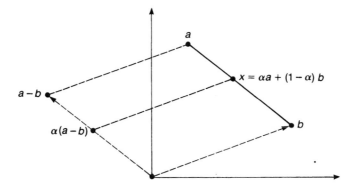

Figure 3.12   Intermediate point on a line segment. Note also that $x = b + \alpha(a - b)$.

· Roughly speaking, preferences are convex when consumers like mixtures. For example, suppose that $a \sim b$, i.e. the consumer is indifferent between a and b. Then a will lie on the indifference curve through b. If preferences are convex, then all the mixtures of **a** and **b** will lie in the preference set S and hence the consumer likes them all at least as much as **a** or **b** (figure 3.13).

Example: Cobb–Douglas preferences
Cobb–Douglas preferences are characterized by indifference curves of the form

$$q_1{}^{\alpha}q_2{}^{\beta} = \gamma$$

where α and β are fixed positive constants and γ is a constant which depends on the level of indifference.

In figure 3.14 the consumer is indifferent between bundles **a** and **b**. She is also indifferent between bundles **c** and **d**. But she strictly prefers either of **c** or **d** to either of **a** or **b**.

In the case when $\alpha = \beta = 1$, the indifference curves are rectangular hyperbolas. The shape of the curves is qualitatively very similar in the general case.

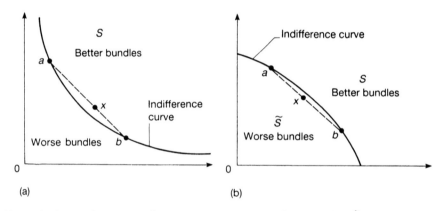

Figure 3.13   (a) Convex preferences; (b) concave preferences (i.e. $\tilde{S}$ is convex).

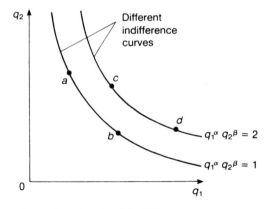

Figure 3.14   Curves for various levels of indifference.

Example: Perfect substitutes
Suppose that the consumer's indifference curves take the form

$$\alpha q_1 + \beta q_2 = \gamma$$

where α and β are fixed positive constants and γ is a constant which depends on the level of indifference. Then the two goods are said to be *perfect substitutes*.

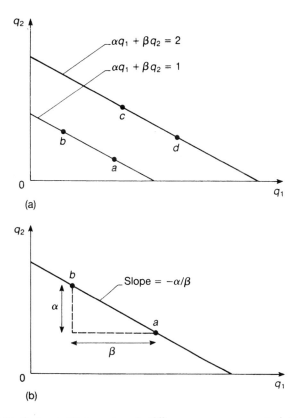

Figure 3.15 (a) Perfect substitutes when indifference curves are straight; (b) slope and substitution rate.

The consumer is indifferent between a and b in figure 3.15(b). She will therefore be ready to trade a for b or the reverse. But to give up a for b is to substitute α units of the second commodity for β units of the first commodity.

As an example, consider bottles of gin. Brand A sells gin in litre bottles. Brand B sells identical gin in pint bottles. A litre is approximately 1.75 pints. A consumer will therefore regard brand A gin and brand B gin as perfect substitutes, since 1 bottle of brand A gin is equivalent to 1.75 bottles of brand B gin. The indifference curves, in this special case, take the form

$$(1)q_A + (1.75)q_B = \gamma$$

where q_A is the number of bottles of brand A gin and q_B is the number of bottles of brand B gin.

Example: Perfect complements
Suppose that the two commodities are gin and vermouth to be used exclusively for mixing martinis and that the consumer will only tolerate martinis in the ratio of 10 parts of gin to 1 part of vermouth. Given 12 litres of gin and 1 litre of vermouth, the consumer will therefore be able to mix 11 litres of martini. This will leave 2 litres of gin for which the consumer has no use. She is therefore indifferent between the bundles $c = (10, 1)'$ and $d = (12, 1)'$.

Applying this argument throughout, we obtain the indifference curves indicated in figure 3.16. Notice that these have 'corners' or 'kinks' along the 'perfect martini line' $q_2 = 10q_1$.

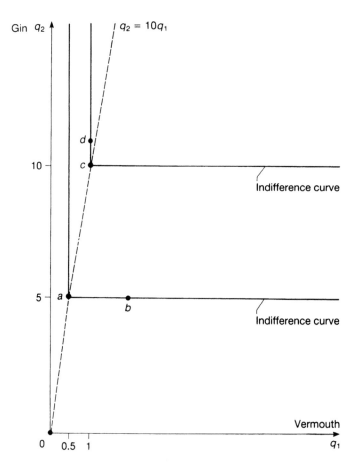

Figure 3.16 Perfect complements give L-shaped indifference curves.

Gin and vermouth are *perfect complements* because neither is worth anything without the right quantity of the other.

3.6   Optimal choice

The consumer wants to choose the bundle she most prefers from her budget set. Usually the optimal bundle **q*** occurs at a point where an indifference curve *touches* the budget line. But this is not always the case as figure 3.17 indicates.

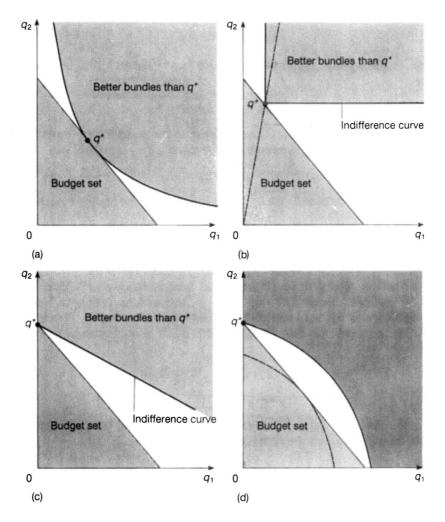

Figure 3.17   (a) Cobb–Douglas preferences; (b) perfect complements; (c) perfect substitutes; (d) concave preferences.

The standard case is illustrated with Cobb–Douglas preferences (figure 3.17(a)). It is easiest to calculate $q*$ using calculus as explained later (section 13.1). Figures 3.17(b), 3.17(c) and 3.17(d) illustrate various types of 'corner solution'. Note that, in figure 3.17(d), an indifference curve touches the budget line but the point of contact is *not* the optimal consumption bundle.

3.7   Sales versus income tax

The government is to tax a consumer. Would the consumer prefer an income tax or a sales tax on one of the commodities she buys, assuming that the revenue raised by the government is to be the same in both cases?

Begin with the sales tax. The budget constraint will then be

$$(p_1 + t_1)q_1 + p_2 q_2 \leqslant I.$$

Suppose the optimal consumption choice is $q*$ (figure 3.18). Then we shall have

$$(p_1 + t_1)q_1* + p_2 q_2* = I. \qquad (3.1)$$

(It cannot be in the interest of the consumer to leave any money unspent.) The revenue raised by the government is therefore

$$R = t_1 q_1*.$$

If this revenue is raised instead by an income tax, the budget constraint will be

$$p_1 q_1 + p_2 q_2 \leqslant I - R.$$

Suppose the optimal consumption choice in this case is $q**$. We shall now argue that the consumer must like $q**$ at least as much as $q*$. The reason is that $q*$ satisfies the budget constraint in the income tax case. Hence the consumer could have chosen $q*$ but preferred to choose $q**$. To see that $q*$ satisfies the income tax case budget constraint, it is only necessary to observe that

$$p_1 q_1* + p_2 q_2* = I - t_1 q_1* \qquad \text{(by equation (3.1))}$$

$$= I - R.$$

Since the consumer likes $q**$ at least as much as $q*$, she must like the income tax at least as much as the sales tax.

3.8   Marginal rate of substitution

When only two commodities are being considered, the slope of an indifference curve at a point Q is called the *marginal rate of substitution* at Q (figure 3.19).

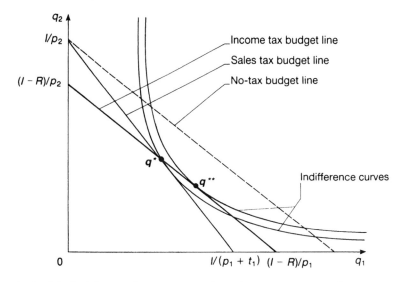

Figure 3.18 Maximizing preference: q^* under sales tax, q^{**} under income tax.

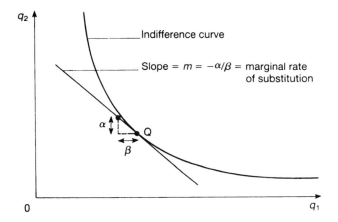

Figure 3.19 The slope is the marginal rate of substitution.

(The slope of a curve at a point Q is simply the slope of the tangent line at Q – assuming that a tangent line can be drawn. If not, then the slope does not exist.)

Close to the point Q, the indifference curve is approximately the same as the tangent line. But we saw in the example on perfect substitutes that, *if* the tangent line *were* the indifference curve, then the consumer would regard the two commodities as perfect substitutes and be willing to substitute α units of the second commodity for β units of the first commodity, or vice versa.

But the tangent line is not the indifference curve. However, it remains true that a consumer in possession of a commodity bundle Q at which the marginal rate of substitution (MRS) is $m = -\alpha/\beta$ will be willing to substitute approximately α of the second commodity for β of the first commodity, or vice versa, *provided that α and β are very small.*

A consequence is that, when the optimal consumption bundle $q*$ is achieved at a point where an indifference curve touches the budget line, it must be the case that

$$\text{MRS} = -p_1/p_2.$$

Mathematically, the equation just records the fact that the slope of the budget line is $-p_1/p_2$. If the budget line touches the indifference curve at $q*$, then it is the tangent line at $q*$. Hence $MRS = -p_1/p_2$ (figure 3.20).

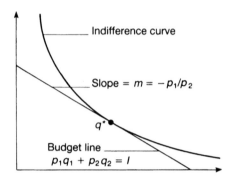

Figure 3.20 At the optimal consumption MRS $= -p_1/p_2$.

The economics are a little more interesting. If the market sets the prices at p_1 and p_2, then the consumer can always sell a small quantity β of the first commodity and use the money $p_1\beta$ to buy a quantity $p_1\beta/p_2$ of the second commodity. If she possesses $q*$ already, she will not want to do this because $q*$ is her optimal bundle. Hence it must be the case that

$$p_1\beta/p_2 \leqslant \alpha$$

where $m = -\alpha/\beta$ is the MRS at $q*$. Similarly, she can always sell a small quantity α of the second commodity and use the money $p_2\alpha$ to buy a quantity $p_2\alpha/p_1$ of the first commodity. As before, it must be the case that

$$p_2\alpha/p_1 \leqslant \beta$$

where $m = -\alpha/\beta$ is the MRS at $q*$. Combining the two inequalities, we obtain that $m = -\alpha/\beta = -p_1/p_2$.

Some remarks on the *sign* of the marginal rate of substitution may be helpful. If both commodities are *goods*, then the sign of the MRS will be *negative*. However, economists are often careless about such matters and omit the sign. You must therefore be prepared to interpret statements about the MRS as possibly referring to $|\text{MRS}|$, i.e. the absolute value of MRS.

This can be confusing. For example, you can see from the figures that, for *convex* preferences, MRS *increases* as q_1 increases (the slope gets less negative). But $|\text{MRS}|$ decreases.

Example
Recall the Cobb–Douglas preferences of the example on page 48. We shall prove later (section 13.1) that the tangent line to the indifference curve through the point Q has equation

$$\frac{\alpha q_1}{Q_1} + \frac{\beta q_2}{Q_2} = \alpha + \beta$$

(figure 3.21). It is therefore easy to work out the marginal rate of substitution at a general point Q since this is just the slope of the tangent line. In fact

$$\text{MRS} = -\frac{\alpha Q_2}{\beta Q_1}.$$

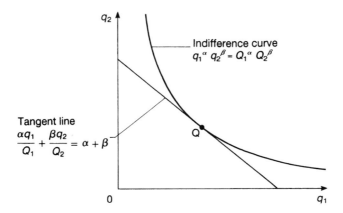

Figure 3.21 MRS $= -\alpha Q_2/\beta Q_1$.

This, in turn, makes it easy to work out optimal consumption bundles. For example, if the budget constraint is $p_1 q_1 + p_2 q_2 \leqslant I$, then the optimal bundle Q occurs where MRS $= -p_1/p_2$ and so

$$-\frac{\alpha Q_2}{\beta Q_1} = -\frac{p_1}{p_2}.$$

There are two unknowns, Q_1 and Q_2, and so a second equation is needed. It is easiest to note that Q must lie on the budget line and thus

$$p_1 Q_1 + p_2 Q_2 = I$$

(figure 3.22).

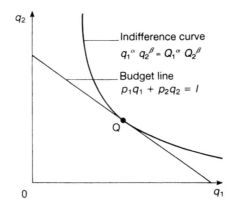

Figure 3.22 The budget line is the tangent line.

Consider the particular case when $\alpha = \beta = 1$, $p_1 = 2$, $p_2 = 3$ and $I = 24$. Our two equations become

$$-\frac{Q_2}{Q_1} = -\frac{2}{3},$$

i.e.

$$2Q_1 - 3Q_2 = 0,$$

and

$$2Q_1 + 3Q_2 = 24.$$

Adding these equations, we obtain that

$$4Q_1 = 24, \quad \text{i.e. } Q_1 = 6,$$

and, subtracting the equations, that

$$6Q_1 = 24, \quad \text{i.e. } Q_2 = 4.$$

The optimal consumption bundle is therefore $Q = (6, 4)'$.

3.9 Factors of production

Producers are normally assumed to seek to maximize profits. One can break their problem down into two steps. The first consists of determining the most profitable output. The second consists of determining the least costly way of producing that output. This second problem is very similar, mathematically, to the problem of consumer choice and so we consider it here.

Inputs to the production process are called factors of production. They are traditionally classified into such categories as land, labour, capital and raw materials. We shall consider only labour (l) and capital (k) to keep things simple. Often the word 'capital' is used to mean the amount of money needed to start a business and to keep it running. Here it means 'capital goods', i.e. production inputs which are themselves produced goods. Machinery is a good example.

Suppose that a producer has decided that the most profitable output level is Q. He will be able to produce this output in various ways using different *technologies*. Each technology will require a different mix of inputs. Some technologies may be labour intensive and require much labour but little capital. Others may automate the production process and use much capital and little labour. An *isoquant* (Greek: 'isos' means equal) is a curve with the property that each point $(k, l)'$ on the curve is an input mix which will produce the same output level (figure 3.23).

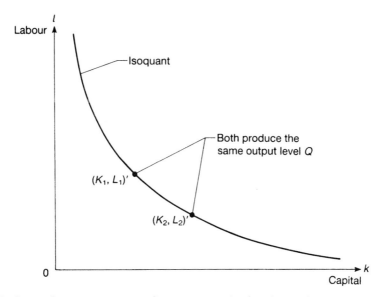

Figure 3.23 An isoquant – curve of constant production (output).

A 'well-behaved' isoquant is just like a 'well-behaved' indifference curve. In particular, a Cobb–Douglas technology producing isoquants of the form

$$k^\alpha l^\beta = \gamma$$

typifies the 'well-behaved' case. However, one does not speak of the marginal rate of substitution for isoquants. One speaks of the *technical rate of substitution* (TRS). This is simply the slope of the isoquant at the point in question. It measures the rate at which labour can be substituted for capital while maintaining the same level of production.

The mix of inputs that a producer chooses to obtain the output level Q will depend on the prices of the inputs. He will choose the input mix which minimizes cost

$$C = pk + wl$$

where p is the price of capital and w is the price of labour (figure 3.24). (Usually l is measured in man-hours so that w is the hourly wage rate and k is measured in machine-hours.)

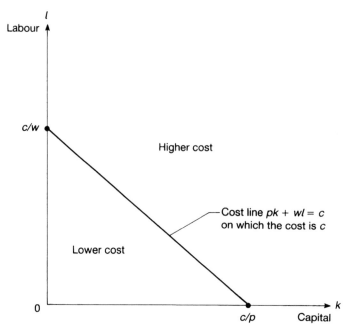

Figure 3.24 An 'isocost' – line of constant cost (of input).

Just as in the consumer choice case, in the well-behaved situation the optimal mix occurs at the point (K, L) where a cost line touches the isoquant corresponding to the output level Q (figure 3.25). The requirement for this is that

$$\text{TRS} = -p/w.$$

Suppose, for example, that the producer believes that the most profitable output level is 12 units, and that the corresponding isoquant is

$$kl = 12.$$

If $p = 2$ and $w = 3$, what is the cost-minimizing input mix $(K, L)'$?

The TRS at $(K, L)'$, i.e. the slope of the isoquant at $(K, L)'$, is obtained as in example 3.10. We have that

$$\text{TRS} = -\frac{\alpha L}{\beta K} = -\frac{L}{K}$$

(since $\alpha = \beta = 1$). In order for a cost line to touch the isoquant $kl = 12$, we need that $\text{TRS} = -p/w$. Hence

$$-\frac{2}{3} = -\frac{L}{K}.$$

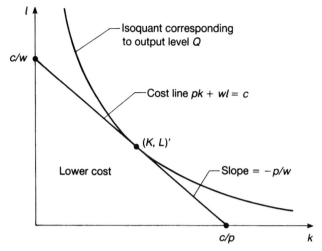

Figure 3.25 Optimal inputs: TRS = − p/w.

There are two unknowns, L and K, and so a second equation is needed. In the example in section 3.8 we used the equation of the budget line, but there we knew the income I and here we do not know the value C of the minimizing cost and so the equation of the cost line is of no immediate help. So we have to use the equation $kl = 12$ of the isoquant, even though this is a little more complicated. Our two equations are therefore

$$2K - 3L = 0$$

(from TRS = − p/w) and

$$KL = 12.$$

The second equation simply says that $(K, L)'$ lies on the isoquant $kl = 12$. Substituting $L = 12/K$ in the first equation, we obtain that

$$2K - 3 \times 12/K = 0$$

$$K^2 - 18 = 0$$

and hence either $K = -\sqrt{(18)}$ or $K = \sqrt{(18)}$. The first possibility is clearly not relevant to the current problem and so the optimum level of capital is $K = \sqrt{(18)} = 3\sqrt{2}$ and the corresponding level of labour is therefore

$$L = 12/K = 12/3\sqrt{2} = 2\sqrt{2}.$$

Hence more capital than labour will be used. The total cost of the optimizing inputs is

$$C = pK + wL = 2 \times 3\sqrt{2} + 3 \times 2\sqrt{2} = 12\sqrt{2}.$$

3.10   Exercises

1*   A consumer's *endowment* is the commodity bundle she has before she trades. If her endowment is q and the price vector is p, where

$$p = \begin{pmatrix} 3 \\ 2 \end{pmatrix} \qquad q = \begin{pmatrix} 1 \\ 4 \end{pmatrix},$$

what is her budget set, if she has no money?

2   A consumer's endowment is q and the price vector is p. If she sells her endowment, can she use the money to buy the commodity bundle r?

$$p = \begin{pmatrix} 1 \\ 2 \\ 3 \end{pmatrix} \qquad q = \begin{pmatrix} 0 \\ 1 \\ 4 \end{pmatrix} \qquad r = \begin{pmatrix} 4 \\ 5 \\ 0 \end{pmatrix}.$$

3*   A consumer's budget constraint is

$$p_1 q_1 + p_2 q_2 \leqslant I.$$

She regards commodities 1 and 2 as perfect substitutes and is always ready to substitute 5 units of commodity 1 for 3 units of commodity 2 or vice versa. What is her optimal consumption bundle in the following cases? Draw diagrams.

(a) $p_1 = 4$, $p_2 = 1$, $I = 10$
(b) $p_1 = 1$, $p_2 = 4$, $I = 15$
(c) $p_1 = 3$, $p_2 = 5$, $I = 30$

4   A consumer's budget constraint is

$$p_1 q_1 + p_2 q_2 \leqslant I.$$

She regards commodities 1 and 2 as perfect complements with the ideal mix consisting of 2 units of commodity 1 for each 3 units of commodity 2. What is her optimal consumption bundle in the following cases? Draw diagrams.

(a) $p_1 = 2$, $p_2 = 2$, $I = 10$
(b) $p_1 = 8$, $p_2 = 3$, $I = 20$

5*   Repeat question 3 for a consumer with Cobb–Douglas indifference curves of the form

$$q_1 q_2^2 = \gamma.$$

6   Repeat question 4 for Cobb–Douglas indifference curves of the form

$$q_1^2 q_2 = \gamma.$$

7*   Find the marginal rate of substitution at the point $(q_1, q_2)'$ for the Cobb–Douglas preferences of question 5. Check that MRS increases as q_1 increases.

8 Repeat question 7 for the Cobb–Douglas preferences of question 6.

9* Repeat question 5 for the case when the government rations the consumption of commodity 2 to a maximum level of 5.

10 Repeat question 6 for the case when the government imposes a sales tax of 50 per cent on consumption of the first commodity above the level of 1.

11* A consumer has concave preferences described by indifference curves of the form

$$q_1{}^2 + q_2{}^2 = \gamma.$$

What is her optimal consumption bundle if her budget constraint is $q_1 + q_2 \leqslant 4$?

12 With the preferences of question 11, how will the consumer feel about a mixture of 1/3 of bundle *a* and 2/3 of bundle *b* if she is indifferent between *a* and *b*? How does this differ from the case of convex preferences?

13* Should a consumer prefer an income tax or a sales tax when both generate the same revenue for the government? Consider the case of *n* commodities with the sales tax applied to each commodity.

14 Should a consumer prefer a straight income subsidy or a price subsidy on one of the two commodities she consumes, assuming that the government donates the same amount of money in each case?

(For the price subsidy, assume that the price of the first commodity to the consumer becomes $p_1 - s_1$ and that the government pays the producer the excess cost $s_1 q_1$ of the consumer's purchase.)

15* Find the optimal input mix and its cost in the case when a producer chooses an output corresponding to the isoquant

$$k^2 l = 16$$

and the prices of capital and labour are respectively $p = 1$ and $w = 2$.

16 Repeat question 15 for the isoquant $k l^2 = 12$.

3.11 Answers

1 The consumer can sell her endowment and obtain its value

$$p \cdot q = p_1 q_1 + p_2 q_2 = 3 \times 1 + 2 \times 4 = 11$$

in money. We can then calculate her budget set as in section 3.3 using $I = 11$ (figure 3.26).

3 First draw some indifference curves. We are told that MRS = $- 3/5$ and so these indifference curves all have slope $- 3/5$ (figure 3.27).

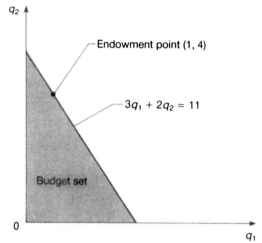

Figure 3.26   Budget set from an endowment of (1, 4).

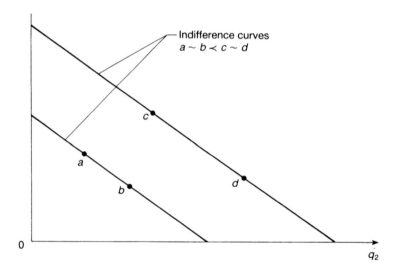

Figure 3.27   Indifference curves.

In cases (a) and (b) a 'corner' solution is obtained (figure 3.28). Case (c) is a case when there is not a unique optimal. Every point on the budget line is optimal.

5   (a) As in the example in section 3.8,

$$\text{MRS} = -\frac{\alpha Q_2}{\beta Q_1} = -\frac{Q_2}{2Q_1}.$$

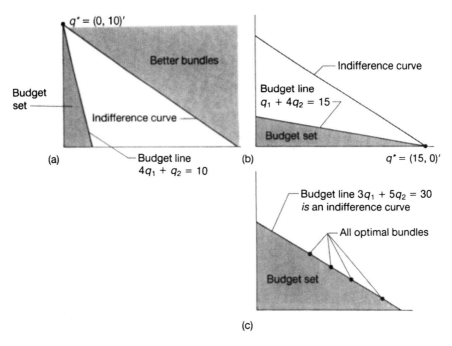

Figure 3.28 Identifying optimal bundles.

Since $p_1 = 4$, $p_2 = 1$ and MRS $= -p_1/p_2$,

$$-\frac{Q_2}{2Q_1} = -\frac{4}{1}.$$

A second equation is provided by the budget line

$$4Q_1 + Q_2 = 10$$

(figure 3.29). Solving these two equations, we obtain that $Q_1 = 5/6$ and $Q_2 = 20/3 = 6\frac{2}{3}$.

(b) The method of (a) yields the equations

$$-\frac{Q_2}{2Q_1} = -\frac{1}{4} \qquad Q_1 + 4Q_2 = 15.$$

Hence $Q_1 = 5$, $Q_2 = 15/6 = 2\frac{1}{2}$.

(c) The method of (a) yields the equations

$$-\frac{Q_2}{2Q_1} = -\frac{3}{5} \qquad 3Q_1 + 5Q_2 = 30.$$

Hence $Q_1 = 10/3 = 3\frac{1}{3}$, $Q_2 = 4$.

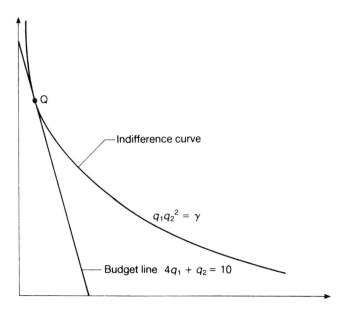

Figure 3.29   Optimal bundle on a Cobb–Douglas indifference curve.

7   As in the example in section 3.8,

$$\text{MRS} = -\frac{\alpha q_2}{\beta q_1} = -\frac{q_2}{2q_1}$$

and we have only to observe that $1/q_1$ gets smaller as q_1 gets bigger, so that $-1/q_1$ gets bigger as q_1 gets bigger.

9   The budget set in case (a) becomes as indicated in figure 3.30. The optimal bundle $(5/6, 6\frac{2}{3})'$ found in question 5(a) is therefore no longer available. The new optimal bundle has $Q_2 = 5$ and so

$$Q_1 = \frac{1}{4}(10 - 5) = \frac{5}{4}.$$

Cases (b) and (c) from question 5 are unaffected because in neither case is $Q_2 > 5$ and so the rationing condition does not bite.

11   The indifference curves are circles (figure 3.31). Note that there are two optimal bundles

$$q^* = (4, 0)' \qquad r^* = (0, 4)'.$$

The bundle $(2, 2)'$ obtained by setting $\text{MRS} = -p_1/p_2$ is *not* optimal.

13   As in section 3.7, optimal consumption q^* with a sales tax satisfies

$$(p + t) \cdot q^* = I$$

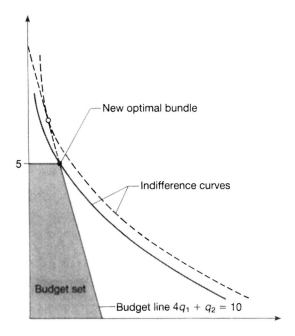

Figure 3.30 Optimal bundle under rationing.

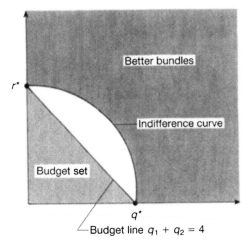

Figure 3.31 Optimal bundles and the corresponding non-convex preference set.

and so the revenue R raised by the government is $R = t \cdot q^*$. If this revenue is raised instead by an income tax, then the new budget constraint is

$$p \cdot q \leqslant I - R.$$

But $q*$ satisfies this new budget constraint because

$$p \cdot q* = I - t \cdot q* = I - R.$$

Hence optimal consumption in the new situation is at least as good as $q*$. Thus the income tax should be preferred.

15   As in section 3.9,

$$\text{TRS} = -\frac{\alpha L}{\beta K} = -\frac{2L}{K}.$$

We need to put $\text{TRS} = -p/w$ where $p = 1$ and $w = 2$. Hence the optimal mix $(K, L)'$ satisfies

$$-\frac{2L}{K} = -\frac{1}{2}$$

$$K - 4L = 0.$$

The second equation is that of the isoquant:

$$K^2 L = 16.$$

Substitute $K = 4L$ from the first equation in the second. Then

$$(4L)^2 L = 16$$

$$16L^3 = 16$$

$$L^3 = 1.$$

It follows that $L = 1$ and hence $K = 4$.

4

Discrete Variables

4.1 Discrete and continuous variables

In previous sections the variables have mostly been continuous. This means that they are allowed to take any value in some interval of real numbers. For example, in the discussion of factors of production (section 3.9), labour appeared as the continuous variable l, allowed to take any value in $\mathbb{R}_+$.

But, of course, this is not entirely realistic. A producer cannot really tell his workers that he requires $\pi^2 - \sqrt{2}$ hours of labour from them next Tuesday. Typically, he will have to work in a whole number of hours. Sometimes the smallest unit allowed will not be hours but days, weeks, months or even years. If the smallest unit allowed is of size h, then labour will have to take one of the values

$$l = nh \qquad (n = 0, 1, 2, \ldots).$$

Labour will then constitute an example of a *discrete variable*. Often, it is convenient to choose the units in which a discrete variable is measured so as to make the smallest unit allowed equal to unity. For example, if workers are paid by the hour, we can measure labour in man-hours and l will then take values in $\mathbb{Z}_+$, i.e. l will be one of the non-negative integers $0, 1, 2, 3, \ldots$.

Why use continuous variables at all if it is true that discrete variables are more realistic? The reason is that the mathematics is usually easier in the continuous case. Consider, for example, the isoquant (see section 3.9) illustrated in figure 4.1 for the case when labour and capital are taken to be discrete variables. (You can think of capital as being measured in machine-hours. The price of capital can then be identified with the hourly rental rate for a machine.)

One of the lessons of economics is supposedly that 'there is no such thing as a free lunch'. A price has to be paid for everything. The price that has to be paid for using the easy mathematics that goes with continuous variables is that the results will only be *approximations*. Consider, for example, the technical rate of substitution (TRS – section 3.9). What is the TRS corresponding to the input bundle $(4, 1)'$ (figure 4.2)?

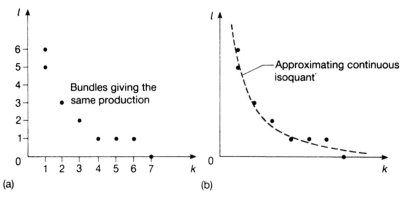

Figure 4.1 (a) Discrete case; (b) continuous approximation.

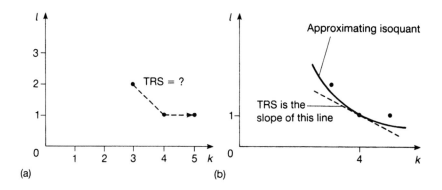

Figure 4.2 (a) Discrete case; (b) continuous approximation.

In the discrete case, one has to say that the TRS depends on whether one *less* unit of capital is to be used or one *more* unit of capital. In the former case, one more unit of labour will be needed to maintain the same production. In the latter case, no fewer units of labour will be required. One might try to express this by saying that the TRS at $(4, 1)'$ is -1 when capital is decreased by 1 unit and 0 when it is increased by 1 unit.

But this is not only clumsy: it is absurdly pedantic in the case when the continuous approximation is a good one. In this case, the difference in the substitution rate when capital is increased or decreased by 1 unit will be very small. Neglecting this difference will therefore generate only small errors and, since there are likely to be measurement errors in the discrete data anyway, there is no point in getting upset about these errors.

When is a continuous approximation likely to be a good one? The answer is that the units of measurement need to be small compared with the quantities measured. If the production of a shipyard is measured in numbers of aircraft carriers produced, this will obviously *not* be the case. On the other hand, it *will* be the case when the output of a distillery is measured in numbers of bottles produced per hour.

Often economists take for granted that the continuous approximation is a good one and speak about such quantities as the TRS without careful regard to what units of measurement are to be used. In such cases, always assume that the unit of measurement is to be understood as very small compared with the quantities involved. The effect on such entities as TRS or MRS (section 3.8) of considering 1 unit more as opposed to 1 unit less will then be negligible.

But, be warned that one cannot always proceed in this way with economic variables. A particularly important example for which going to the continuous case is likely to generate significant errors is that of time. If interest payments are made per annum (i.e. yearly), it will not be adequate to work with a model in which it is assumed that they are paid minute by minute. Compound interest calculations will give significantly different answers.

4.2 Summation

The symbol Σ, which is the Greek letter sigma from which our letter S derives, is used to denote sums. We have that

$$\sum_{k=1}^{n} a_k = a_1 + a_2 + a_3 + \cdots + a_n.$$

For example,

$$\sum_{k=1}^{5} k^2 = 1^2 + 2^2 + 3^2 + 4^2 + 5^2$$

$$= 1 + 4 + 9 + 16 + 25 = 55.$$

Some simple facts are worth remembering.

1

$$\sum_{k=1}^{n} 1 = n.$$

Beginners sometimes find this confusing. Observe that we are told that $a_1 = a_2 = \cdots = a_n = 1$. Write these values in the definition for a sum. The result is that

$$\sum_{k=1}^{n} 1 = \sum_{k=1}^{n} a_k = a_1 + a_2 + \cdots + a_n$$

$$= 1 + 1 + \cdots + 1$$

$$= n \times 1 = n.$$

2 If α and β are constants,

$$\sum_{k=1}^{n} (\alpha a_k + \beta b_k) = \alpha \sum_{k=1}^{n} a_k + \beta \sum_{k=1}^{n} b_k.$$

3

$$\sum_{k=1}^{n} k = 1 + 2 + 3 + \cdots + n = \frac{1}{2} n(n + 1).$$

This can be checked using figure 4.3.

The sum $3 + 5 + 7 + \cdots + 101$ is an example of an *arithmetic progression*. The *common difference* of the terms is $d = 2$ (because $5 - 3 = 2$, $7 - 5 = 2$, ...,

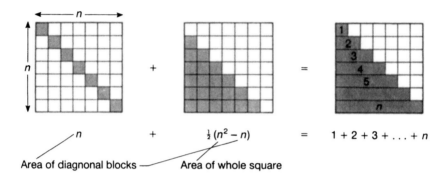

Figure 4.3 Summing the integers.

$101 - 99 = 2$). The first term is $a = 3$ and the last term is $l = 101$. There are $n = 50$ terms because $l = a + (n - 1)d$, i.e. $101 = 3 + 49 \times 2$. The general formula for summing an arithmetic progression is

$$a + (a + d) + (a + 2d) + \cdots + l = \frac{1}{2} n(a + l).$$

This can be deduced from rules 1, 2 and 3 as follows:

$$\sum_{k=0}^{n-1} (a + kd) = a \sum_{k=0}^{n-1} 1 + d \sum_{k=0}^{n-1} k$$

$$= an + d \sum_{k=1}^{n-1} k$$

$$= an + d \frac{1}{2} (n - 1)n$$

$$= \frac{1}{2} n[2a + (n - 1) d]$$

$$= \frac{1}{2} n\{a + [a + (n - 1)d]\} = \frac{1}{2} n(a + l).$$

4   Our next rule is

$$\sum_{k=0}^{n} x^k = 1 + x + x^2 + \cdots + x^n = \frac{1 - x^{n+1}}{1 - x} \qquad (x \neq 1).$$

This is the formula for summing a *geometric progression* with *common ratio* $x \neq 1$. To justify this, we can observe that

$$(1 - x)(1 + x + x^2 + \cdots + x^n)$$

$$= 1(1 + x + x^2 + \cdots + x^n) - x(1 + x + x^2 + \cdots + x^n)$$

$$= 1 + x + x^2 + \cdots + x^n - x - x^2 - x^3 - \cdots - x^{n+1}$$

$$= 1 - x^{n+1}.$$

For example

$$1 + 2 + 2^2 + 2^3 + \cdots + 2^{10} = \frac{2^{11} - 1}{2 - 1} = 2047.$$

4.3 Induction

Suppose that $P(n)$ is an assertion about the integer n. For example, $P(n)$ might be the assertion that

$$1 + x + x^2 + \cdots + x^n = \frac{1 - x^{n+1}}{1 - x}$$

as considered in section 4.2. The *principle of induction* says that, if

(a) $P(N)$ is true and
(b) for each $n \geq N$, $P(n)$ implies $P(n + 1)$,

then $P(n)$ is true for all $n \geq N$. The standard illustration is of a row of dominoes which are stood on end in a row in such a way that if one falls it will knock over the next. The Nth domino is then pushed over. The principle of induction assures us that all subsequent dominoes will fall down. To see this, let $P(n)$ be the assertion that the nth domino will fall and observe that we have arranged for both (a) and (b) to be valid.

In the case when $P(n)$ is the proposition that $1 + x + \cdots + x^n = (1 - x^{n+1})/(1 - x)$, it is easy to check that $P(0)$ is true because this just says that $1 = (1 - x)/(1 - x)$. To use the principle of induction, we need also that $P(n)$ implies $P(n + 1)$, i.e. if $P(n)$ is true, then $P(n + 1)$ is true. We therefore have to check that, if $P(n)$ happens to be true for any particular value of n, then $P(n + 1)$ is necessarily also true. Now, $P(n + 1)$ is the assertion that

$$1 + x + x^2 + \cdots + x^{n+1} = \frac{1 - x^{n+2}}{1 - x}.$$

But

$$1 + x + x^2 + \cdots + x^n + x^{n+1} = (1 + x + x^2 + \cdots + x^n) + x^{n+1}$$

$$= \frac{1 - x^{n+1}}{1 - x} + x^{n+1}$$

provided that $P(n)$ happens to be true for the particular value of n with which we are concerned. But

$$\frac{1-x^{n+1}}{1-x} + x^{n+1} = \frac{1-x^{n+1}+x^{n+1}-x^{n+2}}{1-x} = \frac{1-x^{n+2}}{1-x}.$$

It has therefore been shown that $P(n+1)$ can be deduced from $P(n)$, i.e. $P(n)$ implies $P(n+1)$.

Both (a) and (b) of the principle of induction have been established. Hence $P(n)$ is true for all values of $n \geq 1$.

4.4 Intertemporal choice

Consider a consumer who, unlike the consumers considered so far, wishes to consume in *two* time periods rather than just in one time period. Let her aggregate consumption this year be q_0, measured in dollars, and let her aggregate consumption next year be q_1, measured in dollars. Let the income of the consumer in the current year be I_0 and her income next year be I_1.

If the interest rate is zero and the consumer cannot borrow any money, then her budget set will be as indicated in figure 4.4. Observe that, since consumption is measured in dollars, prices are necessarily equal to unity, i.e. $p_0 = p_1 = 1$, and so the slope of the budget line is -1. She cannot spend more than her income I_0 this year, but she need not spend all of I_0 this year. Instead she can save some of I_0 and spend it next year.

Now suppose, more realistically, that the consumer can borrow and lend at an interest rate of $r > 0$. If the yearly interest rate is $r = 10$ per cent and you

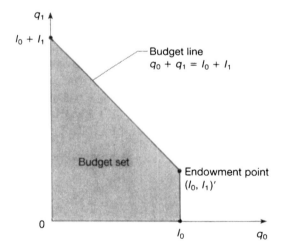

Figure 4.4 Budget set for two-period consumption.

borrow \$20 this year, then, next year, you will owe

$$\$22 = 20 + \frac{10}{100}\, 20.$$

More generally, if the consumer borrows \$$M$ this year, she will have to pay back \$$(1 + r)M$ next year. She will then have $I_0 + M$ to spend this year but only $I_1 - M(1 + r)$ next year. If M is allowed to be negative, we get the corresponding results for lending rather than borrowing. It follows that she can purchase any commodity bundle $(q_0, q_1)'$ for which

$$q_0 = I_0 + M$$
$$q_1 = I_1 - M(1 + r)$$

for some M. Eliminating M between these two equations, we obtain the budget line

$$q_0 - I_0 = \frac{I_1 - q_1}{1 + r}$$

$$q_0 + \frac{1}{1 + r}\, q_1 = I_0 + \frac{1}{1 + r}\, I_1$$

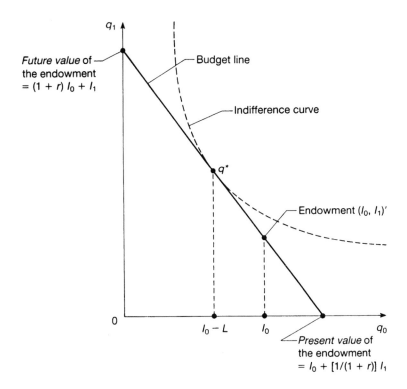

Figure 4.5 Optimal consumption over two periods.

In figure 4.5, first notice that, with an indifference curve like that indicated, the consumer would lend $\$L$ in the current year and consume the bundle q^*. More importantly, observe that *if* she chose to confine her consumption to the current year (and to consume nothing next year), then her consumption this year would be worth

$$PV = I_0 + \frac{1}{1+r} I_1$$

dollars. This is the *present value* of her endowment $(I_0, I_1)'$. To achieve this present value, she will have to borrow this year the maximum amount M that she can pay back next year together with the interest. Since the amount to be paid back is $(1+r)M$, she will be able to borrow M, provided that $(1+r)M = I_1$. Hence $M = I_1/(1+r)$. She will then have $\$PV$ to spend in the current year and $\$0$ to spend next year.

If she chose to confine her consumption to next year (and to consume nothing this year), then her consumption next year would be worth

$$FV = (1+r)I_0 + I_1$$

dollars. This is the *future value* of her endowment $(I_0, I_1)'$. She achieves this by lending her entire income I_0 this year. She will then be paid back $(1+r)I_0$ next year and so have $\$FV$ to spend next year but $\$0$ to spend this year.

4.5   Discounting

You are considering investing $\$J$ in a business enterprise which is certain to generate an income stream of $I_0, I_1, I_2, \ldots$. By this is meant that you will get back $\$I_0$ at the beginning of the first year, $\$I_1$ at the beginning of the second year and so on. Is this a good investment if you can borrow and lend freely at an interest rate of r?

Such problems are trivial. All that is necessary is to reduce everything to its present value. The present value of I_0 is just I_0. The present value of I_1 is

$$\frac{1}{1+r} I_1$$

as explained in section 4.4. For the same reason, the value of I_2 at the beginning of *next* year is

$$\frac{1}{1+r} I_2$$

and so its *present* value is

$$\frac{1}{1+r}\frac{1}{1+r} I_2 = \left(\frac{1}{1+r}\right)^2 I_2.$$

And, in general, the present value of I_k is just

$$\left(\frac{1}{1+r}\right)^k I_k.$$

It follows that the present value of an income stream $I_0, I_1, \ldots, I_n$ is therefore

$$\sum_{k=0}^{n} \delta^k I_k = I_0 + \delta I_1 + \delta^2 I_2 + \cdots + \delta^n I_n$$

where

$$\delta = \frac{1}{1+r}$$

is called the *discount factor* for the interest rate r.

If the income stream $I_0, I_1, I_2, \ldots$ continues for ever, then its present value will be the sum of an infinite series, i.e. the present value is

$$\sum_{k=0}^{\infty} \delta^k I_k = I_0 + \delta I_1 + \delta^2 I_2 + \delta^3 I_3 + \cdots.$$

The investment is therefore a good one only if this present value is at least as big as the required investment of $\$J$.

4.6 Bonds

The seller of a *security* promises to provide the buyer with a specified income stream. A *bond* is a special kind of security sold by both governments and companies to raise money in the present. The seller promises to pay the buyer a fixed amount of $\$I$ at the end of each subsequent year for the next $n-1$ years, after which the bond 'matures' and the seller makes a final payment of F, the 'face value' of the bond, at the end of the nth year.

A *consol* is a bond whose maturity date is postponed for ever. As an example, we shall compute the present value of a consol which pays \$1000 per year. It therefore represents an income stream $I_0, I_1, I_2, \ldots$ in which $I_0 = 0$ and $I_k = 1000$ $(k = 1, 2, 3, \ldots)$. It will be assumed that there is a fixed interest rate of 10 per cent. The relevant discount factor is therefore $\delta = 1/(1+r) = 10/11$.

First it is necessary to say something about limits and infinite series. If $|x| < 1$, then x^n gets closer and closer to zero as n gets larger and larger. We express this by writing

$$x^n \to 0 \text{ as } n \to \infty$$

or, alternatively,

$$\lim_{n \to \infty} (x^n) = 0.$$

For example, $(10/11)^5 = 0.62$, $(10/11)^{10} = 0.39$, $(10/11)^{20} = 0.15$, $(10/11)^{100} = 0.000\,073$ and so on.

Consider now the infinite geometric progression

$$\sum_{k=0}^{\infty} x^k = 1 + x + x^2 + x^3 + \cdots$$

in which $|x| < 1$ (i.e. $-1 < x < 1$). The sum of such an infinite series is defined by

$$\sum_{k=0}^{\infty} x^k = \lim_{n \to \infty} \sum_{k=0}^{n} x^k$$

$$= \lim_{n \to \infty} (1 + x + x^2 + \cdots + x^n)$$

$$= \lim_{n \to \infty} \frac{1 - x^{n+1}}{1 - x} = \frac{1}{1 - x}$$

because $x^n \to 0$ as $n \to \infty$, provided that $|x| < 1$. When $|x| < 1$, we therefore have the formula

$$1 + x + x^2 + x^3 + \cdots = \frac{1}{1 - x}$$

for the sum of an infinite geometric progression. (Do *not* use this when $|x| \geqslant 1$ because it is not valid then.)

As we saw in section 4.5, the present value of an income stream 0, I, I, I, ... is just

$$0 + \delta I + \delta^2 I + \delta^3 I + \cdots = \delta I(1 + \delta + \delta^2 + \delta^3 + \cdots)$$

$$= \delta I \frac{1}{1 - \delta}$$

$$= \frac{1}{1 + r} I \frac{1}{1 - 1/(1 + r)}$$

$$= I/r,$$

because $\delta = 1/(1 + r)$, where r is the interest rate. It follows that the present value of the consol with which we are concerned is

$$\frac{I}{r} = \frac{1000}{10/100} = 10,000.$$

Other things being equal, nobody should therefore pay more than \$10,000 for this consol. However, other things seldom are equal in this context.

4.7   Binomial theorem

If n is a non-negative integer, the number $n!$ (n factorial) is defined by

$$n! = 1 \times 2 \times 3 \times \cdots \times n$$

with $0! = 1$. The number

$$\binom{n}{k} = \frac{n!}{k!(n-k)!} = \frac{n(n-1)(n-2) \cdots (n-k+1)}{k!}$$

is called a *binomial coefficient*.

Figure 4.6(a) is called Pascal's triangle. Each number (except for the 1s) is the sum of the two numbers above it. Each of the entries in Pascal's triangle is a binomial coefficient as indicated in figure 4.6(b).

The *binomial theorem* asserts that, for any non-negative integer n,

$$(p+q)^n = \sum_{k=0}^{n} \binom{n}{k} p^k q^{n-k}.$$

Thus, for $n = 4$,

$$(p+q)^4 = q^4 + 4pq^3 + 6p^2q^2 + 4p^3q + p^4$$

where the binomial coefficients have been read off from the '$n = 4$' line of Pascal's triangle.

The binomial coefficient

$$\binom{n}{k}$$

$n = 0 \ldots$ 　　 1 　　 $\binom{0}{0}$

$n = 1 \ldots$ 　　 1　1 　　 $\binom{1}{0} \binom{1}{1}$

$n = 2 \ldots$ 　　 1　2　1 　　 $\binom{2}{0} \binom{2}{1} \binom{2}{2}$

$n = 3 \ldots$ 　　 1　3　3　1 　　 $\binom{3}{0} \binom{3}{1} \binom{3}{2} \binom{3}{3}$

$n = 4 \ldots$ 　　 1　4　6　4　1 　　 $\binom{4}{0} \binom{4}{1} \binom{4}{2} \binom{4}{3} \binom{4}{4}$

$n = 5 \ldots$ 　　 1　5　10　10　5　1 　　 $\binom{5}{0} \binom{5}{1} \binom{5}{2} \binom{5}{3} \binom{5}{4} \binom{5}{5}$

(a) 　　　　　　 (b)

Figure 4.6 (a) Pascal's triangle; (b) binomial coefficients.

is the number of ways that k objects can be selected from n objects. For example, in how many ways can we select two letters from the list $abcd$? The possible selections are

$$ab, ac, ad, bc, bd, cd$$

and so the answer is 6, which agrees with the fact that

$$\binom{4}{2} = 6.$$

To check this interpretation of a binomial coefficient in the general case, we can appeal to the principle of induction. Let $P(n)$ be the proposition that, for each integer k with $0 \leqslant k \leqslant n$, the number of ways that k objects can be selected from n objects is

$$\binom{n}{k}.$$

Then $P(0)$ is certainly true because there is only one way of selecting no objects from no objects. It remains to show that, for each $n \geqslant 0$, $P(n)$ implies $P(n+1)$. Suppose therefore that $P(n)$ happens to be true for some particular value of n. There is only one way of selecting 0 objects from $n+1$ objects and only one way of selecting $n+1$ objects from $n+1$ objects. We therefore only have to consider $P(n+1)$ in the case when $1 \leqslant k \leqslant n$.

To deduce $P(n+1)$ from $P(n)$, it has to be shown that k objects can be selected from the $n+1$ objects

$$a_1, a_2, \ldots, a_n, a_{n+1}$$

in

$$\binom{n+1}{k} = \binom{n}{k-1} + \binom{n}{k}$$

ways. The equation incorporates the fact that each binomial coefficient in Pascal's triangle (except for the 1s) is the sum of those above it. In selecting k objects from $a_1, a_2, \ldots, a_n, a_{n+1}$, we may either include a_{n+1} or exclude a_{n+1}. If a_{n+1} is included, the remaining $k-1$ objects have to be selected from the n objects $a_1, a_2, \ldots, a_n$. But $P(n)$ tells us that this can be done in

$$\binom{n}{k-1}$$

ways. If a_{n+1} is excluded, then all k objects have to be chosen from the n objects $a_1, a_2, \ldots, a_n$. But $P(n)$ tells us that this can be done in

$$\binom{n}{k}$$

ways. Summing these two results, we obtain the required conclusion: that $P(n+1)$ follows from $P(n)$.

To see why all this is relevant to the binomial theorem, consider the following proof that the coefficient of x^2 in the expansion of $(1+x)^4$ is

$$\binom{4}{2} = 6.$$

The coefficient of x^2 can be found by expanding the expression

$$(1+a)(1+b)(1+c)(1+d)$$

and then writing $a = b = c = d = x$. The terms in the expansion which give rise to x^2 terms after this substitution are

$$ab, \, ac, \, ad, \, bc, \, bd, \, cd.$$

Notice that all we have here is a list of the selections of two letters that can be made from the four letters a, b, c, d. Since there are

$$\binom{4}{2}$$

possible selections, it follows that this must be the coefficient of x^2 in the expansion of $(1+x)^4$.

4.8 Polynomials

The expression

$$(x+1)^4 = x^4 + 4x^3 + 6x^2 + 4x + 1$$

is an example of a polynomial of degree 4. In the general case, a *polynomial* is an expression of the form

$$p(x) = a_n x^n + a_{n-1} x^{n-1} + \cdots + a_1 x + a_0.$$

The constants $a_0, a_1, a_2, \ldots, a_n$ are called the coefficients of the polynomial. If $a_n \neq 0$, the *degree* of the polynomial is n.

Polynomials of degree 0 are just constants. Polynomials of degrees 1, 2, 3, 4 and 5 are called respectively linear, quadratic, cubic, quartic and quintic polynomials.

The most important theorem is that any polynomial of degree n admits a unique factorization into the form

$$p(x) = a_n(x - r_1)(x - r_2) \cdots (x - r_n).$$

The numbers $r_1, r_2, \ldots, r_n$ are called the *roots* of the polynomial. Obviously r is a root of a polynomial $P(x)$ if and only if

$$P(r) = 0.$$

The unique factorization theorem has a difficult proof, much too difficult to be considered here. Also, its conclusion needs to be treated with care for two reasons. The first is that the roots may be complex numbers. For example, the quadratic polynomial $p(x) = x^2 + 1$ is never zero when x is real and so can have no real roots at all. The second reason for care is that roots may be *repeated*. For example, the four roots of the quartic polynomial

$$p(x) = x^4 + 4x^3 + 6x^2 + 4x + 1$$

are all located at -1. We say that -1 is a root of *multiplicity* 4 since it is repeated four times in the factorization of $p(x)$.

We have studied the formula for finding the roots of quadratic polynomials already. There are also formulae for the roots of cubic and quartic polynomials. But these are complicated and involve working with complex numbers even when the coefficients and the roots of the polynomial are all real numbers. The formulae are therefore not much used. The situation for quintic and higher polynomials is even worse. It is a celebrated theorem of the mathematician Abel that *no* formula exists for the roots of quintic and higher polynomials in the general case. Thus although finding the roots of polynomials matters a great deal in many applications, it is a problem which seldom has easy answers.

What we shall describe here is a procedure designed to help *guess* the roots of polynomials in simple cases.

Consider the polynomial

$$p(x) = x^3 - 7x^2 + 16x - 12.$$

We shall never guess the roots of such a polynomial if they are numbers such as 4.973. Let us therefore try some simple numbers. Obviously $r = 0$ is not a root because $p(0) = -12$. Nor is $r = 1$ a root because $p(1) = 1 - 7 + 16 - 12 = -2$. Nor is $r = -1$ a root because $p(-1) = -1 - 7 - 16 - 12 = -36$. (In fact, it is obvious that no $r < 0$ can be a root because we shall have $p(r) < 0$.) But $r = 2$ is a root because $p(2) = 8 - 28 + 32 - 12 = 0$.

It follows that we can factorize $p(x)$ as

$$p(x) = (x - 2)q(x)$$

where $q(x)$ is a polynomial of degree one less than $p(x)$. In this case, $q(x)$ will be a quadratic and so its roots will be easy to find. But first we need to know what the coefficients of $q(x)$ are. Sometimes this is done by working out $p(x)/(x - 2)$ using 'long division' as explained in a later section. But a more efficient method is to make a table, as in figure 4.7(a).

In figure 4.7(a), a_k is the coefficient of x^k in the polynomial $p(x)$ and b_k is the coefficient of x^k in the polynomial $q(x)$. Since $q(x)$ is quadratic, $b_3 = 0$. But the numbers in the shaded squares need to be calculated. We also know that $a_{-1} = 0$ and that our calculations should lead to $b_{-1} = 0$. The final column therefore acts as a check that a mistake has not been made.

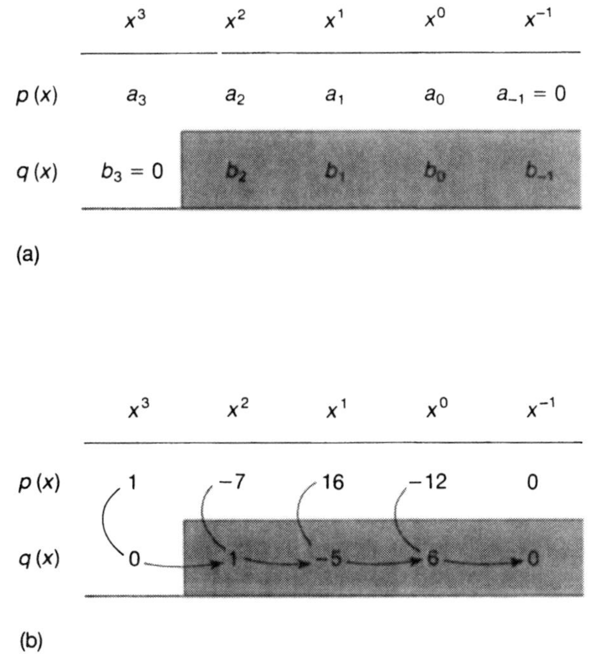

	x^3	x^2	x^1	x^0	x^{-1}
$p(x)$	a_3	a_2	a_1	a_0	$a_{-1} = 0$
$q(x)$	$b_3 = 0$	b_2	b_1	b_0	b_{-1}

(a)

	x^3	x^2	x^1	x^0	x^{-1}
$p(x)$	1	-7	16	-12	0
$q(x)$	0	1	-5	6	0

(b)

Figure 4.7 Factoring $p(x)$ into $x - r$ and $q(x)$: (a) table of coefficients; (b) $a_k = b_{k-1} - rb_k$ obtained from $(x - r)(\cdots + b_k x^k + b_{k-1} x^{k-1} + \cdots)$.

The rule for calculating the coefficients in the shaded boxes when a root r of $p(x)$ is known is as follows:

$$b_{k-1} = a_k + rb_k \qquad (k = 0, 1, 2, \ldots).$$

We know that $b_3 = 0$. Thus, $b_2 = a_3 + rb_3 = 1 + 2 \times 0 = 1$, $b_1 = a_2 + rb_2 = -7 + 2 \times 1 = -5$, $b_0 = a_1 + rb_1 = 16 + 2 \times (-5) = 6$ and $b_{-1} = a_0 + rb_0 = -12 + 2 \times 6 = 0$ (figure 4.7(b)). Thus $q(x) = x^2 - 5x + 6 = (x - 2)(x - 3)$ and so

$$p(x) = (x - 2)q(x) = (x - 2)^2(x - 3).$$

Notice that $r = 2$ turns out to be a root of multiplicity 2.

The justification for the procedure for finding the coefficients of $q(x)$ is very simple. We have that $p(x) = (x - r)q(x)$ and so

$$
\begin{aligned}
a_3 x^3 + a_2 x^2 + a_1 x + a_0 &= (x - r)(b_2 x^2 + b_1 x + b_0) \\
&= (b_2 x^3 + b_1 x^2 + b_0 x) - (rb_2 x^2 + rb_1 x + rb_0) \\
&= b_2 x^3 + (b_1 - rb_2)x^2 + (b_0 - rb_1)x - rb_0.
\end{aligned}
$$

Thus

$a_3 = b_2,$ i.e. $b_2 = a_3 + rb_3$ (recall that $b_3 = 0$)

$a_2 = b_1 - rb_2,$ i.e. $b_1 = a_2 + rb_2$

$a_1 = b_0 - rb_1,$ i.e. $b_0 = a_1 + rb_1$

$a_0 = -rb_0,$ i.e. $b_{-1} = a_0 + rb_0$ (recall that $b_{-1} = 0$).

The procedure has been described for a polynomial $p(x)$ of degree 3, but it works for a polynomial of any degree. And, of course, if $q(x)$ is not quadratic, the whole process will have to be repeated in order to find the roots of $q(x)$.

4.9 Population growth

Suppose that a population contains N_0 individuals at time $t = 0$. The yearly birth rate is $b = 1/100$ and the yearly death rate is $d = 1/101$. This means that, if there are N_t people alive at the end of year t, then $N_t/100$ people will be born and $N_t/101$ people will die in the following year. The number alive at the end of year $t + 1$ will therefore be

$$N_{t+1} = N_t + \frac{1}{100} N_t - \frac{1}{101} N_t.$$

(Of course, N_t is really a discrete variable but it is being treated like a continuous variable because the unit of measurement (i.e. one person) is to be taken as small compared with the quantities involved (i.e. the whole population).)

Write $r = b - d = 1/10,100$ for the rate at which population increases. Then population growth is governed by the *growth equation*

$$N_{t+1} = (1 + r)N_t \qquad (t = 0, 1, 2, \ldots).$$

This is an example of a *difference equation*. A solution is given by

$$N_t = A(1 + r)^t \qquad (t = 0, 1, 2, \ldots)$$

where A is an arbitrary constant. To check this we observe that, if $N_t = A(1 + r)^t$ $(t = 0, 1, 2, \ldots)$, then $N_{t+1} = A(1 + r)^{t+1} = (1 + r)A(1 + r)^t = (1 + r)N_t$, as required.

Observe that A is a constant because it does not vary with t. It is arbitrary because, whatever value is assigned to the constant A, $N_t = A(1 + r)^t$ will still be a solution of the growth equation.

The general solutions of difference equations always involve arbitrary constants. In order to know what values to assign to these arbitrary constants to obtain the particular solution relevant to your problem, *boundary conditions* are required. A boundary condition is just a piece of extra information which allows you to evaluate the arbitrary constants. For example, in the growth model, we might be told that the population at time 0 contains 100 people, i.e. $N_0 = 100$. This means that

$$100 = N_0 = A(1 + r)^0 = A$$

and so the relevant solution of the difference equation is

$$N_t = 100\left(1 + \frac{1}{10,100}\right)^t \qquad (t = 0, 1, 2, \ldots).$$

How did we know that $N_t = A(1 + r)^t$ was the general solution? One way of proceeding is as follows. Start with N_0. Taking $t = 0$ in $N_{t+1} = (1 + r)N_t$ we obtain that

$$N_1 = (1 + r)N_0.$$

Next take $t = 1$ in $N_{t+1} = (1 + r)N_t$. Then $N_2 = (1 + r)N_1$ and so

$$N_2 = (1 + r)^2 N_0.$$

Next take $t = 2$ in $N_{t+1} = (1 + r)N_t$. Then $N_3 = (1 + r)N_2$ and so

$$N_3 = (1 + r)^3 N_0.$$

It is now easy to guess that the general result is

$$N_t = (1 + r)^t N_0 \qquad (t = 0, 1, 2, \ldots).$$

The method provides some bonuses. It shows that *all* solutions must be of the form $N_t = A(1 + r)^t$ and that the arbitrary constant $A = N_0$.

In dynamic situations, it is often useful to look for *equilibrium solutions*. In this context, an equilibrium solution is one which does not depend on time, i.e. $N_t = \bar{N}$ $(t = 0, 1, 2, \ldots)$, where $\bar{N}$ is a constant. Usually, equilibrium solutions can be found without having to determine the general solution first. For example, to find the equilibrium solutions of $N_{t+1} = (1 + r)N_t$, simply write $N_{t+1} = \bar{N}$ and $N_t = \bar{N}$. Then the requirement on $\bar{N}$ is that

$$\bar{N} = (1 + r)\bar{N} \qquad \text{or} \qquad r\bar{N} = 0.$$

There are only two ways in which this equation can be satisfied. Either the growth rate $r = 0$, in which case any value of $\bar{N}$ gives an equilibrium solution; or $r \neq 0$, in which case the only value of $\bar{N}$ which gives an equilibrium solution is $\bar{N} = 0$.

Equilibrium solutions may be stable or unstable. For a *stable equilibrium*, a small change in the equilibrium boundary conditions (in this case $N_0 = \bar{N}$) will lead to a solution which converges back to the original equilibrium, i.e.

$$N_t \rightarrow \bar{N} \text{ as } t \rightarrow \infty.$$

With an *unstable equilibrium* this will fail to be the case.

To study the stability of equilibrium solutions in the growth model, we therefore need to know what happens to $N_t = N_0(1 + r)^t = N_0 c^t$ as $t \rightarrow \infty$. This depends on the value of c.

We know from section 4.6 that

$$c^t \to 0 \text{ as } t \to \infty$$

provided that $|c| < 1$, and so the equilibrium solution $N_t = \bar{N} = 0$ ($t = 0, 1, 2, \ldots$) is stable provided that $-1 < c < 1$ (figure 4.8).

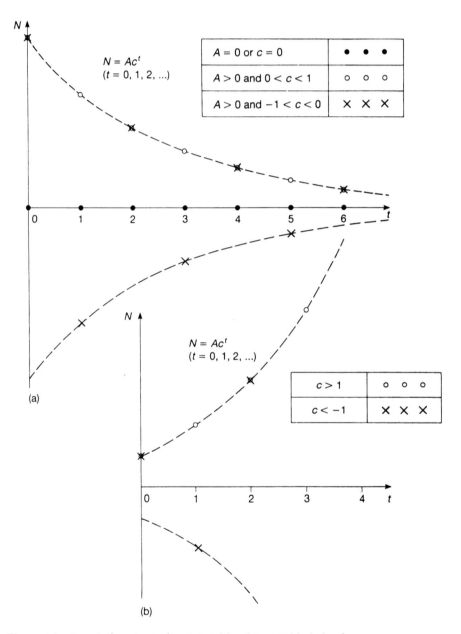

Figure 4.8 Population dynamics: (a) stable; (b) unstable behaviour.

If $c > 1$, then

$$c^t \to +\infty \text{ as } t \to \infty.$$

This formula means that c^t can be made larger than any number you care to name by taking t sufficiently large. For example, $(1.1)^5 = 1.61$, $(1.1)^{10} = 2.59$, $(1.1)^{20} = 6.73$, $(1.1)^{100} = 13,780.60$. Notice how fast $(1.1)^t$ increases, once it gets going.

If $c < -1$, then things are the same as in the case $c > 1$ except that c^t alternates in sign. We say that c^t oscillates infinitely.

There remain the trivial cases $c = 1$ and $c = -1$. When $c = 1$, $c^t \to 1$ as $t \to \infty$. When $c = -1$, c^t oscillates between $+1$ and -1.

Not all of these values of c are strictly relevant to the growth model. A death rate $d > 1$ would not make any sense. Hence $r = b - d \geqslant -1$ and so $c = 1 + r \geqslant 0$. The stability situation is as follows.

$-1 < r < 0$ (negative growth rate)

The only equilibrium solution is $N_t = \bar{N} = 0$. It is *stable* because, for all values of N_0,

$$N_t = N_0(1 + r)^t \to 0 \text{ as } t \to \infty.$$

The reason is that $c = 1 + r$ satisfies $0 \leqslant c < 1$.

$r > 0$ (positive growth rate)

Again, the only equilibrium solution is $N_t = \bar{N} = 0$. It is *unstable* because, for all values of N_0 *except* $N_0 = 0$,

$$N_t = N_0(1 + r)^t \to \infty \text{ as } t \to \infty.$$

The reason is that $c = 1 + r$ satisfies $c > 1$.

Note that, no matter how small the growth rate r may be (for example, $r = 1/10,100$), the population will explode towards infinity provided only that $r > 0$ and $N_0 > 0$.

$r = 0$ (zero growth rate)

In this case, *any* value of $\bar{N}$ provides an equilibrium solution. But none of these is stable. The reason is that, when $r = 0$,

$$N_t = N_0(1 + r)^t = N_0.$$

Thus, if the boundary condition is changed from $N_0 = \bar{N}$ to $N_0 = N^*$, the new solution $N_t = N^*$ does not satisfy $N_t \to \bar{N}$ as $t \to \infty$.

4.10 Cobweb model

This provides an opportunity to discuss the stability of equilibria in a more interesting situation.

Suppose that the price P_t, the demand D_t and the supply S_t of a commodity at times $t = 0, 1, 2, \ldots$ are related by the equations

$$D_t = \alpha - \beta P_t \tag{4.1}$$
$$S_t = D_t \tag{4.2}$$
$$S_{t+1} = \gamma + \delta P_t \tag{4.3}$$

$$(t = 0, 1, 2, \ldots)$$

where α, β, γ and δ are constants with $\beta > 0$ and $\delta > 0$. The idea is that, having produced S_t of the commodity, the producer decides on a price P_t at which to sell. This determines the amount D_t that the consumers will want to buy as described in equation (4.1). (Since $\beta > 0$, demand falls as the price rises.) The producer determines the price so as to sell his entire supply. This explains equation (4.2). Finally, the producer decides how much to supply in period $t + 1$. This will depend on his production costs and on his expectation of what price he will be able to sell at. It is assumed that the producer does not properly understand the way the market works but simply makes a prediction about the price P_{t+1} based on the current price P_t. The amount S_{t+1} supplied in the next period will therefore depend on the current price P_t. Equation (4.3) is the simplest possible relationship between S_{t+1} and P_t which could hold. (Since $\delta > 0$, next period's supply rises as the current price rises.)

An equilibrium solution is found by writing

$$P_t = \bar{P} \qquad D_t = \bar{D} \qquad S_t = \bar{S} \qquad (t = 0, 1, 2, \ldots).$$

Equations (4.1)–(4.3) become

$$\bar{D} = \alpha - \beta \bar{P}$$

$$\bar{S} = \bar{D}$$

$$\bar{S} = \gamma + \delta \bar{P}$$

from which it follows that $\alpha - \beta \bar{P} = \gamma + \delta \bar{P}$. Thus there is a unique equilibrium solution with equilibrium price

$$\bar{P} = \frac{\alpha - \gamma}{\beta + \delta}.$$

Figures 4.9(a) and 4.9(b) begin with a boundary condition $P_0 = P^*$. Then $S_1 = \gamma + \delta P_0$ is found, followed by $D_1 = S_1$ and then $P_1 = (\alpha - D_1)/\beta$. Next we calculate S_2, D_2 and P_2, and so on. The figures show that $P_t \to \bar{P}$ as $t \to \infty$, and so the equilibrium is stable, when $\delta < \beta$. When $\delta > \beta$, P_t oscillates infinitely.

To check these results algebraically, we eliminate terms in S_t and D_t from equations (4.1), (4.2) and (4.3). (This requires rewriting equations (4.1) and

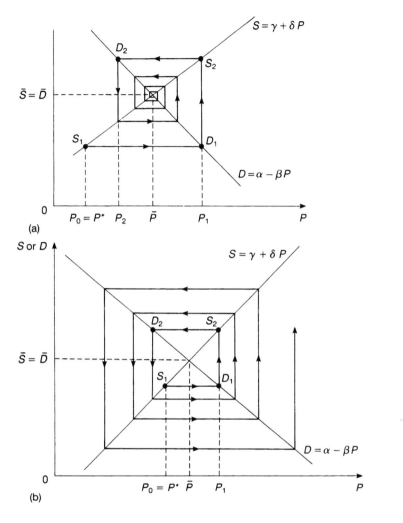

Figure 4.9   Cobweb model: (a) $\delta < \beta$; (b) $\delta > \beta$.

(4.2) as $D_{t+1} = \alpha - \beta P_{t+1}$ and $S_{t+1} = D_{t+1}$.) The result is the difference equation

$$\alpha - \beta P_{t+1} = \gamma + \delta P_t.$$

This becomes easier to deal with on introducing $Q_t = P_t - \bar{P}$. The new equation is

$$\alpha - \beta Q_{t+1} - \beta \bar{P} = \gamma + \delta Q_t - \delta \bar{P},$$

i.e.

$$Q_{t+1} = -\frac{\delta}{\beta} Q_t \qquad (t = 0, 1, 2, \ldots)$$

because $\bar{P} = (\alpha - \gamma)/(\beta + \delta)$. Thus the final difference equation is just the growth equation of section 4.9 but with $c = -\delta/\beta$ replacing $c = 1 + r$. Its solution is therefore

$$Q_t = Q_0 c^t \qquad (t = 0, 1, 2, \ldots)$$

and hence we obtain that

$$P_t = \bar{P} + (P* - \bar{P})c^t \qquad (t = 0, 1, 2, \ldots)$$

in which the boundary condition that $P_0 = P*$ has been incorporated.

Matters differ from section 4.9 in that c is now negative and so c^t oscillates between positive and negative values. However, if $|c| < 1$ (i.e. if $\delta < \beta$), we have the case of *damped* oscillation which means that

$$c^t \to 0 \text{ as } t \to \infty.$$

For example, in the case $c = -1/2$, $c^0 = +1$, $c^1 = -1/2$, $c^2 = +1/4$, $c^3 = -1/8$, $c^4 = +1/16$, $c^5 = -1/32$ and so on.

When $c < -1$ (i.e. if $\delta > \beta$), we have what might be called *explosive* oscillation. For example, in the case $c = -2$, $c^0 = +1$, $c^1 = -2$, $c^2 = +4$, $c^3 = -8$, $c^4 = +16$, $c^5 = -32$ and so on.

With $c = -1$, steady or uniform oscillation is obtained. We have that $c^0 = +1$, $c^1 = -1$, $c^2 = +1$, $c^3 = -1$, $c^4 = +1$, $c^5 = -1$ and so on.

4.11 Linear homogeneous difference equations

If we add 'with constant coefficients', linear homogeneous difference equations can be expressed in the form

$$p(E)y_t = 0 \qquad (t = 0, 1, 2, \ldots)$$

where p is a polynomial and E is the *shift operator*. This is used in the following way. We write $Ey_t = y_{t+1}$, $E^2 y_t = E(Ey_t) = Ey_{t+1} = y_{t+2}$. Similarly, $E^3 y_t = y_{t+3}$ and so on. Thus, for example,

$$(E^2 - 3E + 2)y_t = 0$$

is a shorthand way of writing the difference equation

$$y_{t+2} - 3y_{t+1} + 2y_t = 0.$$

The *order* of such a difference equation is simply the degree of the polynomial p. Thus $y_{t+2} - 3y_{t+1} + 2y_t = 0$ is a difference equation of order 2. The *general solution* of a difference equation of order n is one containing n arbitrary constants.

We have already seen that the growth equation $N_{t+1} = cN_t$, which we can write as

$$(E - c)N_t = 0 \qquad (t = 0, 1, 2, \ldots),$$

has a general solution with one arbitrary constant. The term N_0 can be taken to be anything. But once N_0 has been chosen, its value determines N_1 which, in turn, determines N_2 and so on. With the difference equation

$$y_{t+2} - 3y_{t+1} + 2y_t = 0$$

both the terms y_0 and y_1 can be chosen to be anything. But once y_0 and y_1 have been selected, their values determine y_2. The values of y_1 and y_2 then determine y_3 and so on.

Again, as in the growth model case, the particular values of the arbitrary constants which are relevant to the problem in hand are obtained from boundary conditions. Of course, the larger the order of the difference equation, the more boundary conditions will be needed.

It is easy to write down the general solution of the difference equation

$$p(E)y_t = 0 \qquad (t = 0, 1, 2, \ldots)$$

provided that you can factorize the polynomial $p(x)$. If

$$p(x) = (x - c_1)(x - c_2) \cdots (x - c_n)$$

and the roots $c_1, c_2, \ldots, c_n$ are all *distinct* (i.e. of multiplicity 1), then the general solution is simply

$$y_t = A_1 c_1^t + A_2 c_2^t + \cdots + A_n c_n^t \qquad (t = 0, 1, 2, \ldots)$$

where $A_1, A_2, \ldots, A_n$ are the n arbitrary constants required.

To check this, it is enough to verify that $y_t = A_k c_k^t$ is a solution for each $k = 0, 1, 2, \ldots, n$. We know, from our study of the growth equation, that $y_t = A_k c_k^t$ is a solution of

$$(E - c_k)y_t = 0.$$

But, since c_k is a root of $p(x)$, we may write $p(x) = q(x)(x - c_k)$. It follows that

$$p(E)y_t = q(E)(E - c_k)y_t.$$

But we have seen that $(E - c_k)y_t = 0$. Hence

$$p(E)y_t = q(E)0 = 0$$

and so $y_t = A_k c_k^t$ is a solution of $p(E)y_t = 0$.

Consider the difference equation

$$y_{t+2} - 3y_{t+1} + 2y_t = 0,$$

i.e.

$$(E^2 - 3E + 2)y_t = 0.$$

Since $p(x) = x^2 - 3x + 2 = (x - 1)(x - 2)$, the roots we need are $c_1 = 1$ and $c_2 = 2$. Hence the general solution is

$$y_t = A(1)^t + B(2)^t = A + B2^t$$

where A and B are arbitrary constants.

What happens when roots are repeated? The argument given above remains valid but does not provide enough arbitrary constants. If the root c has multiplicity m, it is necessary to replace the repeating terms Ac^t in the expression for the general solution by a term of the form

$$Ac^t + Btc^t + \cdots + Mt^{m-1}c^t$$

where $A, B, \ldots, M$ are arbitrary constants.

Consider the difference equation

$$y_{t+3} - 7y_{t+2} + 16y_{t+1} - 12y_t = 0,$$

i.e.

$$(E^3 - 7E^2 + 16E - 12)y_t = 0.$$

From section 4.8 we know that

$$p(x) = x^3 - 7x^2 + 16x - 12 = (x-2)^2(x-3)$$

The roots we need are therefore $c_1 = 2$, $c_2 = 2$, $c_3 = 3$, and so the general solution is

$$y_t = A2^t + Bt2^t + C3^t$$

where A, B and C are arbitrary constants.

What happens if roots are complex numbers? Everything described above remains valid. It will be more convenient to take up this point in a later section (section 16.8) when we study an analogous topic: differential equations.

4.12 Multiplier–accelerator models

Consider the following 'macroeconomic' model in which national income Y_t at time t depends on consumption C_t, investment I_t and government expenditure G (which is assumed to be constant). The equations postulated are:

$$Y_t = C_t + I_t + G \tag{4.4}$$
$$C_{t+1} = \gamma Y_t \tag{4.5}$$
$$I_{t+1} = \alpha(C_{t+1} - C_t). \tag{4.6}$$

In these equations, γ $(0 < \gamma < 1)$ is a *multiplier* and α $(\alpha > 0)$ is an *accelerator*. The idea is that consumption C_{t+1} in the next period is proportional to income Y_t in the current period, but that investment I_{t+1} in the next period is proportional to the *increase* $C_{t+1} - C_t$ in consumption.

Consider first the equilibrium values of these variables. Suppose that $Y_t = \bar{Y}$, $C_t = \bar{C}$ and $I_t = \bar{I}$ $(t = 0, 1, 2, \ldots)$. Then

$$\bar{Y} = \bar{C} + \bar{I} + G$$

$$\bar{C} = \gamma \bar{Y}$$

$$\bar{I} = \alpha(\bar{C} - \bar{C}) = 0.$$

Hence $\bar{Y} = \gamma \bar{Y} + 0 + G$. Thus $\bar{Y} = G/(1 - \gamma)$, $\bar{C} = \gamma G/(1 - \gamma)$ and $\bar{I} = 0$. Is this equilibrium stable?

From equation (4.4) we have that

$$Y_{t+1} = C_{t+1} + I_{t+1} + G$$
$$= \gamma Y_t + \alpha(C_{t+1} - C_t) + G.$$

Hence

$$Y_{t+2} = \gamma Y_{t+1} + \alpha(C_{t+2} - C_{t+1}) + G$$

and so from (4.5)

$$Y_{t+2} = \gamma Y_{t+1} + \alpha\gamma(Y_{t+1} - Y_t) + G.$$

This is a difference equation of order 2 that becomes more tractable if, as in section 4.10, we write $Z_t = Y_t - \bar{Y}$. Then

$$Z_{t+2} = \gamma Z_{t+1} + \alpha\gamma(Z_{t+1} - Z_t),$$

i.e.

$$[E^2 - \gamma(1 + \alpha)E + \alpha\gamma]Z_t = 0.$$

The roots of the polynomial $p(x) = x^2 - \gamma(1 + \alpha)x + \alpha\gamma$ are given by

$$c_1 = \frac{1}{2}\{\gamma(1 + \alpha) + \sqrt{[\gamma^2(1 + \alpha)^2 - 4\alpha\gamma]}\}$$

$$c_2 = \frac{1}{2}\{\gamma(1 + \alpha) - \sqrt{[\gamma^2(1 + \alpha)^2 - 4\alpha\gamma]}\}.$$

These are real and distinct provided that $\gamma^2(1 + \alpha)^2 > 4\alpha\gamma$. The general solution of the difference equation is then

$$Z_t = A_1 c_1{}^t + A_2 c_2{}^t \qquad (t = 0, 1, 2, \ldots).$$

For stability, we require that $Z_t \to 0$ as $t \to \infty$, i.e. $Y_t \to \bar{Y}$ as $t \to \infty$. If $A_1 \neq 0$ and $A_2 \neq 0$, it is therefore necessary that $c_1{}^t \to 0$ as $t \to \infty$ and $c_2{}^t \to 0$ as $t \to \infty$. We therefore need that $|c_1| < 1$ and $|c_2| < 1$. This will be satisfied, for example, if $\gamma = 0.9$ and $\alpha = 0.1$. It will fail to be satisfied, and so the equilibrium will be unstable, when, for example, $\gamma = 0.9$ and $\alpha = 2$.

4.13 Summing differences

This last section ties things together. First we explain the term 'difference equation'. This derives from the *difference operator* Δ defined by

$$\Delta y_t = y_{t+1} - y_t.$$

It is easy to express difference equations in terms of the difference operator because

$$Ey_t = y_{t+1} = y_{t+1} - y_t + y_t = \Delta y_t + y_t = (\Delta + 1)y_t$$

and so

$$E = \Delta + 1.$$

For example, the difference equation

$$(E^2 + 3E + 2)y_t = 0$$

can be written as

$$[(\Delta + 1)^2 + 3(\Delta + 1) + 2]y_t = 0,$$

i.e.

$$(\Delta^2 + 5\Delta + 6)y_t = 0.$$

Fortunately, the algebra for such operators is precisely the same as that for numbers in this context.

Expressing difference equations in terms of the difference operator makes it clearer that what we are doing when we solve a difference equation is to carry out one or more *summations*. The basic reason is simply that adding up is the opposite of taking away.

For example, the general solution to the difference equation

$$\Delta y_t = f_t \qquad (t = 0, 1, 2, \ldots)$$

is just

$$y_t = \sum_{k=0}^{t-1} f_k + A \qquad (t = 0, 1, 2, \ldots)$$

where A is an arbitrary constant. To check this, simply observe that

$$y_{t+1} - y_t = \sum_{k=0}^{t} f_k - \sum_{k=0}^{t-1} f_k = f_t.$$

(Note that it is conventional that $\sum_{k=0}^{-1} f_k$ represents 0.)

The summation results of section 4.2 can sometimes therefore be used to good effect in solving difference equations. Consider, for example, the difference equation

$$y_{t+1} - y_t = 2t + 3 \qquad (t = 0, 1, 2, \ldots),$$

i.e.

$$\Delta y_t = 2t + 3.$$

Its general solution is

$$y_t = \sum_{k=0}^{t-1} (2k+3) + A$$

$$= 2\frac{1}{2}(t-1)t + 3t + A$$

$$= t^2 + 2t + A.$$

For a more substantial example, we go back to the discussion of bonds in section 4.6. Recall that a consol pays $I at the end of each year for ever. How much money will the owner of the consol have derived from his ownership if he never spends any of the money and the interest rate is fixed at r? Since he never spends any of the money, the interest will be *compounded*. If the amount of money in year t is M_t, then

$$M_{t+1} = (1+r)M_t + I \qquad (t = 0, 1, 2, \ldots).$$

At the end of year t, the consol owner is paid the interest rM_t on his current capital of M_t plus the 'coupon' of the consol, namely I. This difference equation has to be solved given the boundary condition

$$M_0 = 0.$$

Write $c = 1 + r$ and multiply through the difference equation by the 'summation factor' $c^{-(t+1)}$. We obtain that

$$c^{-(t+1)}M_{t+1} - c^{-t}M_t = Ic^{-(t+1)},$$

i.e.

$$\Delta(c^{-t}M_t) = \frac{I}{c}\left(\frac{1}{c}\right)^t.$$

The general solution is therefore

$$c^{-t}M_t = \frac{I}{c}\sum_{k=0}^{t-1}\left(\frac{1}{c}\right)^k + A.$$

Since the sum is a geometric progression,

$$c^{-t}M_t = \frac{I}{c}\frac{1-(1/c)^t}{1-(1/c)} + A$$

$$= I\frac{c^t - 1}{c - 1}c^{-t} + A$$

and so

$$M_t = I\frac{c^t - 1}{c - 1} + Ac^t.$$

To find the value of the arbitrary constant which is appropriate, we use the boundary condition $M_0 = 0$. When $t = 0$,

$$0 = M_0 = I\frac{c^0 - 1}{c - 1} + Ac^0 = A.$$

The final result is therefore that

$$M_t = I\frac{c^t - 1}{c - 1} \qquad (t = 0, 1, 2, \ldots),$$

i.e.

$$M_t = \frac{I}{r}[(1 + r)^t - 1].$$

The *present value* of this amount of money is

$$V_t = \left(\frac{1}{1+r}\right)^t M_t = \frac{I}{r}\left[1 - \left(\frac{1}{1+r}\right)^t\right]$$

$$\rightarrow \frac{I}{r} \text{ as } t \rightarrow \infty$$

which confirms what was said in section 4.6.

Notice that the present value V of a sum of money M available at time T is the amount you would have to have *now* earning compound interest at rate r in order to end up with M at time T. If you begin with $V_0 = V$ at time 0, then the amount V_t that you will have at time t satisfies the difference equation

$$V_{t+1} = (1 + r)V_t \qquad (t = 0, 1, 2, \ldots).$$

This is just the growth equation of section 4.9 which has general solution

$$V_t = A(1 + r)^t \qquad (t = 0, 1, 2, \ldots)$$

and so, using the boundary condition $V_0 = V$,

$$V_t = V(1 + r)^t.$$

If this is equal to M when $t = T$, it follows that

$$M = V = V(1 + r)^T$$

and so the formula

$$V = \left(\frac{1}{1+r}\right)^T M$$

for the present value of M is recovered.

4.14 Exercises

1* Find the values of the following sums:

(a) $\displaystyle\sum_{k=m}^{n} 1$ (b) $\displaystyle\sum_{k=m}^{n} k$ (c) $\displaystyle\sum_{k=m}^{n} (\alpha k + \beta)$ (d) $\displaystyle\sum_{k=m}^{n} x^k.$

2   Let $p = (p_1, p_2, \ldots, p_n)'$ and $e = (1, 1, \ldots, 1)'$. If y is any n-dimensional vector, define

$$\mathscr{E}y = \sum_{k=1}^{n} p_k y_k$$

and

$$\operatorname{var} y = \sum_{k=1}^{n} p_k y_k^2.$$

Prove the following.

(a)   If α and β are scalars,

$$\mathscr{E}(\alpha x + \beta y) = \alpha \mathscr{E}x + \beta \mathscr{E}y.$$

(b)   If $\mu = \mathscr{E}x$, then

$$\operatorname{var}(x - \mu e) = (\operatorname{var} x) - \mu^2.$$

3*   Prove by induction that

$$\sum_{k=1}^{n} k = \frac{1}{2} n(n+1).$$

4   Prove by induction that

(a) $\displaystyle\sum_{k=1}^{n} k^2 = \frac{1}{6} n(n+1)(2n+1),$

(b) $\displaystyle\sum_{k=1}^{n} k^3 = \frac{1}{4} n^2(n+1)^2.$

5*   Commodity 1 consists of dollar consumption in period 1 and commodity 2 consists of dollar consumption in period 2. A consumer's income in period 1 is $10 and, in period 2, it is $33. The interest rate is 10 per cent. If her preferences are as in section 3.10, question 3, how much will she borrow or lend in period 1?

6   Repeat question 5 for the preferences of section 3.10, question 4.

7*   A shop has a refrigerator for sale at $1000 which you intend to buy. Unfortunately you have no money right now. The shop offers a deal by which you get the refrigerator now in return for 12 payments of $100 at the end of each subsequent month. What rate of interest would you be paying?

8   A bond offers a 'coupon' of I to be paid at the end of each of the next $n - 1$ years after which the bond 'matures' and its owner gets a final payment of F,

the 'face value' of the bond. How much should you be prepared to pay for the bond if $I = 1000$, $n = 21$, $F = 10,000$ and the rate of interest is $r = 8$ per cent?

9* What is the present value of a sum M of money to be paid to you 5 years from now if the rates of interest in the intervening years are respectively r_1, r_2, r_3, r_4 and r_5?

10 A security pays $\$(1.1)^k$ at the end of the kth year for ever. If the interest rate is 10 per cent, what should you be prepared to buy the security for?

11* Check using the definition at the beginning of section 4.7 that, for $1 \le k \le n$,

$$\binom{n+1}{k} = \binom{n}{k} + \binom{n}{k-1}.$$

12 How many ways can three objects be selected from seven objects?

13* Factorize the following polynomials.

(a) $p(x) = x^3 - 3x^2 - 10x$
(b) $p(x) = x^4 + x^3 - 3x^2 - 5x - 2$
(c) $p(x) = x^5 + 3x^4 + 2x^3 - 2x^2 - 3x - 1$

14 Factorize the following polynomials.

(a) $p(x) = x^2 - 3x + 2$
(b) $p(x) = x^3 - 3x^2 + 3x - 1$
(c) $p(x) = x^4 + 4x^3 - 16x - 16$

15* Find the general solutions of the following difference equations.

(a) $y_{t+3} - 3y_{t+2} - 10y_{t+1} = 0$
(b) $y_{t+4} + y_{t+3} - 3y_{t+2} - 5y_{t+1} - 2y_t = 0$
(c) $y_{t+5} + 3y_{t+4} + 2y_{t+3} - 2y_{t+2} - 3y_{t+1} - y_t = 0$

16 Find the general solutions of the following difference equations.

(a) $y_{t+2} - 3y_{t+1} + 2y_t = 0$
(b) $y_{t+3} - 3y_{t+2} + 3y_{t+1} - y_t = 0$
(c) $y_{t+4} + 4y_{t+3} - 16y_{t+1} - 16y_t = 0$

17* An investor has $\$100$ on which he receives compound interest of 10 per cent per year. How much will he have after 20 years?

18 How much was invested at a compound interest rate of 10 per cent per year if the amount which has accumulated after 100 years is $\$1,000,000$?

19* The producer in the cobweb model notices that using the current price as a predictor of the price in the next period always produces a number on the wrong side of $\bar{P}$. He therefore decides to use the average of the price in the current period and the previous period instead. This yields the equations

$$D_t = \alpha - \beta P_t \qquad\qquad (4.7)$$
$$S_t = D_t \qquad\qquad (4.8)$$

$$S_{t+1} = \gamma + \delta \frac{P_t + P_{t-1}}{2} \qquad (4.9)$$

$$(t = 1, 2, 3, \ldots).$$

What is the equilibrium solution? When is this stable? (Assume that $\delta > 8\beta$.)

20   Take $\gamma = 0.9$ and $\alpha = 0.1$ in the multiplier–accelerator model of section 4.12. Taking government expenditure as the unit of measurement (i.e. $G = 1$), what are the equilibrium values of national income, investment and consumption? Show that the equilibrium is stable.

4.15   Answers

1

(a) $\displaystyle\sum_{k=m}^{n} 1 = \sum_{k=1}^{n} 1 - \sum_{k=1}^{m-1} 1 = n - (m-1) = n - m + 1.$

(Note that the answer is *not* $n - m$.)

(b) $\displaystyle\sum_{k=m}^{n} k = \sum_{k=1}^{n} k - \sum_{k=1}^{m-1} k = \frac{1}{2} n(n+1) - \frac{1}{2}(m-1)m = \frac{1}{2}(n^2 + n - m^2 + m)$

$$= \frac{1}{2}[(n-m)(n+m) + (n+m)]$$

$$= \frac{1}{2}(n+m)(n-m+1).$$

(c) $\displaystyle\sum_{k=m}^{n}(\alpha k + \beta) = \alpha \sum_{k=m}^{n} k + \beta \sum_{k=m}^{n} 1 = \frac{\alpha}{2}(n+m)(n-m+1) + \beta(n-m+1)$

$$= (n-m+1)\left[\frac{\alpha}{2}(n+m) + \beta\right].$$

(d) $\displaystyle\sum_{k=m}^{n} x^k = \sum_{k=0}^{n} x^k - \sum_{k=0}^{m-1} x^k = \frac{1-x^{n+1}}{1-x} - \frac{1-x^m}{1-x} = \frac{x^m - x^{n+1}}{1-x}.$

3   Let $P(n)$ be the proposition that

$$\sum_{k=1}^{n} k = \frac{1}{2} n(n+1).$$

Then $P(1)$ is true because this just says that $1 = (1/2)1(1+1)$. Suppose that $P(n)$ happens to be true for some particular value of n. We need to deduce that $P(n+1)$ will then necessarily be true. But

$$\sum_{k=1}^{n+1} k = \sum_{k=1}^{n} k + (n+1)$$

$$= \frac{1}{2} n(n+1) + (n+1)$$

(because $P(n)$ is true). That is,

$$\sum_{k=1}^{n+1} k = \left(\frac{1}{2}n + 1\right)(n + 1) = \frac{1}{2}(n + 1)(n + 2)$$

and so $P(n + 1)$ has been deduced from $P(n)$. It has been shown that (i) $P(1)$ is true and (ii) for any n, $P(n)$ implies $P(n + 1)$. Thus $P(n)$ is true for all $n \geqslant 1$ by the principle of induction.

5 Figure 4.10 shows that the optimal bundle $q*$ requires all consumption in the second period. The consumer therefore lends her initial $10 in the first period and gets back $11 to spend in the second period along with her $33 income.

7 The answer is *not* 20 per cent which is what you would get by reckoning that you borrow $1000 and pay back $1200. You will not have borrowed $1000 for a whole year. After the first month you will have paid some of the amount borrowed back and therefore do not owe interest on the whole $1000.

Your income stream over the 12 months is $I_0, I_1, I_2, \ldots, I_{12}$ where $I_0 = 1000$ and $I_1 = I_2 = \cdots = I_{12} = -100$. From section 4.5, we know that the present value of this income stream is

$$\sum_{k=0}^{12} \delta^k I_k = I_0 + I_1\,\delta + I_2\,\delta^2 + \cdots + I_{12}\delta^{12}$$

$$= 1000 - 100(\delta + \delta^2 + \cdots + \delta^{12})$$

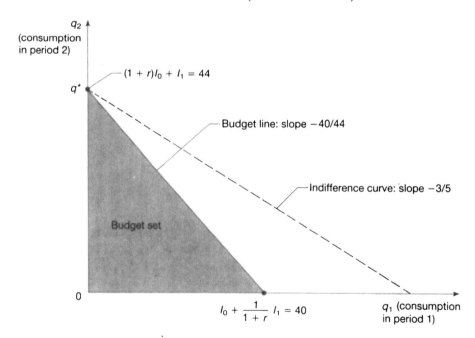

Figure 4.10 Intertemporal choice: corner solution.

$$= 1000 - 100\,\delta(1 + \delta + \cdots + \delta^{11})$$

$$= 1000 - 100\,\frac{\delta(1 - \delta^{12})}{1 - \delta}$$

where $\delta = 1/(1 + r)$ and r is the interest rate. The interest rate you are actually paying is found by setting the present value of your income stream to 0. We therefore require the value of δ such that

$$\delta(1 - \delta^{12}) = 10(1 - \delta)$$

$$\delta^{13} - 11\delta + 10 = 0.$$

One solution is $\delta = 1$ but this is not the solution we want. Approximating techniques exist for estimating the required solution painlessly, but we shall proceed by guessing. First check that $\delta = 0.97$ nearly satisfies our equation. This gives $r = 0.03 = 3$ per cent approximately.

But r is only the *monthly* interest rate. If the yearly rate of interest is R and you borrow \$1 now, then you will have to pay back \$$(1 + R)$ in one year. The present value of this repayment in terms of the monthly interest rate is

$$\left(\frac{1}{1 + r}\right)^{12}(1 + R) = 1.$$

Thus $R = (1 + r)^{12} - 1 \approx 42$ per cent. This is a lot of interest!

9   The value of M at the beginning of year 5 is just

$$\frac{1}{1 + r_5}\,M.$$

Thus the value of M at the beginning of year 4 is

$$\frac{1}{1 + r_4}\frac{1}{1 + r_5}\,M.$$

Proceeding in this way, we find the present value to be

$$\frac{1}{1 + r_1}\frac{1}{1 + r_2}\frac{1}{1 + r_3}\frac{1}{1 + r_4}\frac{1}{1 + r_5}\,M.$$

11   For $1 \leqslant k \leqslant n$,

$$\binom{n}{k} + \binom{n}{k - 1} = \frac{n!}{k!(n - k)!} + \frac{n!}{(k - 1)!(n - k + 1)!}$$

$$= \frac{n!}{(k - 1)!(n - k)!}\left(\frac{1}{k} + \frac{1}{n - k + 1}\right)$$

$$= \frac{n}{(k - 1)!(n - k)!}\frac{n + 1}{k(n - k + 1)}$$

$$= \frac{(n + 1)!}{k!(n + 1 - k)!} = \binom{n + 1}{k}.$$

13

(a) $p(x) = x^3 - 3x^2 - 10x = x(x^2 - 3x - 10) = x(x + 2)(x - 5)$
(b) $p(x) = x^4 + x^3 - 3x^2 - 5x - 2$

Try $x = 1$. $p(1) = 1 + 1 - 3 - 5 - 2 \neq 0$. Hence $x = 1$ is not a root. Try $x = -1$. $p(-1) = 1 - 1 - 3 + 5 - 2 = 0$ and so $x = -1$ is a root. Thus $p(x) = (x + 1)q(x)$. To find $q(x)$, use table 4.1.

Table 4.1

	x^4	x^3	x^2	x^1	x^0	x^{-1}
$P(x)$	1	1	-3	-5	-2	0
$Q(x)$	0	1	0	-3	-2	0
$R(x)$	0	0	1	-1	-2	0

We obtain that $q(x) = x^3 - 3x - 2$. Try $x = -1$. $q(-1) = -1 + 3 - 2 = 0$ and so $x = -1$ is a root of $q(x)$. Thus $q(x) = (x + 1)r(x) = (x + 1)(x^2 - x - 2) = (x + 1)(x + 1)(x - 2)$. Hence

$$p(x) = (x + 1)^3(x - 2).$$

(c) $p(x) = x^5 + 3x^4 + 2x^3 - 2x^2 - 3x - 1$

Try $x = 1$. $p(1) = 1 + 3 + 2 - 2 - 3 - 1 = 0$. Hence $x = 1$ is a root. Thus $p(x) = (x - 1)q(x)$. To find $q(x)$, use table 4.2.

Table 4.2

	x^5	x^4	x^3	x^2	x^1	x^0	x^{-1}
$P(x)$	1	3	2	-2	-3	-1	0
$Q(x)$	0	1	4	6	4	1	0

We obtain that $q(x) = x^4 + 4x^3 + 6x^2 + 4x + 1$ which the alert will recognize as the binomial expansion for $(x + 1)^4$. Thus

$$p(x) = (x - 1)(x + 1)^4.$$

15 (a) $p(E)y_t = (E^3 - 3E^2 + 10E)y_t = 0$

By question 13(a), $p(x) = x(x + 2)(x - 5)$. The general solution is therefore

$$y_t = A(1)^t + B(-2)^t + C(5)^t = A + B(-2)^t + C5^t$$

where A, B and C are arbitrary constants.

(b) $p(E)y_t = (E^4 + E^3 - 3E^2 - 5E - 2)y_t = 0$

By question 13(b), $p(x) = (x + 1)^3(x - 2)$. The general solution is therefore

$$y_t = A(-1)^t + Bt(-1)^t + Ct^2(-1)^t + D2^t.$$

(c) $p(E)y_t = (E^5 + 3E^4 + 2E^3 - 2E^2 - 3E - 1)y_t = 0$

By question 13(c), $p(x) = (x - 1)(x + 1)^4$. The general solution is therefore

$$y_t = A + B(-1)^t + Ct(-1)^t + Dt^2(-1)^t + Et^3(-1)^t.$$

17   Let the amount compounded after t years be M_t. Then we have the difference equation

$$M_{t+1} = (1 + r)M_t \qquad (t = 0, 1, 2, \ldots)$$

in which $r = 1/10$, together with the boundary condition

$$M_0 = 100.$$

The general solution is $M_t = A(1 + r)^t$ $(t = 0, 1, 2, \ldots)$. The boundary condition then yields that

$$M_t = 100(1 + r)^t = 100 \left(\frac{11}{10}\right)^t.$$

The amount we want is

$$M_{20} = 100 \left(\frac{11}{10}\right)^{20} = 673.$$

19   Writing $D_t = \bar{D}$, $S_t = \bar{S}$ and $P_t = \bar{P}$ $(t = 0, 1, 2, \ldots)$ in the given equations, we obtain that

$$\bar{D} = \alpha - \beta \bar{P}$$

$$\bar{S} = \bar{D}$$

$$\bar{S} = \gamma + \delta \frac{\bar{P} + \bar{P}}{2} = \gamma + \delta \bar{P}.$$

Thus the equilibrium values are as in section 4.10. In particular, $\bar{P} = (\alpha - \gamma)/(\beta + \delta)$. Is this equilibrium stable, given that $\delta > 8\beta$?
   First, we obtain a difference equation involving only the price. From equation (4.3),

$$2S_{t+2} = 2\gamma + \delta(P_{t+1} + P_t)$$

and thus

$$2\alpha - 2\beta P_{t+2} = 2\gamma + \delta(P_{t+1} + P_t).$$

Next follow section 4.10 by writing $Q_t = P_t - \bar{P}$. Then we get

$$2\beta Q_{t+2} + \delta Q_{t+1} + \delta Q_t = 0$$

$$(2\beta E^2 + \delta E + \delta)Q_t = 0.$$

The roots of the polynomial $2\beta x^2 - \delta x - \delta$ are

$$c_1 = \frac{-\delta + \sqrt{(\delta^2 - 8\beta\delta)}}{4\beta} \qquad c_2 = \frac{-\delta - \sqrt{(\delta^2 - 8\beta\delta)}}{4\beta}.$$

Thus the general solution is

$$P_t - \bar{P} = Q_t = Ac_1^t + Bc_2^t.$$

For stability, we require that $c_1^t \rightarrow 0$ as $t \rightarrow \infty$ and $c_2^t \rightarrow 0$ as $t \rightarrow \infty$. Thus we need $|c_1| < 1$ and $|c_2| < 1$. It is immediate that $c_2 < 0$ and that $|c_2| > |c_1|$. So when is $|c_2| < 1$? The requirement is that

$$\sqrt{(\delta^2 - 8\beta\delta)} < 4\beta - \delta.$$

Since the left-hand side is positive, we must have $0 < 4\beta - \delta$. Moreover, squaring both sides,

$$\delta^2 - 8\beta\delta < 16\beta^2 - 8\beta\delta + \delta^2.$$

But $0 < 16\beta^2$ is always true (unless $\beta = 0$). Stability is therefore guaranteed provided that $8\beta < \delta < 4\beta$.

5

Functions

5.1 Dependent and independent variables

A function

$$f: x \to y$$

is a rule which assigns a unique object y in the set Y to each object x in the set X. We say that y is the value of the function at x and write

$$y = f(x).$$

In such an equation, the symbol x is often said to be the *independent* variable and y the *dependent* variable. The idea is that we can freely assign to x any value from its range X but this then fixes the corresponding value of y uniquely.

For example, the equation

$$y = x^2$$

defines a function $g: \mathbb{R} \to \mathbb{R}$. To each value of the independent variable x in the set $\mathbb{R}$ of all real numbers, there corresponds just one real number y such that $y = g(x) = x^2$. Figure 5.1 shows the geometric property that a curve in $\mathbb{R}^2$ must satisfy in order to define a function $f: \mathbb{R} \to \mathbb{R}$. Each vertical line must hit the curve in one, and only one, point.

Notice that, in figure 5.1(b), the vertical line through $x = -1$ hits the curve in *three* points. We would therefore not know which of these three points to take to be $f(-1)$. What is more, the vertical line through $x = 2$ does not hit the curve at all. We therefore do not even have any candidate values of y to be $f(2)$.

Some of you will have been taught the term 'multi-valued function'. This is an oxymoron like 'square circle'. It is true that such abuses of language can sometimes avoid the necessity of paying attention to matters of detail which are unimportant in a particular context. But the price which is paid is that one gets confused in other contexts in which the details *do* matter.

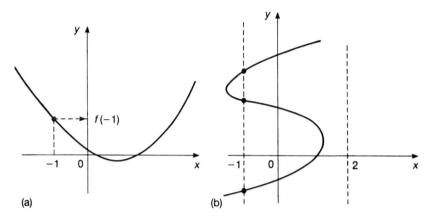

Figure 5.1 (a) Curve defining a function; (b) curve *not* defining a function.

5.2 Production functions

Many synonyms exist for the word 'function'. This is often the case with important mathematical ideas. Some of these synonyms, notably operator and transformation, are used when one is thinking of a function which does something to x in order to make $f(x)$. For example, the function $f: \mathbb{R} \to \mathbb{R}$ defined by

$$f(x) = x^2 + 1$$

can be thought of as the transformation of x into $f(x)$ achieved by the operation of squaring and then adding one.

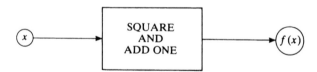

All this is very close to the economist's notion of a production function. Suppose that a producer makes only one output commodity but he can produce this in varying quantities depending on how much of each of m input commodities he decides to use. The precise relationship between the inputs and the output will depend on the *technology* available to the producer. This can be summarized using a *production function* $f: \mathbb{R}^m_+ \to \mathbb{R}_+$. If $x = (x_1, x_2, \ldots, x_m)'$ is an input bundle, then to write

$$q = f(x) = f(x_1, x_2, \ldots, x_m)$$

means that the maximum amount of output that the producer can obtain from x is q.

In section 3.9, we considered the case $m = 2$. The two factors of production were capital (k) and labour (l). A *Cobb–Douglas production function* $F: \mathbb{R}^2_+ \rightarrow \mathbb{R}_+$ is then defined by

$$F(k, l) = k^\alpha l^\beta.$$

Here α and β are positive parameters (i.e. they are constants whose value is left unspecified so that many situations can be studied simultaneously).

If γ is constant, then the set of all values of x which satisfy $f(x) = \gamma$ is called a *contour* of the function. Figure 5.2 shows some contours for a Cobb–Douglas production function. Each of these is just an isoquant (section 3.9). The contour labelled $F(k, l) = 1$ is the set of all input bundles $(k, l)'$ which can be used to produce a maximum output of $q = 1$. That labelled $F(k, l) = 3$ is the set of all bundles which can be used to produce a maximum output of 3.

Contours can also be interpreted in a straightforward geographical sense as on a map. The graph of $q = F(k, l)$ is a *surface* in three dimensions. Part of the surface in the case when $\alpha = \beta = 1/2$ is illustrated in figure 5.3.

Such surfaces are difficult to visualize even for those who are geometrically gifted. Contour maps, however, provide a way of describing the surface which requires only a two-dimensional picture. Figure 5.4 shows three curves of constant height in the surface. The heights are respectively $q = 1$, $q = 2$ and $q = 3$. Vertically below each of these 'level curves' is its corresponding contour.

5.3 Returns to scale

It is natural to think that if you were to double all the inputs, then you would double the output. A production function with this property has *constant returns to scale*. Mathematically, the requirement on a function $f: \mathbb{R}^m_+ \rightarrow \mathbb{R}_+$ is that, for each $c > 1$,

$$f(cx) = f(cx_1, cx_2, \ldots, cx_m) = cf(x).$$

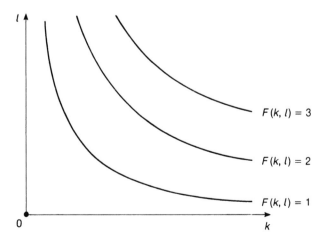

Figure 5.2 Contours of a Cobb–Douglas production function.

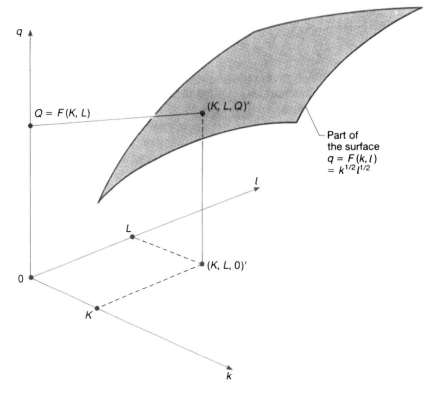

Figure 5.3   The graph of $q = F(k, l)$ is a surface.

A Cobb–Douglas production function has constant returns to scale when $\alpha + \beta = 1$. If $F(k, l) = k^{\alpha}l^{\beta}$, we have that

$$F(ck, cl) = (ck)^{\alpha}(cl)^{\beta} = c^{\alpha + \beta}k^{\alpha}l^{\beta} = cF(k, l).$$

'Increasing' returns to scale can occur in various ways. For example, if the diameter of a tube is doubled, twice as much metal will be needed to make it, but it will carry *four* times as much oil. The mathematical requirement is that, for each $c > 1$,

$$f(cx) > cf(x).$$

A Cobb–Douglas production function has 'increasing' returns to scale when $\alpha + \beta > 1$.

The mathematical requirement of *'decreasing' returns to scale* is that, for each $c > 1$,

$$f(cx) < cf(x).$$

A Cobb–Douglas production function has 'decreasing' returns to scale when $\alpha + \beta < 1$. This case is more problematic than the others. If you get less than

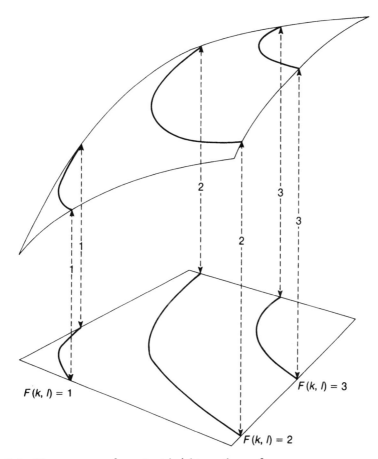

Figure 5.4   Three curves of constant height on the surface.

double the output by doubling the inputs, why not establish two separate factories and run them independently? The reason that 'decreasing' returns to scale can occur is that usually only the inputs you can change get listed. But there may be other *fixed* inputs. For example, suppose your production function is $F(k, l) = k^{1/2}l^{1/2}$ with constant returns to scale. But, if you cannot alter the capital, which stays fixed at $k = 4$, then you will think of your production function as $G(l) = F(l, k) = 2l^{1/2}$ which has 'decreasing' returns to scale. For example,

$$G(4l) = 2(4l)^{1/2} = 4l^{1/2} = 2G(l) < 4G(l).$$

5.4   Utility functions

There is a sense in which a consumer is a special kind of producer. Of course, a consumer does not produce an output commodity to be sold for profit. We think of the consumption bundle chosen by the consumer as producing 'utility' which she enjoys privately.

The contours of a consumer's *utility function* $f: \mathbb{R}^n_+ \to \mathbb{R}$ are then simply her indifference curves (section 3.4). To see this, simply observe that, if $q = q^*$ and $q = q^{**}$ are two commodity bundles on the *same* contour

$$f(q) = \gamma,$$

then the consumer will be indifferent between q^* and q^{**} because they generate the same utility γ.

From the mathematical point of view, it is very convenient to model consumer choice in terms of utility functions. Recall, for example, section 3.10, question 3. The consumer regards commodities 1 and 2 as perfect substitutes and is always willing to substitute 5 units of commodity 1 for 3 units of commodity 2. This can be succinctly expressed by saying that her utility function $F: \mathbb{R}^2_+ \to \mathbb{R}$ is defined by

$$F(q_1, q_2) = 3q_1 + 5q_2.$$

Thus, for example, she is indifferent between the bundles $(5, 0)'$ and $(0, 3)'$ because

$$F(5, 0) = 15 = F(0, 3).$$

If $p_1 = 4, p_2 = 1$ and $I = 10$, so that her budget line is $4q_1 + q_2 = 10$, then we can express the utility she obtains by spending all her income entirely in terms of q_1. The utility is

$$F(q_1, 10 - 4q_1) = 3q_1 + 5(10 - 4q_1) = 50 - 17q_1.$$

When is this largest? Obviously when q_1 is smallest, i.e. when $q_1 = 0$. It follows that the optimal consumption bundle is $q^* = (0, 10)'$.

However, although it is mathematically convenient to work with utility functions, it does not follow that people really have utility generators inside their heads. It is true that 'pleasure and pain centres' exist inside the brain, but what is known about these is too slender to base a theory upon. But economists do not claim that people *actually* maximize something called utility: they only claim that *rational* individuals would behave *as though* they were maximizing a utility function.

This claim is easily defended in the case when the consumer has to choose from a finite set of commodity bundles. Suppose, for example, that there are five bundles, labelled A, B, C, D and E. If the consumer's preference relation is rational in the sense described in section 3.4, then we can rank the five bundles in terms of increasing preference. To be specific, suppose that

$$B < C \sim D < A < E.$$

Thus, if the consumer has to make a choice from the set $\{A, B, C\}$, she will choose A. If she has to make a choice from $\{B, C, D\}$, she will be indifferent between C and D.

To find a suitable utility function $F: \{A, B, C, D, E\} \to \mathbb{R}$ is very easy. First define $F(B) = 0$ and $F(E) = 1$. That is, call the utility of the worst bundle 0 and that of the best bundle 1. Next choose any bundle intermediate between B and E and call its utility 1/2. For example, define $F(D) = 1/2$. Since $C \sim D$, this means that we must also define $F(C) = 1/2$. Only the bundle A is now left. This is intermediate between D and E and so we define $F(A) = 3/4$ because 3/4 is intermediate between $F(D) = 1/2$ and $F(E) = 1$. As table 5.1 shows, the utilities we have assigned to the bundles are ranked in the same way as the bundles themselves. Hence, in making choices, the consumer behaves *as though* maximizing utility.

Table 5.1

Bundles	B	C	D	A	E
Utilities	0	1/2	1/2	3/4	1
Alternative utilities	− 100	20	20	21	1000

Notice that the argument would work no matter how many bundles there were, because there is always another real number between any pair of real numbers. Notice also that there are many ways we could have assigned utility numbers to the bundles consistently with the consumer's preferences. The third row of the table gives an example. A consumer therefore does not have a unique utility function. There will be many utility functions which are equally good at describing her choice behaviour. We usually take the one that seems simplest.

Finally, although we sometimes say that a consumer prefers A to B *because* the utility of A exceeds the utility of B, this is not really true. In fact, we made $F(A) > F(B)$ *because* $A > B$ and so the actual implication is in the other direction! The purpose of utility functions is just to simplify the mathematics, not to provide an explanation of why people choose as they do. In consumer theory utility functions are taken as given and are not explained at all.

5.5   Real variables

This section is about functions $f: X \rightarrow Y$ where X and Y are sets of real numbers.

5.5.1   Constant functions

A function $f: \mathbb{R} \rightarrow \mathbb{R}$ is constant if there is a number c such that, for each $x \in \mathbb{R}$,

$$f(x) = c.$$

For example, the function $F: \mathbb{R} \rightarrow \mathbb{R}$ defined by

$$F(x) = 2 \qquad (x \in \mathbb{R})$$

is constant.

5.5.2 Linear functions

The mathematical definition of a linear function $f: \mathbb{R} \to \mathbb{R}$ requires that

$$f(x) = mx \qquad (x \in \mathbb{R})$$

for some fixed number m. Unfortunately, economists typically abuse the terminology by referring to a function $g: \mathbb{R} \to \mathbb{R}$ defined by

$$g(x) = mx + c \qquad (x \in \mathbb{R})$$

as a 'linear function'. Strictly speaking, the latter is an affine function. However, we shall follow the economists' practice but register some mild disapproval by always writing 'linear function' in quotes when the term is being misused. The reason that an affine function is called 'linear' is because its graph is a straight line (section 2.3).

5.5.3 Polynomial functions

A polynomial function $f: \mathbb{R} \to \mathbb{R}$ is defined by a formula of the type

$$f(x) = a_n x^n + a_{n-1} x^{n-1} + \cdots + a_1 x + a_0 \qquad (x \in \mathbb{R})$$

where the coefficients $a_0, a_1, \ldots, a_n$ are fixed real numbers (section 4.8). For example, the function $F: \mathbb{R} \to \mathbb{R}$ defined by

$$F(x) = (x + 2)^3 = x^3 + 6x^2 + 24x + 8$$

is a polynomial function.

5.5.4 Rational functions

A rational function $f: X \to \mathbb{R}$ is defined by a formula of the type

$$f(x) = \frac{p(x)}{q(x)} \qquad (x \in X)$$

where $p(x)$ and $q(x)$ are polynomials. The set X, on which f is defined, is the set of all values of x for which $q(x) \neq 0$.

Suppose, for example, that $X = (-\infty, -3) \cup (-3, \infty)$. Then the function $F: X \to \mathbb{R}$ defined by

$$F(x) = \frac{x - 1}{x + 3} \qquad (x \neq -3)$$

is rational. Its graph is sketched in figure 1.5 and repeated below in figure 5.5.

(The term rational function is used by way of analogy with rational number. Recall that a rational number has the form p/q, where p and q are integers with $q \neq 0$.)

5.5.5 Increasing functions

The mathematical requirement for an increasing function $f: X \to Y$ is that $f(x) \leqslant f(y)$ whenever $x < y$. The function is strictly increasing provided that $f(x) < f(y)$ whenever $x < y$ (see also section 10.5).

Unfortunately this is another case where the terminology is abused. People sometimes say 'increasing' when they really mean 'strictly increasing'. This is the case, for example, in the definition of 'increasing' returns to scale.

As an example, consider the rational function $F: X \to \mathbb{R}$ defined by

$$F(x) = \frac{x-1}{x+3} \qquad (x \neq -3)$$

(figure 5.5). Notice that, if we restrict our attention to values of x in the interval $(-\infty, -3)$, then the function is strictly increasing; similarly if we restrict attention to $(-3, \infty)$. But the function is not increasing over its whole domain of definition. For example, $f(-4) > f(-2)$ although $-4 < -2$.

5.5.6 Decreasing functions

The mathematical requirement is that $f(x) \geqslant f(y)$ whenever $x < y$. For a strictly decreasing function, the requirement is that $f(x) > f(y)$ whenever $x < y$.

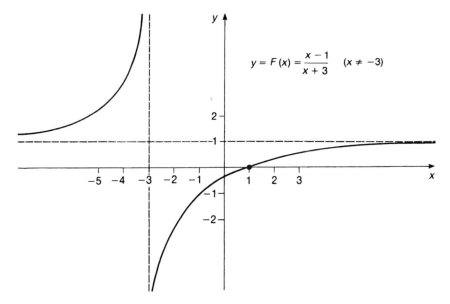

Figure 5.5 Both parts of the graph are increasing, but the function is not.

5.5.7   Continuous functions

A function is continuous if its graph can be drawn without lifting the pencil from the paper. Consider, for example, the function $F: \mathbb{R} \to \mathbb{R}$ defined by

$$F(x) = \begin{cases} \dfrac{x-1}{x+3} & \text{if } x \neq -3 \\ 1 & \text{if } x = -3. \end{cases}$$

This has a discontinuity at $x = -3$ (see figure 5.5).

5.5.8   Differentiable functions

A function is differentiable if its graph has a non-vertical tangent at every point. This is a concept of the utmost importance but, at this point, the only comment that will be made is that a function can be continuous without being differentiable. This can happen, for example, if the graph has a 'kink' as illustrated in figure 5.6.

5.5.9   Convex functions

A function $f: X \to Y$ is convex if the set *above* its graph is convex (section 3.5). For example, the function $F: (-\infty, -3) \to \mathbb{R}$ defined by

$$F(x) = \frac{x-1}{x+3} \qquad (x < -3)$$

is convex. But notice that attention has to be restricted to the interval $(-\infty, -3)$. If we use the same formula to define a function on the interval $(-3, \infty)$, the result will be concave as discussed below.

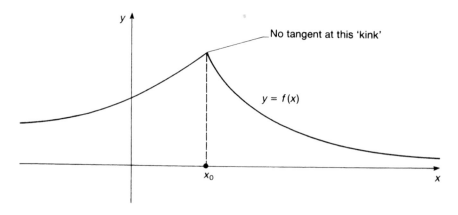

Figure 5.6   A curve that is not differentiable at $x = x_0$.

5.5.10 Concave functions

A function $f: X \to Y$ is concave if the set *below* its graph is convex. As an example, consider the production function $G: \mathbb{R}_+ \to \mathbb{R}_+$ defined by

$$G(l) = 2l^{1/2} \qquad (l \geqslant 0).$$

This was obtained in section 5.3 from a constant-returns-to-scale Cobb–Douglas production function by keeping the capital input fixed. Its graph is illustrated in figure 5.7.

The convex set S below the graph is shaded. Two points should be noted. The first is that a *concave* production function necessarily exhibits *decreasing returns to scale*. To see this, recall from section 3.5 that the point x must lie *inside* the convex set S. Take $\alpha = 1/c$. Then $l = \alpha(cl) + (1 - \alpha)0$. Hence $x = \alpha a + (1 - \alpha)b$. Therefore $H = \alpha G(cl) + (1 - \alpha)0 = G(cl)/c$. Since $H \leqslant G(l)$, it follows that

$$G(cl) \leqslant cG(l).$$

Thus concavity is a stronger condition than decreasing returns to scale (provided that 'decreasing' is interpreted in the proper mathematical sense). Similarly, convexity is stronger than increasing returns to scale.

The other point is that a differentiable function is concave if and only if its slope is *decreasing*. In economics, the word 'marginal' always has a mathematical interpretation as the slope of something (see sections 3.8 and 3.9). Here the slope of the production function when $l = L$ is the *marginal product* (MP).

The diagram shows a production function with marginal product m when $l = L$. This means that the slope when $l = L$ is m. If the input of labour is increased from L by a small amount ΔL, by how much will output increase from Q? The answer

$$\Delta Q = m\Delta L$$

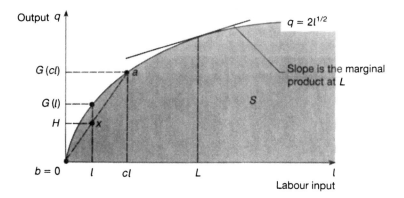

Figure 5.7 A concave production function.

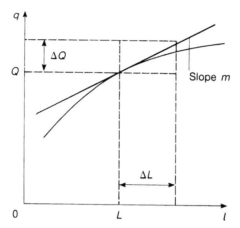

Figure 5.8 Extra output approximately equals slope × extra input.

is not quite right, but it will be *nearly* right if ΔL is very small. Thus, the marginal product m tells us how much extra output we shall get for each extra unit of labour if the current labour force is L. (As explained in section 4.1, this statement requires an understanding that the units being used are small.)

If the marginal product is decreasing (which implies that the production function is concave), then each extra unit of labour produces less extra output than the last unit. Thus, productivity is going down.

Of course, if the production function is convex, then the marginal product increases and so productivity goes up.

5.6 Demand functions

Suppose that a consumer has a fixed income of $I = 24$ and that the price of commodity 2 (which we shall think of as an aggregate of all commodities except commodity 1) is also fixed at $p_2 = 3$. How will the consumer's demand for commodity 1 vary as the price varies?

We shall study the problem in the case when the consumer has a Cobb–Douglas utility function $u: \mathbb{R}_+^2 \to \mathbb{R}$ defined by $u(q_1, q_2) = q_1 q_2$. Her indifference curves are then just as described in example 3.8.1 with $\alpha = \beta = 1$. We have therefore already calculated that her optimal consumption bundle $\boldsymbol{q} = (q_1, q_2)'$, when the price vector is $(p_1, p_2)'$, satisfies

$$\text{MRS} = -p_1/p_2,$$

i.e.

$$-\frac{q_2}{q_1} = -\frac{p_1}{3}.$$

Since q must be on her budget line $p_1 q_1 + 3q_2 = 24$, we also have that $3q_2 = 24 - p_1 q_1$. Thus

$$24 - p_1 q_1 = p_1 q_1$$

and so

$$p_1 = \frac{12}{q_1}.$$

This formula defines the consumer's *demand function* (figure 5.9). That is, her demand function $d: (0, \infty) \to (0, \infty)$ is defined by

$$d(q_1) = \frac{12}{q_1} \qquad (q_1 > 0).$$

Here $d(q_1)$ is the price that must be charged for commodity 1 in order that the consumer buys amount q_1 – other things being equal (i.e. all other variables being held fixed). Note that the demand curve is decreasing. Thus, if you want to sell a lot, you had better charge a low price.

One thing that is a little odd about this formulation is that price is expressed as a function of quantity rather than the reverse. It is natural to think of the price *causing* the demand and hence to look for a function $e: (0, \infty) \to (0, \infty)$ with the property that $q_1 = e(p_1)$ is the amount demanded when the price is p_1. As a consequence, modern economists often refer to $e: (0, \infty) \to (0, \infty)$ as the demand function and call $d: (0, \infty) \to (0, \infty)$ the inverse demand function. But perhaps our somewhat old-fashioned usage will be less confusing for beginners.

Figure 5.10 shows the price p_1 determining the budget line, which then determines the optimal consumption bundle, which then determines the amount $q_1 = e(p_1)$ of commodity 1 demanded.

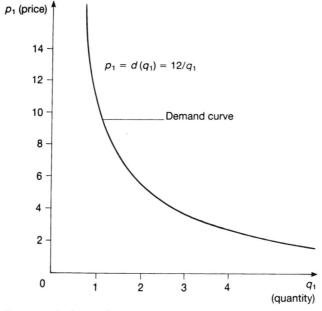

Figure 5.9 Consumer's demand curve.

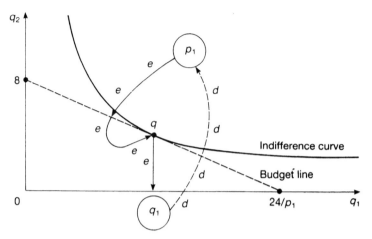

Figure 5.10   Price determines the budget which determines the optimal consumption and hence the demand.

The function e: $(0, \infty) \to (0, \infty)$ is the inverse demand curve. In general, if $f: X \to Y$ is a function, then its inverse function $g: Y \to X$ is what we get by solving the equation

$$y = f(x)$$

to get x in terms of y. It follows that

$$x = g(y)$$

is the same equation as $y = f(x)$ but with its terms rearranged. But remember the definition of a function (section 5.1). For $g: Y \to X$ to be a function, there must be a *unique* value of $x = g(y)$ in X for *every* value of y in Y. Thus, for the inverse function $g: Y \to X$ to be properly defined, the equation

$$y = f(x)$$

must have a *unique* solution on the set X for *every* value of y in the set Y.

The usual notation for the inverse function to $f: X \to Y$ is $f^{-1}: Y \to X$. This does not, of course, mean that $f^{-1} = 1/f$.

To find the inverse function to $d: (0, \infty) \to (0, \infty)$ we have to solve the equation

$$p_1 = 12/q_1$$

to get q_1 in terms of p_1. This is not very difficult. We observe that, for each positive p_1, there is a unique positive q_1 which satisfies the equation:

$$q_1 = 12/p_1.$$

Thus $d^{-1}: (0, \infty) \to (0, \infty)$ is defined by $d^{-1}(p_1) = 12/p_1$. The graph of an inverse function is drawn just by reflecting the graph of the original function across the 45° line (figure 5.11).

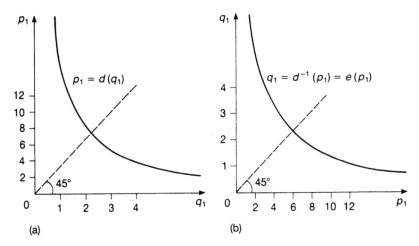

Figure 5.11   (a) Demand curve; (b) inverse demand curve.

5.7   Market demand

A market demand function $D: (0, \infty) \rightarrow (0, \infty)$ gives the total demand in a market, as opposed to the demand of an individual consumer as described in section 5.6. Thus, to write

$$p = D(q)$$

means that p is the price of the commodity in question necessary to generate a total market demand of q. Demand functions are usually assumed to be decreasing.

In principle, a market demand function is found by aggregating all the individual demands. As an example, consider an economy with n consumers. These all have the same utility function as that considered in section 5.6. We shall be considering the market for the first commodity and so $p = p_1$ and $q = q_1$. The second commodity, representing an aggregate of all commodities but the first, will be assumed to have a fixed price $P = p_2$. Although the consumers have the same preferences in this example, we shall assume that they have different incomes $I_1, I_2, \ldots, I_n$.

Adapting the analysis of section 5.6 slightly, we obtain that the demand function $d_k: (0, \infty) \rightarrow (0, \infty)$ for the kth consumer is defined by

$$d_k(q) = \frac{I_k}{2q}.$$

What is aggregate demand? It is certainly *not* $d_1(q) + d_2(q) + \cdots + d_n(q)$. Recall that $d_k(q)$ is the price that will make consumer k buy amount q. We need to look at the inverse demand function $d_k^{-1}: (0, \infty) \rightarrow (0, \infty)$, which is obtained by solving the equation $p = I_k/2q$ to give $q = I_k/2p$. Thus

$$d_k^{-1}(p) = \frac{I_k}{2p}.$$

The quantity $d_1^{-1}(p) + d_2^{-1}(p) + \cdots + d_n^{-1}(p)$ is now the total amount q which will be demanded when the price is p. Hence

$$D^{-1}(p) = d_1^{-1}(p) + d_2^{-1}(p) + \cdots + d_n^{-1}(p) = I/2p$$

where $I = I_1 + I_2 + \cdots + I_n$ is the aggregate income of the consumers. The final demand function is then found by solving the equation $q = I/2p$ to get $p = I/2q$. Thus the market demand function $D: (0, \infty) \rightarrow (0, \infty)$ is defined by

$$D(q) = I/2q.$$

The case when $n = 2$, $I_1 = 12$ and $I_2 = 24$ is illustrated in figure 5.12.

It is obvious that, if there were more consumers, the market demand curve would be shifted to the right. For example, the quantity corresponding to price $p = 4$ in the diagram would cease to be $q_1 + q_2$, if there were a third consumer, and become $q_1 + q_2 + q_3$. Actually, it is not the number of consumers as such which matters in this model but their aggregate income I. The larger the value of I, the greater quantity that is demanded at every price. Thus, increasing the value of I shifts the whole demand curve to the right. Bear in mind that economists nearly always mean such a wholesale shift of the demand curve to the right when they say 'demand goes up' without specifying what the circumstances are. Of course, demand will go up and down in the market as the price changes. But what they mean in saying 'demand goes up' without qualification is that there has been a change in the underlying circumstances which determine how the price and quantity demanded in the market are related (figure 5.13). In our case, for example, it might be that the government decides to tax income more heavily. This will reduce what people have to spend and so shift the whole demand curve to the left. Thus the taxation decision is said to 'reduce demand'.

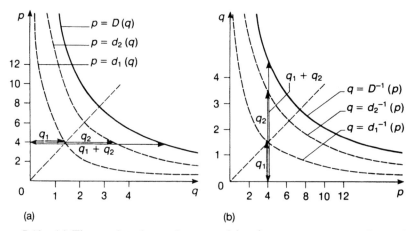

Figure 5.12   (a) The market demand curve arising from two consumer demand curves and (b) its inverse.

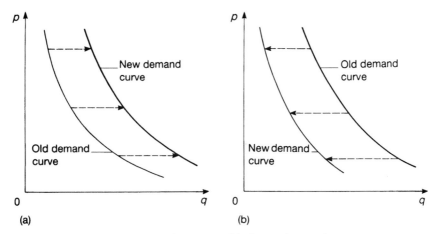

Figure 5.13   (a) (Market) demand goes up; (b) demand goes down.

5.8   Cost functions

To say that a producer's *cost function* is $c: \mathbb{R}_+ \to \mathbb{R}$ means that, for each $q \geqslant 0$, the cost to the producer of manufacturing the output q is equal to $c(q)$.

The construction of a producer's cost function is very similar to the construction of an individual consumer's demand function (section 5.6). Consider, for example, a producer with the Cobb–Douglas production function $F: \mathbb{R}_+^2 \to \mathbb{R}$ defined by

$$F(k, l) = k^{1/2}l^{1/2}.$$

This yields constant returns to scale (section 5.3). Suppose that the price of capital (k) is fixed at $p = 4$ and the price of labour (l) is fixed at $w = 9$. The cost of buying the input bundle $(k, l)'$ is then

$$c = pk + wl = 4k + 9l.$$

If the producer decides to make an amount q of the output, the cost will therefore be $c = 4k + 9l$, where $(k, l)'$ is the input bundle which minimizes the cost of producing q. We saw how to deal with such problems in section 3.9. We need to find the input bundle $(k, l)'$ on the isoquant $k^{1/2}l^{1/2} = q$ at which

$$\text{TRS} = -\frac{p}{w} = -\frac{4}{9}.$$

Proceeding as in section 3.9,

$$-\frac{1}{k} = -\frac{4}{9}$$

and so $l = 4k/9$ and $k = 9l/4$. But $(k, l)'$ must lie on the isoquant $k^{1/2}l^{1/2} = q$ and so

$$k^{1/2}\left(\frac{4k}{9}\right)^{1/2} = q$$

$$\frac{2}{3}k = q$$

$$k = \frac{3q}{2}.$$

Similarly,

$$l = \frac{2}{3}q$$

It follows that the cost of producing q is

$$c = 4k + 9l = 4\frac{3q}{2} + 9\frac{2q}{3} = 12q$$

and thus the formula for the cost function $c: \mathbb{R}_+ \to \mathbb{R}$ is

$$c(q) = 12q \qquad (q \geqslant 0).$$

Cost functions are always assumed to be increasing (figure 5.14). This cost function is linear. Each extra unit costs $12 to make. This uniformity is a consequence of the fact that the production function exhibits constant returns to scale.

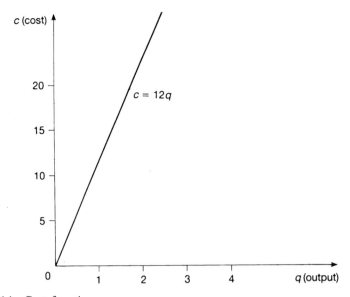

Figure 5.14   Cost function.

Economists distinguish between short-run or variable costs and long-run or fixed costs. The terms 'short run' and 'long run' do not have precise definitions but they are none the less very useful terms. The idea is that, in the long run, everything can be changed. But some things cannot be changed quickly. For example, a producer in a non-unionized industry may well be able to change his labour force fairly readily but he cannot replace his capital goods (machinery, factory buildings etc.) overnight. The term 'short run' signals that some such input is fixed during the time-span being considered, while other inputs may vary.

As an example, we consider the same producer as before but in the short run rather than the long run. As in section 5.3, it will be assumed that capital input is fixed at $k = 4$ but that labour (l) is a variable input. The short-run production function is then $G: \mathbb{R}_+ \to \mathbb{R}_+$, where

$$G(l) = (4)^{1/2} l^{1/2} = 2 l^{1/2}.$$

This short-run production function shows decreasing returns to scale (section 5.3).

If k is held fixed at $k = 4$, then the cost of buying the input bundle $(k, l)'$ is

$$c = pk + wl = 4 \times 4 + 9l = 16 + 9l.$$

If the producer decides to make an amount q of the output, then the amount of labour l required is given by $q = G(l) = 2l^{1/2}$. Thus

$$l = \frac{1}{4} q^2.$$

(Notice, incidentally, that $l = G^{-1}(q)$.) It follows that the cost of producing q is equal to

$$c = 16 + 9l = 16 + \frac{9}{4} q^2$$

and hence the short-run *total cost function* $c: \mathbb{R}_+ \to \mathbb{R}$ is given by

$$c(q) = 16 + \frac{9}{4} q^2 \qquad (q \geq 0)$$

(figure 5.15).

It is no surprise that the total cost curve is increasing. But notice also that it is convex and so its slope is also increasing. The slope of the cost curve when $q = Q$ is the *marginal cost* (MC). To say that marginal cost increases means that each extra unit of output costs more to produce than the last one. Thus unit costs are going up (see section 5.5.10 for comparison). This happens because the short-run production function has decreasing returns to scale.

Sometimes *fixed cost functions* and *variable cost functions* are required. The fixed cost is simply the cost of the fixed inputs and the variable cost is the cost of the variable inputs.

(*Note:* If the capital equipment is fixed in the short run, why is it counted as costing something per hour? The money with which it was bought is a 'sunk

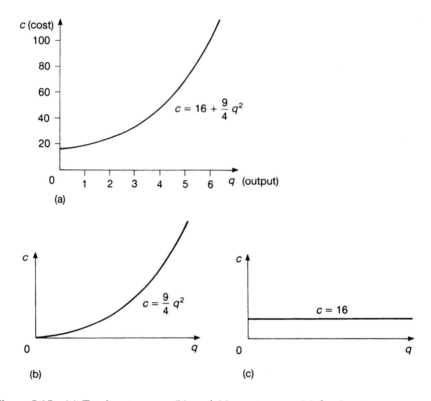

Figure 5.15   (a) Total cost curve; (b) variable cost curve; (c) fixed cost curve.

cost' – it is money which has been spent irrevocably and cannot be recovered. As such, it should be irrelevant to production decisions. This argument is correct but ignores the fact that the capital equipment does not cease to have any value after it is bought. Each hour that it is used in the production process means one hour less that it can be used for its next-best purpose. This might be, for example, renting it by the hour to another producer. The hourly rental rate that the other producer would pay you is then the price that you have to pay if you use the equipment to produce goods. Economists call this the 'opportunity cost' of the equipment.)

5.9   Supply functions

Under perfect competition, each producer assumes that his own output will be so small, compared with the total output in the market, that the effect of his own production on the market price of the product will be negligible. Such a producer is therefore a 'price-taker', i.e. he takes prices as given. Something similar has already been assumed when considering the markets for the factors of production. In treating the prices of labour and capital as fixed, the implicit assumption was that the producer believes his purchases in the labour and capital markets will be so small compared with the total amount purchased that they will not affect the prices he has to pay.

In this section, we shall study the *supply function* s: $\mathbb{R}_+ \to \mathbb{R}_+$ for a price-taking producer with a simple cost function. For each $q \geqslant 0$, the value of $s(q)$ is the market price for the output which will generate a production equal to q. Supply functions are usually increasing.

A producer is assumed to seek to maximize profit. This is the difference between the revenue he gets from selling his output q and the cost of producing q. We discussed the idea of a cost function c: $\mathbb{R}_+ \to \mathbb{R}$ in section 5.8. To say that R: $\mathbb{R}_+ \to \mathbb{R}$ is a *revenue function* means that $R(q)$ is the money that the producer gets from selling the output q. When the price p is fixed, the revenue function is therefore simply defined by

$$R(q) = pq \qquad (q \geqslant 0).$$

It is therefore linear with slope equal to the price.

The *profit function* π: $\mathbb{R}_+ \to \mathbb{R}$ is defined by

$$\pi(q) = R(q) - c(q) \qquad (q \geqslant 0).$$

Figure 5.16 shows a typical situation. Given the price p, profit is largest when $q = q^*$. Thus the value of the supply function at q^* is $s(q^*) = p$.

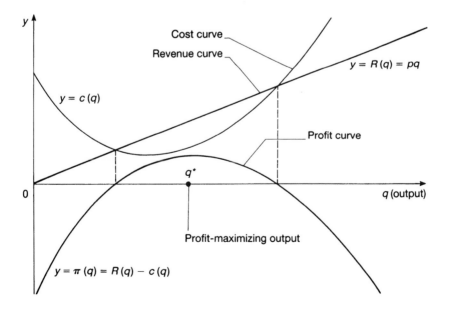

Figure 5.16 Location of the profit-maximizing output for a given price.

Sometimes, unlike figure 5.16, the revenue curve will not intersect the cost curve when the price gets too low. Maximum profit will then be negative, i.e. the producer must make a loss. But he will still produce, in the short run, because he must pay his fixed costs whether or not he produces.

The examples below use cost functions from section 5.8.

5.9.1 $c(q) = 12q$

The profit function $\pi: \mathbb{R}_+ \rightarrow \mathbb{R}$ is given by

$$\pi(q) = pq - 12q = (p - 12)q \qquad (q \geqslant 0).$$

The value of the profit-maximizing output $q = q^*$ depends on the value of the price p. There are three cases (figure 5.17).

1   $p < 12$: profit $\pi(q)$ is negative unless $q = 0$. Hence $q^* = 0$.
2   $p = 12$: profit is always equal to zero for all values of q. Hence q^* can take *any* non-negative value.
3   $p > 12$: profit $\pi(q)$ is strictly increasing. Thus, no matter what value you propose for q^*, I can do better by producing more. Sometimes it is said that the profit-maximizing output is 'infinite'. What this really means is that the producer will want to produce as much as he can. We know, of course, that *something* must stop him producing more and more and more. But what this something is has been left out of this over-simplifed model.

Economists draw the 'supply function' $s: \mathbb{R}_+ \rightarrow \mathbb{R}_+$ as in figure 5.18.

They will also draw the 'inverse supply function' $s^{-1}: \mathbb{R}_+ \rightarrow \mathbb{R}_+$ as in figure 5.19. This does no harm unless you want to use some theorems about functions. Then you have to remember that these 'functions' are not really functions (section 5.1).

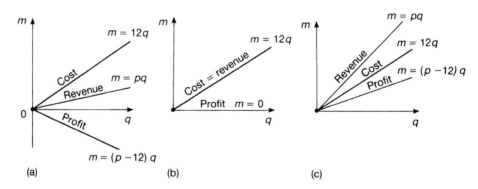

Figure 5.17   Cost ($12q$), revenue (pq) and profit ($(p - 12)q$) curves for (a) $p < 12$, (b) $p = 12$ and (c) $p > 12$.

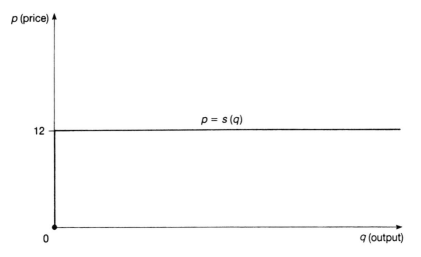

Figure 5.18   Supply function when $c(q) = 12q$.

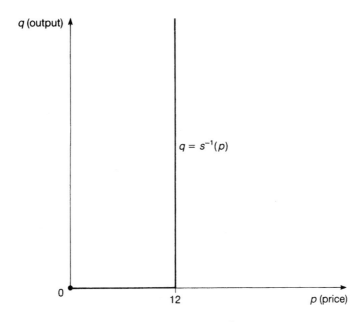

Figure 5.19   Inverse supply function when $c(q) = 12q$.

5.9.2 $c(q) = 16 + 9q^2/4$

The profit function is given by

$$\pi(q) = pq - 16 - 9q^2/4.$$

We can find the profit-maximizing output $q = q^*$, without using calculus, by 'completing the square' (section 1.4). We have that

$$\pi(q) = -\frac{9}{4}\left(q^2 - \frac{4pq}{9}\right) - 16$$

$$= -\frac{9}{4}\left(q - \frac{2p}{9}\right)^2 + \left(-16 + \frac{p^2}{9}\right)$$

$$\leqslant -16 + p^2/9,$$

because squared terms are always non-negative. Hence profit is maximized when

$$q^* = 2p/9.$$

Compare figure 5.20. (Notice that the producer will make a negative profit when $-16 + p^2/9 < 0$, i.e. $p < 12$. Recall that it is not better for him then to produce nothing because he still has his fixed costs to pay.)

The supply function $s: \mathbb{R}_+ \rightarrow \mathbb{R}_+$ is the linear function defined by

$$s(q) = 9q/2$$

because the amount q produced when the price is p is given by $q = 2p/9$.

5.10   Market supply

A market supply function $S: \mathbb{R}_+ \rightarrow \mathbb{R}_+$ gives the *total* supply in a market. Thus to write

$$p = S(q)$$

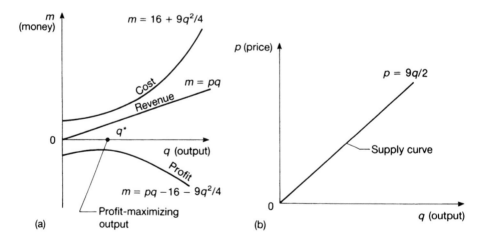

Figure 5.20   (a) Profit-maximizing output; (b) corresponding supply function.

means that p is the price of the commodity in question necessary to generate a total market supply of q.

Market supply functions are obtained by aggregating individual supply functions in exactly the same way that we studied for demand functions in section 5.7. Actually, matters are often simpler in the supply case because it is popular to assume that all the firms in an industry have access to the *same* technology. They will then have the same cost functions and hence the same supply functions.

Nothing could be easier than aggregating n identical supply curves of the type considered in section 5.9.1. This is the case of constant unit cost (each unit of output costs the same to make). Adding n such curves *horizontally* as explained in section 5.7 reproduces precisely the same curve again. It is worth remembering that the market supply curve in a perfectly competitive industry with constant unit cost c is the horizontal line $p = c$ (except when $q = 0$) (figure 5.21).

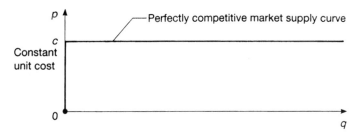

Figure 5.21 Market supply curve under perfect competition.

In the example of section 5.9.2, if the price is p then n identical producers will manufacture a total amount

$$q = ns^{-1}(p) = n2p/9.$$

Hence the market supply function $S: \mathbb{R}_+ \to \mathbb{R}_+$ is defined by

$$p = S(q) = 9q/2n$$

and so is again linear like the individual supply functions $s: \mathbb{R}_+ \to \mathbb{R}_+$ but with a smaller slope.

5.11 Vector variables

This section is about functions $f: X \to Y$ where X and Y are subsets of $\mathbb{R}^m$ and $\mathbb{R}^n$ respectively. Such a function takes an m-dimensional vector x from the set X and transforms it into an n-dimensional vector y in the set Y. Thus the value of $y = f(x)$ is not a number but a vector.

Linear functions $L: \mathbb{R}^n \to \mathbb{R}^m$ occur very frequently indeed. A *linear function* (in the proper mathematical sense) is defined by a formula of the type

$$L(x) = Mx$$

where M is an $m \times n$ matrix.

Consider, for example, the linear function $L: \mathbb{R}^2 \to \mathbb{R}^2$ defined by

$$L(x) = \begin{pmatrix} 0 & 1 \\ 2 & 3 \end{pmatrix} \begin{pmatrix} x_1 \\ x_2 \end{pmatrix}.$$

It is important not to forget that $L(x)$ is a 2×1 column vector. If we write $y = L(x)$, then

$$\begin{pmatrix} y_1 \\ y_2 \end{pmatrix} = \begin{pmatrix} 0 & 1 \\ 2 & 3 \end{pmatrix} \begin{pmatrix} x_1 \\ x_2 \end{pmatrix} = \begin{pmatrix} x_2 \\ 2x_1 + 3x_2 \end{pmatrix}$$

This means that the rule defining the function $L: \mathbb{R}^2 \to \mathbb{R}^2$ can also be expressed as a system of two 'linear' equations:

$$y_1 = x_2$$
$$y_2 = 2x_1 + 3x_2$$

This tells us to calculate $y = L(x)$ in two steps. Begin by computing the first co-ordinate y_1 of y using the formula $y_1 = x_2$. Then compute the second co-ordinate using the formula $y_2 = 2x_1 + 3x_2$.

As an example, consider an economy with n industries producing n different outputs. Outputs from one industry (e.g. machine tools) will serve as inputs to other industries. Leontieff described this situation with a 'linear model' of which the central feature is an $n \times n$ *input–output matrix A* (table 5.2).

The entry a_{12} in this matrix, for example, means that a_{12} dollars' worth of

Table 5.2

		Outputs		
		1	2	n
	1	a_{11}	a_{12} $\quad \cdots$	a_{1n}
	2	a_{21}	a_{22} $\quad \cdots$	a_{2n}
Inputs	:	:	:	:
	n	a_{n1}	a_{n2} $\quad \cdots$	a_{nn}

commodity 1 is necessary in the production of one dollar's worth of commodity 2. Many of the entries in such an input–output matrix will therefore be zero, reflecting the fact that industries do not need the products of all other industries as inputs in their own production process.

At this point, the only comment to be made on Leontieff's model is that, in a planned economy, a central planner who had decided that the total output vector should be x can calculate the necessary input vector y by means of the formula

$$y = Ax.$$

To see this, consider how much of commodity k is required as an input. To get x_1 dollars' worth of commodity 1 as an output, we need $a_{k1}x_1$ dollars' worth of commodity k as input. To get x_2 dollars' worth of commodity 2 as output, we need $a_{k2}x_2$ dollars' worth of commodity k as input. And so on. The total amount of commodity k required is therefore

$$y_k = a_{k1}x_1 + a_{k2}x_2 + \cdots + a_{kn}x_n$$

dollars' worth. But this is just the kth co-ordinate of the column vector Ax.

5.12   Operations on functions

If $f\colon X \to \mathbb{R}$ and $g\colon X \to \mathbb{R}$, then the function $f + g\colon X \to \mathbb{R}$ has the obvious definition

$$(f + g)(x) = f(x) + g(x).$$

Similarly, if α is any scalar (i.e. a real number), the function $\alpha f\colon X \to \mathbb{R}$ has the definition

$$(\alpha f)(x) = \alpha f(x).$$

The same definitions apply to vector-valued functions and it is this fact which explains why matrix addition and scalar multiplication of matrices are defined as in section 2.1. If $f\colon \mathbb{R}^n \to \mathbb{R}^m$ and $g\colon \mathbb{R}^n \to \mathbb{R}^m$ are linear functions, then they are defined by equations

$$f(x) = Ax \qquad g(x) = Bx$$

where A and B are $m \times n$ matrices. It is then very convenient that the function $\alpha f + \beta g\colon \mathbb{R} \to \mathbb{R}$ is simply defined by

$$(\alpha f + \beta g)(x) = (\alpha A + \beta B)x.$$

The idea of composing functions is a little less trivial. If $f\colon Y \to Z$ and $g\colon X \to Y$, then their *composite function* $f \circ g\colon X \to Z$ is defined by

$$f \circ g(x) = f[g(x)].$$

Sometimes a composite function is called a 'function of a function' for obvious reasons.

As an example, consider the functions $F\colon \mathbb{R} \to \mathbb{R}$, $G\colon \mathbb{R} \to \mathbb{R}$ and $H\colon \mathbb{R} \to \mathbb{R}$ defined by

$$F(x) = x + 1 \qquad G(x) = -x \qquad H(x) = x^2.$$

We have that

$$G \circ H(x) = G[H(x)] = G(x^2) = -x^2.$$

On the other hand,

$$H \circ G(x) = H[G(x)] = H(-x) = (-x)^2 = x^2.$$

Thus the functions $G \circ H$ and $H \circ G$ are not the same. On the other hand

$$F \circ (G \circ H)(x) = F[G \circ H(x)] = F(-x^2) = -x^2 + 1$$

while

$$(F \circ G) \circ H(x) = (F \circ G)[H(x)] = F \circ G(x^2) = F[G(x^2)] = F(-x^2) = -x^2 + 1$$

and hence it is true that $F \circ (G \circ H)$ and $(F \circ G) \circ H$ are the same, so that $F \circ G \circ H$ can be written without ambiguity. This is a particular instance of a general result.

Mathematicians think of the composition operation as a peculiar kind of 'multiplication' – one for which it is always true that $f \circ (g \circ h) = (f \circ g) \circ h$ but for which it need *not* be true that $f \circ g = g \circ f$. This observation may remind you of the properties of matrix multiplication described in section 2.1, and there is a good reason for this. Matrix multiplication is defined the way it is in order to make it true that, if $f: \mathbb{R}^m \to \mathbb{R}^l$ and $g: \mathbb{R}^n \to \mathbb{R}^m$ are linear functions given by

$$f(\mathbf{x}) = A\mathbf{x} \qquad g(\mathbf{x}) = B\mathbf{x}$$

where A is an $l \times m$ matrix and B is an $m \times n$ matrix, then the composite function $f \circ g: \mathbb{R}^n \to \mathbb{R}^l$ is given by

$$f \circ g(\mathbf{x}) = AB\mathbf{x}.$$

It is therefore no accident that matrix multiplication always satisfies $(AB)C = A(BC)$, provided that the products are defined, and sometimes fails to satisfy $AB = BA$. Nor, as we shall see, is it any accident that inverse matrices have properties like those of inverse functions.

Suppose that $f: X \to Y$ has an inverse function $f^{-1}: Y \to X$. Recall from section 5.6 that $x = f^{-1}(y)$ is what is obtained by solving $y = f(x)$ to get x in terms of y (provided that a *unique* answer in X is obtained for *each* y in Y).

For example, the function $F: \mathbb{R}_+ \to \mathbb{R}_+$ defined by $F(x) = x^2$ has an inverse function $F^{-1}: \mathbb{R}_+ \to \mathbb{R}_+$. As we learned in section 1.4, for each non-negative value of y, there is exactly one non-negative value of x such that $y = x^2$: namely $x = \sqrt{y}$. The inverse function is therefore given by the formula $F^{-1}(y) = \sqrt{y}$ ($y \geqslant 0$). As explained in section 5.6, the graph of the inverse function can be obtained by reflecting the original graph about the 45° line as illustrated in figure 5.22.

Notice that the function $G: \mathbb{R} \to \mathbb{R}_+$ defined by $G(x) = x^2$ does *not* have an

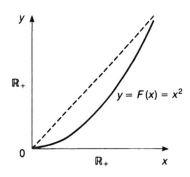 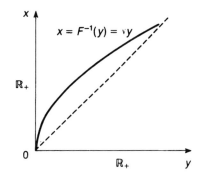

Figure 5.22   On $\mathbb{R}_+$, $F(x) = x^2$ has an inverse $F^{-1}(y) = \sqrt{y}$.

inverse function. For each positive y, there are two values of x in $\mathbb{R}$ such that $y = x^2$: namely $+\sqrt{y}$ and $-\sqrt{y}$. But, to define $G^{-1}(y)$ properly, we need to assign it a *unique* value.

If we think of composition as a form of 'multiplication', then the existence of an inverse function allows a form of 'division'. To see this, suppose that f: $X \rightarrow Y$ has an inverse function f^{-1}: $Y \rightarrow X$. Then $y = f(x)$ says the same as $x = f^{-1}(y)$. It follows that $f^{-1} \circ f$: $X \rightarrow Y$ is given by

$$f^{-1} \circ f(x) = f^{-1}[f(x)] = f^{-1}(y) = x.$$

In this context, the role of the number 1 in ordinary multiplication is taken by the *identity function* e: $X \rightarrow X$ defined by

$$e(x) = x.$$

What has been shown is that $f^{-1} \circ f = e$ – or, in plain English, carrying out one operation and then reversing it gets you back to where you started. It is also true, of course, that $f \circ f^{-1} = e$ (except that here e: $Y \rightarrow Y$).

All this is closely connected with the material on inverse matrices of section 2.1.5. Let f: $\mathbb{R}^n \rightarrow \mathbb{R}^n$ be a linear function defined by

$$f(x) = Ax$$

where A is an $n \times n$ non-singular matrix. To say A is non-singular means that it has an inverse matrix A^{-1}. Such an inverse matrix satisfies the requirement that $A^{-1}A = AA^{-1} = I$, where I is the $n \times n$ unit matrix.

What about an inverse function f^{-1}: $\mathbb{R}^n \rightarrow \mathbb{R}^n$? For this to exist, the equation

$$y = Ax$$

needs to have a unique solution x in $\mathbb{R}^n$ for each y in $\mathbb{R}^n$. Because $A(A^{-1}y) = (AA^{-1})y = Iy = y$, the equation certainly has one solution: namely $x = A^{-1}y$. Moreover, $x = A^{-1}y$ is the *only* solution. To see this, let z be any vector in $\mathbb{R}^n$ which satisfies $y = Az$. Multiplying both sides on the left by A^{-1}, we obtain that $A^{-1}y = A^{-1}Az = Iz = z$ and hence $z = x = A^{-1}y$.

The inverse function $f^{-1}\colon \mathbb{R}^n \to \mathbb{R}^n$ is therefore given by

$$f^{-1}(y) = A^{-1}y.$$

In fact, to write $A^{-1}A = AA^{-1} = I$ is the same as writing $f^{-1} \circ f = f \circ f^{-1} = e$, where the identity function $e\colon \mathbb{R}^n \to \mathbb{R}^n$ in this context is just

$$e(x) = I(x) = x.$$

(Note that a linear function $f\colon \mathbb{R}^m \to \mathbb{R}^n$ can *only* have an inverse when $m = n$. And, even when $m = n$, it has an inverse *only* when its representing matrix is non-singular. See, for example, section 2.4, question 10.)

5.13   Implicit functions

The topic of implicit functions is closely related to that of inverse functions and so only a few remarks are necessary. Suppose, for example, that a function $F\colon \mathbb{R}^2 \to \mathbb{R}$ is given. As we saw in section 5.2, the equation

$$F(x, y) = 0$$

then defines a contour of the function. Suppose that, for each real x, the equation has a unique real solution for y in terms of x. Then an *implicit function* $f\colon \mathbb{R} \to \mathbb{R}$ is defined by the requirement that

$$F(x, f(x)) = 0$$

for each x in $\mathbb{R}$.

Suppose, for example, that $G\colon \mathbb{R}^2_+ \to \mathbb{R}$ is defined by $G(x, y) = x - y^2$. Then the implicit function $g\colon \mathbb{R}_+ \to \mathbb{R}_+$ defined by the equation

$$G(x, y) = x - y^2 = 0$$

is simply $y = g(x) = \sqrt{x}$.

Alternatively, consider the Cobb–Douglas isoquant

$$k^2 l^3 = 8.$$

For each positive k, the equation has a unique positive solution for l in terms of k. It therefore implicitly defines a function $f\colon (0, \infty) \to (0, \infty)$. This implicit function is given by

$$l = f(k) = \left(\frac{8}{k^2} \right)^{1/3} = 2k^{-2/3}.$$

5.14   Discrete variables

Chapter 4 was entirely devoted to discrete variables. All that need be said here is that all this material was about a special kind of function called a *sequence*. This is simply a function whose domain of definition is the set $\mathbb{N}$ of natural numbers.

Consider, for example, the function $f: \mathbb{N} \to \mathbb{R}$ defined by

$$f(n) = (1.1)^n \qquad (n = 1, 2, \ldots)$$

which we encountered in section 4.9. Such a function is called a sequence because we can write its values in a list:

$$f(1), \; f(2), \; f(3), \; f(4), \; f(5), \ldots.$$

The nth number in this list is called the nth *term* of the sequence. For example, the fifth term is

$$f(5) = (1.1)^5 \approx 1.61.$$

5.15   Operators

Functions need not only be defined on sets of numbers. For example, the shift operator E of section 4.11 can be thought of as a function whose domain of definition is the set S of all sequences of real numbers.

Given a sequence $f: \mathbb{N} \to \mathbb{R}$, what is the value of $E(f)$? The shift operator replaces each term $f(n)$ of the sequence f by its successor $f(n+1)$. Thus $E(f) = g$, where $g(n) = f(n+1)$ $(n = 1, 2, 3, \ldots)$. Figure 5.23 illustrates what is going on.

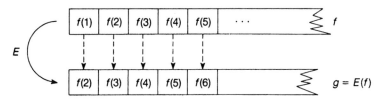

Figure 5.23   The shift operator E.

We have discussed *linear* functions $L: \mathbb{R}^m \to \mathbb{R}^n$. These are defined by $L(x) = Mx$, where M is an $m \times n$ matrix. However, the general requirement for a linear function (or operator) $L: X \to Y$ is simply that

$$L(\alpha x + \beta y) = \alpha L(x) + \beta L(y)$$

for each x and y in X. Both the shift operator E and the difference operator Δ (section 4.13) are therefore linear operators.

*5.16   Probability measures

Suppose a die is rolled. When it comes to rest, it will show one of the numbers 1, 2, 3, 4, 5 or 6. Statisticians call the set

$$S = \{1, 2, 3, 4, 5, 6\}$$

a *sample space* (or event space). They identify the possible events that can result from rolling the die with the subsets of S. Thus the event that the die shows an even number may be identified with the set $E = \{2, 4, 6\}$.

Let $\mathcal{E}$ denote the set of all possible events (i.e. the set of all subsets of S). A *probability measure* is then a function $p: \mathcal{E} \rightarrow [0, 1]$ such that

(a) $p(\varnothing) = 0, p(S) = 1$;
(b) $p(E \cup F) = p(E) + p(F)$ whenever $E \cap F = \varnothing$.

To write $p(\varnothing) = 0$ just means that the probability that nothing will happen is zero. To write $p(S) = 1$ means that the probability that something will happen is 1. Item (b) has more substance. If E and F represent events, the $E \cap F$ represents the event that E *and* F both occur. To write $E \cap F = \varnothing$ therefore means that E and F cannot both occur simultaneously. We say that E and F are *disjoint*. The situation is illustrated in the Venn diagram in figure 5.24. The set $E \cup F$ represents the event that at least one of E and F occurs. Item (b) therefore says that, if two events cannot both occur, then the probability of one or the other occurring is just the sum of their separate probabilities.

Suppose, for example, that the die is 'fair'. Then it will be true that

$$p(\{1\}) = p(\{2\}) = p(\{3\}) = p(\{4\}) = p(\{5\}) = p(\{6\}) = 1/6.$$

The probability that an even number will appear is therefore

$$p(E) = p(\{2, 4, 6\}) = p(\{2\}) + p(\{4\}) + p(\{6\})$$
$$= 1/6 + 1/6 + 1/6 = 1/2.$$

The proper interpretation of probabilities is a subject for philosophers. For our purposes, it will be enough to say that $p(E) = 1/2$ means that there is one chance in two that the event E will occur. To write $p(\{4\}) = 1/6$ means that there is one chance in six that the die will come to rest showing a 4. Or, in gambling terminology, the odds are 5:1 against the die showing a 4.

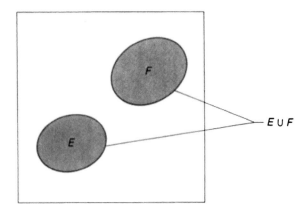

Figure 5.24 E and F are disjoint.

*5.17 Independent events

If A and B are sets, the set $A \times B$ consists of all the 'ordered pairs' (x_1, x_2) with $x_1 \in A$ and $x_2 \in B$. The notation $\mathbb{R}^2 = \mathbb{R} \times \mathbb{R}$ for the set of all two-dimensional vectors is already familiar. Figure 5.25 illustrates the sample space $S^2 = S \times S$ obtained when two independent rolls of the die are observed.

For example, in the figure $(5, 4)$ represents the event that five is rolled the first time and four the second time. Clearly $(5, 4)$ does not represent the same event as $(4, 5)$. The event $E \times F$ is shaded. It is the event that 3 or less is thrown the first time and 2 or more the second time.

There are $36 = 6 \times 6$ entries in the square representing S^2. With the independence assumption, each of these is equally likely. The probability of each is therefore $1/36$. This means that the probability of $E \times F$ must be

$$p(E \times F) = 12/36 = 1/3.$$

Notice that $p(E) = 1/2$ and $p(F) = 2/3$. This illustrates the general rule that

$$p(E \times F) = p(E) \times p(F)$$

whenever E and F are *independent*.

Usually this is expressed by saying that $p(E \cap F) = p(E)p(F)$ when E and F are independent, i.e. the probability that both of two independent events will occur is the product of their separate probabilities. This requires reinterpreting E and F as events in S^2 as indicated in figure 5.26.

Thus E ceases to be the event that a fair die will come to rest showing 1, 2 or 3 and becomes instead the event that the first die will show 1, 2 or 3 and the second die will show 1, 2, 3, 4, 5, or 6. Similarly, F becomes the event that the first die will show 1, 2, 3, 4, 5 or 6 and the second die will show 3, 4, 5 or 6. Such care in interpreting E and F is admittedly pedantic, but a failure to exercise due care can often lead to much confusion.

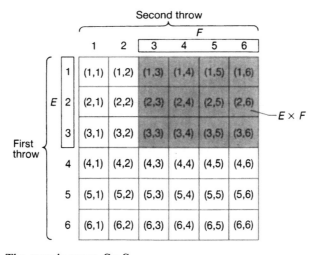

Figure 5.25 The sample space $S \times S$.

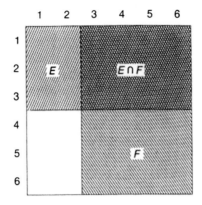

Figure 5.26 E and F reinterpreted in S^2.

Example

A man needs $1000 to pay off the Mafia tomorrow but has only $2. He therefore buys two lottery tickets costing $1 each in two independent lotteries. The prize for the winner in each lottery is $1000 (and there are no second prizes). If the probability of winning in each lottery is $q = 0.0001$, what is the probability that the man will have the money to pay his visitor from the Mafia tomorrow?

SOLUTION   Let W_1 and L_1 respectively be the events that the man wins or loses in the first lottery. Let W_2 and L_2 be defined similarly. Then

$$p(W_1) = q \qquad p(L_1) = 1 - p(W_1) = 1 - q$$
$$p(W_2) = q \qquad p(L_2) = 1 - p(W_2) = 1 - q.$$

What we require is $p(W_1 \cup W_2)$. But this is *not* equal to $p(W_1) + p(W_2)$ because W_1 and W_2 are not disjoint events. They can occur simultaneously. However, $W_1 \cap W_2$, $W_1 \cap L_2$ and $L_1 \cap W_2$ are disjoint events and thus

$$p(W_1 \cup W_2) = p(W_1 \cap W_2) + p(W_1 \cap L_2) + p(L_1 \cap W_2)$$
$$= p(W_1)p(W_2) + p(W_1)p(L_2) + p(L_1)p(W_2)$$
$$= q^2 + q(1 - q) + (1 - q)q$$
$$= 2q(1 - q) = 0.000\ 199\ 98.$$

His prospects with the Mafia are therefore not good. He has less than two chances in 10,000 of coming up with the money.

In such cases, it is often easier to work out the probability that the event required will *not* happen. Here this is the event $L_1 \cap L_2$ that he loses in both lotteries. The required answer is then simply

$$1 - p(L_1 \cap L_2) = 1 - (1 - q)^2 = 2q(1 - q)$$

as before.

*5.18 Random variables

What is the probability that, after an honest deal with a well-shuffled deck, the dealer at bridge will find herself looking at the entire spade suit? The answer is the *very* small number

$$\frac{1}{\binom{52}{13}} = \frac{13!\,39!}{52!} = \frac{1 \times 2 \times 3 \times \cdots \times 12 \times 13}{40 \times 41 \times 42 \times \cdots \times 52}.$$

This remark is made to recall the fact, from section 4.7, that the binomial coefficient

$$\binom{52}{13}$$

is the number of ways in which 13 objects can be selected from 52 objects.

It is seldom useful to know the precise probabilities of specific hands in bridge. But one often needs to know the exact probability that there will be k successes in n independent attempts to achieve some aim. If the probability of achieving a success in each separate attempt is p, the answer is simply

$$\binom{n}{k} p^k (1 - p)^{n-k}.$$

Consider, for example, the probability of achieving exactly two successes in four attempts. If we write, for example, SSFF to indicate success in the first two trials and failure in the second two trials, then the answer is the sum of the following probabilities:

$$p(\text{SSFF}) = p \times p \times (1 - p) \times (1 - p) = p^2(1 - p)^2$$
$$p(\text{SFSF}) = p \times (1 - p) \times p \times (1 - p) = p^2(1 - p)^2$$
$$p(\text{SFFS}) = p \times (1 - p) \times (1 - p) \times p = p^2(1 - p)^2$$
$$p(\text{FSSF}) = (1 - p) \times p \times p \times (1 - p) = p^2(1 - p)^2$$
$$p(\text{FSFS}) = (1 - p) \times p \times (1 - p) \times p = p^2(1 - p)^2$$
$$p(\text{FFSS}) = (1 - p) \times (1 - p) \times p \times p = p^2(1 - p)^2.$$

How many of these are there to be added? The answer is the same as the number of ways of choosing two numbers from the four numbers 1, 2, 3, 4, i.e.

$$\binom{4}{2} = \frac{4!}{2!\,2!} = 6.$$

Each such choice tells us one of the ways in which two successes can occur in four attempts.

The number of successes in n independent trials is an example of a random variable. From the mathematical point of view, this is a very simple idea. If A is a sample space, then a *random variable* is just a function $f \colon A \to X$.

Consider, for example, the case of just two trials (i.e. $n = 2$). Then $A = \{SS, SF, FS, FF\}$. The random variable which counts successes is therefore just the function $X: A \rightarrow \mathbb{Z}$ defined by

$$X(SS) = 2$$

$$X(SF) = X(FS) = 1$$

$$X(FF) = 0.$$

We call X a discrete random variable because it takes discrete values. In this particular case, its values are just integers.

A discrete random variable is often illustrated by drawing a 'bar-chart' or 'histogram'. The area of each bar in the chart represents the probability of the value of the random variable to which it corresponds. The case illustrated in figure 5.27 is for the random variable X which counts the number of successes in three independent trials when the probability of success in each separate trial is $p = 1/3$. Then

$$p(X = 0) = p(FF) = \binom{2}{0} \left(\frac{1}{3}\right)^0 \left(1 - \frac{1}{3}\right)^2 = \frac{4}{9}$$

$$p(X = 1) = p(SF) + p(FS) = \binom{2}{1} \left(\frac{1}{3}\right)^1 \left(1 - \frac{1}{3}\right)^1 = \frac{4}{9}$$

$$p(X = 2) = p(SS) = \binom{2}{2} \left(\frac{1}{3}\right)^2 \left(1 - \frac{1}{3}\right)^0 = \frac{1}{9}.$$

Often a bar-chart like that in figure 5.27 is referred to as the 'probability distribution' of the random variable X. A random variable X which counts the number of successes in n independent trials is said to have a *binomial probability distribution* because, as we have seen,

$$p(x = k) = \binom{n}{k} p^k (1 - p)^{n-k} \qquad (k = 0, 1, 2, \ldots, n)$$

where p is the probability of success in each separate trial. Figure 5.28 illustrates the binomial distribution when $n = 10$ and $p = 1/5$. (The probability of six successes or more is very small indeed.)

The total area of the bars in such a chart is necessarily equal to 1, reflecting the fact that the probability that something will happen is equal to 1.

(*Note:* As has been noted several times already, non-mathematicians are often careless in using mathematical terminology. The notion of a 'probability distribution' provides another example. Properly speaking, the probability distribution of a discrete random variable $X: A \rightarrow \mathbb{Z}$ is the function $F: \mathbb{Z} \rightarrow [0, 1]$ defined by

$$F(k) = p(X \leqslant k)$$

for all integers k. The bar-charts we have been studying are just a device for helping out in computing the values of the probability distribution function.)

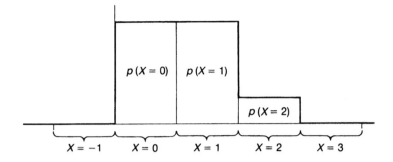

Figure 5.27   Bar-chart: each bar represents a probability.

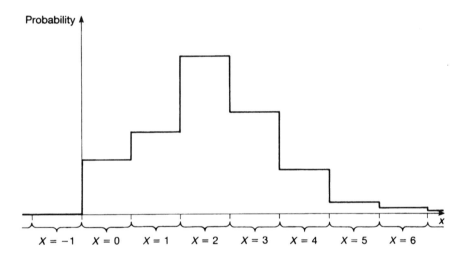

Figure 5.28   The binomial distribution when $n = 10$ and $p = 1/5$.

*5.19 Expectation

The *expected value*, or *expectation*, of a discrete random variable X is defined as

$$\mathscr{E}X = \sum kp(X = k)$$

where the summation extends over all values of k for which $p(X = k)$ is not zero. If many independent observations of the value of X are averaged, then the probability that this 'long-run average' will differ from $\mathscr{E}X$ will be small (provided that the probability distribution of X is not too crazy).

Suppose, for example, that X records the number of pips showing after the roll of a fair die. Then the expected value of X is simply

$$X = \sum_{k=1}^{6} kp(X = k) = \sum_{k=1}^{6} \frac{1}{6}k$$

$$= \frac{1}{6} \sum_{k=1}^{6} k = \frac{1}{6} \times \frac{1}{2} 6(6 + 1) = 3\frac{1}{2}.$$

If you were betting on the outcome of the die roll and win \$5 whenever it shows a six and lose \$1 whenever it shows something else, then your *expected winnings* are

$$(-1)p(X \leqslant 5) + (+5)p(x = 6) = (-1)\frac{5}{6} + (+5)\frac{1}{6} = 0.$$

The expected value of a binomially distributed random variable is often needed. If X is the number of successes in n independent trials with probability p of success in each separate trial, then

$$\mathscr{E}X = \sum_{k=0}^{n} kp(X = k) = \sum_{k=1}^{n} k \binom{n}{k} p^k (1 - p)^{n - k}.$$

(Notice that the term with $k = 0$ is equal to zero.) To simplify this unpleasant formula, we observe that, for $1 \leqslant k \leqslant n$,

$$k \binom{n}{k} = k \frac{n!}{k!(n - k)!} = n \frac{(n - 1)!}{(k - 1)!(n - k)!} = n \binom{n - 1}{k - 1}$$

(because $n - k = (n - 1) - (k - 1)$). It follows that

$$\mathscr{E}X = n \sum_{k=1}^{n} \binom{n - 1}{k - 1} p^k (1 - p)^{n - k}.$$

In the final sum, write $j = k - 1$. Since k ranges from 1 to n, the variable j ranges from 0 to $n - 1$. The expression therefore becomes

$$\mathscr{E}X = n \sum_{j=0}^{n - 1} \binom{n - 1}{j} p^{j + 1} (1 - p)^{n - j - 1},$$

i.e.

$$\mathscr{E}X = np \sum_{j=0}^{n-1} \binom{n-1}{j} p^j (1-p)^{n-1-j}$$

$$= np[p + (1-p)]^{n-1}$$

$$= np$$

by the binomial theorem.

As with many formal mathematical derivations, the final answer is obvious. The quantity X/n is the average number of successes in n trials. The expected value of this must be equal to the probability p of success in a single trial, or probability theory would make no sense.

*5.20 Risky consumer choice

Table 5.3 represents a lottery ticket. The top row represents the prizes available in the lottery and the numbers below are the probabilities of getting the prizes. This is quite a valuable lottery ticket, since the probabilities of winning a prize are quite high. How much should a rational consumer pay for such a ticket?

Table 5.3

Prize	$0	$10	$20	$500	$1000
Probability	0.5	0.3	0.1	0.05	0.05

The naive response is that the ticket must be worth its expected value. That is, if X is the random variable which records the amount won in the lottery, then the consumer should be willing to pay any amount up to $80, because

$$\mathscr{E}X = 0(0.5) + 10(0.3) + 20(0.1) + 500(0.05) + 1000(0.05) = 80.$$

It is likely that this 'answer' makes you feel uneasy. After all, nine times out of ten you will end up with $20 or less. The following story is designed to make you feel even more uneasy.

Before the revolution, so the story goes, a casino in St Petersburg was willing to run any lottery at all, provided the management could set the price of a ticket. Consider the following lottery. A fair coin is tossed repeatedly until it shows 'heads' for the first time. If this occurs on the kth trial, you win 2^k. How much should you be willing to pay in order to play this game?

Assuming that each toss of the coin is independent of other tosses, the probabilities are calculated as indicated below for the case $k = 4$ (table 5.4):

$$p(TTTH) = p(T)p(T)p(T)p(H) = \left(\frac{1}{2}\right)^4 = \frac{1}{16}.$$

Table 5.4

Prizes	$2	$4	$8	$16	$\cdots$	2^k	$\cdots$
Consequence	H	TH	TTH	TTTH	$\cdots$	$\underset{k-1}{\overleftrightarrow{TT \cdots TH}}$	$\cdots$
Probability	$\dfrac{1}{2}$	$\dfrac{1}{4}$	$\dfrac{1}{8}$	$\dfrac{1}{16}$	$\cdots$	$\left(\dfrac{1}{2}\right)^k$	$\cdots$

If the random variable X records the amount won, then

$$\mathscr{E}X = \sum_{k=1}^{\infty} 2^k p(X = 2^k) = \sum_{k=1}^{\infty} 2^k \left(\frac{1}{2}\right)^k$$

$$= \sum_{k=1}^{\infty} 1 = 1 + 1 + 1 + 1 + 1 + \cdots$$

which means that the expected value of X is 'infinite'. Should you therefore be willing to liquidate your entire worldly possessions in order to buy a ticket? Few people would say 'yes' after noting that the probability of ending up with $16 or less is 15/16.

The point of the 'St Petersburg paradox' is that the idea that a rational consumer will necessarily just maximize the expected monetary gain is too simple-minded. Instead it is usual to assume that she will seek to maximize her *expected utility.*

But, for this to make sense, she needs to be equipped with a special kind of utility function called, after its inventors, a *von Neumann and Morgenstern* (VN&M) *utility function.*

To explain this idea, we first need a set S whose members represent the possible final outcomes of an uncertain event after the uncertainty has been resolved. The objects in S, which may, for example, be sums of money or commodity bundles, will then serve as the prizes in hypothetical lotteries. If $p_1 \geqslant 0$, $p_2 \geqslant 0, \ldots, p_n \geqslant 0$ and $p_1 + p_2 + \cdots + p_n = 1$, then the notation

$$L = \begin{array}{|c|c|c|c|c|}
\hline
s_1 & s_2 & s_3 & \cdots & s_n \\
\hline
p_1 & p_2 & p_3 & \cdots & p_n \\
\hline
\end{array}$$

will be used to indicate the lottery L in which the prize s_k is available with probability $p_k (k = 1, 2, \ldots, n)$. The set of all such lotteries is denoted by $\mathscr{L}$.

It will be assumed that the consumer has a rational preference relation $\precsim$, on the set $\mathscr{L}$, with the properties described in section 3.5. In particular, given any two lotteries L and L^*, she is assumed to be able to express a preference between them: either $L < L^*$, $L > L^*$ or $L \sim L^*$. If her preferences are rational, we know from section 5.4 that they can be described by a utility function F: $\mathscr{L} \to \mathbb{R}$ which has the property that writing $L \precsim L^*$ is the same as writing $F(L) \leqslant F(L^*)$. This means that, whenever the consumer makes a rational choice, it is *as though* she were seeking to maximize the value of the utility function. In section 5.4, we also noted that such utility functions are not unique. There will always be many utility functions representing the same preference relation. von Neumann and Morgenstern looked at the utility functions F: $\mathscr{L} \to \mathbb{R}$ which represent the preference relation $\precsim$ and can be expressed as *expectations*.

Some assumptions about rational behaviour beyond those of section 3.5 are necessary. The new assumptions relate to rational behaviour in risky situations. They will be explained as we go along.

The first assumption is that the consumer can identify a best prize b in the set S and a worst prize w. Moreover, she thinks that each intermediate prize s is equivalent to some lottery involving only the best prize and the worst prize. That is, for each prize s in the set S, there is a probability q such that

$$
s \sim
\begin{array}{|c|c|}
\hline
w & b \\
\hline
1-q & q \\
\hline
\end{array}
.
$$

For example, if the best prize is \$100 and the worst prize is \$0, what would be your value of q when $s = \$10$? It is unlikely that you would buy the lottery ticket for \$10 with $q = 1/100$, but you might well do so when $q = 1/4$. If so, then somewhere between 0.01 and 0.25 there is a value of q which will make you just indifferent between buying and not buying.

We can define a function f: $S \to \mathbb{R}$ by defining the value of $f(s)$ to be the probability q in the above discussion. That is, $q = f(s)$ is defined so as to make it true that

$$
s \sim
\begin{array}{|c|c|}
\hline
w & b \\
\hline
1-f(s) & f(s) \\
\hline
\end{array}
.
$$

This function f: $S \to \mathbb{R}$ is a *VN&M utility function*. This means that there is a utility function F: $\mathscr{L} \to \mathbb{R}$ such that, for each lottery L as defined earlier,

$$
F(L) = p_1 f(s_1) + p_2 f(s_2) + \cdots + p_n f(s_n)
$$

$$
= \sum_{k=1}^{n} p_k f(s_k).
$$

Thus, if X is the random variable that records the outcome of the lottery L, then

$$F(L) = \mathcal{E}f(X).$$

In maximizing the value of F, the consumer therefore behaves as though she is maximizing the *expected value* of the VN&M utility function f.

To justify the claim of the preceding paragraph, consider the sequence of lotteries in table 5.5 between each of which von Neumann and Morgenstern

Table 5.5

$$
L = \begin{array}{|c|c|c|c|c|}
\hline
s_1 & s_2 & s_3 & \cdots & s_n \\
\hline
p_1 & p_2 & p_3 & \cdots & p_n \\
\hline
\end{array}
$$

$\approx$

w	b	w	b	w	b		w	b
$1-q_1$	q_1	$1-q_2$	q_2	$1-q_3$	q_3	$\cdots$	$1-q_n$	q_n
p_1		p_2		p_3		$\cdots$	p_n	

$\approx$

w	b
$1-(p_1q_1 + p_2q_2 + \cdots + p_nq_n)$	$p_1q_1 + p_2q_2 + \cdots + p_nq_n$

argue that a rational consumer should be indifferent. At the first step, each prize s_k has been replaced by a lottery which the consumer values equally. That is, $q_k = f(s_k)$ $(k = 1, 2, \ldots, n)$. In the new 'compound lottery', the total probability of getting the best prize is $p_1q_1 + p_2q_2 + \cdots + p_nq_n$. von Neumann and Morgenstern's final assumption is that, when evaluating lotteries with only two prizes, rational consumers will prefer that which assigns greater probability to the better prize. They will therefore behave as though they were maximizing

$$p_1q_1 + p_2q_2 + \cdots + p_nq_n.$$

It follows that the function $F: L \to \mathbb{R}$ defined by

$$F(L) = p_1q_1 + p_2q_2 + \cdots + p_nq_n = \sum_{k=1}^{n} p_k f(s_k)$$

is indeed a utility function, as claimed previously.

(*Notes:* Although one has much less freedom in choosing a VN&M utility function than in the general case, they are not uniquely determined. It is easy to see that, if $f: S \to \mathbb{R}$ is a VN&M utility function representing a consumer's preferences over risky choices, then the function $g: S \to \mathbb{R}$ defined by

$$g(s) = A f(s) + B \qquad (s \in S),$$

where $A > 0$ and B are any constants, is also a VN&M utility function representing the *same* preferences. Sometimes the fact that no functions other than those given in the above equation can represent a preference is expressed by saying that f is a *cardinal* utility function. This term contrasts against the general case where utility functions reflect only a consumer's preference ordering; they are then said to be *ordinal* utility functions.)

*5.21   Risk aversion

A VN&M utility function $f: S \rightarrow \mathbb{R}$ provides information about a rational consumer's attitudes to taking risks. Some people like taking risks. They are said to be *risk loving*. Others dislike taking risks and are said to be *risk averse*. Those who do not care one way or the other are called *risk neutral*.

Consider a lottery ticket

$$L = \begin{array}{|c|c|} \hline q & Q \\ \hline 1-p & p \\ \hline \end{array}$$

in which the prizes q and Q are commodity bundles in $\mathbb{R}^n_+$. Let X be the vector random variable which records the prize which is actually awarded. Then the expected amounts of each commodity for the owner of the ticket are the co-ordinates of the vector

$$\mathscr{E}X = (1 - p)q + pQ$$

(figure 5.29). We saw in section 3.5 that the vector $x = (1 - p)q + pQ$ corresponds to a *physical* mixture of the bundles q and Q in which a fraction $1 - p$ of each of the commodities making up the bundle q is mixed with a fraction p of the same commodity in the bundle Q.

Consider, for example, the case when $n = 1$ and the single commodity is measured by its value in dollars. Take $q = \$3$, $Q = \$9$ and $p = 2/3$. Then the expected dollar value of the lottery ticket is

$$\frac{1}{3} \times 3 + \frac{2}{3} \times 9 = 7.$$

This may be obtained by physically mixing 1/3 of $3 with 2/3 of $9.

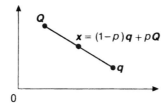

Figure 5.29 x is a mixture of q and Q.

A risk-loving consumer is one who would always rather own the lottery ticket L than the bundle x. A risk-averse consumer would always rather own the bundle x than the lottery ticket L. A risk-neutral consumer would always be indifferent between the two. These definitions correspond to a consumer having respectively a strictly convex, a strictly concave or a 'linear' VN&M utility function $f: \mathbb{R}_+^n \to \mathbb{R}$.

A strictly concave VN&M utility function $f: \mathbb{R}_+ \to \mathbb{R}$ has been drawn in figure 5.30 to illustrate the example given above with $q = 3$, $Q = 9$ and $p = 2/3$. Observe that the utility of the lottery L is

$$F(L) = (1-p)f(q) + pf(Q) = \frac{1}{3}f(3) + \frac{2}{3}f(9),$$

while the utility of the physical mixture is

$$f(x) = f[(1-p)q + pQ] = f\left(\frac{1}{3}\times 3 + \frac{2}{3}\times 9\right) = f(7).$$

Figure 5.31 indicates the case of a risk-neutral consumer.

Usually, consumers are assumed to be risk averse. This is not because it is irrational to be risk loving but because it is commonly observed that real people do buy insurance policies and indulge in other risk-averse activities.

5.22   Exercises

1*   Determine what kinds of 'returns to scale' are shown by the functions f: $\mathbb{R}_+^2 \to \mathbb{R}_+$ defined by

(a) $f(x_1, x_2) = 3x_1 + 4x_2$
(b) $f(x_1, x_2) = x_1^2 + x_2^2$
(c) $f(x_1, x_2) = 3x_1 + 4x_2 + 2$
(d) $f(x_1, x_2) = (x_1 x_2)^{1/2}$

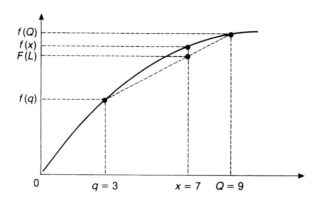

Figure 5.30   Risk aversion: the utility of x exceeds the utility of L.

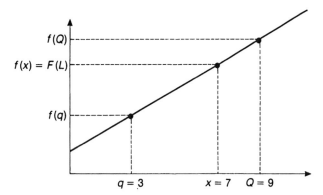

Figure 5.31   Risk neutrality: the utility of *x* equals the utility of *L*.

For each function, sketch the contours $f(x_1, x_2) = 4$, $f(x_1, x_2) = 6$ and $f(x_1, x_2) = 8$ in separate diagrams.

2   Repeat question 1 for the functions defined by

(a) $f(x_1, x_2) = (x_1 + x_2)^{1/2}$
(b) $f(x_1, x_2) = x_1 x_2^2$
(c) $f(x_1, x_2) = (x_1 x_2^2)^{1/3}$
(d) $f(x_1, x_2) = (x_1^2 + x_2^2)^{1/2}$

3*   If the price of the first commodity is $p_1 = 4$ and the price of the second commodity is $p_2 = 3$, find the optimum consumption bundle for a consumer with utility function $f: \mathbb{R}_+^2 \to \mathbb{R}_+$ and income \$12 for each of the functions of question 1.

4   Repeat question 3 for the functions of question 2.

5*   A consumer regards both of two commodities as 'goods'. These can be bought only in one of the following four packages: $A = (1, 2)'$, $B = (8, 4)'$, $C = (2, 16)'$, $D = (4, 8)'$. The consumer's income, when purchasing, is always \$24. If the prices are $p_1 = p_2 = 2$, then she sometimes buys B and sometimes buys D. If the prices are $p_1 = 4$ and $p_2 = 1$, then she always buys C. Find a utility function

$$f: \{A, B, C, D\} \to \mathbb{R}$$

that is consistent with this behaviour.

6   Repeat question 5 on the assumption that the consumer always buys B when the prices are $p_1 = p_2 = 2$ and only sometimes buys C when the prices are $p_1 = 4$ and $p_2 = 1$.

7*   Sketch the graphs of each of the functions $f: \mathbb{R}_+ \to \mathbb{R}$ defined by

(a) $f(x) = 2$ $(x \geq 0)$
(b) $f(x) = 3x - 1$ $(x \geq 0)$
(c) $f(x) = x^2 + 2x + 1$ $(x \geq 0)$

(d) $f(x) = 8/(x^2 + 1)$ $(x \geqslant 0)$
(e) $f(x) = |8x - 8|$ $(x \geqslant 0)$
(f) $f(x) = (16x)^{1/2}$ $(x \geqslant 0)$

Sections 5.5.1–5.5.10 list ten types of function. For each function and for each type, decide whether or not the function is of that type.

8   Repeat question 7 for the following functions:

(a) $f(x) = (x - 1)^3$ $(x \geqslant 0)$
(b) $f(x) = 2 - x$ $(x \geqslant 0)$
(c) $f(x) = (x - 1)/(x + 1)$ $(x \geqslant 0)$
(d) $f(x) = x^2 - x$ $(x \geqslant 0)$
(e) $f(x) = \begin{cases} 2 & \text{if } 0 \leqslant x \leqslant 1 \\ 3 & \text{if } x > 1 \end{cases}$

9*   Suppose that a consumer has a fixed income of \$24 and that the price of the second of two commodities is fixed at $p_2 = 1$. For each of the cases of question 1, find her demand function for the first commodity when her utility function is $f: \mathbb{R}_+^2 \to \mathbb{R}_+$.

10   Repeat question 9 for the functions of question 2.

11*   Find the market demand function for each of the utility functions of question 1, on the assumption that the consumer of question 9 is replicated 100 times.

12   Repeat question 11 for the functions of question 2.

13*   Suppose that $(x_1, x_2)'$ is the input bundle to a production process with production function $f: \mathbb{R}_+^2 \to \mathbb{R}_+$. If the price of the first input is fixed at $p_1 = 4$ and that of the second input is fixed at $p_2 = 3$, find the cost function in each of the cases given in question 1.

14   Repeat question 13 for each of the cases given in question 2.

15*   Find supply functions for producers selling in a perfectly competitive market when their cost functions are as in question 13.

16   Repeat question 15 for the cost functions of question 14.

17*   As described in the example on perfect complements in section 3.5, a consumer regards gin and vermouth as perfect complements, and uses these commodities only for mixing perfect martinis which, according to her definition, consist of 10 parts of gin to 1 part of vermouth. If her income is fixed at \$1000 and the price of gin is fixed at \$10 per litre, find her demand function for vermouth.

18   A bar-owner produces only perfect martinis as defined in question 17. Gin costs \$10 per litre and vermouth costs \$15 per litre. The bar-owner treats other production inputs (e.g. labour) as free. What is his cost function?

19* Consider the linear function $L_1: \mathbb{R}^2 \to \mathbb{R}^2$ and $L_2: \mathbb{R}^2 \to \mathbb{R}^2$ defined by $L_1(x) = M_1 x$ and $L_2(x) = M_2 x$, where M_1 and M_2 are the 2×2 matrices given by

$$M_1 = \begin{pmatrix} 0 & 1 \\ 2 & 3 \end{pmatrix} \qquad M_2 = \begin{pmatrix} 0 & 1 \\ 0 & 2 \end{pmatrix}.$$

In the case of the vector $x = (3, 1)'$, check that

(a) $(L_1 \circ L_2)(x) = (M_1 M_2) x$
(b) $(L_2 \circ L_1)(x) = (M_2 M_1) x$
(c) $L_1^{-1}(x) = M_1^{-1} x$

In the case of the vector $y = (1, 3)'$, check that the equation $y = L_2(u)$ cannot be solved for u. In the case of the vector $z = (2, 4)'$, show that the equation $z = L_2(u)$ has many solutions for u. What conclusions should be drawn about the function $L_2^{-1}: \mathbb{R}^2 \to \mathbb{R}^2$?

20 Sketch the graph of the function $f: \mathbb{R} \to \mathbb{R}$ defined by $f(x) = 1 + x + x^2$. Also sketch the graph of the inverse function $f^{-1}: \mathbb{R} \to \mathbb{R}$.

21* Find the inverse demand functions in the cases considered in question 9.

22 Repeat question 21 for the cases of question 10.

23* A function $f: \mathbb{R}^n \to \mathbb{R}$ is *homogeneous of degree* α if and only if

$$f(cx) = c^\alpha f(x)$$

for all scalars c and all vectors x in $\mathbb{R}^n$. Which of the functions of question 1 are homogeneous and what are their degrees of homogeneity?

24 Repeat question 23 for the functions of question 2.

25* Why does the shift operator E of section 4.11 have no inverse?

26 Explain why the operator E^2 of section 4.11 is the same as $E \circ E$.

5.23 Answers

1 (a) Constant returns to scale (figure 5.32) because

$$f(cx_1, cx_2) = 3cx_1 + 4cx_2 = c(3x_1 + 4x_2) = cf(x_1, x_2).$$

(b) Increasing returns to scale because

$$f(cx_1, cx_2) = (cx_1)^2 + (cx_2)^2 = c^2(x_1^2 + x_2^2) = c^2 f(x_1, x_2)$$

and $c^2 > c$ when $c > 1$.

(c) Increasing returns to scale because

$$f(cx_1, cx_2) = 3cx_1 + 4cx_2 + 2$$

$$= 3cx_1 + 4cx_2 + c2 + 2(1 - c)$$

$$= cf(x_1, x_2) + 2(1 - c) > cf(x_1, x_2)$$

provided that $c > 1$.

3 The contours graphed for question 1 are indifference curves for the consumer in each of the four cases to be considered. Notice that the indifference curves for the utility function in case (a) are also indifference curves in case (b) and vice versa. Both utility functions therefore represent the *same* preferences. Similarly case (d) just represents Cobb–Douglas preferences which could more easily have been represented by the utility function F: $\mathbb{R}^2_+ \to \mathbb{R}_+$ defined by $F(x_1, x_2) = x_1 x_2$.

In each case, the budget set, illustrated in figure 5.33, is the same. The optimal consumption bundle x^* is found as described in section 3.6. We obtain that

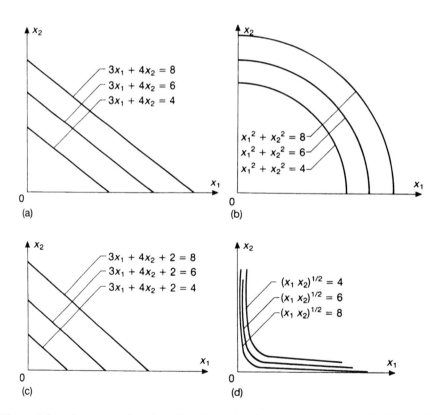

Figure 5.32 Contours of various functions: (a) $f(x_1, x_2) = 3x_1 + 4x_2$; (b) $f(x_1, x_2) = x_1^2 + x_2^2$; (c) $f(x_1, x_2) = 3x_1 + 4x_2 + 2$; (d) $f(x_1, x_2) = (x_1 x_2)^{1/2}$.

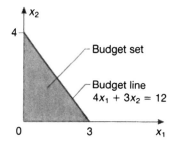

Figure 5.33 The budget set.

(a) $x^* = (0, 4)'$
(b) $x^* = (0, 4)'$
(c) $x^* = (0, 4)'$

(d) Here the preferences are well behaved and the rule MRS $= -p_1/p_2$ applies. For Cobb–Douglas preferences with $\alpha = \beta$, MRS $= -x_2^*/x_1^*$ (example in section 3.8). Thus

$$\frac{x_2^*}{x_1^*} = \frac{p_1}{p_2} = \frac{4}{3}.$$

This has to be solved along with $4x_1^* + 3x_2^* = 12$. On substituting $x_2^* = 4x_1^*/3$ in the latter equation, we obtain that $8x_1^* = 12$ and so $x_1^* = 3/2$. Thus $x_2^* = (4/3) \times (3/2) = 2$. Hence $x^* = (3/2, 2)'$.

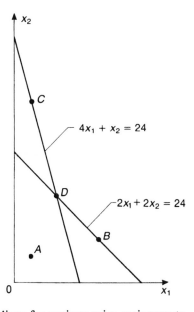

Figure 5.34 Cost lines for various price assignments.

5   The consumer's choices 'reveal' her preferences. As figure 5.34 shows, when the prices are $p_1 = p_2 = 2$, she can buy A, B and D. She sometimes buys B and sometimes buys D. This reveals the preference $A < B \sim D$. When the prices are $p_1 = 4$ and $p_2 = 1$, she can buy A, D and C. She always buys C. This reveals the preferences $A < C$ and $D < C$. Thus, combining the two conclusions,

$$A < B \sim D < C.$$

A suitable utility function $f : \{A, B, C, D\} \to \mathbb{R}$ is defined by

$$f(A) = 0 \qquad f(B) = f(D) = 1/2 \qquad f(C) = 1.$$

An alternative utility function $F : \{A, B, C, D\} \to \mathbb{R}$ is defined by

$$F(A) = -3 \qquad F(B) = F(D) = 0 \qquad F(C) = 75.$$

7   The required graphs are sketched in figure 5.35. In table 5.6, the words 'linear', 'increasing' and 'decreasing' are not used in the precise mathematical sense. If they were, the answers to (b)–5.5.2, (a)–5.5.5 and (a)–5.5.6 would be different.

9   (a)   As we saw in question 3, the indifference curves are lines of slope $-3/4$. The location of the optimal consumption bundle therefore depends on whether the slope $-p_1/p_2$ of the budget line is larger or smaller than $-3/4$ (figure 5.36).

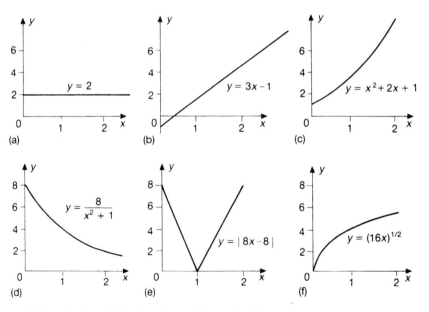

Figure 5.35   Graphs of the functions of question 7.

Table 5.6

	(a)	(b)	(c)	(d)	(e)	(f)
5.5.1	✓	✗	✗	✗	✗	✗
5.5.2	✓	'✓'	✗	✗	✗	✗
5.5.3	✓	✓	✓	✗	✗	✗
5.5.4	✓	✓	✓	✓	✗	✗
5.5.5	'✗'	✓	✓	✗	✗	✓
5.5.6	'✗'	✗	✗	✓	✗	✗
5.5.7	✓	✓	✓	✓	✓	✓
5.5.8	✓	✓	✓	✓	✗	✓
5.5.9	✓	✓	✓	✓	✓	✗
5.5.10	✓	✓	✗	✗	✗	✓

5.5.1, constant; 5.5.2, 'linear'; 5.5.3, polynomial; 5.5.4, rational; 5.5.5, 'increasing'; 5.5.6, 'decreasing'; 5.5.7, continuous; 5.5.8, differentiable; 5.5.9, convex; 5.5.10, concave.

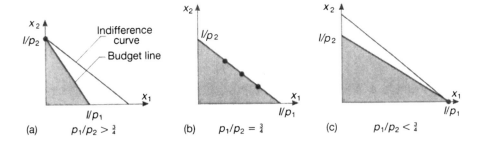

Figure 5.36 Optimal consumption for various price ratios: (a) at $(0, I/p_2)$; (b) all points of the budget line are optimal; (c) at $(I/p_1, 0)$.

We are given that income $I = 24$ and $p_2 = 1$. Hence optimal consumption x of commodity 1 when its price $p_1 = p$ satisfies

$$x = \begin{cases} 0 & \text{when } p > 3/4 \\ 24/p & \text{when } p < 3/4. \end{cases}$$

When $p = 3/4$, anything on the budget line is optimal, which means that x can take any value between 0 and $I/p = 24 \times 4/3 = 32$. We can therefore draw the graph of the inverse demand 'function' as in figure 5.37(a). From this, it is easy to obtain the graph of the demand 'function' itself.

(b) The necessary argument is nearly the same as in part (a). The only difference is that the location of the optimal consumption bundle depends on whether the slope $-p_1/p_2$ of the budget line is larger or smaller than -1 (rather than $-3/4$). In the graph of the demand 'function' for part (a), this means that 32 must be replaced by 24 and 3/4 by 1.

(c) This is exactly the same as part (a).

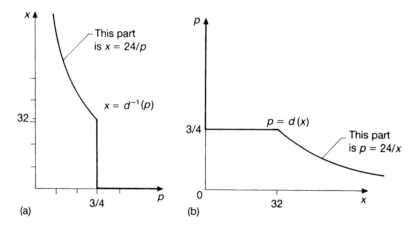

Figure 5.37 (a) Optimal consumption; (b) the inverse demand.

(d) This is the same as section 5.6 except that $p_2 = 1$ (instead of 3). However, the resulting demand function is exactly the same.

11   As in section 5.7,

$$D^{-1}(p) = 100d^{-1}(p).$$

(a) The graph of $x = D^{-1}(p)$ is the same as that of $x = d^{-1}(p)$ (see the answer to question 9(a)) except that 32 has to be replaced by 320.

Similarly for $p = D(x)$.

(b), (c) are just like (a).

(d) This was dealt with in section 5.6.

13 (a) The cost c of buying the input bundle $(x_1, x_2)'$ is equal to $4x_1 + 3x_2$. As figure 5.38 shows, the input bundle $(x_1, x_2)'$ on the isoquant $3x_1 + 4x_2 = q$ which costs least is

$$(x_1, x_2)' = (0, q/4)'.$$

This costs

$$c = 4 \times 0 + 3 \times q/4 = 3q/4$$

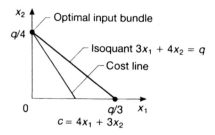

Figure 5.38 Locating the minimum cost on a linear isoquant.

to buy. Hence the required cost function $c: \mathbb{R}_+ \to \mathbb{R}$ is given by

$$c(q) = 3q/4.$$

(b)   This differs from (a) only in that the optimal input bundle is

$$(x_1, x_2)' = (0, \sqrt{q})'$$

(figure 5.39). This costs

$$c = 4 \times 0 + 3 \times \sqrt{q} = 3\sqrt{q}$$

and so the required cost function $c: \mathbb{R}_+ \to \mathbb{R}$ is given by

$$c(q) = 3\sqrt{q}.$$

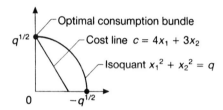

Figure 5.39   Locating the minimum cost on a circular isoquant.

(c)   This is the same as (a) except that q must be relaced by $q - 2$. The cost function $c: \mathbb{R}_+ \to \mathbb{R}$ is then given by

$$c(q) = 3(q - 2)/4.$$

(Of course, unless negative inputs are being considered, this does not make much sense when $q < 2$.)

(d)   This is the same problem as that considered in section 5.8 except that the price of the second input commodity is 3 instead of 9. As in section 5.8, the optimal input bundle $(x_1, x_2)'$ satisfies

$$-\frac{x_2}{x_1} = \text{TRS} = -\frac{p_1}{p_2} = -\frac{4}{3}.$$

If $(x_1, x_2)'$ is required to generate the output q, then $q = (x_1 x_2)^{1/2}$ and so $q^2 = x_1 x_2$. Writing $x_2 = 4x_1/3$ in this equation, we obtain that

$$4x_1^2/3 = q^2$$

$$x_1 = q(3/4)^{1/2}$$

$$x_2 = \frac{4x_1}{3} = \frac{4}{3} q \left(\frac{3}{4}\right)^{1/2} = q \left(\frac{4}{3}\right)^{1/2}.$$

The cost of $(x_1, x_2)'$ is then

$$c = 4x_1 + 3x_2 = 4q\left(\frac{3}{4}\right)^{1/2} + 3q\left(\frac{4}{3}\right)^{1/2} = 2q(12)^{1/2} = 4\sqrt{3}q$$

and so the required cost function $c: \mathbb{R}_+ \rightarrow \mathbb{R}$ is given by

$$c(q) = 4\sqrt{3}q.$$

15   (a)   The case of a linear cost function was considered in section 5.9.1. Just replace 12 in section 5.9.1 by 3/4.

(b)   In this case, the profit function $\pi: \mathbb{R}_+ \rightarrow \mathbb{R}$ is given by

$$\pi(q) = pq - \frac{3}{4}(q - 2) = \left(p - \frac{3}{4}\right)q + \frac{6}{4}.$$

The supply function is therefore the same as in case (a). You just get 6/4 added to the resulting profit.

(c)   The profit function $\pi: \mathbb{R}_+ \rightarrow \mathbb{R}$ is given by

$$\pi(q) = pq - 3\sqrt{q}.$$

Observe that $\pi(q) = q(p - 3/\sqrt{q}) \rightarrow \infty$ as $q \rightarrow \infty$ (unless $p = 0$). At each positive price, the profit-maximizing output is therefore 'infinite'. Representing this in terms of a supply 'function' is not very instructive.

(d)   This is again the same as section 5.9.1 but with 12 replaced by $4\sqrt{3}$.

17   Let the first commodity be vermouth and the second be gin. The consumer is only interested in bundles $(q_1, q_2)'$ with $q_2 = 10q_1$. If the price of vermouth is p_1, her budget line is $p_1q_1 + 10q_2 = 1000$. Substituting for q_2, we obtain that

$$p_1q_1 + 100q_1 = 1000$$

$$p_1 = \frac{1000 - 100q_1}{q_1} = \frac{1000}{q_1} - 100$$

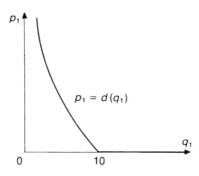

Figure 5.40   Demand function of question 17.

and thus the demand function $d: (0, \infty) \to \mathbb{R}_+$ is given by

$$d(q_1) = \begin{cases} \dfrac{1000}{q_1} - 100 & \text{if } 0 < q_1 < 10 \\ 0 & \text{if } q_1 \geqslant 10 \end{cases}$$

(figure 5.40). (Notice that, if the price of vermouth is zero, that is, vermouth is free, the consumer will spend her \$1000 income on 100 litres of gin. She will then not demand less than 10 litres of gin. If she demands more, it will do her no harm to waste the excess since it comes free.)

19 (a) Observe that

$$M_1 M_2 = \begin{pmatrix} 0 & 1 \\ 2 & 3 \end{pmatrix} \begin{pmatrix} 0 & 1 \\ 0 & 2 \end{pmatrix} = \begin{pmatrix} 0 & 2 \\ 0 & 8 \end{pmatrix}$$

and hence

$$(M_1 M_2)x = \begin{pmatrix} 0 & 2 \\ 0 & 8 \end{pmatrix} \begin{pmatrix} 3 \\ 4 \end{pmatrix} = \begin{pmatrix} 8 \\ 32 \end{pmatrix}.$$

On the other hand

$$(L_1 \circ L_2)(x) = L_1(L_2(x)) = L_1(M_2 x) = M_1(M_2 x).$$

But

$$M_2 x = \begin{pmatrix} 0 & 1 \\ 0 & 2 \end{pmatrix} \begin{pmatrix} 3 \\ 4 \end{pmatrix} = \begin{pmatrix} 4 \\ 8 \end{pmatrix}$$

and hence

$$M_1(M_2) = \begin{pmatrix} 0 & 1 \\ 2 & 3 \end{pmatrix} \begin{pmatrix} 4 \\ 8 \end{pmatrix} = \begin{pmatrix} 8 \\ 32 \end{pmatrix}.$$

(b) We have that

$$(M_2 M_1)x = \begin{pmatrix} 0 & 1 \\ 0 & 2 \end{pmatrix} \begin{pmatrix} 0 & 1 \\ 2 & 3 \end{pmatrix} \begin{pmatrix} 3 \\ 4 \end{pmatrix} = \begin{pmatrix} 2 & 3 \\ 4 & 6 \end{pmatrix} \begin{pmatrix} 3 \\ 4 \end{pmatrix} = \begin{pmatrix} 18 \\ 36 \end{pmatrix}.$$

But

$$(L_2 \circ L_1)(x) = L_2[L_1(x)] = L_2(M_1 x) = M_2(M_1 x)$$

$$= \begin{pmatrix} 0 & 1 \\ 0 & 2 \end{pmatrix} \begin{pmatrix} 0 & 1 \\ 2 & 3 \end{pmatrix} \begin{pmatrix} 3 \\ 4 \end{pmatrix} = \begin{pmatrix} 0 & 1 \\ 0 & 2 \end{pmatrix} \begin{pmatrix} 4 \\ 18 \end{pmatrix} = \begin{pmatrix} 18 \\ 36 \end{pmatrix}.$$

(c) Observe that

$$M_1^{-1}x = \frac{1}{-2} \begin{pmatrix} 3 & -1 \\ -2 & 0 \end{pmatrix} \begin{pmatrix} 3 \\ 4 \end{pmatrix} = -\frac{1}{2} \begin{pmatrix} 5 \\ -6 \end{pmatrix} = \begin{pmatrix} -5/2 \\ 3 \end{pmatrix}.$$

The equation $L_1(u) = x$ means that $M_1 u = x$. This is the same as

$$\begin{pmatrix} 0 & 1 \\ 2 & 3 \end{pmatrix} \begin{pmatrix} u_1 \\ u_2 \end{pmatrix} = \begin{pmatrix} 3 \\ 4 \end{pmatrix}$$

or

$$u_2 = 3 \qquad 2u_1 + 3u_2 = 4.$$

Substitute $u_2 = 3$ in the second equation. This gives $u_1 = (4 - 9)/2$. Thus $L_1(u) = x$ has the unique solution $u = (-5/2, 3)'$. Hence $L_1^{-1}(x) = M_1^{-1}x$.

The equation $y = L_2(u)$ means that $y = M_2 u$. When $y = (1, 3)'$, this is the same as

$$\begin{pmatrix} 0 & 1 \\ 0 & 2 \end{pmatrix} \begin{pmatrix} u_1 \\ u_2 \end{pmatrix} = \begin{pmatrix} 1 \\ 3 \end{pmatrix}$$

or

$$u_2 = 1 \qquad 2u_2 = 3.$$

But it cannot be true that $u_2 = 1$ and $u_2 = 3/2$, and so $y = L_2(u)$ cannot be solved for u.

The equation $z = L_2(u)$ means that $z = M_2 u$. When $z = (2, 4)'$, this is the same as

$$\begin{pmatrix} 0 & 1 \\ 0 & 2 \end{pmatrix} \begin{pmatrix} u_1 \\ u_2 \end{pmatrix} = \begin{pmatrix} 2 \\ 4 \end{pmatrix}$$

or

$$u_2 = 2 \qquad 2u_2 = 4.$$

Thus *any* u with $u_2 = 2$ solves $z = L_2(u)$.

The conclusion to be drawn about $L_2^{-1}: \mathbb{R}^2 \rightarrow \mathbb{R}^2$ is that such a function does not exist.

21   The answers were included in the answer to question 9.

23   (a)   This function is homogeneous of degree 1 because

$$f(cx_1, cx_2) = 3cx_1 + 4cx_2 = c(3x_1 + 4x_2) = cf(x_1, x_2).$$

(b)   This function is homogeneous of degree 2 because

$$f(cx_1, cx_2) = c^2 x_1^2 + c^2 x_2^2 = c^2(x_1^2 + x_2^2) = c^2 f(x_1, x_2).$$

(c)   This function is not homogeneous.

(d)   This function is homogeneous of degree 1 because

$$f(cx_1, cx_2) = (cx_1 cx_2)^{1/2} = c(x_1 x_2)^{1/2} = cf(x_1, x_2).$$

25   If the shift operator had an inverse, there would always be a unique solution $g: \mathbb{N} \to \mathbb{R}$ of the equation

$$f = E(g).$$

But this equation asserts that $f(n) = g(n + 1)$ $(n = 1, 2, \ldots)$. This leaves the value of $g(1)$ free, and hence the equation cannot have a *unique* solution.

6

Equilibrium

6.1 Supply and demand

We met the idea of a market demand function in section 5.7. The idea of a market supply function for the case of a perfectly competitive market was introduced in section 5.10. (Recall that suppliers in a perfectly competitive market are 'price-takers' rather than 'price-setters'. They believe that their own output will be so small, compared with the total output, that it will have a negligible impact on the market price. We have also always implicitly assumed that consumers are 'price-takers' for similar reasons.)

Figure 6.1 shows a 'linear' market demand function $D: \mathbb{R}_+ \to \mathbb{R}$ defined by

$$p = D(q) = A - Bq$$

where A and B are positive constants. It also shows a 'linear' market supply function $S: \mathbb{R}_+ \to \mathbb{R}$ defined by

$$p = S(q) = C + Dq$$

where C and D are non-negative constants and $C < A$. (Notice that, for $q > A/B$, $p = D(q) < 0$. One may interpret this as meaning that the market can be satiated. If too much is produced, consumers will have to be paid to take it away!)

Figure 6.1(a) shows that there will be an *excess demand* (of $D^{-1}(p_1) - S^{-1}(p_1)$) if the market price is p_1. On the other hand, if the market price is p_2, then there will be an *excess supply* (of $S^{-1}(p_2) - D^{-1}(p_2)$).

Economists argue that market forces will act to eliminate such excesses in demand and supply. The argument is that, if demand exceeds supply or supply exceeds demand, then the market will not be in equilibrium. For example, at price p_2, supply exceeds demand. At least one producer will therefore not be able to sell all of his output at this price. Unless he wants to have this unsold surplus left on his hands, he will have to sell it at a lower price. The market price p_2 is therefore not sustainable. Eventually it will be lowered. Similarly, the market price p_1 will eventually have to be raised.

The only price not vulnerable to such an argument is the *equilibrium* or *market-clearing price* $\bar{p}$ at which supply is equal to demand. This is illustrated in figure 6.1(b).

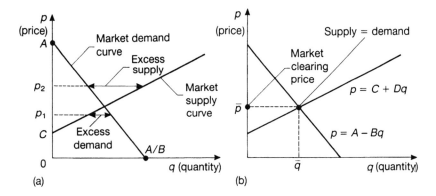

Figure 6.1   (a) Excess supply and excess demand; (b) clearing price.

How does the market go about achieving the equilibrium price? This is not an easy question to answer in the general case. However, the cobweb model of section 4.10 provides a very simplified example of the mechanism that economists have in mind.

Imagine a very perishable good (for example, tomatoes sold on a big-city fruit market). Each day, suppliers decide how much to bring to market. Anything they do not sell on that day will be wasted. Let us assume that the daily demand for tomatoes is given by $D: \mathbb{R}_+ \to \mathbb{R}$, where

$$p = D(q) = A - Bq,$$

and that the daily supply of tomatoes, if the suppliers predict the day's price to be p, is given by $S: \mathbb{R}_+ \to \mathbb{R}$, where

$$p = S(q) = C + Dq.$$

Suppose that the actual market price on day t is equal to p_t. But let us assume that the suppliers always guess that today's price will be the same as yesterday's price. Then the total quantity of tomatoes supplied on day $t + 1$ will be equal to q_{t+1}, where

$$p_t = C + Dq_{t+1}.$$

But, although the suppliers *predict* that the price on day $t + 1$ will be p_t, it will *actually* be p_{t+1}. How is p_{t+1} determined?

Once the suppliers have brought q_{t+1} tomatoes to market, tomatoes are in *fixed supply* on day $t + 1$. The supply curve for tomatoes on day $t + 1$ is therefore necessarily vertical (figure 6.2). It follows that the equilibrium price p_{t+1} for tomatoes on day $t + 1$ is given by

$$p_{t+1} = A - Bq_{t+1}.$$

What has emerged is a version of the cobweb model discussed in section 4.10. If the model is stable, then the price will converge to the market-clearing price $\bar{p}$ (figure 6.3).

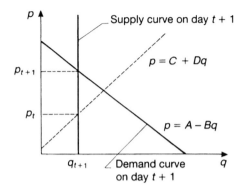

Figure 6.2   On day $t+1$ the guessed price is p_t but the actual price is p_{t+1}, since q_{t+1} is the supply.

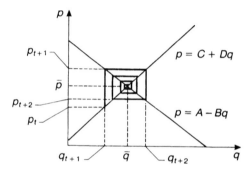

Figure 6.3   A stable cobweb model: prices converge.

Notice that, in this story, nobody works out the market-clearing price. But it operated 'as though' someone had chosen prices so as to clear the market. It was this feature of markets that Adam Smith had in mind when speaking of a 'hidden hand' which acts to equate supply and demand. Indeed, in the story, the suppliers are particularly myopic (short-sighted). If they bring too much to market on one day, they always bring too little on the next day, and vice versa. In real life, suppliers are usually a little cleverer.

If they were very clever, they would be able to predict what the result of the price adjustment process would be before it happened. They would then all turn up on day 0 with exactly the right amounts to generate the equilibrium price $\bar{p}$. Economists refer to such a mental simulation of a market-clearing process as a *tâtonnement* (from the French, *tâtonner*: to grope, to fumble, to feel one's way).

6.2   Comparative statics

A *tâtonnement* would generate an equilibrium immediately. But such an idealization is not to be taken too seriously. It is a picturesque way of expressing the fact that markets get to equilibrium much faster than most other economic processes. In section 5.8, a distinction was drawn between *long-run* decisions about such matters as investment in capital equipment and *short-run* decisions about such matters as how much output to produce given the capital equipment currently installed. By comparison, markets are usually assumed to operate in what might be called the *very short run*.

When thinking about the dynamics of short-run processes (i.e. how things are changing in the short run), it is therefore usual to treat the market-clearing process as a *static* phenomenon. That is, markets are treated as though they were always in equilibrium, without worrying about how this is brought about. Similarly, short-run processes are treated as static when long-run changes are being discussed. This explains the origin of the term *comparative statics* for the study of how equilibria are affected by changes in the underlying parameters.

As an example, suppose that the government imposes a sales tax of 15 per cent in the example of the preceding section. Then, if the consumers are buying at price p, the producers will be selling at price $P = p/1.15$, with the government pocketing the difference. The demand function $D: \mathbb{R}_+ \to \mathbb{R}$ will be as before, i.e.

$$p = D(q) = A - Bq.$$

It will also be true that

$$p = S(q) = C + Dq$$

where $S: \mathbb{R}_+ \to \mathbb{R}$ is the old supply function. But the price P that a producer gets for his product is not the market price p. Replacing p by $p/1.15$, we obtain that

$$p = 1.15S(q) = 1.15(C + Dq).$$

The old situation, with demand and supply functions D and S, is therefore to be compared with a new situation with demand and supply functions $D*$ and $S*$. We have that $D*$ is the same as D but $S*: \mathbb{R}_+ \to \mathbb{R}$ is given by

$$p = S*(q) = 1.15(C + Dq)$$

(figure 6.4). Notice that the sales tax 'decreases supply', i.e. the whole supply curve is shifted to the left (see section 5.7).

The comparative statics problem here is to determine how the equilibrium price and quantity change as a result of the sales tax. It is easy to see that the quantity supplied goes down and the price paid in the market goes up. For a more precise result, some calculations are necessary.

The point $(\bar{q}, \bar{p})$ lies on both the curves $p = D(q)$ and $p = S(q)$. It is therefore found by solving the equations

$$\bar{p} = D(\bar{q}), \qquad \text{i.e. } \bar{p} = A - B\bar{q}$$

$$\bar{p} = S(\bar{q}), \qquad \text{i.e. } \bar{p} = C + D\bar{q}$$

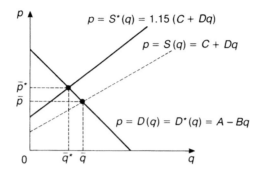

Figure 6.4   A new equilibrium: sales tax alters the supply function.

simultaneously. Subtracting the equations, we obtain that

$$0 = (A - C) - (B + D)\bar{q}$$

$$\bar{q} = \frac{A - C}{B + D} \qquad \bar{p} = A - B\bar{q} = \frac{BC + AD}{B + D}.$$

The point $(\bar{q}*, \bar{p}*)$ is found by solving the equations

$$\bar{p}* = D*(\bar{q}*), \qquad \text{i.e. } \bar{p}* = A - B\bar{q}*$$

$$\bar{p}* = S*(\bar{q}*), \qquad \text{i.e. } \bar{p}* = 1.15(C + D\bar{q}*)$$

simultaneously. We have that

$$\bar{q}* = \frac{A - 1.15C}{B + 1.15D} \qquad \bar{p}* = \frac{1.15(BC + AD)}{B + 1.15D}$$

Examples

In both the following examples, the market demand function D: $(0, \infty) \rightarrow (0, \infty)$ is as calculated in section 5.7, i.e.

$$p = D(q) = \frac{I}{2q}$$

where I is the total income of the consumers. The comparative statics problem to be considered will be to determine the change in equilibrium price and quantity if the government imposes an income tax which reduces I to $I*$.

1   Recall the market supply function $S: \mathbb{R}_+ \rightarrow \mathbb{R}_+$, computed in section 5.10, for the case when each of the (perfectly competitive) producers has to pay a cost of \$12 for each unit of output he produces. This is illustrated in figure 6.5.

The equilibrium price is always 12, i.e. $\bar{p} = \bar{p}* = 12$. The old equilibrium quantity $\bar{q}$ satisfies

$$\bar{p} = I/(2\bar{q})$$

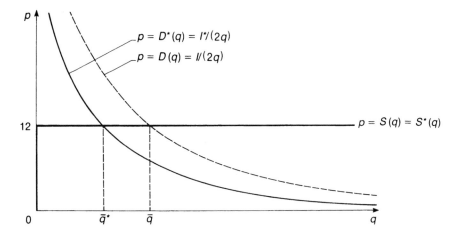

Figure 6.5   A new equilibrium: income tax alters the demand function.

and hence

$$\bar{q} = I/(2\bar{p}) = I/24.$$

Similarly, the new equilibrium quantity is

$$\bar{q}* = I*/24.$$

2   Recall the market supply function $S: \mathbb{R}_+ \rightarrow \mathbb{R}_+$ of section 5.10, defined by

$$p = S(q) = 9q/(2n)$$

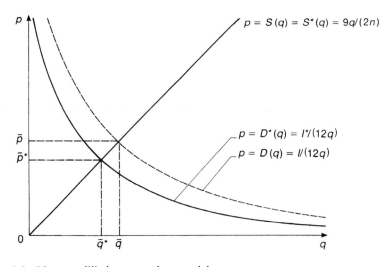

Figure 6.6   New equilibrium: another model.

(figure 6.6). The old equilibrium price and quantity are found by solving the equations

$$\bar{p} = D(\bar{q}), \qquad \text{i.e. } \bar{p} = I/(12\bar{q})$$

$$\bar{p} = S(\bar{q}), \qquad \text{i.e. } \bar{p} = 9\bar{q}/(2n).$$

We obtain that

$$\frac{I}{12\bar{q}} = \frac{9\bar{q}}{2n} \qquad \bar{q}^2 = \frac{In}{54}$$

$$\bar{q} = \left(\frac{In}{54}\right)^{1/2} \qquad \bar{p} = \frac{9}{2n}\left(\frac{In}{54}\right)^{1/2} = \frac{1}{2n}\left(\frac{3In}{2}\right)^{1/2} = \frac{1}{2}\left(\frac{3I}{2n}\right)^{1/2}.$$

Similarly,

$$\bar{q}* = \left(\frac{I*n}{54}\right)^{1/2} \qquad \bar{p}* = \frac{1}{2}\left(\frac{3I*}{2n}\right)^{1/2}.$$

6.3   General equilibrium

So far, our concern has been with *partial equilibrium* models. These are models in which some part of the economy, perhaps the market for a single commodity, is studied in isolation from the rest of the economy. This means that certain parameters are left unexplained.

For instance, in example 2 above, the supply function $S: \mathbb{R}_+ \to \mathbb{R}_+$ was based on the consideration (in section 5.11) of n producers, each with production function $G: \mathbb{R}_+ \to \mathbb{R}$ defined by $g(l) = 2l^{1/2}$ ($l \geq 0$). Thus, only labour l is a variable input, capital being fixed at $k = 4$. Costs were calculated on the assumption that the price of capital is 4 and that of labour is $w = 9$. But no explanation was offered of where these prices came from. Nor was any explanation offered of the source of the consumers' income I in the demand function (from section 5.6).

A *general equilibrium* model seeks to explain *all* relevant parameters. But the price usually paid for the greater generality is a loss of detailed accuracy. Instead of dealing with each economic variable separately, general equilibrium models typically involve only a few aggregated variables.

A very simplified example of what is involved may help. We shall consider an economy with only one consumer and one producer (although it would not complicate matters much if there were 100 identical consumers and 100 identical producers). The producer will have the production function $G: \mathbb{R}_+ \to \mathbb{R}_+$ defined by $G(l) = 2l^{1/2}$ ($l \geq 0$). It will be assumed that he does not have to pay for his capital but that the price of labour is w. His profit function $\pi: \mathbb{R}_+ \to \mathbb{R}$ is then given by

$$\pi(q) = pq - wl$$

$$= pq - wq^2/4$$

$$= -\frac{w}{4}\left(q - \frac{2p}{w}\right)^2 + \frac{p^2}{w}$$

(section 5.9.2). It follows that profit is maximized when $q = 2p/w$, and that the maximum profit is then p^2/w.

The consumer will not only buy the good supplied by the producer, she will also supply the labour he demands as an input. Her budget equation is therefore

$$pq = wl + I$$

where I is her 'unearned' income. This will be taken to be the profit p^2/w of the producer, since we have nobody else around to own the firm. She will be assumed to regard the product good and leisure as perfect complements and to insist on equal amounts of each. Taking the total amount of time available to her as the unit of measurement, she insists that

$$1 - l = q.$$

We can now work out inverse supply and demand functions fairly easily. The inverse supply function must give the total commodity bundle $(q_s, l_s)'$ supplied as a function of the price vector $(p, w)'$ and therefore defined by the equations

$$q_s = \frac{2p}{w} \qquad l_s = \frac{p(w - p)}{w(w + p)}$$

($p \geqslant 0$, $w > 0$). To see this, note that the product good is supplied by the producer, and his profit is maximized when $q_s = 2p/w$. Labour is supplied by the consumer. To find her optimal supply, substitute $q = 1 - l$ in the equation $pq = wl + p^2/w$.

The inverse demand function must give the total commodity bundle $(q_d, l_d)'$ demanded as a function of the price vector $(p, w)'$. It is therefore defined by the equations

$$q_d = \frac{w^2 + p^2}{w(w + p)} \qquad l_d = \left(\frac{p}{w}\right)^2$$

($p \geqslant 0$, $w > 0$). To see this, note that the product good is demanded by the consumer. The amount she demands can be found by substituting $l = 1 - q$ in $pq = wl + p^2/w$. Labour is demanded by the producer. According to his production function, $l_d = q_s^2/4$.

The equilibrium requirement is that supply equals demand. That is,

$$(q_s, l_s)' = (\bar{q}, \bar{l})' = (q_d, l_d)'.$$

The equations $q_s = q_d$ and $l_s = l_d$ both yield the same result:

$$p^2 + 2pw - w^2 = 0.$$

This is a quadratic equation for p/w which has the two solutions $-1 - \sqrt{2}$ and $-1 + \sqrt{2}$. Only the positive solution is meaningful in the current context. Hence the equilibrium prices must satisfy

$$\bar{p} = (\sqrt{2} - 1)\bar{w}.$$

(Notice that we can only expect a result about the *ratio* of the prices because the unit of currency employed in this model is clearly irrelevant.)

The important feature of this general equilibrium model is that nothing is left unexplained. In particular, both the income of the consumer and the price of the factors of production are *endogenous* to the model. That is, their values are determined *within* the model rather than being imposed *exogenously*, i.e. from *without*.

6.4 Linear market equilibrium models

In the previous section the economy studied had only two commodities, a product good and labour. Consider now an economy with n commodities. Then a commodity bundle q and a price vector p will be elements of the set $\mathbb{R}^n_+$. As in the previous section, we may consider the inverse supply function $S^{-1}: \mathbb{R}^n_+ \to \mathbb{R}^n$ and the inverse demand function $D^{-1}: \mathbb{R}^n_+ \to \mathbb{R}^n$. Then the equations

$$q_s = S^{-1}(p)$$

$$q_d = D^{-1}(p)$$

give the commodity bundle q_s supplied and the commodity bundle q_d demanded when the price vector is p. It is important to bear in mind that the amount of a commodity supplied or demanded will depend not only on its own price but on the price of other commodities as well.

The equilibrium condition is that supply equals demand (provided that none of the goods being considered is free). The equilibrium condition is therefore that

$$S^{-1}(\bar{p}) = D^{-1}(\bar{p}).$$

In the case of 'linear' supply and demand curves, this equation reduces to a system of 'linear' equations, whose 'unknowns' are the co-ordinates of the equilibrium price vector $\bar{p} = (\bar{p}_1, \bar{p}_2, \ldots, \bar{p}_n)'$:

$$a_{11}\bar{p}_1 + a_{12}\bar{p}_2 + \cdots + a_{1n}\bar{p}_n = b_1$$

$$a_{21}\bar{p}_1 + a_{22}\bar{p}_2 + \cdots + a_{2n}\bar{p}_n = b_2$$

$$\vdots$$

$$a_{n1}\bar{p}_1 + a_{n2}\bar{p}_2 + \cdots + a_{nn}\bar{p}_n = b_n.$$

Some examples may be of assistance.

Examples
1 Let $S^{-1}: \mathbb{R}^2_+ \to \mathbb{R}^2$ and $D^{-1}: \mathbb{R}^2_+ \to \mathbb{R}^2$ be defined by

$$S^{-1}(p) = \begin{pmatrix} 2p_1 - p_2 \\ 3p_2 - 2p_1 + 2 \end{pmatrix} \qquad D^{-1}(p) = \begin{pmatrix} 3p_2 - 2p_1 + 4 \\ p_1 - p_2 \end{pmatrix}.$$

The equilibrium equations are

$$2\bar{p}_1 - \bar{p}_2 = 3\bar{p}_2 - 2\bar{p}_1 + 4, \qquad \text{i.e. } \bar{p}_1 - \bar{p}_2 = 1$$

$$3\bar{p}_2 - 2\bar{p}_1 + 2 = \bar{p}_1 - \bar{p}_2, \qquad \text{i.e. } 3\bar{p}_1 - 4\bar{p}_2 = 2.$$

We can solve these equations by eliminating variables. To eliminate $\bar{p}_1$, multiply the first equation by 3 and then subtract the equations.

$$3\bar{p}_1 - 3\bar{p}_2 = 3$$

$$\underline{3\bar{p}_1 - 4\bar{p}_2 = 2}$$

$$(-3 + 4)\bar{p}_2 = 3 - 2$$

$$\bar{p}_2 = 1.$$

Substitute this result in $\bar{p}_1 - \bar{p}_2 = 1$. The conclusion is that $\bar{p}_1 = 2$.

2   Let $S^{-1}: \mathbb{R}^2_+ \rightarrow \mathbb{R}^2$ and $D^{-1}: \mathbb{R}^2_+ \rightarrow \mathbb{R}^2$ be defined by

$$S^{-1}(\boldsymbol{p}) = \begin{pmatrix} 2p_1 - p_2 + 1 \\ 2p_2 - p_1 + 3 \end{pmatrix} \qquad D^{-1}(\boldsymbol{p}) = \begin{pmatrix} 2p_2 - p_1 + 2 \\ 2p_1 - p_2 + 4 \end{pmatrix}.$$

The equilibrium conditions are

$$2\bar{p}_1 - \bar{p}_2 + 1 = 2\bar{p}_2 - \bar{p}_1 + 2, \qquad \text{i.e. } 3\bar{p}_1 - 3\bar{p}_2 = 1$$

$$2\bar{p}_2 - \bar{p}_1 + 3 = 2\bar{p}_1 - \bar{p}_2 + 4, \qquad \text{i.e. } 3\bar{p}_1 - 3\bar{p}_2 = -1.$$

Since it is false that $1 = -1$, the equations are inconsistent. No equilibrium exists.

3   Let $S^{-1}: \mathbb{R}^2_+ \rightarrow \mathbb{R}^2$ and $D^{-1}: \mathbb{R}^2_+ \rightarrow \mathbb{R}^2$ be defined by

$$S^{-1}(\boldsymbol{p}) = \begin{pmatrix} 2p_1 - p_2 \\ 2p_2 - p_1 + 3 \end{pmatrix} \qquad D^{-1}(\boldsymbol{p}) = \begin{pmatrix} 2p_2 - p_1 + 3 \\ 2p_1 - p_2 \end{pmatrix}.$$

The equilibrium conditions are

$$2\bar{p}_1 - \bar{p}_2 = 2\bar{p}_2 - \bar{p}_1 + 3, \qquad \text{i.e. } \bar{p}_1 - \bar{p}_2 = 1$$

$$2\bar{p}_2 - \bar{p}_1 + 3 = 2\bar{p}_1 - \bar{p}_2, \qquad \text{i.e. } \bar{p}_1 - \bar{p}_2 = 1.$$

We therefore end up with only one equation. The equations therefore have many solutions. Many equilibria exist.

These examples demonstrate an important point. For the existence of a unique equilibrium, the characterizing equations must be

1   consistent and
2   independent.

When economists seem to deduce the existence of a unique equilibrium from the fact that they have found n equations for n unknowns, they are implicitly appealing to extra information about the workings of the economy that guarantees the consistency and the independence of the equations.

6.5 Homogeneous linear equations

An example of a homogeneous system of linear equations is given below on the left. The same system is expressed in matrix form on the right.

$$
\begin{array}{c}
a + b + c = 0 \\
2a + 2b + 2c = 0 \\
a + 2b + 3c = 0 \\
3a + 4b + 5c = 0
\end{array}
\qquad
\begin{pmatrix} 1 & 1 & 1 \\ 2 & 2 & 2 \\ 1 & 2 & 3 \\ 3 & 4 & 5 \end{pmatrix}
\begin{pmatrix} a \\ b \\ c \end{pmatrix}
=
\begin{pmatrix} 0 \\ 0 \\ 0 \\ 0 \end{pmatrix}
$$

The word 'linear' is used because the left-hand side defines a linear function. The word 'homogeneous' signifies that the right-hand side is the zero vector. (We have already met these words in section 4.11 when discussing difference equations. In the linear homogeneous difference equation $y_{t+2} - 3y_{t+1} + 2y_t = 0$, the 'variables' are to be understood as y_{t+2}, y_{t+1} and y_t.)

Homogeneous equations have the advantage that consistency is not a problem. They always have the trivial solution in which all of the variables are zero. One is therefore interested in when other non-trivial solutions exist. And when they do exist, what are they?

It is not hard to say some general things about the set of all solutions of a system of linear equations

$$Ax = 0$$

where A is an $m \times n$ matrix and x is the $n \times 1$ column vector of unknowns. The most important thing is that the set S of all solutions is a *vector subspace* of $\mathbb{R}^n$. This means that all linear combinations of elements of S are also elements of S. Suppose, for example, that u, v and w are solutions. Then $Au = 0$, $Av = 0$ and $Aw = 0$. A *linear combination* of u, v and w is an expression of the form

$$y = \alpha u + \beta v + \gamma w$$

where α, β and γ are scalars. To check that y is in the set S, we need only observe that

$$Ay = A(\alpha u + \beta v + \gamma w) = \alpha Au + \beta Av + \gamma Aw = 0 + 0 + 0 = 0.$$

To characterize the vector subspace S, we need to find a set of basis vectors for S. For u, v and w to form a *basis* for S, the requirement is that each y in S can be expressed uniquely in the form

$$y = \alpha u + \beta v + \gamma w.$$

The scalars α, β and γ are then said to be the *co-ordinates* of y with respect to the basis u, v and w.

For example, the natural basis for $\mathbb{R}^2$ consists of the vectors $(1, 0)'$ and $(0, 1)'$. Each vector $(\alpha, \beta)'$ in $\mathbb{R}^2$ can be expressed in only one way as a linear combination of these basis vectors:

$$\binom{\alpha}{\beta} = \alpha \binom{1}{0} + \beta \binom{0}{1}.$$

If u, v and w are a basis for S, then we can express 0 as a linear combination of u, v and w in only one way. It follows that the equation

$$0 = \alpha u + \beta v + \gamma w$$

can only hold when $\alpha = \beta = \gamma = 0$. This is the requirement that u, v and w be *linearly independent*. Or, to put the same thing another way, u, v and w are linearly independent when none of them can be expressed as a linear combination of the others. A linearly independent set of vectors in S of maximal size is necessarily a basis for S.

The number of vectors in a basis for S is called the *dimension* of S. Equivalently, the dimension of S is the maximum number of linearly independent vectors that can be chosen from S. Observe that the dimension of $\mathbb{R}^2$ is 2 because it has a basis with two vectors.

(A more exotic example can be found in section 4.11. The set of solutions of the linear homogeneous difference equation

$$y_{t+3} - 7y_{t+2} + 16y_{t+1} - 12y_t = 0$$

consists of all

$$y_t = A2^t + Bt2^t + C3^t$$

where A, B and C are constants. Thus 2^t, $t2^t$ and 3^t (thought of as functions of t) form a basis for the solution set, which therefore has dimension 3. In general, the dimension of the solution set of a linear homogeneous difference equation of order n is equal to n.)

Examples
1   The first example is the same as that above.

(1) $a + b + c = 0$
(2) $2a + 2b + 2c = 0$
(3) $a + 2b + 3c = 0$
(4) $3a + 4b + 5c = 0$

$$\begin{pmatrix} 1 & 1 & 1 \\ 2 & 2 & 2 \\ 1 & 2 & 3 \\ 3 & 4 & 5 \end{pmatrix} \begin{pmatrix} a \\ b \\ c \end{pmatrix} = \begin{pmatrix} 0 \\ 0 \\ 0 \\ 0 \end{pmatrix}.$$

These equations will now be solved in a slow and painful, but very systematic, manner.

Step 1: Replace (4) by (4) – (2).

(1) $a + b + c = 0$

(2) $2a + 2b + 2c = 0$

(3) $a + 2b + 3c = 0$

(4) $a + 2b + 3c = 0$

$$\begin{pmatrix} 1 & 1 & 1 \\ 2 & 2 & 2 \\ 1 & 2 & 3 \\ 1 & 2 & 3 \end{pmatrix} \begin{pmatrix} a \\ b \\ c \end{pmatrix} = \begin{pmatrix} 0 \\ 0 \\ 0 \\ 0 \end{pmatrix}$$

Step 2: Replace (4) by (4) – (3).

(1) $a + b + c = 0$

(2) $2a + 2b + 2c = 0$

(3) $a + 2b + 3c = 0$

(4) $0 + 0 + 0 = 0$

$$\begin{pmatrix} 1 & 1 & 1 \\ 2 & 2 & 2 \\ 1 & 2 & 3 \\ 0 & 0 & 0 \end{pmatrix} \begin{pmatrix} a \\ b \\ c \end{pmatrix} = \begin{pmatrix} 0 \\ 0 \\ 0 \\ 0 \end{pmatrix}$$

Step 3: Replace (2) by $1/2 \times$ (2).

(1) $a + b + c = 0$

(2) $a + b + c = 0$

(3) $a + 2b + 3c = 0$

(4) $0 + 0 + 0 = 0$

$$\begin{pmatrix} 1 & 1 & 1 \\ 1 & 1 & 1 \\ 1 & 2 & 3 \\ 0 & 0 & 0 \end{pmatrix} \begin{pmatrix} a \\ b \\ c \end{pmatrix} = \begin{pmatrix} 0 \\ 0 \\ 0 \\ 0 \end{pmatrix}$$

Step 4: Replace (2) by (2) – (1).

(1) $a + b + c = 0$

(2) $0 + 0 + 0 = 0$

(3) $a + 2b + 3c = 0$

(4) $0 + 0 + 0 = 0$

$$\begin{pmatrix} 1 & 1 & 1 \\ 0 & 0 & 0 \\ 1 & 2 & 3 \\ 0 & 0 & 0 \end{pmatrix} \begin{pmatrix} a \\ b \\ c \end{pmatrix} = \begin{pmatrix} 0 \\ 0 \\ 0 \\ 0 \end{pmatrix}$$

Step 5: Exchange (2) and (3).

(1) $a + b + c = 0$

(2) $a + 2b + 3c = 0$

(3) $0 + 0 + 0 = 0$

(4) $0 + 0 + 0 = 0$

$$\begin{pmatrix} 1 & 1 & 1 \\ 1 & 2 & 3 \\ 0 & 0 & 0 \\ 0 & 0 & 0 \end{pmatrix} \begin{pmatrix} a \\ b \\ c \end{pmatrix} = \begin{pmatrix} 0 \\ 0 \\ 0 \\ 0 \end{pmatrix}$$

Step 6: Replace (2) by (2) – (1).

(1) $a + b + c = 0$

(2) $0 + b + 2c = 0$

(3) $0 + 0 + 0 = 0$

(4) $0 + 0 + 0 = 0$

$$\begin{pmatrix} 1 & 1 & 1 \\ 0 & 1 & 2 \\ 0 & 0 & 0 \\ 0 & 0 & 0 \end{pmatrix} \begin{pmatrix} a \\ b \\ c \end{pmatrix} = \begin{pmatrix} 0 \\ 0 \\ 0 \\ 0 \end{pmatrix}$$

Notice that, in carrying out these operations, one really only needs to write down the matrix. One can then revert to the equations at the end.

After step 6, it is clear that c can be chosen to be *anything*, but then we must have that

$$b = -2c$$
$$a = -b - c = c.$$

Thus, if a, b and c solve the equations, then

$$\begin{pmatrix} a \\ b \\ c \end{pmatrix} = \begin{pmatrix} c \\ -2c \\ c \end{pmatrix} = c \begin{pmatrix} 1 \\ -2 \\ 1 \end{pmatrix}.$$

The solution space consists of all linear combinations of the single vector $(1, -2, 1)'$. One non-zero vector, all by itself, is necessarily linearly independent. Thus $(1, -2, 1)'$ forms a basis for the solution space, which is therefore one dimensional.

2   The second example is the same as the first except that equations (3) and (4) are omitted.

(1) $a + b + c = 0$ $\begin{pmatrix} 1 & 1 & 1 \\ 2 & 2 & 2 \end{pmatrix} \begin{pmatrix} a \\ b \\ c \end{pmatrix} = \begin{pmatrix} 0 \\ 0 \end{pmatrix}$

(2) $2a + 2b + 2c = 0$

Step 1: Replace (2) by $(2) - 2 \times (1)$.

(1) $a + b + c = 0$ $\begin{pmatrix} 1 & 1 & 1 \\ 0 & 0 & 0 \end{pmatrix} \begin{pmatrix} a \\ b \\ c \end{pmatrix} = \begin{pmatrix} 0 \\ 0 \end{pmatrix}$

(2) $0 + 0 + 0 = 0$

No further steps are necessary. The unknowns b and c can be chosen to be anything. But then

$$a = -b - c.$$

The solutions to the equations therefore satisfy

$$\begin{pmatrix} a \\ b \\ c \end{pmatrix} = \begin{pmatrix} -b-c \\ b \\ c \end{pmatrix} = b \begin{pmatrix} -1 \\ 1 \\ 0 \end{pmatrix} + c \begin{pmatrix} -1 \\ 0 \\ 1 \end{pmatrix}.$$

Thus, everything in the solution set can be written as a linear combination of the vectors $(-1, 1, 0)'$ and $(-1, 0, 1)'$. But we ought to check that they are linearly independent before concluding that they form a basis. This follows from the fact that

$$\beta \begin{pmatrix} -1 \\ 1 \\ 0 \end{pmatrix} + \gamma \begin{pmatrix} -1 \\ 0 \\ 1 \end{pmatrix} = \begin{pmatrix} 0 \\ 0 \\ 0 \end{pmatrix}$$

implies $\beta = 0$ and $\gamma = 0$. Since a basis for the solution set has two vectors, it has dimension 2.

6.6 Rank

The procedure of the previous section used the three elementary row operations, namely

1 exchange two rows,
2 multiply a row by a non-zero constant and
3 replace a row by itself plus a constant multiple of another row,

in order to reduce a matrix A to *echelon form*. In this, one gets as many zeros on the left in each row as possible, starting with the bottom and working upwards. The first non-zero term in each row must be 1. An example is given below for an $m \times n$ matrix A with $m = 4$ and $n = 6$.

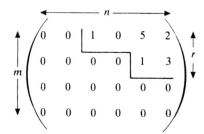

The *rank* of a matrix is the number of non-zero rows in its echelon form. For the matrix given above in the first example, the rank is $r = 2$. A grander way of saying this is that the rank is the dimension of the *row space* of the matrix. The row space is the vector subspace spanned by the rows, i.e. it is the set of all linear combinations of the rows. (Equivalently, the rank is the maximum number of linearly independent rows.)

(The reason why the rank is the dimension of the row space is that the non-zero rows in the echelon form are a basis of the row space of the original matrix. They are linearly independent, and, by reversing the sequence of elementary row operations which led to the echelon form, each row in the original matrix is seen to be a linear combination of the rows in the echelon-form matrix.)

We could, of course, have gone through the same exercise with columns instead of rows (although the interpretation in terms of manipulating equations, as in the examples in section 6.5, would not then apply). The result would be a 'column rank' for the matrix, rather than a 'row rank'. This column rank is the dimension of the *column space* (or, equivalently, the maximum number of linearly independent columns).

It is an important fact that it is always true that

$$\text{row rank} = \text{column rank}.$$

For this reason, we can speak simply of the rank of a matrix without reference to rows or columns.

Let us return to the system of equations with which section 6.5 began to illustrate the significance of the columns of the matrix A (as opposed to the rows). The system can be written as

$$
\begin{aligned}
a + b + c &= 0 \\
2a + 2b + 2c &= 0 \\
a + 2b + 3c &= 0 \\
3a + 4b + 5c &= 0
\end{aligned}
\quad \text{or} \quad
\begin{pmatrix} 1 & 1 & 1 \\ 2 & 2 & 2 \\ 1 & 2 & 3 \\ 3 & 4 & 5 \end{pmatrix}
\begin{pmatrix} a \\ b \\ c \end{pmatrix} =
\begin{pmatrix} 0 \\ 0 \\ 0 \\ 0 \end{pmatrix}
$$

or even

$$
a \begin{pmatrix} 1 \\ 2 \\ 1 \\ 3 \end{pmatrix}
+ b \begin{pmatrix} 1 \\ 2 \\ 2 \\ 4 \end{pmatrix}
+ c \begin{pmatrix} 1 \\ 2 \\ 3 \\ 5 \end{pmatrix}
= \begin{pmatrix} 0 \\ 0 \\ 0 \\ 0 \end{pmatrix}.
$$

The last form allows us to deduce a criterion for the existence of a non-trivial solution without any difficulty.

If the columns of the matrix are linearly independent, it must be the case that $a = b = c = 0$ and hence only the trivial solution exists. Conversely, if a non-trivial solution exists, then the columns of the matrix are linearly dependent.

An $m \times n$ matrix has n columns. These will all be linearly independent unless the rank r of the matrix satisfies $r < n$. The criterion for a non-trivial solution is therefore that $r < n$, and the criterion for only the trivial solution is $r = n$. In face, the dimension of the solution space is always equal to $n - r$.

Examples
1   Consider the homogeneous linear system

$$
\begin{aligned}
(1) \quad a + 2b + 3c &= 0 \\
(2) \quad 3a + b + 2c &= 0 \\
(3) \quad 2a + 3b + c &= 0
\end{aligned}
\quad \text{or} \quad
\begin{pmatrix} 1 & 2 & 3 \\ 3 & 1 & 2 \\ 2 & 3 & 1 \end{pmatrix}
\begin{pmatrix} a \\ b \\ c \end{pmatrix} =
\begin{pmatrix} 0 \\ 0 \\ 0 \end{pmatrix}
$$

Replace (3) by (3) − 2 × (1).
$$
\begin{pmatrix} 1 & 2 & 3 \\ 3 & 1 & 2 \\ 0 & -1 & -5 \end{pmatrix}
$$

Replace (2) by (2) − 3 × (1).
$$
\begin{pmatrix} 1 & 2 & 3 \\ 0 & -5 & -7 \\ 0 & -1 & -5 \end{pmatrix}
$$

Replace (2) by − 1/5 × (2).
$$
\begin{pmatrix} 1 & 2 & 3 \\ 0 & 1 & 7/5 \\ 0 & -1 & -5 \end{pmatrix}
$$

Replace (3) by (3) + (2).
$$\begin{pmatrix} 1 & 2 & 3 \\ 0 & 1 & 7/5 \\ 0 & 0 & -18/5 \end{pmatrix}$$

Replace (3) by $-5/18 \times$ (3).
$$\begin{pmatrix} 1 & 2 & 3 \\ 0 & 1 & 7/5 \\ 0 & 0 & 1 \end{pmatrix} \begin{pmatrix} a \\ b \\ c \end{pmatrix} = \begin{pmatrix} 0 \\ 0 \\ 0 \end{pmatrix}$$

This last equation is equivalent to

$$a + 2b + 3c = 0$$
$$b + 7c/5 = 0$$
$$c = 0.$$

One does not need to solve the final system to see that *only* the trivial solution $a = b = c = 0$ exists. It has been shown that the rank of the 3×3 matrix is 3 and hence $n = r$. (Notice that the dimension of the solution space is $n - r = 0$. The zero-dimensional vector subspace of $\mathbb{R}^3$ consists just of the single vector **0**.)

2   The following system has more unknowns than equations. A homogeneous system with this property *always* has a non-trivial solution. The reason is that the rank r of an $m \times n$ matrix must satisfy both $r \leqslant m$ and $r \leqslant n$ (because row rank = column rank). If $m < n$, it follows that $r < n$ and hence that a non-trivial solution exists. But it is not *necessary* for the existence of a non-trivial solution that there be more unknowns than equations. For instance, example 1 in section 6.5 has a non-trivial solution although there are three equations and four unknowns.

We know that the following system has non-trivial solutions, but what are they?

(1) $a + 2b + 3c = 0$ $\begin{pmatrix} 1 & 2 & 3 \\ 3 & 1 & 2 \end{pmatrix} \begin{pmatrix} a \\ b \\ c \end{pmatrix} = \begin{pmatrix} 0 \\ 0 \\ 0 \end{pmatrix}$
(2) $3a + b + 2c = 0$

Replace (2) by (2) $- 3 \times$ (1).
$$\begin{pmatrix} 1 & 2 & 3 \\ 0 & -5 & -7 \end{pmatrix}$$

Replace (2) by $-1/5 \times$ (2).
$$\begin{pmatrix} 1 & 2 & 3 \\ 0 & 1 & 7/5 \end{pmatrix} \begin{pmatrix} a \\ b \\ c \end{pmatrix} = \begin{pmatrix} 0 \\ 0 \\ 0 \end{pmatrix}$$

Thus we arrive at the equations

$$a + 2b + 3c = 0$$
$$b + 7c/5 = 0.$$

The unknown c can be taken to be anything. Then $b = -7c/5$ and $a = -2b - 3c = -c/5$. Writing $c = 5\gamma$, we obtain that the solutions are of the form

$$\begin{pmatrix} a \\ b \\ c \end{pmatrix} = \begin{pmatrix} -\gamma \\ -7\gamma \\ 5\gamma \end{pmatrix} = \gamma \begin{pmatrix} -1 \\ -7 \\ 5 \end{pmatrix}.$$

The solution set is therefore of dimension 1, with the single vector $(-1, -7, 5)'$ serving as a basis. Notice that the rank of the matrix is 2 and that $n - r = 3 - 2 = 1$.

6.7   Non-homogeneous linear equations

An example of a non-homogeneous system of linear equations is given below:

(1) $a + b + c = 3$

(2) $2a + 2b + 2c = 6$

(3) $a + 2b + 3c = 6$ or

(4) $3a + 4b + 5c = 12$

$$\begin{pmatrix} 1 & 1 & 1 \\ 2 & 2 & 2 \\ 1 & 2 & 3 \\ 3 & 4 & 5 \end{pmatrix} \begin{pmatrix} a \\ b \\ c \end{pmatrix} = \begin{pmatrix} 3 \\ 6 \\ 6 \\ 12 \end{pmatrix}$$

In contrast with the homogeneous case, the first problem to be faced is whether the system is *consistent*. Does it have any solutions at all? The general answer is that a system

$$A\mathbf{x} = \mathbf{y}$$

in which A is an $m \times n$ matrix, $\mathbf{y}$ is an $m \times 1$ vector of constants and $\mathbf{x}$ is an $n \times 1$ vector of unknowns has a solution if and only if $\mathbf{y}$ is in the column space of the matrix A. As we saw in section 6.6,

$$\begin{pmatrix} 1 & 1 & 1 \\ 2 & 2 & 2 \\ 1 & 2 & 3 \\ 3 & 4 & 5 \end{pmatrix} \begin{pmatrix} a \\ b \\ c \end{pmatrix} = a \begin{pmatrix} 1 \\ 2 \\ 1 \\ 3 \end{pmatrix} + b \begin{pmatrix} 1 \\ 2 \\ 2 \\ 4 \end{pmatrix} + c \begin{pmatrix} 1 \\ 2 \\ 3 \\ 5 \end{pmatrix}$$

and so to write $A\mathbf{x} = \mathbf{y}$ is to assert that $\mathbf{y}$ is a linear combination of the columns of A.

Because row rank is the same as column rank, it follows that $A\mathbf{x} = \mathbf{y}$ has a solution if and only if the rank of A is the same as the rank of the *augmented matrix* $(A \mid \mathbf{y})$ defined by

$$(A \mid \mathbf{y}) = \begin{pmatrix} 1 & 1 & 1 & \vdots & 3 \\ 2 & 2 & 2 & \vdots & 6 \\ 1 & 2 & 3 & \vdots & 6 \\ 3 & 4 & 5 & \vdots & 12 \end{pmatrix}.$$

This criterion is not very useful because, to find the ranks of A and $(A|y)$ one has to proceed as though one were solving the equations anyway. The procedure below is identical with that of the examples in section 6.5.

Step 1: Replace (4) by (4) – (2).

(1) $a + b + c = 3$

(2) $2a + 2b + 2c = 6$

(3) $a + 2b + 3c = 6$

(4) $a + 2b + 3c = 6$

$$\begin{pmatrix} 1 & 1 & 1 & | & 3 \\ 2 & 2 & 2 & | & 6 \\ 1 & 2 & 3 & | & 6 \\ 1 & 2 & 3 & | & 6 \end{pmatrix}$$

Step 2: Replace (4) by (4) – (3).

(1) $a + b + c = 3$

(2) $2a + 2b + 2c = 6$

(3) $a + 2b + 3c = 6$

(4) $0 + 0 + 0 = 0$

$$\begin{pmatrix} 1 & 1 & 1 & | & 3 \\ 2 & 2 & 2 & | & 6 \\ 1 & 2 & 3 & | & 6 \\ 0 & 0 & 0 & | & 0 \end{pmatrix}$$

Step 3: Replace (2) by $1/2 \times$ (2).

(1) $a + b + c = 3$

(2) $a + b + c = 3$

(3) $a + 2b + 3c = 6$

(4) $0 + 0 + 0 = 0$

$$\begin{pmatrix} 1 & 1 & 1 & | & 3 \\ 1 & 1 & 1 & | & 3 \\ 1 & 2 & 3 & | & 6 \\ 0 & 0 & 0 & | & 0 \end{pmatrix}$$

Step 4: Replace (2) by (2) – (1).

(1) $a + b + c = 3$

(2) $0 + 0 + 0 = 0$

(3) $a + 2b + 3c = 6$

(4) $0 + 0 + 0 = 0$

$$\begin{pmatrix} 1 & 1 & 1 & | & 3 \\ 0 & 0 & 0 & | & 0 \\ 1 & 2 & 3 & | & 6 \\ 0 & 0 & 0 & | & 0 \end{pmatrix}$$

Step 5: Exchange (2) and (3).

(1) $a + b + c = 3$

(2) $a + 2b + 3c = 6$

(3) $0 + 0 + 0 = 0$

(4) $0 + 0 + 0 = 0$

$$\begin{pmatrix} 1 & 1 & 1 & | & 3 \\ 1 & 2 & 3 & | & 6 \\ 0 & 0 & 0 & | & 0 \\ 0 & 0 & 0 & | & 0 \end{pmatrix}$$

Step 6: Replace (2) by (2) – (1).

(1) $a + b + c = 3$

(2) $0 + b + 2c = 3$

(3) $0 + 0 + 0 = 0$

(4) $0 + 0 + 0 = 0$

$$\begin{pmatrix} 1 & 1 & 1 & | & 3 \\ 0 & 1 & 2 & | & 3 \\ 0 & 0 & 0 & | & 0 \\ 0 & 0 & 0 & | & 0 \end{pmatrix}$$

Notice that the number of zero rows in the echelon form of the augmented matrix $(A \mid y)$ is the same as in the echelon form of the original matrix A. Both matrices therefore have the same rank and hence a solution exists. However, this can just as easily be seen from the reduced form of the equations. In these, c may be taken to be anything. Then

$$b = 3 - 2c$$
$$a = 3 - b - c = 3 - (3 - 2c) - c = c.$$

The solutions are therefore

$$\begin{pmatrix} a \\ b \\ c \end{pmatrix} = \begin{pmatrix} c \\ 3 - 2c \\ c \end{pmatrix} = \begin{pmatrix} 0 \\ 3 \\ 0 \end{pmatrix} + c \begin{pmatrix} 1 \\ -2 \\ 1 \end{pmatrix}$$

where c may take any value.

It is important to observe that, if x^* is some *particular solution* of a consistent system $Ax = y$, then any other solution may be expressed in the form

$$x = x^* + z$$

where z is a solution of the *homogeneous* system $Az = 0$. The reason is simply that, if $Ax^* = y$ and $Ax = y$, then $A(x - x^*) = y - y = 0$, and so $z = x - x^*$ solves $Az = 0$.

In the example we have been considering, $x^* = (0, 3, 0)'$ is a particular solution of the system and, as we saw in example 1 of section 6.5, all solutions of the associated homogeneous system are of the form

$$z = c \begin{pmatrix} 1 \\ -2 \\ 1 \end{pmatrix}.$$

These observations have some useful consequences. If you can guess one particular solution of the system $Ax = y$, then all the others can be found just from looking at the homogeneous system $Ax = 0$. No fuss with the augmented matrix is then necessary. For example, one might easily guess that $x^{**} = (1, 1, 1)'$ is a solution of the system studied in this section. The remaining solutions are then given by

$$\begin{pmatrix} a \\ b \\ c \end{pmatrix} = \begin{pmatrix} 1 \\ 1 \\ 1 \end{pmatrix} + \gamma \begin{pmatrix} 1 \\ -2 \\ 1 \end{pmatrix}.$$

In particular,

$$x^* = \begin{pmatrix} 0 \\ 3 \\ 0 \end{pmatrix} = \begin{pmatrix} 1 \\ 1 \\ 1 \end{pmatrix} + (-1) \begin{pmatrix} 1 \\ -2 \\ 1 \end{pmatrix}.$$

Example

The following non-homogeneous system is *inconsistent*. It has no solutions at all.

(1) $a + b + c = 3$

(2) $2a + 2b + 2c = 6$

(3) $a + 2b + 3c = 6$ or

(4) $3a + 4b + 5c = 6$

$$\begin{pmatrix} 1 & 1 & 1 \\ 2 & 2 & 2 \\ 1 & 2 & 3 \\ 3 & 4 & 5 \end{pmatrix} \begin{pmatrix} a \\ b \\ c \end{pmatrix} = \begin{pmatrix} 3 \\ 6 \\ 6 \\ 6 \end{pmatrix}$$

To verify this assertion, the augmented matrix will be reduced to echelon form, using the same procedure as previously (above and section 6.5).

$$\left(\begin{array}{ccc|c} 1 & 1 & 1 & 3 \\ 2 & 2 & 2 & 6 \\ 1 & 2 & 3 & 6 \\ 3 & 4 & 5 & 6 \end{array} \right)$$

$$\left(\begin{array}{ccc|c} 1 & 1 & 1 & 3 \\ 2 & 2 & 2 & 6 \\ 1 & 2 & 3 & 6 \\ 1 & 2 & 3 & 0 \end{array} \right)$$

$$\left(\begin{array}{ccc|c} 1 & 1 & 1 & 3 \\ 2 & 2 & 2 & 6 \\ 1 & 2 & 3 & 6 \\ 0 & 0 & 0 & -6 \end{array} \right)$$

$$\left(\begin{array}{ccc|c} 1 & 1 & 1 & 3 \\ 1 & 1 & 1 & 3 \\ 1 & 2 & 3 & 6 \\ 0 & 0 & 0 & -6 \end{array} \right)$$

$$\left(\begin{array}{ccc|c} 1 & 1 & 1 & 3 \\ 0 & 0 & 0 & 0 \\ 1 & 2 & 3 & 6 \\ 0 & 0 & 0 & -6 \end{array} \right)$$

$$\left(\begin{array}{ccc|c} 1 & 1 & 1 & 3 \\ 1 & 2 & 3 & 6 \\ 0 & 0 & 0 & 0 \\ 0 & 0 & 0 & -6 \end{array} \right)$$

$$\begin{pmatrix} 1 & 1 & 1 & \vdots & 3 \\ 0 & 1 & 2 & \vdots & 3 \\ 0 & 0 & 0 & \vdots & 0 \\ 0 & 0 & 0 & \vdots & -6 \end{pmatrix}$$

But now further steps are necessary to those of the procedure above. Replace (4) by $-1/6 \times (4)$ and then exchange (3) and (4). The result is the echelon form of the augmented matrix.

$$\begin{pmatrix} 1 & 1 & 1 & \vdots & 3 \\ 0 & 1 & 2 & \vdots & 3 \\ 0 & 0 & 0 & \vdots & 1 \\ 0 & 0 & 0 & \vdots & 0 \end{pmatrix}$$

The rank of the augmented matrix is therefore 3 which is not equal to the rank of the original matrix A, namely 2. (The echelon form of A lies to the left of the vertical line in the augmented matrix.)

It is easy to check that the equations are inconsistent by writing them down in their final reduced form, which is

(1) $a + b + c = 3$
(2) $0 + b + 2c = 3$
(3) $0 + 0 + 0 = 1$
(4) $0 + 0 + 0 = 0.$

We clearly cannot satisfy equation (3)!

*6.8 Non-homogeneous difference equations

Consider the homogeneous difference equation

$$y_{t+2} - 3y_{t+1} + 2y_t = 0. \tag{6.1}$$

We saw in section 4.11 that the equation has a solution of the form $y_t = Ac^t$ provided that $P(c) = 0$, where

$$P(x) = x^2 - 3x + 2$$

is the auxiliary polynomial. As the roots of $P(x)$ are $x = 1$, $x = 2$ we found the general solution of (6.1) to be

$$y_t = A(1)^t + B(2)^t. \tag{6.2}$$

We noted at the end of section 6.5 that these solutions form a two-dimensional vector subspace provided that we are prepared to countenance the functions of t as vectors.

In section 6.7 we saw that the general solution of an non-homogeneous matrix equation $Ax = b$ takes the form

$$x = x^* + z$$

where x^* is some particular solution and z solves the associated or 'complementary' homogeneous equation $Az = 0$. The situation for difference equations is not dissimilar. A non-homogeneous difference equation such as

$$y_{t+2} - 3y_{t+1} + 2y_t = 3^t \tag{6.3}$$

can be written in the general form

$$P(E)y_t = g_t \tag{6.4}$$

where E is the shift operator and in our case $g_t = 3^t$. Let y_t^* be a particular solution of (6.4) and let y_t be any other solution, then we have

$$P(E)(y_t - y_t^*) = P(E)y_t - P(E)y_t^* = g_t - g_t = 0,$$

so that $z_t = y_t - y_t^*$ solves the complementary homogeneous difference equation

$$P(E)z_t = 0. \tag{6.5}$$

Thus again we have

general solution = particular solution + complementary solution.

We apply this result to a number of examples.

Examples
1   Find the general solution of the difference equation

$$y_{t+2} - 5y_{t+1} + 6y_t = 1. \tag{6.6}$$

SOLUTION   We factorize the auxiliary polynomial $P(x) = x^2 - 5x + 6 = (x - 2) \times (x - 3)$. Thus the complementary homogeneous equation

$$y_{t+2} - 5y_{t+1} + 6y_t = 0$$

has the general solution $y_t = A2^t + B3^t$. Next we look for a particular solution of (6.6). The first place to look is for a constant (or 'static') solution $y_t = k$. Substituting into the left-hand side LHS of equation (6.6) we obtain

$$\text{LHS} = k - 5k + 6k = k(1 - 5 + 6) = kP(1) = 2k.$$

This will equal the right-hand side if $2k = 1$, i.e. $k = 1/2$. The general solution is thus

$$y_t = \frac{1}{2} + A2^t + B3^t.$$

Encouraged by the ease with which we solved the equation here, we try a slightly less simple right-hand side.

2   Find the general solution of the difference equation

$$y_{t+2} - 5y_{t+1} + 6y_t = t. \tag{6.7}$$

SOLUTION For want of any other idea we try the same kind of function as appears on the right-hand side, i.e. $y_t = kt$. This does not quite work because

$$\text{LHS} = k[(t + 2) - 5(t + 1) + 6t]$$
$$= k[t(1 - 5 + 6) + (2 - 5)]$$
$$= k(2t - 3). \tag{6.8}$$

But we can overcome the problem of the extra term in (6.8) by using instead $y_t = kt + l$. We then have

$$\text{LHS} = k[(t + 2) - 5(t + 1) + 6t] + l(1 - 5 + 6)$$
$$= k(2t - 3) + 2l$$
$$= 2kt + (2l - 3k).$$

Thus, taking $2k = 1$ and $2l = 3k$, i.e. $k = 1/2$, $l = (3/2)(1/2) = 3/4$, we do obtain a solution. The general solution is therefore

$$y_t = \frac{1}{2}t + \frac{3}{4} + A2^t + B3^t.$$

We rightfully expect this method to work when the right-hand side is a polynomial in t. Though some complications can occur (see example 4 below), we find that the particular solution is again a polynomial – often of the same degree. We now turn our attention to exponential functions on the right-hand side.

3 Find the general solution of the difference equation

$$y_{t+2} - 3y_{t+1} + 2y_t = 3^t. \tag{6.9}$$

SOLUTION Given the special role of the functions c^t we naturally look and hope for a solution in the space spanned by 3^t. Our hopes will be rewarded. We substitute $y_t = k3^t$ into the left-hand side of (6.9):

$$\text{LHS} = k3^{t+2} - 3k3^{t+1} + 2k3^t = k3^t(3^2 - 3 \times 3 + 2) = k3^t \times 2. \tag{6.10}$$

Thus if we take $k = 1/2$ we shall have found a particular solution. Hence by (6.2) the general solution is

$$\frac{1}{2}3^t + A(1)^t + B(2)^t = \frac{1}{2}3^t + A + B2^t.$$

Let us note that equation (6.10) reads

$$\text{LHS} = k3^t P(3) \tag{6.11}$$

and so in fact $k = 1/P(3)$.

We now look at some complications that can occur.

4 Find the general solution of the difference equation

$$y_{t+2} - 3y_{t+1} + 2y_t = 1. \tag{6.12}$$

SOLUTION   Here $P(x) = x^2 - 3x + 2 = (x - 1)(x - 2)$. Since $P(1) = 0$ we must not try $y_t = k(1)^t$ (see (6.11) and compare example 1). We try instead $y_t = kt(1)^t$. Substitution into the equation leads to

$$\text{LHS} = k[(t + 2) - 3(t + 1) + 2t] = k[t(1 - 3 + 2) + (2 - 3)] = k(-1).$$

Taking $k = -1$ solves our problem. Notice that the substitution worked out to be LHS $= k[tP(1) + P'(1)]$ with $P(1) = 0$. The general solution of (6.12) is

$$y_t = -t + A + B2^t.$$

5   Find the general solution of the difference equation

$$y_{t+2} - 3y_{t+1} + 2y_t = 2^t.$$

SOLUTION   We shall be unsuccessful if we try $y_t = k2^t$. Just as in (6.11) we obtain

$$\text{LHS} = k2^t P(2)$$

where $P(x) = x^2 - 3x + 2$. But $P(2) = 0$ and so the left-hand side cannot match the right-hand side. Some inspiration is required. We saw in section 4.11 that when the auxiliary equation has a repeated root c we need to form additional solution functions like tc^t, $t^2 c^t$, ... We try the same trick here. Substituting $kt2^t$ into equation (6.13) on the left gives

$$
\begin{aligned}
\text{LHS} &= k(t + 2)2^{t+2} - 3k(t + 1)2^{t+1} + 2kt2^t \\
&= k2^t[(t + 2)2^2 - 3(t + 1)2 + 2t] \\
&= k2^t[t(2^2 - 3 \times 2 + 2) + (2 \times 2^2 - 3 \times 2)] \\
&= k2^t(0 \times t + 2) \\
&= 2k2^t.
\end{aligned}
\tag{6.13}
$$

Thus for $k = 1/2$ we obtain a particular solution. The general solution is thus

$$y_t = \frac{1}{2} t2^t + A + B2^t.$$

Again you will notice that the left-hand side of (6.13) reads

$$k2^t[tP(2) + P'(2)].$$

A final awkward example follows.

6   Find the general solution of the difference equation

$$y_{t+3} - 7y_{t+2} + 16y_{t+1} - 12y_t = 2^t. \tag{6.14}$$

SOLUTION   As usual we first consider the homogeneous equation

$$y_{t+3} - 7y_{t+2} + 16y_{t+1} - 12y_t = 0. \tag{6.15}$$

The auxiliary polynomial is

$$P(x) = x^3 - 7x^2 + 16x - 12 = (x - 2)^2(x - 3)$$

and so the homogeneous equation has the general solution

$$y_t = A2^t + Bt2^t + C3^t.$$

In view of this it would be unwise to try a particular solution of (6.14) in the form 2^t, or even $t2^t$, since both on substitution on the left-hand side of (6.14) would necessarily yield zero because they are solutions of (6.15). The trick is to 'notch up' by one more power as we have already done previously. Thus we try $y_t = kt^2 2^t$. Substitution into the right-hand side of (6.14) gives

$$2^t k[(t + 3)^2 2^3 - 7(t + 2)^2 2^2 + 16(t + 1)^2 2 - 12t^2]$$

$$= 2^t k[t^2(2^3 - 7 \times 2^2 + 16 \times 2 - 12) + 2t(3 \times 2^3 - 7 \times 2 \times 2^2 + 16 \times 1 \times 2)$$

$$+ (9 \times 8 - 7 \times 4 \times 4 + 16 \times 2)]$$

$$= 2^t k[t^2 P(2) + 2t \times 2P'(2) - 8]$$

$$= -8k2^t.$$

Hence $k = -1/8$ and the general solution is

$$y_t = -\frac{1}{8} t^2 2^t + A2^t + Bt2^t + C3^t.$$

The moral of the uncomplicated examples 1–3 was that a particular solution could be found in the same form as the function on the right-hand side. Complications arose when the function on the right-hand side looked like part of the 'complementary solution'. In that case we needed to notch up the degree of the polynomial.

6.9   Finding the inverse of a matrix

In section 2.1 we explained that division by a matrix M is not always possible. Those for which division is possible, i.e. those for which M^{-1} exists, were called non-singular. We obtained a formula in section 2.1.5 for M^{-1} when M is a 2×2 matrix but we have yet to obtain one for a general square matrix.

Since the main use of M^{-1} is in the solution of a matrix equation like $Mx = b$ we must expect a connection between a formula for M^{-1} and our earlier method of solving a system of simultaneous equations by row operations (i.e. manipulations of the equations). To find the connection we review the calculations in the examples in section 6.6.

$$A = \begin{pmatrix} 1 & 2 & 3 \\ 3 & 1 & 2 \\ 2 & 3 & 1 \end{pmatrix}$$

was reduced to the echelon form

$$\begin{pmatrix} 1 & 2 & 3 \\ 0 & 1 & 7/5 \\ 0 & 0 & 1 \end{pmatrix}$$

by a sequence of elementary row operations and hence was shown to be of rank 3. The calculation of example 1 in section 6.6 is repeated below, together with an explanation of why each elementary row operation is equivalent to multiplication on the left by an 'elementary matrix'.

Step 1: Replace row (3) by row (3) – 2 × row (1).

$$E_1 A = \begin{pmatrix} 1 & 0 & 0 \\ 0 & 1 & 0 \\ -2 & 0 & 1 \end{pmatrix} \begin{pmatrix} 1 & 2 & 3 \\ 3 & 1 & 2 \\ 2 & 3 & 1 \end{pmatrix} = \begin{pmatrix} 1 & 2 & 3 \\ 3 & 1 & 2 \\ 0 & -1 & -5 \end{pmatrix}.$$

Step 2: Replace row (2) by row (2) – 3 × row (1).

$$E_2(E_1 A) = \begin{pmatrix} 1 & 0 & 0 \\ -3 & 1 & 0 \\ 0 & 0 & 1 \end{pmatrix} \begin{pmatrix} 1 & 2 & 3 \\ 3 & 1 & 2 \\ 0 & -1 & -5 \end{pmatrix} = \begin{pmatrix} 1 & 2 & 3 \\ 0 & -5 & -7 \\ 0 & -1 & -5 \end{pmatrix}.$$

Step 3: Replace row (2) by row (–1/5) × row (2).

$$E_3(E_2 E_1 A) = \begin{pmatrix} 1 & 0 & 0 \\ 0 & -1/5 & 0 \\ 0 & 0 & 1 \end{pmatrix} \begin{pmatrix} 1 & 2 & 3 \\ 0 & -5 & -7 \\ 0 & -1 & -5 \end{pmatrix} = \begin{pmatrix} 1 & 2 & 3 \\ 0 & 1 & 7/5 \\ 0 & -1 & -5 \end{pmatrix}.$$

Step 4: Replace row (3) by row (3) + row (2).

$$E_4(E_3 E_2 E_1 A) = \begin{pmatrix} 1 & 0 & 0 \\ 0 & 1 & 0 \\ 0 & 1 & 1 \end{pmatrix} \begin{pmatrix} 1 & 2 & 3 \\ 0 & 1 & 7/5 \\ 0 & -1 & -5 \end{pmatrix} = \begin{pmatrix} 1 & 2 & 3 \\ 0 & 1 & 7/5 \\ 0 & 0 & -18/5 \end{pmatrix}.$$

Step 5: Replace row (3) by (–5/18) × row (3).

$$E_5(E_4 E_3 E_2 E_1 A) = \begin{pmatrix} 1 & 0 & 0 \\ 0 & 1 & 0 \\ 0 & 0 & -5/18 \end{pmatrix} \begin{pmatrix} 1 & 2 & 3 \\ 0 & 1 & 7/5 \\ 0 & 0 & -18/5 \end{pmatrix} = \begin{pmatrix} 1 & 2 & 3 \\ 0 & 1 & 7/5 \\ 0 & 0 & 1 \end{pmatrix}.$$

Because the 3×3 matrix A has rank 3, we can now continue using elementary row operations to reduce the echelon form to the 3×3 unit matrix I. If A had rank less than 3, the echelon form would have a zero row and so such a continuation would be impossible.

Step 6: Replace row (2) by row (2) – (7/5) × row (3).

$$E_6(E_5 E_4 E_3 E_2 E_1 A) = \begin{pmatrix} 1 & 0 & 0 \\ 0 & 1 & -7/5 \\ 0 & 0 & 1 \end{pmatrix} \begin{pmatrix} 1 & 2 & 3 \\ 0 & 1 & 7/5 \\ 0 & 0 & 1 \end{pmatrix} = \begin{pmatrix} 1 & 2 & 3 \\ 0 & 1 & 0 \\ 0 & 0 & 1 \end{pmatrix}.$$

Step 7: Replace row (1) by row (1) – 2 × row (2).

$$E_7(E_6E_5E_4E_3E_2E_1A) = \begin{pmatrix} 1 & -2 & 0 \\ 0 & 1 & 0 \\ 0 & 0 & 1 \end{pmatrix}\begin{pmatrix} 1 & 2 & 3 \\ 0 & 1 & 0 \\ 0 & 0 & 1 \end{pmatrix} = \begin{pmatrix} 1 & 0 & 3 \\ 0 & 1 & 0 \\ 0 & 0 & 1 \end{pmatrix}.$$

Step 8: Replace row (1) by row (1) – 3 × row (3).

$$E_8(E_7E_6E_5E_4E_3E_2E_1A) = \begin{pmatrix} 1 & 0 & -3 \\ 0 & 1 & 0 \\ 0 & 0 & 1 \end{pmatrix}\begin{pmatrix} 1 & 0 & 3 \\ 0 & 1 & 0 \\ 0 & 0 & 1 \end{pmatrix} = \begin{pmatrix} 1 & 0 & 0 \\ 0 & 1 & 0 \\ 0 & 0 & 1 \end{pmatrix} = I.$$

The result of the calculation can be expressed as

$$E_8E_7E_6E_5E_4E_3E_2E_1A = I.$$

Each elementary row operation is *reversible*. (It is to ensure this that the second operation, as described in section 6.6, stipulates that only multiplication by non-zero constants is permitted.) This reversibility means that the elementary matrices necessarily have inverses and hence so does the product $E_8E_7 \cdots E_1$. (Its inverse is equal to $E_1^{-1}E_2^{-2} \cdots E_8^{-1}$.) Thus we can write

$$A = (E_8E_7 \cdots E_1)^{-1},$$

from which it follows, not only that A has an inverse matrix, but that this is equal to

$$A^{-1} = E_8E_7 \cdots E_1.$$

We can therefore calculate A^{-1} by applying to I precisely those elementary row operations which reduce A to I. The mechanics appear in the next example.

This section concludes with table 6.1 which lists a number of equivalent ways of saying that an $n \times n$ matrix is non-singular. Only the last of these will be unfamiliar. Determinants are discussed in section 6.11.

Table 6.1

A is non-singular
$Ax = y$ has a unique solution
A has rank n
A has an inverse matrix A^{-1}
A has non-zero determinant

Example
In the example in section 6.7 it was explained that the same sequence of elementary row operations that reduces A to I will simultaneously reduce I to A^{-1}. The mechanics of the process are given below.

$$A = \begin{pmatrix} 1 & 2 & 3 \\ 3 & 1 & 2 \\ 2 & 3 & 1 \end{pmatrix} \qquad I = \begin{pmatrix} 1 & 0 & 0 \\ 0 & 1 & 0 \\ 0 & 0 & 1 \end{pmatrix}$$

Step 1: Replace row (3) by row (3) – 2 × row (1).

$$\begin{pmatrix} 1 & 2 & 3 \\ 3 & 1 & 2 \\ 0 & -1 & -5 \end{pmatrix} \quad \begin{pmatrix} 1 & 0 & 0 \\ 0 & 1 & 0 \\ -2 & 0 & 1 \end{pmatrix}$$

Step 2: Replace row (2) by row (2) – 3 × row (1).

$$\begin{pmatrix} 1 & 2 & 3 \\ 0 & -5 & -7 \\ 0 & -1 & -5 \end{pmatrix} \quad \begin{pmatrix} 1 & 0 & 0 \\ -3 & 1 & 0 \\ -2 & 0 & 1 \end{pmatrix}$$

Step 3: Replace row (2) by (–1/5) × row (2).

$$\begin{pmatrix} 1 & 2 & 3 \\ 0 & 1 & 7/5 \\ 0 & -1 & -5 \end{pmatrix} \quad \begin{pmatrix} 1 & 0 & 0 \\ 3/5 & -1/5 & 0 \\ -2 & 0 & 1 \end{pmatrix}$$

Step 4: Replace row (3) by row (3) + row (2).

$$\begin{pmatrix} 1 & 2 & 3 \\ 0 & 1 & 7/5 \\ 0 & 0 & -18/5 \end{pmatrix} \quad \begin{pmatrix} 1 & 0 & 0 \\ 3/5 & -1/5 & 0 \\ -7/5 & -1/5 & 1 \end{pmatrix}$$

Step 5: Replace row (3) by (–5/18) × row (3).

$$\begin{pmatrix} 1 & 2 & 3 \\ 0 & 1 & 7/5 \\ 0 & 0 & 1 \end{pmatrix} \quad \begin{pmatrix} 1 & 0 & 0 \\ 3/5 & -1/5 & 0 \\ 7/18 & 1/18 & -5/18 \end{pmatrix}$$

Step 6: Replace row (2) by row (2) –(7/5) × row (3).

$$\begin{pmatrix} 1 & 2 & 3 \\ 0 & 1 & 0 \\ 0 & 0 & 1 \end{pmatrix} \quad \begin{pmatrix} 1 & 0 & 0 \\ 1/18 & -5/18 & 7/18 \\ 7/18 & 1/18 & -5/18 \end{pmatrix}$$

Step 7: Replace row (1) by row (1) – 2 × row (2).

$$\begin{pmatrix} 1 & 0 & 3 \\ 0 & 1 & 0 \\ 0 & 0 & 1 \end{pmatrix} \quad \begin{pmatrix} 16/18 & 10/18 & 14/18 \\ 1/18 & -5/18 & 7/18 \\ 7/18 & 1/18 & -5/18 \end{pmatrix}$$

Step 8: Replace row (1) by row (1) – 3 × row (3).

$$I = \begin{pmatrix} 1 & 0 & 0 \\ 0 & 1 & 0 \\ 0 & 0 & 1 \end{pmatrix} \quad A^{-1} = \begin{pmatrix} -5/18 & 7/18 & 1/18 \\ 1/18 & -5/18 & 7/18 \\ 7/18 & 1/18 & -5/18 \end{pmatrix}$$

To check that an error has not been made, we shall verify that $A^{-1}A = I$. Observe that

$$A^{-1}A = \frac{1}{18} \begin{pmatrix} -5 & 7 & 1 \\ 1 & -5 & 7 \\ 7 & 1 & -5 \end{pmatrix} \begin{pmatrix} 1 & 2 & 3 \\ 3 & 1 & 2 \\ 2 & 3 & 1 \end{pmatrix} = \frac{1}{18} \begin{pmatrix} 18 & 0 & 0 \\ 0 & 18 & 0 \\ 0 & 0 & 18 \end{pmatrix}$$

as required.

6.10 Input–output analysis

In the Leontieff model of section 5.11, the equation

$$y = Ax$$

gives the total input vector y necessary for an economy containing n industries to produce a total output vector of x. An example of a 3×3 input–output matrix A is given in table 6.2.

Table 6.2

		Outputs		
		1	2	3
	1	0.3	0.1	0.2
Inputs	2	0.0	0.4	0.1
	3	0.2	0.0	0.1

$= A$

The matrix describes how the various industries in the economy are related. For example, the production of steel requires coal, iron ore and electricity, which are the outputs of other industries. Even steel itself is used in the production of steel. The entries of the matrix A (called the 'technical coefficients') quantify these relationships. For example, a_{23} is the value in dollars of commodity 2 necessary to produce 1 dollar's worth of commodity 3.

A central planner, who has to organize the economy so as to meet a fixed demand vector d, needs to solve the equation

$$x = Ax + d.$$

The left-hand side is the total supply. The right-hand side is the total demand. This includes not only the amount d demanded for consumption but also the amount $y = Ax$ demanded as input to the production processes.

The equation for the central planner may be conveniently rewritten in the form

$$(I - A)x = d.$$

This is a non-homogeneous linear system of three linear equations in three unknowns, as discussed in section 6.7. The matrix

$$I - A = \begin{pmatrix} 0.7 & -0.1 & -0.2 \\ 0.0 & 0.6 & -0.1 \\ -0.2 & 0.0 & 0.9 \end{pmatrix}$$

is called the Leontieff matrix.

It is seldom computationally efficient to solve a system of linear equations by inverting a matrix. Usually, it is best to eliminate variables systematically, as described in section 6.7. But our central planner will need to solve the equation $(I - A)x = d$ for many values of the demand vector d. It will therefore be worth his while to compute $(I - A)^{-1}$ so that the required total output can be expressed as

$$x = (I - A)^{-1}d.$$

In some cases, it is possible to find tricks which avoid some of the calculations required by systematic methods such as that described in section 6.8. In the case of the Leontieff matrix, for example, we may use the formula

$$(I - A)(I + A + A^2 + \cdots + A^m) = (I - A^{m+1}), \tag{6.16}$$

which is true for exactly the same reason as that given in section 4.2, rule 4, in discussing the formula for summing a geometric progression. If the terms of the matrix A are all sufficiently small, then the terms of the matrix A^{m+1} will be very small indeed for sufficiently large values of m. For the particular matrix A given above,

$$A^2 = \begin{pmatrix} 0.13 & 0.07 & 0.09 \\ 0.02 & 0.16 & 0.05 \\ 0.08 & 0.02 & 0.05 \end{pmatrix} \qquad A^3 = \begin{pmatrix} 0.057 & 0.041 & 0.042 \\ 0.016 & 0.066 & 0.025 \\ 0.034 & 0.016 & 0.023 \end{pmatrix}$$

and so the terms of A^3 are already fairly small. But, if all the terms of the matrix A^{m+1} are nearly zero, then the right-hand side of equation (6.16) is nearly equal to I. Thus $(I - A)^{-1}$ is nearly equal to $I + A + A^2 + \cdots + A^m$, which is relatively easy to compute.

For example, when $m = 2$, $(I - A)^{-1}$ is *approximately* equal to

$$I + A + A^2 = \begin{pmatrix} 1 & 0 & 0 \\ 0 & 1 & 0 \\ 0 & 0 & 1 \end{pmatrix} + \begin{pmatrix} 0.3 & 0.1 & 0.2 \\ 0.0 & 0.4 & 0.1 \\ 0.2 & 0.0 & 0.1 \end{pmatrix} + \begin{pmatrix} 0.13 & 0.07 & 0.09 \\ 0.02 & 0.16 & 0.05 \\ 0.08 & 0.02 & 0.05 \end{pmatrix}$$

$$\approx \begin{pmatrix} 1.4 & 0.2 & 0.3 \\ 0.0 & 1.6 & 0.2 \\ 0.3 & 0.0 & 1.2 \end{pmatrix}$$

(The final approximation to $(I - A)^{-1}$ is given to an accuracy of only one decimal place. It would be unreasonable to claim a greater accuracy, without good reason, when we know that the entries of A^3 differ from I in the second decimal place.)

If the demand vector d happens to be equal to

$$d = \begin{pmatrix} 1,000,000 \\ 2,000,000 \\ 3,000,000 \end{pmatrix}$$

then the required total output $x = (I - A)^{-1}d$ is approximately equal to

$$\begin{pmatrix} 1.4 & 0.2 & 0.3 \\ 0.0 & 1.6 & 0.2 \\ 0.3 & 0.0 & 1.2 \end{pmatrix} \begin{pmatrix} 1,000,000 \\ 2,000,000 \\ 3,000,000 \end{pmatrix} = \begin{pmatrix} 2,700,000 \\ 3,800,000 \\ 3,900,000 \end{pmatrix}.$$

So far, only an open version of the Leontieff model has been presented. A closed version would locate the destination of all outputs and the origin of all inputs *within* the economy being modelled. (The distinction between 'open' and 'closed', in this context, is closely related to that made earlier between partial and general equilibrium. But here prices are taken as fixed.)

The fact that goods, in the open version, are consumed outside the economy is apparent. It is not quite so obvious that the open version assumes the existence of inputs from outside the economy. But notice that the sum of each of the columns in the matrix A is less than unity. For example, the sum of the first column is $0.3 + 0.0 + 0.2 = 0.5$. This means that, to produce 1 dollar's worth of output, the first industry needs only \$0.5 within the economy. The remaining \$0.5 obtained from selling the output must therefore be spent *outside* the economy.

A naive way of closing the model is to treat labour as a missing input. This is assumed to be supplied by a fourth industry which needs consumption goods to operate. The closed model will require a 4×4 matrix B, all of whose columns sum to unity, as in the example in table 6.3.

Since all output is now disposed of within the economy, the central planner obtains the equation

$$x = Bx$$

Table 6.3

		Outputs			
		1	2	3	4
	1	0.3	0.1	0.2	0.0
	2	0.0	0.4	0.1	0.8
Inputs	3	0.2	0.0	0.1	0.1
	4	0.5	0.5	0.6	0.1

$= B$

when he equates supply and demand. This leads to the homogeneous system

$$(I - B)x = 0.$$

From section 6.6, we know that the condition for this system to have a non-trival solution is that the 4×4 matrix $I - B$ has rank less than 4. But, from table 6.4,

$$r_1 + r_2 + r_3 + r_4 = (0, 0, 0, 0),$$

i.e. the rows of $I - B$ yield the zero vector (because the columns of B sum to unity). Thus the rows of $I - B$ are linearly *dependent* and so $I - B$ has rank less than 4. We conclude that $(I - B)x = 0$ has a non-trivial solution.

Table 6.4

$r_1 =$	0.7	$- 0.1$	$- 0.2$	0.0	
$r_2 =$	0.0	0.6	$- 0.1$	$- 0.8$	$= I - B$
$r_3 =$	$- 0.2$	0.0	0.9	$- 0.1$	
$r_4 =$	$- 0.5$	$- 0.5$	$- 0.6$	0.9	

(There is therefore a guarantee that the closed model makes proper sense. Is there a similar guarantee that the open model makes proper sense: that is, that the 3×3 matrix $I - A$ has rank 3 and so $(I - A)^{-1}$ exists? The answer is affirmative, provided that each of the columns of A sums to *less than* unity.

If $y < 1$ is the largest of the column sums of A and C is any 3×3 matrix with largest entry y, then the entry in the ith row and jth column of $D = AC$ is

$$d_{ij} = \sum_{k=1}^{3} a_{ik}C_{kj} \leq y \sum_{k=1}^{3} a_{ik} \leq yy.$$

It follows that the largest entry of A^{m+1} is no larger than $y^m \rightarrow 0$ as $m \rightarrow \infty$ (section 4.6). One may then appeal to equation (6.16) above and obtain not only that $(I - A)^{-1}$ exists but that it satisfies

$$(I - A)^{-1} = I + A + A^2 + A^3 + \cdots$$

(which is the matrix version of the formula for an infinite geometric progression derived in section 4.6).

More cautiously, it can be argued that, if $x = Ax$, then $x = A(Ax) = A^2x$ and, in general, $x = A^{m+1}x$. Since the right-hand side tends to zero as $m \rightarrow \infty$, it follows that $x = 0$. Thus $(I - A)x = 0$ has only the trivial solution. Thus $I - A$ has rank 3 and so is non-singular.)

6.11   Determinants – a tool for solving equations

Let us look carefully at the solution of the pair of equations

$$ax + by = u \qquad (6.17a)$$
$$cx + dy = v. \qquad (6.17b)$$

Eliminating first y and then x between the two equations we obtain

$$x(ad - bc) = ud - vb \qquad y(ad - bc) = uc - va.$$

Thus the solution is

$$x = \frac{ud - vb}{ad - bc} \qquad y = \frac{uc - va}{ad - bc}.$$

These formulae are valid provided that $ad - bc \neq 0$.

A scrutiny of the formulae reveals their structure to be based upon a strange multiplication process. In particular a comparison of the denominator common to both the x and the y formula against the matrix of coefficients suggests some worthwhile notation for this 'cross-product' (it is a difference in product of the diagonal and the anti-diagonal elements; compare the inner product of columns in section 2.2.

Definition

The expression $ad - bc$ is known as the *determinant* of the 2×2 matrix

$$A = \begin{pmatrix} a & b \\ c & d \end{pmatrix}$$

and is written either as $\det(A)$ or as

$$\begin{vmatrix} a & b \\ c & d \end{vmatrix}.$$

Example

$$\begin{vmatrix} 1 & 2 \\ 3 & 4 \end{vmatrix} = 1 \times 4 - 2 \times 3 = -2.$$

In this notation we have the rather satisfying formulation

$$x = \begin{vmatrix} u & b \\ v & d \end{vmatrix} \div \begin{vmatrix} a & b \\ c & d \end{vmatrix}$$

and

$$y = \begin{vmatrix} a & u \\ c & v \end{vmatrix} \div \begin{vmatrix} a & b \\ c & d \end{vmatrix}$$

where the numerator in each case is obtained by replacing the appropriate column of the determinant of A by the constants on the right-hand side of equations (6.17). We shall soon see that some similarly looking formulae can be developed for a system of three equations in three unknowns and also for larger systems. All these formulae go by the name of *Cramer's rule*. Before going ahead with this quest let us note some very simple facts about these determinants.

6.11.1 Simple facts about determinants

Fact 1 $\det(A) = \det(A')$, i.e.

$$\begin{vmatrix} a & b \\ c & d \end{vmatrix} = \begin{vmatrix} a & c \\ b & d \end{vmatrix}.$$

Fact 2

$$\begin{vmatrix} b & a \\ d & c \end{vmatrix} = bc - ad = - \begin{vmatrix} a & b \\ c & d \end{vmatrix},$$

i.e. exchanging two columns changes the sign of the determinant; similarly with exchange of rows (by fact 1). As a corollary we have fact 3.

Fact 3 A determinant with a repeated column (row) is zero.

Since in this case the exchange of two equal columns at once changes the sign and leaves the determinant unaltered, we have $\det(A) = -\det(A)$, and so $\det(A) = 0$. Alternatively, note that

$$\begin{vmatrix} a & a \\ c & c \end{vmatrix} = ac - ac = 0.$$

Fact 4

$$\begin{vmatrix} \lambda a & \lambda b \\ c & d \end{vmatrix} = \lambda ac - \lambda bd = \lambda \begin{vmatrix} a & b \\ c & d \end{vmatrix},$$

i.e. if one row is multiplied by a scalar then the determinant is multiplied by that scalar. Similarly, if one column is multiplied by a scalar then so is the determinant.

Fact 5

$$\begin{vmatrix} a+A & b \\ c+C & d \end{vmatrix} = \begin{vmatrix} a & b \\ c & d \end{vmatrix} + \begin{vmatrix} A & b \\ C & d \end{vmatrix}$$

because the left-hand side is $(a+A)d - b(c+C) = (ad-bc) + (Ad-bC)$ which is the right-hand side.

Taking $A - b\lambda$, $C = d\lambda$ we obtain

$$\begin{vmatrix} a+b\lambda & b \\ c+d\lambda & d \end{vmatrix} = \begin{vmatrix} a & b \\ c & d \end{vmatrix} + \lambda \begin{vmatrix} b & b \\ d & d \end{vmatrix},$$

i.e. the addition of a multiple of another (different) column to a given column of the determinant does not alter the determinant's value.

6.11.2 Solution of three equations

So let us consider the three-variable problem. We shall solve

$$ax + by + cz = u \qquad\qquad (6.18a)$$
$$dx + ey + fz = v \qquad\qquad (6.18b)$$
$$gx + hy + kz = w \qquad\qquad (6.18c)$$

or in matrix form

$$\begin{pmatrix} a & b & c \\ d & e & f \\ g & h & k \end{pmatrix} \begin{pmatrix} x \\ y \\ z \end{pmatrix} = \begin{pmatrix} u \\ v \\ w \end{pmatrix}.$$

We can solve the two equations (6.18b) and (6.18c) for y and z in terms of x to obtain

$$y \begin{vmatrix} e & f \\ h & k \end{vmatrix} = \begin{vmatrix} v - dx & f \\ w - gx & k \end{vmatrix}$$

and

$$\begin{vmatrix} e & f \\ h & k \end{vmatrix} = \begin{vmatrix} e & v - dx \\ h & w - gx \end{vmatrix}.$$

Cross-multiplying equation (6.18a) by

$$\begin{vmatrix} e & f \\ h & k \end{vmatrix}$$

and then substituting for y and z we obtain

$$a \begin{vmatrix} e & f \\ h & k \end{vmatrix} + b \begin{vmatrix} v - dx & f \\ w - gx & k \end{vmatrix} + c \begin{vmatrix} e & v - dx \\ h & w - gx \end{vmatrix} = u \begin{vmatrix} e & f \\ h & k \end{vmatrix}.$$

Now we use facts 4 and 5 to rewrite this as

$$x \left\{ a \begin{vmatrix} e & f \\ h & k \end{vmatrix} - b \begin{vmatrix} d & f \\ g & k \end{vmatrix} - c \begin{vmatrix} e & d \\ h & g \end{vmatrix} \right\} = u \begin{vmatrix} e & f \\ h & k \end{vmatrix} - b \begin{vmatrix} v & f \\ w & k \end{vmatrix} - c \begin{vmatrix} e & v \\ h & w \end{vmatrix}.$$

But by fact 2

$$\begin{vmatrix} e & d \\ h & g \end{vmatrix} = - \begin{vmatrix} d & e \\ g & h \end{vmatrix} \qquad \begin{vmatrix} e & v \\ h & w \end{vmatrix} = - \begin{vmatrix} e & v \\ h & w \end{vmatrix}$$

where we have exchanged columns so that they appear in the same order as in the matrix

$$\begin{pmatrix} a & b & c \\ d & e & f \\ g & h & k \end{pmatrix}.$$ (6.19)

Finally, we obtain

$$x\left\{a\begin{vmatrix} e & f \\ h & k \end{vmatrix} - b\begin{vmatrix} d & f \\ g & k \end{vmatrix} + c\begin{vmatrix} d & e \\ g & h \end{vmatrix}\right\} = u\begin{vmatrix} e & f \\ h & k \end{vmatrix} - b\begin{vmatrix} v & f \\ w & k \end{vmatrix} + c\begin{vmatrix} e & v \\ h & w \end{vmatrix}.$$

Similar formulae could also be obtained for y and z arguing from symmetry, but there is a quicker route to them as we soon see. We are in any case led to the following.

Definition

The determinant of the 3×3 matrix in (6.19) is

$$\begin{vmatrix} a & b & c \\ d & e & f \\ g & h & k \end{vmatrix} = a\begin{vmatrix} e & f \\ h & k \end{vmatrix} - b\begin{vmatrix} d & f \\ g & k \end{vmatrix} + c\begin{vmatrix} d & e \\ g & h \end{vmatrix}.$$

Examples
1

$$\begin{vmatrix} 1 & 0 & 0 \\ 0 & 1 & 0 \\ 0 & 0 & 1 \end{vmatrix} = \begin{vmatrix} 1 & 0 \\ 0 & 1 \end{vmatrix} - 0 + 0 = 1.$$

2

$$\begin{vmatrix} 1 & 2 & 3 \\ 4 & 5 & 6 \\ 7 & 8 & 9 \end{vmatrix} = 1\begin{vmatrix} 5 & 6 \\ 8 & 9 \end{vmatrix} - 2\begin{vmatrix} 4 & 6 \\ 7 & 9 \end{vmatrix} + 3\begin{vmatrix} 4 & 5 \\ 7 & 8 \end{vmatrix}$$

$$= (45 - 48) - 2(36 - 42) + 3(32 - 35)$$
$$= -3 + 14 - 9 = 2.$$

Armed with the definition above, we can write the x solution of the system (6.18) in the format

$$x = \begin{vmatrix} u & b & c \\ v & e & f \\ w & h & k \end{vmatrix} \div \begin{vmatrix} a & b & c \\ d & e & f \\ g & h & k \end{vmatrix}.$$

We therefore see that Cramer's rule is valid once more. Its format enables us to write down y and z easily. The rule is often quoted in the form

$$x = \frac{\Delta_x}{\Delta} \qquad y = \frac{\Delta_y}{\Delta} \qquad z = \frac{\Delta_z}{\Delta}$$

where $\Delta = \det(A)$ and Δ_x denotes the determinant obtained from A by replacing its first column by the column of constants appearing on the right-hand side of the equations (6.18). The formula is valid provided that $\det(A) \neq 0$.

Example
Solve for x using Cramer's rule.

$$\begin{pmatrix} 1 & 2 & 3 \\ 3 & 1 & 2 \\ 2 & 3 & 1 \end{pmatrix} \begin{pmatrix} x \\ y \\ z \end{pmatrix} = \begin{pmatrix} 1 \\ 2 \\ 3 \end{pmatrix}.$$

SOLUTION

$$\Delta = \det(A) = \begin{vmatrix} 1 & 2 & 3 \\ 3 & 1 & 2 \\ 2 & 3 & 1 \end{vmatrix} = 1(1-6) - 2(3-4) + 3(9-2) = -5 + 2 + 21 = 18.$$

Similarly,

$$\Delta_x = \begin{vmatrix} 1 & 2 & 3 \\ 2 & 1 & 2 \\ 3 & 3 & 1 \end{vmatrix} = 1(1-6) - 2(2-6) + 3(6-3) = -5 + 8 + 9 = 12.$$

Hence $x = 12/18 = 1/3$.

6.11.3   More properties of determinants

It is easy to verify facts 2–5 for 3×3 determinants. Fact 1 is less obvious but true nevertheless.
Fact 6 In the formula above the determinant is said to have been expanded 'by its first row'. If we exchange the first and second row the value of the determinant changes sign and we have

$$\begin{vmatrix} a & b & c \\ d & e & f \\ g & h & k \end{vmatrix} = - \begin{vmatrix} d & e & f \\ a & b & c \\ g & h & k \end{vmatrix} = -d \begin{vmatrix} b & c \\ h & k \end{vmatrix} + e \begin{vmatrix} a & c \\ g & k \end{vmatrix} - f \begin{vmatrix} a & b \\ g & h \end{vmatrix},$$

giving an expansion 'by the second row'. Notice that the determinants on the right-hand side are obtained from (6.19) by striking out the row and column of (6.19) corresponding respectively to the entries d, e and f. Such a determinant, i.e. one obtained by striking out the row and column corresponding to an entry, is called that entry's *minor*. The determinant A may be computed by selecting any row or column and summing for each of the entries in the chosen row (or column) terms of the form

$$\pm \text{entry} \times \text{minor},$$

taking care to enter the sign according to the table

$$
\begin{array}{ccc}
+ & - & + \\
- & + & - \\
+ & - & +
\end{array}
$$

The determinant is then said to have been expanded by that row or column.

This idea may be developed to define 4×4 determinants and beyond, again in such a way as to extend the validity of Cramer's rule to four variables. Thus the 4×4 determinant is defined by the equation

$$
\begin{vmatrix}
a & b & c & d \\
e & f & g & h \\
k & l & m & n \\
p & q & r & s
\end{vmatrix}
= a \begin{vmatrix} f & g & h \\ l & m & n \\ q & r & s \end{vmatrix}
- b \begin{vmatrix} e & g & h \\ k & m & n \\ p & r & s \end{vmatrix} + \cdots
$$

The minors multiplying the entries are obtained as before by the deletion of the appropriate row and column. The signs for expansion by an appropriate row or column are taken from the table of signs (extending the previous table)

$$
\begin{array}{cccc}
+ & - & + & - \\
- & + & - & + \\
+ & - & + & - \\
- & + & - & +
\end{array}
$$

6.11.4 A formula for A^{-1}

To find A^{-1} we need to solve the single equation

$$AB = I.$$

Let the columns of B be u, v, w. Then the previous equation asserts that

$$
Au = \begin{pmatrix} 1 \\ 0 \\ 0 \end{pmatrix} \qquad
Av = \begin{pmatrix} 0 \\ 1 \\ 0 \end{pmatrix} \qquad
Aw = \begin{pmatrix} 0 \\ 0 \\ 1 \end{pmatrix}.
$$

Assuming $\det(A) \neq 0$ we can apply Cramer's rule to solve each of these equations. Writing $u = (x, y, z)'$ we obtain

$$
x = \begin{vmatrix} 1 & b & c \\ 0 & e & f \\ 0 & h & k \end{vmatrix} \div \begin{vmatrix} a & b & c \\ d & e & f \\ g & h & k \end{vmatrix}.
$$

Thus expanding by the first row (or column)

$$\det(A) \, x = \left| \begin{pmatrix} e & f \\ h & k \end{pmatrix} \right| = A_{1,1}$$

where $A_{1,1}$ denotes the minor of the (1, 1) entry of A (i.e. a). Similarly

$$\det(A) \, y = \begin{vmatrix} a & 1 & c \\ d & 0 & f \\ g & 0 & k \end{vmatrix} = - \begin{vmatrix} d & g \\ f & k \end{vmatrix} = - A_{1,2}$$

where $A_{1,2}$ denotes the minor of the (1, 2) entry of A (i.e. b). Similarly

$$\det(A) \, z = \begin{vmatrix} a & b & 1 \\ d & e & 0 \\ g & h & 0 \end{vmatrix} = \begin{vmatrix} d & g \\ e & h \end{vmatrix} = - A_{1,3}$$

where $A_{1,3}$ denotes the minor of the (1, 3) entry of A (i.e. c). Thus

$$\det(A) \, \boldsymbol{u} = \begin{pmatrix} A_{1,1} \\ - A_{1,2} \\ A_{1,3} \end{pmatrix}.$$

To cut a long story short we state the answer:

$$B = \frac{1}{\det(A)} \begin{pmatrix} + A_{1,1} & - A_{2,1} & + A_{3,1} \\ - A_{1,2} & + A_{2,2} & - A_{3,2} \\ + A_{1,3} & - A_{2,3} & + A_{3,3} \end{pmatrix}.$$

The matrix appearing on the right is the *transpose* of the *adjugate* matrix, i.e. of the matrix whose entries are obtained from A by replacing the original entries of A by their signed minors. Thus

$$A^{-1} = \frac{1}{\det(A)} \, \mathrm{adj}(A)'. \tag{6.20}$$

Example
Solve the following equation using A^{-1}.

$$\begin{pmatrix} 1 & 2 & 3 \\ 3 & 1 & 2 \\ 2 & 3 & 1 \end{pmatrix} \begin{pmatrix} x \\ y \\ z \end{pmatrix} = \begin{pmatrix} 1 \\ 2 \\ 3 \end{pmatrix}.$$

SOLUTION   Since

$$\begin{pmatrix} x \\ y \\ z \end{pmatrix} = A^{-1} \begin{pmatrix} 1 \\ 2 \\ 3 \end{pmatrix}$$

we compute

$$\mathrm{adj}(A) = \begin{pmatrix} -5 & 1 & 7 \\ 7 & -5 & 1 \\ 1 & 7 & -5 \end{pmatrix}.$$

We know that

$$\det(A) = 1(1-6) - 2(3-4) + 3(9-2) = -5 + 2 + 21 = 18.$$

So

$$A^{-1} = \frac{1}{18} \begin{pmatrix} -5 & 7 & 1 \\ 1 & -5 & 7 \\ 7 & 1 & -5 \end{pmatrix} \begin{pmatrix} 1 \\ 2 \\ 3 \end{pmatrix} = \frac{1}{18} \begin{pmatrix} 12 \\ 12 \\ -6 \end{pmatrix} = \frac{1}{3} \begin{pmatrix} 2 \\ 2 \\ -1 \end{pmatrix}.$$

Formula (6.20) works also for 2×2 matrices.

Example
Find the inverse of

$$A = \begin{pmatrix} a & b \\ c & d \end{pmatrix}.$$

SOLUTION

$$\mathrm{adj}(A) = \begin{pmatrix} d & -c \\ -b & a \end{pmatrix}.$$

Hence

$$A^{-1} = \frac{1}{ad-bc} \begin{pmatrix} d & -b \\ -c & a \end{pmatrix}.$$

Fact An important fact which we shall not prove here is

$$\det(AB) = \det(A)\det(B).$$

An important conclusion is that a matrix A has an inverse if and only if $\det(A) \neq 0$. First suppose $\det(A) \neq 0$. Then we have already established a formula for the inverse of A. Next suppose that A has an inverse. Denoting it by B we have

$$1 = \det(I) = \det(AB) = \det(A)\det(B).$$

Hence $\det(A) \neq 0$.
Deduction

$$\det(A^{-1}) = \det(A)^{-1}$$

when $\det(A) \neq 0$.

6.12   Exercises

1*   Market supply and demand are given by

$$p = S(q) = q/9 \qquad (q \geqslant 0)$$
$$p = D(q) = 100 - q \qquad (q \geqslant 0).$$

Show that the equilibrium price is $\bar{p} = 10$ and the equilibrium quantity is $\bar{q} = 90$. The total amount paid by consumers is then $\bar{p}\bar{q} = 900$.

   The government needs to raise \$90 and so imposes a sales tax of 10 per cent in this market. Why will the government be disappointed?

2   In example 2 in section 6.2, market supply and demand are given by

$$p = S(q) = 9q/(2n)$$
$$p = D(q) = I/(2q) \qquad (q > 0)$$

where n is the number of firms and I is the consumers' income. What will the percentage increase in the equilibrium price be if the number of firms falls by half and the income of the consumers doubles?

3*   Show that the vectors u and v are linearly independent but that the vector w can be expressed as a linear combination of u and v, in the case when

$$u = \begin{pmatrix} 1 \\ 1 \\ 0 \end{pmatrix} \qquad v = \begin{pmatrix} 2 \\ 1 \\ 1 \end{pmatrix} \qquad w = \begin{pmatrix} 1 \\ 0 \\ 1 \end{pmatrix}.$$

Show that the set of all linear combinations of u and v is a subspace of $\mathbb{R}^3$. Find a basis for this subspace. What are the co-ordinates of w with respect to this basis?

4   Repeat question 3 for the case

$$u = \begin{pmatrix} 1 \\ 1 \\ 2 \end{pmatrix} \qquad v = \begin{pmatrix} 2 \\ 3 \\ 1 \end{pmatrix} \qquad w = \begin{pmatrix} 1 \\ 0 \\ 5 \end{pmatrix}.$$

5*   Find all solutions of the following homogeneous system of linear equations:

$$a + 2b + 3c = 0$$
$$2a + 4b + 6c = 0$$
$$3a + 6b + 9c = 0.$$

Find a basis for the solution space and determine the dimension of the solution space.

6   Repeat question 5 for the system

$$a + b + c = 0$$
$$a - b + c = 0$$
$$a + 3b + c = 0.$$

7* Find the rank of the matrix

$$A = \begin{pmatrix} 1 & 0 & 0 \\ 2 & 1 & 1 \\ 0 & 1 & 1 \end{pmatrix}.$$

Do the same for the transpose matrix A' and check that the same result is obtained.

8 Repeat question 7 for the matrix

$$A = \begin{pmatrix} 1 & 1 & 2 \\ 2 & 3 & 1 \\ 1 & 0 & 5 \end{pmatrix}.$$

9* Find all solutions of the non-homogeneous systems

(a) $a + 2b + 3c = 1$ (b) $a + 2b + 3c = 1$
      $2a + 4b + 6c = 1$ $2a + 4b + 6c = 2$
      $3a + 6b + 9c = 1$ $3a + 6b + 9c = 3$

10 Repeat question 9 for the systems

(a) $a + b + c = 1$ (b) $a + b + c = 1$
      $a - b + c = 1$ $a - b + c = 2$
      $a + 3b + c = 1$ $a + 3b + c = 3$

11* Explain why the matrix A of question 7 is singular. Find the inverse matrix B^{-1} of the matrix

$$B = \begin{pmatrix} 1 & 1 & 1 & 1 \\ 1 & 2 & 3 & 0 \\ 0 & 1 & 2 & 3 \\ 0 & 0 & 1 & 2 \end{pmatrix}.$$

12 Find the inverse matrix $(I - A)^{-1}$ of the matrix

$$I - A = \begin{pmatrix} 0.7 & -0.1 & -0.2 \\ 0.0 & 0.6 & -0.1 \\ -0.2 & 0.0 & 0.9 \end{pmatrix}$$

which appears in section 6.10 using the method of the example in section 6.9. Reduce the matrix $I - B$ of section 6.10 to echelon form and so check that it is singular.

6.12.1 Non-homogeneous difference equations

1 Find the general solution of

$$y_{t+2} - 4y_{t+1} + 4y_t = 1.$$

2 Find the general solution of

$$y_{t+2} - 4y_{t+1} + 4y_t = t.$$

3 Find the general solution of

$$y_{t+2} - 4y_{t+1} + 4y_t = 3^t.$$

4 Find the general solution of

$$y_{t+2} - 4y_{t+1} + 4y_t = t2^t.$$

[*Hint:* Try $y_t = kt^2 2^t$.]

5 In year t ($t = 0, 1, 2, \ldots$), the price P_t, demand D_t and supply S_t of a commodity are related by the equations

$$D_t = 20 - 6P_t$$
$$S_t = D_t$$
$$S_t = -15 + 3P_{t-1}.$$

Prove that the price P_t satisfies the difference equation

$$6P_{t+1} + 3P_t = 35.$$

Solve this to find a general expression for P_t. Show that, regardless of the initial price P_0, the price P_t oscillates and approaches a particular value P^* as t increases.

6 If $P(x) = ax^2 + bx + c$ show that substituting $y_t = kt^2 d^t$ into the left-hand side of

$$ay_{t+2} + by_{t+1} + cy_t = g_t \qquad (6.21)$$

leads to

$$d^t[t^2 P(d) + 2tdP'(d) + d(4ad + b)].$$

Deduce that if d is a double root of $P(x) = 0$ then a particular solution of (6.21) when $g_t = d^t$ is $y_t = 1/d(4a + b)$, provided that $d \neq 0$.

6.12.2 Determinants

1 Check facts 1–5 for 3×3 matrices.

2 Show that if E is an elementary matrix then

$$\det(E) = \begin{cases} -1 & \text{if } E \text{ exchanges columns (same for exchange of rows)} \\ \lambda & \text{if } E \text{ scales a column/row by } \lambda \\ +1 & \text{if } E \text{ adds one column to another.} \end{cases}$$

3 Show that $\det(EA) = \det(E)\det(A)$ when E is an elementary row operation.

4 Repeat the exercise to show that $\det(AE) = \det(A)\det(E)$ when E is an elementary column matrix.

5 Show that if I_4 is the 4×4 unit matrix then $\det(I_4) = 1$.

6 Deduce that if A is $n \times n$ and of rank n so that

$$A = E_1 \cdots E_l I,$$

then $\det(A) = \det(E_1) \cdots \det(E_l) \times 1$.

7 Show that if A is non-singular then $\det(AB) = \det(A) \det(B)$ by considering

$$AB = E_1 \cdots E_l B.$$

8 Show that if A is singular then AB is singular.
[Hint: If $Bz = 0$ for some $z \neq 0$ then $ABz = 0$. If B is non-singular, $Ax = 0$ implies $AB(B^{-1})x = 0$.]

9 Deduce that when A is singular $\det(AB) = 0 = \det(A) \det(B)$.

10 Show that $\det(P^{-1}AP) = \det(A)$.

6.13 Answers

1 In section 6.2, $A = 100$, $B = 1$, $C = 0$, $D = 1/9$, and 1.15 must be replaced by 1.10. Then

$$\bar{q}* = \frac{A - 1.10C}{B + 1.10D} = \frac{100}{1 + 11/90} = \frac{9000}{101} = 89.11$$

$$\bar{p}* = \frac{1.10(BC + AD)}{B + 1.10D} = \frac{11}{10} \times \frac{100}{9} \times \frac{1}{1 + 11/90} = \frac{1100}{101} = 10.89.$$

The government revenue is

$$\frac{1}{11} \bar{p}* \bar{q}* = \$88.22.$$

3 For u and v to be linearly independent, we need that

$$\alpha \begin{pmatrix} 1 \\ 1 \\ 0 \end{pmatrix} + \beta \begin{pmatrix} 2 \\ 1 \\ 1 \end{pmatrix} = \begin{pmatrix} 0 \\ 0 \\ 0 \end{pmatrix}$$

to imply that $\alpha = \beta = 0$. The vector equation can be rewritten as

$$\alpha + 2\beta = 0$$
$$\alpha + \beta = 0$$
$$\beta = 0.$$

Substituting $\beta = 0$ in $\alpha + 2\beta = 0$, we obtain that $\alpha = 0$. This concludes the proof that u and v are linearly independent.

For w to be a linear combination of u and v, we need that

$$\begin{pmatrix} 1 \\ 0 \\ 1 \end{pmatrix} = \gamma \begin{pmatrix} 1 \\ 1 \\ 0 \end{pmatrix} + \delta \begin{pmatrix} 2 \\ 1 \\ 1 \end{pmatrix}$$

which can be rewritten as

$$1 = \gamma + 2\delta$$
$$0 = \gamma + \delta$$
$$1 = \delta.$$

These equations are satisfied by $\gamma = -1$ and $\delta = 1$.

Let S be the set of all linear combinations of u and v. We need to show that linear combinations of vectors in S are also in S. This is easy because, if x and y are in S, then $x = \alpha_1 u + \beta_1 v$ and $y = \alpha_2 u + \beta_2 v$. Hence

$$\gamma x + \delta y = (\alpha_1 \gamma + \alpha_2 \delta)u + (\beta_1 \gamma + \beta_2 \delta)v$$

and so $\gamma x + \delta y$ is a linear combination of u and v and therefore is in the set S.

The vectors u and v are a basis for S. The co-ordinates of w with respect to this basis are -1 and 1, because $w = (-1)u + (1)v$.

5   $a + 2b + 3c = 0$ $\begin{pmatrix} 1 & 2 & 3 \\ 2 & 4 & 6 \\ 3 & 6 & 9 \end{pmatrix} \begin{pmatrix} a \\ b \\ c \end{pmatrix} = \begin{pmatrix} 0 \\ 0 \\ 0 \end{pmatrix}$

   $2a + 4b + 6c = 0$

   $3a + 6b + 9c = 0$

   $a + 2b + 3c = 0$ $\begin{pmatrix} 1 & 2 & 3 \\ 2 & 4 & 6 \\ 0 & 0 & 0 \end{pmatrix} \begin{pmatrix} a \\ b \\ c \end{pmatrix} = \begin{pmatrix} 0 \\ 0 \\ 0 \end{pmatrix}$

   $2a + 4b + 6c = 0$

   $a + 2b + 3c = 0$ $\begin{pmatrix} 1 & 2 & 3 \\ 0 & 0 & 0 \\ 0 & 0 & 0 \end{pmatrix} \begin{pmatrix} a \\ b \\ c \end{pmatrix} = \begin{pmatrix} 0 \\ 0 \\ 0 \end{pmatrix}$

Thus b and c can be chosen to be anything, but then a must satisfy

$$a = -2b - 3c.$$

The solutions of the system are therefore of the form

$$\begin{pmatrix} a \\ b \\ c \end{pmatrix} = \begin{pmatrix} -2b - 3c \\ b \\ c \end{pmatrix} = b \begin{pmatrix} -2 \\ 1 \\ 0 \end{pmatrix} + c \begin{pmatrix} -3 \\ 0 \\ 1 \end{pmatrix}.$$

The solution space has dimension 2 and the vectors

$$\begin{pmatrix} -2 \\ 1 \\ 0 \end{pmatrix} \quad \begin{pmatrix} -3 \\ 0 \\ 1 \end{pmatrix}$$

form a basis for this space.

7

$$A = \begin{pmatrix} 1 & 0 & 0 \\ 2 & 1 & 1 \\ 0 & 1 & 1 \end{pmatrix} \qquad A' = \begin{pmatrix} 1 & 2 & 0 \\ 0 & 1 & 1 \\ 0 & 1 & 1 \end{pmatrix}$$

$$\begin{pmatrix} 1 & 0 & 0 \\ 0 & 1 & 1 \\ 0 & 1 & 1 \end{pmatrix} \qquad \begin{pmatrix} 1 & 2 & 0 \\ 0 & 1 & 1 \\ 0 & 0 & 0 \end{pmatrix}$$

$$\begin{pmatrix} 1 & 0 & 0 \\ 0 & 1 & 1 \\ 0 & 0 & 0 \end{pmatrix}$$

Since the echelon form has two non-zero rows in both cases, the matrix has rank 2.

9

(a) $a + 2b + 3c = 1$ $\begin{pmatrix} 1 & 2 & 3 & \vdots & 1 \\ 2 & 4 & 6 & \vdots & 1 \\ 3 & 6 & 9 & \vdots & 1 \end{pmatrix}$

     $2a + 4b + 6c = 1$

     $3a + 6b + 9c = 1$

$$\begin{pmatrix} 1 & 2 & 3 & \vdots & 1 \\ 2 & 4 & 6 & \vdots & 1 \\ 0 & 0 & 0 & \vdots & -2 \end{pmatrix}$$

$$\begin{pmatrix} 1 & 2 & 3 & \vdots & 1 \\ 0 & 0 & 0 & \vdots & -1 \\ 0 & 0 & 0 & \vdots & -2 \end{pmatrix}$$

The equations have no solutions. The augmented matrix does not have the same rank as A.

(b) $a + 2b + 3c = 1$ $\begin{pmatrix} 1 & 2 & 3 & \vdots & 1 \\ 2 & 4 & 6 & \vdots & 2 \\ 3 & 6 & 9 & \vdots & 3 \end{pmatrix}$

     $2a + 4b + 6c = 2$

     $3a + 6b + 9c = 3$

$$\begin{pmatrix} 1 & 2 & 3 & \vdots & 1 \\ 2 & 4 & 6 & \vdots & 2 \\ 0 & 0 & 0 & \vdots & 0 \end{pmatrix}$$

$a + 2b + 3c = 1$ $\begin{pmatrix} 1 & 2 & 3 & \vdots & 1 \\ 0 & 0 & 0 & \vdots & 0 \\ 0 & 0 & 0 & \vdots & 0 \end{pmatrix}$

Here b and c can be chosen to be anything, but then $a = 1 - 2b - 3c$. The solutions are therefore

$$\begin{pmatrix} a \\ b \\ c \end{pmatrix} = \begin{pmatrix} 1 - 2b - 3c \\ b \\ c \end{pmatrix} = \begin{pmatrix} 1 \\ 0 \\ 0 \end{pmatrix} + b\begin{pmatrix} -2 \\ 1 \\ 0 \end{pmatrix} + c\begin{pmatrix} -3 \\ 0 \\ 1 \end{pmatrix}.$$

11 The 3×3 matrix A of question 7 is singular because its rank is only 2. The inverse matrix for B is found using the method of the example in section 6.9.

$$B = \begin{pmatrix} 1 & 1 & 1 & 1 \\ 1 & 2 & 3 & 0 \\ 0 & 1 & 2 & 3 \\ 0 & 0 & 1 & 2 \end{pmatrix} \qquad I = \begin{pmatrix} 1 & 0 & 0 & 0 \\ 0 & 1 & 0 & 0 \\ 0 & 0 & 1 & 0 \\ 0 & 0 & 0 & 1 \end{pmatrix}$$

$$\begin{pmatrix} 1 & 1 & 1 & 1 \\ 0 & 1 & 2 & -1 \\ 0 & 1 & 2 & 3 \\ 0 & 0 & 1 & 2 \end{pmatrix} \qquad \begin{pmatrix} 1 & 0 & 0 & 0 \\ -1 & 1 & 0 & 0 \\ 0 & 0 & 1 & 0 \\ 0 & 0 & 0 & 1 \end{pmatrix}$$

$$\begin{pmatrix} 1 & 1 & 1 & 1 \\ 0 & 1 & 2 & -1 \\ 0 & 0 & 0 & 4 \\ 0 & 0 & 1 & 2 \end{pmatrix} \qquad \begin{pmatrix} 1 & 0 & 0 & 0 \\ -1 & 1 & 0 & 0 \\ 1 & -1 & 1 & 0 \\ 0 & 0 & 0 & 1 \end{pmatrix}$$

$$\begin{pmatrix} 1 & 1 & 1 & 1 \\ 0 & 1 & 2 & -1 \\ 0 & 0 & 1 & 2 \\ 0 & 0 & 0 & 4 \end{pmatrix} \qquad \begin{pmatrix} 1 & 0 & 0 & 0 \\ -1 & 1 & 0 & 0 \\ 0 & 0 & 0 & 1 \\ 1 & -1 & 1 & 0 \end{pmatrix}$$

$$\begin{pmatrix} 1 & 1 & 1 & 1 \\ 0 & 1 & 2 & -1 \\ 0 & 0 & 1 & 2 \\ 0 & 0 & 0 & 1 \end{pmatrix} \qquad \begin{pmatrix} 1 & 0 & 0 & 0 \\ -1 & 1 & 0 & 0 \\ 0 & 0 & 0 & 1 \\ 1/4 & -1/4 & 1/4 & 0 \end{pmatrix}$$

Now that B has been reduced to echelon form, it can be seen to have rank 4. Thus it has an inverse matrix.

$$\begin{pmatrix} 1 & 1 & 1 & 1 \\ 0 & 1 & 2 & -1 \\ 0 & 0 & 1 & 0 \\ 0 & 0 & 0 & 1 \end{pmatrix} \qquad \begin{pmatrix} 1 & 0 & 0 & 0 \\ -1 & 1 & 0 & 0 \\ -1/2 & 1/2 & -1/2 & 1 \\ 1/4 & -1/4 & 1/4 & 0 \end{pmatrix}$$

$$\begin{pmatrix} 1 & 1 & 1 & 1 \\ 0 & 1 & 2 & 0 \\ 0 & 0 & 1 & 0 \\ 0 & 0 & 0 & 1 \end{pmatrix} \qquad \begin{pmatrix} 1 & 0 & 0 & 0 \\ -3/4 & 3/4 & 1/4 & 0 \\ -1/2 & 1/2 & -1/2 & 1 \\ 1/4 & -1/4 & 1/4 & 0 \end{pmatrix}$$

$$\begin{pmatrix} 1 & 1 & 1 & 1 \\ 0 & 1 & 0 & 0 \\ 0 & 0 & 1 & 0 \\ 0 & 0 & 0 & 1 \end{pmatrix} \qquad \begin{pmatrix} 1 & 0 & 0 & 0 \\ 1/4 & -1/4 & 5/4 & -2 \\ -1/2 & 1/2 & -1/2 & 1 \\ 1/4 & -1/4 & 1/4 & 0 \end{pmatrix}$$

$$I = \begin{pmatrix} 1 & 0 & 0 & 0 \\ 0 & 1 & 0 & 0 \\ 0 & 0 & 1 & 0 \\ 0 & 0 & 0 & 1 \end{pmatrix} \qquad B^{-1} = \begin{pmatrix} 1 & 0 & -1 & 1 \\ 1/4 & -1/4 & 5/4 & -2 \\ -1/2 & 1/2 & -1/2 & 1 \\ 1/4 & -1/4 & 1/4 & 0 \end{pmatrix}$$

Notice that three steps were compressed into one in the final stage. A check is always wise:

$$\begin{pmatrix} 1 & 1 & 1 & 1 \\ 1 & 2 & 3 & 0 \\ 0 & 1 & 2 & 3 \\ 0 & 0 & 1 & 2 \end{pmatrix} \begin{pmatrix} 1 & 0 & -1 & 1 \\ 1/4 & -1/4 & 5/4 & -2 \\ -1/2 & 1/2 & -1/2 & 1 \\ 1/4 & -1/4 & 1/4 & 0 \end{pmatrix} = \begin{pmatrix} 1 & 0 & 0 & 0 \\ 0 & 1 & 0 & 0 \\ 0 & 0 & 1 & 0 \\ 0 & 0 & 0 & 1 \end{pmatrix}.$$

7
Eigenvalues and Eigenvectors

7.1 Example: super-power arms race

Two super-powers have defence expenditures x_t and y_t respectively in year t. Suppose that the first super-power sets its defence spending so that

$$\Delta x_t \equiv x_{t+1} - x_t = -ax_t + by_t \qquad (a, b > 0). \tag{7.1}$$

Thus the change in the super-power's spending from one year to the next is positively dependent on the adversary's current budget and negatively dependent on its own current level of spending; note that if $x_t > (b/a)y_t$ (i.e. expenditure is large relative to y_t) defence spending can be cut. Suppose that the second super-power follows the same type of strategy:

$$\Delta y_t \equiv y_{t+1} - y_t = +cx_t - dy_t \qquad (c, d > 0). \tag{7.2}$$

The (hopeful) question arises: since $x_t \equiv 0$, $y_t \equiv 0$ is an equilibrium solution, do the actual defence budgets tend to zero over time? The difference equations (7.1) and (7.2) are said to be *coupled*, since the right-hand sides contain a mixture of the two variables x and y.

It is thus natural to seek a change of variable which will uncouple the equations. Let us introduce two new variables X and Y which, when mixed appropriately, yield x and y. Let

$$x_t = pX_t + uY_t$$

$$y_t = qX_t + vY_t.$$

It will be convenient to go through the uncoupling exercise using matrices. Thus (7.1) and (7.2) read

$$\begin{pmatrix} x_{t+1} - x_t \\ y_{t+1} - y_t \end{pmatrix} = \begin{pmatrix} -a & b \\ c & -d \end{pmatrix} \begin{pmatrix} x_t \\ y_t \end{pmatrix}$$

or even

$$\begin{pmatrix} x_{t+1} \\ y_{t+1} \end{pmatrix} - \begin{pmatrix} x_t \\ y_t \end{pmatrix} = A \begin{pmatrix} x_t \\ y_t \end{pmatrix} \tag{7.3}$$

where

$$A = \begin{pmatrix} -a & b \\ c & -d \end{pmatrix}.$$

Similarly, we write

$$\begin{pmatrix} x_t \\ y_t \end{pmatrix} = \begin{pmatrix} p & u \\ q & v \end{pmatrix} \begin{pmatrix} X_t \\ Y_t \end{pmatrix} = P \begin{pmatrix} X_t \\ Y_t \end{pmatrix} \tag{7.4}$$

where

$$P = \begin{pmatrix} p & u \\ q & v \end{pmatrix}.$$

Substituting from (7.4) into (7.3), we obtain that

$$P \begin{pmatrix} X_{t+1} \\ Y_{t+1} \end{pmatrix} - P \begin{pmatrix} X_t \\ Y_t \end{pmatrix} = AP \begin{pmatrix} X_t \\ Y_t \end{pmatrix}$$

and so, assuming that P^{-1} exists, we obtain that

$$\begin{pmatrix} X_{t+1} \\ Y_{t+1} \end{pmatrix} - \begin{pmatrix} X_t \\ Y_t \end{pmatrix} = P^{-1}AP \begin{pmatrix} X_t \\ Y_t \end{pmatrix}. \tag{7.5}$$

If we can arrange so that

$$P^{-1}AP = \begin{pmatrix} r & 0 \\ 0 & s \end{pmatrix} \tag{7.6}$$

the equations represented by (7.5) will be uncoupled; we have by (7.5) and (7.6)

$$X_{t+1} - X_t = rX_t$$
$$Y_{t+1} - Y_t = sY_t.$$

Alternatively

$$X_{t+1} = (1 + r)X_t$$
$$Y_{t+1} = (1 + s)Y_t$$

so that $X_t = (1 + r)^t X_0$ and $Y_t = (1 + s)^t Y_0$.

We note that the assumption that P is non-singular is simply the assumption that we can solve (7.4) for x_t, y_t when X_t, Y_t are given. Our pacifist question will have an affirmative answer if $-2 < r$, $s < 0$ because then $X_t \to 0$ and $Y_t \to 0$, and hence by (7.4) $x_t \to 0$ and $y_t \to 0$. Conversely, if $x_t \to 0$, $y_t \to 0$, then we also have $X_t \to 0$, $Y_t \to 0$ since

$$\begin{pmatrix} X_t \\ Y_t \end{pmatrix} = P^{-1} \begin{pmatrix} x_t \\ y_t \end{pmatrix}.$$

7.2 Eigenvalues

Let us return to equation (7.6) from the last section. We can rewrite the equation as

$$AP = P\begin{pmatrix} r & 0 \\ 0 & s \end{pmatrix} = \begin{pmatrix} rp & su \\ rq & sv \end{pmatrix} \tag{7.7}$$

On the right-hand side we see that the columns of P have been rescaled. We can compute the left-hand side. We have

$$AP = \begin{pmatrix} -ap + bq & -au + bv \\ cp - dq & cu - dv \end{pmatrix}. \tag{7.8}$$

Concentrating on the columns we see that actually

$$AP = \left(A\begin{pmatrix} p \\ q \end{pmatrix} \quad A\begin{pmatrix} u \\ v \end{pmatrix} \right)$$

Comparing (7.7) and (7.8) we obtain

$$A\begin{pmatrix} p \\ q \end{pmatrix} = \begin{pmatrix} rp \\ rq \end{pmatrix} = r\begin{pmatrix} p \\ q \end{pmatrix}$$

$$A\begin{pmatrix} u \\ v \end{pmatrix} = \begin{pmatrix} su \\ sv \end{pmatrix} = s\begin{pmatrix} u \\ v \end{pmatrix}.$$

This leads us to a very important definition.

Any number λ such that the equation

$$Ax = \lambda x \tag{7.9}$$

has a non-zero solution vector x is called an *eigenvalue* (or characteristic root) of the matrix A. It is important to insist that $x \neq 0$, because when $x = 0$ the equation (7.9) is satisfied for any choice of λ and that is clearly an uninteresting situation.

Any non-zero vector x satisfying (7.9) is called an *eigenvector* of A for the *eigenvalue* λ. (It is sometimes called a characteristic vector.)

Thus our de-coupling procedure calls for computing the eigenvalues. This may be done quite easily. First rewrite (7.9) in the form

$$(A - \lambda I)x = 0 \tag{7.10}$$

where I is the identity matrix. We now see that the matrix $A - \lambda I$ is *singular*; otherwise $(A - \lambda I)^{-1}$ would exist and that would imply from (7.10) that $x = 0$, a contradiction. Hence we have the following theorem.

Theorem

The eigenvalues satisfy the characteristic equation

$$\det(A - \lambda I) = 0.$$

Proof If $\det(A - \lambda I) \neq 0$, the matrix $A - \lambda I$ would have an inverse; we have just seen that this is not the case.

Example
Find the eigenvalues of

$$\begin{pmatrix} -3 & 5 \\ 5 & -3 \end{pmatrix}$$

and their corresponding eigenvectors.

SOLUTION   The characteristic equation is

$$\begin{vmatrix} -3 - \lambda & 5 \\ 5 & -3 - \lambda \end{vmatrix} = (3 + \lambda)^2 - 25 = 0.$$

Hence $(3 + \lambda)^2 = 25$, or $3 + \lambda = \pm 5$. Thus $\lambda = 2$ or $\lambda = -8$. Now we solve (7.9) when $\lambda = 2$. In our particular case, (7.9) reduces to

$$\begin{pmatrix} -3 & 5 \\ 5 & -3 \end{pmatrix} \begin{pmatrix} x_1 \\ x_2 \end{pmatrix} = 2 \begin{pmatrix} x_1 \\ x_2 \end{pmatrix}.$$

This is the same as (7.10) which thus reads

$$\begin{pmatrix} -3 - 2 & 5 \\ 5 & -3 - 2 \end{pmatrix} \begin{pmatrix} x_1 \\ x_2 \end{pmatrix} = \begin{pmatrix} 0 \\ 0 \end{pmatrix},$$

i.e.

$$-5x_1 + 5x_2 = 0$$
$$5x_1 - 5x_2 = 0.$$

Observe that the second equation is redundant. Both equations yield $x_1 = x_2$ so that one eigenvector to the eigenvalue $\lambda = 2$ is

$$\begin{pmatrix} 1 \\ 1 \end{pmatrix}.$$

In the case when $\lambda = -8$ equation (7.10) becomes

$$\begin{pmatrix} -3 - (-8) & 5 \\ 5 & -3 - (-8) \end{pmatrix} \begin{pmatrix} x_1 \\ x_2 \end{pmatrix} = \begin{pmatrix} 0 \\ 0 \end{pmatrix}$$

from which we read off two identical equations:

$$5x_1 + 5x_2 = 0$$
$$5x_1 + 5x_2 = 0$$

Thus $x_1 = -x_2$ and an eigenvector for the eigenvalue $\lambda = -8$ is

$$\begin{pmatrix} 1 \\ -1 \end{pmatrix}.$$

7.3   Arms race revisited

Under what circumstances do the defence budgets of both super-powers tend
to zero? Recall that according to section 7.2, we need the eigenvalues to lie in
the interval $(-2, 0)$. The characteristic equation for our problem is

$$\begin{vmatrix} -a-\lambda & b \\ c & -d-\lambda \end{vmatrix} = (a+\lambda)(d+\lambda) - bc$$

$$= \lambda^2 + (a+d)\lambda + (ad-bc).$$

If the eigenvalues are r and s then the quadratic in λ must factorize as
$(\lambda-r)(\lambda-s)$. But

$$(\lambda-r)(\lambda-s) = \lambda^2 - (r+s)\lambda + rs.$$

Hence

$$rs = ad - bc \qquad \text{and} \qquad -(r+s) = -(a+d).$$

Since we require $-2 < r, s < 0$ we must have $rs > 0$ and $r+s < 0$. Thus we
require

$$ad - bc > 0 \text{ and } a + d > 0.$$

Conversely, if these conditions hold the roots of the characteristic equation are

$$\lambda = \frac{-(a+d) \pm \sqrt{[(a+d)^2 - 4(ad-bc)]}}{2}.$$

We have $(a+d)^2 - 4(ad-bc) = a^2 + d^2 - 2ad + 4bc = (a-d)^2 + 4bc > 0$ since b,
$c > 0$; thus both roots are real. Both roots are negative if $a+d > 0$ and
$ad - bc > 0$, since then

$$(a+d)^2 - 4(ad-bc) < (a+d)^2.$$

(Alternative argument: one root is obviously negative, but their product is
$ad - bc$ which is positive. So both roots are negative.)

In our model $a, d > 0$ so $a + d > 0$ is fulfilled automatically. This leaves the
condition

$$ad - bc > 0.$$

We can confirm this condition by noting from section 7.1 that both military
powers will reduce spending if

$$x_t > \frac{b}{a} y_t \qquad \text{and} \qquad y_t > \frac{c}{d} x_t$$

in which case

$$x_t > \frac{b}{a} y_t > \frac{b}{a}\frac{c}{d} x_t,$$

i.e.

$$x_t > \frac{b}{a}\frac{c}{d}x_t.$$

Cancelling by $x_t > 0$ and cross-multiplying we obtain $ad > bc$.

7.4   Diagonalization

We have been rather remiss in the last sections in that we have studied only the eigenvalues and eigenvectors of the matrix A without asking if a matrix P can be constructed so that

$$P^{-1}AP = \begin{pmatrix} r & 0 \\ 0 & s \end{pmatrix}. \tag{7.11}$$

In section 7.2 we observed that if such a P were to exist, its columns must be eigenvectors. But if the columns of P are eigenvectors we know only that

$$AP = P\begin{pmatrix} r & 0 \\ 0 & s \end{pmatrix}.$$

We do *not* know that P is non-singular (has an inverse). If a non-singular P exists, we say that the matrix A is *diagonalizable*, since the equation on the right-hand side of (7.11) is a '*diagonal*' matrix (i.e. has non-zero entries only on the diagonal).

Theorem

If the eigenvalues of a matrix A are distinct, then the matrix A is diagonalizable.

Proof We need to show that, when

$$P = \begin{pmatrix} p & u \\ q & v \end{pmatrix}$$

where the columns of P are eigenvectors corresponding respectively to the distinct eigenvalues r, s of A, then the rank of P is 2. Equivalently we wish to show that the columns of P are not scalar multiples of each other. Suppose that

$$\begin{pmatrix} p \\ q \end{pmatrix} = \alpha \begin{pmatrix} u \\ v \end{pmatrix}$$

where α is a scaling factor. Then since

$$A\begin{pmatrix} p \\ q \end{pmatrix} = r\begin{pmatrix} p \\ q \end{pmatrix}$$

and

$$A \begin{pmatrix} u \\ v \end{pmatrix} = s \begin{pmatrix} u \\ v \end{pmatrix}$$

we have

$$r \begin{pmatrix} p \\ q \end{pmatrix} = A \begin{pmatrix} p \\ q \end{pmatrix} = \alpha A \begin{pmatrix} u \\ v \end{pmatrix} = \alpha s \begin{pmatrix} u \\ v \end{pmatrix} = s \begin{pmatrix} p \\ q \end{pmatrix}.$$

Thus

$$(r - s) \begin{pmatrix} p \\ q \end{pmatrix} = \begin{pmatrix} 0 \\ 0 \end{pmatrix}.$$

Since $r - s \neq 0$ we may cancel by $r - s$ and obtain

$$\begin{pmatrix} p \\ q \end{pmatrix} = \begin{pmatrix} 0 \\ 0 \end{pmatrix}.$$

This is a contradiction, as eigenvectors are non-zero by definition. Our proof is therefore complete.

Examples
1   Find a matrix P which diagonalizes the matrix

$$A = \begin{pmatrix} -3 & 5 \\ 5 & -3 \end{pmatrix}$$

SOLUTION   We saw that the eigenvectors corresponding to the eigenvalues 2, -8 were respectively

$$\begin{pmatrix} 1 \\ 1 \end{pmatrix} \quad \text{and} \quad \begin{pmatrix} 1 \\ -1 \end{pmatrix}.$$

We take

$$P = \begin{pmatrix} 1 & 1 \\ 1 & -1 \end{pmatrix}$$

and confirm that $\det(P) = -1 - 1 = -2 \neq 0$. Thus P^{-1} exists and in fact

$$P^{-1} = -\frac{1}{2} \begin{pmatrix} -1 & -1 \\ -1 & 1 \end{pmatrix} = \frac{1}{2} \begin{pmatrix} 1 & 1 \\ 1 & -1 \end{pmatrix}.$$

We leave the reader to check that

$$P^{-1}AP = \begin{pmatrix} 2 & 0 \\ 0 & -8 \end{pmatrix}.$$

2 Show that the matrix

$$A = \begin{pmatrix} 1 & 1 \\ 0 & 1 \end{pmatrix}$$

is not diagonalizable.

SOLUTION To find the eigenvalues we solve the equation

$$\begin{vmatrix} 1 - \lambda & 1 \\ 0 & 1 - \lambda \end{vmatrix} = 0$$

or $(1 - \lambda)^2 = 0$. Thus $\lambda = 1$ is a repeated eigenvalue. We now look for eigenvectors and solve

$$\begin{pmatrix} 1 - 1 & 1 \\ 0 & 1 - 1 \end{pmatrix} \begin{pmatrix} x_1 \\ x_2 \end{pmatrix} = \begin{pmatrix} 0 \\ 0 \end{pmatrix},$$

i.e.

$$0x_1 - x_2 = 0 \qquad \text{or} \qquad x_2 = 0.$$

Notice that the second row of the matrix equation contributes only the equation $0 = 0$. We thus see that the eigenvectors to the value $\lambda = 1$ are of the form

$$\begin{pmatrix} x_1 \\ 0 \end{pmatrix} = x_1 \begin{pmatrix} 1 \\ 0 \end{pmatrix},$$

i.e. they are all scalar multiples of the one unit vector. It follows that any matrix P consisting of eigenvectors of A in this case will have rank 1. P^{-1} will not exist.

We note that if two matrices A and B are related by an equation $B = P^{-1}AP$, then A and B are said to be *similar*.

7.5 Boom–bust: a Markov process

An economy is seen to move from year to year between boom state and recession according to a probability law given by the transition matrix in table 7.1. Thus, the probability of staying in the boom state is p and of moving from

Table 7.1

| | | Next state | |
		Boom	Recession
Current state	Boom	p	$1 - p$
	Recession	$1 - q$	q

boom to recession is $1 - p$. What is the long-term prospect of the economy if $0 < p < 1$ and $0 < q < 1$?

Remark

Any system whose state is governed by a probabilistic law given by a 'state transition matrix' T is said to follow a *Markov process*. Note that the transition probabilities do not depend on the past history but only on the current state.

We may use a vector such as

$$p_t = \begin{pmatrix} \pi_t \\ 1 - \pi_t \end{pmatrix}$$

to describe the probabilities of the system being in either of its possible states at period t. Thus in our case π_t denotes the probability of being in boom at period t, while $1 - \pi_t$ denotes the probability of being in recession. In vector notation, the Markov process obeys the transition equation

$$p_{t+1} = \begin{pmatrix} p & 1 - q \\ 1 - p & q \end{pmatrix} p_t.$$

For example, π_{t+1} is the probability of boom at $t+1$ and is equal to (probability of boom at $t \times$ probability of transition to boom) + (probability of recession at $t \times$ probability of transition to boom) $= \pi_t p + (1 - \pi_t)(1 - q)$. Note how the transition matrix T has been transposed. Writing this as

$$p_{t+1} = A p_t$$

we obtain

$$p_{t+1} = A^t p_0 \qquad (t = 0, 1, 2, \ldots). \tag{7.12}$$

Our problem is to find the limiting value of p_t. Assuming that such a limit exists, we may take limits in the transition equation to obtain that

$$p = A p.$$

This result says that p is an *eigenvector* for the eigenvalue $\lambda = 1$. So we look at the characteristic equation of A. In our case, this is

$$\begin{vmatrix} p - \lambda & 1 - q \\ 1 - p & q - \lambda \end{vmatrix} = \lambda^2 - (p + q)\lambda + [pq - (1 - p)(1 - q)]$$

$$= \lambda^2 - (p + q)\lambda + (p + q - 1)$$

$$= (\lambda - 1)[\lambda - (p + q - 1)].$$

Thus $\lambda = 1$ is an eigenvalue. Next we calculate the eigenvectors corresponding to $\lambda = 1$. We have to solve, as in the example in section 7.2, the equation

$$\begin{pmatrix} p-1 & 1-q \\ 1-p & q-1 \end{pmatrix} \begin{pmatrix} u \\ v \end{pmatrix} = \begin{pmatrix} 0 \\ 0 \end{pmatrix}$$

or, equivalently,

$$(p-1)u + (1-q)v = 0$$

$$(1-p)v + (q-1)v = 0.$$

Since $p - 1 \neq 0 \neq 1 - q$ we put $v = \alpha(1 - p)$ and so $u = \alpha(1 - q)$. Thus the eigenvectors for the eigenvalues $\lambda = 1$ are of the form

$$\begin{pmatrix} u \\ v \end{pmatrix} = \alpha \begin{pmatrix} 1-q \\ 1-p \end{pmatrix}.$$

If such an eigenvector is to be a vector of probabilities p we need to have $u = \pi$ and $v = 1 - \pi$ so that $u \geq 0$, $v \geq 0$ and $u + v = 1$. Then

$$p = \begin{pmatrix} \pi \\ 1-\pi \end{pmatrix} = \alpha \begin{pmatrix} 1-q \\ 1-p \end{pmatrix}.$$

Hence $\alpha(1 - q) + \alpha(1 - p) = 1$, i.e.

$$\pi = \frac{1-q}{2-p-q} = \left(1 + \frac{1-p}{1-q}\right)^{-1}.$$

We note that $\pi > 1/2$ if and only if $p > q$. This is the condition for boom being more likely than recession in the long run.

We have left open the problem of whether p_t tends to any limit. To check this, we need by (7.12) to compute A^t. As an exercise in eigenvectors we propose the following neat method. If we can diagonalize A, we should have

$$P^{-1}AP = \begin{pmatrix} 1 & 0 \\ 0 & p+q-1 \end{pmatrix} \quad (= D, \text{ say})$$

since 1 and $p + q - 1$ are eigenvalues. Hence

$$A = PDP^{-1}$$

and

$$A^2 = PDP^{-1} \cdot PDP^{-1} = PD^2P^{-1}.$$

More generally

$$A^n = PD^nP^{-1}$$

and evidently

$$D^n = \begin{pmatrix} 1 & 0 \\ 0 & (p+q-1)^n \end{pmatrix}.$$

Hence

$$p_t = P \begin{pmatrix} 1 & 0 \\ 0 & (p+q-1)^t \end{pmatrix} P^{-1} p_0.$$

Observe that $-1 < p+q-1 < 1+1-1 = 1$. Thus the term $p+q-1$ is numerically less than unity and hence since $(p+q-1)^t \to 0$ we see that

$$D^t \to \begin{pmatrix} 1 & 0 \\ 0 & 0 \end{pmatrix}.$$

Evidently the two eigenvalues 1 and $p+q-1$ are distinct, so A is diagonalizable, and we have justified the implicit assumption that there is a limiting probability vector p.

7.6 Symmetric matrices

We have seen in section 7.4 that not all matrices are diagonalizable. So, which matrices are? There is no simple criterion. However, there is an instantly recognizable class of important matrices which are diagonalizable; these are the *symmetric* matrices defined by the condition

$$A = A'$$

In the 2×2 case, the symmetric matrices are thus of the form

$$\begin{pmatrix} a & c \\ c & b \end{pmatrix}.$$

A wider class of diagonalizable matrices is mentioned at the end of section 7.9.

Theorem

All the eigenvalues of a symmetric matrix are real.

Proof In the 2×2 case the proof is very easy. The characteristic equation here is
$$\lambda^2 - (a+b)\lambda + (ab - c^2) = 0$$

and the discriminant is thus

$$(a+b)^2 - 4(ab - c^2) = a^2 + 2ab + b^2 - 4ab + 4c^2$$
$$= (a-b)^2 + 4c^2 \geqslant 0$$

and so the roots are real.

Notice that the characteristic equation will have equal roots precisely when this discriminant is zero, i.e. when $a = b$ and $c = 0$, and only then; but, in this case, the matrix is in diagonal form, being equal to aI. In general, however, the two eigenvalues are distinct, and so the matrix is diagonalizable by our earlier theorem. We have thus shown the following.

Theorem

Symmetric matrices are diagonalizable.

We shall give a proof for $n \times n$ matrices in section 7.9 after an excursion into quadratic forms.

7.7   Quadratic forms

We have already seen Cobb–Douglas functions $x^\alpha y^\beta$ mixing the two variables by multiplying them together. Another important way of mixing is by way of an expression of the form

$$ax^2 + by^2 + 2cxy.$$

When $ab \neq 0$ this is called a quadratic form in two variables. Such forms are used in modelling, for example, the cost of producing interdependent commodites x and y or the revenue generated from their sale. A rather simple situation arises when $c = 0$, for then the form is composed only of squares; in particular it is instantly clear what iso-curve is represented by the equation

$$ax^2 + by^2 = 1$$

(figure 7.1). When a and b are positive the curve is an ellipse; when a is positive and b is negative the curve is a hyperbola with asymptotes

$$y = \pm \sqrt{\left(\frac{a}{-b}\right)} x$$

Knowing such facts enables us to determine combinations of x and y corresponding to a maximum revenue for fixed cost or alternatively to a minimum input cost achieving a fixed revenue target.

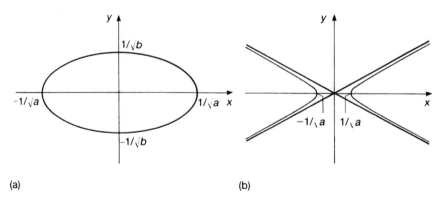

(a)   (b)

Figure 7.1   (a) The ellipse $ax^2 + by^2 = 1$ $(a, b > 0)$; (b) the hyperbola $ax^2 - by^2 = 1$ $(a, b > 0)$.

When $c \neq 0$ it is far from clear what curve is represented by the equation

$$ax^2 + by^2 + 2cxy = 1.$$

It is not even clear whether there are any values where the quadratic form is positive. Both these questions can be resolved by diagonalization of the symmetric matrix

$$\begin{pmatrix} a & c \\ c & b \end{pmatrix}$$

using the identity

$$ax^2 + by^2 + 2cxy = (x, y) \begin{pmatrix} a & c \\ c & b \end{pmatrix} \begin{pmatrix} x \\ y \end{pmatrix}.$$

Following the ideas of section 7.1 we are tempted to make a change of variable:

$$x = pX + uY$$
$$y = qX + vY,$$

i.e.

$$\begin{pmatrix} x \\ y \end{pmatrix} = P \begin{pmatrix} X \\ Y \end{pmatrix}.$$

The quadratic form then becomes

$$(X, Y) P'AP \begin{pmatrix} X \\ Y \end{pmatrix}.$$

It would be convenient if it could be arranged both that $P' = P^{-1}$ and that

$$P^{-1}AP = \begin{pmatrix} r & 0 \\ 0 & s \end{pmatrix}$$

for then the quadratic form simplifies to

$$(X, Y) \begin{pmatrix} r & 0 \\ 0 & s \end{pmatrix} \begin{pmatrix} X \\ Y \end{pmatrix} = rX^2 + sY^2.$$

Now the condition $P' = P^{-1}$ is equivalent to $P'P = I$, i.e.

$$\begin{pmatrix} 1 & 0 \\ 0 & 1 \end{pmatrix} = \begin{pmatrix} p & q \\ u & v \end{pmatrix} \begin{pmatrix} p & u \\ q & v \end{pmatrix} = \begin{pmatrix} p^2 + q^2 & pu + qv \\ pu + qv & u^2 + v^2 \end{pmatrix}$$

or

$$p^2 + q^2 = 1$$
$$u^2 + v^2 = 1$$
$$pu + qv = 0.$$

These three equations assert that the two eigenvectors making up the columns of P are both of *unit* length and that they are perpendicular (*orthogonal*) to each other. A matrix P satisfying $P'P = I$ is called an *orthogonal matrix*.

Now it is easy to rescale eigenvectors so that they are of unit length. But can we arrange for them to be orthogonal? Fortunately, they are often already orthogonal; more precisely, we have the following theorem.

Theorem

Eigenvectors corresponding to distinct eigenvalues of a *symmetric* matrix are orthogonal.

Proof The proof follows similar lines to the theorem of section 7.4. We observe that if

$$A\begin{pmatrix} p \\ q \end{pmatrix} = r\begin{pmatrix} p \\ q \end{pmatrix} \qquad A\begin{pmatrix} u \\ v \end{pmatrix} = s\begin{pmatrix} u \\ v \end{pmatrix}$$

and $A = A'$, then

$$r(p, q) = \left[A\begin{pmatrix} p \\ q \end{pmatrix} \right]' = (p, q)A' = (p, q)A$$

and so

$$r(pu + qv) = r(p, q) \cdot \begin{pmatrix} u \\ v \end{pmatrix}$$

$$= [(p, q)A]\begin{pmatrix} u \\ v \end{pmatrix}$$

$$= (p, q)\left[A\begin{pmatrix} u \\ v \end{pmatrix} \right]$$

$$= (p, q) s\begin{pmatrix} u \\ v \end{pmatrix}$$

$$= s(pu + qv).$$

Thus

$$(r - s)(pu + qv) = 0$$

and so if $r \neq s$ then $pu + qv = 0$ and the eigenvectors are orthogonal.

Example
Check that the eigenvectors corresponding to the eigenvalues $\lambda = 2$ and $\lambda = -8$ of the matrix

$$A = \begin{pmatrix} -3 & 5 \\ 5 & -3 \end{pmatrix}$$

are orthogonal. Determine what curve is represented by

$$10xy - 3x^2 - 3y^2 = 1$$

and sketch the curve.

SOLUTION   We saw in section 7.4 that the eigenvectors were scalar multiples respectively of

$$\begin{pmatrix} 1 \\ 1 \end{pmatrix} \quad \text{and} \quad \begin{pmatrix} 1 \\ -1 \end{pmatrix}.$$

Evidently

$$\begin{pmatrix} 1 \\ 1 \end{pmatrix} \cdot \begin{pmatrix} 1 \\ -1 \end{pmatrix} = 1 \times 1 + 1(-1) = 0$$

and so the two vectors are orthogonal. Both are of length $\sqrt{(1^2 + 1^2)} = \sqrt{2}$. Rescaling them we obtain the orthogonal matrix of eigenvectors:

$$P = \begin{pmatrix} \dfrac{1}{\sqrt{2}} & \dfrac{1}{\sqrt{2}} \\ \dfrac{1}{\sqrt{2}} & \dfrac{-1}{\sqrt{2}} \end{pmatrix}.$$

Hence

$$P'AP = \begin{pmatrix} 2 & 0 \\ 0 & -8 \end{pmatrix}$$

and the change of variable

$$\begin{pmatrix} x \\ y \end{pmatrix} = P \begin{pmatrix} X \\ Y \end{pmatrix} \tag{7.13}$$

leads to

$$1 = 10xy - 3x^2 - 3y^2 = (x, y) A \begin{pmatrix} x \\ y \end{pmatrix}$$

$$= (X, Y) P'AP \begin{pmatrix} X \\ Y \end{pmatrix}$$

$$= 2X^2 - 8Y^2.$$

Thus the curve represents a hyperbola.

To sketch the curve we need to draw the X and Y axes in the x, y diagram. Since $P'P = I$ we have $P^{-1} = P'$ and so

$$\begin{pmatrix} X \\ Y \end{pmatrix} = P^{-1} \begin{pmatrix} x \\ y \end{pmatrix} = P' \begin{pmatrix} x \\ y \end{pmatrix} = \begin{pmatrix} \dfrac{1}{\sqrt{2}} & \dfrac{1}{\sqrt{2}} \\ \dfrac{1}{\sqrt{2}} & \dfrac{-1}{\sqrt{2}} \end{pmatrix} \begin{pmatrix} x \\ y \end{pmatrix}.$$

Thus

$$X = \frac{1}{\sqrt{2}} x + \frac{1}{\sqrt{2}} y$$

$$Y = \frac{1}{\sqrt{2}} x - \frac{1}{\sqrt{2}} y$$

(figure 7.2). Thus $X = 0$ is given by $x + y = 0$, whereas $Y = 0$ is given by $x - y = 0$. If we draw the X and Y axes we find that $Y = 0$ is the line through the eigenvector

$$\begin{pmatrix} 1 \\ 1 \end{pmatrix}$$

and likewise $X = 0$ is the line through the other eigenvector. This is not an accident since any point (x, y) in the plane has X, Y co-ordinates given by

$$\begin{pmatrix} x \\ y \end{pmatrix} = P \begin{pmatrix} X \\ Y \end{pmatrix}$$

$$= X \begin{pmatrix} \dfrac{1}{\sqrt{2}} \\ \dfrac{1}{\sqrt{2}} \end{pmatrix} + Y \begin{pmatrix} \dfrac{1}{\sqrt{2}} \\ \dfrac{-1}{\sqrt{2}} \end{pmatrix}.$$

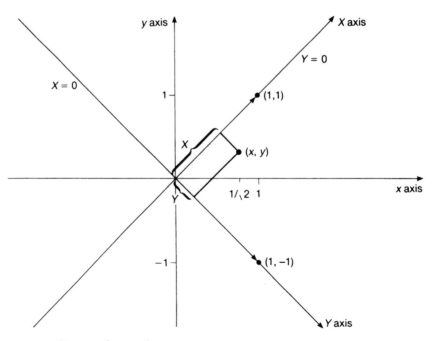

Figure 7.2   Change of co-ordinate system.

It is for this reason that these axes are sometimes referred to as *eigen-lines*.

It is now easy to sketch relative to X, Y axes the hyperbola $2X^2 - 8Y^2 = 1$ bearing in mind that the asymptotes are $8Y^2 = 2X^2$ or $Y = \pm\frac{1}{2}X$ (figure 7.3).

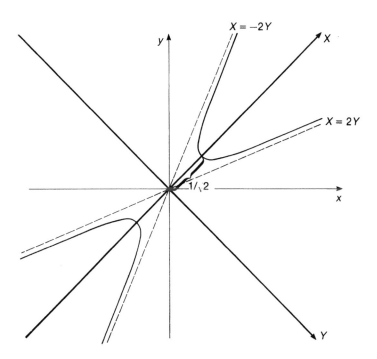

Figure 7.3   Graph of a quadratic form.

7.8   Positive definite forms

The quadratic form

$$z = q(x, y) = ax^2 + by^2 + 2cxy$$

is said to be *positive definite* if $q(x, y) > 0$ for all non-zero x, y. (Obviously $q(0, 0) = 0$, so we must require x and y to be non-zero in this definition.) It is said to be *positive semi-definite* (or non-negative definite) if $q(x, y) \geqslant 0$ for all x, y. In effect we are testing whether zero is a (possibly strict) minimum of the function of two variables $z = q(x, y)$. We know from the last section that we can make a change of variable under which we obtain

$$z = rX^2 + sY^2$$

where r and s are the eigenvalues of

$$\begin{pmatrix} a & c \\ c & b \end{pmatrix}.$$

Hence q is positive definite if and only if both eigenvalues are positive. Notice that in the notation of the last section

$$\begin{pmatrix} x \\ y \end{pmatrix} = P \begin{pmatrix} X \\ Y \end{pmatrix}$$

and since P is non-singular $(x, y) = (0, 0)$ if and only if $(X, Y) = (0, 0)$.

Likewise the quadratic form is positive semi-definite if the eigenvalues are both non-negative.

The two cases can be graphed. In the positive definite case

$$z = rX^2 + sY^2 \qquad (r, s > 0)$$

is a surface whose horizontal sections are ellipses and whose vertical sections are parabolas. In the non-negative definite case if say $s = 0$ we obtain

$$z = rX^2$$

which is a parabolic valley (figure 7.4).

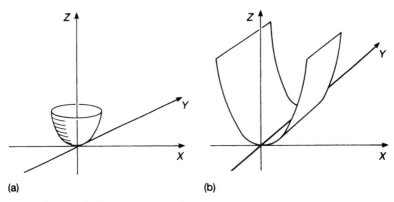

(a)   (b)

Figure 7.4   Quadratic form: (a) both eigenvalues positive; (b) one eigenvalue positive, one zero.

We do not need to know the values of r and s to determine whether the quadratic form is positive definite. It is enough to know their signs. A useful test to check whether r and s are positive can be obtained by looking at the characteristic equation of the matrix A. We have

$$\begin{vmatrix} a - \lambda & c \\ c & b - \lambda \end{vmatrix} = \lambda^2 - (a + b)\lambda + (ab - c^2)$$
$$= (\lambda - r)(\lambda - s)$$

where we have used the roots to factorize the quadratic. Hence

$$r + s = a + b$$
$$rs = ab - c^2.$$

Thus if r and s are both positive $ab - c^2 > 0$ and $a + b > 0$. The converse also holds. For, since A is symmetric, both roots are real. Their product is $ab - c^2 > 0$ and so they are either both positive or both negative. If they were negative their sum would be negative and this contradicts the fact that their sum is $a + b > 0$.

For a final simplification, note that if $ab > c^2$ then either both a and b are positive or both are negative. Hence it is enough to test if $a > 0$. For, if $a > 0$ and $ab > c^2$, then also $b > 0$ and so $a + b > 0$.

Theorem

The eigenvalues of

$$A = \begin{pmatrix} a & c \\ c & b \end{pmatrix}$$

are both positive if and only if $a > 0$ and $\det(A) > 0$.

This theorem generalizes to $n \times n$ matrices as follows.

Test for positive definiteness

The symmetric matrix

$$A = \begin{pmatrix} a_{11} & a_{12} & \cdots \\ a_{21} & a_{22} & \cdots \\ \vdots & \vdots & a_{nn} \end{pmatrix}$$

has positive eigenvalues if and only if all its principal subdeterminants are strictly positive:

$$a_{11} > 0 \qquad \begin{vmatrix} a_{11} & a_{12} \\ a_{21} & a_{22} \end{vmatrix} > 0 \qquad \begin{vmatrix} a_{11} & a_{12} & a_{13} \\ a_{21} & a_{22} & a_{23} \\ a_{31} & a_{32} & a_{33} \end{vmatrix} > 0 \qquad \cdots \qquad \det A > 0.$$

These results will be very important for us in chapter 15 when we discuss testing a general function of two or more variables, e.g. $F(x, y)$, for a minimum.

Remark

In the case of a quadratic form in two variables it is also true that $q(x, y)$ is positive semi-definite if $a \geq 0$ and $ab - c^2 \geq 0$. The general theorem above for quadratic forms in three or more variables does not say anything about semi-definiteness, as the following example shows.

Example
Find the eigenvalues of the symmetric matrix

$$A = \begin{pmatrix} 1 & 1 & 0 \\ 1 & 1 & 0 \\ 0 & 0 & -1 \end{pmatrix}$$

and check that the principal subdeterminants are non-negative. Is its quadratic form semi-definite?

SOLUTION The subdeterminants are 1, 0, 0. The characteristic equation is

$$\begin{vmatrix} 1 - \lambda & 1 & 0 \\ 1 & 1 - \lambda & 0 \\ 0 & 0 & -1 - \lambda \end{vmatrix} = -(1 + \lambda)[(1 - \lambda)^2 - 1]$$

$$= -(1 + \lambda)(\lambda^2 - 2\lambda) = -(\lambda + 1)(\lambda - 2)\lambda$$

where we have expanded the determinant by the bottom row. Thus the eigenvalues are $\lambda = -1, 0, 2$. Hence under a change of variable the quadratic form

$$(x, y, z) A \begin{pmatrix} x \\ y \\ z \end{pmatrix} = x^2 + y^2 - z^2 + 2xy$$

becomes $-X^2 + 2Z^2$ and so is not even semi-definite.

The theorem about positive definiteness can be amended to deal with 3×3 matrices – this is offered as an exercise (see section 7.11, question 17). This amendment becomes too complicated to be worth bothering with for large matrices. We note, however, the following result.

Theorem

The symmetric matrix A has non-negative eigenvalues if and only if the coefficients of its characteristic polynomial

$$p(\lambda) = \det(A - \lambda I) = (-\lambda)^n + (a_{11} + \cdots + a_{nn})(-\lambda)^{n-1} + \cdots + \det(A)$$

are alternately non-negative and non-positive.

Proof If the signs alternate in the characteristic polynomial then

$$p(-t) = (+t)^n + (a_{11} + \cdots + a_{nn})(+t)^{n-1} + \cdots + \det(A) > 0$$

for $t > 0$ since here all the coefficients are non-negative. Hence if $\lambda = -t < 0$, then $p(\lambda) \neq 0$ and so all the eigenvalues (which are necessarily real) must be non-negative.

Conversely, if the eigenvalues of $p(\lambda)$ are $\lambda_1, \lambda_2, \ldots \lambda_n$ and they are all non-negative then (see section 7.11, question 1) we have

$$p(\lambda) = (\lambda_1 - \lambda)(\lambda_2 - \lambda) \cdots (\lambda_n - \lambda)$$

$$= (-\lambda)^n + (-\lambda)^{n-1}\{\lambda_1 + \cdots + \lambda_n\} + (-\lambda)^{n-2}\{\lambda_1\lambda_2 + \lambda_2\lambda_3$$

$$+ \cdots + \lambda_{n-1}\lambda_n + \lambda_n\lambda_1\} + \cdots + \{\lambda_1 \cdots \lambda_n\}.$$

All the expressions occurring in braces are non-negative. Thus the coefficients alternate in sign.

7.8.1   Negative definiteness

The quadratic form $q(x, y)$ is *negative definite* if $q(x, y) < 0$ for all non-zero x and y. It is *negative semi-definite* if $q(x, y) \leqslant 0$ for all x, y. Evidently if $q(x, y)$ is negative definite, $-q(x, y)$ is positive definite. Since the corresponding matrix is

$$-A = \begin{pmatrix} -a & -c \\ -c & -b \end{pmatrix}$$

we require for negative-definiteness of q that

$$-a > 0 \quad \text{and} \quad (-a)(-b) - (-c)^2 > 0,$$

i.e.

$$a < 0 \quad \text{and} \quad ab - c^2 > 0.$$

In general the sequence of principal subdeterminants alternates in strict sign, $-, +, -, \ldots$, if and only if a matrix represents a negative definite matrix.

7.9   Matrices of size $n \times n$

All the theorems discussed in the case of 2×2 matrices are true of larger matrices. Proofs are sometimes more awkward and on one occasion different. The result that needs a different approach follows.

Theorem

The eigenvalues of an $n \times n$ symmetric matrix A with real entries are all real.

Proof Suppose λ is an eigenvalue and $x = (u, v, \ldots)'$ is a corresponding eigenvector of the matrix A. Since we are concerned with the possibility that λ is complex we must also allow the possibility that the components $u, v, \ldots$ of x obtained by solving

$$Ax = \lambda x$$

might also be complex numbers. We shall define that conjugate transpose (or 'transconjugate') to be x^* where

$$x^* = (\bar{u}, \bar{v}, \ldots).$$

Note that if $u = a + ib$ then $\bar{u} = a - ib$ etc. Since $u\bar{u} = a^2 + b^2 = |u|^2$ we see that

$$x^*x = \bar{u}u + \bar{v}v + \cdots = |u|^2 + |v|^2 + \cdots = \|x\|^2 > 0$$

since $x \neq 0$. Taking transposes and conjugates gives us

$$\bar{\lambda}x^* = x^*A'$$

since A is real. Hence, using $A' = A$ we have

$$\bar{\lambda}x^*x = x^*A'x = x^*Ax = x^*\lambda x$$

or

$$(\bar{\lambda} - \lambda)x^*x = 0.$$

But $\|x\|^2 \neq 0$ and so $\bar{\lambda} = \lambda$.

As regards diagonalizability of matrices, those that cannot be diagonalized are termed *defective*. A deep theorem states that for any defective matrix A there is a non-singular matrix P such that $P^{-1}AP$ is in block-diagonal form. This is a matrix of the form

$$\begin{pmatrix} J_1 & & & \\ & J_2 & & \\ & & \ddots & \\ & & & J_m \end{pmatrix}$$

where the non-zero entries are confined to square blocks $J_1, J_2, \ldots$ along the diagonal. In general the blocks themselves take the form

$$\begin{pmatrix} \lambda & 1 & & & \\ & \lambda & 1 & & \\ & & \lambda & 1 & \\ & & & \ddots & \\ & & & & \lambda \end{pmatrix}$$

where λ is an eigenvalue of the matrix A and is repeated along the diagonal with a series of 1s in the diagonal immediately above and zeros elsewhere. Blocks of size 1×1 containing only an eigenvalue as the unique entry are also permitted as Js.

Those non-defective matrices A for which an orthogonal P may be found such that $P'AP$ is diagonal are termed *normal*. The normal matrices are characterized by the property that

$$AA' = A'A$$

Evidently symmetric matrices are normal.

Theorem

If A is a symmetric matrix, there is an orthogonal matrix P such that $P'AP$ is a diagonal matrix.

Remark

We defined orthogonal matrices P in section 7.7 as satisfying $P'P = I$; we saw that this meant that the columns of P were unit vectors and that they were perpendicular to each other. When the symmetric matrix A has all its eigenvalues distinct, the corresponding eigenvectors are linearly independent (section 7.4) and mutually orthogonal (section 7.7). In this case the eigenvectors rescaled to unit length can be arranged as the columns of a matrix P which is orthogonal; moreover, $P'AP$ will be diagonal (see section 7.4). Our method fails when the number of distinct eigenvalues is less than the size of the matrix. The proof below introduces a new method.

Proof We give the proof when A is 3×3, but the method easily adapts to larger matrices.

Let λ be any eigenvalue and let u be a corresponding eigenvector, so that $Au = \lambda u$; we need u to be of unit length (so rescale it, if necessary).

Now choose any two vectors v, w, both of unit length and lying in the plane perpendicular to u but so that they are also perpendicular to each other, as in figure 7.5.

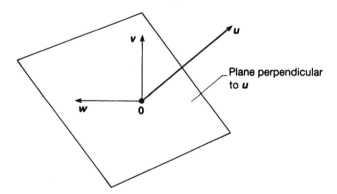

Figure 7.5 v, w are mutually perpendicular and lie in the plane perpendicular to u.

Thus the matrix $P = [u, v, w]$ is orthogonal. Now

$$AP = [Au, Av, Aw]$$

$$= [\lambda u, Av, Aw].$$

Rewrite Av and Aw in terms of u, v, w thus:

$$Av = lu + mv + nw$$

$$Aw = pu + qv + rw.$$

Observe that

$$[u, v, w] \begin{pmatrix} \lambda & l & p \\ 0 & m & q \\ 0 & n & r \end{pmatrix} = (\lambda u, \, lu + mv + nw, \, pu + qv + rw).$$

Hence

$$AP = P \begin{pmatrix} \lambda & l & p \\ 0 & m & q \\ 0 & n & r \end{pmatrix}.$$

But $P^{-1} = P'$ and so

$$P'AP = \begin{pmatrix} \lambda & l & p \\ 0 & m & q \\ 0 & n & r \end{pmatrix}.$$

We notice that $(P'AP)' = P'A'P'' = P'AP$. So $B = P'AP$ is symmetric. It follows that $l = p = 0$ and $n = q$. Thus

$$B = \begin{pmatrix} 1 & 0 & 0 \\ 0 & m & q \\ 0 & q & r \end{pmatrix}.$$

Let

$$C = \begin{pmatrix} m & q \\ q & r \end{pmatrix}.$$

This is a 2×2 symmetric matrix. In section 7.6 we saw that either this is already diagonal (when $q = 0$ and $m = r$) or the eigenvalues are distinct. So there is an orthogonal 2×2 matrix Q_1 such that $Q_1'CQ_1$ is a diagonal matrix D (with the eigenvalues of C as entries).

Let

$$Q = \left(\begin{array}{c|cc} 1 & 0 & 0 \\ \hline 0 & & \\ & & Q_1 \\ 0 & & \end{array} \right)$$

It may be checked that $Q'Q = I$ if $Q_1'Q_1 = I$. Thus Q is orthogonal. It may also be computed that

$$Q'BQ = \left(\begin{array}{c|cc} \lambda & 0 & 0 \\ \hline 0 & & \\ & & D \\ 0 & & \end{array} \right) \tag{7.14}$$

Thus $(PQ)'A(PQ)$ is a diagonal matrix.

Note that the diagonal entries in equation (7.14) are all eigenvalues of A (possibly repeated, if they are not distinct).

7.10 Exercises

1* Find the eigenvalues and corresponding eigenvectors of the following matrices:

(a) $\begin{pmatrix} 1 & 2 \\ 2 & 1 \end{pmatrix}$ (b) $\begin{pmatrix} 1 & 1 \\ 2 & 2 \end{pmatrix}$

(c) $\begin{pmatrix} 1 & 1 & 5 \\ 4 & 1 & 3 \\ 0 & 0 & 1 \end{pmatrix}$ (d) $\begin{pmatrix} 1 & 0 & 1 \\ 0 & 1 & 1 \\ 1 & 1 & 2 \end{pmatrix}$

Hence diagonalize these matrices.

2 Repeat the previous exercise for the matrices

(a) $\begin{pmatrix} 1 & 2 \\ 0 & 3 \end{pmatrix}$ (b) $\begin{pmatrix} 1 & 2 \\ 2 & -2 \end{pmatrix}$

(c) $\begin{pmatrix} 1 & 3 & 0 \\ -3 & -2 & -1 \\ 0 & -1 & 1 \end{pmatrix}$ (d) $\begin{pmatrix} 4 & 0 & 2 \\ 0 & 4 & 2 \\ 2 & 2 & 2 \end{pmatrix}$

3* Which of the matrices in questions 1 and 2 are symmetric? In each case say of the symmetric matrix whether it is positive definite, non-negative definite or neither. For the 2×2 matrices A find the eigen-lines and sketch the curves $x'Ax = 1$.

4 Write down the characteristic polynomial of each of the following matrices:

(a) $\begin{pmatrix} 1 & 3 \\ 3 & 2 \end{pmatrix}$ $\begin{pmatrix} 1 & 2 \\ 2 & 3 \end{pmatrix}$

(b) $\begin{pmatrix} 1 & 4 & 5 \\ 4 & 2 & 6 \\ 5 & 6 & 3 \end{pmatrix}$ $\begin{pmatrix} 4 & 1 & 2 \\ 1 & 5 & 3 \\ 2 & 3 & 6 \end{pmatrix}$

Check whether the matrices are positive definite by reference to (i) the coefficients in the characteristic polynomial and (ii) the principal subdeterminants.

5* Repeat the previous exercise in relation to the symmetric matrices of questions 1 and 2.

6 Let $P(x)$ be a polynomial and let E denote the shift operator (section 4.11). Denoting the function y_t by y let

$$Ay = P(E)y_t.$$

Show that $y = c^t$ is an eigenvector for the eigenvalue $P(c)$ of the transformation A, i.e.

$$Ay = P(c)y.$$

7   Show that the second-order difference equation

$$6y_{t+2} - 5y_{t+1} + y_t = 0 \tag{7.15}$$

is equivalent to the matrix equation

$$\begin{pmatrix} y_{t+1} \\ z_{t+1} \end{pmatrix} = \begin{pmatrix} 0 & 1 \\ -\dfrac{1}{6} & \dfrac{5}{6} \end{pmatrix} \begin{pmatrix} y_t \\ z_t \end{pmatrix}.$$

As this is in the form $p_{t+1} = Ap_t$ show that if $p_t \to p$ then either $p = 0$ or A has 1 as an eigenvalue. Show that the characteristic equation $\det(A - \lambda I) = 0$ is the same as the auxiliary equation of (7.15).

7.11   Further exercises

1   If A is an $n \times n$ symmetric matrix with eigenvalues $\lambda_1, \lambda_2, \ldots, \lambda_n$ show by comparing both sides of the equation

$$\begin{vmatrix} a_{11} - \lambda & a_{12} & \vdots \\ a_{21} & a_{22} - \lambda & \vdots \\ & \cdots & a_{33} - \lambda \end{vmatrix} = (\lambda_1 - \lambda)(\lambda_2 - \lambda) \cdots (\lambda_n - \lambda)$$

that

(a) $\lambda_1 + \lambda_2 + \cdots + \lambda_n = a_{11} + a_{22} + \cdots + a_{nn}$

and

(b) $\lambda_1 \lambda_2 \cdots \lambda_n = \det(A)$.

Verify these results for the examples of question 1 in section 7.10.

2   Check that if A and B are similar (i.e. $B = P^{-1}AP$) then A and B have identical characteristic polynomials and hence the same eigenvalues. [*Hint:* $\det[P^{-1}(A - \lambda I)P] = \det(P^{-1}) \det(A - \lambda I) \det(P)$.]

3   If D is a diagonal matrix, show how to solve

$$X_{t+1} = DX_t + d,$$

where X_t and d are column vectors, by reference to a vector X such that

$$X = DX + d,$$

i.e.

$$(I - D)X = d.$$

[*Hint*: $Z_t = X_t - X$.] Show that $X_t \rightarrow X$ if and only if the diagonal elements of D are in modulus less than unity.

4 Suppose the matrix A can be diagonalized and that

$$P^{-1}AP = \begin{pmatrix} r & 0 \\ 0 & s \end{pmatrix}.$$

Solve, by considering $x_t = PX_t$, the equation

$$x_{t+1} = Ax_t + c$$

assuming that $r \neq 1$, $s \neq 1$.

5* In the Leontieff model of production (section 5.11) an economy meets the consumers' demand for goods $f = (f_1, f_2, \ldots)'$ (where f_i is the demand for the ith commodity) if for some x

$$f + Ax = x$$

where the entries a_{ij} of the matrix A denote the jth firm's output of commodity i per unit input of commodity j. Thus x is the total demand, including the intermediate demand by firms for goods as inputs to the production process.

The economy is closed when $f = 0$ and hence a non-zero demand for intermediate goods can be met if and only if $\lambda = 1$ is an eigenvalue of A.

Show that for any integer n

$$x = f + Af + A^2 f + \cdots + A^n f + A^{n+1} x.$$

Assuming that all the eigenvalues of A are real, show that if they are of absolute value less than unity then

$$(I - A)^{-1} = I + A + A^2 + A^3 + \cdots.$$

[*Hint*: As $x = (I - A)^{-1} f$, show that $\lim A^n x = 0$.]

6 If A is any $n \times n$ transition matrix where each row describes the probabilities of transition from a current state to the possible states in the next period, show that $Ae = e$ where $e' = (1, 1, \ldots)$. (So $\lambda = 1$ is always an eigenvalue.)

7 If A is the transition matrix

$$\begin{pmatrix} p & 1-p \\ 1-q & q \end{pmatrix}$$

find an eigenvector corresponding to the eigenvalue $\lambda = p + q - 1$ and hence find a matrix P such that $P^{-1}AP$ is diagonal. Use this matrix to compute that

$$(2 - p - q)A^t = \begin{pmatrix} 1-q & 1-p \\ 1-q & 1-p \end{pmatrix} + (p + q - 1)^t \begin{pmatrix} 1-p & p-1 \\ q-1 & 1-q \end{pmatrix}.$$

8   At time t the price of corn is p_t^c and the price of hog is p_t^h. The supply and demand for corn at time t are given as in the cobweb model by

$$S_t^c = ap_{t-1}^c + b \qquad D_t^c = kp_t^c + m \qquad (a, b, k, m > 0)$$

whereas the supply and demand for hog are given by

$$S_t^h = \alpha p_{t-1}^h + \beta p_{t-1}^c + \gamma \qquad D_t^h = \kappa p_t^h + \mu \qquad (\alpha, \beta, \kappa, \mu > 0)$$

Thus the two markets are interdependent. Show that if the corn–hog markets are in equilibrium then

$$\begin{pmatrix} p_t^c \\ p_t^h \end{pmatrix} = \begin{pmatrix} \dfrac{a}{k} & 0 \\ \dfrac{\beta}{\kappa} & \dfrac{\alpha}{\kappa} \end{pmatrix} \begin{pmatrix} p_{t-1}^c \\ p_{t-1}^h \end{pmatrix} + \begin{pmatrix} \dfrac{b-m}{k} \\ \dfrac{\gamma-\mu}{\kappa} \end{pmatrix}$$

which is in the form

$$p_t = Ap_{t-1} + c.$$

Show that the eigenvalues of A in this case are a/k and β/κ. Deduce that prices converge if and only if both $|a/k|$ and $|\beta/\kappa|$ are less than unity.

9   A matrix B is skew-symmetric if $B = -B'$. Describe all the 2×2 skew-symmetric matrices.

10   A matrix is said to be normal if $AA' = A'A$. Show that the following are normal matrices:

(a)   symmetric matrices;
(b)   skew-symmetric matrices;
(c)   matrices of the form $\alpha I + B$ where α is a scalar and B is skew-symmetric.

11   Show that a 2×2 matrix is normal if it is either a symmetric matrix or a matrix of the form $\alpha I + B$ with B skew-symmetric.

12   In portfolio analysis, assets are represented in the (x, y) plane where x measures risk and y measures its average (expected) return. A portfolio is made up of two assets (A, a) and (B, b) bought in the proportions t of the first and $1 - t$ of the second. The portfolio is regarded thus as giving a return

$$y = ta + (1 - t)b.$$

Risk x is assessed according to the formula

$$x^2 = t^2 A + (1 - t)^2 B + 2t(1 - t)AB\rho$$

where the number $-1 \leqslant \rho \leqslant 1$ is a measure of risk correlation. By eliminating t between the two equations show that, if $-1 < \rho < 1$, then the equation connecting x and y is a hyperbola. What happens to the hyperbola when $\rho = 1$? What if $\rho = -1$?

[*Remark*:   Risk is in fact measured by the variance (section 4.14, question 2) of the asset's distribution of returns – hence the strange formula for x. You should assume that risk is a positive quantity.]

13   Show that the quadratic form

$$ax^2 + by^2 + cz^2 + 2dxy + 2eyz + 2fxz$$

is non-negative definite, implying and implied by $a \geq 0$, $ab - d^2 \geq 0$ and additionally $bc - f^2 \geq 0$, $ac - e^2 \geq 0$, $\det(A) \geq 0$, where

$$A = \begin{pmatrix} a & d & e \\ d & b & f \\ e & f & c \end{pmatrix}.$$

[*Hint*: For the forward implication, setting one variable to zero gives a quadratic form in two variables. For the converse, check that if λ_1, λ_2, λ_3 are eigenvalues of A then $\lambda_1\lambda_2 + \lambda_2\lambda_3 + \lambda_3\lambda_1 = (ab - d^2) + (bc - f^2) + (ac - e^2)$.]

14   Show that the matrix A has positive eigenvalues if and only if the coefficients of the characteristic polynomial are all non-zero and alternate in sign. (Compare with the theorem of section 7.8.)

15   When $a \neq 0$ use the identity (obtained by completing the square)

$$ax^2 + 2cxy + by^2 = a\left(x + \frac{c}{a}y\right)^2 + \left(b - \frac{c^2}{a}\right)y^2$$

to deduce that this quadratic form is positive definite if and only if $a > 0$ and $ab - c^2 > 0$. What happens if $b = 0$? What conclusions can you draw about non-negative definiteness?

16   What is the connection between the matrices

$$P = \begin{pmatrix} a & c \\ 0 & ab - c^2 \end{pmatrix} \qquad A = \begin{pmatrix} a & c \\ c & b \end{pmatrix}$$

and the identity of the last question.

17   Show that the matrix

$$\begin{bmatrix} a & d & e \\ d & b & f \\ e & f & c \end{bmatrix}$$

is positive definite if and only if

$$a > 0, \; ab - d^2 > 0, \; abd + 2efd > af^2 + be^2 + cd^2.$$

18   Apply the method of completing the square to the quadratic

$$ax^2 + by^2 + cz^2 + 2dxy + 2ezx + 2fyz$$

in order to derive conditions for positive definiteness. Show that your conditions are equivalent to those of the last question.

What conclusions can you draw about non-negative definiteness?

19 Verify the equation

$$\begin{pmatrix} a & c \\ b & d \end{pmatrix}\begin{pmatrix} x \\ y \end{pmatrix} = x\begin{pmatrix} a \\ b \end{pmatrix} + y\begin{pmatrix} c \\ d \end{pmatrix}.$$

How does this generalize to 3×3 matrices?

20 Verify that

$$(u, v, w)\begin{pmatrix} 1 & 0 & 0 \\ 0 & a & c \\ 0 & b & d \end{pmatrix} = (u, av + bw, cv + dw).$$

If the bordered matrix is orthogonal and if u, v, w are mutually orthogonal, then the effect of the bordered matrix is to rotate v and w.

21 Verify that if

$$Q = \left(\begin{array}{c|cc} 1 & 0 & 0 \\ \hline 0 & & \\ & & Q_1 \\ 0 & & \end{array}\right)$$

then $Q'Q = I_{3 \times 3}$ if and only if $Q_1'Q_1 = I_{2 \times 2}$.

7.12 Answers

1

(a)

$$\det\begin{pmatrix} 1 - \lambda & 2 \\ 2 & 1 - \lambda \end{pmatrix} = (1 - \lambda)^2 - 2 \times 2 = \lambda^2 - 2\lambda - 3 = (\lambda - 3)(\lambda + 1)$$

The eigenvalues are $\lambda = -1$ and $\lambda = 3$. We solve $Ax = \lambda x$ in each case, or equivalently $(A - \lambda I)x = 0$. Thus for $\lambda = -1$ we obtain

$$\begin{pmatrix} 1 - (-1) & 2 \\ 2 & 1 - (-1) \end{pmatrix}\begin{pmatrix} x_1 \\ x_2 \end{pmatrix} = \begin{pmatrix} 0 \\ 0 \end{pmatrix}$$

or

$$2x_1 + 2x_2 = 0$$
$$2x_1 + 2x_2 = 0.$$

A second equation is redundant and the general eigenvector is

$$x_1(1, -1)'.$$

For $\lambda = 3$ we obtain

$$\begin{pmatrix} 1-3 & 2 \\ 2 & 1-3 \end{pmatrix}\begin{pmatrix} x_1 \\ x_2 \end{pmatrix}\begin{pmatrix} 0 \\ 0 \end{pmatrix}$$

or

$$-2x_1 + 2x_2 = 0$$
$$2x_1 - 2x_2 = 0.$$

The general eigenvector is

$$x_1(1, 1)'.$$

(b)

$$\det\begin{pmatrix} 1-\lambda & 1 \\ 2 & 2-\lambda \end{pmatrix} = (1-\lambda)(2-\lambda) - 2 = \lambda^2 - 3\lambda - 0 = \lambda(\lambda - 3)$$

For $\lambda = 0$ we solve

$$\begin{pmatrix} 1-0 & 1 \\ 2 & 2-0 \end{pmatrix}\begin{pmatrix} x_1 \\ x_2 \end{pmatrix} = \begin{pmatrix} 0 \\ 0 \end{pmatrix}$$

or

$$x_1 + x_2 = 0$$
$$2x_1 + 2x_2 = 0.$$

Thus the general eigenvector is

$$x_1(1, -1)'.$$

For $\lambda = 3$ we have

$$\begin{pmatrix} 1-3 & 1 \\ 2 & 2-3 \end{pmatrix}\begin{pmatrix} x_1 \\ x_2 \end{pmatrix} = \begin{pmatrix} 0 \\ 0 \end{pmatrix}$$

or

$$-2x_1 + x_2 = 0$$
$$2x_1 - x_2 = 0.$$

The general eigenvector is

$$x_1(1, 2)'.$$

(c) Expanding by the bottom row we obtain

$$\begin{vmatrix} 1-\lambda & 1 & 5 \\ 4 & 1-\lambda & 3 \\ 0 & 0 & 1-\lambda \end{vmatrix} = (1-\lambda)[(1-\lambda)(1-\lambda) - 4]$$

$$= (1-\lambda)(1-\lambda-2)(1-\lambda+2)$$
$$= (1-\lambda)(-1-\lambda)(3-\lambda)$$

and so the eigenvalues are $\lambda = -1, 1, 3$.

Solving $(A - \lambda I)x = 0$ when $\lambda = -1$ we have

$$\begin{bmatrix} 1-(-1) & 1 & 5 \\ 4 & 1-(-1) & 3 \\ 0 & 0 & 1-(-1) \end{bmatrix} \begin{pmatrix} x_1 \\ x_2 \\ x_3 \end{pmatrix} = 0$$

or

$$2x_1 + x_2 + 5x_3 = 0$$
$$4x_1 + 2x_2 + 3x_3 = 0$$
$$2x_3 = 0.$$

Hence $x_3 = 0$ and the other two equations both assert that $2x_1 + x_2 = 0$. The general eigenvector is thus

$$x_1(1, -2, 0)'.$$

When $\lambda = 1$ we must solve

$$\begin{bmatrix} 1-1 & 1 & 5 \\ 4 & 1-1 & 3 \\ 0 & 0 & 1-1 \end{bmatrix} \begin{pmatrix} x_1 \\ x_2 \\ x_3 \end{pmatrix} = 0$$

or

$$x_2 + 5x_3 = 0$$
$$4x_1 + 3x_3 = 0.$$

Note that the last row gives no information. Solving in terms of x_3 we obtain the general eigenvector in the form

$$x_3\left(-\frac{3}{4}, -5, 1\right)'$$

or $\alpha(3, 20, -4)'$, where

$$\alpha = -x_3/4.$$

When $\lambda = 3$ we are to solve

$$\begin{bmatrix} 1-3 & 1 & 5 \\ 4 & 1-3 & 3 \\ 0 & 0 & 1-3 \end{bmatrix} \begin{pmatrix} x_1 \\ x_2 \\ x_3 \end{pmatrix} = 0$$

or

$$-2x_1 + x_2 + 5x_3 = 0$$
$$4x_1 - 2x_2 + 3x_3 = 0$$
$$-2x_3 = 0.$$

Thus $x_3 = 0$ and the other equations both assert that $x_2 = 2x_1$. Hence the general eigenvector is

$$x_1(1, 2, 0)'$$

(d) In the case of the fourth matrix we have

$$\det\begin{pmatrix} 1-\lambda & 0 & 1 \\ 0 & 1-\lambda & 1 \\ 1 & 1 & 2-\lambda \end{pmatrix} = (1-\lambda)[(1-\lambda)(2-\lambda)-1]-0+1[0-(1-\lambda)]$$

$$= (1-\lambda)[(1-\lambda)(2-\lambda)-1-1]$$
$$= (1-\lambda)(\lambda^2 - 3\lambda)$$
$$= (1-\lambda)\lambda(\lambda - 3).$$

Thus $\lambda = 0, 1, 3$ are eigenvalues.
  Solving $(A - \lambda I)x = 0$ for $\lambda = 0$ gives

$$\begin{pmatrix} 1-0 & 0 & 1 \\ 0 & 1-0 & 1 \\ 1 & 1 & 2-0 \end{pmatrix}\begin{pmatrix} x_1 \\ x_2 \\ x_3 \end{pmatrix} = 0$$

or

$$x_1 + x_3 = 0$$
$$x_2 + x_3 = 0$$
$$x_1 + x_2 + 2x_3 = 0.$$

Note that the third equation is redundant, being the sum of the other two. Solving, we obtain the general form of the eigenvector as

$$x_1(1, -1, -1)'.$$

When $\lambda = 1$ we solve

$$\begin{bmatrix} 1-1 & 0 & 1 \\ 0 & 1-1 & 1 \\ 1 & 1 & 2-1 \end{bmatrix}\begin{pmatrix} x_1 \\ x_2 \\ x_3 \end{pmatrix} = 0$$

or

$$x_3 = 0$$
$$x_3 = 0$$
$$x_1 + x_2 - x_3 = 0.$$

Thus $x_3 = 0$ and the eigenvector is of the form

$$x_1(1, -1, 0)'.$$

Finally, when $\lambda = 3$ we obtain

$$\begin{bmatrix} 1-3 & 0 & 1 \\ 0 & 1-3 & 1 \\ 1 & 1 & 2-3 \end{bmatrix} \begin{pmatrix} x_1 \\ x_2 \\ x_3 \end{pmatrix} = 0$$

or

$$-2x_1 + x_3 = 0$$
$$-2x_2 + x_3 = 0$$
$$x_1 + x_2 - x_3 = 0.$$

The last equation may be obtained by adding the previous two; it is thus redundant. Solving the other two in terms of x_3 gives the eigenvector in the form

$$x_3\left(\frac{1}{2}, \frac{1}{2}, 1\right)'$$

or $\alpha(1, 1, 2)'$, where

$$\alpha = x_3/2.$$

To diagonalize the above matrices, we note that in all cases the number of eigenvalues equals the size of the matrix. Hence we put convenient eigenvectors together as the columns of P. We compute P^{-1} and obtain the following identities of the form $P^{-1}AP = $ diagonal matrix.

$$\frac{1}{2}\begin{pmatrix} 1 & -1 \\ 1 & 1 \end{pmatrix}\begin{pmatrix} 1 & 2 \\ 2 & 1 \end{pmatrix}\begin{pmatrix} 1 & 1 \\ -1 & 1 \end{pmatrix} = \begin{pmatrix} -1 & 0 \\ 0 & 3 \end{pmatrix}$$

$$\frac{1}{3}\begin{pmatrix} 2 & -1 \\ 1 & 1 \end{pmatrix}\begin{pmatrix} 1 & 1 \\ 2 & 2 \end{pmatrix}\begin{pmatrix} 1 & 1 \\ -1 & 2 \end{pmatrix} = \begin{pmatrix} 0 & 0 \\ 0 & 3 \end{pmatrix}$$

$$\frac{1}{16}\begin{pmatrix} 8 & -4 & -14 \\ 0 & 0 & -4 \\ 8 & 4 & 26 \end{pmatrix}\begin{pmatrix} 1 & 1 & 5 \\ 4 & 1 & 3 \\ 0 & 0 & 1 \end{pmatrix}\begin{pmatrix} 1 & 3 & 1 \\ -2 & 20 & 2 \\ 0 & -4 & 0 \end{pmatrix} = \begin{pmatrix} -1 & 0 & 0 \\ 0 & 1 & 0 \\ 0 & 0 & 3 \end{pmatrix}$$

$$-\frac{1}{2}\begin{pmatrix} -2 & -2 & 2 \\ 1 & 3 & -2 \\ -1 & -1 & 0 \end{pmatrix}\begin{pmatrix} 1 & 0 & 1 \\ 0 & 1 & 1 \\ 1 & 1 & 2 \end{pmatrix}\begin{pmatrix} 1 & 1 & 1 \\ -1 & -1 & 1 \\ -1 & 0 & 2 \end{pmatrix} = \begin{pmatrix} 0 & 0 & 0 \\ 0 & 1 & 0 \\ 0 & 0 & 3 \end{pmatrix}$$

3   The following are symmetric: 1(a), 1(d), 2(b), 2(c), 2(d) (table 7.2).

Table 7.2

Matrix	Eigenvalues	Definiteness
1(a)	−1, 3	Not at all
1(d)	0, 1, 3	Non-negative definite
2(b)	2, −3	Not at all
2(c)	1, 3, −4	Not at all
2(d)	0, 4, 6	Non-negative definite

For the matrix of 1(a), the eigenvectors are $(1, -1)'$ and $(1, 1)'$, which are orthogonal. Both are of length $(1^2 + 1^2)^{1/2} = \sqrt{2}$. Rescaling and letting

$$P = \begin{pmatrix} \dfrac{1}{\sqrt{2}} & \dfrac{1}{\sqrt{2}} \\ -\dfrac{1}{\sqrt{2}} & \dfrac{1}{\sqrt{2}} \end{pmatrix}$$

we see that

$$P'AP = \begin{pmatrix} -1 & 0 \\ 0 & 3 \end{pmatrix}.$$

So if $x = Py$ then the quadratic form reduces to

$$-y_1^2 + 3y_2^2.$$

Now

$$\begin{pmatrix} y_1 \\ y_2 \end{pmatrix} = P'x = \frac{1}{\sqrt{2}} \begin{pmatrix} 1 & -1 \\ 1 & 1 \end{pmatrix} \begin{pmatrix} x_1 \\ x_2 \end{pmatrix}$$

Thus $y_1 = 0$ is $x_1 - x_2 = 0$ and $y_2 = 0$ is $x_1 + x_2 = 0$ (figure 7.6).

To find the y_i axes we draw the lines through the selected eigenvectors. The hyperbola has asymptotes

$$y_2 = \pm \frac{1}{\sqrt{3}} y_1.$$

For the matrix of 2(b) the eigenvectors corresponding to $\lambda = -3$ and $\lambda = 2$ are $(-1, 2)'$ and $(2, 1)'$. Both are of length $(2^2 + 1^2)^{1/2} = \sqrt{5}$. Thus letting

$$P = \begin{pmatrix} -\dfrac{1}{\sqrt{5}} & \dfrac{2}{\sqrt{5}} \\ \dfrac{2}{\sqrt{5}} & \dfrac{1}{\sqrt{5}} \end{pmatrix}$$

we have

$$P'AP = \begin{pmatrix} -3 & 0 \\ 0 & 2 \end{pmatrix}.$$

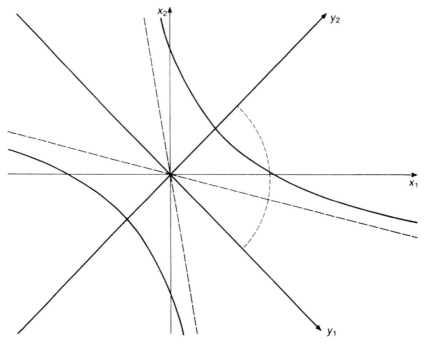

Figure 7.6 $x'Ax = 1$ for A as in question 1(a).

Thus if $Py = x$ the quadratic $x'Ax = 1$ becomes

$$-3y_1^2 + 2y_2^2 = 1.$$

We obtain the asymptotes as

$$y_2 = \pm \left(\frac{3}{2}\right)^{1/2} y_1.$$

Plotting axes through the eigenvectors we obtain figure 7.7.
   Note that

$$\begin{pmatrix} y_1 \\ y_2 \end{pmatrix} = \frac{1}{\sqrt{5}} \begin{pmatrix} -1 & 2 \\ 2 & 1 \end{pmatrix} \begin{pmatrix} x_1 \\ x_2 \end{pmatrix}.$$

5   Table 7.3 shows the results.

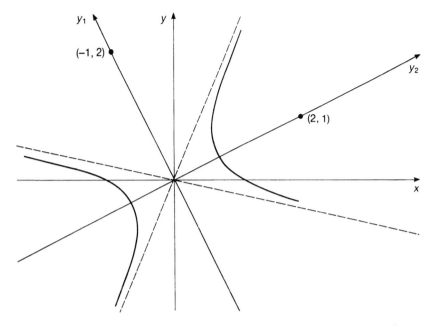

Figure 7.7 $x'Ax = 1$ for A as in question 2(b).

Table 7.3

Matrix	Characteristic	Check sign test	Principal subdeterminant test
1(a)	$\lambda^2 - 2\lambda - 3$	No	1, −3 not definite
1(d)	$-\lambda^3 + 4\lambda^2 - 3\lambda$	Yes, non-negative definite	1, 1, 0 inconclusive
2(b)	$\lambda^2 + \lambda - 6$	No	1, −6 not definite
2(c)	$-\lambda^3 + 0\lambda^2 + 13\lambda - 12$	No	1, 7, −12 not definite
2(d)	$-\lambda^3 + 2\lambda^2 - 24\lambda + 0$	Yes, non-negative definite	4, 16, 0 inconclusive

Part II

Elementary Calculus

In this part of the book we shall be interested in questions of roughly the following sort.

Given an economic model, usually in the form of a number of equations relating several quantities, what can we say about the behaviour of *one* of the quantities when another, or even several others, are changed? Alternatively, if we wish to set a target for one particular quantity (e.g. maximize profit, minimize cost or allocate a resource efficiently), how can this be achieved through selecting or controlling the values of other quantities?

Often, to answer these questions we need to derive a formula with the quantity of interest as its subject. But even when we are lucky enough to get this formula, rarely is our interest immediately gratified. Usually we want *qualitative* information, ideally a curve or graph – better still a curve annotated with numerical information. The qualitative information we seek is usually provided by *calculus* (the curve is rising, falling, it is convexly shaped etc.). We shall spend much time on extending the tools from calculus to deal with situations where there are several variables, as in the case when a firm's revenue R depends on two output commodities, produced in respective amounts q_1, q_2 say, so that

$$R = F(q_1, q_2). \tag{1}$$

Thus R is a function of two variables.

In this case it is natural to investigate the graph of the relationship (1) which is evidently a *surface* (figure 1). If the surface is cut by a vertical plane it traces out a curve in the vertical plane; for example when q_2 is held fixed (*frozen*), say with $q_2 = 1$, the curve is the graph of $R = F(q_1, 1)$ and we are back to a

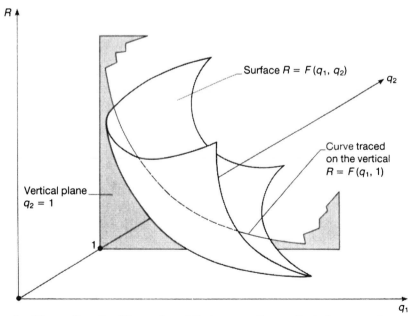

Figure 1   The surface $R = F(q_1, q_2)$ and its trace on the vertical plane $q_2 = 1$.

function of one independent variable. (We shall say that the curve is the *trace* of the surface on the vertical plane.)

We shall uncover many useful facts about surfaces by looking at their traces. In Part I we have already talked about *contours* which are obtained by cutting the surface by a horizontal plane. We shall also find uses for contours when investigating surfaces. All of this begins to sound more like geometry than economics. The bad news is that as soon as economics considers more than one independent variable, qualitative discussions *do require* geometry. But there is some good news.

1   We rarely consider more than two independent variables (and so three-dimensional diagrams can illustrate the goings on).
2   The three-dimensional arguments will be supported by two-dimensional diagrams which have an established home in elementary economics. Contours are, after all, just *isoquants*. Also the vertical traces correspond closely to what is called *partial* analysis (as opposed to *general* analysis). For example, in 'partial equilibrium analysis' (see below) one discusses just *one* commodity to establish a price at which supply balances demand. The customary procedure is to disregard substitution effects for alternative commodities; in effect all the other parts of the market are frozen.
3   The methods which we develop specifically for problems with two independent variables can easily be adapted to deal with more than two independent variables. *Corollary:* We shall usually refrain from dealing with more than two independent variables. *Exhortation:* 'Two-variable' problems can sometimes be solved with methods specific to 'one-variable' problems, but a student who is tempted to use a 'one-variable' method does himself/herself no favours unless he/she also learns how to use the more general method. Don't tempt fate!

8

Limits and their Uses

8.1 Large-scale average cost

Our objective in the examples of this chapter is to introduce the idea of 'limiting behaviour'. A qualitative statement about the actual state of an economic variable will often refer to properties that the variable exhibits approximately or only 'in the limit'. It is therefore important to understand what it is that the more descriptive, qualitative statement is saying.

We begin with a particularly simple context: large-scale average cost. The costs to a firm of producing a quantity of output q will typically fall under two headings: *fixed costs* (perhaps the sunken costs of capital equipment) which do not depend on the level of output selected and the *variable costs* which depend on the selected output q.

Let the fixed cost be k and let us model variable costs as being proportional to output. Thus

$$C(q) = vq + k \qquad (8.1)$$

where v, the constant of proportionality, is the variable cost per unit quantity produced. Our model is thus 'linear' (more properly 'affine').

Hence the average cost AC of producing q is (for $q > 0$)

$$\text{AC} = \frac{C(q)}{q} = \frac{vq + k}{q} = v + \frac{k}{q}.$$

What happens in large-scale production? Perhaps the easiest way to answer this is to draw a graph (figure 8.1). It is clear that the larger q is the nearer AC is to v; the AC curve approaches the horizontal line (asymptote) in the limit.

It is also very instructive to play at number crunching. Take $k = 1$, $v = 3$, and tabulate some very simple calculations:

$$q = 10 \qquad\qquad \text{AC} = 3.1$$
$$q = 100 \qquad\quad\; \text{AC} = 3.01$$
$$q = 1{,}000{,}000 \qquad \text{AC} = 3.000\,001$$

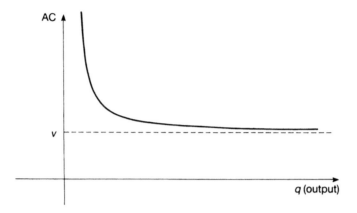

Figure 8.1 For large q average cost approaches v asymptotically.

These numbers are meant to draw your attention to a few rather obvious facts.

1 AC is approximately 3.
2 AC is never equal to 3.
3 The error committed when saying 'for large volume of output AC is 3 (to all intents and purposes)' can be quantified. For example:
   (a) the error is beyond the first decimal place provided that 'large' means 'q is at least a hundred units';
   (b) the error is beyond the fifth decimal place provided that 'large' means 'q is at least a million units'.

Obviously the words 'large scale' and 'large output' are qualitative. In our model these words are quantitively defined in each of the statements (a) and (b) but notice that they can be defined only *after* the 'smallness' of the error has been declared. In ordinary language one often talks of an error being 'negligible', or that a result is true 'to all intents and purposes'. This presupposes that one knows the 'purposes' to which a result is being put and, equally, that one knows what errors may be 'neglected'.

All of these 'ifs and buts' are swept under the carpet when we say that the limiting value of AC 'for large q' (better: 'for q tending to infinity') is 3. In symbols this is written

$$\lim_{q \to \infty} AC(q) = 3.$$

Such, then, is the hidden meaning behind the deceptively simple assertion that, in our model, v is the large-scale average cost.

A slightly more complicated example is also worth looking at. This time we suppose that the variable costs increase more rapidly when output is large than when it is small. We replace the term vq with v constant in (8.1) by $v(q)q$ to indicate that the proportionality factor $v(q)$ varies with q. The simplest idea is to have

$$v(q) = Aq + B \qquad (A, B > 0)$$

so that

$$C(q) = (Aq + B)q + k$$

and the cost is thus quadratic. We have

$$AC = \frac{C(q)}{q} = (Aq + B) + \frac{k}{q}.$$

It is clear, just as before, that the last term on the right is 'small' provided that q is 'large'. Thus the average cost in large-scale production is 'linear' (or 'affine'). This means that in our model $v(q)$ describes the large-scale average cost. Evidently (figure 8.2) the $v(q)$ curve is an asymptote of the AC curve and the asymptote is thus a good approximation of the large-scale behaviour.

8.2   Marginal costs – profitability

A second context in which 'limit behaviour' is highly informative is in checking the profitability of a production process. Let us suppose that a firm faces a quadratic cost function

$$C(q) = \frac{1}{10} q^2 + 3q + 500$$

and that current output q is 100. The market price p is currently 20. Is it desirable to increase production (assuming the market is under-supplied)?

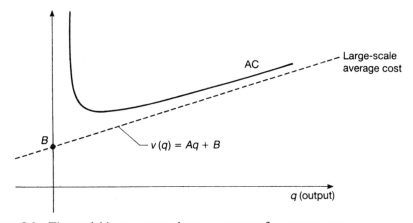

Figure 8.2   The variable cost curve is an asymptote for average cost.

Notice that the variable cost factor $v(q) = (1/10) q + 3$ makes extra production more costly. Is it therefore worth raising output?

Evidently $C(100) = 1800$ so that AC $= 18$ and hence the company is in profit. But consider the average cost not of the *whole* output, but only of a proposed *extra output* h. The average cost of raising production by h is $A(h)$ where

$$A(h) \equiv \frac{C(100 + h) - C(100)}{h} \tag{8.2}$$

$$= \left[\left(\frac{100^2}{10} + \frac{200h}{10} + \frac{h^2}{10} + 300 + 3h = 500 \right) - 1800 \right] h^{-1},$$

i.e.

$$A(h) = 23 + \frac{1}{10} h. \tag{8.3}$$

Thus the average cost is well over 23 (when $h > 0$), so that the extra output would eat into the profit (decrease it) no matter how small h was.

Just as in the example of the last section, let us tabulate $A(h)$ versus h for small h. Notice that $A(0)$ is not defined since the right-hand side of (8.2) would not be meaningful for $h = 0$ (even though (8.3) is!).

$h = 1$	$A(h) = 23.1$
$h = 0.1$	$A(h) = 23.01$
$h = 0.000\ 1$	$A(h) = 23.000\ 1$

The average cost of production in the limit for h tending to zero is 23. The calculations here may be interpreted as saying that 'at the margin of $q = 100$' the production cost is 23. This tells us that the hundredth unit produced is not bringing in profit.

Generally, if the limiting value of the average cost

$$\frac{C(q + h) - C(q)}{h} \qquad (h \neq 0)$$

is well defined, then the limiting value is called the *marginal cost* of q (or the marginal cost of the qth unit).

Evidently, this is the derivative $C'(q)$ and hence is the slope of the cost curve at the corresponding output level q (figure 8.3). Figure 8.3 also serves to remind us that the slope of the curve at E is in fact the limit of the slopes of the chords EF_h as F_h approaches E. In our example

$$C'(q) = \frac{2}{10} q + 3.$$

Thus the qth unit is profitable only if $C'(q) \leqslant 20$, i.e.

$$\frac{1}{5} q + 3 \leqslant 20 \qquad \text{or} \qquad q \leqslant 17 \times 5 = 85.$$

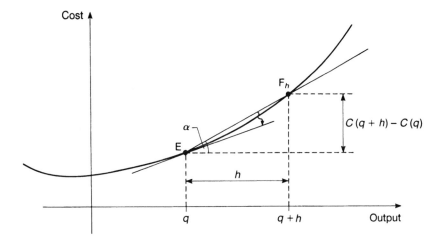

Figure 8.3   The slope of the chord is tan $\alpha = A(h)$, i.e. the average cost of the extra output h. The marginal cost is the limit of the chordal slopes as F_h approaches E, i.e. the slope of the tangent line at E.

8.3   Definition of a limit

This section is merely a formality and may be omitted. It will make profitable reading only if you have fully understood the hand-waving intuitive arguments in the earlier sections. But if you are blind to intuitive parley . . . , then perhaps a purely formal approach might help after all.

In both the earlier sections we were interested in the values $f(x)$ of a chosen function when the variable x was made to behave in a certain way. Thus in section 8.1 x was q and was made to grow indefinitely large: we therefore said that x was tending to infinity (but of course x could not be 'infinity'). In section 8.2 x was h and was made to approach zero (but was not permitted to be zero).

In both sections we referred to the function values and showed that they were close to being a certain value known as 'the limit'. We shall give a formal definition of the formula

$$\lim_{x \to a} f(x) = l$$

where a and l may be either fixed numerical values or the symbol ∞. We split this into a number of steps. The definitions will all sound somewhat legalistic.

Definition of

$$\lim_{x \to \infty} f(x) = l \qquad \text{(when } l \neq \infty) \qquad (8.4)$$

The words below are supposed to say that $f(x)$ will be approximately l 'for all x large enough'. (The problem lies in giving meaning to 'approximately' and to 'large enough'; approximation of course calls for specifying the degree of accuracy.)

To any declaration fixing a decimal position, there corresponds a value X such that for all $x \geq X$ the value $f(x)$ agrees with l at least up to the declared decimal position (figure 8.4).

This says that the graph of $f(x)$ fits into the demanded band when x is restricted to the right of X.

Definition of

$$\lim_{x \to 0} f(x) = l \qquad (\text{when } l \neq \infty) \qquad (8.5)$$

This time we need to say that $f(x)$ is approximately l 'for all x small enough'. Again we need to give meaning to 'approximately' and to 'small enough'.

To any declaration fixing a decimal position there corresponds a value H such that for all $x \neq 0$ with $-H \leq x \leq H$ the value $f(x)$ agrees with l at least up to the declared decimal position (figure 8.5).

This says that the graph of $f(x)$ fits into the demanded band when x is restricted suitably to the left and right of zero. Notice that the statement amounts to finding a measure of closeness between x and zero appropriate to the demanded accuracy.

We can extend definition (8.5) by considering $g(h) = f(a + h)$. Thus

$$\lim_{h \to 0} g(h) = l$$

is then the same assertion as

$$\lim_{x \to a} f(x) = l. \qquad (8.6)$$

This says that the graph of $f(x)$ fits into the demanded band when x is restricted suitably to the left and right of a.

For completeness we have to define the meaning of

$$\lim_{x \to \infty} f(x) = \infty. \qquad (8.7)$$

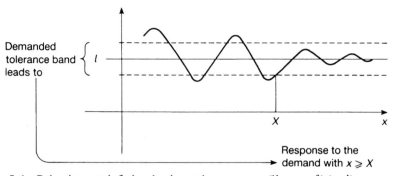

Figure 8.4 Behaviour at infinity: horizontal asymptote ($\lim_{x \to \infty} f(x) = l$).

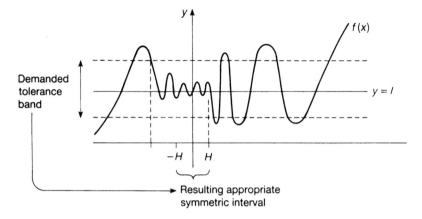

Figure 8.5 Behaviour at the origin ($\lim_{x \to 0} f(x) = l$).

This is supposed to say that $f(x)$ will be as large as we demand provided that x is large enough. We leave legalistic issues as an exercise. The hint is in figure 8.6.

Finally we have to define, for $a \neq \infty$,

$$\lim_{x \to a} f(x) = \infty. \tag{8.8}$$

This is like saying that f has a vertical asymptote at $x = a$ (see figure 8.7 for the implied definition). Since no number appears on the right-hand side of (8.8), only the infinity symbol, it is possible to say that in fact the limit does not exist (compare section 9.6).

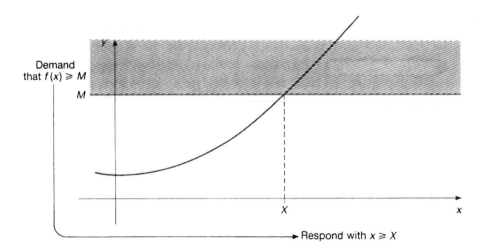

Figure 8.6 Unbounded at infinity: definition of $\lim_{x \to \infty} f(x) = \infty$.

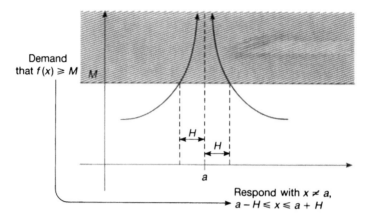

Figure 8.7 Vertical asymptote: definition of $\lim_{x \to a} f(x) = \infty$.

8.4 Exercises

1* If $C = 3q + 5$ how large must q be if $AC \approx 3$ to four places of decimal?

2 How small must q be if

(a) $q^2 \approx 0$ to four places of decimal,
(b) $15q^2 \approx 0$ to four places of decimal?

3* Suppose the proportionality factor in the variable costs of a firm is $v(q) = Aq + B$. Explain why $A, B > 0$. [*Hint*: For small enough q assume $q^2 \approx 0$ (cf. question 2); for large enough q assume $B/q \approx 0$ (cf. question 1).]

4 A firm faces a cost function $C(q) = (Aq + B)q + k$. Currently the demanded output is Q. Write down the condition on the selling price p which ensures that (a) the firm is making a profit and (b) the firm's marginal cost is above p. Show that a selling price can be announced at which the firm is below marginal cost and bringing in profit whenever $AQ^2 > k$. Check that this last condition holds in the model of section 8.2. Construct another such model with $p = 25$.

5* How small must h be if $8h \approx 0$ and $h^2 \approx 0$ each to five places of decimal? How accurate an approximation x is needed for π to ensure that $x^2 \approx \pi^2$ to four places of decimal? Note that here π denotes the ratio of a circle's perimeter to its diameter. [*Hint*: If $\pi = x + h$, then $\pi^2 = x^2 + 2xh + h^2$.]

6 Show that if $0 < r < 1$ then $r > r^2 > r^3 > r^4 > \cdots$ but that if $r > 1$ then $r < r^2 < r^3 < r^4 < \cdots$.

7 This exercise addresses the question if $0 < r < 1$ how large must n be to obtain $r^n \approx 0$ to, for example, five places of decimal (see section 4.6):

(a) when $r = 0.1$,
(b) when $r = 0.2$,
(c) when $r = 0.4$ [*Hint*: $0.4^4 < 0.2$],
(d) when $r = 0.9$ [*Hint*: $0.9^9 < 0.4$].

Use induction (section 4.3) to show that, if $x \geqslant 0$, then $(1 + x)^n \geqslant 1 + nx$ (for $n = 0, 1, 2, \ldots$). Deduce that if $r > 1$ then $r \to \infty$ when $n \to \infty$. [*Hint*: Put $r = 1 + x$.]

Also show that if $x > 0$ then

$$\left(\frac{1}{1+x}\right)^n \leqslant \frac{1}{1+nx}.$$

By considering $r = 1/(1 + x)$ show that if $0 < r < 1$ then $r^n \to 0$ when $n \to \infty$.

8   Recall the sum of the geometric progression (section 4.2):

$$1 + x + x^2 + x^3 + \cdots + x^n = \frac{1 - x^{n+1}}{1 - x}.$$

Deduce that if $|x| < 1$ then the sum to infinity of this progression is

$$1 + x + x^2 + x^3 + \cdots + x^n + \cdots = \frac{1}{1 - x}.$$

Note that if $x > 1$ the terms of the progression become unboundedly large. What happens when (a) $x = -1$ and (b) $x < -1$?

8.5   Answers

1   $C = 3q + 5$ and so $AC = 3 + (5/q)$. We want $AC \approx 3.0000$ to four places of decimal and so $5/q$ must contribute less than 0.0001, i.e. $5/q < 1/10{,}000$ or $q > 10{,}000/5 = 2000$.

3   Here $C(q) = Aq^2 + Bq + k$ where k is the fixed cost. For small q we have $C(q) \approx Bq + k$. Cost must increase with output and so we require $B > 0$. For large q we have $C(q) = Aq^2\{1 + B/q + k/q^2\} \approx Aq^2$ and the cost must remain positive; therefore $A > 0$.

5   To have $8h \approx 0.000\,00$ (five places) we need $8h < 0.000\,01$, and so $h < 0.000\,001\,25$. It will do if $h \approx 0.000\,000$ (six places). To have $h^2 < 0.000\,01$ we note that $(0.1)^2 = 0.01$, $(0.01)^2 = 0.0001$, $(0.001)^2 = 0.000\,001$; thus we need $h < 0.001$. To meet both conditions, it is enough to meet the first. If $\pi = x + h$ then $\pi^2 = x^2 + 2xh + h^2$. For $\pi^2 \approx x^2$ to four places we need $2xh + h^2 \approx 0$ to four places. If $2xh \approx 0$ to five places and $h^2 \approx 0$ to five places then $h^2 + 2xh \approx 0$ to four places. (Note that $0.000\,009 + 0.000\,009 = 0.000\,018$.). With $x < 4$ (since $\pi \approx 3.1$ to one place) we shall be satisfied if $2xh < 8h \approx 0$ to five places. So we need to have π accurate to six places.

9

Continuity and its Uses

9.1 The continuity condition

Let us look back to the computation of the limit occurring in section 8.2. We were interested in

$$\lim_{h \to 0} A(h)$$

where

$$A(h) = \frac{C(q + h) - C(q)}{h}.$$

We noted that $A(0)$ was undefined. However, we saw that for $h \neq 0$

$$A(h) = 23 + \frac{1}{10} h.$$

Now the expression $B(h) = 23 + (1/10)h$ is defined for $h = 0$ and we recognize that

$$\lim_{h \to 0} B(h) = 23 = B(0),$$

which is a rather obvious fact.

If $F(q)$ is a function defined in an interval around $q = Q$ we say that $F(q)$ is 'continuous at $q = Q$' when

$$\lim_{q \to Q} F(q) = F(Q). \tag{9.1}$$

Thus $B(h)$ is continuous at $h = 0$, whereas $A(h)$, since it is not even defined at $h = 0$, is *not* continuous at $h = 0$.

Clearly continuity is a desirable condition when we compute limits. Unfortunately it does not always necessarily hold in economically interesting contexts as the discontinuous examples in the next sections show. However, many functions with which we work in economics satisfy the continuity condition (9.1) at almost all points. The functions which satisfy (9.1) at *all* points include polynomials, sines, cosines, exponentials and logarithms (the latter for positive arguments only).

It is worth pointing out immediately that we often assume continuity – perhaps unwittingly – in quite standard calculations. For example, to compute π^2 (whether by hand or on a calculator), where $\pi = 3.141\,5\ldots$, we make use of a more or less accurate approximation ξ to π (e.g. one to eight figure accuracy) and calculate ξ^2 instead of π^2 itself. This implicitly calls upon the continuity of $f(x) = x^2$ at $x = \pi$; indeed the formula

$$\pi^2 = f(\pi) = \lim_{x \to \pi} x^2$$

asserts that for x close enough to π we shall have x^2 close to π^2 within a demanded accuracy.

9.2   Discontinuous cost function

It is well known that international calls via an operator are charged according to a tariff such as that represented graphically in figure 9.1 (i.e. there is a 3

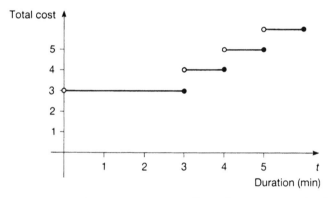

Figure 9.1   Call charges via the operator are discontinuous: ●, attained value; ○, unattained value.

minute minimum; after that charges are by the minute, part of a minute being rounded up to the next minute). The cost curve has breaks and it is natural to say it is *discontinuous*, with discontinuities occurring at $t = 0, 3, 4, 5, \ldots$. The latter are the times at which the cost curve breaks and where immediately after the break the cost rises. Similar situations abound (mail charges, specialist fees etc.).

9.3   Discontinuous stock function

A similar phenomenon occurs in inventory control problems (which we shall study later). A firm may order a fixed quantity of a commodity which it sells. Suppose the annual demand is D and restocking is proposed after complete depletion of stock with the unit cost of storage being d per annum. Assuming a constant rate of depletion and a reordering cost of e, the firm must decide on the regular order size x and the number of times y per annum that the order is to be placed. Evidently $xy = D$, and the graph showing stock versus time is given in figure 9.2.

Although we do not solve this problem here we note that the average stock-holding is $\frac{1}{2}x$; hence the firm faces a cost

$$C = \frac{1}{2}xd + ye$$

and this needs to be minimized subject to $xy = D$.

9.4   Right-sided and left-sided limits

In both examples we can give a precise mathematical statement of the discontinuity or break which features in the graph. For instance, in the case of telephone costs we can say that as t approaches 3 from the left the cost C is 3, whereas as t approaches 3 from the right (i.e. through bigger values) the limiting cost is 4 (figure 9.3). We write this symbolically thus:

$$C(t) \to 3 \quad \text{as} \quad t \to 3-$$

and

$$C(t) \to 4 \quad \text{as} \quad t \to 3+$$

or alternatively

$$\lim_{t \to 3-} C(t) = 3 \quad \text{and} \quad \lim_{t \to 3+} C(t) = 4.$$

The left-sided limiting value of the cost is 3 (which happens also to be the value of $C(3)$) whereas the right-sided limiting value of the cost is 4, so that condition (9.1) of section 9.1 is violated.

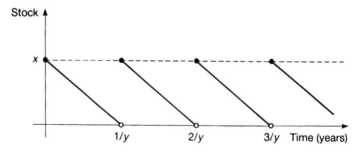

Figure 9.2   Stock chart (goods are ordered y times in a year so the orders arrive at $t = 0, 1/y, 2/y, \ldots, (y - 1)/y$ during the first year): ●, attained value.

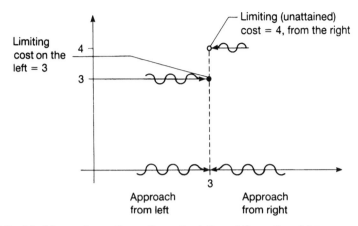

Figure 9.3   Limiting values of cost from the left and from the right.

In the example of section 9.3 suppose that $x = 1$, $y = 2$. There is a discontinuity for $t = 1/2$ and we see that, if $S(t)$ denotes stock at time t,

$$\lim_{t \to 1/2 -} S(t) = 0 \qquad \text{and} \qquad \lim_{t \to 1/2 +} S(t) = 1$$

(figure 9.4).

9.5   Importance of continuity in economic models

We should not have been examining this topic for so long if it were not for the following two crucial properties of continuous functions.

(a)   If $f(x)$ is continuous on the interval $[c, d]$ then $f(x)$ takes on a maximum and a minimum value in $[c, d]$.

This result is fundamental to all optimization work.

(b)   If $f(x)$ is continuous on the interval $[c, d]$ and $f(c) > 0$, whereas $f(d) < 0$, then for some x in the interval, say $x = t$, we have $f(t) = 0$.

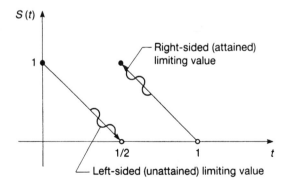

Figure 9.4   Left- and right-sided limits on the stock chart when $x = 1$ and $y = 2$.

This result lies behind the simple argument given in support of market equilibrium, presuming as it does the existence of an intersection of the supply and demand curves. Writing f for the excess demand function, we have

$$f(p) = Q_d(p) - Q_s(p)$$

where $q = Q_d(p)$ is the quantity demanded and $q = Q_s(p)$ is the quantity supplied when the price p prevails (figure 9.5) (see section 5.6, where $Q_d(p)$ is denoted by $e(p)$, and section 5.7). Suppose $f(c) > 0$ and $f(d) < 0$; then provided that $f(p)$ is continuous, we have for some $\bar{p}$ in $[c, d]$ that $f(\bar{p}) = 0$, i.e. $Q_d(\bar{p}) = Q_s(\bar{p})$. Thus if the commodity is over-demanded at low prices and over-supplied at high prices an equilibrium price will exist, at least if we assume that the supply and demand functions are continuous.

The assumption of continuity is important; the functions graphed in figure 9.6 fail to have property (a). See also section 9.7, question 12.

It is perhaps worth considering how formula (9.1) bears on the second property (b). To be specific, suppose $c = 0$, $d = 1$, so that $f(0) > 0$ and $f(1) < 0$. We apply a kind of search algorithm to find a root of f in $[0, 1]$. We test $f(0.5)$. If 0.5 is not the root, then say $f(0.5) > 0$. We now expect to find the root in $[0.5, 1]$ since $f(0.5) > 0$ and $f(1) < 0$. We test $f(0.75)$ for sign. Suppose $f(0.75) < 0$. Then we look for the root in $[0.5, 0.75]$. The process continues, halving the search interval at each stage. Eventually (once the interval is less than $1/10$) the left-hand and right-hand endpoints agree in the first place of decimal. After more steps, when the interval is of length less than $1/100$, the endpoints agree in their second place of decimal. The process thus generates a decimal expansion of a number:

$$t = 0.t_1\, t_2\, t_3 \ldots .$$

It must be that $f(t) = 0$. Suppose instead $f(t) > 0$. For example suppose $f(t) = 0.001$. But for x close enough to t we have $f(x) \approx f(t)$ to three places of decimal and hence $f(x) > 0$. Suppose that 'close enough' means x and t have to agree on the first five places of decimal. Consider the search intervals of size less than $1/100,000$ which contain t. Since both endpoints agree with t on the first five decimal places, f must be positive at both endpoints, a contradiction.

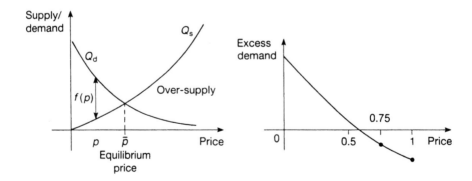

Figure 9.5   Narrowing down the search for zero excess demand.

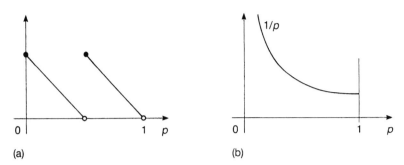

(a) (b)

Figure 9.6 (a) There is no achieved minimum; (b) the function is not defined at the origin and there is no achieved maximum.

9.6 Calculation of limits

Before attempting any examples we state (without proof) some rules concerning limits. In all these rules the limits l and k are supposed to be numerical values and the symbol '∞' is precluded as a value for l or k.

Combination Rule

If

$$\lim_{x \to a} f(x) = l \quad \text{and} \quad \lim_{x \to a} g(x) = k$$

then for any numbers α, β

$$\lim_{x \to a} [\alpha f(x) + \beta g(x)] = \alpha l + \beta k.$$

Product Rule

If

$$\lim_{x \to a} f(x) = l \quad \text{and} \quad \lim_{x \to a} g(x) = k$$

then

$$\lim_{x \to a} f(x)g(x) = lk.$$

This tells us that combinations and products of continuous functions are again continuous functions.

These two rules plus the obvious result that

$$\lim_{x \to a} x = a$$

(literally $x \to a$ as $x \to a$) may be applied several times over to confirm the continuity of any polynomial. Consider, for example, $f(x) = 2x^2 + 3x + 4$.

Evidently $p(x) \equiv 4$ (a constant polynomial) is continuous, and so $3x + 4$ is continuous by the combination rule. Also $x^2 = xx$ is continuous by the product rule; so $2(x^2) + (3x + 4)$ is continuous, again by the combination rule.

The next rule allows us to decide under what circumstances rational functions are continuous on an interval $[c, d]$.

Quotient Rule

If

$$\lim_{x \to a} f(x) = k \quad and \quad \lim_{x \to a} g(x) = l \quad and \quad l \neq 0,$$

then

$$\lim_{x \to a} \frac{f(x)}{g(x)} = \frac{k}{l}.$$

Thus if $Q(x)$ is a polynomial which does not vanish in the interval $[c, d]$, then the rational function

$$\frac{P(x)}{Q(x)}$$

is continuous on $[c, d]$. Here $P(x)$ is any polynomial. In words, division by zero is excluded in this rule.

The rules can be used intelligently to deal even with cases where l or k is infinity. We work a few examples.

Example
1   Show that

$$\lim_{x \to 0} \frac{x^2 + 5x + 2}{x^2 - 6x + 9} = \frac{2}{9}.$$

The numerator tends to 2 and the denominator tends to 9 and so the result follows from the quotient rule.

2   Show that

$$\lim_{x \to \infty} \frac{x^2 + 5x + 2}{x^2 - 6x + 9} = 1.$$

The crucial idea here is to realize that for large x the numerator is essentially x^2. Indeed

$$x^2 + 5x + 2 = x^2 \left(1 + \frac{5}{x} + \frac{2}{x^2}\right)$$

and the term in parentheses is close to unity for large x. A similar idea applies to the denominator. Thus we have for $x \neq 0$

$$\frac{x^2 + 5x + 2}{x^2 - 6x + 9} = \frac{x^2\{1 + 5/x + 2/x^2\}}{x^2\{1 - 6/x + 9/x^2\}} = \frac{1 + 5/x + 2/x^2}{1 - 6/x + 9/x^2}.$$

In the last expression the numerator tends to 1 since $\lim 5/x = 0$ and $\lim 2/x^2 = 0$ (as x tends to infinity). The denominator likewise tends to 1. Now use the quotient rule (with $k = l = 1$) to complete the problem. Also note that carrying out the implied division we have

$$\frac{x^2 + 5x + 2}{x^2 - 6x + 9} = \frac{x^2 - 6x + 9 + (11x - 7)}{x^2 - 6x + 9} = 1 + \frac{11x - 7}{x^2 - 6x + 9} \approx 1 + \frac{11x}{x^2}.$$

3   Examine for continuity at $x = 3$ the rational function

$$f(x) = \frac{x^2 + 5x + 2}{x^2 - 6x + 9}.$$

We observe that the denominator $Q(x) = (x - 3)^2$, and so $\lim_{x \to 3} Q(x) = 0$ whereas $\lim_{x \to 3} P(x) = 9 + 15 + 2 = 26$.

Since division by zero is not valid it follows that f is not defined at $x = 3$. Moreover, since $Q(x)$ is small and positive for x close to 3, $f(x)$ is then large and positive; indeed it is approximately $26/Q(x)$ when x is close to 3 (but note that x is not actually allowed to equal 3). Thus the left- and right-sided limits do not exist; the function $f(x)$ is thus not continuous at $x = 3$.

We have already seen in example 1 that $f(x)$ is close to unity for large values of x. Before plotting a graph of f a word of explanation is required: the three limit rules which we have quoted above are also true for one-sided limits such as $\lim_{x \to a+}$ and $\lim_{x \to a-}$; they are likewise true for the limits $\lim_{x \to \infty}$ and

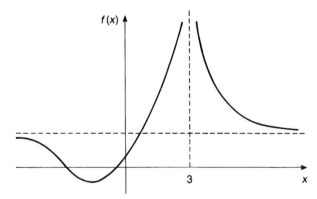

Figure 9.7 $f(x)$ undefined at $x = 3$ and there are no left-sided or right-sided limits.

$$f(x) = \frac{x^2 + 5x + 2}{x^2 - 6x + 9}.$$

$\lim_{x \to -\infty}$. Applying them here shows us that f tends to unity as $x \to \pm\infty$ (figure 9.7). (*Puzzle*: Why is the horizontal asymptote approached from below as $x \to -\infty$?)

9.7   Exercises

1*   Define $f: \mathbb{R} \to \mathbb{R}$ by $f(x) = n$, where n is the greatest integer less than or equal to x. Thus the function describes the process of rounding down to the nearest integer below or equal to x. Graph f for $-2 \leqslant x \leqslant 2$ and discuss its discontinuities. This function is commonly written $[x]$.

2   Graph $x - [x]$, $[1 - x]$, $1 - [x]$, $[2^x]$ and discuss their discontinuities.

3*   Examine for continuity

$$f(x) = \frac{2x + 50}{x - 5}.$$

4   The supply function for a commodity is given by

$$S(p) = \frac{90p + 100}{p + 10} \qquad (p > 0).$$

Find and interpret the limits

$$\lim_{p \to 0+} S(p) \qquad \lim_{p \to \infty} S(p).$$

5*   Find

$$\lim_{x \to 5} \frac{x^2 - 25}{3x - 15}.$$

6   Find

$$\lim_{x \to 2-} \frac{x^2 + 1}{x^2 - x - 2}.$$

7*   The probability distribution function $f(t)$ (see chapter 5, p. 138) based on a sample of distinct numbers x_1, x_2, x_3 is defined by

$$f(t) = \frac{\text{no of indices } i \text{ with } x_i \leqslant t}{3}.$$

Draw a graph of f. [*Hint*: Assume $x_1 < x_2 < x_3$.]

8   Repeat the previous question when the sample is enlarged to x_1, x_2, x_3, x_4.

9*   Find

$$\lim_{t \to \infty} \frac{2^t - 1}{2^t + 1}.$$

[*Hint*: Carry out the implied division (compare section 9.6, example 2).]

10   Find

$$\lim_{x \to \infty} \frac{2^x - 2^{-x}}{2^x + 2^{-x}}.$$

[*Hint*: $t = 2x$ and use the last question.]

11   Do the following limits exist?

$$\lim_{t \to 1} \frac{t^2 - 1}{t - 1} \qquad \lim_{t \to 1} \frac{t^2 - 1}{t^2 - 2t + 1} \qquad \lim_{t \to 1} \frac{t^3 - t^2 - t + 1}{t^2 - 2t + 1}.$$

12   A worker is paid \$10 per hour for the first 8 hours and at time-and-a-half rate (i.e. \$15) for overtime. Derive a formula for the wages owed after time x on the assumption that (a) wages per part of an hour begun are paid pro rata (i.e. proportionally to the time worked), (b) wages per part of an hour begun are paid as for the whole hour.

13   In the inventory problem of section 9.3 suppose that, just as before, the demand for the commodity is constant but that the firm does not restock immediately on depletion of stock. Instead suppose the firm waits for demand (order backlog) to reach a fixed level z and then restocks with quantity $x + z$, of which z (the backlog) is despatched immediately to customers. Draw the new graph for stock.

14   Show that $f(x) = x^3 + 2x^2 + 3x + 4$ is continuous.

15   If the cost function is $C(q) = 1 + |q - 2|$, find MC(3). Investigate $\lim_{h \to 0+} A(h)$ and $\lim_{h \to 0-} A(h)$ for $q = 2$ where $A(h)$ is defined as in section 9.1.

16   Draw graphs of a supply and a demand function which do not give rise to a market equilibrium.

9.8   Answers

1   The discontinuities on $-2 \leqslant x \leqslant 2$ occur at $x = -1, 0, 1, 2$ (figure 9.8). The function is discontinuous from the left (since the limiting value from the left is not attained) but continuous from the right.

3   Provided that $x \neq 5$ the function is continuous. As x approaches 5 from below, the numerator is about $2 \times 5 + 50 = 60$ and the denominator is small and negative. The function takes on negative values unboundedly. (The 'limit' of $f(x)$ is $-\infty$.) As x approaches 5 from above, the numerator as before is about 60 whereas the denominator is small and positive. The function can take arbitrarily large positive values when x is nearly 5. The function is discontinuous from both left and right at $x = 5$ and is not defined for $x = 5$.

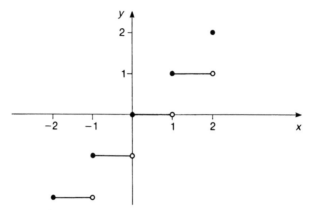

Figure 9.8 Graph of [x].

5 When $x \neq 5$ we may perform a cancellation:

$$\frac{x^2 - 25}{3x - 15} = \frac{(x - 5)(x + 5)}{3(x - 5)} = \frac{x + 5}{3}.$$

The rightmost expression tends to 10/3 as x approaches 5.

7 Without loss of generality we take $x_1 < x_2 < x_3$ (figure 9.9). If x_1, x_2, x_3 are in a different order the discontinuity points on the axis will be, from left to right, least x_i, middle x_i, largest x_i.

9

$$\frac{2^t - 1}{2^t + 1} = 1 - \frac{2}{2^t + 1}$$

Hence as t grows large, the second term becomes small and so the limiting value of the given expression is 1.

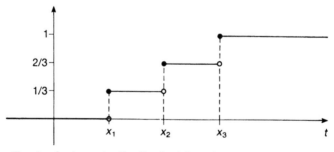

Figure 9.9 Graph of a 'sample distribution' function.

10

Uses of the Derivative

10.1 Instantaneous market indicators

In this chapter we shall learn about two quite distinct roles played by the derivative. The present section dwells on a couple of applications of the same ilk as that of section 8.2 where we used marginal cost to assess profitability of production. An analogy should be made with notions in physics. Speed, such as is indicated on a car's dashboard, is an instantaneous average (increment in distance over a small increment in time) and acts as a guide for the driver to determine such things as whether his trip is running on time and what the estimated time of arrival might be.

Economic activity may likewise be monitored by reference to instantaneous averages, i.e. by observing what effects small changes have. We look at two examples.

Example 1: Elasticity (revision of the product rule)
Our example will make use of the product rule in differentiation which we recall here:

$$\frac{\mathrm{d}}{\mathrm{d}x}(uv) = u'v + uv'.$$

A natural problem for a firm is to consider the effect on revenue of an increase in price. Though the demand itself may be expected to fall the revenue might well either (a) increase, (b) stay put or (c) even decrease, depending on how fast demand declines. In situation (c) demand is said to be *elastic* while in situation (a) it is said to be *inelastic*. The choice of terms may be explained by imagining a string connecting price and revenue and referring to the behaviour of the string when price induces a change in revenue (figure 10.1).

We know that revenue $R = pq = pQ_{\mathrm{d}}(p)$ where $Q_{\mathrm{d}}(p)$ is the quantity of commodity demanded when its price is p (see section 5.6, where $Q_{\mathrm{d}}(p)$ is denoted by $e(p)$, and section 5.7). So

$$\frac{\mathrm{d}R}{\mathrm{d}p} = Q_{\mathrm{d}}(p) + pQ_{\mathrm{d}}'(p) = q + p\frac{\mathrm{d}q}{\mathrm{d}p}.$$

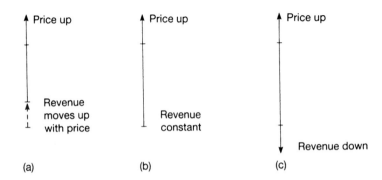

Figure 10.1   (a) Inelastic response; (c) elastic response.

Thus $dR/dp > 0$ if and only if

$$p\frac{dq}{dp} > -q,$$

i.e.

$$-\frac{p}{q}\frac{dq}{dp} < 1 \qquad (\text{as } q > 0).$$

Since the demand curve is downward sloping, $dq/dp < 0$ (figure 10.2) (this is revised in sections 10.3 and 10.5), we see that demand is inelastic if the absolute value of the quantity

$$\varepsilon_d = \frac{p}{q}\frac{dq}{dp}$$

is less than unity. This quantity is known as the 'price elasticity of demand'. Thus small elasticity describes inelasticity, as might be expected. It is when elasticity is greater than unity in absolute value that the demand is elastic.

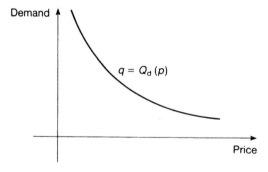

Figure 10.2   Decreasing demand — the slope dq/dp is negative

Caution

Economists as a rule do not use the terms 'elastic' and 'inelastic' with a strict division of the elasticity condition at unity. They will usually apply the term 'elastic' vaguely when elasticity is very much larger than unity. Similarly the term 'inelastic' will be applied when elasticity is small – near zero.

Two points are worth noting. Rewriting

$$\varepsilon_d = \frac{dq}{dp} \bigg/ \frac{q}{p} \qquad (10.1)$$

we see a ratio of the *marginal* demand to the *average* demand. The other point is that, for small increases δp in price, if $\delta q = Q_d(p + \delta p) - Q_d(p)$ we have

$$\frac{dq}{dp} \approx \frac{\delta q}{\delta p},$$

and so

$$\varepsilon_d \approx \frac{\delta q/q}{\delta p/p} \qquad (10.2)$$

which is a ratio of proportionate (and so of percentage) changes in q and p. Thus an elasticity of 2 (more precisely -2) signifies that a 1 per cent price rise entails a 2 per cent fall in demand, and since demand is elastic a fall in revenue occurs.

Remark 1

The right-hand side of (10.1) involves a derivative, i.e. the slope of the tangent to the demand curve at (p, q). It is therefore sometimes called a 'point elasticity' to distinguish it from the quantity on the right-hand side of (10.2). The latter involves the slope of a chord (that joining (p, q) to $(p + \delta p, q + \delta q)$) and is thus a 'chordal elasticity'. It is in fact called a 'line elasticity'. The closeness of the two (see section 10.4) enables us to determine market responses to price changes quickly.

Remark 2

There is a particularly simple geometric argument which enables us to check whether or not a demand curve exhibits elasticity. Rewrite the condition for elasticity as

$$q' < -q/p.$$

The quantity q/p is easily identified as the slope of the line from the origin to (p, q). The mirror image of that line about the horizontal through (p, q) thus has slope $-q/p$ (figure 10.3).

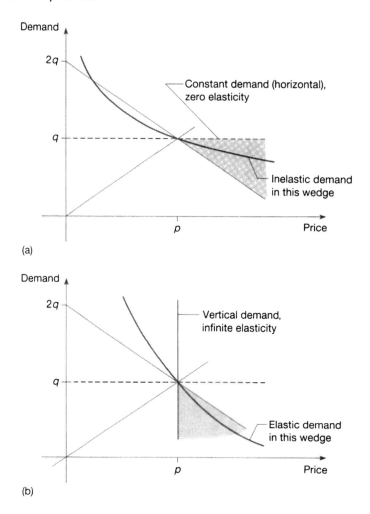

Figure 10.3 (a) Demand falls slowly; (b) demand falls rapidly enough at p to cause a fall in revenue.

Example 2: Elasticity of a linear demand
Suppose $Q(p) = A - Bp$, where A, $B > 0$ and $0 \leqslant p \leqslant A/B$ (see figure 10.4). Since $dq/dp = -B$ we have

$$\varepsilon_d = -B \left| \frac{q}{p} \right. = \frac{-Bp}{A - Bp} .$$

Thus for very low prices ε_d is nearly zero whereas for large admissible prices (i.e. those close to A/B) ε_d is very large (in magnitude). The transition from inelastic to elastic demand occurs when $\varepsilon_d = -1$ whereupon $Bp = A - Bp$, i.e. $p = \frac{1}{2}(A/B)$. That this is halfway to the maximum price is obvious on the basis of the geometric argument of remark 2 above.

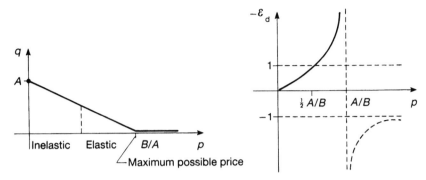

Figure 10.4 Linear demand and its elasticity (graph of $Bp/(A - Bp)$).

Suppose that, in fact, the demand is

$$q = 1000 - \frac{1}{2}p.$$

Then

$$\varepsilon_d = \frac{-\frac{1}{2}p}{1000 - \frac{1}{2}p}.$$

What is the market response to a 5 per cent price change when $p = 500$? In this case

$$\varepsilon_d = \frac{-250}{750} = -\frac{1}{3} \approx -0.33,$$

and so the demand is inelastic (revenue will rise). The demand declines by about 1.6 per cent since

$$\frac{\delta q}{q} \approx \varepsilon_d \frac{\delta p}{p}.$$

We notice that in this example elasticity increases with price. This is in fact true of a wider class of models as we go on to show in the next example.

Warning

In the last example demand is eventually elastic. Such a property might be thought to hold generally: if only it did! A simple decaying 'inverse power' demand exhibits *constant* elasticity; the constant may of course be less than unity (i.e. demand is then constantly inelastic). See section 10.7, question 9.

Example 3: Concave demand functions have increasing elasticity
In the last example we saw that elasticity was (in absolute value) an increasing

function. It is a simple exercise in differentiation to show that this is always the case for a concave demand function. We recall the quotient rule:

$$\frac{d}{dx}\left(\frac{u}{v}\right) = \frac{u'v - uv'}{v^2}.$$

Denoting the absolute value of the elasticity by η we have

$$\eta = -\frac{pq'}{q}.$$

Hence, differentiating with respect to p,

$$\eta' = -\frac{(q' + pq'')q - (pq')q'}{q^2}.$$

Thus $\eta' > 0$ if and only if

$$q' + pq'' < p\frac{q'^2}{q} = q'(-\eta)$$

or

$$pq'' < (-q')(1 + \eta). \tag{10.3}$$

But the left-hand side is negative (since a concave function has negative second derivative), whereas the right-hand side is positive (since $q' < 0$).

Remark

Although the converse statement is certainly *not* true (see section 10.8, question 10) the argument above gives a complementary result: if the elasticity is a decreasing function then necessarily the demand function is convex. (The reverse inequality to (10.3) shows $q'' > 0$.)

Example 4: Behaviour of average cost
We compared average cost AC with marginal cost MC in section 8.2. We can take the story a little further if we invoke the quotient rule. As before let $C(q)$ denote the cost of producing an output q. Thus

$$AC = C(q)/q$$

and, differentiating, we have

$$\frac{d}{dq}(AC) \equiv AC' = \frac{C'(q)q - C(q)}{q^2}.$$

Hence

$$qAC' = C'(q) - \frac{C(q)}{q}$$
$$= MC - AC.$$

For $q > 0$ we deduce that AC declines (i.e. has downward slope, equivalently AC$' < 0$) when MC $<$ AC. Contrarily, AC rises (has upward slope, or AC$' > 0$) when AC is below MC. Notice that AC is stationary (AC$' = 0$) when AC $=$ MC.

This is illustrated in figure 10.5. In figure 10.5(a) we have used the second model of section 8.1 where the marginal cost is linear. For 10.5(b) with a U-shaped MC we evidently need MC to be quadratic and hence C must be cubic (i.e. the variable cost factor is quadratic). See also section 14.8.

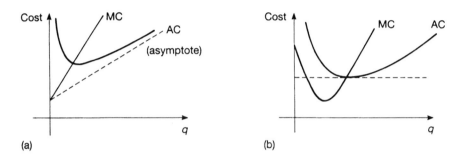

Figure 10.5 Behaviour of average cost: (a) linear MC; (b) quadratic MC.

10.2   Linearization: a tool for simplifying models

In this section we shall analyse the behaviour of national income in a very simple model. The model involves a (national) consumption function $C(Y)$ which depends on national income Y. In a closed economy (i.e. without further source of income) Y is in part consumed (i.e. eaten, or withdrawn from economic activity) and the rest is put to use either as investment I or as government expenditure G. We thus have the identity

$$Y = C(Y) + I + G. \qquad (10.4)$$

We want to solve for Y, but that requires a knowledge of $C(Y)$. We indulge in some trickery. Since our intention is to see how Y will change with G or I, we assume that the current level of Y is known as being $\bar{Y}$ and the current consumption is known as being $\bar{C}$, so that $\bar{C} = C(\bar{Y})$. Now we approximate to the C curve by means of a tangent line. We therefore require to know the derivative $m = C'(\bar{Y})$. This is called the 'marginal propensity to consume', since it represents, in the limit, the increment in consumption over the increment in income.

Now the equation of the line through $(\bar{Y}, \bar{C})$ with slope m is of course

$$C - \bar{C} = m(Y - \bar{Y})$$

or

$$C = mY + c$$

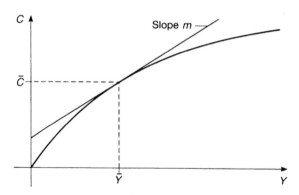

Figure 10.6 $C(Y) \approx mY + c$ near $Y = \bar{Y}$.

where $c = \bar{C} - m\bar{Y}$ and m is the marginal propensity to consume (see figure 10.6). Thus for Y close to $\bar{Y}$ we have the approximate result

$$C(Y) \approx mY + c.$$ (10.5)

Obviously this approximation is only good for a restricted range of values for Y. Let us call this the range of validity of (10.5).

The derivative has provided us with a linearization method. Before proceeding with our problem in economics let us look ahead to functions of more than one variable, for example to a cost function corresponding to the production of two commodities:

$$\text{cost} = F(q_1, q_2).$$

How would we expect to linearize this cost? Evidently by

$$F(q_1, q_2) \approx aq_1 + bq_2 + c.$$ (10.6)

We can make this second approximation take the same form as the first by using matrices. Thus

$$F(q_1, q_2) \approx (a, b) \begin{pmatrix} q_1 \\ q_2 \end{pmatrix} + c$$
$$= Mq + c$$ (10.7)

where M is the 1×2 matrix (a, b) and q is the column vector from the line above. Motivated by the similarity of (10.5) and (10.7) we shall define later (in section 15.1) the derivative of $F(q_1, q_2)$ to be a certain matrix M. These common features will entail thinking of the derivative as the multiplier (m or M) which gives the linear approximation.

To return to our subject, by (10.4) and (10.5) we have

$$Y = mY + c + I + G.$$ (10.8)

Hence, provided that $m \neq 1$, we have

$$Y = \frac{c + (I + G)}{1 - m}.$$ (10.9)

Obviously this equation is only good within a restricted 'range of validity'. We shall see in a moment why $0 < m < 1$. Granted this, we note that increases in I or G in the closed economy (10.4) are possible provided that Y changes according to (10.9). In particular (10.9) tells us the 'gearing' between Y and I (or G), e.g. $dY/dI = 1/(1 - m)$.

10.3 Why the marginal propensity to consume lies between zero and unity

We note that $C(Y)$ is a non-decreasing function of Y – if there is more income, say $Y + h$, then the new consumption will be at least as large as before, so $C(Y + h) \geq C(Y)$, and hence for $h > 0$

$$M(h) \equiv \frac{C(Y + h) - C(Y)}{h} \geq 0.$$

The limiting value thus satisfies $C'(Y) \geq 0$. (Why? If we had $C'(Y) < 0$, then, for small enough h, $M(h)$ would be so close to $C'(Y)$ that $M(h)$ too would be negative.)

The unconsumed part of national income constitutes national savings $S(Y)$. Thus since

$$C(Y) + S(Y) = Y$$

we obtain, after differentiation, that

$$C'(Y) + S'(Y) = 1.$$ (10.10)

It is customary to assume that $S(Y)$ is an increasing function (i.e. $S'(Y) \geq 0$). Hence

$$0 \leq C'(Y) \leq 1.$$

It is also usual to assume both the strict inequalities

$$C'(Y) > 0 \quad \text{and} \quad S'(Y) > 0,$$

so that $C(S)$ and $S(Y)$ are strictly increasing functions (see section 10.5). Finally, we have by (10.10)

$$0 < m = C'(\bar{Y}) < 1.$$

This strict inequality is as much a matter of assumption as a matter of mathematics. To understand this point, note that

$$f(x) = x^2$$

satisfies $f(h) > 0 = f(0)$ for $h > 0$. Yet $f'(0) = 2.0 = 0$ and so the derivative here is not strictly positive. To support the assumption of strictness observe that we might interpret (10.5) as asserting that c represents the 'fixed costs of subsistence'. Lumping c with I and G as the 'costs of running the economy' we see from (10.8) that mY is that fraction of national income set aside for 'quality of subsistence': obviously this is normally a non-zero fraction. (It is a fraction of unity, since unity represents the total.)

10.4   Marginal revenue versus average revenue; the mean value theorem

This section, despite the ominous title, is concerned with a very practical issue. We introduce it by means of an example. A firm assesses its revenue in a two-step calculation – the revenue R is related to output q and the output is related to the labour input L. Thus

$$R = f(q) \qquad \text{and} \qquad q = g(L)$$

so that

$$R = f[g(L)].$$

We wish to compute whether it is worth expanding the labour force.

One instinctively considers the chain rule, which says that if $z = f(y)$ and $y = g(x)$ then

$$\frac{dz}{dx} \equiv \frac{d}{dx} f[g(x)] = \frac{dz}{dy}\frac{dy}{dx} = f'g'.$$

Thus in our case

$$\frac{dR}{dL} = \frac{dR}{dq}\frac{dq}{dL}.$$

Using the names of the three marginal quantities this reads:

marginal revenue product (of labour) = marginal revenue × marginal physical product (of labour),

i.e.

$$\text{MRP} = \text{MR} \times \text{MPP}.$$

Let us set up a model. The function $g(L)$ is a production function which we take in Cobb–Douglas form

$$q = g(L) = L^{1/2}.$$

With a view to later discussion we shall suppose that labour is measured by the number of workers. Also we suppose that this is a hi-tech industry commanding high prices for a small number of goods produced. This is reflected in the coefficients in our linear demand function:

$$q = 30 - \frac{1}{2000} p,$$

i.e.

$$p = 60,000 - 2000q.$$

We evaluate MRP when $L = 25$. Evidently $q = 5$, and hence $p = 60,000 - 10,000 = 50,000$. But $R = pq$, and consequently

$$\frac{dR}{dq} = \frac{d}{dq}(60,000q - 2000q^2) = 60,000 - 4000q. \qquad (10.11)$$

So here MR = 40,000. Also

$$\frac{dq}{dL} = \frac{1}{2}L^{-1/2} = \frac{1}{10}.$$

Thus MRP = 4000 and this needs to be given in appropriate units: presumably dollars per 'worker' (and obviously per month!).

We now argue somewhat vaguely that it is therefore worth expanding the labour force from 25 to 26 assuming a wage can be agreed below 48,000 per annum. Actually, this argument is correct, but only after some contemplation. One criticism that immediately comes to mind is that in our case the increment in labour δL is *not* small.

Let us see what happens if we do not use derivatives and consider the identity

$$\frac{\delta R}{\delta L} = \frac{\delta R}{\delta q}\frac{\delta q}{\delta L},$$

where δq is the increment in output following expansion of L and δR is the corresponding increase in R.

Now $\delta q = \sqrt{(26)} - \sqrt{(25)} \approx 0.099$ and $\delta p = -2000\,\delta q \approx -198$. Finally,

$$\delta R = (p + \delta p)(q + \delta q) - pq$$
$$= p\,\delta q + q\,\delta p + \delta p\delta q$$
$$\approx 50,000 \times 0.099 - 5 \times 198 - 19.8$$
$$\approx 4950 - 990 - 19.8$$
$$= 3940.2$$

and the real answer is in the same ball-park (only about 1.5 per cent out).

A deeper contemplation will unearth a fundamental reason behind the closeness of the two results. Figure 10.7 illustrates R. Note that MR ($= dR/dq$) is decreasing (i.e. the revenue curve is concave) and surely the chord (with slope $\delta R/\delta q$) is parallel to an intermediate tangent. Thus $\delta R/\delta q$ is equal to an intermediate MR between $q = 5$ and $q = \sqrt{(26)} = 5.099$. But for any change Δq the corresponding change ΔMR in MR is ΔMR $= -4000\,\Delta q$ by (10.11). Hence over the interval $[5, \sqrt{(26)}]$ the change in MR is equal to $-4000\delta q \approx -400$, i.e. 1 per cent away from $\delta R/\delta q$. Intuitively we expect the intermediate parallel tangent to be sited halfway between $q = 5$ and $q = \sqrt{(26)}$. Indeed that will be so if the revenue curve is quadratic, which it is here (see section 10.7, question 17). Thus while MR changes by as much as 1 per cent over the whole interval it has changed by only 0.5 per cent midway. Thus in our case MR is 0.5 per cent larger than $\delta R/\delta q$.

Now $dq/dL = 0.1$ is close to $\delta q/\delta L = 0.099$ and is in fact only 1 per cent too large. Hence we see that the calculus answer has over-estimated $\delta R/\delta L$ by at most 1.505 per cent, since the percentage error when multiplying is equal to $0.5 + 1 + 1 \times 0.5/100$ (see section 10.7, question 7). We shall have a lot to say about the errors we commit in our approximations in a separate chapter (Taylor's theorem).

The property just used, that a chord has slope parallel to a tangent at some intermediate position,

$$\frac{f(x + h) - f(x)}{h} = f'(x^*)$$

for some x^* between x and $x + h$, is known as the mean value theorem of differential calculus (figure 10.8). It is this result which allows us to conclude that, if $f'(x) \geq 0$ on an interval $[c, d]$, then $f(x)$ is increasing in that interval (see section 10.5). This is the converse to our earlier remark in section 10.3. We note also that the more nearly the curve of $f(x)$ is quadratic (as a function of x) on the interval in question, the more nearly midway is the intermediate point x^* (see section 10.7, question 21, and section 14.11, question 2).

*10.5   Increasing functions – facts and myths

The issues raised in this section are important although they may seem like nit picking.

The first point concerns a well-known fact: the equivalence of two properties of a function $f(x)$ – that of being non-decreasing ($x_1 < x_2 \Rightarrow f(x_1) \leq f(x_2)$) and that of having a non-negative derivative, i.e. $f'(x) \geq 0$ throughout the domain

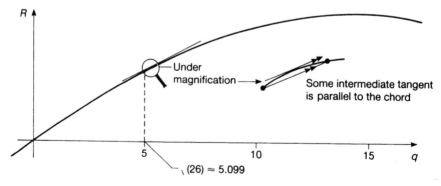

Figure 10.7   The real $\delta R/\delta q$ equals some intermediate marginal cost, but marginal cost changes in $[5, \sqrt{(26)}]$ by at most 400 away from 40,000.

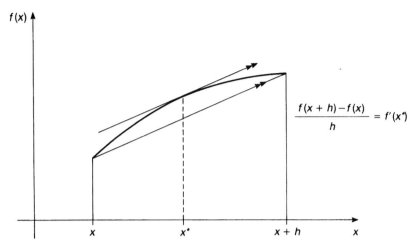

Figure 10.8 The mean value is equal to an intermediate marginal value (mean value theorem), i.e. somewhere a tangent is parallel to the chord.

of the function. The argument in one direction (non-decreasing implies non-negative derivative) was given in section 10.3. The converse is only apparently self-evident, mainly because one usually illustrates $f'(x) \geq 0$ with a diagram showing an increasing function. So what is there in fact to prove? A little more care is needed. Don't draw a curve; just suppose that $x_1 < x_2$ and $f(x_1) > f(x_2)$ and see where that takes you. (This will be an argument by contradiction!) The situation can be illustrated. The chord of the undrawn curve is downward sloping and so the chord has negative slope (figure 10.9). The mean value theorem asserts that for some x^* the mean value is equal to an intermediate marginal value. Thus

$$0 > \frac{f(x_2) - f(x_1)}{x_2 - x_1} = f'(x^*). \tag{10.12}$$

Hence $f'(x^*) < 0$, which is a contradiction, since we assumed $f'(x) \geq 0$ throughout the domain. So the converse is true after all.

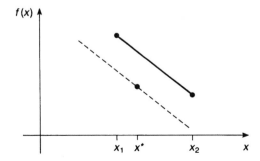

Figure 10.9 Chord of the unknown f curve; a parallel tangent has negative slope (●, points of the f curve).

Before we consider the second point we need to draw a distinction between the non-decreasing functions (often unfortunately, and misleadingly, called increasing functions) and the functions which are (strictly) increasing $(x_1 < x_2 \Rightarrow f(x_1) < f(x_2))$. The argument by contradiction just given will also show that, if $f'(x) > 0$ throughout the domain, then $f(x)$ is strictly increasing. (Adapt the proof above as an exercise.)

This brings us to the second point. There is a widely held belief – a total myth – that the strictly increasing functions are precisely the functions with positive derivative. Obviously not all functions are differentiable and so there is cause for suspicion. More awkwardly we note that $f(x) = x^3$ is a strictly increasing function, and yet $f'(0) = 0$.

If at the outset of this section you thought that converse theorems 'are obvious' you might have been forgiven, but here there is good food for thought. Take sustenance, however, from the observation that $f'(x) > 0$ at all other points; the origin is an exception to the expected rule. Actually there are strictly increasing functions whose derivatives vanish exceptionally more than once! See figure 10.10. Nevertheless, the slope will not be zero throughout a subinterval. Indeed if $f'(x) \equiv 0$ for $a \leqslant x \leqslant b$ then $f(x)$ is constant in that interval. Again this follows from the argument at the beginning. (Try it: if $f(x_1) \neq f(x_2)$ then suppose $f(x_1) > f(x_2)$; (10.12) gives a contradiction.)

The correct conclusion is that if $f(x)$ is strictly increasing then at almost all points the curve has positive slope. We say that $f'(x) > 0$ holds generically. We assumed in section 10.3 in effect that the economy was at a generic position, and so the marginal propensity to consume was strictly between 0 and 1.

10.6   Average revenue, marginal revenue – inverse functions

In section 10.1 we discussed the relationship between average and marginal costs. We look at the corresponding problem on the revenue side.

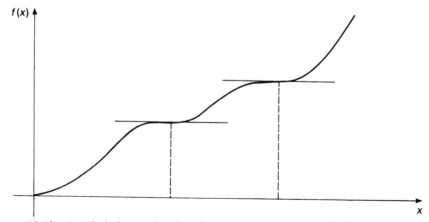

Figure 10.10   A strictly increasing function with many points of inflexion.

We begin by asking: what is average revenue AR? The answer is, of course, revenue over output, i.e. price, since

$$\text{AR} = \frac{R}{q} = \frac{pq}{q} = p.$$

To find marginal revenue we need dR/dq, i.e. $d(pq)/dq$. Using the product rule, formally we get

$$\text{MR} = \frac{d}{dq}(pq) = \frac{dp}{dq}q + p. \tag{10.13}$$

To make sense of the symbol dp/dq we need to know price as a function of output, i.e. we need a relationship in the form $p = f(q)$. In Part I, section 5.6, we conducted our investigations as though the demand curve was given as the graph of a relationship $p = P(q)$ known in that section as the demand function (see the comment there). It is actually often the reverse relationship $q = Q_d(p)$ that is assumed to be given. How do we pass from one to the other? Geometrically this passage is effected by reference to the graph of whichever function is given. If the curve is the graph of $q = Q_d(p)$ then to find $p = P(q)$ we look for the intersection of the ordinate line through q with the demand curve. The price co-ordinate of the intersection point gives p (see figure 10.11). Notice that the demand curve graphing $q = Q_d(q)$ is shown as strictly decreasing so that the construction gives rise to a unique price. In figure 10.12 we see how the geometric construction could fail with more perverse demand curves.

There are two simple ways to generate the graph of the inverse function. The first is to draw the original curve on a transparency: then all that is required is (a) to rotate the transparency counterclockwise by 90°, which interchanges the axes, and (b) to turn the transparency over (i.e. upside down) in order to point the axes in the conventional directions.

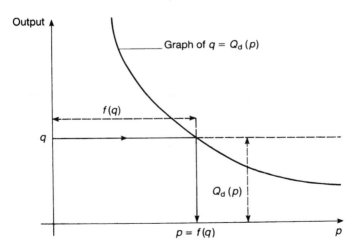

Figure 10.11   Finding the inverse demand.

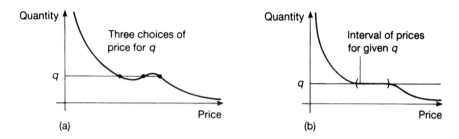

Figure 10.12   Some perverse demand curves: (a) non-decreasing demand; (b) non-strictly-decreasing demand.

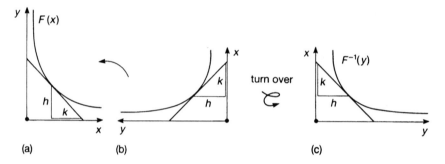

Figure 10.13   Construction of the inverse function: (a) graph of $F(x)$; (b) rotated through 90°; (c) the inverse function $x = F^{-1}(y)$.

This is shown in figure 10.13 starting with a general function $y = F(x)$ and leading to the inverse function, which is conveniently written $x = F^{-1}(y)$. Notice that the displayed tangent line starts with a numerical slope of h/k and after rotation ends up having a numerical slope of k/h. This illustrates the inverse function rule in differentiation:

$$\frac{\mathrm{d}}{\mathrm{d}y} F^{-1}(y) = 1 \left| \frac{\mathrm{d}}{\mathrm{d}x} F(x), \right.$$

more perspicuously rendered in the alternative notation

$$\frac{\mathrm{d}x}{\mathrm{d}y} = 1 \left| \frac{\mathrm{d}y}{\mathrm{d}x} \right. \qquad \left(\text{provided that } \frac{\mathrm{d}y}{\mathrm{d}x} \neq 0 \right).$$

Remark

The condition $\mathrm{d}y/\mathrm{d}x \neq 0$ is worth pausing for. Suppose that in fact $\mathrm{d}y/\mathrm{d}x \equiv F'(x) > 0$ at some x, say at $x = X$. Assuming that F' is continuous, $F'(x) > 0$ is true for all xs near $x = X$. This in turn tells us that $F(x)$ is strictly increasing in the neighbourhood of $x = X$, so that some at least of the F curve gives rise to an inverse. We call this a *local inverse* (figure 10.14).

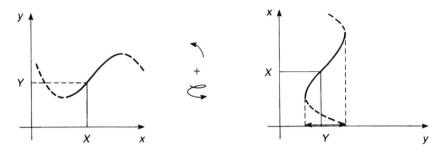

Figure 10.14   (a) Near $x = X$ the full curve is strictly increasing; (b) the full curve has only a *local* inverse available near $y = Y$.

We shall usually construct inverse functions only for strictly increasing (or strictly decreasing) functions. We shall return to this rule when we consider exponential functions.

Observe that an alternative way of getting the inverse function is (section 5.6) to take a reflection about the diagonal line $y = x$ (figure 10.15). In our case the original demand curve graphs $q = Q_d(p)$; the inverted curve is thus the graph of average revenue $AR = f(q)$.

Let us return to our MR problem. According to (10.12) we have

$$MR = q\frac{dp}{dq} + p = q\left|\frac{dq}{dp}\right. + AR,$$

and so

$$MR - AR = q\left|\frac{dq}{dp}\right. < 0$$

since $q' < 0$. Thus $MR < AR$.

Notice the geometrical interpretation of the equation $MR - AR = Qf'(Q)$ based on the parallelogram ABCD (figure 10.16). AB/BD equals numerically the slope of the tangent at D, which is $|f'(Q)|$. (Recall that $f'(Q) < 0$.) But $BD = Q$, and so $AB = DC = Qf'(Q) = MR - AR$.

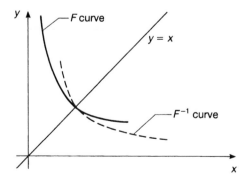

Figure 10.15   Inverting a function by reflection.

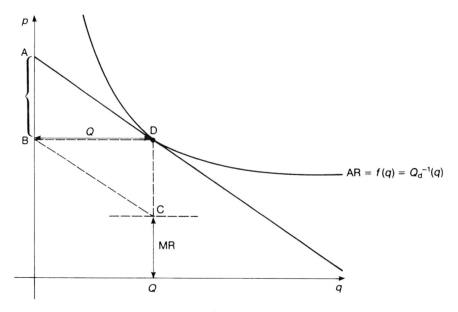

Figure 10.16 MR = AR − $Qf'(Q)$ = DQ − DC (AB/BD = $f'(Q)$ and so AB = $Qf'(Q)$ = DC).

10.7 Exercises

1* Differentiate the following functions:

$$\sin x \qquad x^2 \cos x \qquad \tan x \left(= \frac{\sin x}{\cos x} \right) \qquad \tan^2 x \qquad (1 + x^2)^{1/2}$$

2 Differentiate the following functions:

$$\sin^2 x \qquad \cot x \qquad (1 + x^2)^{1/3}$$

3* Show that the demand function

$$q = 1000 - \frac{1}{2}p - \frac{1}{5}p^2$$

has increasing elasticity by checking for concavity. What is the range of admissible p?

4 Show that the demand function

$$q = 100 - \frac{1}{2}p - \frac{1}{5}p^{3/2}$$

has increasing elasticity by checking for concavity. What is the range of admissible p?

5* If the consumption function is $C(Y) = Y^{1/2}$ what is the marginal propensity to consume when $Y = 1$? What is a good linear approximation to $C(Y)$ in the vicinity of $Y = 1$? Repeat the question for $Y = 4$.

6   Find the derivative of $y = \sin x$ when $x = 0$ and when $x = \pi/4$ (radians). What is a good linear approximation (a) in the vicinity of $x = 0$ and (b) in the vicinity of $x = \pi/4$?

7*   Show that, if $w = uv$ and u, v are approximated by values which are respectively r per cent and s per cent incorrect, then the approximation to w will be

$$\left(r + s + \frac{rs}{100} \right) \text{ per cent}$$

incorrect. [*Hint*: Compute $(u + \delta u)(v + \delta v) - uv$ as in section 10.4.]

8   Show that, when $z = x^2 y$ and x, y change by δx, δy respectively, then the change in z is

$$\delta z \approx 2xy\,\delta x + x^2 \delta y.$$

9*   Verify that if $Q = A/p^k$ with A, k positive constants then $\eta = k$. In the special case $k = 1$ conclude that the segment of the tangent line to the demand curve at (p, q) lying in the positive quadrant is bisected by (p, q). [*Hint*: See remark 2 of section 10.1.] How does this generalize when $k \neq 1$?

10   A production company faces a demand schedule

$$p = 120{,}000 - 12{,}000q$$

and its production function is $q = L^{1/3}$, where L is labour. Currently the company employs 64 staff.

(a)   Compute current values of MR, MPP and hence MRP (see section 10.4 for a definition of these terms).
        At what wage level is it worth expanding the labour force by one person?
(b)   Compute δq when $\delta L = 1$. What is the percentage discrepancy between dq/dL and $\delta q/\delta L$? Compute δR. What is the percentage discrepancy between dr/dL and $\delta R/\delta L$?
(c)   By how many per cent does MR vary over $[4, 4 + \delta q]$?
(d)   How far out is the wage calculation in (a)?

11*   Show that

$$f(x) = \frac{x}{1 - x}$$

is an increasing function (a) in $(-\infty, 1)$ and (b) in $(1, +\infty)$.

12   Show that

$$f(x) = \frac{x + 1}{(x - 3)^2}$$

is (a) increasing in $(0, 3)$ and (b) decreasing in $(3, +\infty)$.

13*   Sketch the curve $y = \tan x$ for $-\pi/2 < x < \pi/2$. Hence draw the inverse function. Use the inverse function rule to show that

$$\frac{dy}{dx} = \frac{1}{1 + y^2}.$$

14   Sketch the curve $y = \cos x$ for $-\pi < x < \pi$. Hence draw the inverse function. Use the inverse function rule to show that

$$\frac{dy}{dx} = -\frac{1}{(1 - y^2)^{1/2}}.$$

15*   If $x = f(t)$, $y = g(t)$ and the inverse function $t = f^{-1}(x)$ exists, explain why $y = g[f^{-1}(x)]$. Use the chain rule to show that

$$\frac{dy}{dx} = \frac{g'(t)}{f'(t)}.$$

Find dy/dx in terms of t when

$$x = t - \sin t \qquad y = 1 - \cos t.$$

16   Repeat the previous exercise when

$$x = \sin t - t \cos t \qquad y = \cos t + t \sin t.$$

17   If $f(x) = ax^2 + bx + c$, show that

$$\frac{f(x + 2h) - f(x)}{2h} = f'(x + h). \tag{10.14}$$

Thus in this case the intermediate point of the mean value theorem is exactly halfway.

18*   Let $g(h) = f(x + 2h) - f(x)$. Show that (10.14) becomes $g'(h) = g(2h)/2h$. Use this equation to show that $g'(h)$ is differentiable for $h \neq 0$ and find $g''(h)$. Deduce that (a) $f(x)$ has a second derivative at any x, and so (b) $g''(h)$ exists also at $h = 0$. Note that this argument extends to higher order derivatives of $g(h)$.

19*   When $q = L^{1/2}$ use the mean value theorem to estimate the change δq when L changes from 25 to 26 by noting that dq/dL changes by at most $\delta q \times d^2q/dL^2$.

20   Repeat the previous exercise with $q = L^{1/3}$, letting L change from 64 to 65.

21*   If $f(x) = Ax^3 + ax^2 + bx + c$, show that

$$\frac{f(x + h) - f(x)}{h} = f'\left(x + \frac{h}{2}\right) + \frac{Ah^2}{4} \tag{10.15}$$

where $A = f'''(0)/3!$

(Note that, if the cubic coefficient is small relative to the quadratic terms, the midpoint is a good approximation for the intermediate point of the mean value theorem. See also section 14.11, question 3.)

22   Show that

$$\frac{f(x+h) - f(x)}{h} = f'(x) + f''(\bar{x})(x^* - x) \qquad (10.16)$$

for some $\bar{x}$, x^* with $x < \bar{x} < x^* < x + h$. Assuming that $f(x)$ is quadratic in x use (10.14) to deduce that the last term in (10.16) is

$$\frac{h}{2} f''\left(x + \frac{h}{4}\right).$$

Deduce that the error in replacing $\delta f/\delta x$ by df/dx for a general $f(x)$ is at most $f''(\bar{x})h$ for some $x < \bar{x} < x + h$ and is likely to be about $f''(x + h/4)h/2$ if f is close to being quadratic between x and $x + h$.

10.8   Further exercises

1   Verify that the function

$$y = \frac{x^{1/2}}{1 - x^{1/2}}$$

satisfies

$$\frac{dy}{dx} = \frac{y(1 + y)}{2x}.$$

2   Draw on one diagram a family of demand curves $q = Q_t(p)$ (corresponding to various time values t) which all pass through a point (p^*, q^*) to illustrate how the response over time to a price rise from p^* to p' leads to a transition from inelastic demand at p^* to elastic demand at p'.

3   Show that if $y = f(x)$ is a strictly increasing function then so is the inverse function $x = f^{-1}(y)$.

4   Show that if $f'(x) > 0$ throughout the domain of $f(x)$ then $f(x)$ is strictly increasing.

5   Show that if $f'(x) = 0$ for $a < x < b$, then $f(x)$ is constant in (a, b).

6   Show that if $y = F(x)$ is a continuous, increasing, convex function then its inverse function $x = F^{-1}(y) \equiv f(y)$ is concave.

7   By 'completing the square' show that for $a > 0$ the quadratic $ax^2 + bx + c$ has a minimum value of $(4ac - b^2)/2a$ achieved when $x = -b/2a$. Deduce that the quadratic is positive for all x if $b^2 < 4ac$. What condition must be placed on b, c if the quadratic is to be positive for all $x > 0$ (i.e. nothing is said for $x \leqslant 0$)?

8   If the variable cost factor is quadratic, say $v(q) = aq^2 + bq + c$, show that the large-scale average cost is approximately a parabola. Since we require $v(q) \geqslant 0$ for $q \geqslant 0$ what restrictions must be placed on a, b, c?

Write down the marginal cost for this $v(q)$. Since this is also a quadratic, check that the restrictions on a, b, c which ensure that AC and MC have graphs as in figure 10.4(b) (i.e. MC_{min} is positive and occurs before AC = MC) are that

$$a > 0 \qquad b < 0 \qquad c > 0 \qquad b^2 < 3ac \qquad k > b^3/27a^2$$

where k represents the fixed costs. [*Hint*: When is $AC' < 0$?]

9 Show that when $a \neq 0$ the quadratic $ax^2 + bx + c$ is positive for all $z > 1$ if and only if $a > 0$, $A + b + c \geq 0$ and either $b^2 - 4ac < 0$ or $2a + b \geq 0$. What is the corresponding condition if $a = 0$?

10 Differentiate $q' = -q\eta/p$ using the quotient rule;

(a) deduce that $\eta' < 0$ implies $q'' > 0$;
(b) if $\eta' > 0$ show that $q'' > 0$ provided that

$$\eta' < \frac{\eta(1 + \eta)}{p}.$$

Note that one way to satisfy the last inequality is to require

$$\eta' = \frac{\eta(1 + \eta)}{2p}.$$

This 'differential equation' may be solved to give the increasing function

$$\eta(p) = \frac{p^{1/2}}{k - p^{1/2}} \qquad \text{for } 0 \leq p < k^2$$

where k is a constant (section 10.8, question 7). The last equation may in turn be solved for q (see chapter 16). For example, if $k = 1$ we obtain

$$q = A(p^{1/2} - 1)^2 \exp(2p^{1/2} - p).$$

(For the definition of 'exp' or 'e' see section 11.1 and the remark before example 2 in section 14.4.)

10.8.1 Linearized models

1 Consider the national income analysis in discrete time with

$$Y_n = C_n + I_n \qquad \text{and} \qquad C_n = mY_{n-1} + c$$

(so that the economy demands a consumption based on the previous year's known output). Assuming $I_n \equiv I$ is constant find Y_n and show that

$$\lim_{n \to \infty} Y_n = Y^*$$

where $Y^* = (c + I)/(m - 1)$. Interpret this result when C_n and I_n are regarded as demands and Y_n is a supply. What happens to $\lim_{n \to \infty} Y_n$ if, instead, $I_0 = I$ and $I_n = I + \Delta I$ ($n = 1, 2, \ldots$) where ΔI is a constant increment to the investment flow.

2 A closed economy produces an income Y_t in year t of which a part C_t is consumed and the remainder I_t is invested. Thus

$$Y_t = C_t + I_t.$$

Planners intend that consumption C_t in year t should be one-half of the current year's income (i.e. $C_t = \frac{1}{2} Y_t$). They believe that a future year's income is proportional to the current investment, i.e. $Y_{t+1} = kI_t$, where k is a constant. Show by eliminating income and consumption that investment I_t satisfies a first-order difference equation. Show also that if investment, and so income, is to rise from year to year then $k > 2$. Find I_t when $I_0 = \frac{3}{2}$ and $k = 2\frac{2}{3}$.

Planners change their minds about consumption, intending now that consumption should be half of the previous year's income ($C_t = \frac{1}{2} Y_{t-1}$), but retain their views as to the relation between future income and current investment. Show by eliminating income and consumption that this time I_t satisfies a second-order difference equation. Solve this difference equation when $I_0 = \frac{3}{2}$, $I_1 = 1$ and $k = 2\frac{2}{3}$.

Is the second model significantly different from the first?

3 If k is a constant, show that the roots of $2z^2 - (k+1)z + k = 0$ are real if $k \geqslant 3 + 2\sqrt{2}$.

4 Yet another scenario. Planners wish to arrange that consumption in any year t be the average of that year's income and the previous year's consumption ($C_t = \frac{1}{2}(Y_t + C_{t-1})$). They continue to believe that the relation between future income and current investment is the same as in question 2.

Show that if $k = 3$ the level of investment will rise and fall periodically. How large must k be if cycling is to be avoided?

10.9 Answers

1 Denoting differentiation by D we have: $D(\sin x) = \cos x$; $D(x^2 \cos x) = 2x \cos x - x^2 \sin x$; $D(\tan x) = D[(\sin x)/(\cos x)] = [\cos^2 x + \sin^2 x]/\cos^2 x = 1 + \tan^2 x = 1/\cos^2 x = \sec^2 x$ (we used the quotient rule); $D(\tan^2 x) = 2 \tan x \sec^2 x$; $D[(1 + x^2)^{1/2}] = x/(1 + x^2)^{1/2}$.

3

$$\frac{dq}{dp} = -\frac{1}{2} - \frac{2}{5}p \quad \text{and} \quad \frac{d^2 q}{dp^2} = -\frac{2}{p} < 0.$$

Thus the demand function is concave and hence the elasticity is increasing. The admissible range for p is

$$0 \leqslant p \leqslant -\frac{1}{2} + \left(\frac{1}{4} + 800\right)^{1/2} \approx 27.7.$$

5 As $C'(Y) = \frac{1}{2} Y^{-1/2} = 1/(2Y^{1/2})$, we have that when $Y = 1$ the marginal propensity to consume is $\frac{1}{2}$. Hence a good approximation near $Y = 1$ is $C - 1 = \frac{1}{2}(Y - 1)$ since $C(1) = 1$. Similarly if $Y = 4$ we have that $C(4) = 2$ and $C'(4) = \frac{1}{4}$ and so a good approximation near $Y = 4$ is given by $C - 2 = \frac{1}{4}(Y - 4)$.

7

$$\delta w = (u + \delta u)(v + \delta v) - uv = u\,\delta v + v\,\delta u + \delta u\,\delta v.$$

Hence

$$\frac{\delta w}{w} = \frac{\delta v}{v} + \frac{\delta u}{u} + \frac{\delta u}{u}\frac{\delta v}{v}$$

$$= \frac{r}{100} + \frac{s}{100} + \frac{rs}{10,000}$$

$$= r + s + \frac{rs}{100}\,\%.$$

9   If $q = A/p^k$ then $q' = (-k)Ap^{-k-1}$. Hence $\eta = -pq'/q = pkAp^{-k-1}A^{-1}p^k = k$. Thus when $k = 1$ the line through $(0, 2q)$ and (p, q) shown in figure 10.3 is actually the tangent line to the demand curve. The point (p, q) is vertically halfway down. Hence (p, q) bisects the segment of the tangent line mentioned in the question.

11   We write $f(x) = (x - 1 + 1)/(1 - x) = -1 + 1/(1 - x)$. Hence $f'(x) = 1/(1 - x)^2 > 0$. Note that neither $f(x)$ nor $f'(x)$ are defined at $x = 1$. Thus we are entitled only to say that $f(x)$ is increasing in $(-\infty, 1)$ since $f'(x) > 0$ in the said interval. Similarly $f(x)$ is increasing in $(1, \infty)$. Figure 10.17 makes it clear why $f(x)$ is not increasing on $(-\infty, \infty)$.

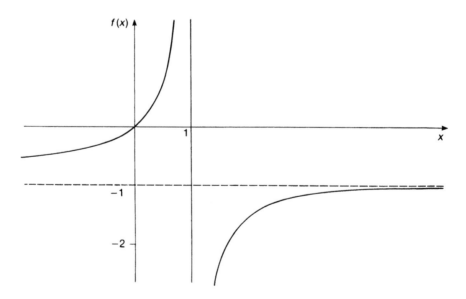

Figure 10.17   Graph of $x/(1 - x)$. The function is increasing in each of $(-\infty, 1)$, $(1, +\infty)$, but $f(0) = 0 > -2 = f(2)$.

13   The curve $y = \tan x$ and its inverse function are shown in figure 10.18. Since

$$\frac{dy}{dx} = 1 + y^2 \qquad \text{(by question 1)},$$

hence

$$\frac{dx}{dy} = \frac{1}{1 + y^2}.$$

15   We have $y = g(t)$, and so substituting for t we obtain $y = g[f^{-1}(x)]$. We may now write by the chain rule

$$\frac{dy}{dx} = \frac{dg}{dt}\frac{df^{-1}}{dx} = \frac{g'(t)}{f'(t)}$$

since by the inverse function rule

$$\frac{df^{-1}}{dx} = \frac{dt}{dx} = 1 \bigg/ \frac{dx}{dt} = \frac{1}{f'(t)}.$$

When $x = t - \sin t$ and $y = 1 - \cos t$ we obtain

$$\frac{dy}{dx} = \frac{\sin t}{1 - \cos t}.$$

18   Since $g(2h)$ is differentiable and $1/2h$ is differentiable for $h \neq 0$, the product is differentiable for $h \neq 0$. The derivative is thus

$$\frac{2g'(2h)2h - 2g(2h)}{4h^2} = \frac{4hg'(2h) - 4hg'(h)}{4h^2} = \frac{g'(2h) - g'(h)}{2h}$$

and this is equal to $g''(h)$.

Now $f(x + h) = f(x) + g(h/2)$ and the right-hand side is twice differentiable with respect to h for $h \neq 0$. Hence $f''(x + h)$ exists for $h \neq 0$. But x is arbitrary and hence so is $x + h$. So $f''(x)$ also exists. But $g''(h) = 4f''(x + 2h)$ and the right-hand side exists for $h = 0$. Hence $g''(0)$ exists.

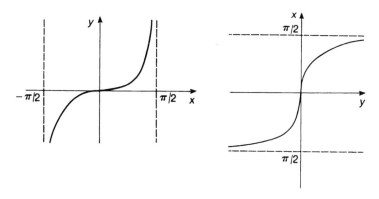

Figure 10.18   (a) $y = \tan x$ for $-\pi/2 < x < \pi/2$; (b) its inverse.

19   We have $dq/dL = \frac{1}{2}L^{-1/2}$ and $d^2q/dL^2 = -\frac{1}{4}L^{-3/2}$. Thus dq/dL changes by at most $1/(4 \times 125) = 1/500$ when $L = 25$, since

$$\frac{dq}{dL}(26) - \frac{dq}{dL}(25) = \frac{d^2q}{dL^2}(\text{intermediate}) \leqslant \frac{1}{500}.$$

21   We have

$$\frac{1}{h}[A(x+h)^3 - Ax^3] = \frac{A(3x^2h + 3xh^2 + h^3)}{h}$$

$$= A(3x^2 + 3xh + h^2)$$

$$= 3A\left(x + \frac{h}{2}\right)^2 + A\left(h^2 - \frac{3h^2}{4}\right)$$

$$= 3A\left(x + \frac{h}{2}\right)^2 + \frac{Ah^2}{4}.$$

Denoting the quadratic terms of $f(x)$ by $g(x)$ we know from question 17 that $[g(x+h) - g(x)]/h = g'(x + h/2)$. Adding to this equation we obtain

$$\frac{A(x+h)^3 - Ax^3 + g(x+h) - g(x)}{h} = 3A\left(x + \frac{h}{2}\right)^2 + g'\left(x + \frac{h}{2}\right) + \frac{Ah^2}{4}$$

$$= f'\left(x + \frac{h}{2}\right) + \frac{Ah^2}{4},$$

as required.

11

Continuous Compounding and Exponential Growth

11.1 Interest compounded with a high frequency

We return to the topic of compound interest begun in section 4.13. Suppose that a sum of money A, known as the *principal*, is allowed to attract interest for one year. We examine how the deposited sum grows when interest is added at regular time intervals during the year (and no withdrawals are made). By decreasing the size of the time intervals we shall increase the frequency with which interest is added. What will stay constant in the process will be the nominal interest rate r, which is applied pro rata, i.e. proportionally to the time interval. For instance, if interest of r per cent per annum is paid monthly, the rate per month is $r/12$ per cent. Thus at the end of the first month the principal increases to $A + Ar/12 = A(1 + r/12)$. Hence, after two months the deposit stands at $A(1 + r/12)^2$ etc. At the year's end the amount in deposit is

$$A\left(1 + \frac{r}{12}\right)^{12}.$$

Evidently, if interest were paid daily at an annual rate of r, the principal after one year would rise to

$$A\left(1 + \frac{r}{365}\right)^{365}. \tag{11.1}$$

In view of these large numbers attention focuses on whether

$$\left(1 + \frac{r}{m}\right)^{m}$$

has a limiting value as m increases unboundedly. The problem amounts to asking how the principal grows in a year when interest is compounded at every instant of time; we are, in effect, dividing a unit of time (the year) into a large number m of instants. On another point of view, since formula (11.1) calls for 365 multiplications, can we estimate the answer by means of an easier calculation? The answer is yes.

To simplify matters, we first investigate what happens if $r = 1$ so that interest is 100%. By the binomial theorem

$$\left(1 + \frac{1}{m}\right)^m = 1 + m\left(\frac{1}{m}\right) + \frac{m(m-1)}{2}\left(\frac{1}{m}\right)^2 + \frac{m(m-1)(m-2)}{3!}\left(\frac{1}{m}\right)^3 + \cdots$$

($m + 1$ terms in all). Now notice that for an increased m we have

$$\left(1 + \frac{1}{m+1}\right)^{m+1} = 1 + (m+1)\left(\frac{1}{m+1}\right) + \frac{(m+1)m}{2}\left(\frac{1}{m+1}\right)^2 + \cdots$$

($m + 2$ terms in all) and this has (a) more terms and (b) larger terms, because for example

$$\frac{1}{2}m(m-1)\left(\frac{1}{m}\right)^2 = \frac{1}{2}(1)\left(1 + \frac{1}{m}\right)$$

whereas

$$\frac{1}{2}(m+1)m\left(\frac{1}{m+1}\right)^2 = \frac{1}{2}(1)\left(1 + \frac{1}{m+1}\right).$$

Similarly

$$\frac{1}{6}m(m-1)(m-2)\left(\frac{1}{m}\right)^3 = \frac{1}{6}(1)\left(1 - \frac{1}{m}\right)\left(1 - \frac{2}{m}\right),$$

while

$$\frac{1}{6}(m+1)m(m-1)\left(\frac{1}{m+1}\right)^3 = \frac{1}{6}(1)\left(1 - \frac{1}{m+1}\right)\left(1 - \frac{2}{m+1}\right).$$

So the expression $(1 + 1/m)^m$ is increasing with m. Does it get unboundedly large? No, because

$$\left(1 + \frac{1}{m}\right)^m \leqslant 1 + 1 + \frac{1}{2} + \frac{1}{3!} + \frac{1}{4!} + \cdots + \frac{1}{m!}$$

$$\leqslant 1 + 1 + \frac{1}{2} + \frac{1}{2.2} + \frac{1}{2.2.2.2} + \cdots + \frac{1}{\underbrace{2 \ldots 2}_{m \text{ times}}}$$

$$< 1 + 1 + \frac{1}{2} + \frac{1}{4} + \frac{1}{8} + \cdots \cdot(ad\ infinitum)$$

$$= 1 + \frac{1}{1 - 1/2} = 3.$$

(Here we have summed the geometric progression – see section 4.2.) There is thus a finite limit. The limiting value is denoted by e, i.e.

$$e = \lim_{m \to \infty}\left(1 + \frac{1}{m}\right)^m. \tag{11.2}$$

Calculation shows that e is approximately 2.718.

Coming back to the original problem with the general value of r and writing $k = m/r$ we have

$$\left(1 + \frac{r}{m}\right)^m = \left(1 + \frac{1}{k}\right)^{kr} = \left[\left(1 + \frac{1}{k}\right)^k\right]^r.$$

The natural conjecture is that

$$\lim_{k \to \infty} \left(1 + \frac{1}{k}\right)^{kr} = e^r. \tag{11.3}$$

However, our previous argument leading to (11.2) required m to be an integer but here there is no guarantee that k is an integer. Nevertheless we can choose an integer n such that $n \leqslant k < n + 1$, so that

$$\frac{1}{n} \geqslant \frac{1}{k} > \frac{1}{n+1},$$

and then we have

$$\left(1 + \frac{1}{n+1}\right)^n \leqslant \left(1 + \frac{1}{n+1}\right)^k \leqslant \left(1 + \frac{1}{k}\right)^k \leqslant \left(1 + \frac{1}{n}\right)^k \leqslant \left(1 + \frac{1}{n}\right)^{n+1}$$

or

$$\left(1 + \frac{1}{n+1}\right)^{-1}\left(1 + \frac{1}{n+1}\right)^{n+1} \leqslant \left(1 + \frac{1}{k}\right)^k \leqslant \left(1 + \frac{1}{n}\right)\left(1 + \frac{1}{n}\right)^n.$$

Since

$$\left(1 + \frac{1}{n+1}\right)^{-1} \to 1$$

both sides of the last inequality tend in the limit to e, and so formula (11.2) is valid for arbitrary k tending to infinity. Note that (11.3) says that when the nominal rate per annum is r the *effective interest rate* per annum is e^r, since $\$1$ after a year grows to $\$e^r$.

Evidently if continuous compounding is computed over a period of time t the value of the principal after t years by (11.3) is

$$\lim_{m \to \infty} A\left(1 + \frac{r}{m}\right)^{mt} = Ae^{rt},$$

since t years contain tm instants (when 1 year contains m).

11.2 Connection with differentiation

Suppose we wish to find the derivative of the function $y = a^x$ (figure 11.1) where $a > 0$ and $a \neq 1$. In fact, we shall consider only $a > 1$ (since if $a < 1$ then $1/a > 1$ and $a^x = (1/a)^{-x}$, and so no loss of generality will be incurred).

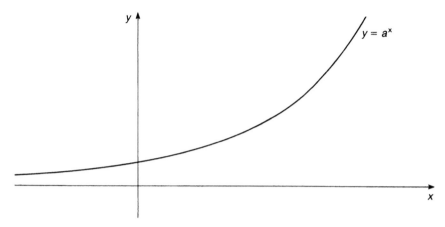

Figure 11.1 Graph of $y = a^x$.

Let us find the derivative when $x = X$. We have

$$\frac{a^{X+h} - a^X}{h} = a^X \frac{a^h - 1}{h}$$

(using $a^{X+h} = a^X a^h$). So all we need to evaluate is

$$l(a) = \lim_{h \to 0} \frac{a^h - 1}{h},$$

assuming that this limit exists, for we may then conclude that

$$\frac{d}{dx}(a^x) = l(a)a^x. \tag{11.4}$$

Obviously $l(a)$ is the slope of the tangent to the curve $y = a^x$ at $x = 0$. We convince ourselves that this limit exists later (see section 11.7.3, question 10). It would be nice to have $l(a) = 1$. We can indeed arrange for this as follows. Take

$$a = 2^{1/l(2)}.$$

Thus from (11.4) we have, using the chain rule (see section 10.4),

$$\frac{d}{dx}(a^x) = \frac{d}{dx}(2^{x/l(2)}) = l(2)2^{x/l(2)} \frac{1}{l(2)} = 2^{x/l(2)} = a^x.$$

Hence if we define $e = 2^{1/l(2)}$ we obtain

$$\frac{d}{dx}(e^x) = e^x. \tag{11.5}$$

We can tie in this last result with the approach of the previous section by considering the slope of e^x at the origin.

By (11.5) the second derivative of e^x is positive, and so the exponential function is *convex*. This tells us that the slope of the chord joining $(0, 1)$ to $(1/n, e^{1/n})$ is greater than the slope of the tangent at $x = 0$ (figure 11.1). But by (11.5) the slope of the tangent is $e^0 = 1$, and so we have

$$1 \leqslant \frac{e^{1/n} - 1}{1/n}$$

which simplifies to

$$1 + \frac{1}{n} \leqslant e^{1/n} \qquad \text{or} \qquad \left(1 + \frac{1}{n}\right)^n \leqslant e. \tag{11.6}$$

This is close to home, but we need inequalities going the other way. Now notice that, if $f(x) \equiv e^x$, then

$$\lim_{n \to \infty} \frac{e^{1/n} - 1}{1/n} = \lim_{h \to 0} \frac{f(h) - f(0)}{h} = f'(0) = 1.$$

Thus if δ is any positive number we shall have for all large n

$$\frac{e^{1/n} - 1}{1/n} \leqslant 1 + \delta. \tag{11.7}$$

Rearrangement leads to

$$e^{1/n} \leqslant 1 + \frac{1 + \delta}{n} \qquad \text{or} \qquad e \leqslant \left(1 + \frac{1 + \delta}{n}\right)^n.$$

Writing k for $n/(1 + \delta)$ we obtain

$$e \leqslant \left[\left(1 + \frac{1}{k}\right)^k\right]^{1 + \delta}. \tag{11.8}$$

To distinguish between the current definition of e and that in the last section, let us temporarily denote the earlier definition by E. Thus

$$E = \lim_{n \to \infty} \left(1 + \frac{1}{n}\right)^n.$$

Then by (11.6) and (11.7) on taking limits we have that

$$E \leqslant e \leqslant E^{1 + \delta}. \tag{11.9}$$

Now let δ approach zero. (Note that we do not allow δ to be zero, because (11.7) fails to be true when $\delta = 0$.) By continuity of the exponential function E^x we have from (11.9) that $E \leqslant e \leqslant E$. The two definitions thus agree.

11.3   Cashing in an appreciating asset

The traditional story goes something like this. A businessman holds an asset which he can sell at time t for a price $V(t)$ where $V(t)$ is an increasing function, i.e. the asset is appreciating in value. At what time should he sell? The answer depends very much on the rate at which the asset is appreciating relative to the bank interest rate. Obviously much depends also on the costs of storing and/or maintaining the asset.

Let us suppose for the moment that storage and maintenance costs are nil and that the nominal annual interest rate is constant at r per cent with the interest compounded continuously. To keep the story simple we suppose that $V(t)$ is a linear function:

$$V(t) = v_0 + at \qquad (a, v_0 > 0).$$

There are a number of ways to solve this timing problem, all of them hinging on a comparison against the return that a deposit in the bank would yield.

One approach is to compute the rate of change

$$\frac{dV}{dt} = a$$

and to consider its ratio to the value $V(t)$. This percentage (or proportional) rate of change is called the *rate of growth* (figure 11.2) which is

$$\frac{1}{V}\frac{dV}{dt} = \frac{a}{at + v_0}.$$

The growth rate is thus decreasing. We compare this growth rate against the growth rate of cash deposited in the bank which is r (see section 11.7.2, question 1). Typically the asset's growth rate begins by exceeding the bank interest rate and then falls to r (when $t = t_0$ say) and continues to decay to zero. After time $t = t_0$ the asset yields a poorer return than cash in the bank. Hence $t = t_0$ is the best time at which to sell, i.e. turn the asset into cash. Thus

$$r = \frac{a}{at_0 + v_0} \qquad \text{or} \qquad t_0 = \frac{a - rv_0}{ar}.$$

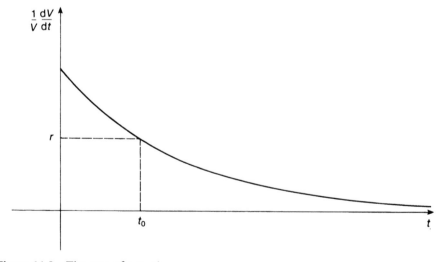

Figure 11.2   The rate of growth.

A less inspired but more predictable argument is to consider the *present value* of selling the asset after an elapse of time t (see section 4.13). Recall that the argument in essence is that a dollar next year is worth less than a dollar this year; after all, 1 dollar deposited until next year yields e^r dollars. So suppose the asset is sold at time t realizing $V(t)$ dollars. Equivalent to this future cash is some amount A_t of cash deposited at present – today (i.e. initially). After time t the principal A_t grows to $A_t e^{rt}$ measured in money at time t. So

$$A_t e^{rt} = V(t) \quad \text{or} \quad A_t = V(t)e^{-rt}.$$

Thus the present value equivalent of cash to be received at a future time t is computed by *discounting* at the nominal rate r. The optimal time is when the present value is maximized (figure 11.3). Obviously the graph is stationary at $t = t_0$. We compute that

$$\frac{d}{dt}[(at + v_0)e^{-rt}] = ae^{-rt} + (at + v_0)e^{-rt}(-r)$$

$$= e^{-rt}[a - r(at + v_0)]$$

and this is zero at t_0 when

$$a = r(at_0 + v_0) \quad \text{or} \quad t_0 = \frac{a - rv_0}{ar}.$$

Clearly our result is valid provided that $a - rv_0 > 0$, i.e. $a/v_0 > r$; otherwise, $dA_t/dt < 0$ for $t > 0$ and the asset is not worth keeping.

Remark

If $V(t)$ is modelled by a polynomial of degree n (which is increasing and positive for all $t \geq 0$) the growth rate declines in much the same way (being a quotient of an $(n-1)$th degree polynomial by an nth degree polynomial). A

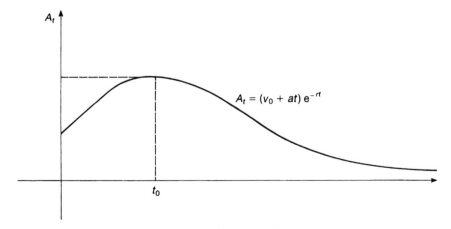

Figure 11.3   The present value of encashment at time t.

different story emerges when we consider $V(t)$ growing exponentially. Clearly $V(t) = v_0 e^{pt}$, which has a growth rate of p, gives a poor model ($p < r$, cash in immediately; $p = r$, cash in any time; $p > r$, never cash in!). Thus a more interesting model must involve the exponential of something slower than a linear function. A favourite is thus $v_0 \exp(t^{1/2})$ (see section 11.7.2, question 6).

11.4   Summing a flow of expenditure

We return to the problem of the last section, wishing now to include a storage and a maintenance cost. Here some new ideas are required. The simplest natural assumption is that the combined storage and maintenance rate is constant. Denoting the cost of combined storage and maintenance charged for the time instant t by $s(t)$ we assume that $s(t) \equiv s$, where s is a constant. Thus each time instant of storage and maintenance has the identical cost s. The present value of the cost of storing for the time duration, between time t and time $t + \delta t$ is $\delta C = e^{-rt} s \, \delta t$. Here, just as before, we have discounted at the rate r. In the limit therefore

$$\frac{dC}{dt} = se^{-rt}.$$

To find the cost we integrate from 0 to T and obtain the present value of storage until $t = T$ to be

$$C(T) = \int_0^T se^{rt} \, dt = -\frac{s}{r}e^{-rT} + \frac{s}{r}.$$

We stop for an important observation. Suppose interest is paid at time instants $t_1, t_2, t_3, \ldots, t_m, \ldots$ where $t_m = m \, \delta t$ (i.e. payment is made after the elapse of each short time interval of length δt). As we have just said the cost of storage over the mth instant is $s \, \delta t$; this has a present value $\delta C_m = s \, \delta t e^{-rt_m}$. Hence the present value of all the costs is

$$\delta C_1 + \delta C_2 + \cdots = \sum_m s \, \delta t e^{-rt_m}.$$

The integral we have just computed is thus the limit of this last sum as δt shrinks to zero. See section 11.7.2, question 9, for a practical application of this idea.

Returning to the problem in hand, in the current situation after including the extra costs the net present value of the asset, if cashed in at time t, is

$$N_t \equiv (at + v_0)e^{-rt} - \left(\frac{s}{r} - \frac{s}{r}e^{-rt} \right)$$

$$= e^{-rt}\left(at + v_0 + \frac{s}{r} \right) - \frac{s}{r}.$$

The N_t curve has much the same shape as the earlier curve. To find its stationary point we differentiate and obtain

$$\frac{d}{dt} N_t = ae^{-rt} + \left(at + v_0 + \frac{s}{r} \right) e^{-rt}(-r)$$

$$= e^{-rt}[(a - rv_0 - s) - rat]$$

so that

$$a - rv_0 - s - rat_0 = 0 \qquad \text{or} \qquad t_0 = \frac{a - rv_0 - s}{ar},$$

which is earlier than before (by s/ar). Again, the result is valid provided that $a \geqslant v_0 r + s$ (for otherwise $dN_t/dt < 0$ for $t > 0$ and the asset is not worth keeping).

We relegate to the exercises models in which storage costs present greater variability.

11.5 Consumer surplus

In the last section we passed from an equation like

$$\frac{dC}{dt} = f(t), \tag{11.10}$$

where $f(t)$ represented the present value of instantaneous storage cost, to the equation

$$C(T) = \int_0^T f(t)\, dt \tag{11.11}$$

and remarked that this integral was in effect the limit of a sum such as

$$\sum_m f(t_m)\, \delta t. \tag{11.12}$$

It is easy to interpret this idea geometrically. The sum (11.12) is an approximation to the area under the graph of $f(t)$ (figure 11.4). Each of the terms $f(t_m)\,\delta t$ represents a strip of height $f(t_m)$ and width δt. This is particularly clear when $f(t)$ is decreasing. The approximation should be good when δt is small. Let us now assume only that $f(t)$ is continuous. If $A(t)$ denotes the area under the graph over the interval $[0, t]$, then clearly for any increment δt we have

$$m\,\delta t \leqslant A(t + \delta t) - A(t) \leqslant M\,\delta t,$$

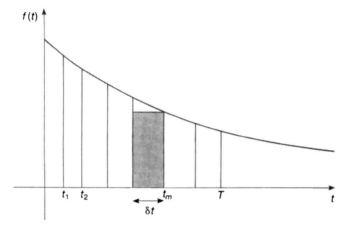

Figure 11.4   The shaded area is equal to $f(t_m)\,\delta t$.

where m and M denote the smallest and largest value of $f(t)$ on the interval $[t, t + \delta t]$ (figure 11.5). Hence

$$m \leqslant \frac{A(t + \delta t) - A(t)}{\delta t} \leqslant M.$$

Thus as $\delta t \to 0$, m and M both approach $f(t)$ and so

$$\frac{\mathrm{d}A}{\mathrm{d}t} = \lim_{\delta t \to 0} \frac{A(t + \delta t) - A(t)}{\delta t} = f(t).$$

We thus see integration as both the inverse operation to differentiation taking us from (11.10) to (11.11) and as a calculation of area taking us in the limit from sums like (11.12) to (11.11). We use both these ideas in the discussion of consumer surplus, which we break up into a number of steps.

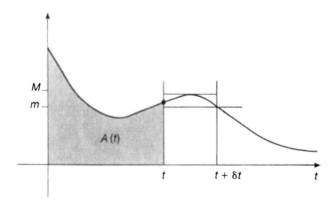

Figure 11.5   The increment in area is numerically between $m\,\delta t$ and $M\,\delta t$.

Example 1: Aggregate demand and consumer surplus

Figure 11.6 shows the market demand curve for a single commodity. Thus if the price is p there is a demand for a quantity $Q_d(p)$. It will also be convenient to refer to the inverse function of $Q_d(p)$ which we denote by $P(q)$. Thus the formula $q = Q_d(p)$ is equivalent to $p = P(q)$ (see section 10.6).

What units is the area under the curve measured in? Clearly the answer is 'price × quantity', i.e. money. In that case, what meaning may be attached to this money? To answer this important question we consider the behaviour of a perfectly discriminating monopolist who intends to sell an amount Q^*. He begins by naming a high price p_1 and releasing for sale a small amount of the commodity, say $\delta q_1 = Q(p_1)$; he knows that there are buyers willing to pay this high price – this is precisely the information conveyed by the demand curve. But he needs to persuade these potential buyers that he will not be supplying any more of the commodity to the market until the current supply is sold. Presumably, as sole supplier, he is able to do so (e.g. by threatening not to produce any more output for the time being). Having secured the sale, he pockets an amount $p_1 \, \delta q_1$ of revenue.

The monopolist can now place another small quantity δq_2 on the market but at a lower price. From the demand curve we see that when the price is p_2 the market can absorb $q_2 = Q_d(p_2)$. So, since part of that demand has already been met, there remains $\delta q_2 = q_2 - \delta q_1$ which can be sold at p_2 – again provided the supplier persuades the new buyers that no further output will be placed on the market until the current offering is taken up. Having effected the next sale the monopolist pockets $p_2 \, \delta q_2$.

The story continues until the monopolist has realized his target output Q^* bit by bit. His total revenue is thus

$$p_1 \, \delta q_1 + p_2 \, \delta q_2 + \cdots + p_n \, \delta q_n.$$

Let us take the increments δq_r all to be equal to δq; then in the limit as $\delta q \to 0$ the monopolist's revenue approaches the value of the integral

$$\int_0^{Q^*} P(q) \, dq.$$

Thus the area under the graph represents the total revenue to a perfectly discriminating monopolist.

Now let us suppose that the supply of the commodity is competitive, instead of monopolist, and that the suppliers sell at the price p^*. From the demand curve we see that the market will absorb an amount Q^*. The expenditure by the consumers is then p^*Q^* which is represented by a rectangle below the demand curve. The difference between the monopolist's takings and p^*Q^*, represented in figure 11.7 by the area between the curve and the horizontal, is thus a net gain to the consumers resulting from the competitive framework. It is known as the *consumers' surplus*. We thus have

$$\text{consumers' surplus} = \int_0^{Q^*} P(q) \, dq - p^*Q^*. \tag{11.13}$$

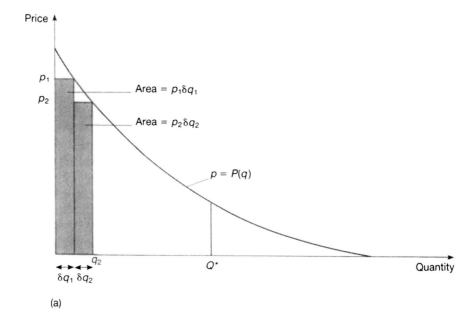

(a)

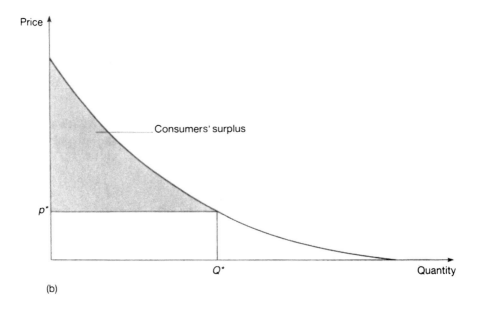

(b)

Figure 11.6 (a) The monopolist extracts revenue equal to the area under the demand curve for $0 \leqslant q \leqslant Q^*$; (b) the shaded area represents the consumers' surplus.

To place this market discussion in perspective we next consider this issue from the point of view of an individual consumer.

Example 2: Individual consumer surplus
Figure 11.7 denotes the demand curve of an individual consumer *i*. As in the previous example we will wish to think of it as graphing the amount *q* demanded by the individual when the price is *p*. It is thus the graph of $Q_d^i(p)$. We shall derive an interesting relationship between the individual's demand and his utility. To do this we assume that the individual evaluates a bundle of goods including an amount *q* of the particular commodity under discussion according to the formula

$$U(q, c) = v(q) + c$$

where *c* is the dollar cost of the remaining commodities. The formula, by implication, measures the utility level *v(q)* in dollars. The function *U(q, c)* is said to be quasi-linear. The usual assumptions are made on *v(q)*, namely that it is an increasing concave function and $v(0) = 0$.

The following calculation assumes that the consumer is a price-taker and the prevailing price of the fixed commodity is *p*. Assuming his budget is *b* he will choose an amount *q* which maximizes $U(q, b - pq)$. The first-order condition for maximization then reads

$$0 = \frac{dU}{dq} = \frac{d}{dq}[v(q) + b - pq] = v'(q) - p.$$

Hence *q* is selected so that $p = v'(q)$, i.e. so that the marginal utility equals the price.

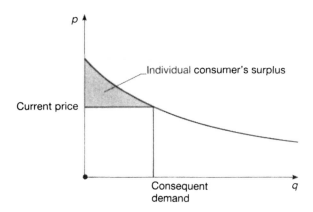

Figure 11.7 Individual's demand curve. The shaded area is equal to the surplus gain.

We have thus deduced that under quasi-linear utility it is the case that

$$p = v'(q)$$

$$q = Q_d{}^i(p).$$

We can eliminate p between these two equations if we make use of the inverse function of $Q_d{}^i(p)$. Denote the inverse function by $P_i(q)$. Thus $p = P_i(q)$ if and only if $q = Q_d{}^i(p)$. We now have

$$\frac{dv}{dq} = P_i(q).$$

Using the notation of the previous example we suppose that the current price is p^* and that the individual consumer i demands Q_i. Integrating with respect to q from 0 to Q_i we obtain

$$v(Q_i) = v(Q_i) - v(0) = [v]_0^{Q_i} = \int_0^{Q_i} \frac{dv}{dq} \, dq = \int_0^{Q_i} P_i(q) \, dq.$$

Thus the utility of the demanded quantity equals the area between the demand curve and the q axis. Subtracting the actual expenditure p^*Q_i we obtain the individual consumer's surplus (this time singular) as the net utility gain of trading. This may be interpreted geometrically as the area between the demand curve and the horizontal corresponding to the current price. We thus have

$$\text{individual's surplus} = \int_0^{Q_i} P_i(q) \, dq - p^*Q_i. \qquad (11.14)$$

Example 3: Aggregate surplus as aggregate of individual surpluses
To establish an immediate connection between the two results assume that the market consists of N identical consumers; thus $P_i(q) = P(q)$ for each i. Hence, in general, if the price is p each individual demands the same quantity $Q_i = q$; thus the aggregate demand Q equals Nq where $p = P(q)$ and evidently $p = P(Q/N)$. Hence, in particular, if the current price is p^* and current total demand is Q^* we can use the formula (11.13) to calculate the aggregate surplus:

$$\text{consumers' surplus} = \int_0^{Q^*} P(Q/N) \, dQ - p^*Q^*$$

$$= \int_0^{q^*} P(q)N \, dq - p^*Nq^*$$

$$= N\left[\int_0^{q^*} P(q) \, dq - p^*q^*\right]$$

$$= N \times \text{individual surplus},$$

where we have used the substitution Nq for Q in the second line (from which it follows that $Ndq = dQ$) and have applied formula (11.14) in the last line.

11.6   Logarithms and how to double your money

We saw in section 10.6 how to invert the demand curve to extract useful information. In this section we consider the inverse of the exponential function. The inverse function of $y = a^x$ for $a > 1$ is known as the *logarithm to the base a*. Thus

$$y = a^x \quad \text{if and only if} \quad x = \log_a y. \qquad (11.15)$$

When $a = e$ we write simply log. Sometimes ln is used for $\log_e$. Its existence is assured because $y = a^x$ for $a > 1$ is a strictly increasing function. We recall from section 10.6 that the logarithm graph is obtained by drawing the exponential graph on a transparency and then rotating counterclockwise through 90° and turning the transparency over (figure 11.8).

Most of this section is devoted to traditional uses of logarithms but before plunging into them our priority is to consider facts which are more prominent in economic modelling.

11.6.1   Differentiation

It is particularly easy to find the derivative of the function $\log_e(y)$, using the inverse function rule of section 10.6. We have

$$y = e^x \qquad \text{or} \qquad x = \log_e y$$

and so

$$\frac{dy}{dx} = e^x.$$

Hence

$$\frac{dx}{dy} = 1 \bigg/ \frac{dy}{dx} = \frac{1}{e^x} = \frac{1}{y}.$$

Thus

$$\frac{d}{dy} \log_e y = \frac{1}{y}.$$

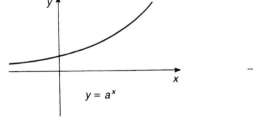

y = a^x

x = log_a(y)

Figure 11.8   Graph of a^x and its inverse $\ln(y)$.

But now we face the more general problem of differentiating a^x and $\log_a y$. In view of the simple form of the answer when $a = e$ we transform the general problem back to the simpler case.

Suppose $y = a^x$. Let $a = e^b$; then $y = (e^b)^x = e^{bx}$. Hence

$$\frac{dy}{dx} = e^{bx}b = ba^x.$$

But $a = e^b$ implies that $\log_e a = \log_e e^b = b$. Thus

$$\frac{d}{dx}(a^x) = (\log_e a)\, a^x.$$

So the number $l(a)$ defined in section 11.2 was just $\log_e a$.

Now suppose $z = \log_a y$; we find dz/dy. We have

$$z = \log_a y \quad \text{if and only if} \quad y = a^z.$$

So

$$\frac{dy}{dz} = a^z \log_e a = y \log_e a.$$

Hence

$$\frac{dz}{dy} = 1 \left/ \frac{dy}{dz} \right. = \frac{1}{y} \frac{1}{\log_e a}.$$

11.6.2 Concavity

Observe that if $z = \log_a y$ then

$$\frac{d^2z}{dy^2} = -\frac{1}{y^2} \log_e a,$$

which is negative for $a > 1$, so that the logarithm functions are all concave. This makes logarithms also favourites for modelling utility functions, especially in the forms

$$u(x) = \log(1 + x) \qquad\qquad (x \geqslant 0)$$

or

$$u(x, y) = \log[(1 + x)^\alpha (1 + y)^\beta] \qquad (x \geqslant 0, y \geqslant 0).$$

These carry some advantages over the Cobb–Douglas functions (see section 15.11, question 15).

11.6.3 Double your money

We return to compounding interest in discrete time. Suppose a principal A is deposited with a bank which offers an annual interest rate r. How long before the principal doubles?

The simple-minded approach is to consider solving

$$2A = A(1 + r)^t \qquad \text{or} \qquad 2 = (1 + r)^t$$

but a glance at the discontinuous graph shows that the equation might never hold for $t = 0, 1, 2, \ldots$. Evidently, if we replace the problem with continuous discounting at an effective rate $1 + r$ (so that $1 + r = e^s$, where s is the nominal rate under continuous compounding), then the curve achieves the value 2 (figure 11.9). We have

$$2 = e^{st} \Leftrightarrow st = \log 2 \Leftrightarrow t = \frac{\log t}{\log(1 + r)}$$

since $s = \log(1 + r)$.

11.6.4   Logarithmic folklore

The logarithmic functions $\log_a y$ have several uses based on one fundamental property. Begin by recalling that

$$a^{x_1} a^{x_2} = a^{x_1 + x_2}. \tag{11.16}$$

Put $y_1 = a^{x_1}$ and $y_2 = a^{x_2}$, so that

$$x_1 = \log_a y_1 \qquad \text{and} \qquad x_2 = \log_a y_2.$$

But now by (11.16)

$$y_1 y_2 = a^{x_1 + x_2} = a^{\log_a y_1 + \log_a y_2}. \tag{11.17}$$

Hence by (11.17)

$$\log_a(y_1 y_2) = \log_a(a^{\log_a y_1 + \log_a y_2})$$

$$= \log_a y_1 + \log_a y_2.$$

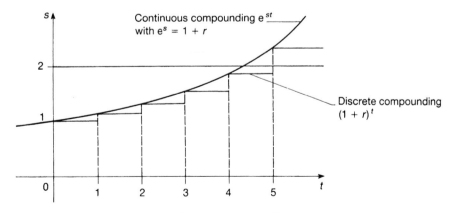

Figure 11.9   Discrete versus continuous compounding.

The basic property of logarithms that

$$\log_a(y_1 y_2) = \log_a y_1 + \log_a y_2$$

was for many years used to simplify calculations involving multiplication; $a = 10$ was commonly used.

How to compute $A \times B$

1 Consult tables to find $\log_{10} A$ and $\log_{10} B$.
2 Obtain $C = \log_{10} A + \log_{10} B$.
3 Consult 'antilogarithm' tables (i.e. tables giving 10^x for various x) to find 10^C, the answer.

Reason

$$\log_{10} 10^C = C = \log_{10} A + \log_{10} B,$$

i.e.

$$\log_{10} 10^C = \log_{10}(AB)$$

and so

$$10^C = AB.$$

Logarithms to the base 10, in view of their practical significance, are called *common* logarithms; those to base e = 2.718 ... are called *natural* because of their simpler derivative (section 11.2). The procedure above is illustrated in figure 11.10. Before electronic calculators became readily available the procedure was implemented on a slide rule, i.e. a ruler with numbers marked along a 'logarithmic scale' containing a central sliding scale also marked up logarithmically. Numbers are marked up according to their logarithmic distance, e.g. 2 is where 0.3010 (= $\log_{10} 2$) might be expected on an ordinary scale.

Before we attempt a worked example, notice that for the base 10 we have by (11.15)

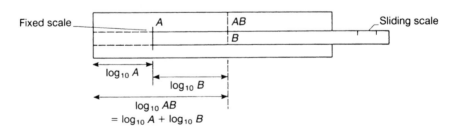

Figure 11.10 Multiplication on a slide rule. Numbers on both scales are marked up according to their logarithmic distance, e.g. 2 is a distance 0.3010 from the beginning of the scale.

$\log_{10} 1 = 0$ since $10^0 = 1$,

$\log_{10} 10 = 1$ since $10^1 = 10$,

$\log_{10} 100 = 2$ since $10^2 = 100$,

$\log_{10} 2 = 0.3010$ by a calculation to be performed in section 14.10, question 4.

Hence

$$\log_{10} 20 = 1.3010$$

as $20 = 2 \times 10$, so add log 2 + log 10, and similarly

$$\log_{10} 200 = 2.3010$$

as $200 = 2 \times 100$. Also

$$\log_{10} 0.1 = -1$$

as $10^{-1} = 1/10$ and

$$\log_{10} 0.2 = -1 + 0.3010$$

as $0.2 = 2 \times 1/10$. In view of the above tricks (involving the moving of the decimal point, as in $0.2 = 2 \times 0.1$ and $20 = 2 \times 10$) it is only necessary for base 10 work to tabulate $\log_{10} x$ for $1 \leqslant x < 10$ and this may be done (using formulae like the ones in section 14.4 say) to some desired accuracy, e.g. in steps of 1/10,000 (giving four-figure accuracy).

Examples
1   Compute 3.1415×1.414.

SOLUTION   We note that

$$\log_{10} 3.1415 = 0.497\ 14$$
$$\log_{10} 1.414 = \underline{0.150\ 44}$$
$$\text{total} = 0.647\ 58.$$

Hence

$$\log_{10}(3.1415 \times 1.414) = 0.647\ 58.$$

Consequently

$$\text{answer} = 4.444.$$

A further example illustrates the power of this method.

2   Find A^B.

SOLUTION   Take logarithms as before to base 10. Let

$$C = \log_{10} A.$$

Then

$$10^C = A.$$

(Recall that $x = \log_a y \Leftrightarrow y = a^x$.) Hence

$$A^B = (10^C)^B = 10^{BC}. \qquad (11.18)$$

Thus the procedure is

1   Compute $C = \log_{10} A$.
2   Obtain $BC = B \times \log_{10} A$ (might involve logs again).
3   Look up 10^{BC} in antilog tables.

Note that by (11.18)

$$\log_a A^B = B \log_a A. \qquad (11.19)$$

This very useful formula allows conversion of logarithms from one base to another.

3   Compute $C = \log_e A$.

SOLUTION   By definition $e^C = A$. Hence

$$\log_{10} A = \log_{10} e^C$$
$$= C \log_{10} e \quad \text{(by (11.19))}.$$

Thus

$$\log_e A = \frac{\log_{10} A}{\log_{10} e}.$$

Similarly we can compute conversions of exponentials, e.g. 2^x in terms of e^x. We have

$$\log_e 2^x = x \log_e 2.$$

Hence, writing $\exp(z)$ for e^z we have

$$2^x = \exp(\log_e 2^x) = \exp(x \log_e 2) \qquad \text{(i.e. } e^{x \log 2}\text{)}.$$

Finally note the alternative treatment of A^B for integer B.

4   Compute A^{27}.

SOLUTION
1   Consult tables to find $\log_{10} A$.
2   Obtain $C = 27 \times \log_{10} A$.
3   Look up 10^C (in antilog tables).

The reasoning is

$$\underbrace{\log_{10} A \times \cdots \times A}_{27 \text{ times}} = \underbrace{\log_{10} A + \log_{10} A + \cdots + \log_{10} A}_{27 \text{ times}}$$
$$= 27 \log_{10} A \text{ etc.}$$

11.6.5 Curve fitting

Suppose we wish to fit a curve of the form $q_1^\alpha q_2^\beta = c$ through some observed (q_1, q_2) data points (figure 11.11); this idea might well arise from the fact that when plotted on graph paper the data points look as though they lie on a curve with some such Cobb–Douglas equation.

Taking logarithms we obtain a linear relationship

$$\alpha(\log_{10} q_1) + \beta(\log_{10} q_2) = \log_{10} c.$$

We now plot the logarithms of the data points and seek a straight line with slope $-\alpha/\beta$ (figure 11.12). This is an altogether easier task, especially if graph paper marked with a logarithmic scale is available.

11.7 Exercises

11.7.1 Exponential functions

1* Find the first derivatives of the following functions:

$$\exp(x^2) \qquad xe^x \qquad \log(1 + x^2) \qquad 2^x.$$

2 Find the first derivatives of the following functions:

$$x \log x \qquad e^x \cos x \qquad \log(1 + e^x) \qquad x^x \, (= e^{x \log x}).$$

3 Show that

$$\frac{d}{dx} \{\log[f(x)]\} = \frac{f'(x)}{f(x)}$$

$$\frac{d}{dx} \{[f(x)]^{1/2}\} = \frac{f'(x)}{2[f(x)]^{1/2}}.$$

4 Use the previous question to find

$$\int \frac{x \, dx}{x^2 + 1} \qquad \int \frac{x \, dx}{(x^2 + 1)^{1/2}}.$$

5 Find the following integrals:

$$\int \log x \, dx \qquad \int \frac{dx}{1 - x^2} \qquad \int x \log x \, dx \quad \left(= \int \frac{1}{2} x \log x^2 \, dx \right).$$

(Note that $2/(1 - x^2) = 1/(1 - x) + 1/(1 + x)$.)

6* Use the definition of the derivative to show that

$$\lim_{h \to 0} \frac{e^h - 1}{h} = 1.$$

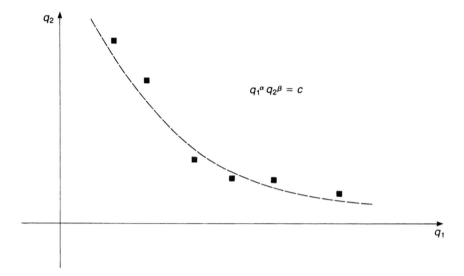

Figure 11.11 Fitting a curve through data points.

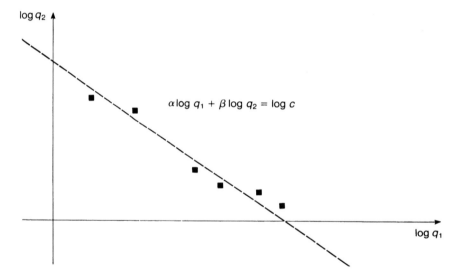

Figure 11.12 Equivalent problem on a logarithmic scale: fitting a line.

Deduce that

$$\lim_{x \to 0} \frac{1 - e^{-x}}{x} = 1.$$

7   If $y = \frac{1}{2}(e^x + e^{-x})$, show that

(a) $y(x) = y(-x),$

(b) $y'(0) = 0,$

(c) $y'(x) > 0$ for $x > 0$ and $y'(x) < 0$ for $x < 0$,
(d) y has a minimum value of 1 at $x = 0$,
(e) $y''(x) = y(x) > 0$, and so y has a convex graph.

Sketch the function.

8*   If $y = Ae^x + Be^{-x}$ and A, $B > 0$, check that y has a minimum value of $2(AB)^{1/2}$ at $x = \xi$ where $\xi = \frac{1}{2} \log B/A$. Show that

$$y(x) = Ae^{\xi}(e^{x-\xi} + e^{-(x-\xi)}).$$

Sketch the graph of y.

9   If $y = \frac{1}{2}(e^x - e^{-x})$, show that

(a) $y(x) = y(-x)$ and $y(0) = 0$,
(b) $y'(x) > 0$ for all x and $y'(0) = 1$,
(c) $y''(x) = y(x) > 0$, so that y is convex for $x > 0$ and concave for $x < 0$.

Sketch the function.

10*   If $y = Ae^x - Be^{-x}$ with A, $B > 0$ check that $y = 0$ at $x = \xi$ where $\xi = \frac{1}{2} \log (B/A)$. Show that

$$y(x) = Ae^{\xi}(e^{x-\xi} - e^{-(x-\xi)}).$$

Also show that

$$y''(\xi) = 0 \qquad y'(\xi) = 2(AB)^{1/2}.$$

Sketch the graph of y.

11   If $y = \frac{1}{2}(e^x + e^{-x})$, then $e^{2x} - 2ye^x + 1 = 0$. Deduce that, if $x > 0$,

$$x = \log [y + (y^2 - 1)^{1/2}].$$

12   If $y = \frac{1}{2}(e^x - e^{-x})$, then $e^{2x} - 2ye^x - 1 = 0$. Deduce that, if $x > 0$,

$$x = \log [y + (y^2 + 1)^{1/2}].$$

13   If y is given by question 11 deduce that

$$\frac{dx}{dy} = \frac{1}{(y^2 - 1)^{1/2}}.$$

[Hint: Show that $(dy/dx)^2 = y^2 - 1$, or use the formula in question 11.]

14*   If y is given by question 12 deduce that

$$\frac{dx}{dy} = \frac{1}{(y^2 + 1)^{1/2}}.$$

[Hint: Show that $(dy/dx)^2 = y^2 + 1$, or use the formula in question 12.]

15 A function is defined for $x \neq 0$ by

$$y = \frac{e^{-x}}{1 - e^{-x}} \quad \left(= \frac{1}{1 - e^{-x}} - 1 \right).$$

Show that $y' < 0$ for $x \neq 0$. Show that $y'' > 0$ for $x > 0$ and $y'' < 0$ for $x < 0$. Plot the curve.

16* Show that $e^x - x > 0$ for $x > 0$. [*Hint*: $e^x - x$ is increasing.] For any A deduce that $c^{2x} > 2Ax$ provided that $x > \log(2A)$ and so $e^z > Az$ for $z > 2 \log(2A)$. Show also that xe^{-x} is decreasing for $x > 1$. Deduce that $xe^{-x} \to 0$ as $x \to \infty$.

17 Show that, if $z = 1 - x - e^{-x}$, then z is decreasing for $x > 0$. Hence for the function defined for $x \geq 0$ by

$$y = \frac{xe^{-x}}{1 - e^{-x}}$$

show that $y'(x) < 0$ for $x > 0$. Hence plot the graph of y.

11.7.2 Present value

1 If $V = Ae^{rt}$ check that the interest rate r is the growth rate of V.

2* Deposits are made continuously (without withdrawals) into an account with a nominal continuous compounding interest r. If the rate of deposit is constant and equal to s, what is the amount in deposit after time t?

3 Suppose maintenance and storage rates increase with time so that the (discounted) present value now satisfies

$$\frac{dC}{dt} = (s + mt)e^{-rt}$$

where s measures storage costs and mt measures the increasing costs of maintenance. Find the optimal time for the model $V(t) = v_0 + at$.

4* A dealer has just acquired an asset whose value, if sold after an elapse of time t, is

$$V(t) = 1 + t^2 \qquad (t \geq 0).$$

If interest is compounded continuously at a rate r what is the present value of the asset if it is to be sold after an elapse of time t. What value of t maximizes this present value? If the rate is 10 per cent estimate this value of t.

5* In the previous question, if storage costs are incurred and the cost at time t is known to be $t + 1$ per unit time, write down the integral giving the present value of storing the asset for the time period $0 \leq t \leq T$ and evaluate this integral.

Obtain the present value of the asset net of storage costs if it is encashed at time T. What is the optimal time for encashment? Estimate the optimal time when the rate of interest is 10 per cent.

6   (A simple model of currency dealing.) A payment of M units in a foreign currency is due at time T. The exchange rate is thought to follow the function $e(t)$ so that $\$e(t)$ buys 1 unit of the foreign currency. The home bank rate is r.

(a) Assuming first that the foreign country has a negligible bank rate, show by minimizing the present value $p(t)$ of buying the M units at time t that either the first-order condition on the optimal time of exchange is obeyed,

$$\frac{e'(t)}{e(t)} = r,$$

or else $t = T$.

(b) Assuming now that the foreign country has a bank rate of s show that the corresponding first-order condition is

$$\frac{e'(t)}{e(t)} = r - s.$$

(c) Taking $e(t) = A + Bt + C \sin t$ (so that fluctuations have a period of 2π), verify that when $A = B = C$ the growth of the exchange rate, namely

$$g(t) = \frac{e'(t)}{e(t)},$$

has a graph as indicated in figure 11.13, so that
(i) $g(t) \geqslant 0$ for $t > 0$,
(ii) $g(t) \to 0$ as $t \to \infty$,
(iii) $g[(2n + 1)\pi] = 0$.

Thus for a given bank rate r the present value $p(t)$ has a finite number of local minima. Hence, depending on the due date T the optimal time of exchange may be either $t = T$ or the largest $t < T$ at which $g(t) = r$.

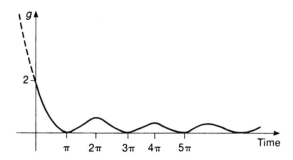

Figure 11.13   Growth of the exchange rate.

(d) Compute the local minimum times when $A = 2$, $B = 0$. [*Hint*: $\cos(t - \alpha) = 2r/(1 - r^2)^{1/2}$ with $\tan \alpha = r$.]

(e) Obtain computer graphs of $p(t)$ when $r = 5$ per cent and $A = 2$, $B = 0.1$, $C = 1$.

7* Find the optimal time for selling an appreciating asset if $V(t) = \exp(t^{1/2})$ when (a) storage costs are zero, (b) storage costs are as in section 11.4. In case (b) plot the curve $\exp(t^{1/2})$ and $2st^{1/2}/(1 - 2rt^{1/2})$ to deduce that the optimal time t_0 satisfies

$$\frac{1}{4(r + s)^2} < t < \frac{1}{4r^2}.$$

8 Repeat the previous problem for $V(t) = 2^t$.

9 What is wrong with the following argument (figure 11.14)? 'For the valuation $V(t) = v_0 + at$ of the appreciating asset, compare the final value, namely $v_0 e^{rt}$, of depositing the initial cash amount v_0 after an elapse of time t with the final $v_0 + at$. Therefore sell when $v_0 + at = v_0 e^{rt}$.'

10 A film society possesses a circular cinema film spool with a hub radius a of 6 cm and an overall radius b of 27.5 cm. Its running time is 50 min. However, the film society wishes to show a film of somewhat greater running time and considers extending the rim of the spool so that the reel has radius $c = 33$ cm; use the fact that $\Sigma_i 2\pi r_i \, \delta r \approx \int 2\pi r \, dr$ to show that the running time T satisfies

$$\frac{T}{50} \approx \frac{c^2 - a^2}{b^2 - a^2},$$

so that $T \approx 73$ min.

11 If the thickness of the film is d show that the length of film on the spool is

$$\pi(a + b)(b - a + d)/d,$$

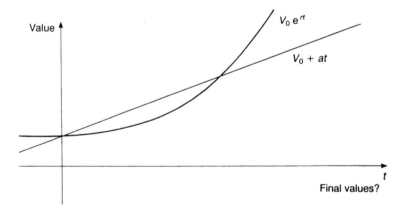

Figure 11.14   In support of a fallacious argument.

so that in fact

$$\frac{T}{50} = \frac{(c+a)(c-a+d)}{(b+a)(b-a+d)}.$$

Show also that the error in the earlier equation is $0.013d$, i.e. less than the twinkling of an eye, and hence not noticeable. [Hint: $(A+d)/(B+d) - A/B = (B-a)\,d/[B(B+d)]$.]

11.7.3 Checking for concavity

1* Plot the logistic curve

$$y = \frac{1}{1 + e^{-kx}}.$$

Verify that $y' = ky(1-y)$. Find y'' and check where the curve is convex and where it is concave.

2* Plot the curve $y = x^{1/2} - rx$ for $x > 0$ and verify that it is concave (i.e. has a negative second derivative).

3 For the cubic curve

$$y = 4r^2x^3 - 4rx^2 + x - 1 \qquad (0 < r < 1)$$

show that the stationary points are at $x = 1/(6r)$ and $x = 1/(2r)$. Check that, when $x = 1/(6r)$, y may be either negative or positive depending on whether $r < 4/54$ or $r > 4/54$. Where is the curve concave and where convex? Sketch the curve for the two cases $r < 4/54$, $r > 4/54$.

4* For the curve

$$y = \exp(x^{1/2} - rx) \qquad (0 < r < 1)$$

find y' and locate the stationary point. Also find y''. Refer to the last question to determine the sign of y'' and sketch the graph of y for the two cases $r < 4/54$, $r > 4/54$. [Hint: You will find the cubic polynomial of the last question if you substitute $z = x^{1/2}$ in y''.]

5 Explain why investment I and capital K are related by the equation $I = dK/dt$. Consider the national income analysis of section 10.2 amended to read

$$Y = C + I \qquad \text{with} \qquad C = mY + c.$$

Suppose national income is driven by investment via the Cobb–Douglas production function $Y = K^{1/2}$ (so that $K = Y^2$). Show that

$$\frac{dt}{dY} = \frac{2Y}{sY - c}$$

where $s = 1 - m$ is the marginal propensity to save. Integrate with respect to Y.

6   Show that

$$m \log_e \left(1 + \frac{1}{m}\right) \rightarrow \log_e(e) = 1 \text{ as } m \rightarrow \infty.$$

Verify that

$$\frac{\log(x+h) - \log x}{h} = \frac{1}{x}\left[\frac{x}{h}\log\left(1 + \frac{h}{x}\right)\right]$$

and so obtain an alternative proof that the derivative of $\log_e x$ is $1/x$.

7   Show that the price elasticity of the demand function $q = Ae^{-p}$ is $\eta = p$. (Recall that $\eta = -(dq/dp)/(p/q)$.) Comment on the convexity of q.

8   Repeat the last problem with $q = A(1 - e^{-1/p})$ and show that

$$\eta = \frac{1}{p}\frac{e^{-1/p}}{1 - e^{-1/p}}.$$

Find q'' and sketch the demand curve. [*Hint*: When $p = 0$, assume $e^{-1/0} = e^{-\infty} = 0$ and $\eta = 0$.]

9   Plot the demand curve

$$q = \frac{2}{1 + e^{kp}} \qquad (p \geqslant 0)$$

and check that it is convex. Find the elasticity η and plot $|\eta|$.

10   Let $m(h) = (a^h - 1)/h$. Show that if $0 < k < h$ then

$$m(-1) < m(k) < m(h).$$

[*Hint*: Refer to figure 11.15. The point (k, a^k) is on the graph and by convexity below the chord. Also the chord slope is increasing.] Hence $m(h)$ decreases to a finite limit as $h \rightarrow 0$.

11.8   Answers

11.8.1   Exponential functions

1   Denoting differentiation by D we have $D[\exp(x^2)] = \exp(x^2) 2x$; $D(xe^x) = e^x + xe^x$; $D[\log(1 + x^2)] = 2x/(1 + x^2)$; $D(2^x) = D(e^{x\log 2}) = e^{x\log 2} \cdot \log 2 = 2^x \cdot \log_e 2$.

6   If $f(x) = e^x$ then

$$1 = e^0 = f'(0) = \lim_{h \to 0} \frac{f(h) - f(0)}{h} = \lim_{h \to 0} \frac{e^h - 1}{h}.$$

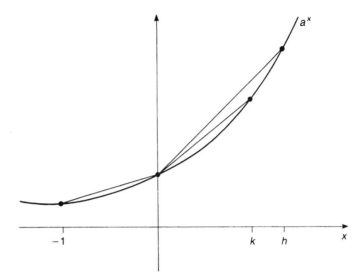

Figure 11.15 Chords of the graph of a^x.

Hence, writing $h = -x$ we obtain

$$1 = \lim_{x \to 0} \frac{e^{-x} - 1}{-x} = \lim_{x \to 0} \frac{1 - e^{-x}}{x}.$$

8   $y' = Ae^x - Be^{-x}$. Thus $y' = 0$ when $e^{2x} = B/A$, or $x = \frac{1}{2} \log (B/A)$. Since $y' = Ae^x + Be^{-x} > 0$ the function is convex and the stationary point is a global minimum. Evidently since $e^{2\xi} = B/A$ we have

$$y = Ae^x + Ae^{2\xi}e^{-x} = Ae^{\xi}(e^{x - \xi} + e^{\xi - x}).$$

Thus the curve is as illustrated in figure 11.16. Note that at $x = \xi$ we have $y = 2Ae^{\xi} = 2A(B/A)^{1/2} = 2(AB)^{1/2}$.

10   Here $y' = Ae^x + Be^{-x} > 0$. Evidently $y = 0$ of $Ae^{2x} = B$ and so $e^{2x} = B/A$. We note that $y'' = y$ and so $x = \frac{1}{2} \log (B/A)$ is a point of inflexion (figure 11.17).

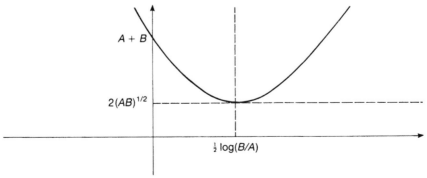

Figure 11.16 Graph of $y = Ae^x - Be^{-x}$.

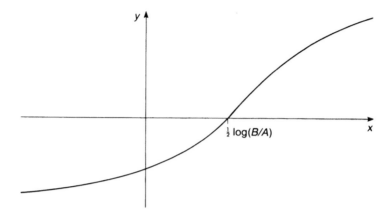

Figure 11.17 Graph of $y = Ae^x + Be^{-x}$.

14 Evidently $y'^2 = \frac{1}{4}(e^{2x} + 2 + e^{-2x}) = \frac{1}{4}(e^{2x} - 2 + e^{-2x}) + 1 = y^2 + 1$.

16 If $y = e^x - x$ then $y' = e^x - 1 > 0$ provided that $e^x > 1$, i.e. $x > 0$. Thus for $x > 0$ the function is increasing. But $e^0 - 0 = 1 > 0$. And so the function remains positive. Hence $e^{2x} \geq e^x e^x = e^x x > 2Ax$ for $e^x > 2A$, i.e. for $x > \log(2A)$. Thus $e^z \geq Az$ for $z > 2 \log(2A)$ $(z = 2x)$.

If $y = xe^{-x}$ then $y' = e^{-x} - xe^{-x} = e^{-x}(1 - x)$. Hence $y' < 0$ for $x > 1$. If $\lim xe^{-x} = k > 0$ then $xe^x \geq k$, i.e. $e^x \leq x/k$ for all x, contradicting the earlier result.

11.8.2 Present value

2

$$\text{balance at time } t = \int_0^t se^{rt}\, dt$$

$$= s\left[\frac{e^{rt}}{r}\right]_0^t = \frac{s}{r}(e^{rt} - 1).$$

4

$$PV = e^{-rt}(1 + t^2).$$

$$PV' = e^{-rt}[-r(1 + t^2) + 2t]$$

$$PV' = 0 \leftrightarrow rt^2 - 2t + r = 0$$

$$\leftrightarrow t = \frac{1 \pm (1 - r^2)^{1/2}}{r}$$

$$PV'' = e^{-rt}[r^2(1 + t^2) - 2tr + 2 - 2tr]$$

$$= e^{-rt}\{-r[2t - r(1 + t^2)] + 2(1 - tr)\}.$$

At $t = t_+$

$$PV'' = e^{-rt}2\{1 - [1 + (1 - r^2)^{1/2}]\} < 0.$$

At $t = t_-$

$$PV'' = e^{-rt}2\{1 - [1 - (1 - r^2)^{1/2}]\} > 0.$$

There is thus a local maximum at $t = t_+$.

$$PV(0) = 1$$

$$PV(t_+) = \exp\{-[1 + (1 - r^2)^{1/2}]\}(1 + t_+^2)$$

$$PV(t_+) > 1 \Leftrightarrow 1 + t_+^2 > \exp[1 + (1 - r^2)^{1/2}].$$

If $r = 0.1$

$$t_+ = \frac{1 + \sqrt{(0.99)}}{0.1} \approx 20.$$

Clearly $e^2 < 9$ and so a maximum occurs at $t_+ \approx 20$.

5   The time interval $(t, t + \Delta t)$ leads to a cost of $(1 + t) \Delta t$ and the present value of this is

$$e^{-rt}(1 + t) \Delta t.$$

Total costs at present value for $[0, T]$ are

$$\int_0^T e^{-rt}(1 + t)dt = \left[\frac{e^{-rt}}{-r}(1 + t)\right]_0^T - \int_0^T \frac{e^{-rt}}{-r} dt$$

$$= \frac{e^{-rT}(1 + T)}{-r} - \frac{1}{-r}\left[\frac{e^{-rt}}{-r^2}\right]_0^T$$

$$= \frac{1}{r} + \frac{1}{r^2} - \frac{(1 + T)e^{-rT}}{r} - \frac{e^{-rT}}{r^2}$$

Net present value including storage costs is

$$N = e^{-rt}\left[(1 + t^2) + \frac{1 + t}{r} + \frac{1}{r^2}\right] - \frac{1}{r} - \frac{1}{r^2}$$

and so

$$N' = e^{-rt}\left[-r(1 + t^2) - (1 + t) - \frac{1}{r} + 2t + \frac{1}{r}\right]$$

$$= e^{-rt}[-r(1 + t^2) + t - 1].$$

$$N' = 0 \Leftrightarrow rt^2 - t + (1 + r) = 0$$

$$\Leftrightarrow t = \frac{1 \pm [1 - 4r(1 + r)]^{1/2}}{2r}.$$

If $r = 0.1$ then

$$t_+ = \frac{1}{2}[1 + (0.56)^{1/2}] \approx 8.7.$$

7   We consider part (b).

$$\text{present value} = v(t)\exp(-rt) = \exp(t^{1/2} - rt).$$

The total storage costs at present value are

$$\int_0^t s \exp(-rt)\, dt = \frac{s}{r}[1 - \exp(-rt)].$$

Thus

$$\text{net value} = \exp(t^{1/2} - rt) - \frac{s}{r}[1 - \exp(-rt)] \equiv N(t).$$

$$N'(t) = \exp(t^{1/2} - rt)\left(\frac{1}{2}t^{-1/2} - r\right) + \frac{s}{r}(-r)\exp(-rt).$$

Hence

$$N'(t) = 0 \leftrightarrow \exp(t^{1/2})\left(\frac{1}{2t^{1/2}} - r\right) = s$$

$$\leftrightarrow \exp(t^{1/2}) = \frac{2st^{1/2}}{1 - 2rt^{1/2}}.$$

When $\exp(t^{1/2}) = 1$ we have $1 - 2rt^{1/2} = 2st^{1/2}$ and so $1 = 2(r + s)t^{1/2}$ (figure 11.18). Here $t^{1/2} = 1/2(r + s)$. Hence

$$\frac{1}{2(r + s)} \leqslant t_0^{1/2} \leqslant \frac{1}{2r}.$$

11.8.3   Checking for concavity

1

$$y = \frac{1}{1 + e^{-kx}}$$

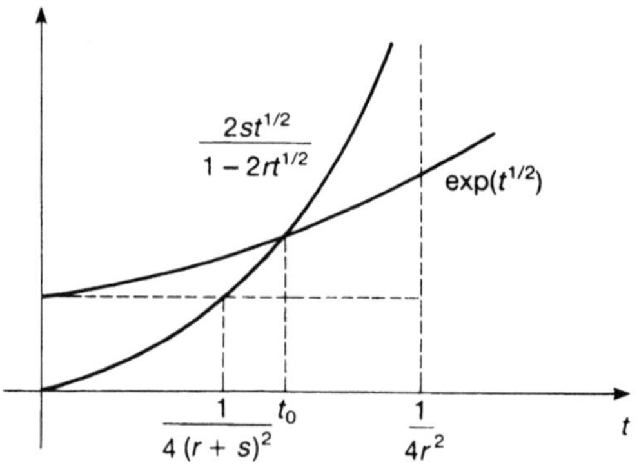

Figure 11.18   Locating the optimal time t_0 in question 7.

We have

$$y' = \frac{-1}{(1+e^{-kx})^2} e^{-kx}(-k)$$

$$= \frac{ke^{-kx}}{(1+e^{-kx})^2} > 0 \quad \text{(function is increasing)}$$

$$\frac{y''}{k} = \frac{(-ke^{-kx})(1+e^{-kx})^2 - e^{-kx}2(1+e^{-kx})e^{-kx}(-k)}{(1+e^{-kx})^4}$$

$$= \frac{-ke^{-kx}(1+e^{-kx}) + 2ke^{-kx}e^{-kx}}{(1+e^{-kx})^3}$$

$$\frac{y''}{k^2} = \frac{e^{-kx}e^{-kx} - e^{-kx}}{(1+e^{-kx})^3} = \frac{e^{-kx}(e^{-kx}-1)}{(1+e^{-kx})^3} = \begin{cases} \text{positive} & x < 0 \\ 0 & x = 0 \\ \text{negative} & x > 0 \end{cases}$$

(figure 11.19).

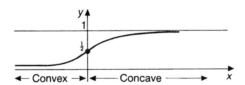

Figure $\leftarrow$ Convex $\rightarrow$ | $\leftarrow$ Concave $\longrightarrow$ x

Figure 11.19   Graph of a logistic curve $y = 1/(1+e^{-kx})$.

2

$$y = x^{1/2} - rx = x^{1/2}(1 - rx^{1/2})$$

and so, near $x = 0$, $y \approx x^{1/2}$.

$$y = x(-r + 1/x^{1/2})$$

and so, for *large* x, $y \approx x(-r) = -rx$.

$$y' = \frac{1}{2}x^{-1/2} - r$$

and so $y' = 0 \Leftrightarrow x = 1/(4r^2)$.

$$y'' = \frac{1}{2}\left(-\frac{1}{2}\right)x^{-3/2} < 0$$

and so y is *concave* for $x > 0$ (figure 11.20).

4

$$y = \exp(x^{1/2} - rx) \qquad y' = y\left(\frac{1}{2}x^{-1/2} - r\right)$$

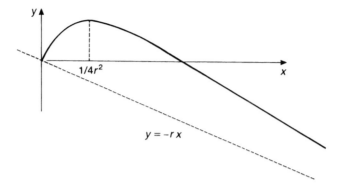

Figure 11.20   Graph of $y = \sqrt{x} - rx \ (r > 0)$.

Note that

$$y' = 0 \text{ if } x^{1/2} = \frac{1}{2r}.$$

$$y'' = y'\left(\frac{1}{2}x^{-1/2} - r\right) + y\left[\frac{1}{2}\left(-\frac{1}{2}\right)x^{-3/2}\right]$$

$$= y\left(\frac{1}{2}x^{-1/2} - r\right)^2 + y\left(-\frac{1}{4}x^{-3/2}\right)$$

$$= y\left(\frac{1}{4x} - \frac{r}{x^{1/2}} + r^2 - \frac{1}{4xx^{1/2}}\right)$$

$$= \frac{y}{4xx^{1/2}}\{x^{1/2} - 4rx + 4r^2xx^{1/2} - 1\}.$$

To determine the sign of y'' we put $z = x^{1/2}$ and consider

$$w = z - 4rz^2 + 4r^2z^3 - 1 \qquad (\text{contents of } \{\ldots\})$$

which is cubic. Now

$$w' = 1 - 8rz + 12r^2z^2 \equiv (6rz - 1)(2rz - 1)$$

$$w'' = -8r + 24r^2z = 24r^2\left(z - \frac{1}{3r}\right).$$

Thus

$$w''\left(\frac{1}{6r}\right) < 0 \ (\text{local maximum}) \qquad w''\left(\frac{1}{2r}\right) > 0 \ (\text{local minimum}).$$

We note that $w(0) = -1$, $w(1/2r) = -1$ and that

$$w\left(\frac{1}{6r}\right) = \frac{1}{6r} - \frac{4r}{36r^2} + \frac{4r^2}{36 \times 6r^3} - 1$$

$$= \frac{9 - 6 + 1}{54r} - 1$$

$$= \frac{4}{54r} - 1$$

$$= \frac{1}{r}\left(\frac{2}{27} - r\right) = \begin{cases} \text{negative} & r \leqslant 2/27 \approx 7.4\% \\ \text{or zero} & \\ \text{positive} & r > 2/27. \end{cases}$$

Two cases arise as illustrated (figure 11.21). Note that

$$w\left(\frac{1}{r}\right) = \frac{1}{r} - 1 > 0.$$

The corresponding shapes of y are sketched in figure 11.22.

Near $x = 0$, y'' is large, negative and therefore concave; for x large, $y'' \approx yr^2 > 0$, and therefore convex.

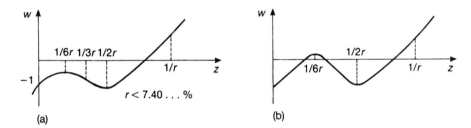

Figure 11.21 Graph of w: (a) $r \leqslant 2/27$; (b) $r > 2/27$.

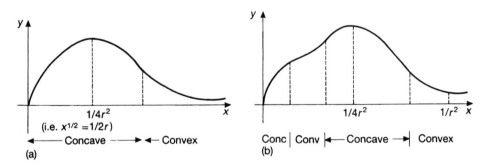

Figure 11.22 Graph of y: (a) $r \leqslant 2/27$; (b) $r > 2/27$.

12

Partial Differentiation

12.1 Total versus partial change: analysis of two input costs

We examine a new situation – how a function of two variables, such as a production cost, depending on two inputs, say $C(q_1, q_2)$, responds to simultaneous changes in both q_1 and q_2. This opens up our quest for a multivariable differential calculus. Although production managers may have to change both q_1 and q_2 we shall analyse the behaviour of cost changes as though each variable had been changed separately. Suppose initially we had

$$q_1 = Q_1 \qquad \text{and} \qquad q_2 = Q_2$$

and that these values have been changed in one step to

$$q_1 = Q_1 + h \qquad \text{and} \qquad q_2 = Q_2 + k.$$

We consider the mathematics of 'partial' changes made up of two steps as follows.

Step 1 $q_1 = Q_1 + h$ and $q_2 = Q_2$.
Step 2 $q_1 = Q_1 + h$ and $q_2 = Q_2 + k$.

This is illustrated in the (q_1, q_2) plane in figure 12.1. Since in each of the steps one variable is held at a fixed (constant) value we can examine the consequence of each of the one-step changes by the one-variable calculus. We thus define the *partial derivative* with respect to q_1 at (Q_1, Q_2) by the formula

$$\frac{\partial C}{\partial q_1} = \lim_{h \to 0} \frac{C(Q_1 + h, Q_2) - C(Q_1, Q_2)}{h},$$

also denoted by

$$C'_{q_1}(Q_1, Q_2) \qquad \text{or} \qquad C'_1(Q_1, Q_2).$$

In the last two notations differentiation is indicated by a prime; the independent variable that is subject to change is referred to in the subscript either by its name or by its position. Such notation reflects the fact that the

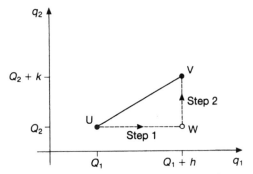

Figure 12.1 Splitting a change into partial changes 1 and 2.

process treats one variable as subject to change and the other as though it were a constant; it also reflects the fact that we are performing ordinary differentiation. Nevertheless, it is sometimes convenient to suppress the prime, on the grounds that the subscript already indicates the differentiation process.

A modified notation proves useful especially when there are more than two variables and the context does not make clear which of them is being held constant; it is

$$\left(\frac{\partial C}{\partial q_1}\right)_{q_2} \qquad \text{or even} \qquad \frac{\partial C}{\partial q_1}\bigg|_{q_2 = Q_2}.$$

We define similarly the partial derivative with respect to q_2 at (Q_1, Q_2) by

$$\frac{\partial C}{\partial q_2} = \lim_{k \to 0} \frac{C(Q_1, Q_2 + k) - C(Q_1, Q_2)}{k}.$$

Warning Three forms of the letter 'd' are used:

- Greek delta (δ or Δ) is usually used to indicate a finite increase in a variable, an increment, which is small (by some standard);
- Roman 'd' is used in one-variable work to denote 'ordinary' differentiation;
- curly or round delta (∂) (or partial ∂) is used to indicate differentiation in the presence of other variables which are held constant.

This convention should be scrupulously followed.

We shall see in section 12.4 how to relate these partial derivatives to the total change in C. The basic idea (to which we shall return) consists in noting the following identity.

$$\begin{aligned}
\Delta C &= \text{total change in } C \text{ (between the points U and V)} \\
&= C(Q_1 + h, Q_2 + k) - C(Q_1, Q_2) \\
&= [C(Q_1 + h, Q_2 + k) - C(Q_1 + h, Q_2)] \\
&\quad + [C(Q_1 + h, Q_2) - C(Q_1, Q_2)] \\
&= \text{partial change between U and W } (q_2 \text{ constant}) \\
&\quad + \text{partial change between W and V } (q_1 \text{ constant}). \qquad (12.1)
\end{aligned}$$

It is this decomposition into partial changes using the intermediate position W that justifies our interest in partial derivatives.

Example
If $F(x, y) = 3x^4 + 6xy - 2y^3$ find the partial derivatives at $x = 1$, $y = 2$.

SOLUTION   Differentiating F with y held fixed, we pretend y is a constant and differentiate in the usual way with respect to x:

$$\frac{\partial F}{\partial x} = 12x^3 + 6y.$$

Similarly holding x fixed and differentiating with respect to y we have

$$\frac{\partial F}{\partial x} = 6x - 6y^2.$$

Thus

$$\frac{\partial F}{\partial x}(1, 2) = 12 + 12 = 24 \qquad \frac{\partial F}{\partial y}(1, 2) = 6 - 6 \times 4 = -18.$$

Higher order partial derivatives follow the same symbolic conventions as ordinary derivatives. Thus we have

$$\frac{\partial^2 C}{\partial q_1^2} = \frac{\partial}{\partial q_1}\left(\frac{\partial C}{\partial q_1}\right) \qquad \text{and} \qquad \frac{\partial^2 C}{\partial q_2^2} = \frac{\partial}{\partial q_2}\left(\frac{\partial C}{\partial q_2}\right).$$

Note the mixed derivatives

$$\frac{\partial^2 C}{\partial q_1 \partial q_2} = \frac{\partial}{\partial q_1}\left(\frac{\partial C}{\partial q_2}\right) \qquad \text{and} \qquad \frac{\partial^2 C}{\partial q_1 \partial q_2} = \frac{\partial}{\partial q_2}\left(\frac{\partial C}{\partial q_1}\right).$$

Amazingly these two are usually equal (provided that $C(q_1, q_2)$ is well behaved).

12.2   Geometric meaning of the partial derivatives

For a function of two variables it is easy to interpret partial derivatives as slopes, by reference to the surface which is a graph in three dimensions of $z = F(x, y)$ (figure 12.2). The plane $y = Y$ intersects the surface $z = F(x, y)$ in a curve which is the graph of $z = F(x, Y)$. When $x = X$ that curve has slope equal to

$$\frac{\partial F}{\partial x}(X, Y).$$

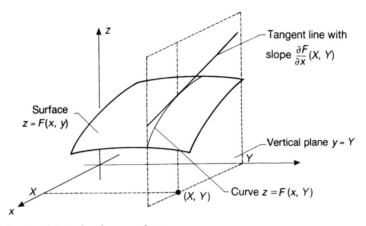

Figure 12.2 Partial derivatives as slopes.

12.3 Comparative statics: national income revisited

We study the effect on national income of varying the tax policy. A simple model for the interrelationship of investment I, government expenditure G, taxes T on national income Y, and consumption C might be (assuming that supply equals demand)

$$Y = C + I + G \qquad (12.2)$$

$$C = C(Y - T) \qquad (12.3)$$

$$T = \gamma + \delta Y \qquad (12.4)$$

where δ is the income tax rate and γ stands for alternative forms of tax revenue, e.g. poll tax. Linearizing the consumption, at the equilibrium values $\bar{Y}, \bar{T}$, we put for (12.3)

$$C = \alpha + \beta(Y - T) \qquad (12.3')$$

where β is the marginal propensity to consume (see section 10.2). Thus by (12.4)

$$C = \alpha + \beta(Y - \gamma - \delta Y)$$
$$= (\alpha - \beta\gamma) + \beta(1 - \delta)Y.$$

Hence by (12.2)

$$Y = (\alpha - \beta\gamma) + \beta(1 - \delta)Y + I + G,$$

i.e. at the equilibrium $Y = \bar{Y}$ we have

$$Y = \bar{Y} = \frac{\alpha - \beta\gamma + I + G}{1 - \beta(1 - \delta)}. \qquad (12.5)$$

The division is valid because $0 < \beta < 1$ (see section 10.2) and the tax rate satisfies $0 \leqslant \delta \leqslant 1$. We may regard the $\bar{Y}$ given in (12.5) as a function of four variables: the taxation variables γ, δ, the government expenditure G and the investment level I. We thus have

$$\frac{\partial \bar{Y}}{\partial \delta} = \frac{0 - \beta(\alpha - \beta\gamma + I + G)}{[1 - \beta(1 - \delta)]^2} = -\frac{\beta\bar{Y}}{1 - \beta(1 - \delta)} < 0$$

$$\frac{\partial \bar{Y}}{\partial \gamma} = \frac{-\beta}{1 - \beta(1 - \delta)} < 0.$$

Also note that

$$\frac{\partial \bar{Y}}{\partial G} = \frac{1}{1 - \beta(1 - \delta)} > 0. \tag{12.6}$$

This last calculation carries a warning. If we differentiate equation (12.2) partially we get the larger answer:

$$\frac{\partial Y}{\partial G} = 1. \tag{12.7}$$

The confusion here arises from the ambiguity of the symbolism used. Properly speaking, differentiation is applied to a function. Thus if $f(C, I, G) = C + I + G$ then $\partial f / \partial G = 1$. Similarly if

$$F(I, G, \gamma, \delta) = \frac{\alpha - \beta\gamma + I + G}{1 - \beta(1 - \delta)}$$

then

$$\frac{\partial F}{\partial G} = \frac{1}{1 - \beta(1 - \delta)}.$$

We have been using Y in (12.7) essentially to denote f; more accurately, in (12.7) we are noting what happens to Y when G is changed while C and I are held fixed. In (12.6), on the other hand, the variables γ, δ and I are held fixed, but C may vary.

We can make the symbols more precise at the cost of a notational mess; we list the variables held fixed. Thus (12.7) becomes

$$\left(\frac{\partial Y}{\partial G}\right)_{C, I} = 1,$$

while (12.6) becomes

$$\left(\frac{\partial Y}{\partial G}\right)_{\gamma, \delta, I} = \frac{1}{1 - \beta(1 - \delta)}.$$

12.4 The chain rule: marginal product revisited

Suppose a firm employs labour l to produce two 'intermediate goods' in quantities q_1 and q_2, where

$$q_1 = g_1(l) \qquad \text{and} \qquad q_2 = g_2(l),$$

and that these as inputs produce revenue

$$R = R(q_1, q_2).$$

We wish to know dR/dl. Suppose therefore that the labour force is changed from $l = L$ to $l = L + \Delta L$. Let the initial levels of the inputs be

$$Q_1 = g_1(L) \qquad \text{and} \qquad Q_2 = g_2(L)$$

and let the corresponding changes in inputs be

$$h = g_1(L + \Delta L) - g_1(L) \qquad k = g_2(L + \Delta L) - g_2(L).$$

Hence initially

$$q_1 = Q_1 \qquad \text{and} \qquad q_2 = Q_2$$

and subsequently

$$q_1 = Q_1 + h \qquad \text{and} \qquad q_2 = Q_2 + k.$$

According to equation (12.1)

$$\Delta R = (\Delta R)_1 + (\Delta R)_2,$$

where ΔR is the total change in R while $(\Delta R)_1$ and $(\Delta R)_2$ denote the two partial changes along $q_2 = Q_2$ and $q_1 = Q_1 + h$ respectively (figure 12.3). (Thus $(\Delta R)_1$ indicates changing value in q_1 only etc.) Therefore

$$\frac{\Delta R}{\Delta L} = \frac{(\Delta R)_1}{\Delta L} + \frac{(\Delta R)_2}{\Delta L}.$$

But we can rewrite this as

$$\frac{\Delta R}{\Delta L} = \frac{(\Delta R)_1}{h} \frac{h}{\Delta L} + \frac{(\Delta R)_2}{k} \frac{k}{\Delta L}.$$

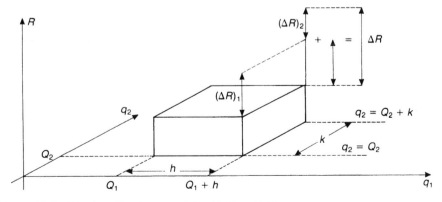

Figure 12.3 Ringing the changes: $\Delta R = (\Delta R)_1 + (\Delta R)_2$.

This becomes even more elegant if we write Δq_1 for h and Δq_2 for k (since h and k represent changes in q_1 and q_2 respectively). We then have

$$\frac{\Delta R}{\Delta L} = \frac{(\Delta R)_1}{\Delta q_1}\frac{\Delta q_1}{\Delta L} + \frac{(\Delta R)_2}{\Delta q_2}\frac{\Delta q_2}{\Delta L}. \tag{12.8}$$

Allowing ΔL to approach zero we obtain a plausibility argument (which we shall improve on) for the chain rule:

$$\frac{dR}{dl} = \frac{\partial R}{\partial q_1}\frac{dq_1}{dl} + \frac{\partial R}{\partial q_2}\frac{dq_2}{dl}.$$

Notice the occurrence of both roman d and curly ∂, especially as applied to R. The reason is simple in the case of the d applied to q_1 and q_2; since both are functions of the one variable l we use dq_1/dl etc. Now on the right-hand side, as expected, R denotes the function $R(q_1, q_2)$ and so curly ∂ is used to indicate this. On the left-hand side, however, something curious is going on; R denotes an altogether different function of one variable, namely $R[g_1(l), g_2(l)]$ and so the straight d is used.

This ambiguous use of R, though clarified by judicious use of d and ∂, is fundamentally naughty but universally practised (not unlike several of the seven deadly sins). Here is what rules of strict conduct require.

1   R is the name of a dependent variable.
2   Thou shalt not have false names for functions.
3   Thou shalt denote the revenue function by another letter, say by $F(q_1, q_2)$. (Thus $R = F(q_1, q_2)$.)
4   Thou shalt denote the composite function $F[g_1(l), g_2(l)]$ by yet another letter $f(l)$.
5   Thou shalt recite the chain rule thus:

$$\frac{df}{dl} = \frac{\partial F}{\partial q_1}\frac{dg_1}{dl} + \frac{\partial F}{\partial q_2}\frac{dg_2}{dl}. \tag{12.9}$$

Thus spake the Lord of Protocol.

In the seventh section (12.7) we shall indeed observe protocol (especially when addressing Euler's theorem) and in some other moving feats. Usually, however, we do not stand on such ceremony, but apply savoir faire, as occasion demands, and mix our symbolic concoctions at will.

Let us now see why the rule holds. We examine the two summands in (12.8) separately. The first of these is

$$\frac{R(Q_1 + h, Q_2) - R(Q_1, Q_2)}{h}\frac{\Delta q_1}{\Delta L}.$$

There is no doubt that $\Delta q_1/\Delta L$ tends to $g_1'(L)$, i.e. dq_1/dl. The factor before it likewise definitely tends to $R_{q_1}'(Q_1, Q_2)$, i.e. $\partial R/\partial q_1$. But there is a difficulty with the other summand of (12.8) which is in full

$$\frac{R(Q_1 + h, Q_2 + k) - R(Q_1 + h, \ Q_2)}{k} \frac{\Delta q_2}{\Delta L}.$$

Of course $\Delta q_2/\Delta L$ tends to dq_2/dl as ΔL tends to zero. But the first factor not only has k tending to zero but also h. We apply the mean value theorem of section 10.4 and we have, fixing h and k,

$$\frac{R(Q_1 + h, Q_2 + k) - R(Q_1 + h, Q_2)}{k} = R'_{q_2}(Q_1 + h, Q'_2)$$

where Q'_2 is somewhere *between* Q_2 and $Q_2 + k$. Thus if ΔL tends to zero we have (vectorially)

$$(Q_1 + h, Q'_2) \rightarrow (Q_1, Q_2). \tag{12.10}$$

Hence

$$R'_{q_2}(Q_1 + h, Q'_2) \rightarrow R'_{q_2}(Q_1, Q_2). \tag{12.11}$$

Note that for (12.10) to imply (12.11) is asking for a continuity condition on R'_{q_2} as in section 9.1 (where formula (9.1) requires the numerical q to be replaced by a vector q).

Example 1
Verify the chain rule by computing dR/dl for $R(q_1, q_2) = q_1 q_2$ when $q_1 = l^{1/4}$ and $q_2 = l^{1/2}$.

SOLUTION   We have for the composite function

$$R = l^{1/4} l^{1/2} = l^{3/4}$$

and so

$$\frac{dR}{dl} = \frac{3}{4} l^{-1/4}.$$

We also have

$$\frac{\partial R}{\partial q_1} = q_2 \qquad \frac{\partial R}{\partial q_2} = q_1$$

and

$$\frac{dq_1}{dl} = \frac{1}{4} l^{-3/4} \qquad \frac{dq_2}{dl} = \frac{1}{2} l^{-1/2}$$

and so

$$\frac{dR}{dl} = q_2 \frac{1}{4} l^{-3/4} + q_1 \frac{1}{2} l^{-1/2} = \frac{1}{4} l^{1/2} l^{-3/4} + \frac{1}{2} l^{-1/2} l^{1/4} = \frac{3}{4} l^{-1/4}.$$

There will inevitably be circumstances where direct computation from the composite function is easier, but that need not always be true.

Example 2: Introducing capital into marginal product
The chain rule can be used when there are several independent variables at the end of the chain of composition. We might have

$$R = R(q_1, q_2)$$

and

$$q_1 = g_1(K, L) \qquad \text{and} \qquad q_2 = g_2(K, L),$$

so that inputs are the product of the two variables capital and labour. We thus have

$$R = R[g_1(K, L), g_2(K, L)]$$

and, for instance, differentiating partially with respect to L

$$\frac{\partial R}{\partial L} = \frac{\partial R}{\partial q_1} \frac{\partial q_1}{\partial L} + \frac{\partial R}{\partial q_2} \frac{\partial q_2}{\partial L}.$$

Properly speaking the partial on the left is

$$\left(\frac{\partial R}{\partial L} \right)_K$$

and the partials on the right include

$$\left(\frac{\partial R}{\partial q_1} \right)_{q_2}.$$

So here again we should obey protocol, but then as usual we do not.

12.5 Implicit differentiation

A very important application of the chain rule is to compute the derivative dy/dx when it is inconvenient to obtain the explicit form of the relationship between y and x, even though it is assumed to exist (say in the shape of $y = g(x)$). A case in point is our constant companion the national income equation:

$$Y = C(Y) + I. \tag{12.12}$$

It is not easy in practice to find Y as a function of I. We can of course make approximations to C (yielding $Y \approx (c + I)/(1 - m)$, as in section 10.2) and in principle a geometric construction can be given to find the explicit function – apply the method of section 10.6 to obtain the inverse of $I = \Phi(Y) \equiv Y - C(Y)$ so that $Y = \Phi^{-1}(I)$. Fortunately all of this is unnecessary if all we want is dY/dI because, of course, we may differentiate (12.12) and obtain

$$\frac{dY}{dI} = C'(Y)\frac{dY}{dI} + 1. \tag{12.13}$$

(Note that the 'function of a function rule' used here is the one-variable case of the chain rule.) Thus

$$\frac{dY}{dI} = \frac{1}{1 - C'(Y)} = \frac{1}{1 - m}. \tag{12.14}$$

This idea may be pursued more generally. Suppose that we have a relationship between x and y given in the form of an equation

$$F(x, y) = 0 \tag{12.15}$$

where $F(x_1, x_2)$ is a function of two variables (e.g. F in the case above could be the excess supply function $F(Y, C) \equiv Y - C(Y) - I$). Then, if we could get our hands on the explicit solution $y = g(x)$, we would have

$$F[x, g(x)] \equiv 0. \tag{12.16}$$

Now consider the composite function (this protocol is necessary!)

$$f(x) \equiv F[x, g(x)].$$

Clearly $f(x)$ is constantly zero by (12.16) so $df/dx = 0$. But by the chain rule we have

$$\frac{df}{dx} = \frac{\partial F}{\partial x_1}\frac{dx_1}{dx} + \frac{\partial F}{\partial x_2}\frac{dx_2}{dx}.$$

Since $x_1 = x$ and $x_2 = y$ this is conventionally written

$$\frac{df}{dx} = \frac{\partial F}{\partial x}\frac{dx}{dx} + \frac{\partial F}{\partial y}\frac{dy}{dx}.$$

We conclude, since $df/dx = 0$ and $dx/dx = 1$, that

$$\frac{dy}{dx} = -\frac{\partial F}{\partial x}\bigg/\frac{\partial F}{\partial y} \qquad \left(\text{provided that } \frac{\partial F}{\partial y} \neq 0\right).$$

The method just introduced is known as implicit differentiation.

Example
Find both directly and implicitly dy/dx when

$$F(x, y) \equiv y^2 - x^3 - x^2 = 0.$$

SOLUTION   Using the *direct approach*, evidently for $x > -1$ it is true that

$$y = \pm[x^2(1 + x)]^{1/2}.$$

We take a closer look at what is going on. We first sketch a graph of $z = x^2(1 + x)$ and then imagine ourselves finding the two square roots. The graphical idea needs a couple of explanations. Evidently we get a graph symmetric about the x axis (figure 12.4). Near $x = 0$ we have $y^2 \approx x^2$ and so

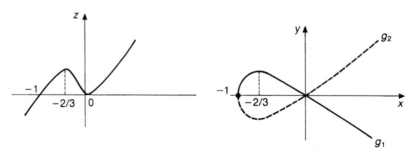

Figure 12.4   Graph of (a) $z = x^2(1 + x)$ and (b) $y = z^{1/2}$.

$y = \pm x$ and the two bits of the curve have slope ± 1. Near $x = -1$ put $x = -1 + u$ with $u \approx 0$. Now $y^2 = (-1 + u)^2 (1 - 1 + u) \approx u$ so that y locally looks like the graph of the square root function $x^{1/2}$ translated back to $x = -1$. We thus arrive at *two* differentiable solutions of

$$F(x, y) = 0$$

defined for $x > -1$, namely the solid curve and the broken curve. Thus, for instance,

$$g_1(x) = \begin{cases} x(1 + x)^{1/2} & -1 \leqslant x \leqslant 0 \\ -x(1 + x)^{1/2} & 0 \leqslant x. \end{cases}$$

We leave the reader the easy calculation of $g_1'(x)$. Our discussion shows that even the direct approach need not be simple!

In the *implicit approach* we apply the chain rule:

$$-3x^2 - 2x + 2y \frac{dy}{dx} = 0$$

or

$$\frac{dy}{dx} = \frac{2x + 3x^2}{2y} \qquad \text{(provided that } y \neq 0\text{)}.$$

What happens when $\partial F/\partial y = 0$, i.e. $y = 0$? The answer is that $x = 0$ or $x = -1$. These were the two sticking points of the direct approach. When $x = -1$ clearly $2x + 3x^2 = -2 + 3 = 1$, so that in fact $dy/dx = \infty$. To see what is happening at $x = 0$ we note that

$$\left(\frac{dy}{dx}\right)^2 = \frac{4x^2 + 12x^3 + 9x^4}{4(x^2 + x^3)} = \frac{4 + 12x + 9x^2}{4(1 + x)}$$

and this tends to 1 when x approaches zero.

Remark

We do not stop to consider in any depth the *implicit function theorem* which is connected with our discussion above. This is the theorem (see also section 5.13) which asserts that for any relation connecting x and y in the form

$$F(x, y) = 0$$

and for any (x_0, y_0) such that $F(x_0, y_0) = 0$, there is an explicit solution valid locally, i.e. near $x = x_0$, provided that $\partial F/\partial y \neq 0$ at (x_0, y_0). Thus there is a function of the form $y = g(x)$ with $y_0 = g(x_0)$ defined in an interval around $x = x_0$ such that

$$F[x, g(x)] \equiv 0.$$

Compare also the remark of section 10.6 on local inverses.

The implicit function theorem would thus fall foul of $(-1, 0)$ and $(0, 0)$ where $\partial F/\partial y = 0$. The reasons should be clear.

12.6 Implicit differentiation: economic applications

Example 1
Suppose that all we are given is a relationship satisfied by production (output), capital and labour in the form

$$F(Q, K, L) = 0. \tag{12.17}$$

Suppose, further, that we know that (12.17) unambiguously defines Q (implicitly) in terms of K and L; say

$$Q = g(K, L).$$

We require $\partial Q/\partial L$, the marginal physical product of labour.

SOLUTION We use the trick in section 12.5. Put $z = F[g(K, L), K, L]$. Thus $z \equiv 0$, and hence

$$\frac{\partial z}{\partial L} = 0.$$

But, as in section 12.4, example 2, since K is constant

$$\frac{\partial z}{\partial L} = \frac{\partial F}{\partial Q} \frac{\partial g}{\partial L} + \frac{\partial F}{\partial L} \frac{dL}{dL},$$

i.e.

$$0 = \frac{\partial F}{\partial Q} \frac{\partial Q}{\partial L} + \frac{\partial F}{\partial L}$$

and so

$$\frac{\partial Q}{\partial L} = -\frac{\partial F}{\partial L} \Big/ \frac{\partial F}{\partial Q}.$$

Example 2: A worked example
Suppose that $F(Q, K, L) \equiv Q^3 K^2 + L^3 + QKL - 3 = 0$ is the given relationship, as in example 1. Thus

$$\frac{\partial Q}{\partial L} = -\frac{\partial F}{\partial L} \Big/ \frac{\partial F}{\partial Q} = -\frac{3L^2 + QK}{3Q^2 K^2 + KL}$$

$$\frac{\partial Q}{\partial K} = -\frac{\partial F}{\partial K} \Big/ \frac{\partial F}{\partial Q} = -\frac{2Q^3 K + QL}{3Q^2 K^2 + KL}.$$

For instance, if $K = L = 1$ then $Q^3 + Q - 2 = 0$. Since $Q^3 + Q - 2 = (Q - 1) \times (Q^2 + Q + 2)$, we have $Q = 1$. So

$$\frac{\partial Q}{\partial L} = -\frac{4}{4} = 1 \qquad \text{and} \qquad \frac{\partial Q}{\partial K} = -\frac{3}{4}.$$

12.7   Euler's theorem for homogeneous functions

Recall that a function such as $Q = F(K, L)$ is homogeneous of degree α if

$$F(tK, tL) = t^\alpha F(K, L) \qquad (t > 0).$$

We think of ourselves as applying the chain rule as in equation (12.9) to $F(q_1, q_2)$ where

$$q_1 = g_1(t) \equiv Kt \qquad \text{and} \qquad q_2 = g_2(t) \equiv Lt.$$

We regard K and L to be fixed at some constant values and t as variable so that

$$\frac{dq_1}{dt} = g_1'(t) \equiv K \qquad \text{and} \qquad \frac{dq_2}{dt} = g_2'(t) = L.$$

Thus if $f(t) = F(tK, tL)$, then

$$\frac{df}{dt} = \frac{\partial F}{\partial q_1}\frac{dq_1}{dt} + \frac{\partial F}{\partial q_2}\frac{dq_2}{dt}.$$

But also

$$\frac{df}{dt} = \frac{d}{dt}[t^\alpha F(K, L)] = \alpha t^{\alpha-1} F(K, L).$$

Comparing the two formulae for df/dt when $t = 1$ we obtain

$$\alpha F(K, L) = \frac{\partial F}{\partial q_1} K + \frac{\partial F}{\partial q_2} L$$

or, unfixing K and L and treating them now as variables again,

$$\alpha F(K, L) = \frac{\partial F}{\partial K} K + \frac{\partial F}{\partial L} L. \qquad (12.18)$$

This result is known as Euler's theorem. When $\alpha = 1$ the production function F is often, albeit erroneously, said to be 'linearly homogeneous'. A case in point is when F is a production function with constant returns to scale. Note that in such a case, i.e. when F is indeed homogeneous of degree 1, we have

$$K\frac{\partial Q}{\partial K} + L\frac{\partial Q}{\partial L} = Q.$$

Thus if the returns to scale are constant, the product Q is exactly exhausted if each of the factors of production K, L is paid a price equal to its marginal product. This is known as the Clark–Wicksell theorem. See C. E. Ferguson, *Neo-classical Theory of Production and Distribution* (Cambridge: Cambridge University Press, 1969), for a comment regarding the once prevailing theory that, since this is the observed behaviour at equilibrium in a competitive environment, production functions must be linearly homogeneous. The latter deduction is based on the following remark.

Fact It may be shown (see for instance Ostaszewski, *Advanced Mathematical Methods*, Cambridge: Cambridge University Press, 1990, page 337) that, if equation (12.18) above holds, then F is homogeneous of degree α.

Example
Verify Euler's theorem for the generalized Cobb–Douglas function $F(K, L) = KL^2$ when $K = 2$ and $L = 5$.

SOLUTION   We follow through the entire argument as given above, where now we have the data $K = 2$, $L = 5$. Thus

$$F(2t, 5t) = 2t(5t)^2 = t^3 \times 2 \times 5^2 = t^3 F(2, 5),$$

so that F is of degree 3. We differentiate each side separately starting with the extreme right-hand side (RHS).

$$\frac{d}{dt}(\text{RHS}) = 3t^2 F(2, 5) = 3t^2 \times 50. \qquad (12.19)$$

We differentiate the extreme left-hand side (LHS) using the chain rule; we think of the rule as being applied to

$$F(q_1, q_2) = q_1 q_2^2$$

with the substitutions

$$q_1 = 2t \qquad \text{and} \qquad q_2 = 5t,$$

so that

$$\frac{d}{dt}(\text{LHS}) = \frac{\partial F}{\partial q_1}\frac{dq_1}{dt} + \frac{\partial F}{\partial q_2}\frac{dq_2}{dt}$$

$$= q_2{}^2 \times 2 + 2q_1q_2 \times 5$$

$$= (25t^2) \times 2 + (2 \times 10t^2) \times 5. \tag{12.20}$$

Clearly (12.19) and (12.20) are both equal to $150t^2$. Setting $t = 1$ we obtain the identity

$$150 = 2 \times 25 + 5 \times 20.$$

This agrees with (12.18) when $\alpha = 3$, $Q = 50$, $K = 2$, $L = 5$, since $\partial Q/\partial K = 25$ and $\partial Q/\partial L = 20$.

12.8   Exercises

1   Find the first-order and second-order partial derivatives of the following functions:

(a) $x^{1/4}y^{3/4}$ (b) $(x^2 + y^2)^{1/2}$

(c) $x^\alpha y^\beta$ (d) $(x^\gamma + y^\gamma)^{1/\gamma}$

2*   Verify the chain rule when $F(x, y) = x^2y + y^3x$ and $x = t^2$, $y = t^3$.

3*   If $z = F(x, y)$ and x, y respectively change from X, Y to $X + \Delta x$, $Y + \Delta y$, then provided that Δx, Δy are small enough formula (12.8) asserts that

$$\Delta z \approx \frac{\partial F}{\partial x}\Delta x + \frac{\partial F}{\partial y}\Delta y.$$

Compute the right-hand side when $F(x, y) = xy$. Show that if x, y change respectively by r per cent and s per cent then z changes by approximately $r + s$ per cent. By how much is this answer wrong? (See section 10.7, question 9.)

4*   Find the first-order partial derivatives when $z = x^y$. [*Hint*: $\log z = y \log x$.] Show that if x, y are changed by 1 per cent each, then the percentage change in z is about $y + y \log x$ per cent.

5   Repeat the previous question when $z = x^{y^{1/2}}$.

6*   Let $x(t) = X + th$, $y(t) = Y + tk$, and let $g(t) = F[x(t), y(t)]$. Use the chain rule to show that

$$g'(t) = \frac{\partial F}{\partial x}[x(t), y(t)]h + \frac{\partial F}{\partial y}[x(t), y(t)]k.$$

Writing $h = \Delta x$, $k = \Delta y$ and using the mean value theorem of section 10.4 show that in fact

$$\Delta z = \frac{\partial F}{\partial x}\Delta x + \frac{\partial F}{\partial y}\Delta y,$$

where the partial derivatives are evaluated at $(X + t^*\Delta x, Y + t^*\Delta y)$. [Hint: $\Delta z = g(1) - g(0) = g'(t^*)$.]

7 Find $\partial Q/\partial L$ and $\partial Q/\partial K$ when Q, K and L are related by the equation $Q^3 K^2 + L^2 + 2QKL = 4$.

8 Find $\partial Q/\partial L$ and $\partial Q/\partial K$ when Q, K and L are related by the equation $Q^5 + 2Q^2 KL^2 + QK^2 L^3 = 4$.

9* A production function is defined for $K, L > 0$ by the formula

$$Q = (K^{1/2} + L^{1/2})^2.$$

Use implicit differentiation to show that the isoquant Q = constant satisfies

$$\frac{dK}{dL} = -\frac{K^{1/2}}{L^{1/2}}.$$

Differentiate this result to obtain

$$\frac{d^2 K}{dL^2} = \frac{Q}{2K^{3/2}}$$

and deduce that the isoquant is convex.

10 Follow through and verify Euler's theorem when $F(K, L) = K^{1/4} L^{3/4}$.

11 Fruity Juices plc markets two products A (apple juice) and B (orange juice) at prices p_A and p_B respectively in quantities q_A and q_B. Suppose the demand schedules for A and B are

$$q_A = 500 - 100p_A{}^2 - 50p_B{}^2$$

$$q_B = 4000 - 300p_B{}^{4/5} + 300p_A{}^{2/3}.$$

Determine whether the two products are complementary or competitive by investigating the effect of a price change in either one on the demand for the other. (Consider $\partial q_A/\partial p_B$ and $\partial q_B/\partial p_A$.)

12* With reference to section 12.3 find

$$\left(\frac{\partial Y}{\partial G}\right)_{T,I}.$$

Is it different from the following?

$$\left(\frac{\partial Y}{\partial G}\right)_{\gamma, \delta, I}$$

13 With reference to section 12.4 find

$$\left(\frac{\partial R}{\partial K}\right)_L.$$

14 Why is the stationary point of $z = x^2(1 + x)$ at the same x value ($x = -2/3$) as the stationary value of $y = x(1 + x)^{1/2}$? Give a general reason based on the function of a function rule.

12.9   Answers

2

$$\frac{\partial F}{\partial x} = 2xy + y^3 = 2t^5 + t^9.$$

$$\frac{\partial F}{\partial y} = x^2 + 3y^2x = t^4 + 3t^6t^2 = t^4 + 3t^8.$$

By the chain rule

$$\frac{dF}{dt} = \frac{\partial F}{\partial x}\frac{dx}{dt} + \frac{\partial F}{\partial y}\frac{dy}{dt}$$

$$= (2t^5 + t^9)2t + (t^4 + 3t^8)3t^2$$

$$= 4t^6 + 2t^{10} + 3t^6 + 9t^{10}$$

$$= 11t^{10} + 7t^6.$$

By direct computation we have

$$F = (t^2)^2t^3 + (t^3)^3t^2 = t^7 + t^{11}$$

$$\frac{dF}{dt} = 7t^6 + 11t^{10}$$

and the two answers agree.

3   With $F(x, y) = xy$ we obtain

$$\frac{\partial F}{\partial x} = y \qquad \frac{\partial F}{\partial y} = x$$

and so

$$\Delta z \approx y\Delta x + x\Delta y.$$

Hence

$$\frac{\Delta z}{z} = \frac{\Delta z}{xy} \approx \frac{\Delta x}{x} + \frac{\Delta y}{y}.$$

Since $\Delta x/x = r/100$ and $\Delta y/y = s/100$ we have

$$\frac{\Delta z}{z} \approx \frac{r + s}{100}.$$

By section 10.7, question 9, the true answer differs from this by

$$\frac{rs}{10,000} = \frac{rs}{100} \text{ per cent.}$$

4   Since $\log z = y \log x$ we have

$$\frac{\partial}{\partial x}(\log z) = \frac{1}{z}\frac{\partial z}{\partial x} = y\frac{1}{x}$$

and

$$\frac{1}{z}\frac{\partial z}{\partial y} = \log x.$$

By the formula

$$\frac{\Delta z}{z} \approx \frac{1}{z}\frac{\partial z}{\partial x}\Delta x + \frac{1}{z}\frac{\partial z}{\partial y}\Delta y$$

$$\frac{\Delta z}{z} \approx \frac{y}{x}\Delta x + \log x\,\Delta y$$

$$= y\frac{\Delta x}{x} + y\log x\frac{\Delta y}{y}$$

$$= y + y\log x \quad \text{per cent}$$

6

$$g'(t) = \frac{\partial F}{\partial x}\frac{\mathrm{d}}{\mathrm{d}t}(X + th) + \frac{\partial F}{\partial y}\frac{\mathrm{d}}{\mathrm{d}t}(Y + tk)$$

$$= \frac{\partial F}{\partial x}h + \frac{\partial F}{\partial y}k$$

$$= \frac{\partial F}{\partial x}\Delta x + \frac{\partial F}{\partial y}\Delta y$$

as asserted.

$$\Delta z = F(X + \Delta x, Y + \Delta y) - F(X, Y)$$

$$= g(1) - g(0) = g'(t^*) \times 1$$

for some $0 < t^* < 1$.

12   We must find Y in terms of G, T, I. By equation (12.2) we need to eliminate C in favour of G, T, I, Y. But

$$C = C(Y - T) = \alpha + \beta(Y - T).$$

Thus

$$Y = \alpha + \beta(Y - T) + I + G$$

and so

$$(1 - \beta)Y = \alpha - \beta T + I + G$$

$$Y = \frac{\alpha - \beta T + I + G}{1 - \beta}.$$

Hence

$$\left(\frac{\partial Y}{\partial G}\right)_{T,I} = \frac{1}{1-\beta}.$$

Next we must find Y in terms of G, γ, δ and I (i.e. eliminate C from (12.2) in favour of G, γ, δ, I, Y). This has already been done in equation (12.5) of section 12.3. Thus

$$\left(\frac{\partial Y}{\partial G}\right)_{\gamma,\delta,I} = \frac{1}{1-\beta(1-\delta)}.$$

The two results are equal only when δ (income tax) is zero.

9 $Q = (K^{1/2} + L^{1/2})^2$. Treating Q as constant we differentiate with respect to L assuming that K is a function of L. Thus since $dQ/dK = 0$ we have

$$0 = 2(K^{1/2} + L^{1/2})\left(\frac{1}{2}K^{-1/2}\frac{dK}{dL} + \frac{1}{2}L^{-1/2}\right)$$

Assuming that $K^{1/2} + L^{1/2} \neq 0$ (i.e. K and L are not both zero)

$$-K^{-1/2}\frac{dK}{dL} = L^{-1/2} \quad \text{or} \quad \frac{dK}{dL} = -L^{-1/2}K^{+1/2}.$$

Differentiating the last result with respect to L gives by the product rule

$$\frac{d^2K}{dL^2} = -\left(-\frac{1}{2}\right)L^{-3/2}K^{1/2} - L^{-1/2}\left(\frac{1}{2}K^{-1/2}\frac{dK}{dL}\right)$$

$$= \frac{1}{2}L^{-3/2}K^{1/2} - \frac{1}{2}L^{-1/2}K^{-1/2}(-K^{1/2}L^{-1/2})$$

$$= \frac{1}{2}(L^{-3/2}K^{1/2} + L^{-1})$$

$$= \frac{1}{2L}\left(1 + \frac{K^{1/2}}{L^{1/2}}\right) > 0.$$

Hence the isoquant is convex.

13

The Gradient

13.1 Tangent budget lines

In an earlier chapter we discussed the maximization of utility $u(q_1, q_2)$ subject to the budget constraint

$$p_1 q_1 + p_2 q_2 = m \qquad (13.1)$$

which restricts the available commodity pairs (q_1, q_2). The argument of section 3.8 showed that, if utility contours are convex, maximization of utility occurs at a point (Q_1, Q_2) where the budget line is tangent to a utility isocurve. This translated into the condition that the marginal rate of substitution MRS between the two commodities is equal to the inverse ratio of their prices (see section 13.3 for a mnemonic).

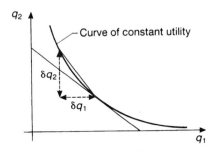

Figure 13.1 A very small decrease δq_1 in the first commodity is balanced in utility by an increase of δq_2 in the second.

In the language of calculus, a reduction from Q_1 to $Q_1 - \delta q_1$ is balanced in utility by an increase from Q_2 to $Q_2 + \delta q_2$ (figure 13.1). The ratio $-\delta q_2 / \delta q_1$ is the slope of a chord. Passing to the limit we obtain the slope of the tangent at (Q_1, Q_2), but that is the marginal rate of substitution. Thus

$$\mathrm{MRS} = -\frac{dq_2}{dq_1}.$$

Now the slope of the budget line is $-p_2{}^{-1}/p_1{}^{-1}$, and hence

$$\frac{dq_2}{dq_1} = \frac{p_2{}^{-1}}{p_1{}^{-1}}. \tag{13.2}$$

We can of course obtain dq_2/dq_1 at (Q_1, Q_2) quite easily in the case of the Cobb–Douglas utility function. Since an isocurve is given by the equation

$$q_1{}^\alpha q_2{}^\beta = k,$$

where k is a constant, we can differentiate implicitly to obtain

$$\alpha q_1{}^{\alpha-1} q_2{}^\beta + \beta q_1{}^\alpha q_2{}^{\beta-1} \frac{dq_2}{dq_1} = 0.$$

Thus at (q_1, q_2) we have

$$\frac{dq_2}{dq_1} = -\frac{\alpha \, q_1{}^{\alpha-1} q_2{}^\beta}{\beta \, q_1{}^\alpha q_2{}^{\beta-1}} = -\frac{\alpha q_2}{\beta q_1}$$

and so we need to solve simultaneously

$$-\frac{\alpha Q_2}{\beta Q_1} = \frac{p_2{}^{-1}}{p_1{}^{-1}}$$

$$p_1 Q_1 + p_2 Q_2 = m.$$

We leave this to the reader.

The critical question we need to consider now is how this argument extends to more variables; for instance, if there are three commodities, then we require to maximize $u(q_1, q_2, q_3)$ subject to a budget constraint

$$p_1 q_1 + p_2 q_2 + p_3 q_3 = m.$$

This evidently depicts a plane in three-space (figure 13.2).

Presumably the isoquant surface looks somewhat akin to a piece of orange peel stuck to the maximization point $Q = (Q_1, Q_2, Q_3)$ and is tangent to the budget plane. What is the isoquant tangency condition? Evidently the budget plane no longer has a single well-defined slope. A moment's thought will nevertheless convince you that we can repeat the earlier analysis leading to (13.2) both in the q_1, q_2 plane through (Q_1, Q_2, Q_3) and the q_1, q_3 plane to obtain

$$\frac{dq_2}{dq_1} = \frac{p_2{}^{-1}}{p_1{}^{-1}} \qquad \frac{dq_3}{dq_1} = \frac{p_3{}^{-1}}{p_1{}^{-1}} \tag{13.3}$$

(see figure 13.3).

This may be neatly summarized in the ratio formula

$$dq_1 : dq_2 : dq_3 = p_1{}^{-1} : p_2{}^{-1} : p_3{}^{-1} \tag{13.4}$$

(where the intended meaning of $dq_1 : dq_2$ is of course dq_1/dq_2 etc.). The point about formula (13.4) as opposed to (13.3) is the equal footing of all three

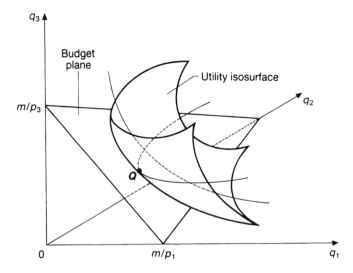

Figure 13.2 Utility isosurface touching the budget plane at the point of maximum utility.

variables q_1, q_2, q_3. Actually there is another way to arrange formula (13.4) if we agree to break up the derivative quotient notation:

$$\frac{dq_1}{p_1^{-1}} = \frac{dq_2}{p_2^{-1}} = \frac{dq_3}{p_3^{-1}}. \tag{13.5}$$

This formula is even more elegant than (13.4) and is meaningful once we agree to interpret the broken-up derivatives via (13.3). But let us throw caution to the wind and suppose that we can make sense of dq_1, dq_2, dq_3 as numbers (indeed we can, but an explanation will have to wait until section 13.8). If the common value of the quantities in (13.5) is λ then we may rewrite (13.5) in vector notation thus:

$$(dq_1, dq_2, dq_3) = \lambda(p_1^{-1}, p_2^{-1}, p_3^{-1}). \tag{13.6}$$

If challenged to interpret (13.6) we can always claim that we are only computing ratios of the three co-ordinates on both sides of (13.6) to obtain (13.3); such a claim evidently also eliminates reference to the proportionality factor λ.

Equation (13.6) is not just another way of saying (13.3) in neat form using the language of vectors. It carries with it two challenging questions:

1 interpret the vector (p_1, p_2, p_3);
2 attach meaning to the left-hand side of (13.6).

We attack the first question immediately in the next section. Our approach will be, as always, to ask the same question in two dimensions: interpret the vector (p_1, p_2). Where did the brute first turn up? Evidently, in the budget constraint (13.1); so that is where our enquiries will begin. As for the second question – the answer must wait until section 13.8.

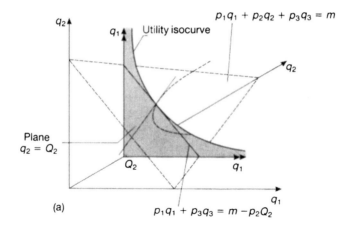

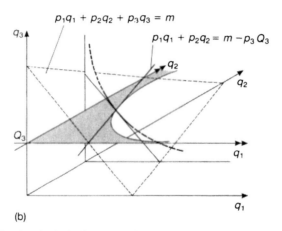

Figure 13.3 (a) In the shaded plane $q_2 = Q_2$ the budget line $p_1q_1 + p_3q_3 = m - p_2Q_2$ is tangent to the isocurve and so $dq_3/dq_1 = p_1/p_3$; (b) working in the horizontal plane $q_3 = Q_3$ we see that the budget line $p_1q_1 + p_2q_2 = m - p_3Q_3$ is tangent to the isocurve and so $dq_2/dq_1 = p_1/p_2$.

13.2 Price vectors and normals

Our objective is to interpret geometrically the price vector associated with the budget line

$$p_1q_1 + p_2q_2 = m.$$

The obvious place to begin (when ideas are lacking) is 'experimental evidence'. So let us plot the line

$$x + 2y = 4 \tag{13.7}$$

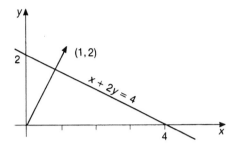

Figure 13.4 The vector $(1, 2)'$ is perpendicular to the line.

and draw the vector $(1, 2)'$. It is immediately clear from figure 13.4 that the vector of coefficients $(1, 2)'$ is orthogonal (perpendicular) to the line. Now, why? A quick reference to section 2.2 tells us that a vector $(x, y)'$ is perpendicular to $(1, 2)'$ if

$$(x, y)'(1, 2)' = 0 \qquad \text{or} \qquad 1 \times x + 2 \times y = 0.$$

Hence it is obvious that $(1, 2)$ is perpendicular to any vector $(x, y)'$ lying on the line

$$x + 2y = 0 \qquad (13.8)$$

(figure 13.5). Of course we recognize that the line with equation (13.8) is parallel to our original line with equation (13.7). But, why? The quick answer is that they both have slope equal to $-1/2$. But isn't the quick answer restating that both equations have an identical vector of coefficients? So let's find a more satisfying answer. We would like to refer only to the coefficient vector so as to make the opposite assertion, namely that (13.7) and (13.8) are parallel lines because both lines are perpendicular to the coefficient vector.

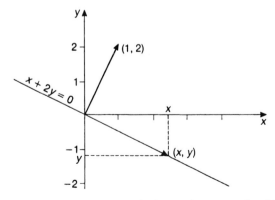

Figure 13.5 The vector $(1, 2)'$ is perpendicular to the vector $(x, y)'$ which lies on $x + 2y = 0$.

Here is the alternative argument. The vector $(1, 2)'$ does not lie on (13.7) because

$$1 \times 1 + 2 \times 2 = \| (1, 2) \|^2 = 5. \tag{13.9}$$

Cross-multiplying (13.9) by 4/5 we see that

$$1 \times \frac{4}{5} + 2 \times \frac{8}{5} = \frac{4}{5} \times 5 = 4$$

and so, if $(a, b)'$ is the rescaled version of $(1, 2)'$,

$$(a, b)' = \frac{4}{5}(1, 2)',$$

then that does lie on the line (13.7). Thus we may rewrite the equation of the line as

$$x + 2y = 4 = 1 \times a + 2 \times b$$

and this is equivalent to

$$(x - a) + 2(y - b) = 0, \tag{13.10}$$

i.e.

$$(1, 2)' \cdot (x - a, y - b)' = 0. \tag{13.11}$$

Equation (13.11) asserts that $(1, 2)'$ is perpendicular to the vector $(x - a, y - b)'$. But the parallelogram law for the addition of vectors tells us that $(x - a, y - b)'$ is parallel to QP (figure 13.6).

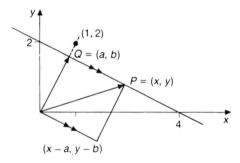

Figure 13.6 $(a, b)' = \frac{4}{5}(1, 2)'$ lies on $x + 2y = 4$ and $(x - a, y - b)'$ is parallel to QP.

Notice that when $(x, y)'$ lies on the line with equation (13.7) then $(u, v)' = (x - a, y - b)'$ lies on the line with equation

$$x + 2y = 0,$$

because $u + 2v = 0$ (see (13.10)). This can be more effectively restated: every vector (x, y) on the line (13.7) is the translate by (a, b) of a vector (u, v) lying on the parallel line through the origin, i.e.

$$(x, y) = (u, v) + (a, b).$$

Remark

All the manipulations and ideas of this section may be performed on three (or more) variables. In particular we conclude, in answer to question 1 at the end of the last section, that (p_1, p_2, p_3) is orthogonal to the budget plane (figure 13.7).

Any vector which is perpendicular to a plane is said to be a normal to the plane, or is said to point normally to the plane. In two dimensions we similarly say that a vector is normal to a line when that vector is perpendicular to the line. In the multivariable context normals carry the information which in the two-dimensional context we are accustomed to getting from slopes.

13.3   Normals to isoquant curves: the gradient

Let us solve the utility maximization problem more generally. If the utility function is $u(q_1, q_2)$ then its isoquants satisfy

$$u(q_1, q_2) = k, \tag{13.12}$$

where k is a constant. This time we go beyond computing the marginal rate of substitution and ask for the equation of the tangent to (13.12) at $q_1 = Q_1$, $q_1 = Q_2$. (The follow-up question will be: when does this tangent coincide with the budget line?) Differentiating (13.12) implicitly we obtain (see section 12.5)

$$\frac{\partial u}{\partial q_1} + \frac{\partial u}{\partial q_2} \frac{dq_2}{dq_1} = 0,$$

so that

$$\frac{dq_2}{dq_1} = -\frac{\partial u}{\partial q_1} \bigg/ \frac{\partial u}{\partial q_2}. \tag{13.13}$$

Expression (13.13) is of course evaluated at $q_1 = Q_1$, $q_2 = Q_2$. Note that the marginal rate of substitution $-dq_2/dq_1$ equals the appropriate ratio of marginal utilities. We promised in section 13.1 to comment in a memorable way on this ratio. Thinking of q_1, q_2 as apples and oranges observe the rule:

$$\frac{\text{utiles}}{\text{apples}} \div \frac{\text{utiles}}{\text{oranges}} = \frac{\text{oranges}}{\text{apples}}.$$

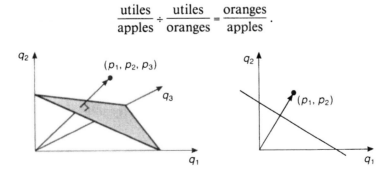

Figure 13.7   The price vector points normally to the budget plane/line.

Returning to our main purpose: by (13.13) the equation of the tangent is

$$q_2 - Q_2 = \left(\frac{dq_2}{dq_1}\right)_{\substack{q_1 = Q_1 \\ q_2 = Q_2}} (q_1 - Q_1)$$

or

$$(q_2 - Q_2)\left(\frac{\partial u}{\partial q_2}\right) = -\left(\frac{\partial u}{\partial q_1}\right)(q_1 - Q_1).$$

Thus finally the tangent has equation

$$\frac{\partial u}{\partial q_1}(q_1 - Q_1) + \frac{\partial u}{\partial q_2}(q_2 - Q_2) = 0$$

where the partials are evaluated at $q_1 = Q_1$, $q_2 = Q_2$.

Example 1
For the Cobb–Douglas utility function $u = q_1^{1/4} q_2^{3/4}$ find the tangent at $(1, 1)'$ to the isoquant $u = 1$.

SOLUTION   We have

$$\frac{\partial u}{\partial q_1} = \left(\frac{1}{4} q_1^{-3/4} q_2^{3/4}\right)_{\substack{q_1 = 1 \\ q_2 = 1}} = \frac{1}{4} \qquad \frac{\partial u}{\partial q_2} = \left(\frac{3}{4} q_1^{1/4} q_2^{-1/4}\right)_{\substack{q_1 = 1 \\ q_2 = 1}} = \frac{3}{4}.$$

Hence the tangent has the equation

$$\frac{1}{4}(q_1 - 1) + \frac{3}{4}(q_2 - 1) = 0.$$

Example 2
Repeat the previous example with the general Cobb–Douglas utility $u = q_1^{\alpha} q_2^{\alpha}$ for $q_1 = Q_1$, $q_2 = Q_2$.

SOLUTION   We have

$$\frac{\partial u}{\partial q_1} = \alpha Q_1^{\alpha - 1} Q_2^{\beta} \qquad \text{and} \qquad \frac{\partial u}{\partial q_2} = \beta Q_1^{\alpha} Q_2^{\beta - 1}.$$

Thus the tangent has the equation

$$\alpha Q_1^{\alpha - 1} Q_2^{\beta}(q_1 - Q_1) + \beta Q_1^{\alpha} Q_2^{\beta - 1}(q_2 - Q_2) = 0$$

or, dividing by $Q_1^{\alpha} Q_2^{\beta}$,

$$\frac{\alpha}{Q_1}(q_1 - Q_1) + \frac{\beta}{Q_2}(q_2 - Q_2) = 0.$$

Finally we have

$$\frac{\alpha q_1}{Q_1} + \frac{\beta q_2}{Q_2} = \alpha + \beta. \tag{13.14}$$

Remarks

Equation (13.14) asserts that a normal direction to the tangent at (Q_1, Q_2) (known as a normal to the curve) is given by the vector of partial derivatives

$$\left(\frac{\partial u}{\partial q_1}, \frac{\partial u}{\partial q_2}\right). \tag{13.15}$$

Note that the components here are the marginal utilities of the two goods. If the tangent coincides with the budget line this normal points in the same direction as the normal to the budget line, i.e. for some scaling factor λ

$$\left(\frac{\partial u}{\partial q_1}, \frac{\partial u}{\partial q_2}\right) = \lambda(p_1, p_2). \tag{13.16}$$

Clearly this agrees with the condition that the marginal rate of substitution equals the corresponding price ratio.

Condition (13.16) generalizes to more variables, as might be expected. Of course one reason for expecting this will be that the various marginal rates of substitution, such as dq_3/dq_2, continue to be equal to the inverse ratio of the corresponding marginal utilities, e.g. $(\partial u/\partial q_2)/(\partial u/\partial q_3)$ (see section 13.9, question 8). In view of this wide applicability some more general notation is in order.

Definition

If $u = u(q_1, q_2, \ldots)$ is a function of several variables its gradient, denoted ∇u (or grad u), is the vector

$$\nabla u = \left(\frac{\partial u}{\partial q_1}, \frac{\partial u}{\partial q_2}, \ldots\right)$$

whose components are the marginal utilities.

Thus the utility maximization condition takes on the elegant form

$$\nabla u = \lambda p,$$

where $p = (p_1, p_2, \ldots)$ is the price vector and λ is a constant of proportionality.

The gradient notation also helps to give a condition for two curves

$$u(q_1, q_2) = k \qquad v(q_1, q_2) = l$$

to touch at a point $q_1 = Q_1$, $q_2 = Q_2$. By assumption the two curves share a common tangent line. They must therefore also have normals pointing in the same (or opposite) directions (figure 13.8). It follows that for some scaling factor λ

$$\nabla u = \lambda \nabla v.$$

We will call this the *co-tangency* condition. It will be useful for us when we come to our analysis of barter in the Edgeworth box (see section 13.4).

Example
Verify that $x^2 + y^2 = 2$ and $xy = 1$ touch at $x = 1$, $y = 1$.

Geometric considerations

One way to see that this is true is to note that the hyperbola has a constant elasticity of 1 (section 10.7, question 9). By symmetry the segment PQ of the tangent to $xy = 1$ at $R = (1, 1)'$ is bisected at R and $PR = RQ$ (figure 13.9). But $OR \perp PQ$, since elasticity is 1; $OR = \sqrt{2}$, and hence PQ is a tangent to the circle. (Recall that the radius is perpendicular to the tangent.)

Co-tangency condition

We have $u(x, y) = xy$ and $v(x, y) = x^2 + y^2$. Hence $\nabla u = (y, x)'$ and $\nabla v = (2x, 2y)'$. At $x = 1$, $y = 1$ we have $\nabla u = (1, 1)'$ and $\nabla v = (2, 2)'$ and so $\nabla u = \frac{1}{2} \nabla v$.

Remark

It may seem perverse to call a normal direction a gradient; however, the components of the gradient are after all the slopes in the $q_1, q_2, \ldots$ directions (see section 12.2). So once more it is life that has teased us by making the gradient point at right angles to the slope. Count your blessings that it points somewhere useful and note how neatly it shoulders the directional work. We shall see later that ∇u points in the direction of greatest utility increase (section 13.7).

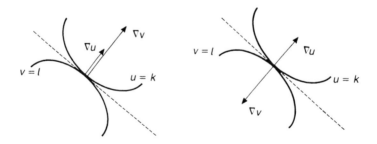

Figure 13.8 Condition for touching curves (co-tangency): $\nabla u = \lambda \nabla v$. Note that ∇u and ∇v point in the direction of increase in u and in v respectively.

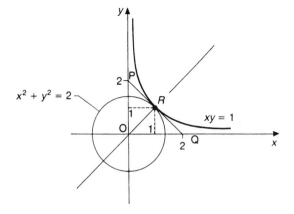

Figure 13.9   The circle $x^2 + y^2 = 2$ and hyperbola $xy = 1$ touch at $R = (1, 1)'$.

13.4   An application: the Edgeworth box

The traditional exposition has Robinson Crusoe bartering wheat for fish with Man Friday. Robinson has an amount W of wheat, but no fish; Friday has an amount F of fish and no wheat; no money is involved so that Robinson assesses a deal giving him (w, f), i.e. an amount w of wheat and an amount f of fish, where $0 \leqslant w \leqslant W$ and $0 \leqslant f \leqslant F$, by reference to its utility $u_R(w, f)$. Evidently such a deal gives Friday an amount $W - w$ of wheat and $F - f$ of fish which he assesses by reference to its utility $u_F(W - w, F - f)$.

We shall assume a Cobb–Douglas utility function:

$$u_R(w, f) = wf^2$$
$$u_F(w, f) = w^2 f \tag{13.17}$$

so that

$$u_F(W - w, F - f) = (W - w)^2 (F - f). \tag{13.18}$$

The indifference curves may be illustrated in the usual way (figure 13.10). Possible trades may be further investigated by superimposing the two diagrams so that Friday's origin is placed at (W, F) in the Robinson diagram and rotated

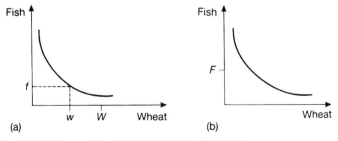

Figure 13.10   (a) Robinson diagram; (b) Friday diagram.

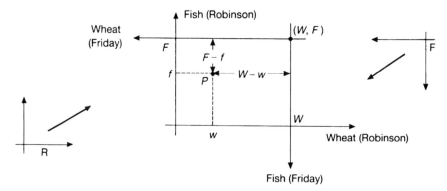

Figure 13.11 Superposition of the Friday diagram on the Robinson diagram produces the Edgeworth box. Note how $P = (w, f)$ also represents $(W - w, F - f)$ in Friday co-ordinates.

so that a box is formed, known as the *Edgeworth box* (figure 13.11). The advantage of such a trick is that the point P representing a trade for Robinson of w wheat and f fish simultaneously represents, relative to the superimposed axes, a trade for Friday of $W - w$ wheat and $F - f$ fish.

We examine a general point P in the box and the indifference curves for Robinson and Friday which pass through it (figure 13.12). If the curves cross over at P as shown, then a trade such as Q inside the lens-shaped region represents utility levels higher than at P for both Robinson and Friday. Hence neither would wish to agree a contract for P.

The points (w^*, f^*) at which the corresponding two indifference curves are tangential, rather than crossing over, are thus *possible* deals. They form what is known as a *contract curve*. To find its equation we note that, since the indifference curves share a tangent line, section 13.3 tells us that the vectors

$$\left(\frac{\partial u_R}{\partial w}(w, f), \quad \frac{\partial u_R}{\partial f}(w, f)\right)$$

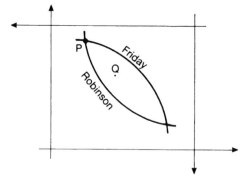

Figure 13.12 The point Q represents an improved allocation over P for both Robinson and Friday. P is thus inefficient.

and

$$\left(\frac{\partial u_F}{\partial w}(W-w, F-f), \ \frac{\partial u_F}{\partial f}(W-w, F-f)\right)$$

are proportional. This is because the common tangent may be expressed in the form

$$0 = \frac{\partial u_R}{\partial w}(w^*, f^*)(w-w^*) + \frac{\partial u_R}{\partial f}(w^*, f^*)(f-f^*)$$

or the form

$$0 = \frac{\partial v_F}{\partial w}(w^*, f^*)(w-w^*) + \frac{\partial v_F}{\partial f}(w^*, f^*)(f-f^*),$$

where we have written $v_F(w, f)$ for $u_F(W-w, F-f)$ for convenience.

Now comparing coefficients, we have for some λ (a constant of proportionality)

$$\frac{\partial u_R}{\partial w}(w^*, f^*) = \lambda \frac{\partial u_F}{\partial w}(W-w^*, F-f^*)$$

$$\frac{\partial u_R}{\partial f}(w^*, f^*) = \lambda \frac{\partial u_F}{\partial f}(W-w^*, F-f^*).$$

(13.19)

Notice that if $v_F(w, f) = u_F(W-w, F-f)$ we are saying, at (w^*, f^*), that

$$\left(\frac{\partial u_R}{\partial w}, \frac{\partial u_R}{\partial f}\right) = \lambda\left(\frac{\partial v_F}{\partial w}, \frac{\partial v_F}{\partial f}\right).$$

Geometrically, the equation says that the 'normal vectors' ∇u_R, ∇v_F (compare formula 13.16) are parallel. Actually, since ∇u_R and ∇v_F point in the direction of fastest increase in utility (section 13.7), they must point in opposite directions (figure 13.13).

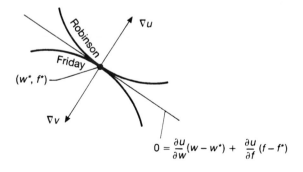

Figure 13.13 At the efficient point (w^*, f^*) the Robinson and the Friday indifference curves share a tangent.

Let us take $W = 2$ and $F = 1$. We solve (13.19). First note that

$$\frac{\partial u_R}{\partial w} = f^2 \qquad \frac{\partial u_R}{\partial f} = 2wf$$

and

$$\frac{\partial}{\partial w} u_F(W - w, F - f) = \frac{\partial}{\partial w}(2 - w)^2(1 - f) = -2(2 - w)(1 - f)$$

$$\frac{\partial}{\partial f} u_F(W - w, F - f) = \frac{\partial}{\partial f}(2 - w)^2(1 - f) = -(2 - w)^2.$$

Thus (13.19) becomes

$$f^2 = -2\lambda(2 - w)(1 - f)$$

$$2wf = -\lambda(2 - w)^2.$$

Dividing gives

$$\frac{f}{2w} = \frac{2(1 - f)}{2 - w}$$

or

$$2f - wf = 4w - 4wf,$$

i.e.

$$3wf + 2f - 4w = 0.$$

13.5   Tangent planes to surfaces

In the last two sections we examined the condition for tangency between a line and a curve in terms of their normals. We have already hinted that the same formula is applicable for tangency between a plane and a surface. We shall now see why this is so.

For this purpose we need to compute the equation of the tangent plane to a surface $z = F(x, y)$. Our argument is based on the geometrical interpretation of partial derivatives as slopes in the x and y directions (see section 12.2) and will involve taking vertical sections both of the surface and of its tangent plane.

We begin by selecting a point (X, Y, Z) on the surface $z = F(x, y)$ so that $Z = F(X, Y)$. We know from section 2.3 that a plane in xyz space has an equation of the form

$$ax + by + cz = d. \tag{13.20}$$

Let us suppose that (13.20) is the equation of the tangent plane to the surface at (X, Y, Z). Substituting X, Y, Z into (13.20) then tells us that

$$aX + bY + cZ = d. \tag{13.21}$$

We eliminate d by subtracting (13.21) from (13.20) and obtain

$$a(x - X) + b(y - Y) + c(z - Z) = 0. \tag{13.22}$$

It will be convenient to reorganize this equation as follows. We suppose that the tangent plane is *not* vertical so that $c \neq 0$ (why?). Dividing the last equation by c and renaming coefficients appropriately, we have

$$z - Z = l(x - X) + m(y - Y). \tag{13.23}$$

To interpret the slopes l and m we take vertical slices of three-space. First put $y = Y$. The vertical section of the surface is evidently a curve (see figure 13.14(b)) whose equation is

$$z = F(x, Y). \tag{13.24}$$

The slope of this curve (the x slope) when $x = X$ is equal, by section 12.2, to the partial derivative $\partial F/\partial x$ evaluated at $x = X$, $y = Y$. Now the same vertical section of our tangent plane is a line which touches the curve (13.24). We can obtain the equation of this line by setting $y = Y$ in (13.23). Evidently the equation is

$$z - Z = l(x - X).$$

The slope in xz space of this line is equal to l. Hence

$$l = \frac{\partial F}{\partial x}.$$

Similar considerations when applied to the vertical slice $x = X$ lead to

$$m = \frac{\partial F}{\partial y}.$$

Thus the equation of the tangent plane is

$$z - Z = \frac{\partial F}{\partial x}(x - X) + \frac{\partial F}{\partial y}(y - Y) \tag{13.25}$$

where the partial derivatives are evaluated at $x = X$, $y = Y$.

Example
Find the equation of the tangent plane at $(2, 3, 12)'$ to the surface $z = G(x, y) \equiv x^2 y$. Also find a normal to the tangent plane.

SOLUTION   We compute the partial derivatives when $x = 2$, $y = 3$.

$$\frac{\partial G}{\partial x} = 2xy \Big|_{\substack{x=2 \\ y=3}} = 2 \times 2 \times 3 = 12$$

$$\frac{\partial G}{\partial y} = x^2 \Big|_{\substack{x=2 \\ y=3}} = 2^2 = 4.$$

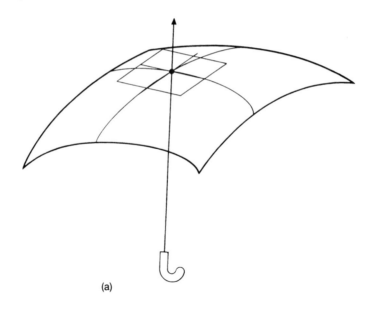

(a)

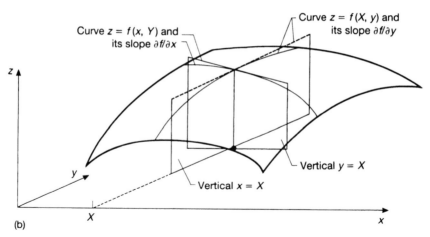

(b)

Figure 13.14 (a) Mathematician's impression of an umbrella? The two ridges/spokes run parallel to the x and y axes. (b) The serious view.

Thus the required equation is

$$z - 12 = 12(x - 2) + 4(y - 3).$$

Rearranging, we have

$$12x + 47y - z = 24.$$

The coefficient vector $(12, 4, -1)'$ is thus a normal to the plane (see the closing remark of section 13.2).

Remark 1

What we have just done in the last example can be done quite generally. Rewrite (13.25):

$$\frac{\partial F}{\partial x} x + \frac{\partial F}{\partial y} y - z = \frac{\partial F}{\partial x} X + \frac{\partial F}{\partial y} Y - Z.$$

The coefficient vector is

$$\left(\frac{\partial F}{\partial x}, \frac{\partial F}{\partial y}, -1 \right). \tag{13.26}$$

Thus the gradient vector ∇F augmented by -1, which we might write as $(\nabla F, -1)$, is a normal to the tangent plane. This is a little counterintuitive at first, since earlier arguments lead us to expect just a gradient operation, not one augmented with a -1 (cf. the case of a normal to a curve as in section 13.3). We have been misled by a formatting discrepancy.

In section 13.3 curves were given as u isoquants and the normal was given by ∇u. The curves there were not presented in the explicit form $y = f(x)$ which is the format corresponding to our surface $z = F(x, y)$. The curves were in fact presented in the implicit form

$$u(x, y) = \text{constant}.$$

We can call this the *isoquant format*. All points along the curve have equal u value. (Note in passing that *isos* in Greek means 'equal' and *quantum* in Latin means 'how much'.) In the present section the surface was presented in the explicit form $z = F(x, y)$. We can of course rewrite this equation in isoquant format by way of a new function $U(x, y, z)$ defined by

$$U(x, y, z) \equiv F(x, y) - z.$$

Then the surface satisfies the equation

$$U(x, y, z) = 0$$

and the points along the surface have equal U value (namely zero). The surface is thus a U isoquant. The normal accordingly is ∇U. But notice that we have

$$\frac{\partial U}{\partial x} = \frac{\partial F}{\partial x} \qquad \frac{\partial U}{\partial y} = \frac{\partial F}{\partial y} \qquad \frac{\partial U}{\partial z} = -1$$

and so $\nabla U = (\nabla F, -1)$ and the two formats yield answers that do agree.

Remark 2

We can continue this line of thought. The surface $z = F(x, y)$ in three dimensions gives rise to 'isoquant curves' in two dimensions (i.e. curves of constant F value), namely those points (x, y, z) on the surface which are at a predetermined fixed height z, i.e. contours.

In particular if we take the horizontal plane $z = Z$, which evidently passes through (X, Y, Z), we obtain the F isoquant curve

$$F(x, y) = Z. \tag{13.27}$$

The plane $z = Z$ intersects the tangent plane (13.25) in a line which is the tangent line to (13.27) (figure 13.15). What is its equation? Put $z = Z$ in (13.25) and we obtain

$$0 = \frac{\partial F}{\partial x}(x - X) + \frac{\partial F}{\partial y}(y - Y).$$

Thus ∇F which we might have expected in place of (13.26) is actually a normal to the F isoquant given by (13.27).

In summary:

1 a curve/surface given in isoquant form $U(x, y, \ldots) = $ constant has as normal ∇U;
2 a curve/surface given in explicit form $z = F(x, \ldots)$ has as normal $(\nabla F, -1)$.

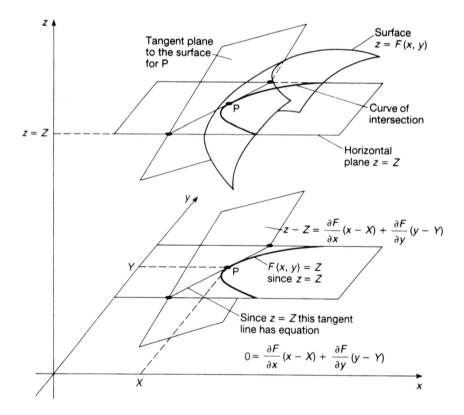

Figure 13.15   The tangent plane to $z = F(x, y)$ intersects with $z = Z$ to give a tangent line to the contour $F(x, y) = Z$ at (X, Y).

13.6   A directional marginal utility

We begin our discussion with a concrete example.

Example
An economic agent assesses a commodity bundle (x, y) according to the utility function $u(x, y) = x^2y$. He currently holds the two commodities in the amounts $x = 1$, $y = 2$. What is his marginal utility when he is offered simultaneously increments in both commodities as follows?

(a)   The increments are equal ($\delta x = \delta y$).
(b)   The increments in y and x are in the ratio $4 : 3$ (i.e. $\delta y : \delta x = 4 : 3$).

Before answering the question we pause to illustrate the situation in figure 13.16. The initial holding is at P. After receipt of the increments δx and δy, the agent's holding is at $Q = (1 + \delta x, 2 + \delta y)$. The path followed by Q (as δx is varied) forms what we might call the *increment path*. It is a straight line through P with gradient 1 in case (a) and with gradient 4/3 in case (b). Since a direction of increase is implicitly involved in this question, it is natural to speak of a directional marginal utility. But how should it be defined? In case (a) it would be tempting to let $\delta x = \delta y = h$ and to consider the limit of

$$\frac{u(1 + h, 2 + h) - u(1, 2)}{h}$$

as h tends to zero, just as in ordinary differentiation. However, there is a difficulty since the length PQ is actually $h\sqrt{2}$ (apply Pythagoras's theorem). So, if marginal utility is to measure the change in utility per unit change in input, we ought in case (a) to consider the limit of

$$\frac{u(1 + h, 2 + h) - u(1, 2)}{h\sqrt{2}}.$$
$$(13.28)$$

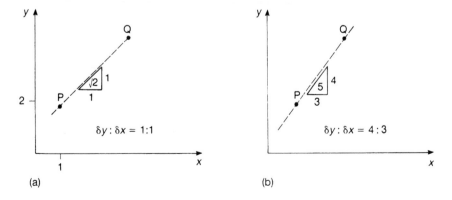

Figure 13.16   The increment path: (a) the increments are equal; (b) the increments are in the ratio $\delta y : \delta x = 4 : 3$.

Similarly in case (b) we could take $\delta x = h$, $\delta y = \frac{4}{3} h$. Then PQ is of length $\frac{5}{3} h$ and the marginal utility is presumably the limit of

$$\frac{u(1 + h, 2 + \frac{4}{3} h) - u(1, 2)}{\frac{5}{3} h}. \tag{13.29}$$

All of this is extremely inelegant. The more elegant approach is surely to hand over the central role to PQ. Thus if PQ is of length t, then in case (a)

$$\delta x = t \cos 45° = t\sqrt{2} \quad \text{and} \quad \delta y = t\sqrt{2}.$$

The corresponding marginal utility MU is as follows.

Case (a) $MU = \lim_{t \to 0} \dfrac{u(1 + t/\sqrt{2}, 2 + t/\sqrt{2}) - u(1, 2)}{t}$ (13.30)

Case (b) $MU = \lim_{t \to 0} \dfrac{u(1 + \frac{3}{5} t, 2 + \frac{4}{5} t) - u(1, 2)}{t}$. (13.31)

Before attempting to compute either of these quantities let us refer to figure 13.17 which shows the graph of $z = x^2 y$ and the utility paths in cases (a) and (b) when Q travels along the increment paths of figure 13.16.

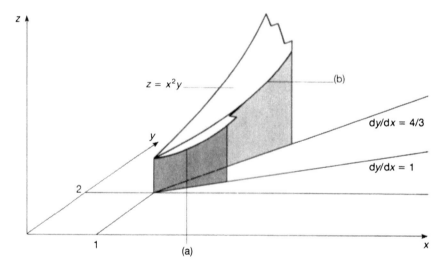

Figure 13.17 A piece of the surface $z = x^2 y$ showing the utility paths (a) and (b) corresponding to the increment paths of figure 13.16.

A glance at the figure shows that in each case the marginal utility is the slope at P of the corresponding utility path. Let us take a closer look at case (a). Since t measures distance along the increment path from P, we can treat it as the t axis with origin at P (figure 13.18). Relative to this t axis the utility path has the equation

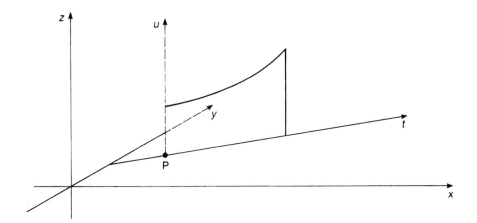

Figure 13.18 The increment path acts as a t axis with origin at P.

$$u = u\left(1 + \frac{t}{\sqrt{2}}, 2 + \frac{t}{\sqrt{2}}\right).$$

The marginal utility is therefore du/dt evaluated at $t = 0$. We can proceed to compute it in one of two ways.

By direct substitution we obtain

$$u = \left(1 + \frac{t}{\sqrt{2}}\right)^2\left(2 + \frac{t}{\sqrt{2}}\right).$$

Hence

$$\frac{du}{dt} = 2\left(1 + \frac{t}{\sqrt{2}}\right)\left(2 + \frac{t}{\sqrt{2}}\right)\frac{1}{\sqrt{2}} + \left(1 + \frac{t}{\sqrt{2}}\right)^2\frac{1}{\sqrt{2}}.$$

Thus in case (a)

$$MU = 2 \times 1 \times 2\frac{1}{\sqrt{2}} + \frac{1}{\sqrt{2}} = \frac{5}{\sqrt{2}}.$$

Alternatively, we can apply the chain rule to $u = x^2 y$:

$$\frac{du}{dt} = \frac{\partial u}{\partial x}\frac{dx}{dt} + \frac{\partial u}{\partial y}\frac{dy}{dt}.$$

Here by (13.30) $x = 1 + t\sqrt{2}$ and $y = 2 + t/\sqrt{2}$. Hence at P

$$MU = (2xy)_{\substack{x=1\\y=2}}\frac{1}{\sqrt{2}} + (x^2)_{\substack{x=1\\y=2}}\frac{1}{\sqrt{2}}$$

$$= 4\frac{1}{\sqrt{2}} + 1\frac{1}{\sqrt{2}} = \frac{5}{\sqrt{2}}.$$

Similarly in case (b), when $x = 1 + \frac{3}{5}t$ and $y = 2 + \frac{4}{5}t$ we have

$$MU = 4\frac{3}{5} + 1\frac{4}{5} = \frac{16}{5}.$$

13.6.1   General discussion

We are now in a position to define the directional marginal utility when $x = X$ and $y = Y$. This requires first that we specify a direction for the increment path. Although we first spoke of the ratio of the increments and hence of the slope of the increment path, we eventually found ourselves referring to

$$\delta x = t \cos \alpha \qquad \text{and} \qquad \delta y = t \sin \alpha,$$

where $\tan \alpha$ is the slope of the increment path (figure 13.19). Thus $x = X + t \times \cos \alpha$ and $y = Y + t \sin \alpha$ along the increment path. Notice that the increment path is parallel to the vector $v = (\cos \alpha, \sin \alpha)'$, which is therefore referred to as the *direction vector* for the increment path. Evidently the length of v is unity (since $\cos^2 \alpha + \sin^2 \alpha = 1$).

Definition

A vector v of length 1 is called a *direction*.

Suppose $v = (v_1, v_2)'$ has length 1. Using inner products (section 2.2) we notice from figure 13.20 that

$$v_1 = \begin{pmatrix} v_1 \\ v_2 \end{pmatrix} \cdot \begin{pmatrix} 1 \\ 0 \end{pmatrix} = \| v \| \cdot \| e_1 \| \cos \alpha = 1 \times 1 \cos \alpha$$

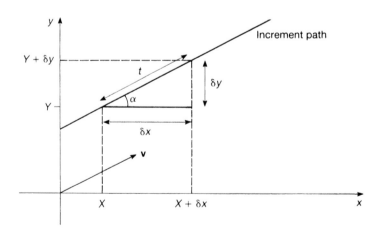

Figure 13.19   Along the increment path $x = X + t \cos \alpha$, $y = Y + t \sin \alpha$.

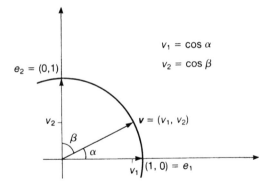

Figure 13.20 A vector v of unit length and its direction cosines.

$$v_2 = \begin{pmatrix} v_1 \\ v_2 \end{pmatrix} \cdot \begin{pmatrix} 0 \\ 1 \end{pmatrix} = \| v \| \cdot \| e_2 \| \cos \alpha = 1 \times 1 \cos \beta$$

where α and β are the corresponding angles between v and the x and y axes. The components of v are therefore often called its *direction cosines*.

Definition

If v is a direction vector the directional derivative in direction v of $z = F(x, y)$ at $x = X$, $y = Y$, denoted $D_v F(X, Y)$, is

$$\left. \frac{\mathrm{d}}{\mathrm{d}t} F(X + tv_1, Y + tv_2) \right|_{t = 0}.$$

By the chain rule we have

$$D_v F(X, Y) = \frac{\partial F}{\partial x} v_1 + \frac{\partial F}{\partial y} v_2 = \nabla F \cdot v. \tag{13.32}$$

Thus, if F is a utility function, its directional derivative is what we earlier called the directional marginal utility.

13.7 Direction of fastest growth

We return to the example of the previous section and ask in what ratio increments should be offered to the agent to maximize his marginal utility. Equivalently: what direction of increase should x and y follow if the growth in utility is to be largest? The answer is extremely simple. We have by (13.32) for any direction v that

$$D_v u(x, y) = \nabla u \cdot v$$
$$= \| \nabla u \| \cos \theta \tag{13.33}$$

where θ is the angle between v and ∇u (figure 13.21) and $\| \nabla u \|$ is the length of the vector ∇u (refer to section 2.2, especially figure 2.3). The quantity in (13.33) is therefore largest when $\cos\theta = 1$, i.e. $\theta = 0$. The fastest growth in utility is achieved when v points in the same direction as ∇u. Thus

$$v = \frac{\nabla u}{\|\nabla u\|}.$$

In our example of section 13.6 we have

$$\nabla u = (2xy, x^2)' \Big|_{\substack{x=1 \\ y=2}} = (4, 1)'.$$

Hence the fastest growth in utility occurs when

$$v = \frac{1}{\sqrt{(17)}}\begin{pmatrix} 4 \\ 1 \end{pmatrix}.$$

Evidently we are asking for the increments to satisfy $\delta x : \delta y = 4 : 1$. We have arrived at the general principle that at any point utility grows fastest in a direction normal to the utility isoquant through the point (figure 13.22).

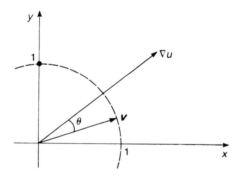

Figure 13.21 θ is the angle between ∇u and v.

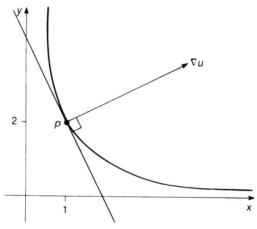

Figure 13.22   At any point utility grows fastest in a direction normal to the utility isoquant.

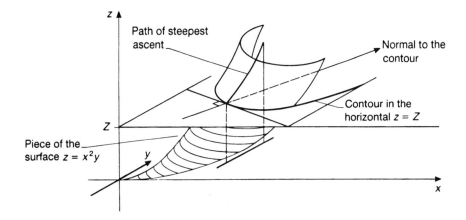

Figure 13.23 The steepest path is encountered when climbing in a compass direction normal to the contour.

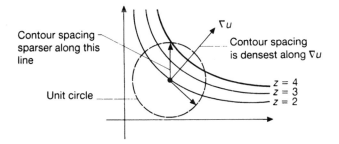

Figure 13.24 A contour map shows contours for every unit rise in height. The steepest ascent crosses more contour lines.

Obviously the same principle applies to revenue curves, cost curves etc. We may imagine the surface $z = u(x, y)$, graphed in figure 13.23, as depicting a mountain. The geographer's contour is of course a path of constant height which has zero steepness. The steepest path (i.e. the path with greatest physical gradient) occurs in a direction normal to the contour. On a geographical map the direction of steepest ascent crosses more contour lines than do other directions of ascent. At the other extreme is the direction tangential to the contour, which crosses no contour lines (figure 13.24).

*13.8 Breaking the convention: differentials

In section 13.1 we suggested breaking the convention which says that dy/dx is meaningful only as a symbol denoting the limiting quotient, and we temporarily allowed ourselves the separate use of dy and dx. As promised, we explain how breaking the taboos can be done consistently with the quotient notation.

To talk about dy/dx we must first have y as a function of x. Let us be specific. Suppose $y = x^2$, so that $dy/dx = 2x$. What meaning can we give the equation

$$dy = 2x\ dx?$$

To focus our thoughts better we take $x = 1$ and ask to interpret the equation

$$dy = 2dx$$

with reference to the curve $y = x^2$ (figure 13.25). Now 2 is the slope of the tangent, but it is certainly *not* true that when $x = 1 + \delta x$ the increment δy in y obeys $\delta y = 2\delta x$; in fact $\delta y = (1 + \delta x)^2 - 1 = 2\delta x + (\delta x)^2$. However, the corresponding increment in the y value on the tangent line is precisely $2\delta x$. So if we let dx be an increase in x, the increase in y on the tangent line is actually precisely $2dx$. This tangent line then *defines* dy.

Definition

The differentials dx and dy associated with the function $y = f(x)$ and with a chosen point of the graph, say $x = X$, $y = Y$ (where $Y = f(X)$), are two new variables connected by the equation

$$dy = f'(X)\ dx \qquad (13.34)$$

where dx is an independent variable.

It is usual to represent differentials on a Cartesian axis system with origin at (X, Y) (figure 13.26). It is then convenient to regard (13.34) as approximating linearly the true relation $y + \delta y = f(x + \delta x)$ between δy and δx, and therefore to

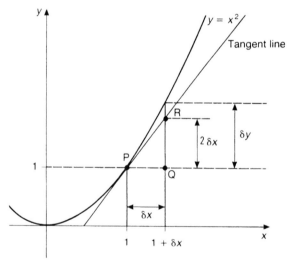

Figure 13.25 Interpreting $dy = 2dx$ at $x = 1$; $\delta y \neq 2\delta x$ but $RQ = 2\delta x$ with R on the tangent line. We define $dx = \delta x = PQ$ and $dy = QR = 2dx$.

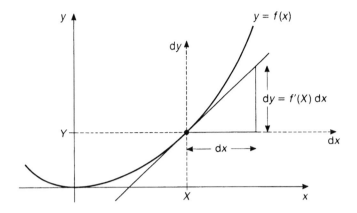

Figure 13.26 Differentials are represented by Cartesian axes through a point (X, Y) of a curve and related via $dy = f'(X)dx$.

restrict dx to be small (though in fact dx, as defined above, is an independent and unrestricted variable).

We note that if the function $y = f(x)$ is known only implicitly through the equation

$$F(x, y) = 0,$$

then equivalent to (13.34) is the equation

$$\frac{\partial F}{\partial x} dx + \frac{\partial F}{\partial y} dy = 0, \tag{13.35}$$

obtained via implicit differentiation (since $-(\partial F/\partial x)/(\partial F/\partial y)$ is the slope of the tangent line).

In the context of section 13.1 we can now legitimately write

$$(dq_1, dq_2) = \lambda(p_1^{-1}, p_2^{-1}),$$

since in fact dq_1 and dq_2 are the differentials associated at (Q_1, Q_2) with the implicit relation

$$u(q_1, q_2) = k.$$

Thus by (13.35) dq_1 and dq_2 are connected by the equation

$$\frac{\partial u}{\partial q_1} dq_1 + \frac{\partial u}{\partial q_2} dq_2 = 0.$$

The obvious generalization to, say, two variables runs like this. If $z = F(x, y)$ represents a surface, then its tangent plane at $x = X$, $y = Y$, $z = Z$ (where $Z = F(X, Y)$), as we have learnt, is given by

$$z - Z = \frac{\partial F}{\partial x}(x - X) + \frac{\partial F}{\partial y}(y - Y). \tag{13.36}$$

The partial derivatives here are evaluated at $x = X$, $y = Y$. We let dx, dy, dz be three new variables connected by the equation

$$dz = \frac{\partial F}{\partial x} dx + \frac{\partial F}{\partial y} dy. \tag{13.37}$$

The differentials dx and dy are regarded as independent variables. The equation (13.37) approximates to the true relation $Z + \delta z = F(X + \delta x, Y + \delta y)$ between δz and the increments δx, δy. Again, it is normal to think of dx and dy as small, although (13.37) does not restrict them. When dx and dy are small, dz is approximately the total change δz (take $\delta x = dx$, $\delta y = dy$). Hence dz is called the *total differential*. Clearly (13.37) describes the tangent plane (13.36) in different co-ordinates.

Notice the connection with the chain rule. If $x = g(t)$ and $y = h(t)$ we have for $t = T$ that

$$dx = g'(T) \, dt \qquad dy = h'(T) \, dt.$$

Substituting in (13.35) gives

$$dz = \frac{\partial F}{\partial x} g' \, dt + \frac{\partial F}{\partial y} h' \, dt.$$

Division by dt shows that the ratio of differentials dz/dt is, by the chain rule, also equal to the derivative dz/dt.

13.9   Exercises

1* $F(x, y) = x^2 y + y^3 x$. Find $\nabla F(1, 2)$. Also find the rate of increase in the direction of the vectors $(1, 2)'$ and $(3, 4)'$. [*Hint*: Scale them down to unit length!]

2   If $u = x^2 y^5$, which is the direction of fastest utility growth when $x = 1$, $y = 2$?

3* Find the equation of the chord joining the points $(0, 1)$ and $(\frac{1}{2}, 0)$ of the ellipse $4x^2 + y^2 = 1$. Use the co-tangency condition to find at what point of the ellipse its tangent is parallel to this chord.

4* If $y = f(x)$ describes a curve, write down in terms of $f'(x)$ a normal vector at (X, Y). Check that your answer is correct by reference to the $u = 0$ contour when $u(x, y) \equiv f(x) - y$.

5* Robinson barters wheat for fish with Friday. Robinson initially has 2 units (sacks) of wheat and Friday 1 unit (netfull) of fish. Both have the same Cobb–Douglas utility $u(w, f) = (wf)^{1/2}$ for a bundle of goods comprising w units of wheat and f units of fish. Find the set of possible contracts (w, f). You should explain carefully the condition $\nabla u = \lambda \nabla v$ where $v = u(2 - w, 1 - f)$ by reference to a diagram of the Edgeworth box.

6   Repeat the analysis in the Edgeworth box of section 13.4 when

$$u_R(w, f) = u_F(w, f) = (w + 1)(f + 1)$$

and $W = 2$, $F = 1$, i.e. find the contract curve.

(a) The point (W, O) is the 'no-trade' point for Robinson. Why is it also the 'no-trade' point for Friday?

(b) If prices p_1, p_2 for wheat and fish respectively prevail, write down Robinson's budget line equation. Why is this also Friday's budget line in the Edgeworth box?

(c) For what values $w = \bar{w}$, $f = \bar{f}$ is $u(w, f) = (\bar{w} + 1)(\bar{f} + 1)$, i.e. the indifference curve through $(\bar{w}, \bar{f})$, tangential to the budget line?

(d) For what values of (p_1, p_2) is $(\bar{w}, \bar{f})$ also on the contract curve? Interpret the economic significance of this pricing structure.

7*   He and She negotiate without reference to money for an exchange of goods X and Y of which each is the sole holder. Each is known to behave as though the preference for holding amounts x of X and y of Y was measured by $u = \log[(x + 1)(y + 1)]$. He holds 3 units of X and She holds 2 units of Y. Explain why the only feasible contracts for an exchange satisfy the condition $\nabla u = \lambda \nabla v$, where $v(x, y) = u(3 - x, 2 - y)$. If prices p for X and q for Y are announced what does the condition

$$\nabla u = \mu \begin{pmatrix} p \\ q \end{pmatrix}$$

signify? At what price ratio would a feasible exchange contract satisfy their optimal requirements (subject to the budget constraint imposed by the sale of their initial holdings)?

8*   Find the equation of the tangent plane at $(1, 1, 1)$ to the surface $z = F(x, y) \equiv x^2 y^5$. Also write down the equation of the tangent line to the contour $x^2 y^5 = 1$. What are the normal vectors in each case?

9   With reference to the example of section 13.6, suppose an economic agent currently holding a commodity bundle of $(x, y) = (4, 1)$ assesses utility by the formula $u(x, y) = (xy)^{1/2}$. Find the increment paths when increments are offered in the ratio $\delta y : \delta x = 1 : 1$ and when they are offered in the ratio $2 : 1$. What are the corresponding marginal utilities for these increments? What incremental ratio maximizes marginal utility?

10   Use the chain rule to verify formula (13.32) when $w = F(x, y, z)$ and $v = (v_1, v_2, v_3)$.

11*   Show that if $x/z = u/w$ and $y/z = v/w$, then for some λ

$$(x, y, z) = \lambda(u, v, w).$$

[Hint: $(x, y, z) = z(x/z, y/z, 1)$.]

12   Prove that if utility $u(q_1, q_2, q_3)$ is maximized subject to $p_1 q_1 + p_2 q_2 + p_3 q_3 = m$, then for some λ

$$\left(\frac{\partial u}{\partial q_1}, \frac{\partial u}{\partial q_2}, \frac{\partial u}{\partial q_3} \right) = \lambda(p_1, p_2, p_3).$$

[*Hint:* By equation (13.16) $(\partial u/\partial q_i)/(\partial u/\partial q_j) = p_i/p_j$ holds when the third variable is held fixed. Apply the previous exercise.]

13   Figure 13.27 shows how the directional derivative in direction v falls off as θ increases to $90°$. The tip of the vector $D_v F(X, Y)$ describes a circle – why?

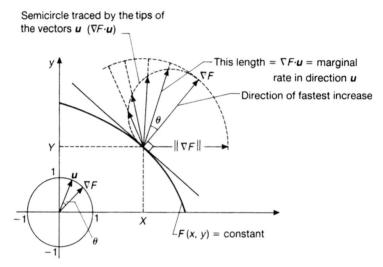

Figure 13.27   The vector in direction u of length equal to ∇u (the directional derivative) traces a semicircle.

13.10   Answers

1   $\nabla F = (2xy + y^3, x^2 + 3y^2 x)'$. So $\nabla F(1, 2) = (12, 13)'$.

The unit vector in direction $(1, 2)'$ is $u = (1/\sqrt{5})(1, 2)'$. The directional derivative in direction u is

$$\frac{1}{\sqrt{5}} 12 + \frac{2}{\sqrt{5}} 13 = \frac{38}{\sqrt{5}} = \frac{38\sqrt{5}}{5}.$$

The unit vector in direction $(3, 4)'$ is $v = (1/5)(3, 4)'$. The corresponding directional derivative is

$$\frac{3}{5} 12 + \frac{4}{5} 13 = \frac{88}{5}.$$

3   The join of $(0, 1)$ and $(\frac{1}{2}, 0)$ is given by

$$\frac{y - 1}{0 - 1} = \frac{x - 0}{\frac{1}{2} - 0} \qquad \text{or} \qquad 2x + y = 1.$$

This has normal $(2, 1)'$. The ellipse $4x^2 + y^2 = 1$ is a contour of $F(x, y) = 4x^2 + y^2$. A normal at any point of the contour is $\nabla F(x, y) = (8x, 2y)'$ and it will be parallel to the other normal if $(8x, 2y)' = \lambda(2, 1)'$. Thus $8x/2y = 2/1$ or

$4x = 2y$, i.e. $y = 2x$. But $(x, y)'$ is to lie on the ellipse and so $1 = 4x^2 + y^2 = 4x^2 + (2x)^2 = 8x^2$. Thus if

$$x = \frac{1}{\sqrt{8}} = \frac{\sqrt{2}}{4} \qquad \text{and} \qquad y = \frac{\sqrt{2}}{2}$$

we obtain a point of the ellipse where the normal to its tangent is parallel to the given chord.

4 If $u(x, y) = f(x) - y$ then $\nabla u(X, Y) = (f'(X), -1)'$. Also the tangent to $y = f(x)$ at (X, Y) is $y - Y = f'(X)(x - X)$, or $f'(X)x - y = f'(X)X - Y$, and here the gradient is also $(f'(X), -1)'$.

5 $u = (wf)^{1/2}$, $v = (2 - w)^{1/2}(1 - f)^{1/2}$:

$$\nabla u = \left(\frac{1}{2} w^{-1/2} f^{1/2}, \frac{1}{2} w^{1/2} f^{-1/2} \right)'$$

$$\nabla v = \left(-\frac{1}{2} (2 - w)^{-1/2}(1 - f)^{1/2}, -\frac{1}{2} (2 - w)^{1/2}(1 - f)^{-1/2} \right)'.$$

u and v are mutually tangential at $(w, f)'$ and so satisfy $\nabla u = \lambda \nabla v$, i.e.

$$\frac{1}{2} \left(\frac{f}{w} \right)^{1/2} = -\frac{\lambda}{2} \left(\frac{1 - f}{2 - w} \right)^{1/2}$$

and

$$\frac{1}{2} \left(\frac{w}{f} \right)^{1/2} = -\frac{\lambda}{2} \left(\frac{2 - w}{1 - f} \right)^{1/2}.$$

Eliminating λ:

$$\frac{f}{w} = \frac{1 - f}{2 - w}$$

or

$$2f - wf = w - wf$$

and so

$$w = 2f.$$

The explanation is as follows.

(a) (w, f) represents simultaneously (i) itself as an allocation to Robinson and (ii) $(2 - w, 1 - f)$ as the complementary allocation to Friday. In terms of (w, f) Friday's utility is $v = u(2 - w, 1 - f)$.

(b) If u and v contours through a point (w, f) are not tangential then improvements may be made by moving into the lens area (both u and v values are greater there), as in figure 13.28.

(c) ∇u, ∇v are normal vectors to the tangent lines to the u, v contours.

7 We make use of the Edgeworth box illustrated in figure 13.28. Each point (x, y) with $0 \leq x \leq 3$ and $0 \leq y \leq 2$ represents an allocation of (x, y) to Him and an allocation of $(3 - x, 2 - y)$ to Her. His utility is thus $u(x, y)$. Hers is $u(3 - x, 2 - y) \equiv v(x, y)$.

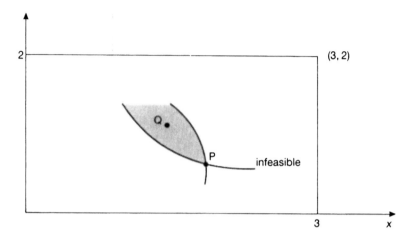

Figure 13.28 The Edgeworth box for question 7.

At a point $P = (x, y)$ where a u curve is *not* tangential to the v curve we may find Q in the shaded area where they are both better off (because the u and v curves are convex/concave respectively). The co-tangency condition is thus that the normal vectors are parallel, i.e.

$$\nabla u = \lambda \nabla v.$$

Here $u = \log[(1 + x)(1 + y)]$, $v = \log[(4 - x)(3 - y)]$ and so

$$\left(\frac{1}{1 + x}, \frac{1}{1 + y}\right)' = \lambda\left(\frac{-1}{4 - x}, \frac{-1}{3 - y}\right)'.$$

Hence

$$\frac{y + 1}{x + 1} = \frac{3 - y}{4 - x}$$

$$4 + 4y - x - xy = (4 - x)(1 + y)$$

$$= (1 + x)(3 - y)$$

$$= 3 - y + 3x - xy.$$

$$1 = 4x - 5y. \tag{13.38}$$

The condition

$$\nabla u = \mu\binom{p}{q} \tag{13.39}$$

signifies that the budget line

$$px + qy = 3p \tag{13.40}$$

is parallel to the tangent line to the u contour. Thus if the contour through $(x, y)'$ is tangential to the budget line He is *maximizing his utility*. If the point lies on (13.38) we have by (13.39)

$$4x - 5y = 1$$

$$\frac{p}{q} = \frac{y+1}{x+1} \tag{13.41}$$

and of course

$$px + qy = 3p. \tag{13.42}$$

This may also be written as follows (since (13.38) implies and is implied by $(y+1)/(x+1) = (3-y)/(4-x)$). Rewriting (13.41) as

$$k \equiv \frac{p}{q} = \frac{y+1}{x+1} \tag{13.43}$$

and (13.38) as

$$k \equiv \frac{p}{q} = \frac{3-y}{4-x}, \tag{13.44}$$

by (13.43) and (13.44)

$$kx + k - y - 1 = 0$$
$$\underline{- kx + 4k + y - 3 = 0}$$

Adding:

$$5k - 4 = 0$$

$$k = \frac{4}{5}.$$

8   $\nabla F(x, y) = (2xy^5, 5x^2y^4)'$, and so $\nabla F(1, 1) = (2, 5)'$. The required tangent plane is thus

$$z - 1 = 2(x - 1) + 5(x - 2).$$

Setting $z = 1$ we obtain a vertical section (a) of the surface $z = x^2y^5$ in the form of the contour $1 = x^2y^5$, and (b) of the tangent plane above in the form of the line $0 = 2(x - 1) + 5(x - 2)$ which is tangent to the contour.

11   $(x, y, z) = z(x/z, y/z, 1) = z(u/w, v/w, 1) = zw(u, v, w)$. Taking $\lambda = zw$ gives the required conclusion.

14

Taylor's Theorem – An Approximation Tool

14.1 'Double your money' – approximation and relative smallness

In section 11.5 we used logarithms to determine how long it takes for an initial deposit to double when interest is compounded annually at a rate r. We needed in particular to solve the equation

$$(1 + r)^t = 2 \tag{14.1}$$

for t. We shall solve (14.1) approximately without recourse to logarithms. Though some of what we do may at first seem a little dubious, we shall find later that all is well. Justifying inspired hunches is the better part of mathematical valour (if not of mathematics generally). We imagine t is a natural number (wince!), and then the binomial theorem allows us to bring down the exponent t. Our new equation is

$$2 = 1 + rt + \frac{1}{2} t(t-1) r^2 + \cdots \text{ (terms of order } r^3 t^3 \text{ and higher).} \tag{14.2}$$

Clearly the right-hand side is unmanageable as it stands. However, if we are prepared to drop most of the summands we can solve for t approximately. By (14.2) we see that $rt < 1$. (Notice that this inequality already tells us something about t; when r ranges between 0.1 and 0.2, it follows from the inequality that t is of the order of 10 at most.) As for the powers $(rt)^2$, $(rt)^3$ etc. these are dropping off in size. We shall think of $(rt)^3$ and higher powers as 'small' (whatever that might mean). This leads to the approximate version of (14.2) in the form

$$2 \approx 1 + rt + \frac{1}{2} r^2 t^2 - \frac{1}{2} r^2 t. \tag{14.3}$$

This formula needs explaining: we have ignored not only terms like $r^3 t^3$ but also $r^3 t^2$, $r^3 t$, $r^3 t$ etc. Why? Because they are also 'small': e.g. $r^3 t^2 = r(rt)^2$ and $r^3 t = r^2(rt)$, and the factor r, which in the case of interest rates is usually below 0.2, reduces the contribution due to the powers of rt still further. We return to

384

this point in a moment. Now the equation (14.3) is almost quadratic in rt. In fact, let us drop the term $r^2t = r(rt) < r$ which is 'small'. Put $rt = x$ and we have

$$2 = 1 + x + \frac{1}{2}x^2$$

or

$$x^2 + 2x - 2 = 0.$$

Hence $x = \sqrt{3} - 1 = 0.732\,05\ldots$. This gives us something known as the *73 rule*:

$$rt \approx 0.73. \tag{14.4}$$

Thus if $r = 10$ per cent we have $t \approx 7$ years.

In the next section we take up in earnest the problem of estimating an error made in the course of an approximation. For the moment let us discuss only the earlier use of the word 'small'. You might smile and ask: how small, how short is a piece of string? However, we can make sense of the word. Smallness is after all a relative matter. For instance the last term of (14.3) which we dropped should be compared with the term rt which we regard as significant. We have

$$\frac{r^2t/2}{rt} = \frac{r}{2} \approx 5 \text{ per cent} \quad (\text{perhaps!}).$$

Consider a few of the other terms of (14.2). We make free use of (14.4):

$$\frac{r^2t^2/2}{rt} = \frac{1}{2}rt \approx 36 \text{ per cent}$$

(not negligible and included in (14.3)),

$$\frac{r^3t^3/6}{rt} = \frac{1}{6}r^2t^2 \approx 9 \text{ per cent},$$

$$\frac{r^4t^4/(4!)}{rt} \approx 2 \text{ per cent}.$$

Later terms in (14.2) will exhibit even smaller percentages – we leave any unconvinced reader to play some finger exercises on a calculator. The terms in (14.2) are not so numerous as to allow the omitted terms to build up a very large error. At any event it should now be clear how smallness can be reckoned within the course of an approximation. What remains unclear is whether the use of the binomial expansion formula in (14.2) is justifiable when t is not an integer. The justification will soon come in section 14.3.

14.2 Estimating error via the derivatives

This section is an introduction to an extremely important theorem known as Taylor's theorem. We really need only its statement – both this introduction and the proof in section 14.3 are not essential to an understanding of the various applications which follow. In that sense this section may 'safely' be omitted. The purpose here is to motivate the result and to avoid the impression of producing a rabbit out of a hat.

Our task is to provide tools for estimating the error made in replacing an object X by an object $X + h$ during the course of a computation. What is a 'computation'? For our purposes it has to be a function $f(x)$ because we must be dealing with a rule which associates a number not only with the object $x = X$ but also with various 'substitutes' such as $x = X + h$. An example to have in mind is the computation of π^2, where $\pi = 3.1415 \ldots$; the computation here is represented by the function $f(x) \equiv x^2$ and in practice instead of using π we necessarily use approximations to π (as when we supply π to a certain number of decimals only). In the case of that example we appeal to the continuity of x^2 (see section 8.4, question 5, and section 9.1) in order to guarantee the accuracy of our final computation.

It is important to grasp the logic of such a continuity argument. Our starting point is an intuitive statement along the lines

$$f(X + h) \approx f(X) \quad \text{for small } h.$$

Of course, taken at face value this is meaningless. To attach any meaning to an 'approximate equality' requires a precise statement about the error, i.e. about the discrepancy, or difference, between the objects concerned. Denote the error by $e(h)$. Thus we have the identity

$$f(X + h) = f(x) + e(h).$$

The appeal to continuity of f is then the following claim about the behaviour of the error $e(h)$:

$$\lim_{h \to 0} e(h) = 0. \tag{14.5}$$

This says that we can limit/control the error by using appropriately small h. That is the long and short of it.

But can we say anything more about how small $e(h)$ is? In the last section we learnt to treat 'small' in a relative way by making comparisons against a significant quantity. Here we may deem h to be the significant quantity against which to make comparisons. We therefore seek information about $e(h)/h$. But

$$\frac{e(h)}{h} = \frac{f(X + h) - f(x)}{h} \tag{14.6}$$

and immediately we have differentiability thrust upon as. So, assuming that $f'(x)$ exists,

$$\lim_{h \to 0} \frac{e(h)}{h} = f'(X), \tag{14.7}$$

which leads us to claim that $e(h) \approx f'(X)h$. We make this into a more precise statement by measuring, as before, the discrepancy between the two sides of this latest approximate identity. Let

$$e(h) = f'(X)h + e_1(h). \tag{14.8}$$

Then from (14.7) we have

$$\frac{e_1(h)}{h} = \frac{e(h)}{h} - f'(X) \to 0. \tag{14.9}$$

Hence $e_1(h)$ is small relative to h (i.e. its size relative to h may be made as small as we will, when appropriately small h are considered). Thus knowing that $f(x)$ is better behaved, e.g. that it is differentiable, gives better information about the error $e(h)$.

Naturally we ask: can we do better? The mean value theorem gives the estimate

$$\frac{e(h)}{h} = f'(X_h)$$

for some X_h between X and $X + h$ so that

$$\frac{e_1(h)}{h} = f'(X_h) - f'(X),$$

and here we come to a dead end. The best we can do with our earlier approach is to write $X_h = X + k$ and to assert, again by the mean value theorem (applied to f'), that

$$\frac{e_1(h)}{h} = f''(X^*)k \qquad \text{(with } |k| < |h|), \tag{14.10}$$

where X^* is somewhere between X and $X + k$. How well does this compare with a concrete example?

Example
Analyse the error term $e_1(h)$ when $f(x) \equiv x^3$ and $X = 1$.

SOLUTION   We have $f'(x) = 3x^2$ and so $f'(1) = 3$. But

$$f(X + h) \equiv (1 + h)^3$$
$$= 1 + 3h + 3h^2 + h^3$$
$$= f(X) + f'(1)h + h^2(3 + h).$$

Thus $e_1(h) \approx 3h^2$ whereas according to (14.10) we were able to say only that $|e_1(h)/h^2| < f''(1) = 6$.

Remark

Presumably we expect $e_1(h) \approx ch^2$ for some constant c, i.e.

$$\lim_{h \to 0} \frac{e_1(h)}{h^2} = c.$$

What should the constant c be? For a hint we look at the simplest functions $f(x)$, namely the polynomials. We can look upon $f(X + h)$ as a polynomial in h – just expand the powers $(X + h)^2$, $(X + h)^3$ etc. using the binomial theorem. Thus,

$$f(X + h) = a + bh + ch^2 + \text{terms in } h^3 \text{ and higher powers.}$$

Setting $h = 0$ we obtain $f(X) = a$. Differentiating once with respect to h we have

$$f'(X + h) = b + 2ch + \text{terms in } h^2 \text{ plus higher powers}$$

and setting $h = 0$ gives $f'(X) = b$. Differentiating one more time

$$f''(X + h) = 2c + \text{terms in } h \text{ plus higher powers}$$

and so $\frac{1}{2}f''(X) = c$. Taylor's theorem confirms this result for more general functions.

14.3   Taylor's theorem: second-order error

In this section we prove the following assertion.

If $f(x)$ is twice differentiable in an interval around $x = X$, then for any point $X + h$ in that interval

$$f(X + h) = f(X) + hf'(X) + \frac{1}{2}f''(X*) h^2 \tag{14.11}$$

where $X*$ is a point somewhere between X and $X + h$. In effect this is a strong form of the mean value theorem and is a special case of Taylor's theorem to be quoted in the next section.

To simplify the presentation we shall prove (14.11) when $X = 0$. Our objective is thus to obtain a formula for the (error) term E_0 in the equation

$$f(h) = f(0) + hf'(0) + E_0. \tag{14.12}$$

We note the geometric interpretation of E_0 in figure 14.1, namely as the amount by which the graph overshoots the tangent line at $x = h$.

To test the dependence of E_0 on h we introduce an intermediate point z between 0 and h. The tangent line at $x = z$ to the curve produces an overshoot $E(z)$ at $x = h$. Thus when $z = 0$ we have $E(0) = E_0$. More interestingly $E(h) = 0$. We must determine how $E(z)$ depends on z. Notice that the introduction of the intermediate tangent line puts $f'(z)$, its slope, into consideration. As this z varies we can expect $f''(z)$ also to appear in our calculation.

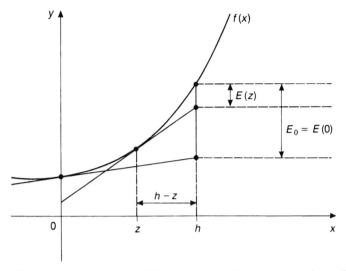

Figure 14.1   Varying the position z of the tangent produces an overshoot $E(z)$. We test the dependence of $E(z)$ on $h - z$.

We need a formula for the overshoot. The equation of the intermediate tangent line is

$$y = f(z) + f'(z)(x - z).$$

Hence the overshoot $E(z)$ is obtained by substituting $x = h$ in the right-hand side here and subtracting from $f(h)$. Thus

$$E(z) = f(h) - f(z) - f'(z)(h - z). \tag{14.13}$$

This equation confirms that indeed $E(h) = 0$ while, by (14.12), $E(0) = E_0$. Since we expect a quadratic dependence of the overshoot $E(z)$ on the quantity $h - z$, we manufacture a quadratic approximation to $E(z)$. Now the quadratic expression in z

$$Q(z) = E_0 \frac{(h - z)^2}{h^2}$$

has the property $Q(0) = E_0$ and $Q(h) = 0$, and so we assess the difference

$$F(z) = E(z) - Q(z)$$

by asking where the difference is largest (figure 14.2). If it is largest at $z = z^*$ then $F'(z^*) = 0$. Evidently $F(0) = 0 = F(h)$ and so z^* is between 0 and h.

We compute that

$$\begin{aligned}
F'(z) &= E'(z) - Q'(z) \\
&= -f'(z) - f''(z)(h - z) - f'(z)(-1) \\
&\quad - \frac{E_0}{h^2} 2(h - z)(-1).
\end{aligned}$$

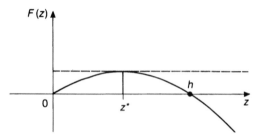

Figure 14.2   The discrepancy between $E(z)$ and the quadratic approximation $Q(z)$ is largest at a stationary point.

But $F'(z^*) = 0$ and so

$$f''(z^*)(h - z^*) = \frac{2E_0}{h^2}(h - z^*).$$

Since $z^* \neq h$ we have

$$E_0 = \frac{h^2}{2}f''(z^*)$$

and this is the asserted formula.

14.4   Taylor's theorem: higher order terms and $(1 + x)^t$

Suppose a function $f(x)$ is known to have derivatives to the nth order in an interval (c, d) containing $x = X$. Then Taylor's theorem asserts that for any h with $X + h$ in the interval (c, d)

$$f(X + h) = f(X) + f'(X)h + \frac{h^2}{2}f''(X) + \cdots + \frac{h^{n-1}}{(n-1)!}f^{(n-1)}(X)$$

$$+ \frac{h^n}{n!}f^{(n)}(u)$$

for some u, where u lies strictly between X and $X + h$. Here $f^{(r)}(x)$ denotes $d^r f(x)/dx^r$.

In other words, we can attempt to express $f(X + h)$ as a polynomial in h, say of degree $n - 1$, whereupon the error may be computed in terms of the nth derivative and the nth power of h. This thus generalizes the linear approximation with quadratic error term developed in section 14.3. Notice that if a function $f(x)$, such as for example $\sin x$, can be differentiated indefinitely many times in any interval, then we can contemplate an infinite series, rather like the geometric progressions of section 4.2, of the form

$$f(X) + f'(X)h + \frac{h^2}{2}f''(X) + \cdots + \frac{h^n}{n!}f^{(n)}(X) + \cdots,$$

and we might hope to have it equal to $f(X + h)$. This is really asking whether the error term, which now depends on n,

$$\frac{h^n}{n!} f^{(n)}(u_n),$$

tends to zero. Quite often it does. In fact if it does so whenever $X + h$ is in our interval (c, d) we say that $f(x)$ is *analytic*.

Example 1

Show that

$$e^z = 1 + z + \frac{z^2}{2!} + \frac{z^3}{3!} + \cdots .$$

SOLUTION We consider $f(x) = e^x$ with $X = 0$ and $h = z$. Of course $f(x) = f'(x) = f''(x) = \cdots = e^x$ and so $f(0) = f'(0) = \cdots = 1$. Thus

$$e^z = f(0 + z) = 1 + z + \frac{z^2}{2!} + \cdots .$$

The nth error term takes the form

$$\frac{z^n}{n!} e^{X*}$$

where $X*$ is between 0 and z. We assume $z > 0$. The error is thus no greater than

$$\frac{z^n}{n!} e^z.$$

Let N be the first integer greater than $|z|$. Then $|z/N| < 1$ and so for $n > N$

$$\frac{z^n}{n!} = \frac{z}{1} \cdots \frac{z}{N} \frac{z}{N+1} \cdots \frac{z}{n}$$

$$\leq \frac{z}{1} \cdots \frac{z}{N} \frac{z}{N} \cdots \frac{z}{N}$$

$$= \frac{z^N}{N!} \left(\frac{z}{N}\right)^{n-N}$$

But $0 < |z/N| < 1$ and so the last factor tends to zero as n tends to infinity.

Remark

This expression for e^x is a very useful formula which we shall apply in the next section when we look at a generalization of the Cobb–Douglas function.

Remark

Recall our derivation of e as the limit of $(1 + 1/m)^m$. We noted that by the binomial theorem

$$\left(1 + \frac{1}{m}\right)^m = 1 + m\,\frac{1}{m} + \frac{m(m-1)}{2!}\,\frac{1}{m^2} + \frac{m(m-1)(m-2)}{3!}\,\frac{1}{m^3} + \cdots$$

$$= 1 + 1 + \frac{1}{2!}\,1\left(1 - \frac{1}{m}\right) + \frac{1}{3!}\,1\left(1 - \frac{1}{m}\right)\left(1 - \frac{2}{m}\right) + \cdots.$$

As m tends to infinity the terms on the right-hand side tend to

$$1 + 1 + \frac{1}{2!} + \frac{1}{3!} + \cdots,$$

i.e. to e^1.

Example 2
Estimate the error when $(1 + r)^t$ is approximated by $1 + rt + \frac{1}{2}r^2t(t-1)$, as in section 14.1, for $r = 10$ per cent.

SOLUTION Some care is needed here: t is of course fixed and so the function is $f(x) = x^t$ while $X = 1$ and $h = r$. We have $f'(x) = tx^{t-1}$, $f''(x) = t(t-1)x^{t-2}$, $f'''(x) = t(t-1)(t-2)x^{t-3}$. Hence $f(1) = 1$, $f'(1) = t$, $f''(1) = t(t-1)$, so that

$$(1 + r)^t = 1 + tr + \frac{t(t-1)}{2!}\,r^2 + \frac{t(t-1)(t-2)}{3!}\,r^3(X*)^{t-3}$$

where $X*$ is between 1 and $1 + r$. In section 14.1 the approximation we took led to $t \approx 7.3$. By implication we want the accuracy of this expression when $t = 7.3$ (although of course $t = (\log 2)/(\log 1.1) \approx 7.27$). Our estimate for the error using the over-estimate $X* = 1.1$ is thus

$$\frac{1}{3!} \times 7.3 \times 6.3 \times 5.3 \times (0.1)^3(1.1)^{4.3} \approx 0.06.$$

Using the more likely $X* = 1.05$ gives an error estimate of 0.05 – not much different.

Example 3
Find the Taylor expansion of $(1 + r)^t$ for general r and t positive.

SOLUTION This is really a continuation of the last example with a view to justifying the equality (14.2) of section 14.1. Applying Taylor's theorem for n terms we do of course get the expected formula. In fact if t is an integer n, so that $f(x) = x^n$, then $f^{(n+1)}(x) \equiv 0$ and we get the binomial theorem since the $(n+1)$th error is zero. For general t, however, we can generate an infinite number of terms. The series expansion is valid as the error term tends to zero for $|r| < 1$ when n tends to infinity; the argument is a little tricky and we give it just for interest. The error term when we expand up to r^n is of course

$$\frac{t(t-1) \cdots (t-n+1)}{1 \times 2 \times \cdots \times n} r^n (X*)^{t-n}.$$

Assuming $0 < r < 1$ we may over-estimate $(X*)^t$ by $(1+r)^t$ and likewise over-estimate $(X*)^{-n} = (1/X*)^n$ by $1^n = 1$ (since $X* > 1$). Clearly r^n tends to zero (section 8.4, question 6). We are left with an ugly coefficient. We can show that the ugly coefficient remains bounded as n increases. Rewrite it as a product

$$\frac{t}{1} \frac{t-1}{2} \cdots \frac{t-m+1}{m} \cdots \frac{t-n+1}{n}$$

and observe that eventually

$$-1 < \frac{t-m+1}{m} < 1.$$

The inequality on the left is clear because $-m < t - m + 1$; that on the right holds as soon as $m > \frac{1}{2}(t + 1)$. Thus, apart from the first $\frac{1}{2}(t + 1)$ factors, all later factors are numerically less than 1. If N is the first integer larger than $\frac{1}{2}(t + 1)$, then the first N factors contribute less than

$$\frac{t}{1} \frac{t}{2} \cdots \frac{t}{N} = \frac{t^N}{N!}$$

and this is a fixed bound on the coefficients.

*14.5 The constant elasticity of substitution production function in the limit as ρ approaches zero

The following production function is also considered in economics:

$$F(q_1, q_2) = [\alpha q_1^\rho + (1 - \alpha)q_2^\rho]^{1/\rho} \qquad (\rho \leqslant 1). \qquad (14.14)$$

This is not defined when $\rho = 0$. We shall show that in the limit as ρ approaches zero the right-hand side becomes $q_1^\alpha q_2^{1-\alpha}$. We take the ρth power of each side and note that

$$\alpha q_1^\rho + (1 - \alpha)q_2^\rho = \alpha \exp(\rho \log q_1) + (1 - \alpha) \exp(\rho \log q_2)$$
$$\approx \alpha(1 + \rho \log q_1) + (1 - \alpha)(1 + \rho \log q_2)$$
$$= 1 + \rho[\alpha \log q_1 + (1 - \alpha) \log q_2]$$

where we have used the Taylor expansion for $\exp(x)$ (see example 1 of the last section). Thus

$$F(q_1, q_2)^\rho \approx 1 + \rho \log(q_1^\alpha q_2^{1-\alpha}).$$

Rewriting the left-hand side as $\exp[\rho \log F(q_1, q_2)]$ we can approximate it in the same way to obtain

$$1 + \rho \log F(q_1, q_2) \approx 1 + \rho \log(q_1{}^\alpha q_2{}^{1-\alpha}). \tag{14.15}$$

Hence, as promised, we obtain

$$\lim_{\rho \to 0} F(q_1, q_2) = q_1{}^\alpha q_2{}^{1-\alpha}.$$

We have been somewhat remiss by not including in our calculation the remaining terms of the series. We leave the reader to work out the exact statement, satisfying ourselves with the sloppy assertion that the error in (14.15) may be written in the form $\rho^2 f(\rho)$ where the function $f(\rho)$ depends on q_1 and q_2 and remains finite as ρ approaches zero.

Thus the function (14.14) is a generalization of the Cobb–Douglas function.

14.6 Concavity of $f(x)$ from $f''(x) \leqslant 0$

We are in a position to show, as promised in section 10.1 (example 3), that a function, say with domain an interval $c < x < d$, is concave (section 5.5.10) if and only if $f''(x) \leqslant 0$ in (c, d). Recall that a function is concave if chords joining points of the graph are below the graph. This is the same as saying that the subgraph (i.e. the set of points below the graph) is convex.

With reference to figure 14.3, if $x < y < z$ are three points in (c, d) then concavity requires $B = (y, f(y))$ to be above the chord AC. We observe (and this is easy to prove) that therefore

$$\text{slope BC} \leqslant \text{slope AC} \leqslant \text{slope AB}.$$

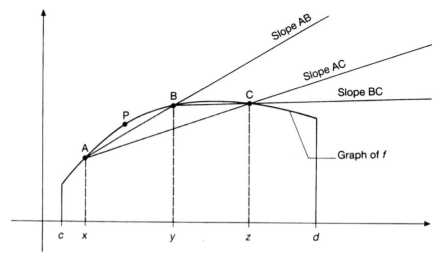

Figure 14.3 Comparing chordal slopes of a concave function.

If we think of A as fixed, we see that as P approaches A first through C and then through B the slope of AP increases up to the gradient at A, i.e. $f'(x)$. Similarly as P approaches C first through A and then through B, the slope of the chord PC decreases down to the gradient at C, i.e. $f'(z)$. Thus $f'(z)$ = gradient at C ⩽ slope BC ⩽ slope AC ⩽ slope AB ⩽ gradient at A = $f'(x)$, i.e.

$$f'(z) \leqslant f'(x).$$

Thus $f'(x)$ is a non-increasing function; hence $f''(x) \leqslant 0$ for all x in (c, d). This condition is (conversely) also sufficient.

We have for any X and h by Taylor's theorem that

$$f(X + h) = f(X) + hf'(X) + \frac{1}{2} h^2 f''(u)$$

for some u; but $f''(u) \leqslant 0$ and so

$$f(X + h) \leqslant f(X) + hf'(X).$$

So the points below the curve are also below the tangent. Hence

$$\text{subgraph} = \bigcap_{c < x < d} A_x$$

where A_x denotes the points below the tangent line (the 'subtangent' sets shown in figure 14.4). Equality holds because no point above $f(X)$ is included in A_x on the ordinate line $x = X$. As an intersection of convex sets the subgraph is convex.

14.7 Classification of stationary points: revision

This revision section is intended by way of an introduction to our optimization work with functions $F(x, y)$ of two variables.

Here we wish to note

1 why and when a maximum of $f(x)$ occurs at a stationary point (i.e. $f'(x) = 0$) and
2 which stationary points are local maxima or local minima and which are not.

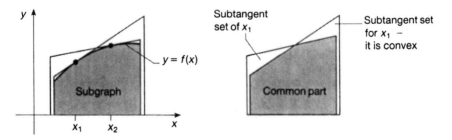

Figure 14.4 The graph is an envelope of tangent lines. The part common to *all* the subtangent sets is the subgraph and so is convex.

Suppose that $f(x)$ is defined in an interval I. The interval may possibly be half-infinite, e.g. $[0, \infty)$, as might be the case for a cost function $C(q)$ where clearly we permit only $q \geqslant 0$. We are interested in either maximizing $f(x)$, as in the case of profits, or minimizing $f(x)$, as in the case of costs. To cover both cases with one name we speak of optimizing, or extremizing, $f(x)$. Suppose for the moment, however, that we wish to minimize $f(x)$ and that the minimum occurs when $x = X$.

Consider the effect on $f(x)$ when x is changed to $x = X + h$ and $h \neq 0$. Evidently $X + h$ has to be in the interval I for our discussion to make sense. We have

$$f(X) = \min f(x) \leqslant f(X + h). \tag{14.16}$$

Thus, for $h > 0$,

$$\frac{f(X + h) - f(X)}{h} \geqslant 0.$$

Assuming that f is differentiable at $X = h$, we take limits as h tends to zero through positive values and obtain

$$f'(X) \geqslant 0. \tag{14.17}$$

Since for $h < 0$ we have

$$\frac{f(X + h) - f(X)}{h} \leqslant 0,$$

we may also take limits as h tends to zero through negative values and obtain

$$f'(X) \leqslant 0. \tag{14.18}$$

Hence

$$f'(X) = 0, \tag{14.19}$$

i.e. X is a 'stationary point'.

The familar technique of checking the stationary points for optimality requires care over the following issues.

1 Is the function to be optimized differentiable? The example of $f(x) = 1 + |x - 1|$ has its minimum at a non-stationary point (figure 14.5). Indeed at $x = X = 1$ there is no derivative to speak of and so (14.19) is deprived of meaning.
2 If the domain of x is an interval, does the optimum occur at an endpoint? For the case illustrated in figure 14.6 the minimum is at $x = X = 1$. Evidently (14.18) holds since $f'(1) \leqslant 0$. However, (14.17) does not hold because $X + h$ for $h > 0$ is not in the domain of the problem and so already (14.19) is false. Nevertheless for small negative h we do have (14.16) and hence (14.18).

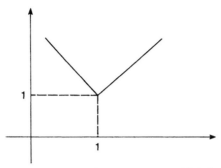

Figure 14.5 $f(x) = 1 + |x - 1|$ has a minimum at $x = 1$ which is not stationary since there is no derivative at $x = 1$.

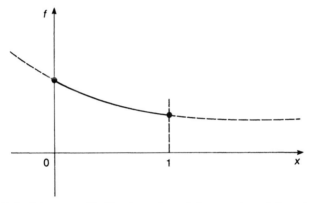

Figure 14.6 Minimizing over $[0, 1]$ – here the minimum at $x = 1$ is not stationary.

3   A stationary point might be only a 'relative' (or 'local') minimum (figure 14.7). Worse still, it might be a 'point of inflexion'; or it could be a maximum when a minimum is sought.

To determine what is happening at a stationary point $x = X$ we examine $f(x)$ near $x = X$ using Taylor's theorem. We have

$$f(X + h) = f(X) + f'(X) h + \frac{1}{2} h^2 f''(X_h)$$

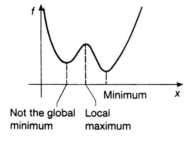

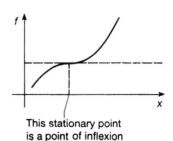

Figure 14.7 Non-minimizing stationary points.

where $f'(X) = 0$ and X_h is between X and $X + h$. Since we do not usually know X_h the strategy is to consider $f''(X)$ instead and to assume that $f''(x)$ is continuous. We note that (figure 14.8)

1 if $f''(X) > 0$, then for small h also $f''(X_h) > 0$;
2 if $f''(X) < 0$, then for small h also $f''(X_h) < 0$;
3 if $f''(X) = 0$, we cannot draw any conclusions about the sign of $f''(X_h)$.

Thus if $f''(X) > 0$ we have a *local minimum*. (This is because

$$f(X) = f(X + h) - \frac{1}{2} h^2 f''(X_h) < f(X + h)$$

and for small enough h the coefficient at h^2 is positive.)

If $f''(X) < 0$ we have a *local maximum*. (This time the coefficient at h^2 is negative and so

$$f(X) = f(X + h) - \frac{1}{2} h^2 f''(X_h) > f(X + h)$$

for small enough h.)

If $f''(X) = 0$ we need more information. To obtain more information we assume that f has higher derivatives and we take the Taylor expansion one term further. Thus if $f'(X) = f''(X) = 0$ we have

$$f(X + h) = f(X) + \frac{h^3}{3!} f'''(X_h)$$

for some X_h between X and $X + h$. Again we use the continuity argument.

(a) If $f'''(X) > 0$ then $f'''(x) > 0$ close to $x = X$. Hence $f'''(X_h) > 0$ and thus

$$f(X) = f(X + h) - \frac{1}{3!} h^3 f'''(X_h) \begin{cases} < f(X + h) & \text{for} \quad h > 0 \\ > f(X + h) & \text{for} \quad h < 0. \end{cases}$$

We thus have a *point of inflexion* if $f'''(X) > 0$ since on the left $f(x)$ decreases and on the right $f(x)$ increases (figure 14.9). This is because the power of h is odd this time.

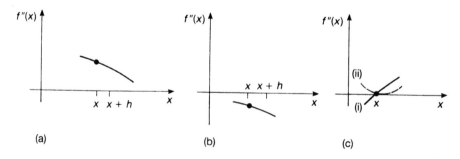

Figure 14.8 Drawing conclusions about the sign of $f''(X_h)$ from $f''(X)$: (a) $f''(x)$ stays positive near $x = X$; (b) $f''(x)$ stays negative near $x = X$; (c) $f''(x)$ could change sign (curve (i)), or equally well might not (curve (ii)).

(b) If $f'''(X) < 0$ then, for small h, $f'''(X_h) < 0$ and the argument is similar.
(c) If $f'''(X) = 0$ we need more information. Again Taylor's theorem may be applied to give

$$f(X + h) = f(X) + \frac{h^4}{4!} f''''(X_h).$$

Since the power of h is even, the story is as above. Of course if $f''''(X) = 0$ we need yet more terms in the Taylor theorem.

The pattern should now be clear: an odd power of h gives a point of inflexion whereas an even power will give a local maximum or minimum depending on the sign of its coefficient. We have thus proved the following.

14.7.1   The Nth derivative test

If $f'(X) = f''(X) = \cdots = f^{(N-1)}(X) = 0$ and $f^{(N)}(X) \neq 0$ *and $f^{(N)}(x)$ is continuous at $x = X$* then

1   for N odd, $x = X$ is a point of inflexion,
2   for N even and $f^{(N)}(X) < 0$, $x = X$ is a local minimum,
3   for N even and $f^{(N)}(X) < 0$, $x = X$ is a local maximum.

Examples
1   $f(x) = x^3$. We have $f'(0) = 0$; $f''(x) = 6x$ and so $f''(0) = 0$ and $f'''(0) = 6 \neq 0$ – hence a point of inflexion.

2   $f(x) = x^4$. We have $f'(0) = 0$, $f''(x) = 12x^2$, $f'''(x) = 24x$, $f''''(x) = 24$. Thus $f'(0) = f''(0) = f'''(0)$ and $f''''(0) > 0$. Hence $x = 0$ is a local minimum.

These results are confirmed by the familiar graphs in figure 14.10.

14.8   Modelling a cost curve with a cubic

As an example of stationary point classification we consider the problem of finding a function $f(q)$ describing a cost curve C whose marginal cost behaves as in figure 14.11. The simplest function with a U-shaped curve is a quadratic.

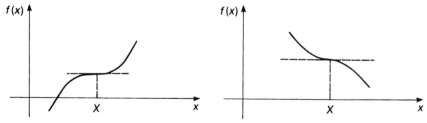

Figure 14.9   If $f'(X) = f''(X) = 0$ and $f'''(X) \neq 0$ there is a point of inflexion at $x = X$.

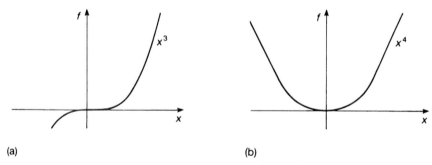

(a)   (b)

Figure 14.10 Nth derivative test confirmed for x^3 and x^4: (a) $f'''(0) = 6$;
(b) $f''''(0) = 12$.

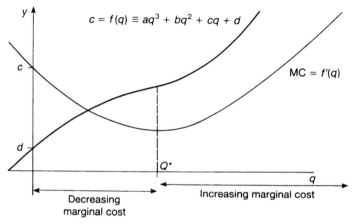

Figure 14.11   A marginal cost curve: note the inflexion (with positive slope) in the
cost curve at $q = Q^*$.

If MC is to be quadratic we need C to be modelled by a cubic. Consider

$$C = f(q) \equiv aq^3 + bq^2 + cq + d.$$

Evidently we wish costs to be large when q is large. Hence $a > 0$. Since $f(0)$
represents the fixed costs of production we need $d > 0$. We consider the
quadratic

$$MC = f'(q) = 3aq^2 + 2bq + c.$$

We find the stationary point $q = Q^*$ of MC. Since

$$\frac{d}{dq}(MC) = f''(q) = 6aq + 2b, \tag{14.20}$$

we have $Q^* = -2b/(6a) = -b/(3a)$. We require the minimum marginal cost to be *positive*; but

$$MC(Q^*) = 3a\frac{b^2}{9a^2} + 2b\frac{-b}{3a} + c = \frac{3ac - b^2}{3a}.$$

Thus we require $3ac - b^2 > 0$.

Notice that by (14.20) $f''(Q^*) = 0$ and $f'''(q) = 6a \neq 0$ so that the cost curve has a point of inflexion at $q = Q^*$. Notice too that since $3ac > b^2$ the value of c is also positive.

*14.9 An exotic application: monopolistic barter

We return to the discussion of barter conducted in the Edgeworth box (see section 13.4) and suppose that Robinson Crusoe is bartering his supply W of wheat with several, say n, natives each like Friday in all respects, so that each has a supply F of fish. Thus the $n + 1$ participants in this bartering arrangement all have identical utility functions, i.e. $U(w, f)$. We assume that the utility function is concave. We stop to consider the significance of this assumption.

14.9.1 Jensen's inequality for concave functions

Suppose we graph the surface $u = U(w, f)$. To say that the function is concave (section 14.6) is to say that the set of points below the surface is convex. In particular the chord joining two points on the surface lies under the surface as shown in figure 14.12.

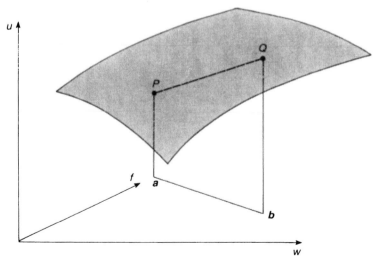

Figure 14.12 A concave function: the chord joining P and Q lies below the surface.

It is useful to express this fact in the form of an inequality. Consider two points $P = (w_1, f_1, u_1)$ and $Q = (w_2, f_2, u_2)$ of the surface, where $u_1 = U(w_1, f_1)$ and $u_2 = U(w_2, f_2)$. Vertically below them are the points $a = (w_1, f_1)$ and $b = (w_2, f_2)$, where we have dropped the third co-ordinate which is zero. We may now refer to a two-dimensional diagram in (w, f) space which tells us that a point on the line segment between a and b will have co-ordinates

$$(w, f) = \alpha(w_1, f_1) + (1 - \alpha)(w_2, f_2)$$

where $0 \leqslant \alpha \leqslant 1$. This is because

$$(w, f) = (w_2, f_2) + \alpha(w_1 - w_2, f_1 - f_2)$$
$$= b + \alpha(a - b)$$

and thus α, being a stretching factor, is non-negative and less than unity (figure 14.13).

The value at the intermediate point is $U[\alpha(w_1, f_1) + (1 - \alpha)(w_2, f_2)]$, i.e. $U(\alpha w_1 + (1 - \alpha)w_2, \alpha f_1 + (1 - \alpha)f_2)$. On the other hand, the height of the point on the chord is

$$\alpha U(w_1, f_1) + (1 - \alpha) U(w_2, f_2)$$

(figure 14.14). Since this is below the surface we obtain the following inequality:

$$\alpha U(w_1, f_1) + (1 - \alpha) U(w_2, f_2) \leqslant U[\alpha(w_1, f_1) + (1 - \alpha)(w_2, f_2)].$$

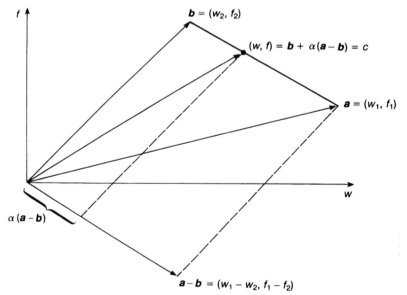

Figure 14.13 An intermediate point is a fraction α of the way along the segment, measuring from b in the direction $b - a$.

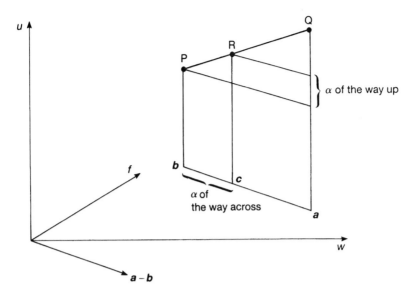

Figure 14.14   The point R on the chord above the intermediate point c is the same fraction α of unity vertically up from P to Q.

We may rewrite this inequality by setting $\beta = 1 - \alpha$:

$$\alpha U(w_1, f_1) + \beta U(w_2, f_2) \leq U[\alpha(w_1, f_1) + \beta(w_2, f_2)]$$

or, using vector notation,

$$\alpha U(a) + \beta U(b) \leq U(\alpha a + \beta b)$$

where $0 \leq \alpha \leq 1$, $0 \leq \beta \leq 1$ and $\alpha + \beta = 1$. It is instructive to view the left-hand side as a weighted average of two utilities and the right-hand side as the utility of the weighted average of two commodity bundles.

The above inequality can be shown to imply a more general result known as Jensen's inequality: for a concave utility function, a weighted average of the utilities of a number of commodity bundles is less than or equal to the utility of the same weighted average of the bundles or, in symbols, for the case of m commodity bundles

$$\alpha_1 U(a_1) + \cdots + \alpha_m U(a_m) \leq U(\alpha_1 a_1 + \cdots + \alpha_m a_m)$$

where $0 \leq \alpha_1 \leq 1, \ldots, 0 \leq \alpha_m \leq 1$ and $\alpha_1 + \cdots + \alpha_m = 1$.

We are now in a position to discuss the bartering arrangements. With n Fridays the total supply of goods is (W, nF). If this is distributed between the participants so that Robinson gets (w_0, f_0) while Friday 1 gets (w_1, f_1) and Friday 2 gets (w_2, f_2) etc., then we have

$$(W, nF) = (w_0, f_0) + (w_1, f_1) + \cdots + (w_n, f_n).$$

Hence

$$\left(\frac{W}{n+1}, \frac{n}{n+1} F\right) = \frac{1}{n+1}(w_0, f_0) + \frac{1}{n+1}(w_1, f_1) + \cdots + \frac{1}{n+1}(w_n, f_n).$$

Here the $n+1$ weights $1/(n+1)$ occurring on the right-hand side add up to unity and so using Jensen's inequality we conclude that

$$U\left(\frac{W}{n+1}, \frac{n}{n+1} F\right) \geq \frac{1}{n+1} U(w_0, f_0) + \frac{1}{n+1} U(w_1, f_1) + \cdots + \frac{1}{n+1} U(w_n, f_n)$$

or

$$(n+1)U\left(\frac{W}{n+1}, \frac{n}{n+1} F\right) \geq U(w_0, f_0) + U(w_1, f_1) + \cdots + U(w_n, f_n).$$

The last inequality asserts that the total utility for any distribution of wheat and fish among the parties is never greater than when the total supply (W, nF) is equally distributed amongst them.

But now Robinson reckons it would be unfair on him if this maximal total utility were to be received in equal amounts by all the parties; he feels that his is a more arduous and more skilled contribution than that of mere fishermen. He therefore intends to extract a reward for his participation in the barter in the form of a greater than average transfer to himself of the total utility. Thus Robinson sets about computing the total utility available for transfer when he agrees to barter with just m of the natives, where $m \leq n$. We denote this total utility by U_m. Evidently

$$U_m = (m+1)U\left(\frac{W}{m+1}, \frac{m}{m+1} F\right),$$

since the total resource for redistribution among $m+1$ is (W, mF). This is of the form $(m+1)U(tW, (1-t)F)$, where $t = 1/(m+1)$ would be 'small' for m large. We shall apply Taylor's theorem to the function

$$U(t) = U(tW, (1-t)F),$$

where W and F are regarded as fixed. We obtain

$$U(t) = U(0) + tU'(0) + \frac{t^2}{2} U''(h)$$

where the number h depends on t and lies between zero and t. Evidently $U(0) = U(0, F)$ which is the 'no-trade' utility for a Friday. Taking in turn $t = 1/n$ and $t = 1/(n+1)$ and denoting the corresponding h values by h_n and h_{n+1} we have

$$U_n = (n+1)U\left(\frac{1}{n+1}\right)$$

$$U_{n-1} = nU\left(\frac{1}{n}\right)$$

and so

$$U_n - U_{n-1} = (n+1)U(0) + (n+1)\,\frac{1}{n+1}\,U'(0) + \frac{n+1}{2(n+1)^2}U''(h_{n+1})$$

$$-\left[nU(0) + n\,\frac{1}{n}\,U'(0) + \frac{n}{2n^2}\,U''(h_n)\right]$$

$$= U(0) + \frac{1}{2(n+1)}\,U''(h_{n+1}) - \frac{1}{2n}\,U''(h_n). \qquad (14.21)$$

Let us suppose that $U''(t)$ is continuous at $t = 0$. Then since, for sufficiently large n, h_n and h_{n+1} are as close to zero as we please (because $0 < h_n < 1/n$, $0 < h_{n+1} < 1/(n+1)$), we can write

$$U''(h_n) = U''(0) + \varepsilon_n \qquad U''(h_{n+1}) = U''(0) + \varepsilon_{n+1}$$

where ε_n, ε_{n+1} may be made small. Substituting the above into (14.21) we obtain

$$U_n - U_{n-1} - U(0) \le \frac{1}{2}\,U''(0)\left(\frac{1}{n+1} - \frac{1}{n}\right) + \frac{1}{2}\left(\frac{\varepsilon_{n+1}}{n+1} - \frac{\varepsilon_n}{n}\right)$$

$$\le \frac{1}{2}\left\{\frac{-1 \times U''(0)}{n(n+1)} + \frac{\varepsilon_{n+1}}{n} - \frac{\varepsilon_n}{n}\right\}$$

$$\le \frac{1}{2n}\left\{\frac{|U''(0)|}{n+1} + \varepsilon_{n+1} - \varepsilon_n\right\}.$$

We conclude that, if $\varepsilon > 0$ is any small number, we can choose n so large that

$$U_n - U_{n-1} - U(0, F) < \frac{\varepsilon}{n}. \qquad (14.22)$$

Indeed this will be so if we arrange for the contents of the braces $\{\cdots\}$ each to be less than $\varepsilon/3$. In particular we would require $n+1 > 3\,|\,U''(0)\,|\,/\varepsilon$.

The inequality (14.22) is significant. Let v_0 be the maximum utility which Robinson can obtain from distributions which leave all the natives at their original utility level of $U(0, F)$. The case $n = 1$ is illustrated in the Edgeworth box of figure 14.15. Evidently, the natives would hardly be motivated to enter into a trade with such a utility outcome for themselves. That would be a doubtful bargain, even though it would maximize total utility. However, Robinson could claim just a little less than v_0 for himself and offer the leftovers as an enticement to trade.

This simple argument can be used to show that, if n is large, a barter deal which is optimal for all concerned must give Robinson almost all of v_0. To see this, suppose that a deal is reached in which Robinson receives less than $v_0 - \varepsilon$ for some $\varepsilon > 0$. Assume n is so large that (14.22) holds. In this case there will be a native who gets more than $U(0, F) + \varepsilon/n$. Why? Because otherwise each

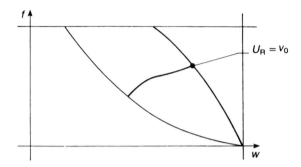

Figure 14.15   The contract awarding Robinson maximal utility v_0 and Friday minimal utility $U(0, F)$.

native has a utility of less than $U(0, F) + \varepsilon/n$ and also Robinson has a utility of less than $v_0 - \varepsilon$; hence the total of these utilities would be less than

$$(v_0 - \varepsilon) + n \left[U(0, F) + \frac{\varepsilon}{n} \right] = v_0 + nU(0, F).$$

The right-hand side here represents a feasible total utility, and so the sum of the utilities which we just considered, being less, does not correspond to an optimal deal. This contradiction leads us to conclude that there is after all a native with more than $U(0, F) + \varepsilon/n$. A bartering group excluding that native but including Robinson and all the others can have a total utility of U_{n-1}. Now referring to the original deal we have

utility of Robinson + utility of $n - 1$ natives included in second trade

$$= U_n - \text{utility of excluded native}$$

$$< U_n - \left[U(0, F) + \frac{\varepsilon}{n} \right] < U_{n-1}.$$

Thus the first deal being considered is not good for Robinson and the $n - 1$ natives, since it gives them in sum less utility than they can already obtain by bartering among themselves and sharing the resulting utility U_{n-1}.

14.10   Exercises

1*   Compute the relative size of omitted items in section 14.1 such as $r^5 t^5/5!$ relative to rt. (Assume $rt \approx 0.73$.)

2*   Consider the cubic approximation for 'double your money':

$$2 = 1 + x + \frac{1}{2} x^2 + \frac{1}{6} x^3.$$

What percentage error is being committed in ignoring other terms? (Assume $r = 10$ per cent.) Show that the cubic brings a 3 per cent improvement to the quadratic expansion. On a calculator (or computer) perform the iteration

$$x_{n+1} = (3 - x_n^3/3)^{1/2} - 1 \qquad x_0 = 0 \qquad (14.23)$$

and hence obtain the cubic approximation $x = 0.698\,885$. Note that $\log_e 2 = 0.694\,147\,1$ (cf. question 4 below). When is the 72 rule that $rt \approx 0.72$ likely to be true?

3* Taking $X = 0$, $h = x$ in section 14.4 find the Taylor expansion for $1/(1 - x)$. Compare your result with the formula for summing a geometric progression. Is the infinite Taylor series expansion valid for $x > 1$? What is the error term exactly when the expansion is to the nth power of x? Compare section 8.4, question 8.

4 Find the Taylor expansion for $\log_e(1 + x)$. Use it to compute $\log_e 2$ by taking $x = -\frac{1}{2}$ in your expansion.

5* Find the Taylor expansion of $\cos x$ and $\sin x$. Check that $e^{ix} = \cos x + i \sin x$ (where $i = \sqrt{(-1)}$) by substituting ix into the series for e^z.

6 Find the Taylor expansion for (a) $(1 - x^2)^{1/2}$ for $|x| < 1$ and (b) $\tan x$ (the first few terms only).

7* If $C(q) = q^3 - 3q^2 + 3q$ and the prevailing price p is 4/3 find the output level which maximizes profit. (Be careful to distinguish between local maxima and local minima.)

8* Repeat the previous question with $p = 1/3$. (Careful: $q \geq 0$ so consider $q = 0$ also.)

9 Find and classify the stationary points of $f(x) = x^3 - 3x^2 + 2x$. Does the function have a global maximum or minimum?

10 Show that if $f'(X) = f''(X) = 0$ but $f''(x) > 0$ for all $x \neq X$ with x near X, then $x = X$ is a local minimum. (This applies to $f(x) = x^4$ where $f''(x) = 12x^2 > 0$ for $x \neq 0$.)

11* Show that $\lim_{h \to 0} (\sin h)/h = 1$ (use the Taylor series for $\sin x$).

12* Use the mean value theorem to show that, if $f(0) = g(0) = 0$ but $g'(0) \neq 0$, then

$$\lim_{h \to 0} \frac{f(h)}{g(h)} = \frac{f'(0)}{g'(0)}. \qquad (14.24)$$

What happens when $f'(0) \neq 0$ but $g'(0) = 0$. (Assume that $f''(x), g''(x)$ are continuous at $x = 0$.)

13   Use Taylor's theorem to show that if $f(0) = g(0) = 0$ and $f^{(r)}(0) = g^{(r)}(0) = 0$ for $r = 1, 2, \ldots, n - 1$, but $g^{(n)} \neq 0$, then

$$\lim_{h \to 0} \frac{f(h)}{g(h)} = \frac{f^{(n)}(0)}{g^{(n)}(0)}. \qquad (14.25)$$

Note that these formulae are known under the name of L'Hôpital's rule, usually quoted in the form

$$\lim_{h \to a} \frac{f(h)}{g(h)} = \lim_{h \to a} \frac{f'(h)}{g'(h)}. \qquad (14.26)$$

They are valid for a finite or $\pm\infty$ on the assumption that $f(a) = g(a)$ and the common value is either 0 or $\pm\infty$.

14*   Use L'Hôpital's rule (14.24) to show that

$$\lim_{h \to 0} \frac{\sin h}{h} = 1$$

$$\lim_{x \to 0} \frac{e^x - 1}{x} = 1$$

$$\lim_{x \to 0} \frac{\log(1 + x)}{x} = 1.$$

15*   Use L'Hôpital's rule (14.25) to show that

$$\lim_{x \to 0} \frac{1 - \cos x}{x^2} = \frac{1}{2}$$

$$\lim_{x \to 0} \frac{x - \sin x}{x^3} = \frac{1}{6}.$$

16   Use L'Hôpital's rule (14.26) to show that

$$\lim_{x \to \infty} x e^{-x} = 0.$$

[*Hint*: Rewrite the expression as a quotient x/e^x] and

$$\lim_{x \to 0} x \log x = 0$$

[*Hint*: Rewrite the expression as a quotient $\log x/(1/x)$].

17   Use L'Hôpital's rule (14.26) to show that

$$\lim_{x \to \infty} x^2 e^{-x} = 0$$

$$\lim_{x \to \infty} x \log x^2 = 0.$$

14.11   Further exercises

1   If $g(2h) = 2hg'(h)$ and $g(0) = 0$ show by applying Taylor's theorem to both $g(h)$ and $g'(h)$ that $g'''(0) = 0$.

2   Deduce from the last question that the only functions which satisfy

$$\frac{f(x + 2h) - f(x)}{2h} = f'(x + h)$$

for all x and h are quadratic. (Show $f'''(x) = 0$.) This resolves a problem left open in section 10.4.

3   Let $g(h) = f(x + 2h) - f(x) - 2hf'(x + h)$. Show that the Taylor series for $g(h)$ has first term

$$g(h) = \frac{f'''(0)}{3!} 2h^3.$$

(This extends the result in section 10.7, question 21.) What is the error term?

4   Show that if (14.23) of section 14.10, question 2, holds then $0 \leqslant x_n \leqslant 1$ implies $0 \leqslant x_{n+1} \leqslant 1$. Use the identity

$$(x_{n+1} - x_n)(x_{n+1} + x_n + 2) = -\frac{1}{3}(x_n - x_{n-1})(x_n^2 + x_n x_{n-1} + x_{n-1}^2)$$

to deduce that

$$|x_{n+1} - x_n| \leqslant \frac{1}{2}|x_n - x_{n-1}|.$$

Conclude that

$$|x_{n+1} - x_n| \leqslant \frac{1}{2^n}|x_1 - x_0|.$$

(This shows that the iteration of section 14.10, question 2, must converge.)

The iteration offered in the question runs along the lines of the cobweb model with the two intersecting curves being $y = x^3$ and $y = 6 - 6x - 3x^2$; compare figure 14.16.

5   Analyse the error terms $e(h)$ and $e_1(h)$ when $f(x) = x^4$ and $X = 1$.

6*   It is thought appropriate to model the average revenue (AR) curve by the cubic relation

$$AR = aQ^3 + bQ^2 + cQ + d \qquad (14.27)$$

where Q is the quantity produced.

(a)   Show that, if the AR curve is to be downward sloping for all $Q \geqslant 0$, then $a < 0$, $c \leqslant 0$ and either (i) $b \leqslant 0$ or (ii) $b > 0$ and $b^2 \leqslant 3ac$.
(b)   Obtain a formula for the marginal revenue (MR) from (14.27). Show that for $a < 0$ the MR curve will initially be downward sloping and then

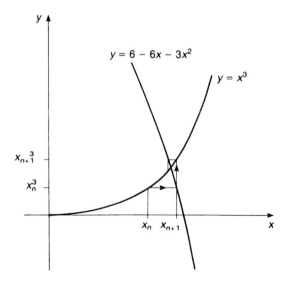

Figure 14.16 The cobweb model for question 4.

upward sloping for a finite range of positive values of Q if $3b^2 > 8ac$, $b > 0$ and $c < 0$. [Recall that AR $= R/Q$.]

(c) Conclude that it is possible for (14.27) to model a downward sloping AR curve consistently with having part of the MR curve upward sloping.

7 Give a precise statement about the error term for the 'constant elasticity of substitution' function in the calculation of section 14.5.

8 Why would it not be appropriate to use the approximation

$$(1 + h)^{1/\rho} \approx 1 + \frac{1}{\rho} h$$

in section 14.5. (Check the error term here when $h = \rho \log(q_1{}^\alpha q_2{}^{1-\alpha})$.)

14.12 Answers

14.12.1 Exercises

1 $(r^5 t^5/5!) \div rt = r^4 t^4/5! = (0.73)^4/120 = 0.0024$ or 0.24 per cent.

2 The error is best estimated using Taylor's theorem as in section 14.4, example 2. We have

$$2 = 1 + rt + \frac{1}{2} r^2 t(t-1) + \frac{1}{6} r^3 t(t-1)(t-2)$$

$$+ \frac{1}{24} r^4 t(t-1)(t-2)(t-3)(X^*)^{t-4}.$$

The given approximation omits the terms

$$-\frac{1}{2}r^2t \qquad \frac{1}{6}r^3(-3t^2+2t) \qquad \frac{1}{24}r^4t(t-1)(t-2)(t-3)(X*)^{t-4}.$$

Their sizes relative to rt are

$$\frac{1}{2}\frac{r^2t}{rt} = \frac{1}{2}r \approx 5 \text{ per cent}$$

$$-\frac{1}{6}\frac{r^3t(2-3t)}{rt} = -\frac{1}{6}r^2(2-3t)$$

$$= -\frac{1}{3}r^2 + \frac{1}{2}r \times rt$$

$$\approx -0.003 + \frac{1}{20}0.73$$

$$= -0.003 + 0.0365 \approx 3 \text{ per cent}$$

We estimate the last term, which is bound to be small (see example 2):

$$\frac{(0.1)^4}{24}(7.3)(6.3)(5.3)(4.3)(1.1)^{3.3} = 0.006.$$

The total error is at most 8 per cent, an improvement of 3 per cent over the quadratic.

The iteration is based on the 'quadratic' equation

$$x^2 + 2x - 2(1 - x^3/6) = 0$$

whose positive root we seek:

$$x = -1 + [1 + 2(1 - x^3/6)]^{1/2}.$$

The formula is used iteratively. We obtain $x_0 = 0$, $x_1 = \sqrt{3} - 1 = 0.732\,05\ldots$ (as before), $x_2 = 0.693\,880\,6$, $x_3 = 0.699\,599\,6$, $x_4 = 0.698\,782\,7$, $x_5 = 0.698\,900\,2$, $x_6 = 0.698\,883\,3$, $x_7 = 0.698\,885\,8$.

3   If $f(x) = (1-x)^{-1}$ then $f'(x) = (-1)(1-x)^{-2}(-1) = (1-x)^{-2}$; $f''(x) = (-2) \times (1-x)^{-3}(-1) = 2(1-x)^{-3}$; $f'''(x) = 2.3(1-x)^{-4}$; $\ldots$ $f^{(n)} = n!(1-x)^{-(n+1)}$. Hence

$$\frac{1}{1-x} = f(0+x) = 1 + x + x^2 + x^3 + \cdots.$$

On the right-hand side we recognize the geometric progression here and see that the series converges only if $|x| < 1$ (cf. section 8.4, question 6). We already know that

$$1 + x + \cdots + x^n = \frac{1-x^{n+1}}{1-x} = \frac{1}{1-x} + \frac{x^{n+1}}{1-x}.$$

The error term is thus

$$\frac{x^{n+1}}{x-1}$$

whereas Taylor's theorem gives $x^{n+1}(1-x^*)^{-(n+2)}$. Since the error term approaches infinity for $x > 1$ the *infinite* series is not a valid expansion.

5 If $f(x) = \sin x$ then $f'(x) = \cos x$, $f''(x) = -\sin x$ etc. Thus $f(0) = f''(0) = f''''(0) = \cdots = 0$ and $f'(0) = 1$, $f'''(0) = -1$, $f'''''(0) = 1, \ldots$ leading to

$$\sin(0+x) = 0 + x + 0 - \frac{x^3}{3!} + 0 + \frac{x^5}{5!} + \cdots.$$

(The error term

$$\frac{x^n}{n!}(\sin \text{ or } \cos)(x^*)$$

is numerically less than $x^n/n!$, which we saw in example 1 of section 14.4 tends to zero.) The same calculation shows that

$$\cos(0+x) = 1 + 0 - \frac{x^2}{2!} + 0 + \frac{x^4}{4!} + \cdots.$$

By section 14.4

$$e^{ix} = 1 + ix + \frac{i^2 x^2}{2!} + \frac{i^3 x^3}{3!} + \frac{i^4 x^4}{4!} + \cdots$$

$$= 1 + ix - \frac{x^2}{2!} - \frac{ix^3}{3!} + \frac{x^4}{4!} + \cdots$$

$$= \left(1 - \frac{x^2}{2!} + \frac{x^4}{4!} + \cdots\right) + i\left(x - \frac{x^3}{3!} + \cdots\right).$$

7 Profit $\pi = pq - C(q) = 4/3q - 3q + 3q^2 - q^3$. Here the first-order condition is

$$0 = -\frac{5}{3} - 3q^2 + 6q \quad \text{or} \quad q^2 - 2q + \frac{5}{9} = 0$$

so that

$$q = 1 \pm \left(1 - \frac{5}{9}\right)^{1/2} = 1 \pm \frac{2}{3} = \frac{1}{3}, \frac{5}{3}.$$

$\pi'' = 6 - 6q = 6(1-q)$ so that $q = 1/3$ is a local minimum and $q = 5/3$ is a local maximum. At $q = 5/3$ we have

$$\pi = q\left(-\frac{5}{3} + 3q - q^2\right) = \frac{5}{3}\left[-\frac{5}{3} - \left(\frac{5}{3}\right)^2 + 3\frac{5}{3}\right] = \frac{5}{3}\left(-\frac{15+25}{9} + 5\right) > 0.$$

8 Profit $\pi = pq - C(q) = 1/3q - 3q + 3q^2 - q^3$. The stationary points satisfy

$$0 = -\frac{8}{3} - 3q^2 + 6q \quad \text{or} \quad q^2 - 2q + \frac{8}{9} = 0.$$

Hence

$$q = 1 \pm \left(1 - \frac{8}{9}\right)^{1/2} = 1 \pm \frac{1}{3} = \frac{2}{3}, \frac{4}{3}$$

$$\pi'' = -6q + 6 = 6(1 - q).$$

Thus $q = 2/3$ is a local minimum whereas $q = 4/3$ is a local maximum.

$$\pi(4/3) = q\left(3q - q^2 - \frac{8}{3}\right) = \frac{4}{3}\left[3\frac{4}{3} - \left(\frac{4}{3}\right)^2 - \frac{8}{3}\right] = \frac{4}{3}\left(4 - \frac{16 + 24}{9}\right) < 0.$$

Hence production is not profitable. Notice that $\pi(0) = 0$ and so in fact zero is the maximum for $q \geqslant 0$.

11 We saw that

$$\sin h = h + \frac{h^2}{2!} \sin X_h.$$

Thus

$$\frac{\sin h}{h} = 1 + \frac{h}{2} \sin X_h.$$

Since $\sin X_h$ is numerically less than unity the right-hand side is numerically not greater than $1 + h/2$. In the limit as h tends to zero we obtain

$$\lim_{h \to 0} \frac{\sin h}{h} = 1.$$

12 We have

$$f(h) = f'(0) h + \frac{h^2}{2} f''(X_h)$$

$$g(h) = g'(0) h + \frac{h^2}{2} g''(Z_h)$$

where X_h, Z_h are between 0 and h. Thus as $h \to 0$

$$\frac{f(h)}{g(h)} = \frac{f'(0) + (h/2)f''(X_h)}{g'(0) + (h/2)g''(Z_h)} \to \frac{f'(0)}{g'(0)}$$

since $f''(X_h) \to f''(0)$ and $g''(Z_h) \to g''(0)$. Evidently the calculation is meaningless if $f'(0) = g'(0) = 0$. If $f'(0) \neq 0$ and $g'(0) = 0$ the numerator tends to $f'(0)$ whereas the denominator is very small. The ratio thus tends to infinity.

14

$$\lim_{h \to 0} \frac{\sin h}{h} = \frac{\cos 0}{1} = 1$$

$$\lim_{x \to 0} \frac{e^x - 1}{x} = \frac{e^0}{1} = 1$$

$$\lim_{x \to 0} \frac{\log(1 + x)}{x} = \frac{1/(1 + 0)}{1} = 1.$$

15

$$\lim_{x \to 0} \frac{1 - \cos x}{x^2} = \lim_{x \to 0} \frac{\sin x}{2x} = \lim_{x \to 0} \frac{\cos x}{2} = \frac{1}{2}$$

$$\lim_{x \to 0} \frac{x - \sin x}{x^3} = \lim_{x \to 0} \frac{1 - \cos x}{3x^2} = \lim_{x \to 0} \frac{\sin x}{6x} = \frac{1}{6}.$$

14.12.2 Further exercises

6   If $AR = aQ^3 + bQ^2 + cQ + d$ then

(a) $AR' = 3aQ^2 + 2bQ + c$.

If this is to be negative for large Q we obtain $a < 0$. At $Q = 0$ we get $c < 0$. The AR' curve is concave.

Either the maximum of AR' is to the left of $Q = 0$ and then, since $AR'' = 6aQ + 2b = 0 \Leftrightarrow Q = -2b/6a = -b/3a$, we require $b \leqslant 0$, *or* the maximum is to the right of $Q = 0$ and the maximum value is negative, i.e.

$$3a\left(-\frac{b}{3a}\right)^2 + 2b\left(-\frac{b}{3a}\right) + c \leqslant 0,$$

i.e.

$$\frac{b^2 - 2b^2 + 3ac}{3a} \leqslant 0,$$

i.e. $b > 0$ and $3ac - b^2 \geqslant 0$.

(b) $R = aQ^4 + bQ^3 + cQ^2 + dQ$.

So

$$MR = 4aQ^3 + 3bQ^2 + 2cQ + d.$$

We want $MR' > 0$ for some range of Q. But

$$MR' = 12aQ^2 + 6bQ + 2c.$$

This is again a concave quadratic/parabola since $a < 0$. We want two real positive roots.

We obtain two real roots if and only if

$$(6b)^2 - 4 \times 12a \times 2c > 0$$

or

$$36b^2 - 8 \times 12ac > 0$$

i.e.

$$3b^2 > 8ac.$$

Note that $MR'' = 24aQ + 6b$ and so if

$$Q' = -\frac{6b}{24a} = -\frac{b}{4a} > 0$$

MR' will be positive at Q'; indeed

$$MR'_{max} = 12a\left(-\frac{b}{4a}\right)^2 + 6b\left(-\frac{b}{4a}\right) + 2c$$

$$= \frac{3b^2 - 6b^2 + 8ac}{4a} > 0$$

$$\Leftrightarrow 8ac - 3b^2 < 0.$$

Note that the product of the roots is $2c/12a$. Thus both roots are positive if $c < 0$. Or note that $MR'(0) = c < 0$.

(c)   Taking $b > 0$, $(8/3)ac \leqslant b^2 < 3ac$, we satisfy both conditions.

15

Optimization in Two Variables

15.1 Interior optimum: stationarity

In this chapter we pursue the problem of maximizing or minimizing a function $z = F(x, y)$; inevitably, the point (x, y) will often be required to lie in a restricted part of the xy plane known as the constraint set of the problem. Our insistence on two variables is purely to keep arguments simple. The ideas which we develop need only some minor adjustments when there are more than two variables; we shall outline these adjustments at the end of the chapter.

Our objective will be to reduce the two-variable problem to a one-variable problem; this will not prove disingenuous, but we shall see a great variety of complications. The first complication relates to whether or not the optimum point, denote it (X, Y), is on the boundary of the constraint set. Whatever the circumstances we shall always end up by looking for a stationary point (though possibly not of $F(x, y)$). The easier case is when the optimum is not on the boundary of the constraint set; (X, Y) is then an *interior point* of the constraint set. This is defined to mean that the whole of some rectangle centred at (X, Y)

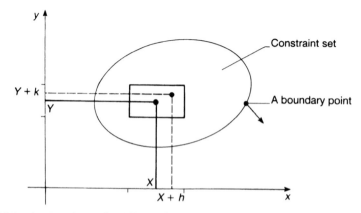

Figure 15.1 An interior point (X, Y) sits in a rectangle contained in the constraint set; from a boundary point all small movements in any direction lead *out* of the set.

lies entirely in the constraint set (figure 15.1). In particular, for all (small enough) h and k the points $(X+h, Y+k)$ are also in the constraint set, i.e. we can move away from (X, Y) in any direction by small amounts and still stay within the constraint set. By contrast a *boundary point* is characterized by the fact that in some direction all (even small) movements from that point lead out of the constraint set.

If $F(x, y)$ has a minimum at an interior point (X, Y) of the constraint set then it is to be expected that

$$\frac{\partial F}{\partial x} = 0 \quad \text{and} \quad \frac{\partial F}{\partial y} = 0, \tag{15.1}$$

provided that these partial derivatives exist. It is easy to see why. Evidently, at all points (x, y) of the constraint set we have

$$F(X, Y) \leqslant F(x, y). \tag{15.2}$$

Consider the function $A(x) = F(x, Y)$. For an interval I of values of x near X the points (x, Y) are in the constraint set (figure 15.2). From (15.2) we conclude that on this interval I the function $A(x)$ satisfies

$$A(X) \leqslant A(x).$$

So $x = X$ is a local minimum for A. Hence $A'(X) = 0$. A similar argument shows that $B(y) = F(X, y)$ has a local minimum at $y = Y$. The result (15.1) is known as the *first-order condition*. (X, Y) is said to be a *stationary point*.

Notice that $(\partial F/\partial x, \partial F/\partial y)$ is just ∇F, or even DF, and so the definition of 'stationary' is still formally that the derivative vanishes. Geometrically the condition says that the tangent plane to $z = F(x, y)$ at (X, Y, Z) where $Z = F(X, Y)$ is just

$$z - Z = 0,$$

i.e. the tangent plane is horizontal (figure 15.3). If (X, Y) is an interior point at which $F(x, y)$ has a maximum then likewise (X, Y) will be a stationary point.

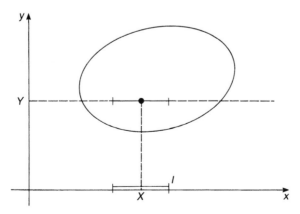

Figure 15.2   An interval of x values near X for which (x, Y) is in the constraint set.

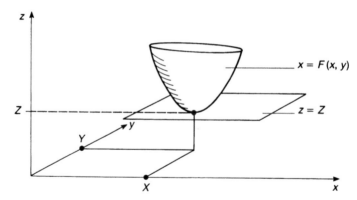

Figure 15.3 The tangent plane at a stationary point is horizontal.

We now have to face the problem of classifying stationary points. We shall turn to Taylor's theorem in order to examine $f(X + h, Y + k)$ for h and k small. We expect this to involve an approximation of the form

$$F(X + h, Y + k) \approx F(X, Y) + ak^2 + 2bhk + ch^2$$

since the linear terms $F'_x h + F'_y k$ are zero. We must therefore examine the surface

$$z = Q(x, y) = ay^2 + 2bxy + cx^2.$$

15.2 Classifying quadratic surfaces

What does the surface

$$z = Q(x, y) = ay^2 + 2bxy + cx^2$$

look like? If the constants a, b, c were given, how would we set about sketching it? We do this in a number of steps.

First step: decomposition As usual in mathematics, we try to reduce an unfamiliar problem to a familiar one involving only one free variable. We shall first plot the curves obtained by slicing the surface vertically and then we shall build up the surface by 'sticking' the curves together. One option is to examine the vertical sections $x = $ constant. There is nothing wrong with such an approach, but there is something better to be done: always think before you leap! $Q(x, y)$ is homogeneous of degree 2, i.e.

$$Q(kx, ky) = k^2 Q(x, y).$$

Hence

$$Q(x, y) = x^2 Q(1, y/x).$$

But $Q(1, y/x)$ is really a function of the one variable y/x. Our search for a one-variable approach should surely take this into account.

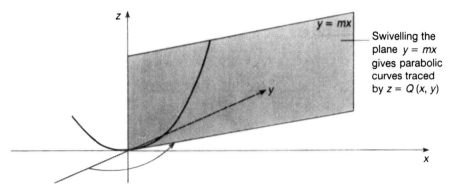

Figure 15.4 A section of the surface $z = Q(x, y)$ traced on the vertical plane $y = mx$. The plane swivels around the z axis from $m = -\infty$ (where $x = 0$) through $m = 0$ (where $y = 0$) back to $m = +\infty$.

So we put

$$y = mx$$

and look at the various vertical sections of the surface by this plane as it swivels round the z axis (figure 15.4).

$$z = Q(x, mx)$$
$$= x^2(am^2 + 2bm + c)$$

or $z = q(m)x^2$ where $q(m) = a + 2bm + cm^2$. Unless $q(m) = 0$ the curve $z = q(m)x^2$ is a parabola. Evidently,

1 if $q(m) < 0$, the parabola has an inverted-U shape;
2 if $q(m) = 0$, the parabola degenerates into a straight line;
3 if $q(m) > 0$, the parabola is U-shaped.

Second step: fitting the curves together – a general case In general as m ranges from $-\infty$ to $+\infty$ we expect $q(m)$ to change sign (figure 15.5). Thus as m changes (and the plane $y = mx$ swivels around the z axis) we obtain U-shaped parabolas which get progressively flatter until they degenerate to a straight line (when $m = m_1$) (figure 15.6). They then reverse their shape to inverted-U parabolas of progressively slimmer proportions, reaching their slimmest at the midpoint m^* between m_1 and m_2. Thereafter the parabolas flatten until they degenerate to a line (when $m = m_2$). Again they reverse shape to the familiar U-shape. These parabolas fit together to form the surface sketched in figures 15.7 and 15.8 (upside down).

We can reconstruct the surface shown in figure 15.7 from the individual curves by imagining that we are stitching together an old-fashioned flip-book (with spine along the z axis) from individual leaves each containing a curve (figure 15.9). The surface is delimited side to side by $x = \pm X$ and also vertically by having $z = Z$ at the top. The side edges are illustrated as parabolas and the top edges as a pair of hyperbolas (why?). The surface resembles a *saddle*.

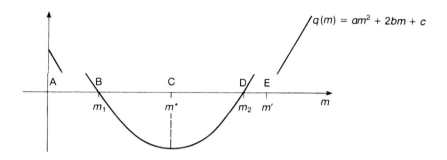

Figure 15.5 For the case illustrated the coefficient $q(m)$ decreases to zero, changes sign, goes back to zero and thereafter increases through positive values.

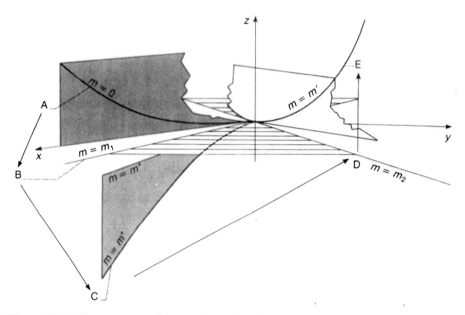

Figure 15.6 The corresponding parabolas (see figure 15.5): when $m = m_1$ or $m = m_2$ the parabolas are lines (B, D); when $m = m^*$ the parabola has an inverted-U shape (C), when $m = 0$ and $m = m'$ the parabolas are U-shaped (A, E).

Third step: other cases We have described the general case when $q(m)$ is as graphed in figure 15.5. However, there are altogether six cases to deal with, as figure 15.10 reminds us. Clearly the sign of a affects only which way up the quadratic surface should be drawn (figure 15.9 with the z axis re-oriented gives the surface $-Q(x, y)$). So there are really only three types of behaviour to consider, as follows:

1   $q(m)$ has two real roots, i.e. $b^2 - ac > 0$,
2   $q(m)$ has a repeated root, i.e. $b^2 - ac = 0$,

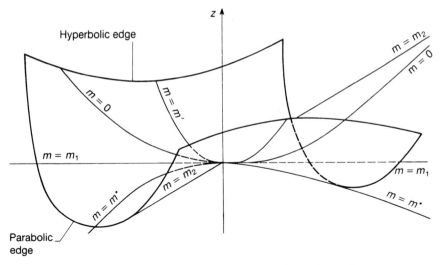

Figure 15.7   Reconstruction of the surface $z = Q(x,y)$ from the various curves $z = q(m)x^2$.

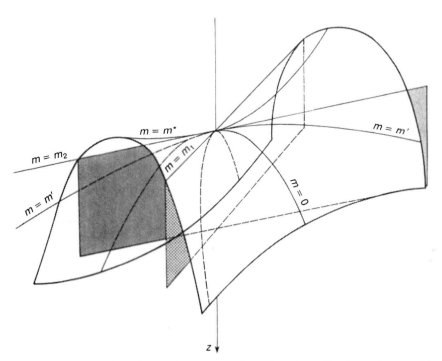

Figure 15.8   Alternative view – the same surface viewed upside down; it resembles a saddle.

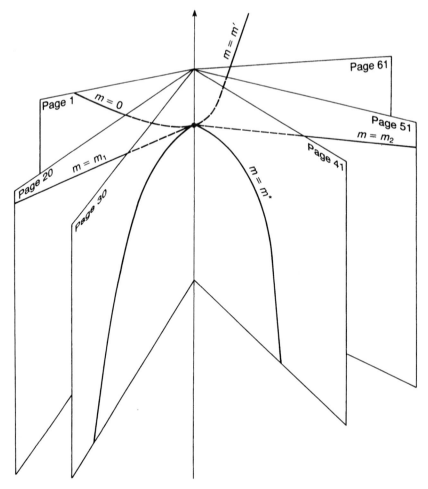

Figure 15.9   As we leaf through the vertical pages of a book whose spine is the z axis we see parabolas flattening to a line and reversing shape etc.

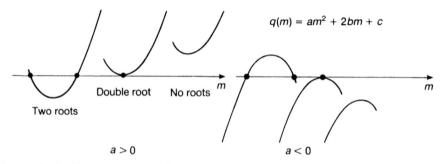

Figure 15.10   Six cases to consider.

3 $q(m)$ has no real roots, i.e. $b^2 - ac < 0$.

Thus the type depends on the discriminant $(2b)^2 - 4ac = 4(b^2 - ac)$. We have already dealt with the first type. The other two types are illustrated in figure 15.11. In the repeated root case the top edges straighten out to lines in preparation for the transition to type 3 where the top edge is elliptical. The valley in the type 2 case has a bottom consisting of a straight line along $y = \bar{m}x$ where $\bar{m}$ is the repeated root:

$$\bar{m} = \frac{-2b \pm \sqrt{0}}{2a} = -\frac{b}{a} \qquad (\text{since } b^2 - ac = 0).$$

We shall refer to this line as the *valley bottom*.

This concludes our classification of the quadratic surface $Q(x, y)$ into *saddles*, *valleys* and *bowls* for $a > 0$. For $a < 0$ we obtain saddles, ridges and inverted bowls.

15.3 Quadratic approximation of a surface locally

Our main aim is still to classify stationary points of $F(x, y)$. This requires us to make good approximations to $F(X + h, Y + k)$ when h, k are small. We shall

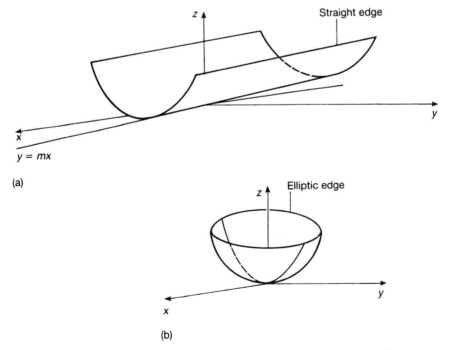

Figure 15.11 (a) A repeated root of $q(m)$ gives a single ridged valley ($b^2 = ac$, $a > 0$); (b) if there are no real roots, then there are no degenerate parabolas: the surface is bowl shaped ($b^2 - ac < 0$, $a > 0$).

need a one-variable approach if we are to apply Taylor's theorem. This is where a geometric outlook helps. The two points of interest, (X, Y) and $(X + h, Y + k)$, determine a line. We make that line the axis for a new variable t. We take (X, Y) as our origin and so $t = 0$ there (figure 15.12), and we establish our unit point at $(X + h, Y + k)$. A general point P_t on the new axis thus has co-ordinates $(X + th, Y + tk)$ in the xy plane. We examine the trace of $z = F(x, y)$ on the vertical plane through the t axis. (Compare also figure 13.18 in connection with directional derivatives.) The curve of intersection satisfies the equation

$$z = F(X + th, Y + tk) \tag{15.3}$$

(figure 15.13). Let

$$f(t) = F(X + th, Y + tk). \tag{15.4}$$

Taylor's theorem tells us that

$$f(1) = f(0 + 1)$$

$$= f(0) + 1 f'(0) + \frac{1}{2} f''(t*) \tag{15.5}$$

where $t*$ lies between 0 and 1.

Example 1
Find $f'(t)$ from (15.4).

SOLUTION   We apply the chain rule to $F(x, y)$ with $x = X + th$, $y = Y + tk$. Thus

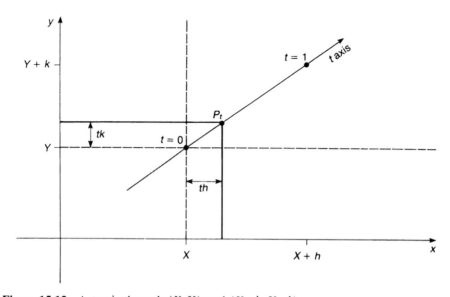

Figure 15.12 A t axis through (X, Y) and $(X + h, Y + k)$.

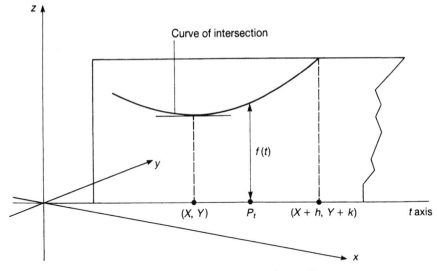

Figure 15.13 Curve of intersection $z = f(t) \equiv F(X + th, Y + tk)$.

$$\frac{df}{dt} = \frac{\partial F}{\partial x}\frac{dx}{dt} + \frac{\partial F}{\partial y}\frac{dy}{dt},$$

$$= \frac{\partial F}{\partial x} h + \frac{\partial F}{\partial y} k.$$

To show the precise dependence on t we write this out in full:

$$f'(t) = hF'_x(X + th, Y + tk) + kF'_y(X + th, Y + tk). \tag{15.6}$$

In particular

$$f'(0) = hF'_x(X, Y) + kF'_y(X, Y). \tag{15.7}$$

Example 2
Find $f''(t)$ from (15.6).

SOLUTION We take each of the two terms of (15.6) separately. First we apply the chain rule to $F'_x(X + th, Y + tk)$. Thus, since again $x = X + th$, $y = Y + tk$, we have

$$\frac{d}{dt} F'_x = \frac{\partial F'_x}{\partial x}\frac{dx}{dt} + \frac{\partial F'_x}{\partial y}\frac{dy}{dt}$$

$$= \frac{\partial F'_x}{\partial x} h + \frac{\partial F'_x}{\partial y} k$$

$$= F''_{xx} h + F''_{xy} k.$$

Similarly

$$\frac{d}{dt} F'_y = F''_{yx} h + F''_{yy} k.$$

Putting this together gives

$$f''(t) = h \frac{d}{dt} F'_x + k \frac{d}{dt} F'_y$$

$$= h(F''_{xx}h + F''_{xy}k) + k(F''_{yx}h + F''_{yy}k).$$

Hence

$$f''(t) = h^2 F''_{xx} + 2hk F''_{xy} + k^2 F''_{yy} \tag{15.8}$$

since $F''_{xy} = F''_{yx}$ (see section 12.1).

Remark

It is convenient to write this in matrix form thus:

$$f''(t) = (h, k) \begin{pmatrix} F''_{xx} & F''_{xy} \\ F''_{xy} & F''_{yy} \end{pmatrix} \begin{pmatrix} h \\ k \end{pmatrix}.$$

The 2×2 matrix is called the *Hessian* $F(x, y)$ and is denoted by $D^2 F$. It is quite properly the second derivative of F for reasons which we shall not go into. Formula (15.8) of course is evaluated at P_t.

We can now compute an approximation for $F(X + h, Y + k) = f(1)$. By (15.5) and (15.8) we obtain Taylor's theorem for two variables, namely

$$F(X + h, Y + k) = F(X, Y) + [hF'_x(X, Y) + kF'_y(X, Y)]$$

$$+ \frac{1}{2}(h^2 F''_{xx} + 2hk F''_{xy} + k^2 F''_{yy})$$

where the second-order derivatives on the right-hand side are evaluated at $t = t^*$ and t^* lies between 0 and 1.

Remark

For h and k small we note that $(X + t^*h, Y + t^*k)$ is close to (X, Y).

Thus, assuming the partial derivatives are continuous at (X, Y), we obtain

$$F(X + h, Y + k) \approx F(X, Y) + [hF'_x(X, Y) + kF'_y(X, Y)]$$

$$+ \frac{1}{2}[h^2 F''_{xx}(X, Y) + 2hk F''_{xy}(X, Y) + k^2 F''_{yy}(X, Y)].$$

This is an important formula because it says that to improve on the linear approximation we should add on a term

$$\frac{1}{2} Q(k, h)$$

where $Q(x, y)$ is the quadratic function studied in the last section with $x = k$, $y = h$ and

$$a = F''_{xx} \qquad b = F''_{xy} \qquad c = F''_{yy}.$$

Example
Find the Taylor expansion for $F(x, y) = x^3 y^2$ when $X = 1$, $Y = 1$. Is the quadratic part a saddle, a valley or a bowl?

SOLUTION   We have

$$F'_x = 3x^2 y^2 \qquad F'_y = 2x^3 y$$

$$F''_{xx} = 6xy^2 \qquad F''_{yy} = 2x^3$$

and

$$F''_{xy} = \frac{\partial}{\partial y}(3x^2 y^2) = 6x^2 y = \frac{\partial}{\partial x}(2x^3 y) = F''_{yx}.$$

(Note that we have verified $F''_{xy} = F''_{yx}$.) Thus

$$F(1 + h, 1 + k) \approx 1 + (3h + 2k) + \frac{1}{2}(6h^2 + 12hk + 2k^2).$$

The quadratic here has discriminant $4(6^2 - 6 \times 2) = 4 \times 24$. The quadratic $q(m)$ thus has two real roots and hence the quadratic part of the Taylor expansion is a saddle-shaped surface.

15.4   Classifying stationary points: local concavity

We can apply the Taylor expansion to $F(x, y)$ at a stationary point (X, Y) to yield

$$F(X + h, Y + k) = F(X, Y) + \frac{1}{2}\{h^2 F''_{xx} + 2hk F''_{xy} + k^2 F''_{yy}\} \qquad (15.9)$$

where the partial derivatives are evaluated at some point P^* on the line segment between (X, Y) and $(X + h, Y + k)$. Let us write

$$F''_{xx}(P^*) = F''_{xx}(X, Y) + e_1(h, k)$$

$$F''_{xy}(P^*) = F''_{xy}(X, Y) + e_2(h, k)$$

$$F''_{yy}(P^*) = F''_{yy}(X, Y) + e_3(h, k).$$

Thus, denoting by $Q(k, h)$ the terms of (15.9) in braces $\{\cdots\}$ but evaluated at (X, Y) instead of at P^*, we have

$$F(X + h, Y + k) = F(X, Y) + \frac{1}{2}Q(k, h)$$

$$+ \frac{1}{2}\{e_1 h^2 + 2e_2 kh + e_3 k^2\}.$$

Provided that h and k are small enough the last term (in braces) will be small relative to the preceding term; but this is true only if the preceding term, i.e. $\frac{1}{2}Q(k, h)$, is not equal to zero. (If $Q(k, h) = 0$ no comparison may be made!)

We have the following important conclusions (figure 15.14).

1 If $F''_{xx} > 0$ and $(F''_{xy})^2 - F''_{xx}F''_{yy} < 0$ the surface $z = F(x, y)$ is in the shape of a bowl near (X, Y) and we have a *local minimum*.

2 If $F''_{xx} < 0$ and $(F''_{xy})^2 - F''_{xx}F''_{yy} < 0$ the surface is in the shape of an upturned bowl close to (X, Y) and so this is a *local maximum*.

Remark

The conditions for a local maximum or minimum repeat the one-variable condition on F''_{xx} but are only valid provided also that a second condition

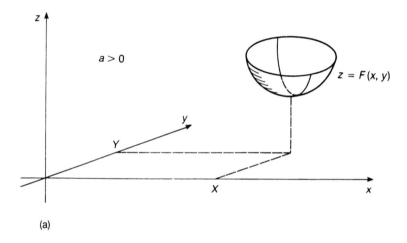

(a)

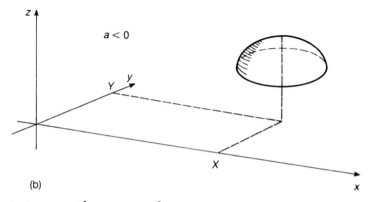

(b)

Figure 15.14   When $b^2 - ac \equiv (F''_{xy})^2 - F''_{xx}f''_{yy} < 0$ the surface is either (a) a bowl when $a \equiv F''_{xx} > 0$ (local minimum) or (b) an overturned bowl when $a \equiv F''_{xx} < 0$ (local maximum).

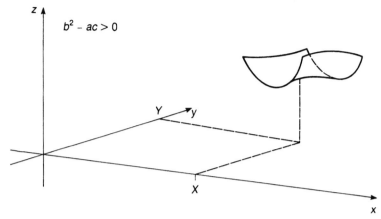

Figure 15.15   The strictly reversed concavity condition yields a local saddle.

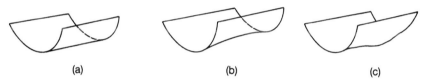

Figure 15.16   The valley bottom in (a) consists of a line of local minima; distortions create (b) a local saddle and (c) a single local minimum.

holds, namely $b^2 - ac < 0$. Note that the inequality is *strict* here and gives the two possibilities of local convexity in 1 and local concavity in 2.

   If the condition $b^2 - ac < 0$ is violated there are two possible scenarios.

3   If the concavity condition is strictly reversed, i.e. $b^2 - ac > 0$, the surface is locally a *saddle* (figure 15.15).

4   If on the other hand the condition $b^2 - ac = 0$ holds at (X, Y) then the error terms $e_1(h, k)$, $e_2(h, k)$, $e_3(h, k)$ in (15.9) will play a significant role. $Q(k, h)$, if *not* identically zero, is a valley. The valley bottom will be distorted, however, by the extra terms which may create either minima (maxima if the valley is upside down, i.e. actually a ridge) or saddle points (figure 15.16). We *cannot tell* what the situation is without examining the function more closely.

15.4.1   Examining the valley bottom when *a, b, c* are not all zero

If $a \neq 0$, then it will suffice to examine $F(x, y)$ only along the valley bottom (section 15.2):

$$y - Y = -\frac{b}{a}(x - X).$$

If $a = 0$ then $b^2 = ac$ implies $b = 0$. Thus $Q = ck^2$ and so if $c \neq 0$ the valley bottom is parallel to the y axis, since $Q(k, h)$ is independent of $y = h$; the valley bottom is therefore along $x = X$. If $c = 0$ the quadratic part degenerates and ingenuity is called for (see the example below).

The conditions given above may be more easily remembered by reference to the Hessian

$$H = \begin{pmatrix} F''_{xx} & F''_{xy} \\ F''_{xy} & F''_{yy} \end{pmatrix}.$$

Since $\det H = F''_{xx}F''_{yy} - (F''_{xy})^2$ we can form the Hessian decision table (table 15.1). A positive decision from the Hessian is followed by an examination of F''_{xx} just as in the one-variable case.

Table 15.1

Hessian determinant positive	Local maximum/minimum	Positive decision
Hessian determinant negative	Saddle	Negative decision
Hessian determinant zero	Insufficient information	Indecisive

Remark 1

The observant reader will notice that the conditions $F''_{xx} > 0$ and $\det H > 0$ are precisely the positive definiteness conditions of section 7.8.

Remark 2

When the Hessian is positive we have

$$F''_{xx}F''_{yy} > (F''_{xy})^2 \geq 0$$

and so $F''_{xx} > 0$ if and only if $F''_{yy} > 0$. We may therefore test either of the unmixed second-order derivatives.

Example 1
Find and classify the stationary points of

$$F(x, y) = x^3 - 3xy^2 + y^4.$$

SOLUTION

$$\frac{\partial F}{\partial x} = 3x^2 - 3y^2 = 3(x - y)(x + y)$$

$$\frac{\partial F}{\partial y} = -6xy + 4y^3 = 2y(2y^2 - 3x).$$

Setting $\partial F/\partial x = 0$ gives either

$$x = y \tag{15.10}$$

or

$$x = -y. \tag{15.11}$$

Similarly $\partial F/\partial y = 0$ gives either

$$y = 0 \tag{15.12}$$

or

$$y^2 = \frac{3}{2} x. \tag{15.13}$$

In principle we have to solve (15.10) and (15.12); (15.10) and (15.13); (15.11) and (15.12); (15.11) and (15.13).

Equations (15.10) and (15.12) give $x = y = 0$; thus $(0, 0)$ is stationary. Equations (15.10) and (15.13) give $y^2 = 3/2x = 3/2y$, and hence

$$y^2 - \frac{3}{2} y = 0$$

or

$$y\left(y - \frac{3}{2}\right) = 0.$$

The solution $y = 0$ (implying $x = 0$) is already known. The other solution is thus $x = y = 3/2$.

Equations (15.11) and (15.12) give $x = -y = 0$, adding nothing new. Equations (15.11) and (15.13) give $y^2 = \frac{3}{2}(-y)$, i.e.

$$y^2 + \frac{3}{2} y = 0$$

or

$$y\left(y + \frac{3}{2}\right) = 0.$$

Again $y = 0$ implies $x = 0$, a known solution. This leaves $y = -3/2, x = 3/2$. The three stationary points are

$$(0, 0) \qquad \left(\frac{3}{2}, \frac{3}{2}\right) \qquad \left(\frac{3}{2}, -\frac{3}{2}\right).$$

We have

$$\frac{\partial^2 F}{\partial x^2} = 6x \qquad \frac{\partial^2 F}{\partial x \, \partial y} = -6y \qquad \frac{\partial^2 F}{\partial y^2} = -6x + 12y^2.$$

Thus

$$D^2 F = 6 \begin{bmatrix} x & -y \\ -y & 2y^2 - x \end{bmatrix}$$

and so

$$\det D^2 F = 36[x(2y^2 - x) - y^2] = 36(2xy^2 - y^2 - x^2).$$

Consequently

$$D^2 F\left(\frac{3}{2}, \frac{3}{2}\right) = 36\left(2\frac{27}{8} - 2\frac{9}{4}\right) = \frac{36 \times 2}{8}(27 - 18) > 0$$

since

$$\frac{\partial^2 F}{\partial x^2} = 6\frac{3}{2} = 9 > 0.$$

We see that (3/2, 3/2) is a local minimum.
Next, we have

$$\det D^2 F\left(\frac{3}{2}, -\frac{3}{2}\right) = D^2 F\left(\frac{3}{2}, \frac{3}{2}\right)$$

(since the terms involving y in fact involve y^2). We still have

$$\frac{\partial^2 F}{\partial x^2} = 9 > 0.$$

Thus (3/2, – 3/2) is also a local minimum.
Finally $\det D^2 F(0, 0) = 0$ and we have no decision. Nevertheless, we easily see that

$$F(x, 0) = x^3 \qquad \text{and} \qquad F(0, y) = y^4.$$

So the surface does not have a local maximum, nor a local minimum at the stated point.
Notice that $D^2 F(0, 0)$ consists entirely of zeros, i.e. there is no quadratic approximation near the origin (the function is actually cubic plus quartic) and so there is no valley bottom to investigate.

Example 2: Two-product profit maximization
A firm acting under 'pure competition', i.e. a price-taker, produces two products A and B in quantities q_A, q_B for which prevailing prices are p_A, p_B. Hence the revenue is

$$R = p_A q_A + p_B q_B.$$

We assume a cost function

$$C(q_A, q_B) = 2q_A{}^2 + q_A q_B + 2q_B{}^2.$$

The profit is thus

$$\pi = \pi(q_A, q_B)$$
$$= R(q_A, q_B) - C(q_A, q_B)$$
$$= p_A q_A + p_B q_B - 2q_A{}^2 - q_A q_B - 2q_B{}^2.$$

At a stationary point

$$\frac{\partial \pi}{\partial q_A} = p_A - 4q_A - q_B = 0$$

$$\frac{\partial \pi}{\partial q_B} = p_B - q_A - 4q_B = 0.$$

We solve

$$4q_A + q_B = p_A$$

$$q_A + 4q_B = p_B$$

so

$$(1 - 16)q_A = p_B - 4p_A \qquad q_A = \frac{4p_A - p_B}{15}.$$

Similarly

$$(1 - 16)q_B = p_A - 4p_B \qquad q_B = \frac{4p_B - p_A}{15}.$$

Thus if $p_A = 12$, $p_B = 18$ then

$$q_A = \frac{48 - 18}{15} = 2 \qquad q_B = \frac{72 - 12}{15} = 4.$$

Here $\pi(2, 4) = 24 + 72 - (8 + 8 + 32) = 48$. We note that

$$D^2 F = \begin{bmatrix} -4 & -1 \\ -1 & -4 \end{bmatrix},$$

and hence det $D^2 F = 16 - 1 = 15 > 0$. Thus since

$$\frac{\partial^2 \pi}{\partial q_A{}^2} = -4 < 0$$

we conclude that we have found a local maximum.

    May we conclude that this is the global maximum? Actually the function π is concave and hence the answer is yes. We defer discussion of this point to a later section.

Example 3
Find and classify the stationary points of $F(x, y) = x^2 + 2xy + y^2 + x^2 y^2$.

SOLUTION

$$\frac{\partial F}{\partial x} = 2x + 2y + 2xy^2 = 0,$$

i.e.

$$x + y + xy^2 = 0.$$

$$\frac{\partial F}{\partial y} = 2x + 2y + 2x^2 y = 0,$$

or

$$x + y + x^2 y = 0.$$

In view of symmetry multiply the first result by x, the second by y.

$$x^2 + xy + x^2 y^2 = 0$$

$$xy + y^2 + x^2 y^2 = 0.$$

Subtracting we obtain

$$x^2 - y^2 = 0.$$

So $x = \pm y$. Now note that

1 $x = y \Rightarrow 2x + x^3 = 0 \Rightarrow x = 0$ (as $x^2 + 2 \neq 0$), and
2 $x = -y \Rightarrow x^3 = 0 \Rightarrow x = 0.$

Thus there is a unique stationary point $x = 0$, $y = 0$. We have

$$D^2F = \begin{bmatrix} 2 + 2y^2 & 2 + 4xy \\ 2 + 4xy & 2 + 2x^2 \end{bmatrix}.$$

Hence if $x = y = 0$

$$D^2F = \begin{bmatrix} 2 & 2 \\ 2 & 2 \end{bmatrix},$$

giving $F'_x = 2$ with a zero Hessian determinant. We check the valley bottom. Here $\bar{m} = -b/a = -1/1 = -1$, and so the bottom is $y = -x$. Then

$$F(x, -x) = x^2 - 2x^2 + x^2 + x^4 = x^4.$$

We note that $F(x, y) \equiv (x + y)^2 + x^2y^2 \geqslant 0$, showing that there is a local minimum at $x = 0$, $y = 0$.

Example 4
Find and classify the stationary points of $F(x, y) = x^2 + 2xy + y^2 - x^2y^2$.

SOLUTION The same argument as above gives a unique stationary point at $x = 0$, $y = 0$. Here again $\bar{m} = -b/a = -1$. But

$$F(x, -x) = -x^4.$$

We thus get a saddle-point since the valley bottom is deformed to be inverted U-shaped. We note that

$$F(x,x) = 4x^2 - x^4 = 4x^2(4 - x^2)$$

so that near the origin $F(x, -x) = -x^4$ whereas $F(x, +x) \approx 4x^2$ (figure 15.17).

15.5 Global concavity

The condition for a local maximum/minimum obtained in the previous section in effect referred to the concavity/convexity of a piece of the surface $z = F(x, y)$. This section allows us to test whether the whole of the surface $z = F(x, y)$ is concave or convex. This issue is important, because if $z = F(x, y)$ is concave then a local maximum is necessarily a global maximum (figure 15.18). We shall see why this is so in a moment.

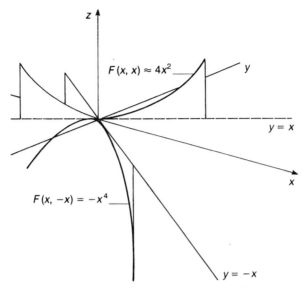

Figure 15.17   The trace of $F(x, y)$ on $y = x$ and $y = -x$.

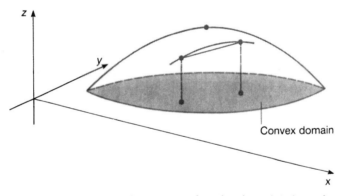

Figure 15.18   A local maximum of a concave function is a global maximum.

Let us first recall that a function $F(x, y)$ defined on a convex domain is said to be concave if the set of points lying on or below the surface is a convex set. This is the same as saying that the chord joining two points of the surface lies on or below the surface.

The definition is also equivalent to saying that any vertical section of the surface yields a curve which is the graph of a concave function in the one-variable sense (see figure 15.19).

We use this observation to establish a condition on the second derivative $D^2 F(x, y)$ of a (twice differentiable) function necessary and sufficient for F to be concave. We fix a point (X, Y) in the domain of F. Let $(X + h, Y + k)$ be any other point in the domain. Just as in section 15.3 we let the line through (X, Y) and $(X + h, Y + k)$ be the t axis for a new variable t. The origin is again to be

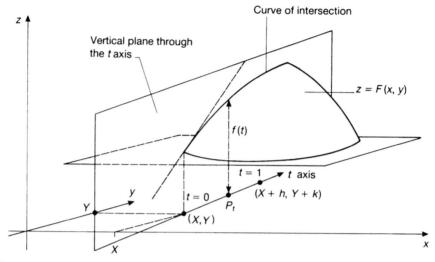

Figure 15.19　Vertical curves of intersection of a concave surface are concave and so $f''(t) \leqslant 0$.

at (X, Y) and the unit point at $(X + h, Y + k)$. Hence, just as before, the general point P_t on the t axis has x and y co-ordinates

$$x = X + ht \qquad \text{and} \qquad y = Y + kt.$$

The curve of intersection between the vertical plane through the t axis and the surface $z = F(x, y)$ is thus the graph of

$$z = f(t) \equiv F(X + ht, Y + kt).$$

Just as before (section 15.3, examples 1 and 2) we have

$$f'(t) = hF'_x + kF'_y$$

and

$$f''(t) = h^2 F''_{xx} + 2hk F''_{xy} + k^2 F''_{yy},$$

the partial derivatives being evaluated at $P_t = (X + ht, Y + kt)$. Now this curve is concave if and only if

$$f''(t) \leqslant 0$$

(see section 5.5.10) for all t such that P_t is in the domain of $z = F(x, y)$. In particular

$$f''(0) \leqslant 0.$$

This last condition asserts that for all h, k

$$h^2 F''_{xx}(X, Y) + 2hk F''_{xy}(X, Y) + k^2 F''_{yy}(X, Y) \leqslant 0. \tag{15.14}$$

Let us put $h = mk$, $a = F''_{xx}$, $b = F''_{xy}$, $c = F''_{yy}$. Then (15.14) requires that for all k and m

$$k^2(am^2 + 2bm + c) \leq 0$$

or, since $k^2 \geq 0$, that

$$q(m) \equiv am^2 + 2bm + c \leq 0,$$

i.e. the quadratic $q(m)$ is non-positive definite (figure 15.20). This requires the quadratic $q(m)$ to have an inverted U-shape (compare figure 15.9), so that $a < 0$, and to have either no real roots or only a repeated root. Referring to the discriminant of $q(m)$ we thus require $b^2 - ac \leq 0$. Thus, if the function $F(x, y)$ is concave, the following conditions are satisfied at all points of the domain of $F(x, y)$:

$$F''_{xx} \leq 0 \qquad\qquad (15.15)$$

$$(F''_{xy})^2 - F''_{xx}F''_{yy} \leq 0.$$

They are almost the same as those for a local maximum except that the inequalities here are weak.

Notice that if (15.15) holds at all points (X, Y) then $f''(0) \leq 0$. Since (X, Y) is arbitrary, $f'' \leq 0$ at all points of the curve of intersection. Thus $f(t)$ is concave. Hence the chord joining any two points of the surface $z = F(x, y)$ is below the corresponding curve through the vertical plane containing the two points. But this says that the chord is on or below the surface. Thus the condition is both necessary and sufficient.

Example 1
Check that the Cobb–Douglas function $z = x^\alpha y^\beta$ for $0 < \alpha, \beta < 1$ and $\alpha + \beta \leq 1$ is concave for $x, y > 0$.

SOLUTION Writing $F(x, y) = x^\alpha y^\beta$ we have $F'_x = \alpha x^{\alpha-1} y^\beta$ and $F'_y = \beta x^\alpha y^{\beta-1}$. Hence

$$D^2 F(x, y) = \begin{pmatrix} \alpha(\alpha-1)x^{\alpha-2}y^\beta & \alpha\beta x^{\alpha-1}y^{\beta-1} \\ \alpha\beta x^{\alpha-1}y^{\beta-1} & \beta(\beta-1)x^\alpha y^{\beta-2} \end{pmatrix}.$$

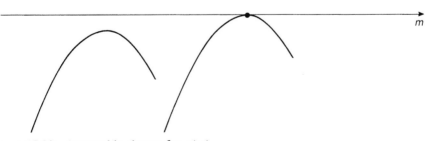

Figure 15.20 Acceptable shapes for $q(m)$.

For concavity we require

$$0 \geqslant F''_{xx} = \alpha(\alpha - 1)x^{\alpha - 2}y^{\beta}$$

(which is true if $0 < \alpha < 1$) and a positive Hessian determinant, i.e.

$$\alpha(\alpha - 1)\beta(\beta - 1)x^{2\alpha - 2}y^{2\beta - 2} - \alpha^2\beta^2 x^{2\alpha - 2}y^{2\beta - 2} \geqslant 0$$

or

$$\alpha\beta[(\alpha - 1)(\beta - 1) - \alpha\beta] \geqslant 0,$$

i.e.

$$\alpha\beta(1 - \alpha - \beta) \geqslant 0.$$

Example 2
Check that the 'constant elasticity of substitution' (CES) production function

$$z = F(x, y) = [\alpha x^{\gamma} + (1 - \alpha)y^{\gamma}]^{1/\gamma}$$

is concave for $x, y \geqslant 0$ when $0 < \alpha < 1$ and $\gamma > 1$.

SOLUTION   We have

$$F'_x = \frac{1}{\gamma}[\alpha x^{\gamma} + (1 - \alpha)y^{\gamma}]^{1/\gamma - 1}\alpha\gamma x^{\gamma - 1}$$

$$= \alpha x^{\gamma - 1}[\alpha x^{\gamma} + (1 - \alpha)y^{\gamma}]^{(1 - \gamma)/\gamma}. \qquad (15.16)$$

Hence

$$F''_{xx} = \alpha(\gamma - 1)x^{\gamma - 2}[\alpha x^{\gamma} + (1 - \alpha)y^{\gamma}]^{(1 - \gamma)/\gamma}$$

$$+ \alpha x^{\gamma - 1}\frac{1 - \gamma}{\gamma}[\alpha x^{\gamma} + (1 - \alpha)y^{\gamma}]^{1/\gamma - 2}\alpha\gamma x^{\gamma - 1}$$

$$= \alpha(1 - \gamma)x^{\gamma - 2}[\alpha x^{\gamma} + (1 - \alpha)y^{\gamma}]^{1/\gamma - 2} \times$$

$$\{-[\alpha x^{\gamma} + (1 - \alpha)y^{\gamma}] + \alpha x^{\gamma}\}.$$

Thus

$$F''_{xx} = -\alpha(1 - \alpha)(1 - \gamma)x^{\gamma - 2}y^{\gamma}[\alpha x^{\gamma} + (1 - \alpha)y^{\gamma}]^{1/\gamma - 2}$$

which is non-positive if $0 < \alpha < 1$ and $\gamma > 1$. Similarly

$$F''_{yy} = -(1 - \alpha)\alpha(1 - \gamma)x^{\gamma}y^{\gamma - 2}[\alpha x^{\gamma} + (1 - \alpha)y^{\gamma}]^{1/\gamma - 2}.$$

By (15.16) we also have

$$F''_{xy} = \alpha x^{\gamma - 1}\left(\frac{1}{\gamma} - 1\right)[\alpha x^{\gamma} + (1 - \alpha)y^{\gamma}]^{1/\gamma - 2}(1 - \alpha)\gamma y^{\gamma - 1}$$

$$= (1 - \gamma)\alpha(1 - \alpha)x^{\gamma - 1}y^{\gamma - 1}[\alpha x^{\gamma} + (1 - \alpha)y^{\gamma}]^{1/\gamma - 2}.$$

Clearly

$$F''_{xx}F''_{yy} = (F''_{xy})^2$$

and so the Hessian determinant, being zero, is non-positive.

15.6   Boundary optimum: Lagrange multipliers

So far we have considered problems such as extremizing $F(x, y)$ where the variables x and y are allowed to take any values. Some problems, however, require us to maximize $F(x, y)$ while placing conditions connecting the variables x and y. One such example was considered in section 9.3: the inventory control problem. This requires us to

$$\text{minimize}\quad C(x, y) = \frac{1}{2}\,xd + ey$$

$$\text{subject to}\quad xy = X$$

where e, d, X are constants.

One approach to this problem is to solve for y and then substitute into C, yielding

$$\text{minimize}\ \frac{1}{2}\,xd + \frac{eX}{x}\,.$$

Differentiating, we obtain the condition for stationarity

$$\frac{1}{2}\,d - \frac{eX}{x^2} = 0$$

or

$$x^2 = 2eX/d.$$

Thus

$$x = (2eX/d)^{1/2}\,.$$

In general, however, it may not be easy to 'solve for y'. An alternative method fortunately exists. Suppose we wish to

$$\text{extremize}\quad F(x, y)$$

$$\text{subject to}\quad G(x, y) = 0.$$

Let us only suppose that y *may* be obtained as a function of x, say $y = \phi(x)$, but let us proceed as though ϕ is not easily obtainable. We try to solve the problem without having ϕ at our disposal.

To, say, minimize $F[x, \phi(x)]$ with x unconstrained, write down the condition for stationarity. Let

$$z = F[x, \phi(x)]$$

and applying the chain rule we have the condition

$$\frac{dz}{dx} = \frac{\partial F}{\partial x} + \frac{\partial F}{\partial y}\frac{d\phi}{dx} = 0$$

and so

$$\frac{d\phi}{dx} = -\frac{\partial F}{\partial x}\bigg/\frac{\partial F}{\partial y} \qquad \left(\text{assuming } \frac{\partial F}{\partial y} \neq 0\right). \tag{15.17}$$

But we have the identity

$$G[x, \phi(x)] \equiv 0$$

which we may also differentiate. Thus

$$\frac{\partial G}{\partial x} + \frac{\partial G}{\partial y}\frac{d\phi}{dx} = 0.$$

Hence

$$\frac{d\phi}{dx} = -\frac{\partial G}{\partial x}\bigg/\frac{\partial G}{\partial y} \qquad \left(\text{assuming } \frac{\partial G}{\partial y} \neq 0\right). \tag{15.18}$$

We may now eliminate $\phi'(x)$ between (15.17) and (15.18) to obtain

$$\frac{\partial F}{\partial x}\bigg/\frac{\partial F}{\partial y} = \frac{\partial G}{\partial x}\bigg/\frac{\partial G}{\partial y}$$

or

$$\frac{\partial F}{\partial x}\bigg/\frac{\partial G}{\partial x} = \frac{\partial F}{\partial y}\bigg/\frac{\partial G}{\partial y}. \tag{15.19}$$

Calling the common value in (15.19) λ, we have

$$\frac{\partial F}{\partial x} = \lambda\frac{\partial G}{\partial x}$$

$$\frac{\partial F}{\partial y} = \lambda\frac{\partial G}{\partial y}. \tag{15.20}$$

Thus

$$\frac{\partial}{\partial x}(F - \lambda G) = 0$$

$$\frac{\partial}{\partial y}(F - \lambda G) = 0. \tag{15.21}$$

The conditions (15.21) assert that the expression in x, y, λ

$$L(x, y, \lambda) \equiv F(x, y) - \lambda G(x, y)$$

known as the *Lagrangian* of the problem has a stationary point. We have thus converted a constrained optimization problem to an unconstrained one. The term λ is called a *Lagrange multiplier*. Notice that the problem of identifying the optimum reduces now to solving the three equations

$$\frac{\partial L}{\partial x} \equiv \frac{\partial F}{\partial x} - \lambda \frac{\partial G}{\partial x} = 0$$

$$\frac{\partial L}{\partial y} \equiv \frac{\partial F}{\partial y} - \lambda \frac{\partial G}{\partial y} = 0$$

$$\frac{\partial L}{\partial \lambda} \equiv G(x, y) = 0$$

for the three unknowns. This may, in principle at least, be carried out and need not require the calculation of $\phi(x)$. The beauty of the method lies in the fact that it easily generalizes to problems involving more variables and more constraints. For instance, to solve the problem

$$\text{maximize} \quad F(x, y, z)$$

$$\text{subject to} \quad G_1(x, y, z) = 0$$

$$\text{and} \quad G_2(x, y, z) = 0$$

we introduce two Lagrange multipliers, say λ_1 and λ_2, one for each constraint, and look for stationary points of the Lagrangian

$$L(x, y, z, \lambda_1, \lambda_2) = F(x, y, z) - \lambda_1 G_1(x, y, z) - \lambda_2 G_2(x, y, z).$$

15.7   Worked examples

Example 1

$$\text{maximize} \quad xy$$

$$\text{subject to} \quad x^2 + 4y^2 = 1.$$

SOLUTION   Put

$$L = xy - \lambda(x^2 + 4y^2 - 1).$$

Then

$$\frac{\partial L}{\partial x} = y - 2\lambda x = 0 \qquad \text{or} \qquad \lambda = \frac{y}{2x}$$

$$\frac{\partial L}{\partial y} = x - 8\lambda y = 0 \qquad \text{or} \qquad \lambda = \frac{x}{8y}.$$

Multiplying together we obtain

$$\lambda^2 = \frac{1}{16} \qquad \text{or} \qquad \lambda = \pm\frac{1}{4}.$$

Hence

$$y = 2\lambda x = \pm \frac{1}{2} x.$$

Substituting into the constraint equation

$$x^2 + 4\left(\pm \frac{1}{2} x\right)^2 = 1$$

gives

$$2x^2 = 1$$

or

$$x = \pm \frac{1}{\sqrt{2}}$$

and

$$y = \pm \frac{1}{2\sqrt{2}}.$$

Evidently xy is maximized at the points $(1/\sqrt{2}, 1/2\sqrt{2})$ and $(-1/\sqrt{2}, -1/2\sqrt{2})$, where its value is $1/4$. It is minimized at the other two points, i.e. $(1/\sqrt{2}, -1/2\sqrt{2})$, $(-1/\sqrt{2}, 1/2\sqrt{2})$, where the value of xy is $-1/4$.

It is instructive to plot a diagram of the constraint curve and the various contours $xy = k$ (figure 15.21). The contour $xy = 1/4 = $ maximum is seen to be tangential to the constraint curve. This is because the co-tangency condition of section 13.3 asserts that

$$\nabla F = \left(\frac{\partial F}{\partial x}, \frac{\partial F}{\partial y}\right)' = \lambda \left(\frac{\partial G}{\partial x}, \frac{\partial G}{\partial y}\right)' = \lambda \nabla G,$$

i.e. the normal to the contour $F = $ maximum is proportional to the normal to the contour $G = 0$.

This last point is not accidental. Imagine tracing contours $F(x, y) = k$ in the (x, y) plane for various increasing values of k. In general one might expect the contour $F(x, y) = k$ to cut the contour $G(x, y) = 0$ in two points P, Q. Thus PQ is a chord to both the F contour and the G contour (figure 15.22). As k increases to max $F(x, y)$, P and Q might be expected to approach each other; PQ would then swing into a limiting tangential position for the G contour. It is equally plausible that PQ, in the limit, should also be a tangent to $F(x, y) = $ maximum.

Example 2: Least cost inputs

A customer's special order for an output of Q_0 needs to be processed. We assume a production function $Q(a, b)$ using two raw materials as inputs. The cost is assumed to be

$$C(a, b) = pa + qb.$$

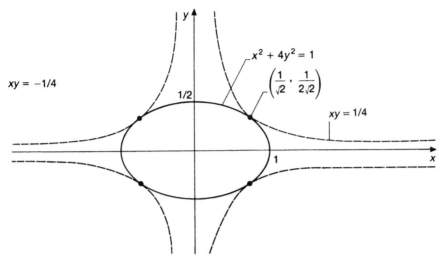

Figure 15.21 The contours $xy = 1/4$ and $xy = -1/4$ are tangential to the constraint curve.

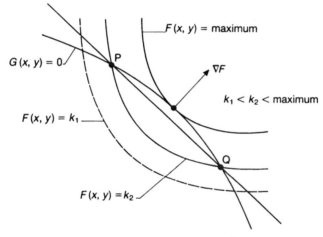

Figure 15.22 As k increases the common chord PQ of the contour $F(x, y) = k$ and $G(x, y) = 0$ becomes a common tangent at the optimum point.

The problem is to find a, b such as to

$$\text{minimize} \quad C(a, b)$$

$$\text{subject to} \quad Q(a, b) = Q_0 \qquad (\text{i.e. } Q(a, b) - Q_0 = 0).$$

SOLUTION The Lagrangian is

$$L(a, b, \lambda) = C(a, b) - \lambda[Q(a, b) - Q_0]$$
$$= pa + qb - \lambda[Q(a, b) - Q_0].$$

We now seek a stationary point.

$$\frac{\partial L}{\partial a} = p - \lambda Q_a = 0 \qquad \text{or} \qquad p = \lambda Q_a$$

$$\frac{\partial L}{\partial b} = q - \lambda Q_b = 0 \qquad \text{or} \qquad q = \lambda Q_b.$$

Hence

$$\frac{Q_a}{Q_b} = \frac{p}{q}.$$

For example, if we take the Cobb–Douglas production function $Q(a, b) = Aa^\alpha b^\beta$ we obtain the condition

$$\frac{p}{q} = \frac{A\alpha a^{\alpha-1}b^\beta}{A\beta a^\alpha b^{\beta-1}} = \frac{\alpha b}{\beta a}.$$

Thus the optimal quantities $(\bar{a}, \bar{b})$ lie on the intersection of the line

$$b = \left(\frac{\beta p}{\alpha q}\right)a$$

with the isoquant $Q(a, b) = Q_0$ (figure 15.23). The line is known as the *expansion path*, since its points correspond to different possible values of Q_0.

Note that, as usual, the *isocost line* $pa + qb =$ constant corresponding to minimum cost is tangential to the isoquant.

Evidently the ratio $-Q_a/Q_b$ is equal to the slope of the tangent line to the isoquant $Q(a, b) = Q_0$, since the tangent line at $(\bar{a}, \bar{b})$ is

$$0 = \frac{\partial Q}{\partial a}(a - \bar{a}) + \frac{\partial Q}{\partial b}(b - \bar{b}).$$

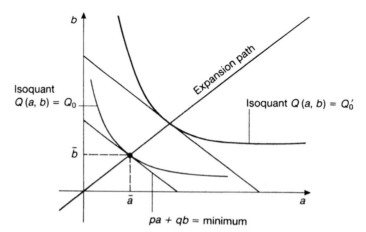

Figure 15.23   As Q_0 changes, the optimal point on the isoquant $Q = Q_0$ traces out the expansion path.

By analogy with our interpretation of the marginal rate of substitution, $-Q_a/Q_b$ may be identified as the marginal rate of technical substitution of the first raw material for the second.

15.8 Lagrange multiplier as the marginal utility of money

We have already discussed in Part I how a consumer reacts when faced with the problem of spending an amount b on two commodities priced p and q. The amounts he is able to buy, say x and y respectively of the first and second commodity, satisfy $px + qy = b$ (figure 15.24). If he acts so as to maximize a utility function $u(x, y)$, his problem

$$\text{maximize} \quad u(x, y)$$

$$\text{subject to} \quad px + qy = b$$

has the Lagrangian formulation

$$L(x, y, \lambda) = u(x, y) - \lambda(px + qy - b).$$

At an optimum,

$$\frac{\partial L}{\partial x} = \frac{\partial u}{\partial x} - \lambda p = 0$$

$$\frac{\partial L}{\partial y} = \frac{\partial u}{\partial y} - \lambda q = 0$$

or, equivalently,

$$\nabla u = \left(\frac{\partial u}{\partial x}, \frac{\partial u}{\partial y}\right)' = \lambda(p, q)'.$$

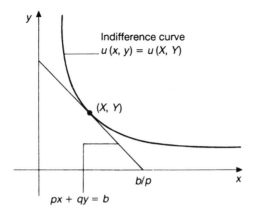

Figure 15.24 The commodity choice (X, Y) maximizes utility subject to the budget constraint.

Thus the budget line is tangential to the indifference curve. Notice that the slope of the tangent line to the indifference curve is

$$-\frac{\partial u}{\partial x}\Big/\frac{\partial u}{\partial y},$$

since its equation, if (X, Y) is the optimum point, is

$$0 = \frac{\partial u}{\partial x}(x - X) + \frac{\partial u}{\partial y}(y - Y),$$

and this was identified (apart from the minus sign) as the marginal rate of substitution between the two commodities (see section 3.8).

Now we may regard the values of X, Y, λ at the optimum to be functions of b. The Lagrangian L is then also a function of b. We have at X, Y that

$$L(b) \equiv L[X(b), Y(b), \lambda(b)] = u[X(b), Y(b)] - \lambda(b)[pX(b) + qY(b) - b].$$

Differentiating with respect to b (and using the chain rule), we obtain

$$\frac{dL}{db} = \frac{\partial u}{\partial x}\frac{dX}{db} + \frac{\partial u}{\partial y}\frac{dY}{db} - \frac{d\lambda}{db}(pX + qY - b) - \lambda\left(p\frac{dX}{db} + q\frac{dY}{db} - 1\right)$$

$$= \frac{dX}{db}\left(\frac{\partial u}{\partial x} - \lambda p\right) + \frac{dX}{db}\left(\frac{\partial u}{\partial y} - \lambda q\right) + \lambda,$$

i.e.

$$\frac{dL}{db} = \lambda.$$

Thus λ measures the sensitivity of L at the optimum to changes in b. Evidently $L(b) \equiv u[X(b), Y(b)]$ (since $pX(b) + qX(b) = b$). Thus

$$\lambda = \frac{d}{db}u[X(b), Y(b)]$$

and so λ is the marginal utility of (budget) money.

15.9   More than two variables

This is where the crunch comes – to deal with three variables or more requires very definitely some matrix algebra. Say we wish to minimize $F(x, y, z)$ with no constraints placed on the variables x, y, z. The minimum point (X, Y, Z) will satisfy just as before

$$\frac{\partial F}{\partial x} = \frac{\partial F}{\partial y} = \frac{\partial F}{\partial z} = 0,$$

in other words

$$DF(X, Y, Z) = \left(\frac{\partial F}{\partial x}, \frac{\partial F}{\partial y}, \frac{\partial F}{\partial z}\right) = 0.$$

This is the first-order condition and is easily checked. Just as in section 15.4 in order to investigate $F(X + h, Y + k, Z + l)$ for arbitrary increments h, k, l we set

$$g(t) = F(X + th, Y + tk, Z + tl)$$

and obtain a one-variable approach. If (X, Y, Z) is a local minimum of $F(X, Y, Z)$ then $g(t)$ has a local minimum at $t = 0$. Hence $g'(0) = 0$. We can also obtain a second-order condition by computing $g''(t)$. Just as in section 15.3, example 2, we obtain

$$
\begin{aligned}
g''(t) = \frac{d}{dt} [& F'_x(X + th, Y + tk, Z + tl)h \\
& + F'_y(X + th, Y + tk, Z + tl)k + F'_z(X + th, Y + tk, Z + tl)l] \\
= (& F''_{xx}h^2 + F''_{xy}hk + F''_{xz}hl) + (F''_{yx}hk + F''_{yy}k^2 + F''_{yz}kl) \\
& + (F''_{zx}hl + F''_{zy}kl + F''_{zz}l^2)
\end{aligned}
$$

where the partials are evaluated at the point $P_t = (X + th, Y + tk, Z + tl)$. We shall have a local minimum provided that $g''(0) > 0$ (cf. section 14.7). The above quadratic in h, k, l is best written out in matrix form as follows:

$$
(h, k, l)
\begin{bmatrix}
F''_{xx} & F''_{xy} & F''_{xz} \\
F''_{yx} & F''_{yy} & F''_{yz} \\
F''_{zx} & F''_{zy} & F''_{zz}
\end{bmatrix}
\begin{pmatrix} h \\ k \\ l \end{pmatrix}.
$$

Notice that this Hessian matrix is symmetric about the diagonal since $F''_{xy} = F''_{yx}$ etc. We need to know conditions on this matrix under which the quadratic expression $g''(0)$ is positive for all h, k, l. We thus want the quadratic expression to be a positive definite form. Let us recall some of these terms. In section 7.6 we defined a matrix A to be symmetric if $A = A'$. If x is a vector of variables, e.g. $x = (x_1, x_2)'$ or $x = (x_1, x_2, x_3)'$, of the same size as the matrix A, then

$$x'Ax$$

is a quadratic form. See section 7.7.

Example 1

$$
(x_1, x_2)
\begin{bmatrix} 1 & 3 \\ 3 & 2 \end{bmatrix}
\begin{pmatrix} x_1 \\ x_2 \end{pmatrix}
= x_1^2 + 6x_1x_2 + 2x_2^2.
$$

Example 2

$$
(x_1, x_2, x_3)
\begin{bmatrix} 1 & 4 & 5 \\ 4 & 2 & 6 \\ 5 & 6 & 3 \end{bmatrix}
\begin{pmatrix} x_1 \\ x_2 \\ x_3 \end{pmatrix}
= x_1^2 + 2x_2^2 + 3x_3^2 + 8x_1x_2 + 10x_1x_3 + 12x_2x_3.
$$

Remark

To help in multiplying out the matrix expressions appearing on the left in both the above examples note that the matrix entry a_{ij} 'multiplies with' x_i and x_j (figure 15.25).

A quadratic form $x'Ax$ is positive definite if $x'Ax > 0$ for all $x \neq 0$. In section 7.8 we examined the simplest quadratic forms, i.e. those which consist of squared terms, e.g. $x_1^2 - 2x_2^2 + 3x_3^2$ or, in matrix form,

$$(x_1, x_2, x_3) \begin{bmatrix} 1 & 0 & 0 \\ 0 & -2 & 0 \\ 0 & 0 & 3 \end{bmatrix} \begin{pmatrix} x_1 \\ x_2 \\ x_3 \end{pmatrix}.$$

This matrix contains entries only on its diagonal and so is said to be a diagonal matrix. For such quadratic forms $x'Ax$ it is particularly easy to determine whether $x'Ax > 0$: the diagonal entries must all be positive. In section 7.6 we looked for a change of variable which turns the quadratic form into a sum or difference of squares. Let A be as in example 1. Thus

$$A = \begin{bmatrix} 1 & 3 \\ 3 & 2 \end{bmatrix}.$$

The substitution

$$x_1 = ay_1 + by_2$$
$$x_2 = cy_1 + dy_2,$$

which we may write in matrix form as $x = Py$, transforms the quadratic to

$$x'Ax = (Py)'APy = y'P'APy.$$

We found that if P consists of orthogonal eigenvectors of unit length then $P' = P^{-1}$ and $P^{-1}AP$ is the diagonal matrix with the eigenvalues of A on its diagonal. To find the eigenvalues in the case of example 1 we must first compute the determinant of

$$\begin{pmatrix} 1 - \lambda & 3 \\ 3 & 2 - \lambda \end{pmatrix}.$$

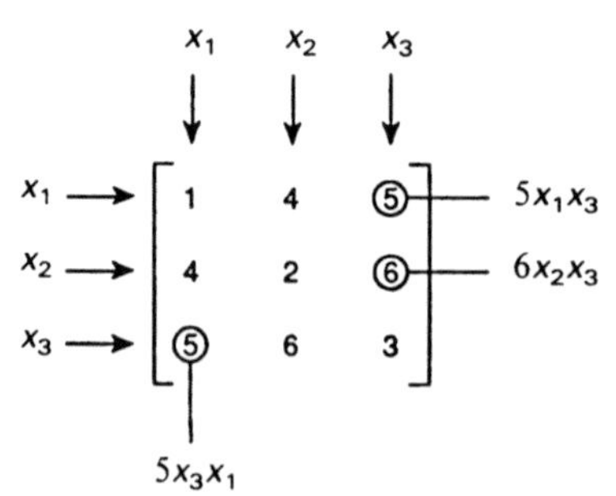

Figure 15.25 Assigning factors to coefficients.

This is known as the *characteristic polynomial*. Thus λ is an eigenvalue when

$$(1 - \lambda)(2 - \lambda) - 9 = 0$$

$$\lambda^2 - 3\lambda - 7 = 0$$

so that

$$\lambda = \frac{3 \pm \sqrt{(9 + 28)}}{2} = \frac{3 \pm \sqrt{(37)}}{2}.$$

After we have found P we shall have

$$x'Ax = y'P'APy = \frac{3 + \sqrt{(37)}}{2} y_1^2 + \frac{3 - \sqrt{(37)}}{2} y_2^2.$$

Note that the first coefficient is positive while the second is negative and so the quadratic form here can take both positive values (e.g. for $y_2 = 0$) and negative values (e.g. for $y_1 = 0$); thus it is not positive definite. When A is as in example 2 the characteristic equation is

$$
\begin{aligned}
p(\lambda) &= \begin{vmatrix} 1 - \lambda & 4 & 5 \\ 4 & 2 - \lambda & 6 \\ 5 & 6 & 3 - \lambda \end{vmatrix} \\
&= (1 - \lambda)(\lambda^2 - 5\lambda - 30) + 4(4\lambda + 18) + 5(14 + 5\lambda) \\
&= -\lambda^3 + 6\lambda^2 + 25\lambda - 30 + 16\lambda + 72 + 70 + 25\lambda \\
&= -\lambda^3 + 6\lambda^2 + 66\lambda + 122 \\
&= 0.
\end{aligned}
$$

Fortunately, however, to check for positive definiteness we only need to know the signs of the eigenvalues. If we factorize the characteristic polynomial

$$
\begin{aligned}
p(\lambda) &= -\lambda^3 + 6\lambda^2 + 66\lambda + 122 \\
&= (\lambda_1 - \lambda)(\lambda_2 - \lambda)(\lambda_3 - \lambda) \\
&= -\lambda^3 + (\lambda_1 + \lambda_2 + \lambda_3)\lambda^2 - (\lambda_1\lambda_2 + \lambda_2\lambda_3 + \lambda_3\lambda_1)\lambda + \lambda_1\lambda_2\lambda_3,
\end{aligned}
$$

we see that, had all three roots λ_i been positive, the coefficients of $p(\lambda)$ would need to alternate in sign. But they do not. So not all the eigenvalues are positive. Since $\lambda_1\lambda_2\lambda_3 = 112$ in fact two of the eigenvalues are negative and only one is positive.

Actually, the calculation of $p(\lambda)$ was itself unnecessary. In section 7.8 we learnt the following two facts:

1 $x'Ax$ is positive definite if the principal subdeterminants of A are all positive, i.e.

$$a_{11} > 0, \qquad \begin{vmatrix} a_{11} & a_{12} \\ a_{21} & a_{22} \end{vmatrix} > 0, \qquad \dots \ .$$

2   $x'Ax$ is negative definite if the sequence of successively higher ordered principal subdeterminants alternate in sign, i.e.

$$a_{11} < 0, \qquad \begin{vmatrix} a_{11} & a_{12} \\ a_{21} & a_{22} \end{vmatrix} > 0, \qquad \ldots \ .$$

In our last example the principal subdeterminants of A are

$$1, \qquad \begin{vmatrix} 1 & 4 \\ 4 & 2 \end{vmatrix} = 2 - 16 = -14 < 0, \qquad \begin{vmatrix} 1 & 4 & 5 \\ 4 & 2 & 6 \\ 5 & 6 & 3 \end{vmatrix} = 112,$$

and so neither 1 nor 2 is satisfied.

We may now deduce the second-order conditions for a local minimum or maximum. In the two-variable case $F(x, y)$ we obtain

1   for a minimum,

$$F''_{xx} > 0, \qquad \begin{vmatrix} F''_{xx} & F''_{xy} \\ F''_{xy} & F''_{yy} \end{vmatrix} = F''_{xx}F''_{yy} - (F''_{xy})^2 > 0,$$

2   for a maximum,

$$F''_{xx} < 0, \qquad \begin{vmatrix} F''_{xx} & F''_{xy} \\ F''_{xy} & F''_{yy} \end{vmatrix} = F''_{xx}F''_{yy} - (F''_{xy})^2 > 0.$$

These are precisely the conditions of section 15.4.

In the three-variable case we deduce that the stationary point (X, Y, Z) is a local minimum if the matrix

$$\begin{bmatrix} F''_{xx} & F''_{xy} & F''_{xz} \\ F''_{yx} & F''_{yy} & F''_{yz} \\ F''_{zx} & F''_{zy} & F''_{zz} \end{bmatrix}$$

has positive principal subdeterminants. However, if the principal subdeterminants listed in ascending order have the signs negative, positive, negative, i.e.

$$F''_{xx} < 0, \qquad \begin{vmatrix} F''_{xx} & F''_{xy} \\ F''_{xy} & F''_{yy} \end{vmatrix} = F''_{xx}F''_{yy} - (F''_{xy})^2 > 0, \qquad \begin{vmatrix} F''_{xx} & F''_{xy} & F''_{xz} \\ F''_{yx} & F''_{yy} & F''_{yz} \\ F''_{zx} & F''_{zy} & F''_{zz} \end{vmatrix} < 0,$$

the stationary point is a local maximum.

15.10   Constrained optimization: a second-order condition

We examine the problem

$$\text{extremize} \quad F(x, y)$$
$$\text{subject to} \quad G(x, y) = 0 \tag{15.22}$$

We suppose that $G(x, y) = 0$ may be solved in the form $y = h(x)$, so that we are extremizing $f(x) = F[x,h(x)]$ without constraint on x. We look for $f''(x)$. Using the chain rule we have

$$f'(x) = F_x[x, h(x)] + F_y[x, h(x)]h'(x)$$

$$f''(x) = F_{xx} + F_{xy}h'(x) + [F_{yx} + F_{yy}h'(x)]h'(x) + F_y h''(x). \qquad (15.23)$$

But

$$G(x, h(x)) \equiv 0 \qquad \text{for all } x.$$

Differentiating this identity we have

$$G_x[x, h(x)] + G_y[x, h(x)]h'(x) = 0 \qquad \text{for all } x. \qquad (15.24)$$

Differentiating this last equation a second time gives, as in (15.23),

$$G_{xx} + G_{xy}h'(x) + G_{yx}h'(x) + G_{yy}h'(x)^2 + G_y h''(x) = 0$$

and so

$$h''(x) = -\frac{1}{G_y}[G_{xx} + 2h'(x)G_{xy} + G_{yy}h'(x)^2]. \qquad (15.25)$$

Recalling that $F_y/G_y = \lambda$, where λ is the Lagrange multiplier, we have from (15.23) and (15.25)

$$f''(x) = (F_{xx} - \lambda G_{xx}) + 2h'(x)(F_{xy} - \lambda G_{xy}) + h'(x)^2(F_{yy} - \lambda G_{yy}).$$

Noting that the Lagrangian is $L(x, y, \lambda) = F(x, y) - \lambda G(x, y)$ we have

$$f''(x) = L_{xx} + 2h'(x)L_{xy} + h'(x)^2 L_{yy}.$$

Eliminating $h'(x)$ by using (15.24) we obtain

$$f''(x) = \frac{1}{G_y^2}(G_y^2 L_{xx} - 2G_x G_y L_{xy} + G_x^2 L_{yy}).$$

This equals $-1/G_y^2$ times the determinant

$$\begin{vmatrix} 0 & G_x & G_y \\ G_x & L_{xx} & L_{xy} \\ G_y & L_{xy} & L_{yy} \end{vmatrix},$$

known as the *bordered Hessian*. Thus if the bordered Hessian is positive at a stationary point of F, that point is a local maximum for (15.22).

15.11 Exercises

1* Find and classify the stationary points of

(a) $F(x, y) = x^3 - 3x^2y - y^2 + 10y$
(b) $F(x, y) = x^3 - y^3 - 3xy$

2   Find and classify the stationary points of

(a) $F(x, y) = x^3 + y^3 - 3x - 12y + 10$
(b) $F(x, y) = -x^3 + y^3 + 3xy$

3   If $F(x, y) = x^2 y$, find $f'(t)$ when

$$f(t) = F(1 + th, 2 + tk).$$

4   Find the Taylor expansion for $F(x, y) = x^2 y$ when $X = 1$ and $Y = 2$.

5*   An individual proposes to divide 60 hours between work, for which he is rewarded \$16 per hour, and leisure. His utility of earning \$w and taking l hours of leisure is $u(w, lw^{3/4} l^{1/4}$. How should he do so optimally?

6   The production of an amount q of a high technology good requires the input of capital K and labour L where

$$q = 10K^{1/4}L^{1/4}.$$

If the price of capital is \$300 per unit and the cost of labour is \$100 per unit find the minimum cost $C(q)$ of producing q. If the commodity can be sold at a price of \$2000 per unit what amount q maximizes the profit $2000q - C(q)$?

7   A consumer buys two goods, X and Y. The price of one unit of X is \$1 and the price of one unit of Y is \$16. The consumer's utility function, which describes how he values x units of X and y units of Y, is given by

$$U(x, y) = x^{3/4} y^{1/4}.$$

He has a budget of \$1280 in total each year to spend on X and Y, so that his budget constraint is

$$x + 16y = 1280. \qquad\qquad (15.26)$$

Using the method of Lagrange multipliers, find the values of x, y which maximize the consumer's utility function $U(x, y)$ subject to the budget constraint, equation (15.26).

8*   A consumer is known to have a Cobb–Douglas utility of the form

$$u(x, y) = x^\alpha y^{1 - \alpha}$$

where the parameter α is not known. However, it is known that when faced with the utility maximization problem

$$\text{maximize} \quad x^\alpha y^{1 - \alpha}$$
$$\text{subject to} \quad x + y = 3,$$

the consumer chooses $x = 1$, $y = 2$. Find the value of α.

9   A consumer with a Cobb–Douglas utility function in the same form as in question 8 chooses to buy two apples and one orange for \$1 when the fruits are equally priced. If the price of oranges falls by one-half and the price of apples remains unchanged, how many apples and oranges will the consumer now buy for \$10?

10* The weekly production of a commodity is modelled by the Cobb–Douglas function

$$Q = L^{1/4}K^{3/4}$$

where L denotes labour and K is capital. If the wage rate is £5 per hour find the minimum weekly cost of producing 5000 units of the commodity (per week). If the production is running at this minimum cost level, in what ratio should capital and labour be initially increased to obtain fastest production growth? Assume the price of capital is 1.

11* (Three-variable Lagrange multiplier problem.)

$$\text{maximize} \quad (x + y)z$$

$$\text{subject to} \quad \frac{1}{x^2} + \frac{1}{y^2} + \frac{2}{z^2} = 4.$$

12 (a) Find the minimum cost $C(q)$ of producing q when the input cost is $p_1 x + p_2 y$ and the production function is $q = Ax^\alpha y^\beta$.
   (b) If the selling price is p what quantity q maximizes the profit $pq - C(q)$? Obtain the supply function.

13 Repeat the previous problem when the production function is $q = (x^\gamma + y^\gamma)^{1/\gamma}$.

14 Show that $z = x^2 + y^2$ is convex.

15 Verify that $F(x, y) = (x^{1/2} + y^{1/2})^2$ is a concave function.

16 Is the function $z = x^2 y$ convex? Concave? How about $z = \log(x^2 y)$?

17 Show that the function

$$F(x, y) = x^3 + xy + y^2$$

is convex for $x \geqslant 1/12$.

18 For what values of p and q is the function

$$F(x, y) = \frac{1}{x^p} + \frac{1}{y^q}$$

defined in the region $x > 0$, $y > 0$ (a) convex, (b) concave?

15.12 Further exercises

1 Solve the inventory problem proposed in section 9.7, question 13, i.e.

$$\text{minimize} \quad C(x, y, z) \equiv \frac{1}{2} xd\left(\frac{x}{x + z}\right) + ey + fz$$

$$\text{subject to} \quad (x + z)y = X$$

where the constants are d, the cost per annum of holding a unit of goods in stock; e, the reordering cost; and f, the cost of instantaneous clearance of a unit of backlog order; and the variables are x, the quantity reordered; y the annual frequency of reordering; and z, the level of backlog required to trigger the reordering of stock.

2 Let $\bar{x}, \bar{y}, \bar{\lambda}$ solve the equations

$$F_x(\bar{x}, \bar{y}) = \bar{\lambda} G_x(\bar{x}, \bar{y})$$

$$F_y(\bar{x}, \bar{y}) = \bar{\lambda} G_y(\bar{x}, \bar{y})$$

$$G_y(\bar{x}, \bar{y}) = c$$

corresponding to the constrained optimization problem: maximize $F(x, y)$ subject to $G(x, y) = c$ (i.e. $G(x, y) - c \equiv 0$). Treating $\bar{x}, \bar{y}, \bar{\lambda}$ as functions of c differentiate the Lagrangian

$$\bar{L} = F(\bar{x}, \bar{y}) - \bar{\lambda}[G(\bar{x}, \bar{y}) - c]$$

with respect to c using the chain rule (see section 12.4, page 336). Deduce that

$$\bar{\lambda} = \frac{d}{dc} F(\bar{x}, \bar{y}).$$

Interpret the Lagrange multiplier.

3 (Least-cost inputs.) Suppose Q_0 (section 15.7, example 2) is fixed but that prices p, q vary. Let $v = p/q$ be the price ratio and let $u = \bar{b}/\bar{a}$ be the ratio of the least-cost inputs. Compute for the Cobb–Douglas production function $Q(a, b) = Aa^\alpha b^\beta$ the value of

$$\sigma = \frac{du}{dv} \bigg/ \frac{u}{v}.$$

Interpret this as an elasticity along the lines of section 10.1.

4 (Two Lagrange multipliers.)

$$\text{maximize} \quad xyz$$
$$\text{subject to} \quad x + 2y + 3z = 1$$
$$3x + 2y + z = 1.$$

5 Minimize $(x - z)^2 + (y - t)^2$ subject to

$$xy = 1$$
$$z + 2t = 1$$

and interpret your result geometrically.

6 A function $z = F(x, y)$ is quasiconcave if for any k the set $\{(x, y): F(x, y) \geq k\}$ is convex (e.g. the Cobb–Douglas functions).

(a) Show that if $F(x, y) \leq F(X, Y)$ then F remains greater than $F(x, y)$ along the line segment from (x, y) to (X, Y), i.e. $G(t) = F[x + t(X - x),$

$y + t(Y - y)]$ for $0 \le t \le 1$ is greater than $F(x, y)$. [*Hint*: See figure 15.26. l is the line through (x, y) and (X, Y), k is any number such that

$$F(x, y) \le k \le F(X, Y).$$

Remember that a convex subset of a line is an interval.]

(b) Deduce that if $u = (X, Y)' - (x, y)'$ and $F(x, y) \le F(X, Y)$ then

$$\nabla F(x, y) \cdot u \ge 0.$$

[*Hint*: Directional derivatives.]

(c) Verify the above condition when $F(x, y) = xy$.
(d) Suppose condition (b) holds whenever

$$F(x, y) \le F(X, Y)$$

for any pair of points (x, y) and (X, Y). Deduce that the property in (a) holds. [*Hint*: If $G(t) < F(x, y)$ then for some s with $0 < s < t$ we have $G(s) < F(x, y)$ and $G'(s) < 0$.]

(e) If F remains greater than $F(x, y)$ along the line segment from (x, y) to (X, Y) whenever $F(x, y) \le F(X, Y)$ show that F is quasiconcave (figure 15.27). [*Hint*: Suppose $F(\bar{x}, \bar{y}) = k$ and $F(X, Y) \ge k$; F remains greater than $F(\bar{x}, \bar{y})$ from $(\bar{x}, \bar{y})$ to (X, Y), and so the line segment joining the two points is contained in $\{(x, y) : F(x, y) \ge k\}$.]

15.13 Answers

1 (a) $F = x^3 - 3x^2 y - y^2 + 10y$

$$\frac{\partial f}{\partial x} = 3x^2 - 6xy = 0 \Rightarrow x = 0 \qquad or \qquad x = 2y.$$

$$\frac{\partial F}{\partial y} = -3x^2 - 2y + 10 = 0.$$

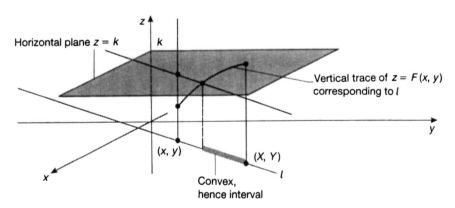

Figure 15.26 On l the set of points where $F \ge k$ is an interval.

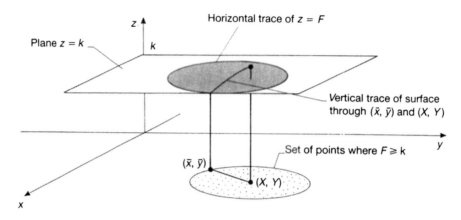

Figure 15.27 The line segment from $(\bar{x}, \bar{y})$ to (X, Y) lies in the shaded area if F is increasing over the segment.

If $x = 0$, we obtain $-2y + 10 = 0$, i.e. $y = 5$. If $x = 2y$ we have $-3 \times 4y^2 - 2y + 10 = 0$ or $12y^2 + 2y - 10 = 0$, i.e. $6y^2 + y - 5 = 0$. So

$$y = \frac{-1 \pm \sqrt{(1 + 4 \times 6 \times 5)}}{12}$$

$$= \frac{-1 \pm \sqrt{(121)}}{12}$$

$$= \frac{-1 \pm 11}{12} = -1, \frac{5}{6}$$

Thus $(-2, -1)$ and $(5/3, 5/6)$ are stationary.
   We classify these points. We have

$$D^2f = \begin{bmatrix} 6x - 6y & -6x \\ -6x & -2 \end{bmatrix}$$

Thus at $(-2, -1)$ we obtain from

$$\begin{bmatrix} -6 & +12 \\ +12 & -2 \end{bmatrix}$$

the principal subdeterminants -6, $12 - 144 < 0$, giving a saddle-point. At $(5/3, 5/6)$ we obtain from

$$\begin{bmatrix} 10 - 5 & -10 \\ -10 & -2 \end{bmatrix}$$

the sequence 5, $-10 - 100 < 0$, giving another saddle-point. The stationary point $(0, 5)$ is a local maximum since the Hessian matrix is

$$\begin{bmatrix} -30 & 0 \\ 0 & -2 \end{bmatrix}$$

and we have the sign sequence $-30, +60$.

(b) $F(x, y) = x^3 - y^3 - 3xy$.

$$\frac{\partial F}{\partial x} = 3x^2 - 3y = 0, \qquad \text{i.e. } y = x^2$$

$$\frac{\partial F}{\partial y} = -3y^2 - 3x = 0, \qquad \text{i.e. } -x = y^2.$$

Thus $x^4 = y^2 = -x$, and so $x = 0$ or $x = -1$. Hence $y = 0$ or $y = 1$ correspondingly.

$$\frac{\partial^2 F}{\partial x^2} = 6x \qquad \frac{\partial^2 F}{\partial x \partial y} = -3 \qquad \frac{\partial^2 F}{\partial y^2} = -6y$$

$$H = \begin{bmatrix} 6x & -3 \\ -3 & -6y \end{bmatrix}.$$

At $(-1, 1)$, $F''_{xx} = -6$, $|H| = +36 - 9 = 27$, a local maximum. At $(0, 0)$, $F''_{xx} = 0$, $H = -9$, and we cannot tell. But $F(0, y) = -y^3$ and so this is a saddle-point.

5   £w earned requires $w/16$ hours. The constraint on time is $60 = w/16 + l$. We eliminate one variable. (Alternatively use the Lagrangian.)

$$u(w, l) = w^{3/4}l^{1/4}$$

$$= w^{3/4}(60 - w/16)^{1/4}$$

$$\frac{du}{dw} = \frac{3}{4}w^{-1/4}\left(60 - \frac{w}{16}\right)^{1/4} + w^{3/4}\left(60 - \frac{w}{16}\right)^{-3/4}\frac{1}{4}\left(\frac{-1}{16}\right)$$

$$\frac{du}{dw} = 0 \leftrightarrow \frac{1}{4}\frac{w^{3/4}}{16}\left(60 - \frac{w}{16}\right)^{-3/4} = \frac{3}{4}w^{-1/4}\left(60 - \frac{w}{16}\right)^{1/4}$$

$$\leftrightarrow \frac{w}{16} = 3\left(60 - \frac{w}{16}\right)$$

$$\leftrightarrow \frac{w}{16} = 180 - \frac{3}{16}w$$

$$\leftrightarrow \frac{4w}{16} = 180 \leftrightarrow w = 4 \times 180.$$

Hence the number of hours of work is $180/4 = 45$ and the number of hours of leisure is 15.

   Alternative solution: the Lagrangian is

$$L = w^{3/4}l^{1/4} + \lambda\left(\frac{w}{16} + l - 60\right)$$

$$\frac{\partial L}{\partial w} = \frac{3}{4}w^{-1/4}l^{1/4} + \frac{\lambda}{16} = 0$$

$$\frac{\partial L}{\partial l} = \frac{1}{4}l^{-3/4}w^{3/4} + \lambda = 0.$$

Hence

$$\lambda = -\frac{1}{4}\frac{w^{3/4}}{l^{3/4}} = -16\frac{3}{4}\frac{l^{1/4}}{w^{1/4}}$$

and so

$$w = 16 \times 3 \times l.$$

Thus

$$60 = l + \frac{w}{16} = l + 3l = 4l$$

$$l = 15$$

$$w = 45.$$

8   At the maximum we have

$$\left(\frac{\partial u}{\partial x}\ \frac{\partial u}{\partial y}\right) = \lambda(1,\ 1)$$

or

$$\frac{\alpha x^{\alpha-1}y^{1-\alpha}}{(1-\alpha)x^{\alpha}y^{-\alpha}} = \frac{1}{1}$$

Thus at $(1,\ 2)$

$$\frac{\alpha}{1-\alpha} = \frac{x}{y} = \frac{1}{2}$$

or

$$2\alpha = 1 - \alpha,$$

yielding

$$\alpha = 1/3.$$

10   Form the Lagrangian $H = K + 5L + \lambda(L^{1/4}K^{3/4} - 5000)$.

$$\frac{\partial H}{\partial K} = 1 + \frac{3}{4}\lambda L^{1/4}K^{-1/4} = 0$$

$$\frac{\partial H}{\partial L} = 5 + \frac{1}{4}\lambda L^{-3/4}K^{3/4} = 0.$$

Hence

$$L^{1/4}K^{-1/4} = -\frac{4}{3\lambda}$$

$$L^{-3/4}K^{3/4} = -\frac{20}{\lambda}.$$

Eliminating λ:

$$\frac{L^{1/4}K^{-1/4}}{L^{-3/4}K^{3/4}} = \frac{4}{60} = \frac{1}{15},$$

i.e. $K = 15L$. Hence

$$C = 20L = K + 5\frac{K}{15} = \frac{4}{3}K.$$

Moreover $5000 = L^{1/4}K^{3/4} = L^{1/4}(15L)^{3/4} = 15^{3/4}L$. So

$$C_{min} = \frac{20 \times 5000}{[(15)^{1/4}]^3}$$

11   Form the Lagrangian

$$L = (x + y)z + \lambda\left(\frac{1}{x^2} + \frac{1}{y^2} + \frac{2}{z^2} - 4\right).$$

Thus

$$\frac{\partial L}{\partial x} = z - 2\lambda x^{-3} = 0 \tag{15.27}$$

$$\frac{\partial L}{\partial y} = z - 2\lambda y^{-3} = 0 \tag{15.28}$$

$$\frac{\partial L}{\partial z} = (x + y) - 4\lambda z^{-3} = 0. \tag{15.29}$$

By (15.27) and (15.28) we have

$$\frac{2\lambda}{x^3} = \frac{2\lambda}{y^3} = z.$$

If $\lambda = 0$ then $z = 0$; this is not possible. Hence $x = y$.
   Now by (15.29), since $2x = 4\lambda/z^3$,

$$x = \frac{2\lambda}{z^3}.$$

But

$$z = \frac{2\lambda}{x^3}.$$

Divide to eliminate λ. Then

$$\frac{x}{z} = \frac{x^3}{z^3}.$$

Since $x \neq 0$, $z \neq 0$ we have

$$1 = \frac{x^2}{z^2},$$

i.e. $x^2 = z^2$. Hence

$$\frac{4}{x^2} = 4,$$

i.e. $x^2 = 1$, $x = \pm 1$. Say $x = 1$; if $z = +1$ we obtain a maximum of $(1 + 1) \times 1 = 2$ and if $z = -1$ we obtain a minimum of $(1 + 1) \times (-1) = -2$.

16

Economic Dynamics: Differential Equations

16.1 Domar's growth model

We wish to model the growth of an economy over time with a view to deciding how to plan at any moment the level of investment $I(t)$. The simplest framework relates investment $I(t)$ both to the income $Y(t)$ at time t (from which the investment originates) and to the ability of that same investment to generate further income.

If a change δI in investment is contemplated, this must be presumed to arise as a fraction saved from an increase δY in income. Assume that the fraction saved is always the same (no matter what the current level of Y) and denote this fraction by s; thus the change δI needs to be financed by the saved part s of the increment δY in income, i.e.

$$s \, \delta Y = \delta I.$$

We therefore postulate a 'demand condition' relating a change in investment to a change in income modelled by the equation

$$s \frac{dY}{dt} = \frac{dI}{dt} \tag{16.1}$$

where the constant s is called the marginal propensity to save.

We now examine how investment influences the economy's ability to produce income. Let $\kappa(t)$ denote the maximum possible output of income at time t; this is called its (production) capacity. The simplest formula connecting capacity to investment relates it to the capital stock $K(t)$ directly; thus

$$\kappa(t) = \rho K(t)$$

where ρ is a constant of proportionality. We are thus assuming a constant capacity-to-capital ratio. But, by definition, the rate of capital formation dK/dt is the (net) investment I. Consequently, we have

$$\frac{d\kappa}{dt} = \rho \frac{dK}{dt} = \rho I. \tag{16.2}$$

We now need to link the demand equation (16.1) with the capacity-generation effect of investment given by (16.2). This is done by postulating that the productive capacity is fully utilized; the economy is then said to be in equilibrium. The equilibrium condition reads

$$Y(t) = \kappa(t). \tag{16.3}$$

The three equations can be used to eliminate $Y(t)$ and $\kappa(t)$, yielding an equation for $I(t)$:

$$\frac{dI}{dt} = s\frac{dY}{dt} = s\frac{d\kappa}{dt} = \rho sI,$$

i.e.

$$\frac{dI}{dt} = \rho sI. \tag{16.4}$$

This differential equation can be solved in two ways.

The first method 'separates' the two variables I and t by placing them on different sides of the equation:

$$\frac{1}{I}dI = \rho s\, dt$$

(Is all on the left; t on the right). Each side is then integrated:

$$\int \frac{dI}{I} = \int \rho s\, dt.$$

Hence

$$\log I = \rho st + \text{constant}$$

and so

$$I(t) = Ae^{\rho st}$$

where A is a constant. In fact, if the initial investment is $I(0)$ we have

$$I(0) = Ae^0 = A$$

and so

$$I(t) = I(0)e^{\rho st}.$$

The model thus requires investment to grow at a rate ρs. Indeed equation (16.4) asserts that

$$\frac{1}{I}\frac{dI}{dt} = \rho s$$

and the left-hand side is by definition 'the rate of growth' of I, i.e. the percentage (or proportional) rate of change (see also section 11.3).

Let us note another method of solving (16.4), known as the *method of integrating factors*. Rewrite (16.4) as

$$\frac{dI}{dt} - psI = 0. \tag{16.5}$$

We now multiply by e^{-pst} to obtain

$$e^{-pst}\frac{dI}{dt} - ps\,e^{-pst}I = 0.$$

Notice that the left-hand side is the derivative of Ie^{-pst}, since by the product rule

$$\frac{d}{dt}(Ie^{-pst}) = e^{-pst}\frac{dI}{dt} + Ie^{-pst}(-ps).$$

Hence

$$\frac{d}{dt}(Ie^{-pst}) = 0$$

and so, integrating,

$$Ie^{-pst} = A.$$

Thus

$$I = Ae^{pst}.$$

16.2   Off-equilibrium: a paradox

What happens if instead of following a growth rate of ps the economy grows at a rate τ? ($\tau > 0$.) According to equation (16.2) we can determine what is happening to the capacity. We have

$$I(t) = I(0)e^{\tau t}. \tag{16.6}$$

Hence

$$\frac{d\kappa}{dt} = pI(0)e^{\tau t}.$$

Integrating from 0 to t we obtain

$$\kappa(t) - \kappa(0) = pI(0)\left(\frac{e^{\tau t} - 1}{\tau}\right).$$

On the other hand to sustain a growth rate τ the income demanded satisfies, according to (16.1),

$$\frac{dY}{dt} = \frac{1}{s}\frac{dI}{dt}.$$

Hence integrating we obtain

$$Y(t) - Y(0) = \frac{1}{s}[I(t) - I(0)] = \frac{I(0)}{s}(e^{\tau t} - 1).$$

The 'utilization ratio' is

$$u(t) = \frac{Y(t)}{\kappa(t)} = \frac{Y(0) + (1/s)I(0)(e^{\tau t} - 1)}{\kappa(0) + (p/\tau)I(0)(e^{\tau t} - 1)}$$

$$\rightarrow \frac{\tau}{ps} \quad \text{as } t \rightarrow \infty.$$

Thus if $\tau > ps$, eventually $Y(t) > \kappa(t)$ and there is a shortage of capacity in the economy. This leads to a paradox: one might think that to overcome a shortage, capacity should be increased by increasing I (see equation (16.2)) but this demands a still higher growth rate in (16.6). (In fact τ should be *cut* to ps.) A similar paradox occurs when $\tau < ps$ and there is surplus capacity.

The Solow model in section 16.4 will get us out of this paradox – obviously at the price of some amendments to the original model.

16.3   Price adjustment in the market

Recall the derivation of an equilibrium price $\bar{p}$ for a commodity whose supply and demand functions are given by

$$Q_d(p) = \alpha - \beta p$$

$$Q_s(p) = -\gamma + \delta p$$

$(\alpha, \beta, \gamma, \delta > 0)$. At equilibrium, when supply balances demand, the equilibrium price satisfies

$$\alpha - \beta\bar{p} = -\gamma + \delta\bar{p},$$

i.e.

$$\bar{p} = \frac{\alpha + \gamma}{\beta + \delta}.$$

But suppose the market is not in equilibrium initially (i.e. at time $t = 0$) and that the price at the outset is instead $p(0)$. We wish to study the way in which price varies over time in response to the inequalities between supply and demand. The easiest way to do this is to suppose that the price change follows the direction of the excess demand (so that price increases for positive excess and decreases for negative excess, i.e. surplus) and obeys a simple law of proportion. Thus

$$\frac{dp}{dt} = \theta[Q_d(p) - Q_s(p)] \tag{16.7}$$

where θ is a *positive* constant of proportionality. Substituting for Q_d and Q_s gives

$$\frac{dp}{dt} = \theta(\alpha - \beta p + \gamma - \delta p).$$

Thus

$$\frac{dp}{dt} + \theta(\beta + \delta)p = \theta(\alpha + \gamma).$$

This is just like equation (16.5) of section 16.1 (except for the constant on the right-hand side). We use the method of integrating factors and multiply by the factor $e^{\theta(\beta + \delta)t}$ to get

$$e^{\theta(\beta + \delta)t}\frac{dp}{dt} + \theta(\beta + \delta)e^{\theta(\beta + \delta)t}p = \theta(\alpha + \gamma)e^{\theta(\beta + \delta)t}.$$

Thus

$$\frac{d}{dt}(e^{\theta(\beta + \delta)t}p) = \theta(\alpha + \gamma)e^{\theta(\beta + \delta)t}.$$

Integrating, we obtain

$$e^{\theta(\beta + \delta)t}p = \theta(\alpha + \gamma)\frac{e^{\theta(\beta + \delta)t}}{\theta(\beta + \delta)} + c$$

where c is a constant. To find c put $t = 0$. Then

$$e^0 p(0) = \frac{\alpha + \gamma}{\beta + \delta} + c \equiv \bar{p} + c.$$

Hence $c = p(0) - \bar{p}$ and so

$$p(t) = \frac{\alpha + \gamma}{\beta + \delta} + ce^{-\theta(\beta + \gamma)t}$$

or

$$p(t) = \bar{p} + [p(0) - \bar{p}]e^{-\theta(\beta + \delta)t}.$$

Evidently, since θ, β, $\delta > 0$, we see that $p(t) \to \bar{p}$ as $t \to \infty$. Thus a market adjusting itself according to the rule (16.7) moves with time towards the static equilibrium price $\bar{p}$. We say that the equilibrium price $\bar{p}$ is *asymptotically stable* to describe the fact that a disturbance of the price from $\bar{p}$ to $p(0)$ gives rise to a price $p(t)$ which approaches $\bar{p}$ in the limit as t tends to ∞.

16.4 Solow's growth model

To overcome the paradox in Domar's model we enrich the framework by introducing labour L as well as capital K into the productive process.

If the output of the economy is Q, we assume, as before, that investment is a constant fraction s of output, i.e.

$$\frac{dK}{dt} \equiv I = sQ, \qquad (16.8)$$

but we write quite generally

$$Q = F(K, L). \qquad (16.9)$$

Notice that we no longer consider 'demanded' income Y nor the capacity κ of the economy, preferring instead the actual output/income Q. In other respects (16.8) and (16.9) closely follow (16.1) and (16.2) of section 16.1. Evidently, if the variable L is introduced, we must also describe its behaviour over time. A simple assumption is that of a constant growth rate:

$$\frac{1}{L} \frac{dL}{dt} = \lambda \qquad (16.10)$$

where λ is a constant.

So far the model is rather general because of the unspecified function $F(K, L)$ in equation (16.6). Solow took the traditional view that $F(K, L)$ is 'linearly homogeneous' (see section 12.7). Recall that this means that

$$F(\mu K, \mu L) = \mu F(K, L) \qquad \text{for } \mu > 0.$$

Taking $\mu = L^{-1}$ we obtain

$$F(K, L) = LF(K/L, 1).$$

Writing $k = K/L$ we define a function $\phi(k)$ of one variable by setting

$$\phi(k) = F(k, 1).$$

Notice that if $F(K, L)$ is the Cobb–Douglas function $K^\alpha L^{1-\alpha}$, then

$$\phi(k) = k^\alpha.$$

We return to this specialization in a moment.

We have three equations (16.8), (16.9) and (16.10) in the three variables K, L and Q. We use the equations to eliminate all three variables in favour of the one variable k. We have

$$K = kL$$

and so

$$I \equiv \frac{dK}{dt} = L \frac{dk}{dt} + k \frac{dL}{dt}.$$

This and (16.8) together imply

$$sF(K, L) = L \frac{dk}{dt} + k \lambda L$$

or

$$sL\phi(k) = L\frac{dk}{dt} + k\lambda L.$$

Cancelling by L, we arrive at *Solow's equation*

$$\frac{dk}{dt} + \lambda k = s\,\phi(k).$$

This equation may be discussed qualitatively for a general ϕ, but we prefer not to do this and instead now specialize down to the Cobb–Douglas form where $\phi(k) = k^\alpha$. Thus we need to solve

$$\frac{dk}{dt} + \lambda k = sk^\alpha.$$

A trick is used here (due to Bernoulli) which reduces the equation to an easier format. Since we have

$$k^{-\alpha}\frac{dk}{dt} + \lambda k^{1-\alpha} = s,$$

we try the substitution $z = k^{1-\alpha}$. We have

$$\frac{dz}{dt} = (1 - \alpha)k^{-\alpha}\frac{dk}{dt}.$$

Hence

$$\frac{1}{1-\alpha}\frac{dz}{dt} + \lambda z = s$$

or

$$\frac{dz}{dt} + (1-\alpha)\lambda z = s(1-\alpha).$$

Now we can use an integrating factor $e^{(1-\alpha)\lambda t}$. Thus multiplying each side we have

$$e^{(1-\alpha)\lambda t}\frac{dz}{dt} + z(1-\alpha)\lambda e^{(1-\alpha)\lambda t} = s(1-\alpha)e^{(1-\alpha)\lambda t}$$

or

$$\frac{d}{dt}(ze^{(1-\alpha)\lambda t}) = s(1-\alpha)e^{(1-\alpha)\lambda t}.$$

Hence

$$ze^{(1-\alpha)\lambda t} = s(1-\alpha)\frac{e^{(1-\alpha)\lambda t}}{(1-\alpha)\lambda} + c$$

where c is a constant. Hence

$$k^{1-\alpha} = \frac{s}{\lambda} + ce^{-(1-\alpha)\lambda t}.$$

To find c put $t = 0$. Then

$$k(0)^{1-\alpha} = \frac{s}{\lambda} + c.$$

Thus

$$k(t)^{1-\alpha} = \frac{s}{\lambda} + \left[k(0)^{1-\alpha} - \frac{s}{\lambda} \right] e^{-(1-\alpha)\lambda t}.$$

Assuming as usual that $0 < \alpha < 1$ and $\lambda > 0$, we see that

$$\left(\frac{K}{L} \right)^{1-\alpha} \to \frac{s}{\lambda}, \qquad \text{i.e. } \frac{K}{L} \to \left(\frac{s}{\lambda} \right)^{1/(1-\alpha)} \qquad \text{as } t \to \infty. \qquad (16.11)$$

Notice that

$$\frac{1}{K} \frac{dK}{dt} = \frac{1}{K} I = \frac{sQ}{K} = \frac{sLk^\alpha}{K} = sk^{\alpha-1}.$$

Hence in the limit the rate of growth of capital is $s\lambda/s = \lambda$, i.e. is equal to the growth rate of labour. Less obvious is the fact that the same holds of the growth rate of investment. We have

$$I = sQ = sLk^\alpha.$$

Hence

$$\log I = \log s + \log L + \alpha \log k.$$

Differentiating we obtain

$$\frac{1}{I} \frac{dI}{dt} = \frac{1}{L} \frac{dL}{dt} + \alpha \frac{1}{k} \frac{dk}{dt}$$

$$= \lambda + \frac{\alpha}{k} (sk^\alpha - \lambda k) \qquad \text{(Solow's equation)}$$

$$= \lambda + \alpha s \left(k^{\alpha-1} - \frac{\lambda}{s} \right)$$

$$\to \lambda \text{ as } t \to \infty.$$

Actually, both these results are true for general (economically significant) functions ϕ. The point of this model is that the economy approaches a state k_∞ which corresponds to static equilibrium. The static case, when $dk/dt = 0$, simply gives

$$0 + \lambda k = sk^\alpha,$$

i.e.

$$k^{1-\alpha} = s/\lambda.$$

Reference to (16.11) demonstrates that the economy approaches its static equilibrium without any need for the kind of fine tuning of investment which was characteristic of the Domar model.

16.5   Résumé on differential equations

The dynamic models of the previous sections involved solving equations of one of the following formats:

$$\frac{dy}{dx} + f(x)y = g(x) \tag{16.12}$$

$$h(y)\frac{dy}{dx} = f(x). \tag{16.13}$$

These equations are of order 1, since only the first-order derivative occurs; they are also of degree 1 since dy/dx is not raised to any power other than 1. We shall consider higher order differential equations but shall stay with degree 1.

Equation (16.12) is treated by the method of integrating factors as follows (compare the 'summation factor' of section 4.13). Let

$$F(x) = \int f(x)\, dx$$

and multiply (16.12) through by $e^{F(x)}$. Thus

$$e^{F(x)}\frac{dy}{dx} + e^{F(x)}F'(x)y = g(x)e^{F(x)},$$

since $F'(x) = f(x)$. By the product rule we have therefore

$$\frac{d}{dx}(e^{F(x)}y) = g(x)e^{F(x)}.$$

Hence

$$e^{F(x)}y = \int g(x)e^{F(x)}dx + \text{constant.}$$

In all our previous examples $f(x)$ was actually constant, so let us solve a more awkward example.

Example
Solve

$$\frac{dy}{dx} = x^2 + \frac{2y}{x}.$$

SOLUTION

$$\frac{dy}{dx} - \frac{2}{x}y = x^2.$$

Thus

$$F(x) = \int -\frac{2}{x} dx = -2 \log x.$$

Therefore

$$\exp[F(x)] = \exp(-2 \log x) = \exp[\log(x^{-2})] = \frac{1}{x^2}.$$

Hence

$$\frac{d}{dx}\left\{\frac{1}{x^2} y\right\} = \frac{1}{x^2} x^2 = 1$$

and so

$$\frac{1}{x^2} y = x + c,$$

yielding

$$y = x^3 + cx^2.$$

The differential equation (16.13) is solved by the method of separating variables. Thus

$$\int h(y) dy = \int f(x) dx$$

(see section 16.1).

Example
Solve

$$\frac{dy}{dx} = \frac{y^3}{x+3}.$$

SOLUTION   Separating the variables we have

$$\int \frac{1}{y^3} dy = \int \frac{dx}{x+3}$$

or

$$-\frac{1}{2} y^{-2} = \log(x+3) + c$$

$$y^2 = \frac{-1}{\log[(x+3)^2] + 2c}.$$

Evidently the constant c must be such that the right-hand side is actually positive.

In section 16.4 we used *Bernoulli's substitution* to solve a special case of Solow's equation. In fact the substitution $z = y^{1-\alpha}$ is useful in solving the equation

$$\frac{dy}{dx} + f(x)y = g(x)y^\alpha, \tag{16.14}$$

since division by y^α gives

$$y^{-\alpha}\frac{dy}{dx} + f(x)y^{1-\alpha} = g(x).$$

Setting $z = y^{1-\alpha}$ we have

$$\frac{dz}{dx} = (1-\alpha)y^{-\alpha}\frac{dy}{dx}.$$

Hence

$$\frac{1}{1-\alpha}\frac{dz}{dx} + f(x)z = g(x)$$

or

$$\frac{dz}{dx} + (1-\alpha)f(x)z = (1-\alpha)g(x)$$

and this is again in the same format as (16.12).

Example
Solve

$$\frac{dy}{dx} + xy = 3xy^2.$$

SOLUTION   Here $\alpha = 2$. Setting

$$z = y^{1-2} = \frac{1}{y}$$

gives

$$\frac{dz}{dx} = -\frac{1}{y^2}\frac{dy}{dx}.$$

Hence, since

$$\frac{1}{y^2}\frac{dy}{dx} + \frac{x}{y} = 3x,$$

we have

$$-\frac{dz}{dx} + xz = 3x$$

or

$$\frac{dz}{dx} - xz = -3x.$$

The integrating factor here is $\exp(-x^2/2)$ since $F(x) = -x^2/2$. Thus

$$\exp\left(-\frac{x^2}{2}\right)\frac{dz}{dx} - x\exp\left(-\frac{x^2}{2}\right)z = -3x\exp\left(-\frac{x^2}{2}\right)$$

and so

$$\frac{d}{dx}\left[\exp\left(-\frac{x^2}{2}\right)z\right] = -3x\exp\left(-\frac{x^2}{2}\right).$$

Integrating we obtain

$$\exp\left(-\frac{x^2}{2}\right)z = -3\int \exp\left(-\frac{x^2}{2}\right)x\,dx = 3\exp\left(-\frac{x^2}{2}\right) + c.$$

Thus

$$y = \frac{1}{3 + c\exp(-x^2/2)}.$$

It is time we considered the general problem of solving a differential equation in the form

$$F(x, y) + G(x, y)\frac{dy}{dx} = 0.$$

The ground we have covered so far is this:

1 $F(x, y) = f(x)$ and $G(x, y) = h(y)$ (separation of variables);
2 $F(x, y) = f(x)y$ and $G \equiv 1$ (integrating factor);
3 $F(x, y) = f(x)y + g(x)y^\alpha$ and $G \equiv 1$ (Bernoulli substitution).

A fourth general circumstance with which we are able to deal arises when the differential equation is in exact form. Other than this and some inspired trickery (presented in the next section) only numerical methods may be applied – a topic beyond the scope of this book.
    We say that the equation

$$F(x, y) + G(x, y)\frac{dy}{dx} = 0 \qquad (16.15)$$

is *exact* if

$$\frac{\partial F}{\partial y} = \frac{\partial G}{\partial x}. \qquad (16.16)$$

The idea behind this definition is the hope of finding a solution of (16.15) in the form

$$H(x, y) = 0$$

for some function H. Differentiation of the last equation gives

$$\frac{\partial H}{\partial x} + \frac{\partial H}{\partial y}\frac{dy}{dx} = 0. \tag{16.17}$$

We thus hope to find a function $H(x, y)$ satisfying

$$F(x, y) = \frac{\partial H}{\partial x}$$

$$G(x, y) = \frac{\partial H}{\partial y} \tag{16.18}$$

which is what we obtain on comparing (16.15) and (16.17). Assuming that (16.18) has a solution for H we conclude that

$$\frac{\partial F}{\partial y} = \frac{\partial^2 H}{\partial x\,\partial y} = \frac{\partial G}{\partial x}$$

and hence the condition (16.16). It turns out, although we do not prove this, that condition (16.16) guarantees the existence of a function $H(x, y)$ satisfying (16.18). Such an H provides a solution of (16.15) in the form $H(x, y) = 0$.

Example
Solve

$$2xy + x^2\frac{dy}{dx} = 0.$$

SOLUTION   We have

$$\frac{\partial}{\partial y}(2xy) = 2x$$

$$\frac{\partial}{\partial x}(x^2) = 2x$$

and so the equation is exact. We now seek a function $H(x, y)$ satisfying (see (16.18))

$$\frac{\partial H}{\partial x} = 2xy \tag{16.19a}$$

$$\frac{\partial H}{\partial y} = x^2. \tag{16.19b}$$

We solve (16.19a) by 'partial integration'; since $\partial H/\partial x$ is the result of differentiating as though y was a constant, we reverse the process and integrate with respect to x treating the variable y as though it was a constant. This gives

$$H(x, y) = x^2 y + \text{constant}.$$

However, the 'constant' term is only a constant relative to x being varied. For different values of y the constant term could be different and so might depend on y. So we write

$$H(x, y) = x^2y + C(y).$$

Similarly we may integrate equation (16.19b) partially to obtain

$$F(x, y) = x^2y + D(x),$$

where again the constant of integration is constant relative to y and may depend on x. Comparing both results gives

$$x^2y + C(y) = x^2y + D(x)$$

or

$$C(y) = D(x).$$

Since the left-hand side is independent of x we see that here $D(x) \equiv k$, a constant. Thus finally we have $F(x, y) = x^2y + k$ and the differential equation has the solution

$$x^2y + k = 0$$

for some constant k.

Note that our example can also be solved using integrating factors. (Exercise!)

A further example
Solve

$$(x + y + 1) + (x - y^2 + 3)\frac{dy}{dx} = 0.$$

SOLUTION   We have

$$\frac{\partial}{\partial y}(x + y + 1) = 1$$

$$\frac{\partial}{\partial x}(x - y^2 + 3) = 1$$

and hence the equation is exact. We need to solve for H the two equations

$$\frac{\partial H}{\partial x} = x + y + 1$$

$$\frac{\partial H}{\partial y} = x - y^2 + 3.$$

Integrating partially we obtain

$$H(x, y) = \frac{1}{2}x^2 + xy + x + C(y)$$

$$H(x, y) = xy - \frac{1}{3}y^3 + 3y + D(x).$$

Setting the two results equal (for consistency), we get

$$\frac{1}{2}x^2 + xy + x + C(y) = xy - \frac{1}{3}y^3 + 3y + D(x).$$

Notice that the mixed term xy cancels (this is precisely because of the exactness condition) and we are able to separate the variables x and y thus:

$$\frac{1}{2}x^2 + x - D(x) = -\frac{1}{3}y^3 + 3y - C(y).$$

Now each side must be constant. (Why? Put $y = 0$ for example and we have $\frac{1}{2}x^2 + x - D(x) = -C(0) = $ constant.) Let the common value of each side be k. Then

$$\frac{1}{2}x^2 + x - D(x) = k$$

or

$$D(x) = \frac{1}{2}x^2 + x - k.$$

Thus

$$H(x, y) = xy - \frac{1}{3}y^3 + 3y + \left(\frac{1}{2}x^2 + x - k\right).$$

Hence our solution is $H(x, y) = 0$, i.e.

$$xy - \frac{1}{3}y^3 + 3y + \frac{1}{2}x^2 + x = k. \tag{16.20}$$

It is usual to regard this equation connecting x and y as constituting the solution to the differential equation even though we have not made y the subject of the formula. We are thus content if we have arrived at a relationship between x and y which is 'free of calculus', i.e. contains no differentiation or integration symbols. Essentially, we are 'passing the buck' in that it is no mean task to solve the cubic in y of equation (16.20). Obviously that can be done for each x on a computer, which is ultimately where every buck always stops.

16.6 Some more tricks for order 1

16.6.1 'The homogeneous in x and y' case

A very special case of the equation

$$F(x, y) + G(x, y)\frac{dy}{dx} = 0$$

occurs when $F(x, y)$ and $G(x, y)$ are homogeneous functions of the same order. We then use the substitution

$$v = y/x,$$

i.e.

$$y = vx.$$

Note that

$$\frac{dy}{dx} = x\frac{dv}{dx} + 1v.$$

Example
Solve

$$(xy - x^2 - y^2) + xy\frac{dy}{dx} = 0.$$

SOLUTION   Notice that both $F(x, y) = xy - x^2 - y^2$ and $G(x, y) = xy$ are homogeneous of degree 2. Indeed we have

$$F(\lambda x, \lambda y) = \lambda^2 xy - \lambda^2 x^2 - \lambda^2 y^2 = \lambda^2 F(x, y)$$

$$G(\lambda x, \lambda y) = \lambda^2 xy = \lambda^2 G(x, y).$$

Put $v = y/x$, then $y = vx$ and hence

$$vx^2 - x^2 - v^2 x^2 + vx^2\left(x\frac{dv}{dx} + v\right) = 0.$$

Cancelling by x^2 gives

$$v - 1 - v^2 + vx\frac{dv}{dx} + v^2 = 0$$

or

$$vx\frac{dv}{dx} = 1 - v.$$

We can now solve by separation of variables:

$$\int \frac{v\, dv}{1 - v} = \int \frac{dx}{x}.$$

Rewriting this as

$$\int \left(-1 + \frac{1}{1 - v}\right) dv = \int \frac{dx}{x}$$

we obtain

$$-v - \log(1 - v) = \log x + C.$$

Write $C = \log c$. Then

$$-v = \log(1 - v) + \log x + \log c$$
$$= \log[cx(1 - v)].$$

Hence

$$e^{-v} = cx(1 - v).$$

Finally, substituting for v we obtain

$$e^{-y/x} = cx(1 - y/x) = c(x - y).$$

Thus

$$e^{-y/x} = c(x - y).$$

Notice again that this is regarded as the 'solution' to the differential equation (i.e. we do not seek to make y the 'subject of the formula').

16.6.2 Change of variable inspired by context

Here we are in the domain of ingenuity.

Example
Solve

$$\frac{dy}{dx} = \frac{1}{x - y} + 1.$$

SOLUTION   Put $z = x - y$ so that

$$\frac{dz}{dx} = 1 - \frac{dy}{dx}.$$

Hence

$$1 - \frac{dz}{dx} = \frac{1}{z} + 1.$$

Thus

$$\frac{dz}{dx} = -\frac{1}{z}$$

and so

$$\int z \, dz = -\int dx$$

or

$$\frac{1}{2} z^2 = -x + c.$$

Thus

$$x - y = [2(c - x)]^{1/2}$$

and

$$y = x - [2(c - x)]^{1/2}.$$

Example
Solve

$$\frac{dy}{dx} = \frac{y}{2x + y^3}.$$

SOLUTION   None of the methods described so far seem to apply here. However, if we 'interchange variables', i.e. treat y as the independent variable, then we are better off. Recalling that

$$\frac{dx}{dy} = \left(\frac{dy}{dx}\right)^{-1}$$

(assuming $dy/dx \neq 0$) we have, reciprocating the equation,

$$\frac{dx}{dy} = \frac{2x + y^3}{y}$$

or

$$\frac{dx}{dy} - \frac{2}{y}x = y^2.$$

But this is the first example of section 16.5 with x and y interchanged; the solution, using an integrating factor, is thus

$$x = y^3 + cy^2.$$

This concludes our survey of elementary methods for order 1, degree 1. We introduce higher order equations with some examples from economics.

16.7   A market with price trend anticipation

It is not unreasonable to expect buyers and sellers in a market to adapt their behaviour not just to the current price but also to the underlying trend in the behaviour of the price over time. Both may be supposed to take into account the current rate of change in price (its velocity, or more precisely its inflation), i.e. dp/dt, and also its 'acceleration' d^2p/dt^2 (the rate of change of inflation). The simplest way of including these two quantities is to suppose that at any time t the demand and supply functions take the form

$$Q_d = \alpha - \beta p + m\frac{dp}{dt} + n\frac{d^2p}{dt^2}$$

$$Q_s = -\gamma + \delta p + u \frac{dp}{dt} + v \frac{d^2 p}{dt^2}$$

where α, β, γ, $\delta > 0$ (as before). Notice that, for example, $m > 0$ implies that rising prices cause demand to increase relative to the initial model ($\alpha - \beta p$). The economic interpretation is that buyers will prefer to 'buy early' in anticipation of higher prices later; by bringing forward their orders they boost current demand.

Let us assume that the market is in equilibrium over all time t. Thus market clearance occurs when

$$\alpha - \beta p + m \frac{dp}{dt} + n \frac{d^2 p}{dt^2} = -\gamma + \delta p + u \frac{dp}{dt} + v \frac{d^2 p}{dt^2}$$

or

$$(n - v) \frac{d^2 p}{dt^2} + (m - u) \frac{dp}{dt} - (\beta + \delta)p = -(\alpha + \gamma).$$

We are thus faced with an equation of the form

$$a_0 \frac{d^2 p}{dt^2} + a_1 \frac{dp}{dt} + a_2 p = -(\alpha + \gamma)$$

where a_0, a_1, a_2 are constants.

16.8   Second-order differential equations with constant coefficients

We first consider the 'homogeneous' equation

$$a_0 \frac{d^2 y}{dt^2} + a_1 \frac{dy}{dt} + a_2 y = 0. \tag{16.21}$$

We try to solve this equation by substituting the exponential function $y = e^{rt}$. Thus

$$a_0 r^2 e^{rt} + a_1 r e^{rt} + a_2 e^{rt} = 0$$

and we shall have a solution if r satisfies

$$a_0 r^2 + a_1 r + a_2 = 0. \tag{16.22}$$

We call this the *auxiliary equation*. If its roots are α, β and they are distinct, it may be shown that the solution of (16.21) takes the form

$$y(t) = A e^{\alpha t} + B e^{\beta t}. \tag{16.23}$$

Here A and B are constants whose values need to be determined by reference to, say, the initial conditions of the dynamical system represented by (16.21).

If, however, the roots are equal (i.e. a double root occurs), then the situation is somewhat different, in that the solution of (16.21) now takes the form

$$y(t) = (A + Bt)e^{\alpha t} \qquad\qquad (16.24)$$

where A and B are constants (as before). Let us look at some examples.

Example 1
Solve

$$\frac{d^2y}{dt^2} + \frac{dy}{dt} - 2y = 0.$$

SOLUTION   The auxiliary equation is

$$r^2 + r - 2 = 0.$$

The roots are

$$\alpha, \beta = \frac{-1 \pm \sqrt{(1 + 4 \times 2)}}{2} = \frac{-1 \pm 3}{2} = 1,\ -2.$$

The solution of the equation is thus

$$y(t) = Ae^t + Be^{-2t}.$$

Example 2
Solve

$$\frac{d^2y}{dt^2} + 6\frac{dy}{dt} + 9y = 0.$$

SOLUTION   The auxiliary equation is

$$r^2 + 6r + 9 = 0$$

or

$$(r + 3)^2 = 0.$$

Thus we have a repeated root and our solution is

$$y(t) = (A + Bt)e^{-3t}.$$

Example 3
Solve

$$\frac{d^2y}{dt^2} + 2\frac{dy}{dt} + 17y = 0.$$

SOLUTION   The auxiliary equation is

$$r^2 + 2r + 17 = 0$$

with roots

$$\alpha, \beta = \frac{-2 \pm \sqrt{(4 - 4 \times 17)}}{2} = -1 \pm \sqrt{(1 - 17)} = -1 \pm 4i$$

where $i = \sqrt{(-1)}$. The roots are *complex*. Let us see where that takes us. According to formula (16.20) our solution is of the form

$$y(t) = Ae^{(-1 + 4i)t} + Be^{(-1 - 4i)t}$$

$$= e^{-t}(Ae^{4it} + Be^{-4it}).$$

We expect our solution to be real. Presumably, A and B are themselves complex, allowing the final answer to be real. This is indeed true. Let us see why. Recall our Taylor series for e^z:

$$e^z = 1 + z + \frac{z^2}{2!} + \frac{z^3}{3!} + \frac{z^4}{4!} + \cdots .$$

Assuming that we may put $z = i\theta$ we get

$$e^{i\theta} = 1 + i\theta + \frac{i^2\theta^2}{2!} + \frac{i^3\theta^3}{3!} + \frac{i^4\theta^4}{4!} + \frac{i^5\theta^5}{5!} + \cdots$$

$$= 1 + i\theta - \frac{\theta^2}{2!} - i\frac{\theta^3}{3!} + \frac{\theta^4}{4!} + i\frac{\theta^5}{5!} + \cdots$$

$$= \left(1 - \frac{\theta^2}{2!} + \frac{\theta^4}{4!} - \cdots\right) + i\left(\theta - \frac{\theta^3}{3!} + \frac{\theta^5}{5!} - \cdots\right)$$

$$= \cos \theta + i \sin \theta$$

(see section 14.4). We thus have the identity

$$e^{i\theta} = \cos \theta + i \sin \theta. \qquad (16.25)$$

Hence our solution may now be rewritten

$$y(t) = e^{-t}[A(\cos 4t + i \sin 4t) + B(\cos 4t - i \sin 4t)]$$

$$= e^{-t}[(A + B) \cos 4t + i(A - B) \sin 4t].$$

Put $C = A + B$, $D = i(A - B)$. Then

$$y(t) = e^{-t}(C \cos 4t + D \sin 4t)$$

and for C, D real this is the real form of our solution. Notice that

$$A + B = C$$
$$A - B = iD.$$

Hence $A = \frac{1}{2}(C + iD)$, $B = \frac{1}{2}(C - iD)$ and C, D are thus the real and imaginary parts of $2B$.

One other observation is useful in the complex case. If $\alpha, \beta = a \pm ib$, then the solution (16.23) has the alternative form

$$y(t) = e^{at}(C \cos bt + D \sin bt) \qquad (16.26)$$

This is $Ae^{at+ibt} + Be^{at-ibt} = e^{at}(Ae^{ib} + Be^{-ib})$ and the argument above for $4t$ can be repeated for bt. Formula (16.26) allows us to see that the sinusoidal fluctuations are either damped by the factor e^{at} for $a < 0$ or exacerbated if $a > 0$ (figure 16.1).

We now briefly turn to the inhomogeneous case

$$a_0 \frac{d^2y}{dt^2} + a_1 \frac{dy}{dt} + a_2 y = g(t). \tag{16.27}$$

Suppose we are fortunate enough to find one (so-called particular) solution of (16.27), say $y_p(t)$, and seek further solutions to (16.27). Since we have

$$a_0 \frac{d^2y_p}{dt^2} + a_1 \frac{dy_p}{dt} + a_2 y_p = g(t), \tag{16.28}$$

we may subtract (16.28) from (16.27) in order to eliminate $g(t)$. We are thus left with

$$z(t) = y(t) - y_p(t)$$

satisfying

$$a_0 \frac{d^2z}{dt^2} + a_1 \frac{dz}{dt} + a_2 z = 0. \tag{16.29}$$

Thus, since $y(t) = y_p(t) + z(t)$ we see that the general solution of (16.27) is the sum of any *particular solution* and the solution of the *complementary equation* (16.29). The complementary equation is homogeneous and we call $z(t)$ the complementary function. We shall use this observation in the next two economic models.

16.9 The market with price trend anticipation (continued)

Recall that the equation for market clearance was

$$a_0 \frac{d^2p}{dt^2} + a_1 \frac{dp}{dt} + a_2 p = -(\alpha + \gamma).$$

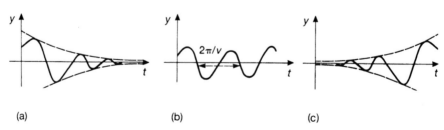

(a) (b) (c)

Figure 16.1 Sinusoidal fluctuations are damped by e^{at} for $a < 0$ in (a), of constant amplitude for $a = 0$ in (b) or exacerbated for $a > 0$ in (c).

We look for a particular solution. There is an obvious candidate – a constant price $p(t) \equiv \bar{p}$. Since the first and second derivatives vanish we have

$$0 + a_2\bar{p} = -(\alpha + \gamma).$$

Recall that here $a_2 = -(\beta + \delta)$. Thus

$$\bar{p} = \frac{\alpha + \gamma}{\beta + \delta},$$

yielding yet again the static equilibrium price; this should be no surprise. Thus the price path is in general

$$p(t) = \bar{p} + P(t)$$

where $P(t)$ is the complementary function and satisfies

$$a_0 \frac{d^2 P}{dt^2} + a_1 \frac{dP}{dt} + a_2 P = 0.$$

Section 16.8 describes how to solve it; however, our immediate question is now: does $P(t) \to 0$, because if so then $p(t) \to \bar{p}$ and the market will exhibit asymptotic stability (see section 16.3). An examination of the possible forms of $P(t)$, i.e. equations (16.23), (16.24) and (16.26) of section 16.8, yields a very quick answer: (a) if both roots of the auxiliary equation are real and negative $P(t) \to 0$ by virtue of the exponential decay terms $e^{\alpha t}$, $e^{\beta t}$; (b) if the roots of the auxiliary equation are complex and their real part is negative then $P(t) \to 0$ by virtue of the decay term e^u.

It is a simple exercise to check that (a) or (b) occurs if and only if:

$$\text{either} \qquad a_0 > 0,\, a_1 > 0,\, a_2 > 0$$
$$\text{or} \qquad a_0 < 0,\, a_1 < 0,\, a_2 < 0$$

Since $a_2 < 0$ the model will be asymptotically stable if $n - v < 0$ and $m - u < 0$, i.e. $n < v$ and $m > u$. One might say then that the buyers need to be less responsive to the trend than the sellers.

Example
Suppose that

$$Q_d = 42 - 4p - 4\frac{dp}{dt} + \frac{d^2 p}{dt^2}$$

$$Q_s = -6 + 8p.$$

(Thus $m = -4$, $n = 1$, $u = v = 0$.) For market clearance we require $Q_s = Q_d$ and so

$$\frac{d^2 p}{dt^2} - 4\frac{dp}{dt} - 12p = -48.$$

The static solution $p \equiv \bar{p}$ has $-12\bar{p} = -48$ or $\bar{p} = 4$. The complementary function satisfies

$$\frac{d^2z}{dt^2} - 4\frac{dz}{dt} - 12z = 0.$$

The auxiliary equation thus reads

$$r^2 - 4r - 12 = 0$$

with roots

$$\frac{4 \pm \sqrt{(4^2 + 4 + 12)}}{2} = 2 \pm \sqrt{(4 + 12)} = 6, \ -2.$$

Hence

$$p(t) = 4 + Ae^{6t} + Be^{-2t}.$$

The market will be stable only if the initial conditions are such that $A = 0$. Suppose for example that $p(0) = 6$ and $p'(0) = 4$. We need to find A, B.

$$6 = p(0) = 4 + A + B \qquad \text{or} \qquad A + B = 2$$

$$4 = p'(0) = 6A - 2B \qquad \text{or} \qquad 3A - B = 2.$$

Thus $4A = 4$ and so $A = 1$ and $B = 1$. For the given initial conditions we thus have

$$p(t) = 4 + e^{6t} + e^{-2t}$$

and so prices soar; the market is unstable.

Remark

The stability condition $n < v$, $m < u$ is not satisfied here ($-4 < 0$ but $1 \not< 0$); thus stability depends upon the initial market conditions.

16.10 Finding particular solutions

We briefly return to the question of finding a particular solution to

$$a_0 \frac{d^2y}{dt^2} + a_1 \frac{dy}{dt} + a_2 y = g(t).$$

There is a body of literature concerned with this problem (e.g. Laplace transform theory). We limit ourselves to a small table of functions which should be tried as solutions (table 16.1).

The basic idea of the table is as follows. Try for a similar kind of function to $g(t)$ (e.g. if $g(t)$ is a polynomial, try a polynomial of the same degree) unless $g(t)$ is of the same form as the complementary function, in which case notch

Table 16.1

Case	$g(t)$	What to try
Roots $\alpha \neq \beta$ are *real* Complementary function is $Ae^{\alpha t} + Be^{\beta t}$	$e^{\gamma t}$ γ real	$Ce^{\gamma t}$ unless $\gamma = \alpha$ or $\gamma = \beta$; then use $Cte^{\gamma t}$
	Constant	C unless $\alpha = 0$ or $\beta = 0$; then use Ct
	Polynomial of degree n	Polynomial of degree n unless $\alpha = 0$ or $\beta = 0$; then use a polynomial of degree $n + 1$ without constant term
	$e^{\delta t} \cos \gamma t$ or $e^{\delta t} \sin \gamma t$ γ, δ real	$e^{\delta t}(C \cos \gamma t + D \sin \gamma t)$
Roots $\alpha = \beta$ Complementary function $(At + B)e^{\alpha t}$	$e^{\gamma t}$ γ real	$Ce^{\gamma t}$ unless $\gamma = \alpha = \beta$; then use $Ct^2 e^{\gamma t}$
	Constant	C unless $\alpha = 0$; then use Ct^2
	Polynomial of degree n	Polynomial of degree n unless $\alpha = 0$; then use polynomial of degree $n + 2$ without linear terms
	$e^{\delta t} \cos \gamma t$ or $e^{\delta t} \sin \gamma t$ γ, δ real	$e^{\delta t}(C \cos \gamma t + D \sin \gamma t)$
α, β complex $= a \pm ib$ Complementary function is $e^{at}(A \cos bt + B \sin bt)$	$e^{\gamma t}$ γ real	$Ce^{\gamma t}$
	Polynomial of degree n	Polynomial of degree n
	$e^{\delta t} \cos \gamma t$ or $e^{bt} \sin \gamma t$ γ, δ real	$e^{\delta t}(C \cos \gamma t + D \sin \gamma t)$ unless $\delta = a$ and $\gamma = b$; then use $te^{at}(C \cos bt + D \sin bt)$

up by one power of t when $\alpha \neq \beta$ and by two powers of t when $\alpha = \beta$ (where α, β are roots of the auxiliary equation). We saw a similar phenomenon in section 6.8 during our discussion of inhomogeneous difference equations. There is a very good reason for this notching up, but its proper appreciation would require us to set up a good deal of extra mathematical machinery. Those interested are referred to K. G. Binmore's *Calculus* (Cambridge: Cambridge University Press, 1983).

Example 1
Solve

$$\frac{d^3 y}{dt^2} + 5\frac{dy}{dt} + 3y = 6t^2 - t - 1.$$

SOLUTION   The auxiliary equation is $r^2 + 5r + 3 = 0$ with roots

$$r = \frac{-5 \pm \sqrt{(25-12)}}{2} = \frac{-5 \pm \sqrt{(13)}}{2}.$$

The table instructs us to try $y_p = at^2 + bt + c$. Thus on substitution we have

$$2a + 5(2at + b) + 3(at^2 + bt + c) = 6t^2 - t - 1$$

or

$$3at^2 + (10a + 3b)t + (2a + 5b + 3c) = 6t^2 - t - 1.$$

By comparison of both sides $3a = 6$, and so $a = 2$; $10a + 3b = -1$ and so $3b = -1 - 20$ and $b = -7$; $2a + 5b + 3c = -1$ and so $3c = -1 - 4 + 35 = 30$. Thus $y_p = 2t^2 - 7t + 10$. Hence

$$y = 2t^2 - 7t + 10 + A\exp(-\{[5 + \sqrt{(13)}]/2\}t) + B\exp(\{[\sqrt{(13)} - 5]/2\}t).$$

Example 2
Solve

$$\frac{d^2y}{dt^2} + 5\frac{dy}{dt} = 6t^2 + e^{-5t}.$$

SOLUTION   We solve this problem by tackling two problems: (a)

$$\frac{d^2y}{dt^2} + 5\frac{dy}{dt} = e^{-5t}$$

and (b)

$$\frac{d^2y}{dt^2} + 5\frac{dy}{dt} = 6t^2.$$

Note that the auxiliary equation is $r^2 + 5r = 0$ with roots $r = 0$, -5 and so the complementary function is $Ae^{0t} + Be^{-5t}$. For (a) we therefore try $y_p = Cte^{-5t}$; thus

$$e^{-5t} = 5[Ce^{-5t} + Ct(-5)e^{-5t}] + [C(-5)e^{-5t} + C(-5)e^{-5t}$$
$$+ Ct(-5)(-5)e^{-5t}],$$

i.e.

$$e^{-5t} = e^{-5t}(5C - 10C) + te^{-5t}(-25C + 25C).$$

Thus $-5C = 1$ or $C = -1/5$, giving $y_p = -(1/5)te^{-5t}$.
For (b) we try $y_p = at^3 + bt^2 + ct$ (since $\alpha = 0$). Substituting we obtain

$$6t^2 = 5(3at^2 + 2bt + c) + (6at + 2b)$$

or

$$6t^2 = 15at^2 + (10b + 6a)t + (5c + 2b).$$

Thus $15a = 6$ or $a = 2/5$. Also $10b + 6a = 0$ or $10b = -12/5$, and so $b = -6/25$. Furthermore $5c + 2b = 0$ or $5c = +12/25$, so $c = 12/125$. Thus

$$y_p = \frac{2}{5}t^3 - \frac{6}{25}t^2 + \frac{12}{125}t.$$

In conclusion a particular solution to our original problem is

$$y_p = -\frac{1}{5}te^{-5t} + \frac{2}{5}t^3 - \frac{6}{25}t^2 + \frac{12}{125}t.$$

The reasoning is this. Suppose

$$\frac{d^2y_1}{dt^2} + 5\frac{dy_1}{dt} = e^{-5t}$$

and

$$\frac{d^2y_2}{dt^2} + 5\frac{dy_2}{dt} = 6t^2.$$

Then

$$\frac{d^2}{dt^2}(y_1 + y_2) + 5\frac{d}{dt}(y_1 + y_2) = e^{-5t} + 6t^2,$$

i.e. the sum solves the equation

$$\frac{d^2y}{dt^2} + 5\frac{dy}{dt} = e^{-5t} + 6t^2.$$

Returning to our problem we see that the general solution is

$$y = y_p + Ae^{0t} + Be^{-5t},$$

i.e.

$$y = A + Be^{-5t} - \frac{1}{5}te^{-5t} + \frac{2}{5}t^3 - \frac{6}{25}t^2 + \frac{12}{125}t.$$

16.11   Higher orders

The situation for higher order differential equations is very similar. The equation

$$a_0\frac{d^ny}{dt^n} + a_1\frac{d^{n-1}y}{dt^{n-1}} + \cdots + a_ny = 0 \tag{16.30}$$

is solved by finding the roots $\alpha_1, \ldots, \alpha_n$ of the auxiliary equation

$$a_0r^n + a_1r^{n-1} + \cdots + a_n = 0.$$

If the roots are all distinct the solutions of (16.30) are of the form

$$y(t) = A_1 e^{\alpha_1 t} + A_2 e^{\alpha_2 t} + \cdots + A_n e^{\alpha_n t} \tag{16.31}$$

where $A_1, \ldots, A_n$ are constants. If any one of the roots is repeated, for instance say α_1 is a multiple root of multiplicity m, then the formula needs to be amended and the terms

$$A_1 e^{\alpha_1 t} + A_2 t e^{\alpha_1 t} + \cdots + A_m t^{m-1} e^{\alpha_1 t}$$

must replace the terms $A_1 e^{\alpha_1 t} + \cdots + A_m e^{\alpha_m t}$ of (16.31) (where we have assumed $\alpha_1 = \alpha_2 = \cdots = \alpha_m$). Similar amendments apply to all other multiple roots.

To find particular solutions of the inhomogeneous equation a method similar to that of section 16.10 is applied. The 'notching-up' corresponds to a coupling effect between the multiplicity m of a root α of the auxiliary equation and the occurrence of a function $t^k e^{\alpha t}$ in $g(t)$; the presence of $t^k e^{\alpha t}$ means that the trial function should contain terms $t^s e^{\alpha t}$ for powers s with $m \leq s \leq m + k$. Compare with table 16.1 when $\alpha = 0$ ($m = 1$, $k = n$ and so $1 \leq s \leq n + 1$; or $m = 2$, $k = n$ and $2 \leq s \leq n + 2$).

16.12 A final example: the Phillips relation

A second-order differential equation appears in the modelling of inflation and unemployment. The basic model presupposes, on empirical evidence, a relationship between the 'rate of inflation' (i.e. the rate of growth of price levels) and the rate of growth of the money-wage. The relationship builds on an observation by Phillips that the rate of growth of the money-wage depends on the unemployment rate. Let us write this as

$$\frac{1}{W}\frac{dW}{dt} = f(U)$$

where W is the money-wage, U is the rate of unemployment and f is assumed to be decreasing, i.e. $f'(U) < 0$. The rate of inflation is then deemed to be the difference between wage growth and labour productivity T. Thus

$$\frac{1}{P}\frac{dP}{dt} = \frac{1}{W}\frac{dW}{dt} - T$$

where P is the general price level.

The simplest model then takes $f(U) = \alpha - \beta U$ with $\alpha, \beta > 0$ and the Phillips relation now reads

$$\alpha - \beta U = \frac{1}{W}\frac{dW}{dt} = \frac{1}{P}\frac{dP}{dt} + T,$$

i.e.

$$\frac{1}{P}\frac{dP}{dt} = \alpha - \beta U - T. \tag{16.32}$$

This basic model, however, suffers a defect: once an inflationary trend is observed inflationary expectations become incorporated in money-wage demands. The basic model is adapted to reflect this fact. We assume that

$$\frac{1}{W}\frac{dW}{dt} = f(U) + h\pi$$

where π is the expected rate of inflation (at time t) and h satisfies $0 < h \leqslant 1$. The coefficient h is a 'weighting' factor which gives expectations a higher or lesser prominence in the model. Equation (16.32) in modified form now reads

$$\frac{1}{P}\frac{dP}{dt} = \alpha - \beta U - T + h\pi. \tag{16.33}$$

The simplest model for the evolution of the expected rate of inflation (as in the dynamic market model of section 16.3) assumes that the rate of change of π follows directly the *excess* of the true rate of inflation over the expected rate. Thus

$$\frac{d\pi}{dt} = \theta\left(\frac{1}{P}\frac{dP}{dt} - \pi\right) \tag{16.34}$$

where the constant of proportionality θ is positive. In fact we may suppose that $0 < \theta \leqslant 1$. (Why?)

The model is further enriched by considering the effects of a monetary policy. Let the nominal money balance be M so that real money is measured by $R = M/P$. Now

$$\frac{1}{R}\frac{dR}{dt} = \frac{d}{dt}\log R = \frac{d}{dt}[\log (M/P)],$$

i.e.

$$\frac{1}{R}\frac{dR}{dt} = \frac{d}{dt}(\log M - \log P)$$

$$= \frac{1}{M}\frac{dM}{dt} - \frac{1}{P}\frac{dP}{dt}.$$

Let us further assume that

$$\frac{1}{P}\frac{dP}{dt} = \frac{1}{M}\frac{dM}{dt} + \frac{1}{k}\frac{dU}{dt} \tag{16.35}$$

where $k > 0$ is a constant. This equation requires some motivation. If unemployment were constant (so that $dU/dt = 0$) equation (16.35) would be a statement of the standard monetarist view that in equilibrium the rate of growth of price equals the rate of growth of nominal money. Equation (16.35) allows, though somewhat crudely, for out of equilibrium behaviour. When unemployment rises the level of real output will fall and it follows that the rate of increase in price levels will run ahead of the rate of increase in money supply and vice versa. After some rearrangement the equation may be seen as saying that the unemployment rate changes at a rate which negatively follows the growth rate of real money.

Assuming that productivity T is constant, it is possible to use equations (16.33)–(16.35) to eliminate any two of the variables U, π, $p = (1/P)\,dP/dt$. We do this here for U and p. We make a final assumption – that $m = (1/M)\,dM/dt$, the growth rate of nominal money, is constant.

It will be convenient to use dot notation for differentiation, so that, for instance, $\dot{U} = dU/dt$ and $\ddot{U} = d^2U/dt^2$.

16.12.1 An equation for U

We have

$$\dot{U} = k(p - m) \tag{16.36}$$

$$\dot{\pi} = \theta(p - \pi) \tag{16.37}$$

$$p = \alpha - \beta U - T + h\pi. \tag{16.38}$$

Thus

$$\frac{1}{k}\dot{U} + m = \alpha - \beta U - T + h\pi. \tag{16.39}$$

Differentiating (16.39) yields

$$\frac{1}{k}\ddot{U} = -\beta\dot{U} + h\dot{\pi}. \tag{16.40}$$

But substituting into (16.37) from (16.36) gives

$$h\dot{\pi} + \theta\pi h = \theta ph$$

$$= h\theta\left(\frac{\dot{U}}{k} + m\right). \tag{16.41}$$

Using (16.39) and (16.40) the left-hand side of (16.41) may be rewritten thus:

$$h\dot{\pi} + \theta\pi h = \left(\frac{1}{k}\ddot{U} + \beta\dot{U}\right) + \theta\left(\frac{1}{k}\dot{U} + m - \alpha + \beta U + T\right).$$

Hence by (16.41)

$$h\theta\dot{U} + mkh\theta = \ddot{U} + k\beta\dot{U} + \theta(\dot{U} + mk - \alpha k + \beta kU + Tk)$$

or

$$\ddot{U} + \dot{U}(k\beta + \theta - h\theta) + U(\theta\beta k) = \theta(mhk - mk + \alpha k - Tk)$$

or

$$\ddot{U} + \dot{U}[k\beta + \theta(1 - h)] + U(\theta\beta k) = k\theta[\alpha - m(1 - h) - T].$$

Using the asymptotic stability criterion explained in section 16.9 we see that the roots of

$$r^2 + [k\beta + \theta(1 - h)]r + \theta\beta k = 0$$

either have negative real part or are negative. Thus the complementary function tends to zero with time. We can obtain a static particular solution $U = \bar{U}$; this must satisfy

$$\bar{U}\theta\beta k = k\theta[\alpha - m(1 - h) - T]$$

so

$$\bar{U} = \frac{\alpha}{\beta} - m\frac{1 - h}{\beta} - \frac{T}{\beta}. \tag{16.42}$$

Thus in general $U(t) \to \bar{U}$. Notice that for $h = 1$ the limiting unemployment rate is independent of the growth rate of nominal money.

16.12.2 An equation for p

We have by (16.38) $\dot{p} = -\beta\dot{U} + h\dot{\pi}$. Hence by (16.36)

$$\dot{p} = h\dot{\pi} - \beta k(p - m). \tag{16.43}$$

Thus

$$\ddot{p} = h\ddot{\pi} - \beta k\dot{p}. \tag{16.44}$$

Now by (16.37) $\dot{\pi} + \theta\pi = \theta p$, and so $\ddot{\pi} + \theta\dot{\pi} = \theta\dot{p}$ and $h\ddot{\pi} + \theta h\dot{\pi} = \theta h\dot{p}$. From (16.44) and (16.43) we obtain

$$(\ddot{p} + \beta k\dot{p}) + \theta(\dot{p} + \beta kp - \beta km) = \theta h\dot{p}.$$

Finally $\ddot{p} + \dot{p}[\beta k + \theta(1 - h)] + \beta\theta kp = \theta\beta km$. Again the complementary function tends to zero. The static solution $p(t) \equiv \bar{p}$ requires

$$\beta\theta k\bar{p} = \theta\beta km,$$

i.e.

$$\bar{p} = m.$$

Hence over time the inflation rate $p(t)$ approaches m, the constant growth rate of nominal money.

16.12.3 The long-run Phillips relation

The long-run Phillips relation is defined to be the relationship between the limiting (static equilibrium) unemployment rate and the limiting (equilibrium) rate of inflation; we have calculated in (16.42) that the relationship is

$$\bar{U} = \frac{\alpha - T}{\beta} - \frac{1 - h}{\beta}\bar{p}.$$

Its graph, the long-run Phillips curve, is a straight line and is seen to be vertical when $h = 1$. The constant value $(\alpha - T)/\beta$ is termed the *natural rate of unemployment*.

Remark

The long-run Phillips relation can be obtained directly from equation (16.33) by assuming rather than proving that over time the variables tend to a static equilibrium. Evidently in static state $\dot{\pi} = 0$ so that $p = \pi \ (= \bar{p})$ by (16.37), i.e. price inflation is correctly anticipated in equilibrium. Hence in static equilbrium

$$\bar{p} = \alpha - \beta \bar{U} - T + h\bar{p}$$

which is the same long-run relation as above (figure 16.2).

16.13 Exercises

1 Solve the following equations by separation of variables:

*(a)
$$x\frac{dy}{dx} + \frac{1}{y^2} = y$$

(b)
$$y = x\frac{dy}{dx} + \frac{1}{y}$$

2 Solve the following equations by the method of integrating factors:

*(a)
$$\frac{dy}{dx} = x^3 + \frac{y}{x}$$

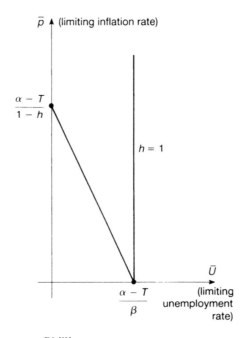

Figure 16.2 The long-run Phillips curve.

(b)
$$x\frac{dy}{dx} + 2 + 3y = xy$$

(c)
$$\frac{dy}{dx} - \frac{2y}{x} = x^2$$

(d)
$$\frac{dy}{dx} - \frac{y}{x(x+1)} = x$$

3   Solve the following equations of homogeneous type by the substitution $y = vx$:

*(a)
$$\frac{dy}{dx} = \frac{y + (x^2 - y^2)^{1/2}}{x}$$

(b)
$$4x^2 + 2y^2 - xy\frac{dy}{dx} = 0$$

(c)
$$\frac{dy}{dx} = \frac{y^2 + x(x^2 + y^2)^{1/2}}{xy}$$

4   Solve the following exact equations:

*(a)
$$(2x^3 - xy^2 - 2y + 3) - (x^2y + 2x)\frac{dy}{dx} = 0$$

*(b)
$$2xy - 1 + (x^2 + 1)\frac{dy}{dx} = 0$$

(c)
$$3x^2y^2 + 2xy + (2x^3y + x^2)\frac{dy}{dx} = 0$$

(d)
$$(3x^2y^2 + y^2\cos x) + (2x^3y + 2y\sin x)\frac{dy}{dx} = 0$$

5   Solve (cf. section 16.5) the following equation:

$$x^2\frac{dy}{dx} + 2xy = y$$

(a) by integrating factors and also (b) by separation of variables.

6*   Solve:

(a)
$$\frac{dy}{dx} = (x + y + 2)^2 \qquad [\text{Put } z = (x + y + 2)]$$

(b)
$$3x\frac{d^2y}{dx^2} + 2\frac{dy}{dx} = 0 \qquad \left[\text{Put } z = \frac{dy}{dx}\right]$$

(c)
$$\frac{d^2y}{dx^2} - 2\frac{dy}{dx}y = 0 \qquad \left[\text{Note that } \frac{d}{dx}(y^2) = 2y\frac{dy}{dx}\right]$$

(d)
$$\frac{dy}{dx} = \frac{y}{x+y} \qquad [\text{Exchange } x \text{ and } y]$$

7   Find *all* solutions of the following homogeneous differential equations.

(a)
$$3\frac{d^3y}{dx^3} + 7\frac{d^2y}{dx^2} + 2\frac{dy}{dx} = 0$$

(b)
$$\frac{d^2y}{dx^2} - 2\frac{dy}{dx} - 3y = 0$$

(c)
$$\frac{d^3y}{dx^3} - 7\frac{dy}{dx} - 6y = 0$$

(d)
$$\frac{d^4y}{dx^4} - 2\frac{d^3y}{dx^3} + \frac{d^2y}{dx^2} = 0$$

(e)
$$\frac{d^4y}{dx^4} + 2\frac{d^3y}{dx^3} - 3\frac{d^2y}{dx^2} - 4\frac{dy}{dx} + 4y = 0$$

(f)
$$\frac{d^2y}{dx^2} - \frac{dy}{dx} + y = 0$$

8   Find *all* solutions of the differential equation

$$3\frac{d^3y}{dx^3} + 7\frac{d^2y}{dx^2} + 2\frac{dy}{dx} = f(x)$$

in the following cases.

(a) $f(x) = e^x$
(b) $f(x) = \sin x$
(c) $f(x) = x^2$
(d) $f(x) = e^{-2x}$

9*   Solve

$$\eta = -\frac{p}{q}\frac{dq}{dp} = k$$

and so deduce that the only demand functions with constant elasticity are of the form

$$q = Ae^{-kp}.$$

16.14   Further exercises

1   A market for a commodity is modelled by taking the demand and supply functions as

$$D(p) = 1 - p$$

$$S(p) = 2p^2$$

so that when the price p prevails the amount of commodity demanded by the market is $D(p)$ and the amount producers are willing to supply is $S(p)$. Price adjusts over time t in response to excess of demand over supply according to the equation

$$\frac{dp}{dt} = D(p) - S(p).$$

Show by solving this equation that for some constant A

$$\frac{p+1}{2p-1} = Ae^{3t}.$$

Hence find the price $p(t)$ if initially the price level is $p = 1/4$. Show that over time the price adjusts towards the clearing value (i.e. the price at which supply and demand are equal).

2   Repeat the previous question when

$$D(p) = 1 - p^2$$

$$S(p) = 3p^2$$

and the initial price is $p = 3/4$. Plot the graph of $p(t)$.

3   A company's profit $P(t)$ (which, if negative, represents a loss) at time t satisfies the differential equation

$$\frac{dP}{dt} = g(t) + KP(t)$$

where $K > 0$ is a constant and g is a function of t. Prove that, for any $t \geqslant 0$,

$$P(t) = e^{Kt}P(0) + e^{Kt} \int_0^t g(x)e^{-Kx}\, dt.$$

Suppose $g(t) = e^t$ and that $P(0) = 0$. Prove that

$$P(t) = te^t \quad \text{if } K = 1$$

and

$$P(t) = \frac{e^t}{1-K}(1 - e^{(K-1)t}) \quad \text{if } K \neq 1.$$

4   Suppose that the amount $A(t)$ of money in an investor's account at time t satisfies the differential equation

$$\frac{dA}{dt} = f(t) + rA(t)$$

where $r > 0$ is a constant and f is a function of t. Show that, for any $t \geqslant 0$,

$$A(t) = e^{rt}A(0) + e^{rt} \int_0^t f(x)e^{-rx}\, dt.$$

If $f(t) = t$ and $A(0) = 0$, show that

$$A(t) = \frac{e^{rt} - (1 + rt)}{r^2}.$$

Suppose instead that $r = 2$, $A(0) = 0$ and $f(t) = e^t$. Find an expression for $A(t)$ in this case.

5*   A primitive economy depends upon imports $M = M(t)$ to sustain its recently acquired technology. Exports $X = X(t)$ are a fraction of the output $Y = Y(t)$, i.e.

$$X = aY \qquad (0 < a < 1)$$

and output is thought to grow according to the law

$$\frac{dY}{dt} = bM \qquad (0 < b < 1).$$

Current debt satisfies

$$\frac{dD}{dt} = rD + M - X$$

where r, the interest rate, is constant. Creditors have in mind to allow debt growth to be exactly balanced by export growth, i.e.

$$\frac{dD}{dt} = \frac{dX}{dt}.$$

Find a differential equation for D by eliminating M, X and Y and hence determine the behaviour of debt. What initial debt-to-output ratio D_0/Y_0 allows steady state debt?

6   With reference to section 11.7.3, question 5, solve the system of equations

$$Y = C + I \qquad C = mY + c$$
$$I = dK/dt \qquad Y = K^{1/2}.$$

7   With reference to the elasticity topic of exercises 10.8, question 10, solve

(a) $\dfrac{dy}{dp} = \dfrac{y(1 + y)}{2p}.$

(b)   If $h(p)$ is your solution to (a) solve the equation

$$-\frac{q}{p}\frac{dp}{dq} = h(p).$$

8   In the model of section 16.12 verify that the real wage W/p grows exponentially.

9   Verify that the roots of

$$a_0 r^2 + a_1 r + a_2 = 0$$

are real and negative, or complex with real part, if either a_0, a_1, $a_2 > 0$ or a_0, a_1, $a_2 < 0$.

16.15   Answers

1 (a)

$$x\frac{dy}{dx} = y - \frac{1}{y^2} = \frac{y^3 - 1}{y^2}$$

Separating the variables gives

$$\int \frac{y^2 dy}{y^3 - 1} = \int \frac{dx}{x}$$

and so

$$\frac{1}{3} \log(y^3 - 1) = \log x + \log c = \log(cx)$$

Thus

$$y^3 - 1 = (cx)^3.$$

2(a)

$$\frac{dy}{dx} - \frac{y}{x} = x^3 \qquad\qquad (16.45)$$

The integrating factor is obtained from $\int -1/x\, dx = -\log x$ as $e^{-\log x} = 1/x$.
We check that

$$\frac{d}{dx}\left(\frac{1}{x} y\right) = \frac{1}{x}\frac{dy}{dx} - \frac{1}{x^2} y = \frac{1}{x} \times (\text{LHS of } (16.45)).$$

Thus

$$\frac{d}{dx}\left(\frac{1}{x} y\right) = \frac{1}{x} x^3 = x^2$$

and so

$$\frac{1}{x} y = \frac{1}{3} x^3 + c$$

and

$$y = \frac{1}{3} x^4 + cx.$$

3(a)   If $y = vx$ then

$$\frac{dy}{dx} = x\frac{dv}{dx} + v.$$

Thus

$$x^2 \frac{dv}{dx} + vx = vx + (x^2 - v^2 x^2)^{1/2}.$$

Hence

$$x^2 \frac{dv}{dx} = x(1 - v^2)^{1/2}.$$

Thus

$$\int \frac{dv}{(1 - v^2)^{1/2}} = \int \frac{dx}{x}$$

$$\text{arcsin } v = \log x + c$$

giving

$$y = x \sin(\log x + c).$$

4

(a) We check for exactness.

$$\frac{\partial}{\partial y}(2x^3 - xy^2 - 2y + 3) = -2xy - 2$$

$$\frac{\partial}{\partial x}(-x^2y - 2x) = -2xy - 2.$$

Solve

$$\frac{\partial F}{\partial x} = 2x^3 - xy^2 - 2y + 3$$

$$\frac{\partial F}{\partial y} = -x^2y - 2x.$$

Thus

$$F = \frac{2}{4}x^4 - \frac{x^2}{2}y^2 - 2xy + 3x + C(y)$$

and

$$F = -\frac{x^2y^2}{2} - 2xy + D(x).$$

Hence $\frac{1}{2}x^4 + 3x + C(y) = D(x)$ and so $C(y) = D(x) - \frac{1}{2}x^43x = k$ say. Thus the solution is $F = 0$ or

$$-\frac{x^2y^2}{2} - 2xy + \frac{1}{2}x^4 + 3x + k = 0.$$

(b) We check for exactness.

$$\frac{\partial}{\partial y}(2xy - 1) = 2x = \frac{\partial}{\partial x}(x^2 + 1).$$

We solve

$$\frac{\partial F}{\partial x} = 2xy - 1$$

giving

$$F = x^2y - x + C(y)$$

and

$$\frac{\partial F}{\partial y} = x^2 + 1$$

giving

$$F = x^2y + y + D(x).$$

For consistency we require

$$x^2y - x + C(y) = x^2y + y + D(x)$$
$$C(y) - y = D(x) + x.$$

Thus both sides of the last equation (being independent of each other) are constant. If $D(x) + x = k$ we obtain

$$0 = F(x, y) \equiv x^2y + y - x + k$$

as the solution.

6   (a)   Put $z = x + y + 2$. Then

$$\frac{dz}{dx} = 1 + \frac{dy}{dx}$$

and so

$$\frac{dz}{dx} - 1 = z^2$$

or

$$\frac{dz}{dx} = 1 + z^2.$$

Hence

$$\int \frac{dz}{1 + z^2} = \int dx$$

and so

$$\arctan z = x + c,$$

i.e.

$$x + y + 2 = \tan(x + c),$$

giving

$$y = \tan(x + c) - x - 2.$$

(b)   Let

$$z = \frac{dy}{dx}.$$

Then

$$3x\frac{dz}{dx} + 2z = 0$$

or

$$\int \frac{3\,dz}{z} = -\int 2\frac{dx}{x}$$

so that

$$3\log z = -2\log x + 2\log C,$$

i.e.

$$z^3 = \left(\frac{C}{x}\right)^2.$$

Thus

$$\frac{dy}{dx} = \left(\frac{C}{x}\right)^{2/3} = Cx^{-2/3},$$

i.e.

$$y = 3Cx^{1/3} + D.$$

(c)

$$\frac{d^2y}{dx^2} = 2y\frac{dy}{dx}.$$

Hence

$$\frac{dy}{dx} = y^2 + c$$

or

$$\int \frac{dy}{y^2 + c} = \int dx.$$

If $c > 0$, we let $c = a^2$. Then

$$\frac{1}{a}\arctan\left(\frac{y}{a}\right) = x + b.$$

Thus $y = a\tan[a(x + b)]$.

If $c < 0$, we let $c = -a^2$. Then since

$$\frac{1}{y^2 - a^2} = \frac{1}{(y - a)(y + a)} = \frac{1}{2a(y - a)} - \frac{1}{2a(y + a)}$$

$$\frac{1}{2a}[\log(y - a) - \log(y + a)] = x + b.$$

Thus

$$\log\left(\frac{y - a}{y + a}\right) = 2a(x + b)$$

giving

$$\frac{y-a}{y+a} = Ae^{2ax}.$$

(d)

$$\frac{dy}{dx} = \frac{y}{x+y}$$

or

$$\frac{dx}{dy} = \frac{x+y}{y} = \frac{x}{y} + 1.$$

Thus

$$\frac{dx}{dy} - \frac{x}{y} = 1.$$

If x and y replace one another we get

$$\frac{dy}{dx} - \frac{y}{x} = 1.$$

The integrating factor is obtained from $\int -1/x \, dx = -\log x$ as $e^{-\log x} = 1/x$.
Hence

$$\frac{d}{dx}\left(y\frac{1}{x}\right) = \frac{1}{x}$$

and so

$$y\frac{1}{x} = \log x + \log c$$

$$y = x \log cx$$

$$e^y = (cx)^x.$$

The solution of the original equation is thus

$$e^x = (cy)^y.$$

9   First suppose that $q = Ap^{-k}$. Then

$$\frac{dq}{dp} = A(-k)p^{-k-1}$$

$$+\frac{p}{q}\frac{dq}{dp} = -\frac{kAP^{-k}}{Ap^{-k}} = -k$$

Now we solve $+(p/q) \, dq/dp = -k$. Separating the variables we obtain

$$\int \frac{dq}{q} = -k \int \frac{dp}{p}$$

$$\log q = -k \log p + \log B.$$

Thus

$$q = Bp^{-k},$$

as required.

5 (of Exercises 16.14)

$$X = aY$$
$$Y' = bM$$
$$D' = rD + M - X$$
$$D' = X'.$$

Hence $D(t) - D_0 = X(t) - X_0 = X - aY_0$. Thus

$$D' = rD + \frac{1}{b}\frac{1}{a}X' - (D - D_0 + aY_0)$$

$$= rD + \frac{1}{ab}D' - D + D_0 - aY_0$$

$$\left(1 - \frac{1}{ab}\right)D' + (1 - r)D = (D_0 - aY_0)$$

$$D' + \frac{ab(1 - r)}{ab - 1}D = \frac{(D_0 - aY_0)ab}{ab - 1}.$$

The particular solution $\bar{D}$ (at the steady state) satisfies

$$\frac{ab(1 - r)}{ab - 1}\bar{D} = \frac{(D_0 - aY_0)ab}{ab - 1}$$

i.e.

$$\bar{D} = \frac{D_0 - aY_0}{1 - r}.$$

The general solution is $D = \bar{D} + Ae^{+\lambda t}$, $\lambda = ab(1 - r)/(1 - ab)$. We find A:

$$D_0 = \bar{D} + A$$

$$A = D_0 - \bar{D}$$

$$= \frac{D_0(1 - r) - D_0 + aY_0}{1 - r}$$

$$= \frac{aY_0 - rD_0}{1 - r}.$$

Since $ab < 1$ there is a steady state if $aY_0 = rD_0$, i.e. $D_0/Y_0 = a/r$.

Index of symbols

Index

Index

Printed in the United States
208008BV00005B/1-10/P